LAW, LAW REFORM
AND THE FAMILY

Law, Law Reform and the Family

STEPHEN CRETNEY

Fellow of All Souls College, Oxford

CLARENDON PRESS · OXFORD
1998

Oxford University Press, Great Clarendon Street, Oxford OX2 6DP

Oxford New York

Athens Auckland Bangkok Bogota Bombay Buenos Aires
Calcutta Cape Town Dar es Salaam Delhi Florence Hong Kong Istanbul
Karachi Kuala Lumpur Madras Madrid Melbourne Mexico City
Nairobi Paris Singapore Taipei Tokyo Toronto Warsaw
and associated companies in
Berlin Ibadan

Oxford is a registered trade mark of Oxford University Press

Published in the United States
by Oxford University Press Inc., New York

British Library Cataloguing in Publication Data
Data available

Library of Congress Cataloging in Publication Data
Cretney, Stephen Michael.
Law, law reform, and the family / Stephen Cretney.
p.   cm.
Includes bibliographical references and index.
1. Domestic relations—Great Britain.   2. Law reform—Great
Britain.   I. Title.
KD750.C695   1998
346.4101'5—dc21   98–38625

ISBN 0–19–826871–8

1 3 5 7 9 10 8 6 4 2

Typeset by Graphicraft Limited, Hong Kong
Printed in Great Britain
on acid-free paper by
Biddles Ltd., Guildford and King's Lynn

FOR
ANTONIA
MATTHEW
and
EDWARD

Preface

The history of law reform is the history of strong differences of opinion between those who wanted a change and those who did not, and on the whole progress has been made by these means.

(Sir John Simon, then Home Secretary, to the Chief Magistrate, Sir Rollo Graham Campbell, 13 July 1936.)

The importance of studying the law in its social and historical context has been part of the conventional wisdom for many years; but surprisingly little detailed work by lawyers on the background to legislation has been published. For the past five years the matchless research environment provided by All Souls College has enabled me to work on the development of English family law, and to draw on the rich deposits preserved in the Public Record Office as well as other sources, official and unofficial. I intend to publish a comprehensive study of *Law, Lawmakers and the Family in 20th Century Britain* in due course which the present collection of research papers and essays to some extent anticipates.

There is always a danger that such collections will lack any common or unifying theme; but I hope this is not true of the contents of this volume. Chapter 1, 'The Law Commission: True Dawns and False Dawns', exposes the difficulties of reconciling traditional principles of ministerial responsibility for legislation with the Labour Party's 1964 commitment to create—as part of the skilled professionalism intended to supplant decades of dilettante amateurism—an independent body to have full charge of the machinery for law reform. This Chapter also demonstrates the difficulty which a non-governmental body such as the Law Commission has in securing the legitimacy necessary in any democratic law-making process.

Chapter 2 ('Putting Asunder and Coming Together: Church, State and the 1969 Divorce Reforms') has (unlike the others in this Collection) not previously been published. It describes the circumstances in which Archbishop Ramsey set up a small group to consider whether a new kind of divorce law, 'free from the most unsatisfactory features of the matrimonial offence based law but not weakening the status of marriage in the community', might be devised; and describes the part subsequently played by the Law Commission in securing the apparent consensus on which the 1969 Divorce Reform Act was founded. The 'concordat' between the Archbishop's Group and the Law Commission is a matter of published record; but it is now apparent that the two sides had very different notions of what it was they had agreed. The Archbishop's Group's papers (preserved at Lambeth Palace) and the surviving Law Commission internal records (in the Public Record Office) throw some light on how two inconsistent views of the divorce process were apparently reconciled. They also reveal the role played by Government Ministers and Civil Servants in encouraging the Church of England to act and thereby remove from the agenda of political controversy an issue which had become politically embarrassing.

Legislation is often said to reflect the intention of Parliament; and one of the successes of the Law Commission has been in producing thoroughly researched Consultation Papers and Reports dealing with the relevant issues—even if, as in the 1969 divorce reforms, the Commission's stance of disinterested objectivity does not bear close scrutiny. In this country, law reform has usually to be by consent or not at all; and it is sometimes tempting for those concerned to take care that potentially controversial matters do not capture the glare of public attention and media coverage since reform is only likely to be achieved by a certain degree of economy with the truth. Chapter 3, 'The Forfeiture Act 1982: A Case Study of the Private Member's Bill as an Instrument of Law Reform' puts on record what is in one view a lamentable example of law reform by stealth. Would it have been better to leave to the judiciary the task of finding a remedy for the injustice sometimes caused by the application of the so-called forfeiture rule (that is, the rule that no one is entitled to benefit from his own wrong)?

The next three Chapters deal with reforms of the divorce process. The presenting issue in 'Disgusted, Buckingham Palace . . . : Divorce, Indecency and the Press, 1926' is the question of how far proceedings affecting the family should be like other court proceedings and thus open to public scrutiny. It also shows how a single sensational case—the *Russell* divorce—can create an irresistible demand for legislation; and in this respect, by demonstrating the overriding importance of pressure from public opinion (or at least 'informed' public opinion) in determining what is and what is not put on the statute book, takes up a recurrent theme of this volume. The Chapter may also have some value in providing a vivid (if mercifully unusual) illustration of some of the serious defects of the matrimonial offence doctrine of divorce, and the harsh consequences which the law could have for those—however apparently privileged—ensnared in it.

In recent years, the creation of 'family courts' and the development of 'conciliation' as an alternative to adversarial litigation have come to be seen as providing relief for the family confronted with breakdown; and mediation has now received the stamp of legislative approval in the Family Law Act 1996. But it is often forgotten that these are not new ideas. 'Marriage Saving and the Early Days of Conciliation: The Role of Claud Mullins' is a study of the background to a statute enacted more than sixty years ago—and, in 1998, still in substance in force—which was intended to ensure that family disputes between wage earners should be dealt with by means of conciliation rather than litigation. It also records the contribution of a remarkable, but now almost forgotten, London magistrate to family law reform—a story which loses nothing by the poignancy of Mullins's struggles with his magisterial colleagues and others.

Lord Denning's influence on the development of English law is widely acknowledged. But few today appreciate the decisive importance in the development of English family law of the Committee which he chaired in 1947 into the apparently unalluring subject of Procedure in Matrimonial Causes—not least in defining the proper roles of the courts on the one hand and marriage support, child welfare and other social work services on the other. I have tried to give an account of these matters—which have a topical relevance in the light of the policies adopted by the Family Law Act 1996—in ' "Tell me the Old, Old Story": The Denning Report, Divorce and Reconciliation'. This Chapter may yet again have something of interest for those who see judges as Olympian figures able to rise above the personal jealousies and hostilities to which others are subject.

The law is obviously important when disputes have to be resolved, but how significant is it in the routine functioning of families? Do social practices need to be underwritten by (or at least be consistent with) legal norms? The view that the law influences opinion and behaviour is, of course, often used in discussions about divorce and illegitimacy, for example. But lawyers perhaps exaggerate the extent to which people even know what the law is. For example, for more than fifty years, the law—in defiance of skilfully marshalled pressure groups, but reflecting bureaucratic notions of what was required for the efficient administration of such things as public health and education services—continued to refuse wives the right to parental authority over their children. The question whether this had any practical significance is highlighted by the Chapter entitled ' "What will the Women Want Next?" The Struggle for Power within the Family, 1925–1975'— which again demonstrates the sometimes ambivalent role played by civil servants in the process of law reform, and provides another illustration of both the advantages and disadvantages of compromise on issues of principle.

The legal institution of adoption provides today a striking illustration of the law effecting a change in legal status and the legal relationships which flow from such status. Chapter 8, 'Adoption—from Contract to Status?' traces the evolution of adoption in English law from a court-ratified contract dependent on an informed consent by the child's parents and yet with only limited impact on the child's status within the family to a process in which the crucial decisions are taken by professional social workers applying their perception of how best to serve the child's welfare. Although the formal decision is still taken by a court, it may be questioned how far the process is still one of judicial adjudication.

The way in which both the technicalities of legal classification—is adoption primarily a matter of legal status or a matter of welfare provision, for example —as well as considerations of departmental interests and responsibility are raised again in Chapter 9, 'The State as a Parent: The Children Act 1948 in Retrospect'. This tells the story of the background to what is by any standards one of the major pieces of post-World War II social legislation; and illustrates dramatically the influence which media publicity and public opinion can have on the development of the law. But in the present context it is noteworthy that the reason the Act gave a statutory priority to one particular form of child care ('boarding-out' or foster care) as against adoption (which was the preference of the Curtis Committee to whose recommendations the Children Act purported to give effect) is a particularly striking illustration of how departmental responsibilities for legislation can have a significant impact on the content of the law: the Lord Chancellor's Department was responsible for adoption (because it was to do with legal status) whereas the Home Office was responsible for child care. The Act was essentially a Home Office Bill, and so adoption was outside its scope. This Chapter also again demonstrates the importance of individuals—including civil servants such as Sir Sidney Harris and Sir Claud Schuster—not to say the impact of group rivalries (in this case between the Home Office and the Departments of Health and Education) in determining the outcome of law reform proposals. The role of the determined individual is indeed a recurrent theme in these essays.

The final Chapter deals with division of family property on death; and may demonstrate how even the most elaborate attempts to inform—in this case by detailed analysis, public consultation, attitude surveys, and the collection of empirical data—may still leave the solution dependent very much on the decision taker's own scale of values. At first sight it might seem almost self-evident that if a man dies without leaving a will his widow should be entitled to his property. But is this really appropriate as a universal solution in a divorce-prone society where the widow will often have had no relationship with the deceased's children, and indeed where the deceased's children may strongly resent the property they regard as their family's passing to strangers and even enemies? The Law Commission undoubtedly had a more difficult task than did the Morton Committee forty years earlier; but some things—not least the difficulty of translating general policies into legislation and the difficulties of ensuring that reform is consistent with public expectations—do not change.

I have tried to insert sufficient introductory material to make the essays comprehensible to readers who are not necessarily expert in the field, I have taken the opportunity to correct some factual and typographical errors, and I have revised some passages which had been overtaken by subsequent events; but in principle the papers are printed as originally published.

The author acknowledges Crown Copyright in statutory materials, the official reports of parliamentary proceedings, and in the archives deposited in the Public Record Office; and he acknowledges the rights of the Church of England in relation to the papers cited in Chapter 2. Copyright subsists in the Law Reports published by the Incorporated Council of Law Reporting, and in Family Law Reports published by Jordan Publishing.

The author wishes to pay tribute to the help provided by the staff of the Public Record Office, the Lambeth Palace Library, the British Library Newspaper Library at Colindale, the Parliamentary Papers collection in the Bodleian

Library, the Bodleian Law Library in Oxford, and the Codrington Library in All Souls College. Mr Michael Sayers (Secretary of the Law Commission) and the Record Officers in the Home Office and Lord Chancellor's Department have also provided invaluable assistance in the search for relevant papers.

Acknowledgement of the help generously provided by friends and colleagues is made at the beginning of the relevant Chapters. The author is grateful to the publishers for arranging the preparation of the Index and Tables.

S.M.C.

The Feast of the Venerable Bede, 27 May 1998

Acknowledgements

The author acknowledges the interest of the editors and publishers of *The Modern Law Review*, the *Oxford Journal of Legal Studies*, the *Denning Law Journal*, the *Law Quarterly Review*, the *Child and Family Law Quarterly Review*, and of Sweet & Maxwell Ltd., in respect of material first published as shown at the beginning of Chapters 1, and 3–10.

Table of Contents

Table of Cases

Table of U.K. Statutes and Statutory Instruments

1*

The Law Commission:
True Dawns and False Dawns

INTRODUCTION

The Law Commission was established by the Law Commissions Act 1965[1] which requires the Commission—five lawyer Commissioners, assisted by a support staff— to take and keep the law under review, to see to its 'systematic development and reform', and to work towards the simplification and modernisation of the law. The broad terms of the Act require the Commission to concern itself with a wide range of legal issues—ranging from such arcane topics as the *Classification of Limitation in Private International Law*[2] through ambitious schemes for the *Codification of the Criminal Law*[3] to potentially controversial issues such as the law relating to *Rape within Marriage*.[4] For nearly thirty years[5] family law was 'one of the most important and productive areas' of the Commission's work;[6]

---

* This title was suggested by an article by the then Chairman of the Law Commission, Sir Henry Brooke, in the Oct. 1994 issue *The House Magazine* (the 'parliamentary weekly magazine which prides itself on being the most widely read magazine in Parliament': *Law Commission Twenty-Ninth Annual Report 1994* (Law Com. No. 232, 1995) para. 5.9, fn. 19). Sir Henry (whose outstanding contribution to modernising the Commission's image is described in the opening pages of the original paper) wrote that the 'recent past has been wintry. There is now a rosy hue on the horizon, but should I fear a false dawn?' The rosy dawn referred to improvements in the relationships between the Commission and the Legislature; but perhaps the rosy hue should have conveyed the proverbial warning: a sudden and violent storm was about to break in the form of the attack on the Commission's Family Homes and Domestic Violence Bill: see below.

[1] There is a separate Scottish Law Commission, based in Edinburgh.

[2] Law Com. No. 114 (1982).

[3] See *Law Commission Twenty-Seventh Annual Report 1992* (Law Com. No. 210, 1993) paras. 2.14–2.16 where the history of this project is summarised.   [4] Law Com. No. 205 (1992).

[5] When Professor B. M. Hoggett (who had for nearly ten years been primarily responsible for the Law Commission's family law work) left the Commission on 31 Dec. 1993 'the very success of the Commission's work in the field of family law . . . meant that it was difficult to justify having a new Commissioner who would lead work exclusively on family law': Law Commission's *Twenty-Eighth Annual Report 1993* (Law Com. No. 223, 1994) para. 1.33; and the Commission's *Thirty-Second Annual Report 1997* (Law Com. No. 250, 1998) did not include any family law projects among the 'Major Targets' for the year set out at p. 16. For a critical view of the decision to give a lower priority to family law see Dame B. Hale (formerly B. Hoggett) 'Family Law Reform: Wither or Whither' (1995) 48 CLP 217.

[6] Dame B. Hale has recorded her view that 'family law has historically been the most successful area for the Law Commission': see 'Family Law Reform: Wither or Whither' (1995) 48 CLP 217, 232. Between 1965 and 1993 the Commission published 31 reports on the reform of family law; and all but two of these were implemented: see the Law Commission's *Twenty-Eighth Annual Report 1993* (Law Com. No. 223, 1994) p. 42, and (for a useful summary of the Commission's activities in the field) Part III.

and the Commission could justly regard its record of achievement in this area as a 'formidable success story'.[7] Although from time to time the Commission expressed concern about delay in implementing its Reports (of which there are more than two hundred) the overall rate of implementation is high;[8] and for many years there was almost universal agreement that the Law Commissions Act had been a landmark in the history of English Law.[9]

But in November 1995 the Commission's family law work suddenly made the Commission the centre of a major political storm. A Bill to implement the Law Commission's *Report on Domestic Violence and Occupation of the Family Home*,[10] put forward as a largely technical measure designed to increase the effectiveness of legal protection for victims of domestic violence, was denounced by a small number of backbench Conservative MPs as a 'charter for live-in lovers'; and a campaign by one tabloid newspaper[11] portrayed the Commission as a 'trendy, left-wing academic quango'[12] exercising a dubious and even dangerous influence. 'Legal commissars subverting family values'[13] warned the headline; and readers were reminded of the Commission's origins in the early days of the 1964 Labour Government. The Commission (they were told) was the 'last relic of old labour';[14] and it should be 'consigned to the graveyard of the Wilson era, together with Neddy and the Department of Economic Affairs'.[15] The Government yielded, and—in a, today, almost unprecedented retreat—was compelled to withdraw the Bill for reconsideration.[16] Not surprisingly, this caused much embarrassment to an already vulnerable Government.[17]

---

[7] Ibid.

[8] The Commission's *Thirty-Second Annual Report 1997* (Law Com. No. 250), para. 1.10, states that the overall rate of implementation of law reform reports is now over 70 per cent. For a discussion of the record of implementation see S. M. Cretney, 'The Politics of Law Reform—A View from the Inside' (1985) 48 MLR 493.

[9] Chorley and Dworkin, 'The Law Commissions Act, 1965' (1965) 28 MLR 675; and see n. 22 below.   [10] Law Com. No. 207, 1992.

[11] The *Daily Mail*. It is right to record that the *Mail's* campaign was—as pointed out by other newspapers, such as the *Guardian*, 2 Nov. 1995—in some respects based on misunderstandings; and few if any would condone the *Mail's* personal attacks on the former commissioner who had been in charge of one aspect of the law reform programme. But, as Michael White wrote in the *Guardian* (above), the *Mail* is 'in many ways, Fleet Street's most politically sophisticated newspaper' orchestrating its campaigns 'more effectively—and more blatantly—than most'; and some of the issues raised by the success of the campaign are important.   [12] The *Daily Mail*, 22 Feb. 1996.

[13] The campaign was not restricted to the Law Commission's work on family law: the *Daily Mail's* coverage of the Commission's Consultation Paper No. 139, *Consent in the Criminal Law*, was headlined 'Law Chiefs propose "licence" for sex perverts'.   [14] The *Daily Mail*, 1 Nov. 1995.

[15] The *Daily Mail*, 1 Nov. 1995.

[16] Lord Irvine of Lairg said that the Government had allowed the Bill to be 'killed off at the eleventh hour . . . by succumbing to a campaign of misinformation by a tabloid newspaper backed up by a tiny and unthinking minority' in the Conservative Party: *Official Report* (HL) 15 Nov. 1995, vol. 567, col. 142. The relevant provisions (with some comparatively minor amendments no doubt intended to placate critics) were reintroduced in the 1995–6 session of Parliament, and now form Part IV of the Family Law Act 1996.

[17] On 27 Oct. the *Daily Telegraph* front page led with an account by its political editor of the pressures which had 'forced the Government into an embarrassing retreat'.

It is easy to dismiss such a campaign as a sensation-seeking attempt to gain support for a 'tiny unrepresentative minority' on the extreme right of the political spectrum;[18] and the Commission itself appeared to believe that silence was the most appropriate response to such criticism.[19] But subsequent parliamentary debates[20] (in which a former Attorney-General[21] described the Commission in the House of Lords as an 'unrepresentative quango' whose proper role was confined to making 'technical improvements in branches of the law', whilst other right-wing members of each House of Parliament expressed reservations[22] about the Commission's part in formulating policy) may be a reminder that even three decades after the enactment of the Law Commissions Act 1965, there are still questions to be asked about the Commission's place in the political structure. For example: what exactly should be the relationship between the Commission and the executive and the legislature? Is the Commission's role to be[23] primarily a 'planning, research and consultative body'? How far should the Commission seek to engage in long-term and systematic reviews as against seizing pragmatically on the opportunities which present themselves? How far are the political and

[18] By the Labour Shadow Lord Chancellor, Lord Irvine of Lairg, *Official Report* (HL) 30 Jan. 1996, vol. 568, cols. 1397–8.

[19] The Law Commission's *Thirtieth Annual Report 1995* (Law Com. No. 239, 1996) does not name the *Daily Mail* and stated simply that the Bill was criticised 'by a small minority of commentators in the national press', but that 'other press commentators'—credited in a footnote as the *Guardian*, the *Independent* and the *Daily Telegraph*—'saw the benefits that the changes would bring'. The author was told by a highly placed Law Commission source that the attention given to the Commission by the *Mail* did not deserve the 'high profile' given to it in the present essay. Mrs Josephine Hayes, a barrister of London SW1, complained to the Press Complaints Commission that the *Mail*'s coverage was inaccurate and misleading; but the Commission regarded 'almost all the specific matters on which the complaint was made to be matters of opinion which the newspaper or the columnists concerned were entitled to express in a vigorous way on a matter of current public debate'. The *Mail*'s columnist was 'entitled to express his view as to the history of the establishment of the Law Commission', although 'in alleging that the provisions of the Bill were unprecedented, the newspaper misdescribed some of its effects' and gave a misleading account of existing legislation. Except to that extent, the complaint was rejected: *Press Complaints Commission, Report No. 34* (1996).

[20] On the Family Law Bill (which incorporated the provisions of the Family Homes and Domestic Violence Bill, modified in some respects to meet the concerns referred to above). The Bill also contained provisions originating in Law Commission reports to reform the ground for divorce.

[21] Lord Rawlinson of Ewell (Attorney-General 1970–4), *Official Report* (HL) 11 Jan. 1996, col. 290. Lord Rawlinson's views are not held by the great majority of lawyers who have commented on the role of the Law Commission; and indeed any comprehensive list of the tributes paid to the Commission by informed judicial, academic and other commentators would fill many pages. The Commission's *Thirtieth Annual Report 1995* (Law Com. No. 239, 1996, para. 1.9) gives references to comments made in 1995 by members of both Houses of Parliament expressing support for the Commission's work in simplifying and modernising the law.

[22] See notably Baroness Young, *Official Report* (HL) 30 Nov. 1995, vol. 567, col. 732: 'members of the Law Commission are clearly living in a completely different world from the one in which I find myself living'. For similarly critical comments on the Law Commissioners' role in relation to divorce reform, see Lord Coleraine, *Official Report* (HL) 20 Nov. 1995, vol. 567, cols. 195–6; Lord Moran, *Official Report* (HL) 30 Nov. 1995, vol. 567, col. 765; Mr Edward Leigh, *Official Report* (HC) 24 Apr. 1996, col. 450; Dame Jill Knight, *Official Report* (HC) 24 Apr. 1996, cols. 770–1.

[23] As the Permanent Secretary in the Lord Chancellor's office assured his Treasury colleague in 1964: see n. 54 below.

moral preferences and social attitudes of the Commissioners to influence the Commission's work?

This is not the first time these questions have been asked. As the departmental papers now available for inspection[24] under the thirty-year rule[25] show, many of them were asked as long ago as 1965. The papers also show that the birth of the Commission was a much more difficult process than has previously been understood; and they throw light not only on the difficulties perhaps implicit in the Commission's mandate but also on the nature of the law-making process.

This essay is primarily an account, drawing on those papers, of the background to the enactment of the Law Commissions Act 1965. It seeks to highlight the matters which at the time seemed important to the officials and Ministers involved. It will become apparent that there was real concern—not previously fully revealed—about significant constitutional issues, and that the Act now on the statute book was far more of a compromise than has been appreciated. It will also become apparent that some of the problems discussed thirty years ago still remain unsolved.

1965: THE BILL WHICH GARDINER BROUGHT TO THE WOOLSACK[26]

The proposal that a body of Law Commissioners be established to take charge of the planning and drafting of law reform[27] measures had first been publicised in 1963 in a collection of essays, *Law Reform NOW* edited by Gerald Gardiner

---

[24] The papers (files reference 3697A/3) in the Lord Chancellor's Department include a file of Lord Chancellor Gardiner's private correspondence on the subject. The author is indebted to Enid Smith (at the time the Departmental Records Officer) for her assistance in producing these papers. The only Home Office file deposited at the Public Record Office under the title 'The Law Commission' (HO307/106) contains no more than prints of the Bill and Act; and—notwithstanding the assistance of the Home Office's Departmental Records department—I have not discovered any Home Office files dealing primarily with the events leading up to the creation of the Commission. There are, however, relevant papers in the Home Office files (HO291/582–635—some of which remain closed under the thirty-year rule) dealing with the Criminal Law Revision Committee.

[25] The author acknowledges the Crown copyright subsisting in respect of these documents.

[26] The Bill as first discussed by officials was so described by Sir George Coldstream (Permanent Secretary to the Lord Chancellor and Clerk to the Crown in Chancery, 1954–68) to the Treasury Solicitor W. A. H. Druitt, 4 Nov. 1964.

[27] For the machinery of law reform before the creation of the Law Commissions, see E. C. S. Wade, 'The Machinery of Law Reform' (1961) 24 MLR 1. For a full account of the work of the Lord Chancellor's Law Reform Committee (established by Lord Chancellor Sankey in 1934, and reactivated on the initiative of Lord Chancellor Jowitt in 1952) see M. C. Blair, 'The Law Reform Committee: The First Thirty Years' [1982] CJQ 64, and 'More legislation from the Law Reform Committee' [1982] CJQ 289. Gardiner had forcefully exposed what he saw as the limitations on the existing part-time bodies. Although they produced recommendations for effective reform in technical areas of the law, Gardiner believed that it was impossible to reform the law of England 'in your spare time on an occasional afternoon', with the result that they 'hardly did more than scratch the soil': see *Official Report* (HL) 1 Apr. 1965, vol. 264, col. 1153.

QC[28] and Dr Andrew Martin.[29] In June 1964—no doubt in anticipation of the General Election in the event held on 15 October—Martin sent Gardiner a draft of a Law Reform (Miscellaneous Provisions) Bill;[30] and this—after[31] the return, with a tiny overall majority,[32] of a Labour Government and the appointment of Gardiner as Lord Chancellor—immediately engaged the attention of officials.[33] In fact, the Law Commissions Act 1965 is recognisably based on Martin's draft;[34] but some central issues of policy proved highly contentious. The first of these issues concerned control of the highly skilled parliamentary draftsmen.

THE DRAFTING OF LEGISLATION: WHO IS IN CHARGE?

For the authors of *Law Reform NOW* it was clear almost beyond argument that it should be for the Law Commissioners to oversee the drafting of all government legislation; and Martin's draft Bill would have required them to ensure that legislative proposals from Government Departments, whatever the topic, should

[28] Gerald Gardiner (1900–90), perhaps the leading advocate of his day, had a long and active involvement in law reform and humanitarian causes: reference may be made to the biography written by his second wife (M. Box, *Rebel Advocate* (1983)) to R. F. V. Heuston, *Lives of the Lord Chancellors 1940–1970* (1987) and to the obituary in *The Times* 9 Jan. 1990. Created a life peer in 1963 on the nomination of the leader of the Labour Party, he had urged the need for the whole of English law to be subjected to systematic and continuous review undertaken by four or five Law Commissioners: *Official Report* (HL) vol. 258 col. 1088. The then Lord Chancellor, Lord Dilhorne, thought that the existing machinery for law reform was 'much to be preferred': col. 1098.

[29] (1906–85). Martin, after a cosmopolitan education in Budapest, Paris and Vienna, had settled in England in 1937, and was called to the English Bar in 1940. Although the object of some disparaging comment (the *Observer* stated that he was 'mainly known among lawyers' as the co-author of *Law Reform NOW* and that he combined a 'part time practice in private international law' with an academic appointment, whilst the former Lord Chancellor Viscount Dilhorne questioned whether Martin could be said to be 'actively engaged in practice': *Official Report* (HL) 14 Apr. 1965, vol. 265 col. 443) Martin in fact had a substantial if specialised practice (see further n. 100 below) and had been appointed to a Chair in International and Comparative Law at the University of Southampton in 1963. He was certainly a man of wide culture (whose musical skills had been developed under the tuition of both Bartok and Dohnanyi) and personal charm; whilst his contribution to law reform in this country speaks for itself: see *The Times* obituary, 2 Mar. 1985.

[30] Martin to Gardiner, 27 July 1964.

[31] No doubt, in accordance with practice, officials in the Lord Chancellor's office had previously considered the commitment to create a Law Commission which had been made in the Labour Party's election manifesto.

[32] Only four, according to the Table in D. Butler and G. Butler, *British Political Facts 1900–1994* (7th edn. 1994) p. 217.

[33] The Labour Party's Election Manifesto, *The New Britain*, had given a commitment to the creation of such a body; and it appears that law reform was the subject of one of the party's election broadcasts: see the reference to Dr H. J. Beynon's unpublished thesis, *Independent Advice on Legislation* (Oxford, 1982) in S. M. Cretney, 'The Politics of Law Reform—a View from the Inside' (1985) 48 MLR 493, 494.

[34] This is a considerable tribute to Martin's skills, particularly in the light of the critical approach traditionally taken by Parliamentary Counsel to the efforts of outsiders.

be 'in harmony with the programmes of the Law Commission for the reform of the law'.[35] Further evidence of the dominant role intended for the Commission was provided by a clause in Martin's draft which would have required[36] courts to have regard to memoranda to be published by the Lord Chancellor explaining the policy underlying each public general Act.

This last proposal was too much for Gardiner, who noted that it would effectively give the Executive power to dictate to the courts the meaning of legislation.[37] But, although that provision was dropped, Gardiner remained determined to secure greater control of the drafting process. He thought it anomalous that the government draftsmen should be the responsibility of the Treasury.[38] Accordingly, he circulated a proposal that ministerial responsibility for the Parliamentary Counsel

[35] Gardiner himself clearly saw the Lord Chancellor's Office as having a central and controlling role in the formulation of all government legislation. 'The new Labour Government goes into action with a very ambitious programme of social and economic legislation, in addition to a number of carefully prepared projects for the reform of the "general law" . . . It is imperative that the Lord Chancellor's Department should be able, right from the start of this great legislative programme, to express an opinion on the best way in which all these projects can be made to fit each other and at the same time to fit into a general trend of development . . .': draft Annex A to Memorandum to the Home Affairs Committee, Nov. 1964.

[36] The courts were also to be expressly *permitted* to have regard to Law Commission or Royal Commission reports.

[37] The Lord Chancellor's officials discussed the proposal with the First Parliamentary Counsel, Sir Noel Hutton. He considered that the provision was 'very interesting'; but repeated the objection (already made by Gardiner) that it seemed difficult to allow Parliament to pass an Act and 'then proceed to tell them what they have done'; and he also pointed out that the American practice (on which Martin had relied) had evolved over a long period of time: Hutton to Coldstream, 4 Nov. 1964. Hutton got 'one of the particularly able people in his office, Francis Bennion' to draft a paper, and the result (dated 17 Dec. 1964) is both erudite and interesting. Coldstream eventually minuted Gardiner: 'At the official level it has been suggested that this question as a whole might be referred to the Law Commission for consideration. They would certainly have an opportunity of making a comparative study of the attitudes of Commonwealth and foreign courts to this problem. But in any event I would not advise you to introduce a Bill with a clause of this kind in it unless you had first given the Judges, particularly the Law Lords, a very full opportunity of considering the implications.' This suggestion was adopted; and the Law Commissions eventually published a *Report on the Interpretation of Statutes* (Law Com. No. 21, Scot. Law Com. No. 11, 1969). But change—of a radical and controversial nature—was brought about by judicial rather than legislative means: *Pepper (Inspector of Taxes)* v. *Hart* [1993] AC 593, HL (critically analysed by F. Bennion, *Second Cumulative Supplement* (1995) to *Statutory Interpretation* (2nd. edn. 1992) Section 217). For a discussion of other attempts to improve the drafting of statutes, see the Renton Committee's Report on *Preparation of Legislation* (Cmnd. 6053, 1975); the Report of the Hansard Society Commission on the Legislative Process (Chairman: Lord Rippon of Hexham) *Making the Law* (1992); and note the Report by the Inland Revenue, *The Path to Tax Simplification* (made under Finance Act 1965 s.160) which envisages a complete rewrite of the primary tax legislation in 'simpler, more user-friendly language, which will be easier for everyone to understand'.

[38] Gardiner's paper accurately stated that the reason why the Office of Parliamentary Counsel to the Treasury had been established by Treasury Minute in 1869 was because of the disproportionate expense, and lack of uniform language and legislative technique, which had previously characterised the drafting of legislation; while there was also 'as far as the Treasury was concerned, considerable difficulty in exercising that close control over all legislative proposals which in the late 1860's was considered to be one of the Treasury's natural responsibilities': Annex A, para. 3. For accounts of the history of the office of Parliamentary Counsel, see F. Bennion, *Statute Law* (3rd edn., 1990) ch. 2; and note the article by Sir Noel Hutton, 'Mechanics of Law Reform' (1961) 24 MLR 18.

be 'transferred forthwith to the Lord Chancellor'.[39] If this were not done, the Lord Chancellor's Department would be seriously impeded in carrying out some of its most important functions.[40] But—notwithstanding Gardiner's assurance that the Treasury's own essential functions would remain unaffected—this apparently mild suggestion for rationalisation immediately aroused a storm of protest in Whitehall. The Secretary of the Home Affairs Committee and the Second Secretary at the Treasury were 'certain'—so Sir George Coldstream, Permanent Secretary in the Lord Chancellor's Department, informed Gardiner[41]—that Ministers would 'take strong exception' to the memorandum intended to be circulated to the Home Affairs Committee in which the proposal had been developed. In Coldstream's view, such a transfer was properly a matter for discussion with the Prime Minister, the Chancellor of the Exchequer and the Lord President of the Council. In any event, matters affecting the machinery of government ought to be discussed by the Ministers most closely concerned before being submitted—as Gardiner had wished to do—to a Cabinet Committee. Sir George Coldstream had no doubt: 'we must accept these views' lest 'our main thesis on the Law Commission be bedevilled at the outset by dissensions on a machinery of government issue not strictly relevant to it'. Gardiner agreed that the offending annex be withdrawn from the agenda for the time being.

In spite of this procedural reverse, Gardiner did not drop the matter. But even his practised advocacy could not outweigh the opposition of the Chancellor of the Exchequer, James Callaghan. In Callaghan's view,[42] there was no reason why the needs of the Law Commission for draftsmen should not be met without making any change in departmental responsibility for deployment of resources. In any case, the fact that Parliamentary Counsel provided a vital common service

---

[39] Draft Annex to Memorandum to Home Affairs Committee, Nov. 1964, para. 6. Sir George Coldstream told the First Parliamentary Counsel—by way of apology for the absence of any prior discussion—that Gardiner had drafted the Annex himself: Coldstream to Hutton, 2 Nov. 1964.

[40] Notably the improvement of the statute book, and advising whether legislation originating in other Departments fitted 'into the overall trend that, in the opinion of the Government, the development of our legal system ought to follow': Annex A, para. 3. It is not easy to imagine how Gardiner would have reacted to the Major Government's initiative (most fully explained in *Official Report* (HC) 14 Mar. 1995, *Written Answers* cols. 464–5) to establish a pilot project for using the private sector in drafting legislation. The potential benefits of this initiative were said to include reducing time pressures caused by the volume of work facing existing draftsmen; widening the range of talent available to Government Departments; bringing relevant specialist skills into the drafting process, and providing fresh thinking as to how laws should be drafted. It appears that outside agencies (two firms of solicitors, one set of barristers' chambers, and a draftsman in private practice) were employed to produce 32 pages of the Finance Act 1996 at a cost (up to publication of the Bill) of £130,000: *Official Report* (HC) 30 Jan. 1996, *Written Answers* col. 614. There are respectable precedents for employing draftsmen from outside the office of Parliamentary Counsel (not least the use of Sir Benjamin Cherry in connection with the 1925 property legislation); and the Government's initiative leaves responsibility for 'ensuring that the clauses and schedules drafted by the contractors are fitted into the Bill in the appropriate place': *Official Report* (HC) 14 Mar. 1995, *Written Answers* col. 465.

[41] Minute of 10 Nov. 1964.

[42] See his letter to Gardiner of 10 Dec. 1994, indicating that he did not accept that the case for change had been made out.

for *all* Government Departments meant that Counsel naturally found their place, for establishment purposes, in the Treasury as the central civil service department. But more important issues (Callaghan thought) were at stake: the matter was one of principle. It was the responsibility of Parliamentary Counsel to advise the Prime Minister, as First Lord of the Treasury, on legal questions affecting ministerial powers and responsibilities and parliamentary procedures. The Prime Minister (Callaghan continued) might well need this advice, not only at the beginning of a new Administration, but on any occasion where there were changes in the machinery of government. It would 'seem anomalous' that the Prime Minister should have to 'turn for this advice to the servants of another Minister. On such occasions, the Prime Minister would wish to keep very much in his own hands the timing of any consultation with his colleagues, and should have directly available to him the services of his own expert advisers.'

Eventually, Gardiner had a meeting with the Prime Minister, Harold Wilson (apparently without any of Gardiner's officials being present); and the outcome was a compromise of the kind for which Wilson was renowned. It would be right (Wilson decided[43]) for ministerial responsibility for Parliamentary Counsel to stay with the Treasury; but, on the other hand, it was important that the Law Commissioners should have the full-time services of draftsmen physically situated with them in the same building. There should indeed be 'some interchange' between the draftsmen at the Commission and the main body of draftsmen in Whitehall 'but this can—and must—be done without putting the Law Commission at risk of draftsmen being taken away from them at short notice at an inconvenient time'. The First Parliamentary Counsel would ensure that the Commission's needs were met; and Wilson insisted that he be told 'right away' should any difficulties arise, and in particular should there be a problem 'about your not having enough men of the right quality to do the job at the pace you consider desirable'. And so there came into being the organisational[44] arrangements which have worked satisfactorily[45] for thirty years. Indeed, it has been said[46] that 'it was a stroke of genius . . . to obtain a permanent detachment at the Commission's offices of draftsmen from the Office of Parliamentary Counsel'.[47] But the notion that the Lord

[43] Prime Minister's Personal Minute No. M.4/65, 11 Jan. 1965.

[44] This is not to deny that there have from time to time been cultural and personal difficulties in the relationships between the Commission's lawyers and individual draftsmen: see R. T. Oerton, *A Lament for the Law Commission* (Chichester: Countrywise Press, 1987) pp. 47–59.

[45] There have, however, been occasional problems in keeping a full complement of draftsmen, e.g. the Law Commission's *Twenty Seventh Annual Report 1992* (Law Com. No. 210, 1993, para. 3.3) reports that although five Parliamentary Counsel had assisted the Commission in that year 'only four of these have been draftsmen serving on secondment from the Office of the Parliamentary Counsel, and at one time the number of these went down to three'.

[46] By Professor Aubrey Diamond, 'The Law Commission and Government Departments' in G. Zellick (ed.), *The Law Commission and Law Reform* (London: Sweet & Maxwell, 1988) p. 27. Professor Diamond attributes this stroke of genius to Lord Scarman, the first Chairman of the Commission; but it is apparent from the text that the real credit belongs to Harold Wilson.

[47] The senior draftsman seconded to the Commission on its creation was Sir John Twistleton-Wykeham-Fiennes (1911–96), a man of legendary intellectual brilliance who (as *The Times*'s obituarist put it on 23 Apr. 1996) 'laid the foundations of what has proved an amicable and mutually

Chancellor and the Law Commission were to be in charge of the drafting of all legislation had gone for good. It was already a far cry from the new Jerusalem originally envisaged by Gardiner and Martin.

THE COMMISSION AND MINISTERIAL RESPONSIBILITY

Even deeper waters lay ahead. Gardiner put his proposal for the establishment of a body of Law Commissioners 'with the standing and salaries of judges of the Supreme Court and supported by a suitable staff of legally qualified officers'[48] to the Cabinet's Home Affairs Committee.[49] He envisaged that the Commissioners would be answerable to the Lord Chancellor; but that they would be left to plan their own work. In practice, he said, the work would fall into a number of 'fairly well-defined categories':[50]

First, the planning of a systematic review of the law . . . This will involve, among other things, devising a more intensive programme of statute law revision and consolidation; examining the possibilities of codification of certain fields of the law; considering proposals received from representative organisations and other bodies for reform of the law; making recommendations as to the appointment of Royal Commissions and other committees to inquire into particular branches of the law and assisting these bodies in

productive partnership'. As Norman Marsh pointed out in lectures given in 1973 at the International Centre of European Studies and Research, Luxembourg, 'something in the nature of a dialogue . . . develops between the Commission and the draftsman, with whom they are in daily contact' and this dialogue may have had a 'fruitful effect so far as what can be called the *prima facie* comprehensibility' of the Commission's draft bills. However, as pointed out at n. 44 above, the relationship between counsel and others concerned is not always easy; and it is to be noted that Fiennes's obituarist records that persistent 'adherence to a bad point could make [Fiennes] tremble with rage'.

[48] Memorandum by the Lord Chancellor, considered by the Home Affairs Committee on Friday 13 Nov. 1964, para. 6.

[49] A draft of the paper had been discussed with First Parliamentary Counsel and officials from the Home Office, the Board of Trade, Housing, the Treasury, the Cabinet Office, the Law Officers' Department, the Treasury Solicitor, the Scottish Office and the Lord Advocate's Department at a meeting held on 5 Nov. 1964. A large number of substantial objections to the original proposals were made; and officials from the Lord Chancellor's Department (Coldstream, Denis Dobson, R. E. K. Thesiger, and J. W. Bourne) put up to Gardiner suggestions for meeting them. These suggestions included the imposition of close ministerial control over priorities by requiring the Commission to submit a planning programme to a ministerial committee for decision on how far it should be carried out; restricting the Commission's freedom to make positive recommendations on policy matters on its own initiative; and the elimination of any suggestion that Departments be required to submit legislative proposals to the Commission: see the note 'Results of Preliminary Departmental Consideration' dated 6 Nov. 1964 (drafted by Bourne). In a letter of 10 Nov. 1964 Coldstream apologised to Sir Philip Allen (the Second Secretary at the Treasury) for the fact that time did not permit a further meeting to consider a revised draft paper, assured him that every point made at the officials' meeting had been 'put to, and personally considered by, the Lord Chancellor' and regretted that the original draft had not brought out sufficiently clearly the Lord Chancellor's view of the Commission as primarily a consultative body which need not interfere with work currently undertaken by Departments. But Coldstream underlined that the Lord Chancellor, although aware of the considerable misgivings felt by Departments, regarded the proposal that the Commission should plan the review of the *whole* of English law and be free to make recommendations affecting any branch of the law as 'an essential part of the plan'. [50] Op. cit. para. 7.

carrying out their tasks; and obtaining information about foreign laws and their operation where such information is relevant to the work of the Commission.

Secondly, the making—on the basis of the review carried out and the information and proposals collected—of positive recommendations concerning the reform of certain branches or topics of the 'general law', i.e. of common law and equity, and also that part of the statute law which does not fall within the province of any particular Government Department.

Thirdly, the drafting of Bills and of detailed explanatory memoranda thereon (which, it is suggested, should in future be, together with certain other authoritative materials, admissible evidence of the purpose that any given piece of legislation is intended to serve).

These proposals were not well received either by officials in other Departments or by the Ministers they advised. The main objection—which seems to have brought the plans for a Law Commission near to collapse—centred on the relationship between the Commissioners and Government Departments. It was (perhaps) all very well for the Law Commissioners to review the law as a whole; but if, having done so, they considered reform to be necessary the appropriate procedure would be for the Commissioners to make a recommendation to the relevant Minister (for example, the Home Secretary in relation to the criminal law[51]); and it would then be for the Minister to decide what further action (if any) should be taken.[52] Although Gardiner had taken pains[53] to still fears that the Commission would

---

[51] The 1964 Home Office files dealing with a request from the BBC for permission to interview the Chairman of the Criminal Law Committee, Sellers LJ, 'on law reform' reveal a background of some hostility to Gardiner. Officials noted that Gardiner had 'contrived early in [a television] interview to give the impression . . . that the Lord Chancellor's Department . . . was responsible for the whole of the law'. Particular offence seems to have been caused by Gardiner's claim to have written to the Lord Chancellor about a criminal law matter to be told by him that this was for the Home Secretary, and then to be told by the Home Secretary that the matter was for the Lord Chancellor. (The Official minuted that he had 'not tried to identify this enquiry: I doubt if the facts are as suggested', but Gardiner continued to use the anecdote: see *Official Report* (HL) 1 Apr. 1965, vol. 264, col. 1146, and 'The Role of the Lord Chancellor in the Field of Law Reform' (1971) 87 LQR 326, 327.) Moreover, Gardiner had 'showed no awareness' of the existence of the Criminal Law Revision Committee; and the writer doubted whether the BBC had appreciated the divided responsibility for the criminal and civil law. The Secretary of State, Henry Brooke (see n. 145 below) took a more liberal line than his officials, minuting that he saw 'no reason why Lord Justice Sellers should not receive or accept an invitation from the B.B.C.'. However, Brooke agreed that it would be 'advisable to make perfectly clear . . . where the Ministerial responsibility lies; and also (if possible) to suggest to Lord Justice Sellers that the B.B.C. may well ask him point blank whether he agrees with Mr Gardiner about the inadequacy of the reform effort, and that we hope he would refuse to get embroiled in controversy of that sort': HO291/586, 10 Jan. 1964.

[52] This point of view is most clearly expressed in a minute by Sir Charles Cunningham (then Permanent Under-Secretary of State at the Home Office) to the Home Secretary dated 24 Nov. 1964 and copied by Cunningham to Coldstream on a personal and confidential basis. Cunningham was prepared to accept that Departments should inform the Commission about their own law reform measures in case the Commission wished to offer any comments, and that in some cases a Department might 'wish to use [the Commission's] services to obtain information, or to ask . . . for advice'.

[53] To the extent that his Memorandum to the Home Affairs Committee proposed the retention of the Criminal Law Revision Committee, thereby abandoning the view put forward in *Law Reform NOW* at p. 10 that the Committee would no longer be needed as a permanent institution but rather that it (along with the Lord Chancellor's Law Reform Committee and Private International Law Committee) be re-established *ad hoc* whenever the need arose to consider any 'major project that the Law Commission . . . might decide to refer to them'.

usurp the governmental function of the Executive,[54] there remained a suspicion that the Commission was intended not merely to be a consultative advisory body but also to have some kind of executive power.[55] And this, as Richard Crossman put it, was something which Whitehall would not have.[56]

What was to be done? An *ad hoc* Committee, chaired by the Lord President of the Council[57] was established[58] to consider the issues and try to find solutions.[59] It is quite clear that the officials involved would have wished to confine the Commission's remit to the Lord Chancellor's own departmental responsibilities and to those parts of the substance of the civil law which were outside the responsibility of any other Department.[60] The Commission might have a role to play in

[54] See in particular para. 9 of the Memorandum by the Lord Chancellor, considered by the Home Affairs Committee on Friday 13 Nov. 1964: the Commissioners would 'draft and comment on proposals for legislation; it will remain for the Ministers to decide whether to act on them and for Parliament to decide whether to accept them . . .'. Gardiner also urged that the Commission could not interfere with other Ministers or Departments, because it would be under the Lord Chancellor and responsible only to him.

[55] R. Crossman, *The Diaries of a Cabinet Minister*, vol. 1 (London: Hamish Hamilton and Jonathan Cape, 1975) p. 75. The account of the Home Affairs Committee's meeting by the then Minister of Housing is revealing. Crossman wrote: 'Gardiner is an extraordinarily inept politician . . . [At] the end of an hour it was clear that his Bill would be totally rejected unless it was sent to a sub-committee and saved there. He had the Home Secretary, Frank Soskice, saying he wasn't going to have his criminal law mucked about by law commissioners and he also had Douglas Jay making the same kind of objection for the Board of Trade . . . we saved the Lord Chancellor from himself by setting up the sub-committee and I found myself a member of it.' It appears that Soskice continued to remain sensitive to criticism of the Home Office's discharge of its responsibilities for the criminal law: on 16 Feb. 1965 he wrote to Sir Eric Fletcher (who as Minister without Portfolio had the carriage of the Law Commissions Bill in the Commons) that he was 'a good deal concerned about the attack which [Fletcher] had made . . . on the Home Office, and by implication on Lord Justice Sellers' Criminal Law Revision Committee'. Although 'slanging the Home Office is an old English custom which I should be sorry to see fall into desuetude' the members of the Criminal Law Revision Committee would 'resent—and justifiably resent—the implications of your reference to them'.

[56] Ibid. It appears that the Lord Chancellor's own officials saw that Gardiner's failure to appreciate the extent to which 'the law' embodied government policy was 'a rock on which [his] proposal might founder'. [57] Herbert Bowden.

[58] The Departments involved were the Lord Chancellor's Office, the Treasury, the Home Office, Foreign Office, Ministry of Agriculture, Ministry of Housing and Local Government, the Board of Trade, the Scottish Office, the Law Officers, the Parliamentary Counsel, the Treasury Solicitor and the Cabinet Office.

[59] The answer to Professor Aubrey Diamond's question (see 'The Law Commission and Government Departments' in G. Zellick (ed.), *The Law Commission and Law Reform* (London: Sweet & Maxwell, 1988) p. 21) whether much thought was given to the relationship that would exist between the Commission and Departments at the time the Law Commissions Act 1965 was being drafted can be seen in the light of this evidence to be 'a great deal'; and with the benefit of access to the papers (which Professor Diamond did not have) it can be seen that his suggestion that the Lord Chancellor's officials may have said to themselves 'We will let Lord Gardiner get on with this. We will not tell him of the problems that lie ahead. He will find out the difficulties in the fullness of time' is not merely cynical but wrong: see in particular the note (drafted by J. W. Bourne) 'Results of Preliminary Departmental Consideration' dated 6 Nov. 1964 which asks Gardiner to consider and give instructions about the 'precise ambit of the Law Commission's functions in regard to departmental responsibility for legislation' as well as many other matters.

[60] A view forcefully expressed from the Law Officers' Department by G. E. Dudman, who pointed out that the 'introduction of a true capital gains tax' was one of the 'law reforms' proposed in *Law Reform NOW*. Dudman suggested that the fields of law in which the Commission was to operate be

formulating the law as an instrument giving effect to given objectives; but the formulation of those objectives was to remain the responsibility of the Departments concerned.[61]

Perhaps unsurprisingly, it proved impossible to resolve this conflict of principle at official level.[62] Fortunately a compromise eventually emerged from the Lord President's ministerial sub committee.[63] On the one hand, the Commissions[64] were to provide the machinery for 'the systematic reform of the law'. On the other hand, there was to be no departure from constitutional propriety. The Commissions were to operate under the ultimate authority of the Cabinet, and Departmental Ministers were to remain responsible to Parliament[65] for any law reform within the field for which they were answerable. These objectives were to be achieved in the following way:[66]

(1)   The Commission would operate under the authority of the Lord Chancellor. It would keep the whole law under review. It would submit to the Lord Chancellor periodically a programme covering a convenient period—say of five or ten years—for the detailed examination of particular aspects of the law or of the law within particular fields. It would recommend how the topics included in the programme should be examined—for example (a) by the Commission itself; (b) by the Home Secretary's Criminal Law Revision Committee; (c) by a body appointed *ad hoc*; or (d) by the relevant Department in consultation with outside experts.

(2)   The Lord Chancellor before approving the proposed programme would consult the Ministers departmentally concerned. It was noted that such consultation might result in some adjustment of the timetable 'e.g. to avoid taking on the examination of a contentious topic at a time which might prejudice

set out in detail. (He presciently identified the law of divorce as an appropriate subject for the Commission's enquiries—a suggestion which might have alarmed Sir Eric Fletcher whose vocal opposition to divorce reform had made him unpopular in sections of the Labour Party: see *The Times*, obituary, 12 June 1990; E. G. M. Fletcher, *Random Reminiscences* (1968).)

   [61]   See Dudman to Coldstream, 30 Nov. 1964.
   [62]   See the Report of the Committee of Officials instructed to report to the Lord President's subcommittee, para. 11.   [63]   It reported on 11 Dec. 1964.
   [64]   Although Gardiner's original view expressed in his Memorandum to the Home Affairs Committee had been that it would be better at the outset to confine the Commission to England and Wales it had soon come to be accepted that there should be a separate Commission for Scotland.
   [65]   This was the principal point on which the Committee of Officials reported that 'some Departments still feel difficulty': see the Committee's Report, para. 2. The Committee of Officials also noted particular concerns of some Departments 'particularly the Home Office: first, that it was impracticable to separate reform of the law from responsibility for its administration; secondly, that the Departmental Minister was alone in a position to weigh the many considerations affecting the desirability of undertaking a particular project of reform; thirdly, if the Commission's plans are to be published (and it seems inevitable that they should be) it is the responsible Minister who will be liable to be criticised for failure to undertake a project which the Commission had proposed to him and it would accordingly be only right that he, and no other Minister, should be responsible for dealing with the Commission. It is plain that some embarrassment is likely to be caused in any event if a Minister is seen to be rejecting the proposals of a body of the high standing of the Law Commission.'
   [66]   Set out in the annex to the Report of the Lord President's Committee 11 Dec. 1964.

the development of the Government's policy in the field in question . . . Failing agreement the issue would be referred to the Cabinet'.

(3)   The programme of work, when approved, would be published; and thereafter, subject to any change in circumstances, the projects for which the programme called would be put in hand by the Commission or the relevant Minister according to the method agreed. Within an approved plan, the Commission would be responsible for (a) putting in hand a comprehensive programme of consolidation and statute law revision; and (b) undertaking the specific projects of law reform which had been agreed (including, where appropriate, the drafting of a Bill).

(4)   Reform recommendations made by the Commission would be considered by the Lord Chancellor if they fell within the areas for which the Lord Chancellor was responsible. If they did not, the Lord Chancellor would transfer the Commission's Reports to the relevant Departmental Minister.[67]

(5)   The Commission's Reports would be published; but it would be made clear that the proposals emanated from the Commission, and accordingly the Lord Chancellor would not be committed to them. In this way there would be no apparent breach of the principle of collective responsibility if, in the event, the Departmental Minister disagreed with the Lord Chancellor.

(6)   Departments were to be under no obligation to consult the Commission on Bills within the Government's main programme of legislation; but the Commission would be available for consultation by Departments in connection with their own examination of particular fields of the law. The Commission would also provide a research and advisory service on Commonwealth[68] and foreign law.

(7)   The Commission would make an annual report on its work to the Lord Chancellor; and the reports would be presented to Parliament.

PROGRAMMES CONTROLLED BY GOVERNMENT

The key element in this compromise is the notion of the 'programme' of law reform. On the one hand (and, as we have seen, against the opposition of some officials) it retained the principle (to which Gardiner and Martin attached so much importance[69]) that it was to be for the Commission to undertake a comprehensive

---

[67] In the event of disagreement amongst the Ministers concerned about implementation of reform proposals affecting their departmental interests the matter was to be referred to the Cabinet.

[68] It should be recorded that Sir William Dale, then Legal Adviser in the Commonwealth Relations Office, had been a powerful proponent of the mutual benefits for Commonwealth and British legal systems which would flow from the establishment of the Law Commission.

[69] Evidenced in the eloquent passage in the Memorandum by the Lord Chancellor, considered by the Home Affairs Committee on Friday 13 Nov. 1964: 'Although there have been from time to time comprehensive and useful revisions of isolated branches of the law (for example, the reviews of property law which led to the legislation of 1925, and of company law which led to Companies Acts of

review of the whole of the law[70] irrespective of departmental responsibility. On the other hand, it was to be for Ministers to decide whether to give effect to the Commission's view that particular areas of the law should be examined with a view to reform and if so by what agency (whether the Commission itself or some other agency such as the Criminal Law Revision Committee[71]). In the result, although significant concessions had been made to departmental susceptibilities[72]— for example, the Criminal Law Revision Committee was to remain the direct responsibility of the Home Secretary[73]—the main institutional structure of Gardiner's

1929 and 1948) there has been no programme of reform leading to a systematic and continuous review of the whole of English law. I am convinced that such a review is needed and that it will never be undertaken unless it is made the principal function of a permanent whole-time organisation. It is quite useless to expect men, however talented and industrious, to undertake such a task if they can devote to it only such odd days as they can take off from their regular work. What is required is a body in permanent being, with proper offices and expert staff to assist them, who can plan the work for a number of years ahead and supervise its execution . . .'

[70] 'The law' was carefully defined so as not to include the law of Scotland (which was to be the preserve of the Scottish Law Commission) 'or any law of Northern Ireland which the Parliament of Northern Ireland has power to amend': see Law Commissions Act 1965, s. 1(5). The intention was (in the words of the Notes on Clauses dated 27 Jan. 1965) 'to ensure that the Commission is responsible not only for the law of England but the whole of the law within the competence of the Parliament of the United Kingdom except the law of Scotland and any law which the Parliament of Northern Ireland has power to amend'. This was of particular significance in the context of consolidation and statute law revision (where the English and Scottish Commissions would act together); but it was also important that the English Commission should be able to deal with Acts applying outside Great Britain, for example, in case amendment of the Fugitive Offenders Act were contemplated. Although the Commission would be responsible for any part of the law of Northern Ireland reserved under the Government of Ireland Act 1920 it was 'not contemplated that the Commission should in practice have to concern itself with the law in force in Northern Ireland, but it is desirable that there should be no doubt as to the extent of the Commission's jurisdiction'. Against this background it is noteworthy that the Law Commission's Report on *Illegitimacy* (Law Com. No. 118, 1982, para. 11.20) explains that provisions amending the British Nationality Act 1981 so as to confer British citizenship on illegitimate children on the same basis as legitimate children had not been included because any 'such amendment would have to await the outcome of consultation with those responsible for the reform of the law in other parts of the United Kingdom'.

[71] This was a matter to which the Home Office attached particular importance: see the Permanent Under-Secretary's minute to the Home Secretary dated 24 Nov. 1964. It is noteworthy that the Criminal Law Revision Committee's remit had been carefully restricted to matters specifically referred to it by the Home Secretary in order to protect Ministers from the embarrassment that would result if the Committee 'pursued questions that raise inopportune issues of policy and to protect the Committee from wasting time on unprofitable topics suggested both by outside correspondents and by some of their own members': PRO file HO291/582. Home Office officials were not prepared to advise acceptance of the suggestion made by the Lord Chief Justice that the Committee be allowed on its own initiative to consider 'minor points . . . on the day to day working of the courts' on the ground that even minor points might raise issues of policy, not merely of administration or machinery.

[72] Departmental fears of publicity had also been taken into account. Dobson minuted the Lord Chancellor on 18 Jan. 1965 that 'a good deal of trouble was taken to ensure that the programmes should not be published until they had been approved'. (Gardiner publicly put a different emphasis on the issue, assuring the House of Lords that the only thing which was not to be published was the Commission's original draft programme: *Official Report*, 27 Apr. 1965, vol. 265, col. 579.)

[73] The Home Office view (as stated by the Committee of Officials) was that the machinery of the Criminal Law Revision Committee, had 'proved satisfactory (so far as it has gone) precisely because that Committee reports to, and works throughout in close contact with, the Home Secretary and his department'.

proposal remained intact. Instructions were given to Parliamentary Counsel to draft the Bill.[74]

LEGISLATION UNNECESSARY?

But the Lord Chancellor's problems were not over. First in point of time was the question (raised, surprisingly, by Sir Noel Hutton[75]) whether legislation was necessary at all.[76] The advantages of proceeding without legislation—the Commissioners could be appointed and get to work immediately, no need to debate in Parliament the precise wording of the Commissions' functions, flexibility to make changes in the light of experience[77]—were obvious. But Hutton must surely have known[78] that the arguments to the contrary[79] carried much more weight with Gardiner. In particular, the fact that a Commission established without a Bill could equally be dissolved by a stroke of a future Government's pen was (and remained) a powerful influence. The draft of a Bill was settled, Gardiner obtained the approval of the Legislation Committee[80] to its introduction in the House of Commons,[81]

[74] At the suggestion of the Lord President a White Paper, *Proposals for Law Commissions for England and Scotland* (1966) Cmnd. 2513, was prepared for publication at the same time as the Bill. Appointments to the Scottish Commission were to be made jointly by the Secretary of State for Scotland and the Lord Advocate; and it was contemplated that the Scottish Commission would be under the 'joint direction' of those two Ministers: Report of the Committee of Officials, para. 12. The Lord President's Committee noted in para. viii of the annex to its report that the Scottish Commission 'while at liberty to make privately to those Ministers suggestions as to the areas of law which in their opinion need detailed examination, would not themselves embark on an examination in depth of any suggested area unless those Ministers (i) agreed with the suggestion, and (ii) did not consider that the subject matter called for examination by some other body'.

[75] The First Parliamentary Counsel, who (as seen above) had been actively involved in the earlier discussions.

[76] Hutton considered that the convention requiring new permanent heads of public expenditure to be warranted by specific statutory authority other than the Appropriation Acts could be met by a single clause Bill.

[77] Probably Hutton was most impressed by the general principle: if 'the Parliamentary convention [i.e. relating to new permanent heads of public expenditure: see n. 76 above] does not apply in this case and we are not altering the law, then prima facie we ought not to have a Bill'.

[78] Hutton's seven-page letter to Dobson dated 4 Jan. 1965 deployed the arguments for and against express statutory provision. He concluded 'we shall have a Bill and . . . the Bill that we shall have is substantially the Bill described in your instructions'; but he thought the question 'ought not to go by default'.

[79] Leaving on one side the fact that a specific commitment to legislation had been given in the Queen's Speech: see *Official Report* (HL) 3 Nov. 1994, vol. 261, col. 13.

[80] At its meeting on 19 Jan. 1995.

[81] The Bill was given a first reading on 20 Jan. 1965. Detailed work on finding the staff and premises for the Commission had already been put in hand by R. E. K. Thesiger: see his letter of 4 Jan. to C. C. Lucas at the Treasury. Thesiger's plan for staffing the Commission was based on the creation of sections, each charged with responsibility for one of the heads of activity to be specified in the Act, i.e. a section dealing with Review of the law, a Reform section, a Consolidation and Revision section, and a Research section. In practice, Consolidation and Revision did come to be treated as a distinct activity, but Review/Reform/ and Research were divided between sections (or Teams, as they came to be called) established by reference to subject matter (e.g. Contract, Criminal Law) rather than function.

and the Bill received a second reading on 8 February[82]—little more than a month after Hutton had questioned the need for legislation.

ALL COMMISSIONERS EQUAL?

Questions of finance, and in particular the question of the level of the Commissioners' remuneration, proved much more difficult to resolve. Parliamentary Counsel was originally instructed to include express provision that the Commissioners should all be paid the salary of a High Court judge;[83] but there was an immediate protest from the Treasury.[84] Gardiner reacted vigorously. The high standing of the Commissioners[85] should be made plain on the face of the Bill. Practising lawyers of appropriate calibre would undoubtedly have been earning incomes substantially in excess of judicial salaries and would not be attracted by anything less than the salary of a High Court judge. Although it might be possible to recruit 'top class academics' for a smaller salary it would be invidious to discriminate between Commissioners of equal status and responsibilities. In any event only small sums of money were involved.[86] But once again his advocacy made little impression on Treasury Ministers and officials. First, it would be wrong in principle to 'follow the quite exceptional procedure of specifying in the statute itself the salaries of the Law Commissioners'; and secondly, on the merits, it would be wrong to pay Commissioners who did not hold judicial office on appointment a salary 'fixed with the special demands of judicial office' in mind.[87]

---

[82] *Official Report* (HC) vol. 706, col. 47. The Bill was considered by Standing Committee A at four meetings between 2 Mar. and 11 Mar. 1965; and subsequent debates are to be found in *Official Report* (HC) 22 Mar. 1965, vol. 709, col. 181 (Report and Third Reading); *Official Report* (HL) 1 Apr. 1965, vol. 264, col. 1140 (2nd Reading); 4 May 1965, vol. 265, col. 830 (Report); 6 May 1965, vol. 265, col. 1029 (Third Reading); and finally *Official Report* (HC) 14 June 1965, vol. 714, col. 175.

[83] Although the suggestion in Martin's Bill (circulated by Coldstream on 4 Nov. 1964) that the salaries should be charged on the consolidated fund in the same way as judicial salaries had been dropped.

[84] 'I was surprised to see that instructions had been sent in regard to the salaries of members of the Commission before the proposals had been cleared with us . . . these proposals give us considerable difficulty—we do not see why a university professor, for example, should be paid the salary of a high court judge for work which is not really comparable': Sir Philip Allen to D. Dobson, 5 Jan. 1996.

[85] Gardiner had emphasised, in his Memorandum to the Home Affairs Committee (13 Nov. 1964), that if the Commission was to be effective, it 'must be composed of men sufficiently eminent in the legal world to command the confidence of the Bench, the legal profession, the civil service and last, but not least, Parliament and the general public . . .'.

[86] Memorandum dated 7 Jan. 1965 putting the case for Gardiner's proposal. Perhaps by a coincidence, on the same day *The Times* published a comment suggesting that there would be difficulty in recruiting lawyers of the standing of those who had served on the Law Reform Committee; and Gardiner forwarded this to the Chief Secretary with a letter reiterating his view that any barrister who was on his 'short-list for a' High Court judicial appointment would expect a judicial salary, so that the only question was whether the three other Commissioners were to be paid 'different amounts for bearing exactly the same responsibility and doing exactly the same work'.

[87] J. Diamond, Financial Secretary to the Treasury, to Gardiner, 14 Jan. 1965. Diamond's letter went on to say that judicial salaries were already 'relatively high compared with others paid in the public service' and that an impending increase could well take a puisne judge's salary above that of

The Treasury had its way: the Act provided[88] that Commissioners (other than a person holding high judicial office[89]) be paid salaries or remuneration at a rate determined by the Lord Chancellor with the approval of the Treasury; and, as envisaged,[90] the rates were eventually set at a rate lower than the salary of a High Court judge.[91]

THE COMMISSIONERS: SOCIAL AND POLITICAL BIAS?

There were other problems about the tenure and qualifications[92] of the Commissioners which did not fully emerge until the Bill was being debated in Parliament. Gardiner had told the Cabinet's Legislation Committee that he intended all the appointments to be full-time[93] but that the Bill had been drafted to permit him to make whatever arrangements about the length of time for which a person should hold office as a Commissioner he considered appropriate in the particular case; and he had in fact envisaged that some of the appointments might

a Permanent Secretary or Cabinet Minister. The amounts involved might be small; but to concede a judicial salary to the Commissioners would 'have wide-ranging repercussions in other fields'. It was 'unrealistic to think that we are concerned here solely with the cost of the salaries of the five Law Commissioners themselves'.

[88] Law Commissions Act 1965, s. 4(2).

[89] As defined by the Appellate Jurisdiction Act 1876 as amended: Law Commissions Act 1965, s. 6(2).   [90] In Diamond's letter to Gardiner of 14 Jan. 1965.

[91] The Minutes of a Meeting held at the Treasury on 8 Jan. 1965 record that the Financial Secretary did 'not completely rule out the possibility of paying' a high salary 'on a personal basis if it could be established that this was necessary to attract a particular individual (for example, a barrister with high current earnings looked [sic] forward to the High Court Bench)'; and it appears that higher rates were at one time paid to practitioners than to those appointed to the Commission from academic life. In the event (see R. F. V. Heuston, *Lives of the Lord Chancellors 1940–1970* (1987) p. 233) the Chairman continued to be paid £8,000 as a High Court judge, the two practising barristers were paid £7,000, and the two academics £6,000 (some £57,000 in 1996 money terms). It is understood that the existence of the differential was not known to those concerned, and that the discovery caused great offence.

[92] The formal qualifications now embodied in the Law Commissions Act 1965, s. 1(2) are that the Commissioners should 'appear to the Lord Chancellor to be suitably qualified' for appointment 'by the holding of judicial office or by experience as a barrister or solicitor or as a teacher of law in a university'. The Notes on Clauses dated 18 Jan. 1965 state that the expression 'judicial office' is not defined, and the Lord Chancellor would be able to appoint to the Commission a person whose judicial experience had been acquired in Northern Ireland or in one of the Commonwealth countries or as a member of the colonial judiciary. However, it was unlikely that the Lord Chancellor would wish to appoint someone whose judicial experience had been acquired outside the Commonwealth. It was also thought unlikely that the Lord Chancellor would wish to appoint a barrister or solicitor whose professional qualification had not been acquired in England; but, in contrast, the Lord Chancellor 'might well wish to appoint to the Commission for a period an academic lawyer with experience of the teaching of the common law in a university outside England and Wales, whether in Northern Ireland, the Commonwealth or even the United States'.

[93] Memorandum by the Lord Chancellor for the meeting of the Legislation Committee on 19 Jan. 1965, para. 1.

be permanent.[94] However, in response to pressure in the House of Lords the Bill was amended to limit the period of appointment to a term not exceeding five years,[95] but with the possibility of reappointment.[96]

Perhaps the most uncomfortable episode for the Government came with a revelation[97] in the *Guardian*[98] of the names of the individuals who were in fact eventually appointed to be the first five Commissioners.[99] There were two sources of embarrassment: first, the absence of any practising[100] solicitor[101] amongst the names mentioned;[102] and secondly, the left-wing bias apparent to some in the proposed appointments. An attempt was made to meet the first problem by appointing

[94] Minutes of the Meeting held in the Chief Secretary's Room at the Treasury on 8 Jan. 1965, p. 1.

[95] An amendment limiting Commissioners' tenure was carried against the Government in the House of Lords: see *Official Report* (HL) 14 Apr. 1965, vol. 265, col. 472. For the compromise, see *Official Report* (HL) 4 May 1965, vol. 265, col. 833. In response to Viscount Dilhorne's expressed concern about Commissioners being suddenly overtaken by premature ageing, Gardiner pointed out that appointments could be made expressly to terminate on incapacity, and it is understood that this is routinely done.

[96] This power has been frequently exercised. The record for long service as a member of the Law Commission is currently held by Norman Marsh QC, who was appointed in 1965 and remained in office until 1978.

[97] J. Churchill of the Lord Chancellor's Office minuted Coldstream that the article was no doubt 'another of Michael Zander's'. Churchill explained that he always tried to give Zander (then Legal Correspondent of the *Guardian* and a lecturer at the London School of Economics) 'anything to which we wish publicity to be given . . . He has always observed any embargo as to time of publication.' This did nothing to allay Coldstream's fury at 'a shocking leak—of which I know the source'. 'Take care vis-a-vis Zander', he counselled.   [98] 'Five Likely Law Commissioners', 17 Mar. 1965.

[99] Sir Leslie Scarman (then a judge of the Probate, Divorce and Admiralty Division), Professor L. C. B. Gower (sometime Cassell Professor of Commercial Law at the London School of Economics), Neil Lawson QC (a practising barrister, who belonged to what the *Observer* described as 'the very left-wing Haldane Society'), Norman Marsh (Director of the British Institute of International and Comparative Law), and Professor Andrew Martin.

[100] The allegation that academic lawyers were over-represented on the Commission evidently worried Gardiner—a man whose subsequent commitment to higher education would not have been predicted by the Oxford examiners who in 1923 placed him in the fourth class in the Final Honour School of Jurisprudence. Stung by an outspoken attack on Martin by Viscount Dilhorne, Gardiner recorded that Martin had had substantial earnings at the bar 'in a type of practice similar to that which Lord Justice Diplock used to have, and which itself requires real brains, and this is why I was rather upset at his being called "a don"'. The passage seems to have been omitted from the final version of the letter sent to the prominent City solicitor Lord Tangley (who, as Sir Edwin Herbert, had been President of The Law Society).

[101] The *Observer* commented that Gower had been trained as a solicitor, but 'in the last few years he has been far from England, telling the Nigerians how to run their law schools'.The absence of a practising solicitor was no doubt all the more embarrassing to Gardiner because Scarman had written 'in confidence' to Coldstream on 1 Mar. 1965 to the effect that the 'Commission may be dangerously weakened if its membership fails to include a distinguished practising solicitor . . . if we are to get whole-hearted co-operation from the solicitors [*sic*] profession I think such an appointment is needed; and I would like to suggest that the Law Society be consulted'.

[102] The Prime Minister had already been embarrassed by the divisions within the structure of the profession: his intention that Sir Eric Fletcher be appointed Solicitor-General had been frustrated by advice that it was constitutionally impossible for a solicitor to hold this office; while suggestions that Fletcher be appointed 'Queen's Solicitor' were also deemed unacceptable: see R. F. V. Heuston, *Lives of the Lord Chancellors 1940–1970* (1987) p. 231; and E. G. M. Fletcher, *Random Reminiscences* (1968).

a practising solicitor[103] to be Special Consultant to the Law Commission;[104] but little could be done at this stage to correct the perception of political and academic bias—the verdict of the profession was no doubt that the Commission consisted of a judge, a practising barrister and three leftish dons.[105] Gardiner protested privately[106] that only one of the people concerned 'had taken any active part in politics, certainly for the last ten years' and that in any event Law Commissioners 'doing a professional job of work, could, as men of integrity be trusted not to play party politics' so that it would not matter if 'three of them were Conservatives, or Liberal, or Labour'. This is, of course, a respectable point of view recognising that many of those active in public life are capable of detachment from party political considerations. But there is surely force in Viscount Dilhorne's reminder that if it is known that members of a committee have political views the usual practice should be 'to try to secure that there is a balance . . . If you have a body with a known political bias, its conclusions may be attacked on that ground and be generally less acceptable than if made by a balanced body.'[107]

THE COMMISSION'S ROLE: ADVISE OR ASSIST?

In one respect, it appears that the Government failed to make a full disclosure of the reasons which led to its accepting amendments to the Bill. As originally drafted the Bill contained a provision that the Commission should provide 'assistance' to Government Departments and others concerned with proposals for the reform of any branch of the law; and the fear that such a provision 'might seem to require the Commissions to provide assistance to such bodies as the National Council of Civil Liberties' led to the insertion in the draft Bill of a condition that such provision be subject to the approval of the Lord Chancellor.[108] But this did not suffice to still criticism. The Government responded by accepting

---

[103] The appointment of Arthur Stapleton Cotton, a prominent Surrey solicitor and member of the Council of the Law Society, was announced in *The Times* on 26 June 1965. Scarman, as Chairman, wrote to the *Law Society's Gazette* that it was intended that Cotton's voice be heard in the inner councils of the Commission: Aug. 1965, p. 463; and the author has been informed by Norman Marsh that Cotton 'functioned exactly like the other Commissioners and was absolutely invaluable with the kind of constructively critical comment which a body of inexperienced reformers needs'.

[104] The retirement of Professor Andrew Martin in 1970 enabled a practising solicitor (Claud Bicknell of Newcastle-upon-Tyne) to be appointed as a Commissioner, and since then there has always been one Commissioner (Stephen Edell, 1975–83; Trevor Aldridge, 1984–93; and Diana Faber, 1994 to date) recruited from private practice as a solicitor.

[105] As Tangley memorably expressed it in the Second Reading debate in the House of Lords: *Official Report* (HL) 1 Apr. 1965, vol. 264, col. 1203. In the circumstances it is surprising that Tangley should have written to Gardiner deploring that the debate had 'degenerated into a party political battle' and offered help in putting down suitable amendments.

[106] In a letter dated 3 May 1965 to his Conservative predecessor Viscount Dilhorne.

[107] Dilhorne to Gardiner, 4 May 1965.

[108] See para. 1 of Dobson's minute of 18 Jan. 1965 to the Lord Chancellor for the meeting of the Legislation Committee on the following day.

amendments substituting 'advice and information' for 'assistance' and confining
the bodies eligible for such help to those whose concern was 'at the instance of
the Government'.[109] It has been suggested[110] (on the basis of the parliamentary
debates) that in doing so—albeit with bad grace—the Lord Chancellor gave way
to 'the rather silly apprehensions of the Opposition' that the Commission might
be used as a method of subsidising political bodies. But one presumably weighty
consideration was not revealed to Parliament. This was that Sir Leslie Scarman
had expressed the view[111] that the inclusion in the Act of a duty to give 'assistance' to the Government would make it impossible for a judge to accept office
as chairman of the Commission: in Scarman's view, the 'only assistance which
a judge can properly offer is *advice*'. In the circumstances, it is strange that Gardiner
should have continued to tell Parliament that he could see no difference between
'advice' and 'assistance'.[112]

THE NEW DAWN: 15 JUNE 1965

There was comparatively little discussion in Parliament of the matters of high
constitutional principle which had so nearly brought Gardiner's original proposals
to collapse; and, although as we have seen the Government had some uncomfortable moments, the Bill, substantially unamended, received the Royal Assent
on 15 June 1965.[113] The Act, in provisions which merit verbatim quotation, embodied the inspirational language of the original Martin draft skilfully adapted to
meet departmental concerns. The Commissions are charged with the duty of taking and keeping the law under review:

with a view to its systematic development and reform, including in particular the
codification of [the] law, the elimination of anomalies, the repeal of obsolete and unnecessary enactments, the reduction of the number of separate enactments and generally the
simplification and modernisation of the law, and for that purpose—

---

[109] Law Commissions Act 1965, s. 3(1)(e).

[110] By Chorley and Dworkin, 'The Law Commissions Act, 1965' (1965) 28 MLR 675, 685.

[111] *Mr Justice Scarman's Memorandum on the Law Commission Bill* dated 28 Mar. 1965, paras.
3–5: 'It is . . . fundamental that a judge must remain independent of the executive. He must not accept
any appointment which would compromise his independence, involve him in responsibility for the
making of policy decisions, or appear to put him in the position of an executive assistant to those
who are responsible for making policy decisions . . . "To provide assistance to government departments" are dangerous words. The only assistance which a judge can properly offer is *advice*. If the
Commission's function be allowed to go beyond that of advice, a judge cannot accept office as chairman. This would, I think, be a disaster. All difficulty disappears if the word "advice" be substituted
for "assistance" . . . [P]rovided the advisory character of the Commission's function is made clear,
the appointment of a judge as its chairman would be a development consistent not only with the traditional role of H. M. Judges but with the part they in fact play in modern society.'

[112] See *Official Report* (HL) 1 Apr. 1965, vol. 264, col. 1222, and 27 Apr. 1965, vol. 265, col. 568.

[113] For the circumstances in which the Bill received the Royal Assent on that day see Chorley
and Dworkin, 'The Law Commissions Act, 1965' (1965) 28 MLR 675, 681, n. 30.

(a) to receive and consider any proposals for the reform of the law which may be made or referred to them;

(b) to prepare and submit to the Lord Chancellor[114] from time to time programmes for the examination of different branches of the law with a view to reform, including recommendations as to the agency (whether the Commission or another body) by which any such examination should be carried out;

(c) to undertake, pursuant to any such recommendation approved by the Lord Chancellor, the examination of particular branches of the law and the formulation, by means of draft Bills or otherwise, of proposals for reform therein;

(d) to prepare from time to time at the request of the Lord Chancellor comprehensive programmes of consolidation and statute law revision, and to undertake the preparation of draft Bills pursuant to any such programme approved by the Lord Chancellor;

(e) to provide advice and information to government departments and other authorities or bodies concerned at the instance of the Government with proposals for the reform or amendment of any branch of the law;

(f) to obtain such information as to the legal systems of other countries as appears to the Commissioners likely to facilitate the performance of any of their functions.

Thus for the first time in history the country had a statutory and professional body charged with the mission of reforming and modernising its law; and, as a result of the determination and effective planning of the Lord Chancellor and his officials, the Commission was able to begin work immediately.[115] Even more remarkably, its *First Programme of Law Reform*[116] was ready little more than a month after Royal Assent.[117] The assessment made by the *Modern Law Review*[118] that the Law Commissions Act provided machinery which, if effectively used, would enable legal rules devised to meet the requirements of earlier ages in which needs were different, to be changed or moulded to provide a

---

[114] The text of Law Commissions Act 1965, s. 3(1)(b) refers to 'the Minister'; but this expression is defined by s. 6(2) to mean the Lord Chancellor in relation to the Law Commission (and the Secretary of State and Lord Advocate in relation to the Scottish Law Commission).

[115] 'The Law Commissions Act, 1965' (1965) 28 MLR 675, 681. But it may be that the decision to base the Commission in offices in Theobalds Road had unfortunate consequences. 'It meant', a long-serving official has written to the author, 'that any meeting with Departmental officials from the Whitehall/Westminster area took up half a day. The Civil Service would never authorise payment for taxis and the available bus service was slow . . . So there were *no* meetings if they could possibly be avoided. Experience has led me to the conclusion that absence of personal *rapport* with Departmental lawyers and administrators has been a major reason for the failure to accept, or implement, some of the Commission's more important Reports. [Lord Gardiner] would have disagreed strongly; but I have come to regard the Commission as an institution complementary to, though independent of, Government.'

[116] Law Com. No. 1 (1965). For comment on the remarkable breadth of the Commission's achievements in its first year, see C. P. Harvey (1966) 29 MLR 649.

[117] The Commissioners had started work with vigour (one being at his desk at 8a.m. on the first working day) and (as the author has been told by Mrs Ruth Deech) their enthusiasm infected all who worked in the Commission. For a sadly different perspective on the Commission in the years after 1972, see R. T. Oerton, *A Lament for the Law Commission* (Chichester: Countrywise Press, 1987), particularly Chs. 5 and 6.

[118] By Chorley and Dworkin, 'The Law Commissions Act, 1965' (1965) 28 MLR 675.

flexible and suitable system for the present, and, indeed, for periods to come[119] seemed to reflect informed and progressive opinion.

Thirty years later it is apparent that, for almost all lawyers, the Commission has been a triumphant success;[120] but, as Chorley and Dworkin also pointed out,[121] the Commission had to live down a 'rather unfortunate start' in the debating chambers of Parliament. The present essay cannot and does not attempt a general assessment of the Commission's role, but it has demonstrated that the really 'unfortunate start' was in the corridors of Whitehall. How far does experience suggest that the concerns expressed in Whitehall and Westminster at the time of the Commission's creation had any substance?

THE COMMISSION AND THE DEPARTMENTS

The archives make it clear that the most powerfully voiced objection to the plans for a Law Commission were based on Gardiner and Martin's claims that it should undertake a central planning role extending to the whole of English law irrespective of departmental responsibilities. Certainly, those concerned to uphold constitutional orthodoxy would have had their worst fears confirmed had they seen the order of battle (apparently produced by Martin[122]) which envisaged, for example, that one Commissioner and his subordinate staff would be concerned with 'Economic Law' (a term which extended to commercial and trade union law) and with 'proposals for, and scrutiny of legislation concerning subjects in the care of other Departments', whilst another Commissioner was to be concerned with Constitutional and Administrative Law (a term which included such topics as the 'legal organisation of the planned economy').[123] The archives make it clear that the often stated view[124] that the 'founding fathers' of the Law

[119] This optimistic view may have been widespread amongst academic lawyers; but others thought the prospects were unappealing. *New Society* commented on 28 Jan. 1965 that a law commissioner would need to possess 'saintly qualities' given that the job was likely to be a 'dead end and frustrating one'; while one senior official has told the author he considered Scarman unwise to accept appointment as chairman since the Commission looked likely to be a 'backwater which would ruin his judicial career'.

[120] It has enjoyed the consistent support of lawyers with widely differing social and political attitudes: see, for example, S. M. Cretney, 'The Politics of Law Reform—A View from the Inside' (1985) 48 MLR 493; whilst it would be superfluous to reproduce judicial tributes to the high quality of the Commission's work.

[121] Chorley and Dworkin, 'The Law Commissions Act, 1965' (1965) 28 MLR 675, 688.

[122] To be found (undated and without accompanying correspondence) in the file of Lord Gardiner's Personal Correspondence: see n. 24 above.

[123] Even after the enactment of the Law Commissions Act 1965, there might have been concern about a rather obscure passage in the *Note by the Commissioners* to the *First Programme of Law Reform* (1965, Law Com. No. 1) which referred to the great respect which English law exhibited for 'both the concept and the application of the rule of Law', but warned that if 'our law is to survive as one of the great legal systems of the world, it is necessary that a proper balance be struck between that concept and the administrative techniques of a highly developed industrial society' (para. 5).

[124] See most recently Dame B. Hale, 'Family Law Reform: Wither or Whither' (1995) 48 CLP 217, 218.

Commission[125] expected the Commission to be principally involved in 'lawyers' law' is simply untrue.

But it is true that, from the outset, the Commissioners in practice exercised considerable restraint in dealing with topics falling within the responsibilities of Whitehall Departments: the broad general statement[126] that a 'great deal would have to be done before it could be justly said that the legal system was in harmony with the social and economic requirements and aspirations of a modern state' led in practice to no more than proposals for review of topics such as strict liability in tort, exclusion clauses and the doctrine of fundamental breach in contract,[127] and even the financial limits then governing magistrates' orders in affiliation proceedings.

It is true that when the Commission did, after consultation, venture into topics for which Whitehall Departments had responsibility, the outcome—in terms of implementation of the resultant Reports[128]—was often disappointing;[129] but there is no evidence that the Commission attempted to seize control of policy making from the unwilling.[130] The Commission has never undertaken reform in such sensitive areas as employment, trade union, or tax law;[131] whilst its approach to reform

---

[125] There were of course, then as now, those outside the Commission who did take this restricted view of the Commission's province.

[126] *Note by the Commissioners* to the *First Programme of Law Reform* (1965, Law Com. No. 1) para. 6.

[127] *Note by the Commissioners* to the *First Programme of Law Reform* (1965, Law Com. No. 1) para. 6. Work on the ill-fated proposal to codify the Law of Contract (which became Item I in the First Programme) was discontinued; but work continues to be done on some aspects of contract law.

[128] The Commission traditionally refuses to regard 'lobbying' Departments about implementation as part of its legitimate function (although it gives assistance to Departments once a decision has been taken): see J. Beatson, *Home Affairs Committee: the Work of the Law Commission* (Minutes of Evidence, 18 May 1994, HC Session 1993–4, 418-i, p. 14).

[129] The Home Office and Department of the Environment seemed to emerge as contenders for the doubtful honour of success in pigeon-holing Law Commission reports; but the extent of the problem of non-implementation is a topic on which different views were held: see M. Kerr, 'Law Reform in Changing Times' (1980) 96 LQR 515; Hailsham, 'Obstacles to Law Reform' [1981] CLP 281; S. M. Cretney, 'The Politics of Law Reform—A View from the Inside' (1985) 48 MLR 493; P. M. North, 'Law Reform, Process and Problems' (1985) 101 LQR 338; and G. Drewry, 'The Legislative Implementation of Law Reform Proposals' in G. Zellick (ed.), *The Law Commission and Law Reform* (London: Sweet & Maxwell, 1988). The emphasis placed on non-implementation in some of the Law Commission's recent Annual Reports (see the account in the Law Commission's *Twenty-Ninth Annual Report 1994* (Law Com. No. 232, 1995, Part V)) also became sharper: contrast the view (expressed in the Law Commission's *Twentieth Annual Report 1984–1985* (Law Com. No. 155, 1986, para. 1.9)) that it is to misunderstand the nature of the Commission's work to judge its success or shortcomings merely by the extent to which its recommendations have been implemented.

[130] On two occasions disagreement about the scope of the Commission's work has been publicly revealed: it was not allowed to include an investigation into the principles governing liability for personal injury, nor did Government accept the Commission's view that Administrative Law should be reviewed by a Royal Commission: see the references cited in S. M. Cretney, 'The Politics of Law Reform—A View from the Inside' (1985) 48 MLR 493, 497, n. 18.

[131] *Law Commission Twentieth Annual Report 1984–1985* (Law Com. No. 155, 1986, para. 1.5). In fact, some effort was put into attempts to improve the form, as distinct from the substance of the Revenue law statutes: see S. M. Cretney, 'The Politics of Law Reform—A View from the Inside' (1985) 48 MLR 493, 499, n. 25; and major consolidation within these areas has been undertaken.

of the criminal law has long been to choose topics and procedures in collaboration with the Home Office.

It is also true that the Commission's insistence on the need to preserve its independence may, even in the very recent past, have led to it adopting procedures which (at least to the outsider unaware of the historical background) seem surprising.[132] But, for their part, Departments came to realise (as one exceptionally well-placed observer[133] has put it) that the Law Commission was not a revolutionary body which would overturn the tables in the Temple.

Over the years, collaboration became the order of the day—notwithstanding fears voiced at one time[134] that this tendency could undermine the Commission's watchdog role, and occasional reminders of the burden placed on the Commission by requests for advice from Government Departments.[135] Thus, the

But it may be significant that the Report by the Inland Revenue, *The Path to Tax Simplification* (made under Finance Act 1965 s. 160) discusses the possibility of establishing a 'new Government body—such as a Tax Law Commission' to rewrite the relevant statutes—and does not envisage that the Law Commissions would have any role in this. The Commission has made recommendations for a statutory right of recovery of taxes in the course of its work on *Restitution: Mistakes of Law and Ultra Vires Public Authority Receipts and Payments* (1994) Law Com. No. 227, and for the tax treatment of structured settlements in its work on *Structured Settlements and Interim and Provisional Damages* (1994) Law Com. No. 224; and these have been given effect in part by the Finance Act 1995: *Law Commission Twenty-Ninth Annual Report 1994* (Law Com. No. 232, 1995, para. 2.17–2.18); *Thirtieth Annual Report 1995* (Law Com. No. 239, 1996, para. 1.16).

[132] For example, the outsider might think it odd that the Commission published Reports on Land Registration only (it seems) subsequently to discover that there was 'significant opposition' to some of the recommendations made therein, 'not least from HM Land Registry', and that it took five years from the publication of the Report for a meeting to try to resolve these difficulties to be convened. The eventual outcome was the establishment of a Joint Working Group which has produced one Report (with draft legislation) and intends to publish a Second Report seeking views on much more extensive reforms to the land registration system with a view to the complete replacement of the Land Registration Act 1925: see *First Report of a Joint Working Group on the Implementation of the Law Commission's Third and Fourth Reports on Land Registration* (Law Com. No. 235, 1995); the Law Commission's *Twenty-Ninth Annual Report 1994* (Law Com. No. 232, 1995, paras. 2.67–2.70 and 3.3–3.6).

[133] H. Knorpel QC (at the time Solicitor to the DHSS, from 1966–7 a member of the Law Commission's legal staff, and latterly Counsel to the Speaker of the House of Commons), in G. Zellick (ed.), *The Law Commission and Law Reform* (London: Sweet & Maxwell, 1988) p. 68.

[134] See in particular Lord Scarman's Jawaharlal Nehru Memorial Lecture, *Law Reform: the British Experience* (1979).

[135] The *Law Commission Thirteenth Annual Report 1977–1978* (Law Com. No. 92, 1978, para. 1.5) forcefully drew attention to the burdens imposed on the Commission by requests for advice on proposals with an international element. The Commission pointed out that, whilst it was impossible always to make a positive response in such cases, sometimes the international initiative was potentially so important for the development of English law that the matter should be formally referred to the Commission under Law Commissions Act 1965, s. 3(1)(e). For a positive account of the value of the work undertaken in the 1970s in relation to the European Community, see P. M. North in *Thirty Years of the Law Commission 1965–1995* (1996), at p. 11. But the *Law Commission Twenty-Ninth Annual Report 1994* (Law Com. No. 232, 1995, paras. 1.21–1.23 and 3.3–3.6) points out the burden of negotiation with Departments on Commission projects, both before and after Report; while the *Law Commission Thirtieth Annual Report 1995* (Law Com. No. 239, 1996, para. 1.10) points out that the 'Jellicoe' procedure 'makes great demands' on those involved.

Commission has included in its *Sixth Programme of Law Reform*[136] 'an examination of such aspects of company law as may from time to time appear to the Law Commission and to the Department of Trade and Industry[137] to require examination' (and it seems that the Commission is increasingly giving assistance to the DTI on the Department's own work[138]) while the Commission has accepted a Reference[139] from the Home Secretary on Evidence in Criminal Cases. There can be no doubt that such collaboration can be remarkably fruitful, as demonstrated by the involvement of the Commission with the Department of Health in work which made possible the enactment of the Children Act 1989[140] and thereby achieved what may well be regarded as a significant contribution to the Commission's committed goal of codification.[141] Even the Commission's Programmes of Law Reform have moved towards identifying detailed items of work to be undertaken over a comparatively short period,[142] rather than the long-term planning of systematic reform to which Gardiner and Martin attached such importance.

In short, in this respect at least, the fears expressed by Departments in 1965 have proved groundless: Ministers and officials remain in charge. The influence of the decision, contrary to the original Gardiner/Martin plan, to underline

[136] Law Com. No. 234, 1995, Item 9. At the time of writing the Commission has a Seventh Programme of Law Reform—apparently to be in the form of a two-year rolling programme—under consideration; and in formulating this programme it will bear in mind its published 'project selection criteria'. The Commission has stated that its 'longer-term aims' include promoting 'good relations between the Law Commission and Government Departments . . .': *Thirty-Second Annual Report 1997* (1998), para. 1.34.

[137] With whom (according to J. Beatson: see *Home Affairs Committee: the Work of the Law Commission* (Minutes of Evidence, 18 May 1994, HC Session 1993–4, 418-i, p. 14)) the Commission had a very fruitful relationship. Cf the view of Lord Gardiner that the Department had 'always acted as if Parliament had conferred on them an exclusive right to propose reforms of our commercial law': (1971) 87 LQR 326, 333.

[138] See e.g. the work on Electronic Data Interchange referred to in the *Law Commission Twenty-Ninth Annual Report 1994* (Law Com. No. 232, 1995) paras. 2.28–2.29.

[139] Under Law Commissions Act 1965, s. 3(1)(e).

[140] See *Law Commission Twenty-Fifth Annual Report 1990* (1991, Law Com. No. 195, para. 2.26); and generally *Law Commission Twenty-Eighth Annual Report 1993* (1994, Law Com. No. 223, Part III).

[141] See Dame B. Hale, 'Family Law Reform: Wither or Whither' (1995) 48 CLP 217. Although codification is one of the statutory objectives of the Commission, it appears that Government does not normally attach priority to measures which merely restate the law (e.g. on confidentiality): see *Home Affairs Committee: the Work of the Law Commission* (Minutes of Evidence, 18 May 1994, HC Session 1993–4, 418-i) p. 9. No. doubt political pressure is responsible for the commitment to simplify taxation statutes referred to in n. 131 above.

[142] See n. 136 above; and note that in its *Sixth Programme of Law Reform* (1995, Law Com. No. 234, para. 1.2) the Law Commission asserted that while the proper performance of the Commission's statutory duties 'necessarily involves . . . long term thinking and planning' concentration on the agenda for a three-year period might help the Lord Chancellor's Department 'to ensure that [the Commission is] furnished with the resources to meet what are comparatively short term targets'. In a *Supplementary Memorandum* to the *Home Affairs Committee: the Work of the Law Commission* (Minutes of Evidence, 18 May 1994, HC Session 1993–4, 418-i) the Commission noted that it was no longer engaged on some of the earlier schemes for major codification (e.g. of landlord and tenant law) but instead was concentrating its resources on 'compact, relatively small proposals for law reform on a scale which Parliament might conceivably handle'.

by statute the Commission's subordination to the Executive[143] on subsequent relationships is a matter for speculation; but there no longer seems to be any substantial risk that the constitutional relationship between the Commission and Whitehall Departments will cause the problems so anxiously discussed at the time.

THE UNSOLVED PROBLEMS: (I) THE COMMISSION AND
THE PARLIAMENTARY PROCESS

The same cannot be said about legislative implementation of the Commission's recommendations. The words of the Home Office's Permanent Under-Secretary in 1964[144] have a distinctly contemporary resonance:[145] 'Whatever theoretical arrangements are made, the limiting factors in law reform will be the availability of draftsmen and Parliamentary time. Discussions about Parliamentary time are in progress; but there must be a limit to what can be done even with a special procedure.' So too does the warning given in 1964[146] to the Lord Chancellor by his own officials:[147] 'in the nature of things Bills with political contents will always get priority' over law reform measures.[148]

In the three decades of the Commission's life there has been extensive discussion of these matters.[149] As recently as 1993, Part I of the Commission's *Twenty-Eighth Annual Report*[150] was headed 'Serious Problems with the Parliamentary

---

[143] i.e. in particular by the provisions requiring ministerial approval to the implementation of programmes: see above p. 92.

[144] Minute by Sir Charles Cunningham dated 24 Nov. 1964: see n. 52 above.

[145] As do the words of the Rt.Hon. Henry Brooke MP (Home Secretary in Harold Macmillan's Cabinet 1962–4, and father of the Commission's most recently retired Chairman) responding to criticism of the Home Office record in making faster progress on implementation of reforms of the criminal law. He explained that the principal difficulty was the lack of parliamentary time, and pointed out that the Law Commission's Bill did 'not appear to tackle' this: see *Official Report* (HC) 8 Feb. 1965, vol. 706, col. 51. See also the response of Lord Chancellor Dilhorne to Gardiner's 1964 speech advocating the creation of a Law Commission: *Official Report* (HL) vol. 258 col. 1105.

[146] The continued validity of the warning seems to be confirmed by the evidence of J. Beatson to the *Home Affairs Committee: the Work of the Law Commission* (Minutes of Evidence, 18 May 1994, HC Session 1993–4, 418-i, p. 14): the Department of Trade are 'much more interested in what trading and consumer interests have to say than what we say'.

[147] 'Results of Preliminary Departmental Consideration' dated 6 Nov. 1964: see n. 49 above.

[148] See also the statement in the Report of the Committee of Officials to the Lord President's sub-committee (n. 62 above) para. 14 that they had made no attempt to consider the possibility of reform in the procedure of the House of Commons to facilitate the passage of Law Reform Bills; but that it was 'obvious . . . that reform on these lines is crucial if a comprehensive plan for law reform is to be realised'; and note the accurate summary by Chorley and Dworkin, 'The Law Commissions Act, 1965' (1965) 28 MLR 675, 682, that the main contention of opposition speakers in the debates on the Bill was that the new Commissions would 'prove abortive unless more effective arrangements were made for passing their measures through the legislative machine . . .'.

[149] See notably G. Drewry, 'The Legislative Implementation of Law Reform Proposals' in G. Zellick (ed.), *The Law Commission and Law Reform* (London: Sweet & Maxwell, 1988).

[150] Law Com. No. 223, 1994.

Process'[151] and the Report complained[152] that the Commission's law reform measures 'however small the measure and however glaring the mistake they are correcting, all face the same titanic struggle for parliamentary time'.[153] But it is clear that some progress—notably the use of Special Standing Committees and Second Reading Committees in the House of Commons and the Jellicoe Special Public Bill procedure in the House of Lords—has been made; and further modest progress may be made by adoption of the specific proposals of the Select Committee set up by the incoming New Labour Government[154] to make proposals for improvement in the procedures for examining legislative proposals. Certainly, the need to have improved parliamentary procedures available to facilitate the expert scrutiny of technical Bills is incontestable; but the question of what is a 'technical' measure remains one on which opinions are likely to differ.[155] Whether the Commission is right to discount the effect of the controversies surrounding the Domestic Violence Bill[156] or whether—as the author inclines to believe—the controversy is likely to have a long-term effect on the plausibility of the Commission's work in areas involving social and moral judgements[157] remains to be seen. That controversy may have destroyed the image, carefully fostered (as the next Chapter of this book[158] demonstrates) at the time of the family law reforms of the late sixties, of the Commission as a dispassionate body of experts advising primarily on matters of technical feasibility.[159]

[151] It is true that the Commission's *Twenty-Ninth Annual Report 1994* (Law Com. No. 232, 1995, para. 1.15) recorded that the 'political climate has now altered, and there seems to be a much sounder understanding at Westminster of the value of the work we do'; and that each House had adapted its procedures to facilitate examination and implementation of the Commission's Reports. But these words were written before the withdrawal of the Family Homes and Domestic Violence Act.

[152] Para. 1.23.

[153] Note also the view of Sir Thomas Bingham MR that the Commission's 'well-argued and compelling proposals for improving the law . . . gather dust not because their value is doubted but because there is inadequate parliamentary time to enact them': 'The European Convention on Human Rights: Time to Incorporate' (1993) 109 LQR 390.

[154] *Select Committee on Modernisation of the House of Commons, First Report, The Legislative Process* (1997–8) HC 190. The Law Commission's *Thirty-Second Annual Report 1997* (1998), para. 1.22 notes that the Select Committee considered many of the points made in a submission by the Law Commission 'could be met by specific but generally applicable proposals which they made'; but the Commission asserted that it would still 'continue to press for more fundamental change'.

[155] Note that the Family Homes and Domestic Violence Bill was thought to be sufficiently technical to make it apt for the Jellicoe procedure; and the embarrassing withdrawal occurred after that procedure had been completed. [156] See text to n. 11 above.

[157] It may be significant that the Government was quick to announce that it did not intend to proceed with legislation recommended by the Commission in its *Report on Mental Incapacity* (1995) Law Com. No. 231 which had also been the subject of some—as the Commission point out, uninformed—press criticism: *Official Report* (HL) 16 Jan. 1996, vol. 568, WA 43. However, the Government subsequently published its own consultation paper (drawing extensively on the Commission's work, which was of exceptionally high quality) into these matters, although one of the issues to be considered is whether legislation in some areas is appropriate at all.

[158] 'Putting Asunder and Coming Together: Church, State and the 1969 Divorce Reforms', Ch. 2 below.

[159] In this context, it is tempting to speculate on the reasons which have apparently led the Law Commission to reclassify its examination of 'the property rights of home-sharers' (which appeared as part of Item 8 'Family Law' in the Commission's *Sixth Programme of Law Reform* (Law Com.

THE UNSOLVED PROBLEMS: (II) THE LAW COMMISSION
AS A POLITICAL INSTITUTION

The first appointments to the Law Commission[160] of what some saw as an unrepresentative group of left-wing intellectuals gave rise to concern that the
Commission would manipulate the development of the law in accordance with
the Commissioners' own political philosophy. Experience soon demonstrated that
there was no foundation for fears that the Commissioners would engage in political activity as traditionally understood: the Commission hardly needs to assert
that it is 'totally outside party politics'[161] but it is much more difficult convin-
cingly to meet concerns that the Commissioners would go beyond the task of
simplifying the complex and stray into areas of policy formation which ought to
be resolved by Parliament.[162] Indeed, the Commission has—with Reports on
Blasphemy and other contentious areas of the criminal law, Landlord and Tenant,
and Family Law—almost defiantly ignored suggestions made in 1965 that it should
confine its work to what is usually called lawyers' law.[163] Of course, on one view[164]

No. 234, 1995)) as a matter of 'Property and Trust Law': see *Law Commission Thirty-First Annual
Report 1996* (Law Com. No. 244, 1997, Part V). The Commission has noted that a 'wide range of
opinions' are held and that 'some people view with concern proposals which might seem to support
or encourage couples to enter into non-marital cohabitation instead of marriage' (*Law Commission
Thirtieth Annual Report 1995* (Law Com. No. 239, 1996, para. 6.10)); but this seems unlikely to
allay the concern expressed in a letter from the Chairman of the Conservative Christian Fellowship
to *The Times* (6 Feb. 1998) about the 'libertine Law Commission's advocacy of increased rights for
cohabiting couples'.

[160] See p. 18 above.

[161] As the Law Commission's *Thirty-Second Annual Report 1997* (1998) states in para. 1.30.

[162] As Sir Ivan Lawrence put it in the course of evidence to the *Home Affairs Committee: the
Work of the Law Commission* (Minutes of Evidence, 18 May 1994, HC Session 1993–4, 418-i,
q. 12); and see generally the discussion at pp. 5–7.

[163] See notably Sir J. Hobson, *Official Report* (HC) 8 Feb. 1965, vol. 706, col. 59; Sir Hugh Lucas
Tooth, at col. 98; Leo Abse (expressing—paradoxically in view of his subsequent success in achiev-
ing divorce law reform with the collaboration of the Law Commission—reservations about the
Commission undertaking legislation impinging on human relationships) at col. 128; and Viscount
Dilhorne, *Official Report* (HL) 1 Apr. 1965, vol. 264, col. 1166. But it was not only professional
politicians who expressed such views: Lord Tangley (see n. 100 above) said that if the Law
Commission either initiated or considered changes in the law dealing with deep moral or political
problems 'they might as well finish their work altogether because they would lose all power and
respect' at col. 1203; while Lord Denning (at col. 1213) thought the Commission should not seek
to take over broad questions of policy in the law (such as the emancipation of women) but rather
confine itself to filling gaps in the law.

[164] Which the author tried to develop in his Inaugural Lecture at Bristol University on 25 Oct.
1984: see S. M. Cretney, 'The Politics of Law Reform—A View from the Inside' (1985) 48 MLR
493. It must be conceded that there are some exceptions; for example, it is not easy to identify scope
for controversy in the proposal made by the Law Commission in its report on *Property Law: Title
on Death* (1989, Law Com. No. 184) that the legal estate in land vest in the Public Trustee rather
than in the President of the Family Division: see now Law of Property (Miscellaneous Provisions)
Act 1994. On the other hand it remains the author's view that even highly technical law reform may
become controversial: for example, some may think reform of the Rules against Perpetuities and

all law reform must (in so far as it will involve value judgements and change in legal rights and duties) have a political element;[165] but even those who would not go so far find difficulty in explaining what mandate the Commissioners have to recommend change in the law affecting their fellow citizens' lives; and this is all the more so in those areas—such as the circumstances in which medical treatment may be withdrawn—in which strong (if not always particularly well-informed or sophisticated) views are held. The Commission is wont to justify its role by reference to its consultation process; but whether such consultation can fairly be regarded as reflecting public opinion is questionable. The Law Commission's Consultation Paper on *Domestic Violence and Occupation of the Family Home*, for example, attracted responses from thirty-three national and local organisations and twenty-three individuals (most of whom were academic and practising lawyers or members of the judiciary); and it may well be asked just how representative such a sample could be.[166] The Commission has, from time to time—for example in its work on Family Property, Intestate Succession, and Divorce—made use of attitude surveys but the data provided by such surveys may be capable of more than one interpretation.[167]

Accumulations (as recommended in the Law Commission's *Report on The Rule against Perpetuities and Excessive Accumulations* (1998, Law Com. No. 251)) could raise difficult issues of economic policy, but see the discussion at paras. 2.30–2.38.

[165] Hence, consolidation measures and statute law revision should usually be (and have traditionally been) uncontroversial and are dealt with by special procedures. There are, however, exceptions even here: see the difficulties encountered in the consolidation of the Chronically Sick and Disabled Persons Act 1970: S. M. Cretney, 'The Politics of Law Reform—A View from the Inside' (1985) 48 MLR 493, 502; and note that the Attorney-General's statement in the proceedings leading to the Marriage Act 1949—the first consolidation measure to be dealt with under the Consolidation of Enactments (Procedure) Act 1949 allowing 'minor corrections and improvements' in consolidation measures—that the vellum industry was 'dead or dying' and that accordingly the historic requirement for certain certificates to be on 'vellum or parchment' ought to be replaced by a provision stipulating merely the use of 'durable materials' led to a furious protest by Messrs Band & Co. to the effect that they could themselves supply an almost unlimited amount of the traditional materials: PRO file LCO2/6674.

[166] See S. M. Cretney, 'Family Law: A Bit of a Racket?' (The Joseph Jackson Memorial Lecture) (1996) 146 New LJ 91, 92.

[167] For example, the Public Opinion Survey on the Ground for Divorce revealed that 84 per cent of the sample thought that the present law was satisfactory because one person could start proceedings at once if the other had committed adultery or behaved intolerably (see *The Ground for Divorce* (Law Com. No. 192, 1990) App. D para. 1.4); and the same percentage thought fault-based divorce to be acceptable; while overall there was an equal division of opinion on whether the law should be changed at all. It may be questioned whether these findings support recommendations for change involving a compulsory period of delay however intolerable the respondent's behaviour, yet those were the Commission's recommendations. Again, the Commission's survey into *Intestacy* (Law Com. No. 187, 1989) suggested that, although the whole of an intestate's estate should generally pass to a surviving spouse rather than to children, less than a third of the sample thought that this principle should apply to cases in which the surviving spouse was the deceased's second wife. Yet the Commission recommended that the whole estate should pass to a surviving spouse, irrespective of how many children the intestate might have had by others. Even more surprisingly, the Commission expressed strong disapproval of the Government's decision to reject their proposal: see *Twenty-Eighth Annual Report 1993*, para. 3.6–3.9 and Ch. 10 below.

The dilemma is certainly worrying; but possibly the most persuasive answer to the problems of authority and accountability is, paradoxically, to be found in the subordination, already explained, to accountable Ministers. The Commission —like a Royal Commission or a Departmental Committee—advises; Ministers and Parliament decide. In taking their decision they will of course be influenced by the evidence marshalled by the Commission in support of the recommendations; but the judgement about whether that evidence is convincing remains a matter for those who are directly accountable to the community.

The difficulty with this approach is that it tends towards non-implementation. If there is any fear of controversy, or even if officials can plausibly suggest the possibility of controversy,[168] Ministers may simply take no action.[169] In that event, the fate of the recommendations depends on the chance of whether or not a private member of either House of Parliament is able to take up the Bill;[170] and even if such a member is found, the possibility of opposition may at worst kill the Bill or at best lead to its being significantly amended.[171]

Some modest progress has been made in agreeing procedures whereby Government Departments will give a speedy response to Law Commission Reports;[172]

[168] See, for example, the remarks of the Lord Chancellor on the Bill for the Land Registration Act 1988 (*Official Report* (HL) 25 Nov. 1987, vol. 490, col. 691): 'Although the principle of an open register presents many attractions . . . it was felt this was a decision which should not be hurried.'

[169] As noted above, some 70 per cent of all Law Commission Reports recommending reform have been implemented in whole or in part, but in evidence to the House of Commons Home Affairs Committee (*The Work of the Law Commission*, Minutes of Evidence, 18 May 1994, HC Session 1993–4, 418-i, p. 16) the Commission stated that only eleven of the forty-six then unimplemented reports had been in terms rejected.

[170] There have been some significant achievements in this respect—in recent years the Land Registration Act 1988 was introduced by Lord Templeman; the Computer Misuse Act 1990 by Mr Michael Colvin MP; the Access to Neighbouring Land Act 1992 by Lord Murton of Lindisfarne; the Carriage of Goods by Sea Act 1992 by Lord Goff of Chieveley; and the Sale of Goods (Amendment) Act 1995 by Lord Mustill. The role of peers will be noted (cf. *Parliamentary Procedures and the Law Commission, A Research Study*, by P. Hopkins with a foreword by the Law Commission (1994), Parts V and VI); and it will also be seen that difficulties in giving effect to the Commission's recommendations were revealed in the course of parliamentary debates on these measures.

[171] As in the case of the Access to Neighbouring Land Bill, introduced by Mr John Ward MP and taken through the House of Commons as a Private Members Bill 'on the nod'. Opposition to some features of the Bill was voiced in the Second Reading Debate in the House of Lords on 16 July 1991; and for this and other reasons the Bill did not make further progress in that session. In the following session Lord Murton of Lindisfarne reintroduced a Bill amended to take account of those objections (from bodies such as the Country Landowners' Association, the Royal Institute of Chartered Surveyors, and the National Trust: see *Official Report* (HL) 11 Dec. 1991, vol. 533, col. 822) and this became law. The Law Commission expressed sorrow that 'pressure from certain landowning interests . . . forced changes to our recommendations in two significant respects' (*Twenty-Seventh Annual Report 1992* (Law Com. No. 210, 1993) para. 1.7)—thereby displaying a degree of commitment to its own assessment of the balance of competing interests almost as surprising as its continued and forcefully expressed commitment to its proposals for changing the rules of intestate distribution: see further Ch. 10 below.

[172] See the Law Commission's *Thirty-Second Annual Report 1997* (1998), paras. 1.11–1.12. Relevant Departments have agreed that they will normally give the Law Commission an initial response to a Report within six months and a final response 'without unreasonable delay', and that they will

and it may be that these procedures will over the years be effective in reducing what appears to be the main problem—i.e. the Executive's failure on occasion to grasp the nettle and give proper consideration to carefully prepared reform proposals. It may also be that some further progress can be made[173] by developing formal links between the Law Commission and a Parliamentary Committee overseeing the machinery of law reform which would have an input from members of both Houses of Parliament and might be able to identify on the one hand those issues which are controversial or raise sensitive issues of policy and substance and are thus meet for full debate[174] and, on the other hand, those which can properly be regarded as uncontroversial and thus suitable for some special streamlined legislative process. But it would be unwise to minimise the temptation for politicians to manipulate for party advantage any procedure which could be devised,[175] whilst it is also clear that the preferences and priorities of a professional law reform agency will often be markedly different from those of practising politicians.[176] The fundamental problem remains that law reform is essentially a political act, and that in a parliamentary democracy it is for the elected government to take decisions and assume the responsibility for doing so. Trust in the Law Commission[177] is unlikely to be reinforced by perpetuating the pretence—so effective, as we see in the next Chapter, in the early days of the Commission's work on family law—that the Commission's function was

give the Commission an opportunity to comment on any major obstacle they see to implementing the Report.

[173] As suggested by Lord Irvine when 'shadow' Lord Chancellor: 'The Legal System and Law Reform under Labour', D. Bean (ed.), *Law Reform for All* (1996) pp. 28–9.

[174] But it is not always realised that the impact of apparently technical legislation may only appear when proposals are critically examined; and in this respect the adversarial system has something to offer. The history of the Family Homes and Domestic Violence Bill may suggest that any committee should be serviced by a secretariat specifically concerned to probe the implications of what is proposed and to seek out those with views not necessarily represented in formal consultation on law reform exercises.

[175] See, for example, the breakdown in collaboration between the political parties which, in 1993, led to the frustration of plans to bring forward five 'small but useful law reform measures': The Law Commission's *Twenty-Eighth Annual Report 1993* (1994, Law Com. No. 223). It may also be thought that Lord Irvine's speech on 30 Jan. 1996 on the Committee stage of the Family Law Bill evidences how fragile such collaboration may be. He claimed that the Government's actions in withdrawing the Family Homes and Domestic Violence Bill (after the Bill had been fully considered by a Public Bill Committee in the House of Lords) and subsequently reintroducing a Bill amended to take account of the criticisms made by some of the Government's supporters imperilled the use of the Public Bill Committee in the future. 'Assuaging uninformed minorities does not facilitate all-party agreements which alone can be the foundation for utilising the Jellicoe procedure in the future': *Official Report* (HL) vol. 568, cols. 1397–8.

[176] Note the statement in the Law Commission's *Twenty-Ninth Annual Report 1994* (Law Com. No. 232, 1995, para. 1.19) that the difficulty in the way of using a special procedure for such matters was that 'the House of Commons has always interested itself in the criminal law' and that 'some way must be found whereby the needs of members of the House of Commons can be effectively reconciled with the need to convert the bedraggled state of the criminal law into an efficient working tool for law enforcement'.

[177] Which, as Sir Henry Brooke put it in the Foreword to the *Law Commission Twenty-Ninth Annual Report 1994* (Law Com. No. 232, 1995), it is 'vitally important to preserve'.

simply to give objective and disinterested advice on technical matters. Law Commissioners have their own values[178]—political, moral and philosophical— which must inevitably affect the content of the Commission's proposals.[179]

[178] As pointed out above, the first Commissioners were appointed on the basis of Lord Chancellor Gardiner's personal knowledge; but over the years the system has gradually evolved and latterly vacancies have been advertised and filled after formal interview with officials of the Lord Chancellor's Department, the Chairman of the Commission, and others. Information about Commissioners has usually been confined to bland articles in the professional press, and it is rare for Commissioners to reveal much about their own values. Exceptionally, on 16 Feb. 1984 *The Times* quoted the newly appointed Mrs Brenda Hoggett (then a Reader in Law at the University of Manchester) as saying 'I am a feminist of the kind who would like to see changes in the way society is organised, rather than wanting women to conform to male-determined roles' and reported that Mrs Hoggett (who after some ten years' service as a Law Commissioner was appointed to the High Court bench as Dame Brenda Hale) saw the law as 'dominated by men and their concerns'.

[179] This Chapter reproduces, with minor amendments, a paper originally published in (1996) 59 MLR 631. Two of the original Law Commissioners (Mr Norman Marsh CBE QC and the late Professor L. C. B. Gower OBE QC FBA), one recently retired Law Commissioner (Professor Jack Beatson), one of the first members of the Law Commission's legal staff (Mrs Ruth Deech), two former officials of the Lord Chancellor's Department (Sir Wilfrid Bourne KCB QC and Sir Derek Oulton GCB QC), a practising solicitor with great experience of the working of the Lord Chancellor's Department (Mr Cyril Glasser), and two academic lawyers with interests in public law (Miss A. L. C. Davies and Professor David Feldman) kindly read a draft; but the statement that the author is solely responsible for any errors and for all statements of opinion is in this case more than conventional since at least one of those named strongly disagrees with some of the views expressed.

2*

Putting Asunder and Coming Together: Church, State and the 1969 Divorce Reforms

INTRODUCTION

In 1963 the law still denied divorce except to those who could provide evidence sufficient to convince a court[1] of a partner's adultery or other matrimonial offence.[2] In that year, a determined attempt was made to change the law to allow divorce where a couple had lived apart for at least seven years. The attempt failed. But less than a decade later the Divorce Reform Act 1969 allowed divorce if the parties had lived apart for two years (and both consented) or five years (if one did not consent). How did such a dramatic change come about in what, in this context,[3] seems a remarkably short time?

One answer no doubt lies in what could be called 'the spirit of the age'. 1963 was, after all, the year in which (according to Philip Larkin[4]) 'sexual intercourse began'. It was also the year of the so-called Profumo affair in which a Minister of the Crown admitted lying to Parliament about his relationship with a woman;[5] and unprecedented press publicity was given to the surrounding events and rumours. (For example, another Minister was said to indulge in 'weird sexual practices' involving his appearing naked—save for a mask—at parties.[6]) Lord Denning's exhaustive investigation[7] into these matters (concluding[8] that although there had

---

* This Chapter (which has not been published elsewhere) draws in particular on the *Ramsey Papers* and the Papers of the Archbishop's Group preserved in Lambeth Palace Library. The author has also benefited from discussion with the late Professor L. C. B. Gower and comments on a draft made by J. M. Cartwright Sharp, P. S. C. Lewis and Mrs Ruth Deech (all of whom were members of the Legal Staff of the Law Commission at the relevant time), Mr Leo Abse and Sir William van Straubenzee (both then Members of Parliament) and Professor David McClean QC.

[1] In theory, the court required a high standard of proof, but in practice divorce could usually be obtained if both husband and wife were agreed on this outcome: see the evidence of L. C. B. Gower to the *Royal Commission on Marriage and Divorce, Minutes of Evidence*, Paper No. 3 and First Day 20 May 1952; and see further n. 44 below.

[2] 'To end dead marriages, adultery had to be committed or affected, the mutuality of partings had to be masked under the pretence of desertion, and puffed-up allegations of sadistic conduct had to be mounted to establish proof of cruelty': L. Abse, *Private Member* (1973) p. 159.

[3] It had taken a quarter of a century for reforms—adding cruelty, desertion, and incurable insanity to adultery as grounds for divorce—recommended by the Royal Commission on Divorce and Matrimonial Causes (1912) Cd. 6478 to be enacted in the Matrimonial Causes Act 1937: see for the background S. Redmayne, 'The Matrimonial Causes Act 1937: A lesson in the art of compromise' [1993] OJLS 183.　　　　　　　　　　　　　　　　　　　　　　[4] *Annus Mirabilis* (1967).

[5] Described on television by another Minister as a 'strumpet'.

[6] *Lord Denning's Report* (Cmnd. 2152, Sept. 1963) para. 319.

[7] *Lord Denning's Report* (Cmnd. 2152, Sept. 1963).

[8] *Lord Denning's Report* (Cmnd. 2152, Sept. 1963) paras. 319–27.

indeed been orgies where guests indulged in 'sexual activities of a vile and revolting nature' and that it was true dinner had been served by a naked masked man
yet there was not a 'shred of evidence' that the man in question was a Minister)
did little to calm the fevered atmosphere.[9] In the circumstances, it became
increasingly difficult to believe that civilisation would be endangered by allowing the thousands of (often elderly and usually eminently respectable) couples
living together in what came to be called 'stable illicit unions' to crush the 'empty
legal shell' of an earlier marriage so that they could become in law what they
had long been in fact.

The way in which attitudes change on such issues is a fascinating subject but
one which must be left to the social historian.[10] This essay is concerned with a
much narrower topic: how the Report of a committee set up by the Archbishop
of Canterbury[11] was used to influence opinion and provide a justification for the
changes made in the law in 1969—changes which in a number of important respects
can be seen to have been inconsistent with the fundamental principles underlying the committee's thinking. The Records of the Archbishop's Group,[12] and Official
Papers deposited in the Public Records Office for the relevant period,[13] have recently
come into the public domain, and throw some light on these matters.

It is necessary to put the setting up of the Archbishop's Group into context,
and for this purpose first to go back to the 1950s.

THE BACKGROUND—(I) THE GENESIS OF 'IRRETRIEVABLE
BREAKDOWN' AS GROUNDS FOR DIVORCE: MRS EIRENE WHITE'S
MATRIMONIAL CAUSES BILL 1951

The massive increase in divorce associated with the two twentieth-century
World Wars[14] had been a source of grave anxiety to conventional opinion, which

---

[9] An excellent account of the events 'in that strangely hysterical year of 1963' is given in Prime
Minister Macmillan's official biography, A. Horne, *Macmillan 1957–1986*, pp. 471–97.

[10] Leo Abse (for whose role in bringing about reform see below) has provided his own fascinating
account of the 'powerful but [not] easily definable forces' working on the side of reform: L. Abse,
Private Member (1973) p. 167.

[11] *Putting Asunder, A Divorce Law for Contemporary Society* (1966).

[12] The Records, impeccably catalogued and preserved at the Lambeth Palace Library, include the
Minutes of the Archbishop's Group on Reform of the Divorce Laws (MS 3460) and material in the
Ramsey Papers vols. 43, 62, 82, 102, and 117.

[13] Regrettably, many of the relevant Law Commission papers have been destroyed; whilst
searches of the Lord Chancellor's Department's records for the relevant period suggest that much
material from that source has also been destroyed. As will emerge, it has proved possible to fill many
of the gaps from the Lambeth Palace archive. The author gratefully acknowledges the considerable
assistance given by the Secretary of the Law Commission and the Departmental Records Officer in
the Lord Chancellor's Office in identifying the files which have survived and those which were destroyed.

[14] See Ch. 6, below. The 1956 *Royal Commission on Marriage and Divorce* (Chairman: Lord Morton
of Henryton) (1956, Cmd. 9678) took a particularly gloomy view of the fact that the increase had
been far greater after World War II than the 'comparatively modest' increase after World War I. The

saw in the 'insidious growth' in the divorce rate a 'tendency to take the duties and responsibilities of marriage less seriously than formerly' and a threat to the 'whole stability of marriage' as the 'basis of a secure and stable family life'.[15] At a somewhat less lofty level, those concerned with the administration of the family justice system became preoccupied with avoiding its collapse under the apparently relentless pressure of divorce petitions.[16] But even amongst those who firmly believed the ideal of marriage—in particular as a way of providing children the 'settled and harmonious life on which so much of their future happiness depends'[17]—to be the traditional union 'for better for worse, for richer for poorer . . . till death us do part'[18] there was concern about the lot of the hundred thousand or more people[19] living apart from their legal spouses in stable unions to which the law denied recognition. The impossibility of legalising such relationships against the will of an 'innocent' legal spouse denied many men and women (and in particular the children they bore) adequate social and financial protection.[20]

In 1951 in an attempt to meet this concern, Mrs Eirene White had introduced a Private Member's Bill[21] into the House of Commons,[22] avowedly intended 'to deal with marriages in which the spouses have lived separately for seven years, but in which no hitherto recognised ground for divorce exists or in which one partner, having grounds for action, declines to take it and keeps the other partner tied against his or her will, generally for life'. The Bill did this by invoking 'a new principle, in that it looks to the breakdown of the marriage as the ground for divorce'[23] (whilst not prejudicing the right of an injured party to seek divorce

---

Commission quoted the Registrar-General as saying that 'the effect of the First World War was to cause fifteen *hundred* more petitions to be filed each year and of the Second World War to cause 20 *thousand* more petitions to be filed each year' and was particularly alarmed that the hopes that the increase would be merely temporary seemed to have been falsified.

[15] *Report of the Royal Commission on Marriage and Divorce* (Chairman: Lord Morton of Henryton) (1956, Cmd. 9678) paras. 47, 49 and 37.   [16] See Ch. 6, below.

[17] Mrs Eirene White MP, moving the Second Reading of the Matrimonial Causes Bill: *Official Report* (HC) 9 Mar. 1951, vol. 485, col. 926; see further below.

[18] The vow prescribed by the Book of Common Prayer and taken by those marrying in the Church of England. In Register Office weddings the man had simply to say to the woman that he took her to be his 'lawful wedded wife' and vice versa (Marriage Act 1949, s. 44(3), now modernised by Marriage Ceremony (Prescribed Words) Act 1996) but administrative steps were taken (see Registrar-General's Circular No. 8 of 1947)—following the recommendation of the *Committee on Procedure in Matrimonial Causes* (Chairman: the Hon. Mr Justice Denning) (1947, Cmd. 7024) paras. 29(xiii) and 87, I, 4—'to emphasise the solemnity of the occasion and clearly to express the fundamental principle that marriage is the personal union, for better or for worse, of one man with one woman, exclusive of all others . . . so long as both shall live'.

[19] Mrs White's estimate: *Official Report* (HC) 9 Mar. 1951, vol. 485, col. 927.

[20] Mrs Eirene White MP, *Official Report* (HC) 9 Mar. 1951, vol. 485, col. 928.

[21] The Matrimonial Causes Bill, Bill No. 22, 1950–1.

[22] *Official Report* (HC) 9 Mar. 1951, vol. 485, col. 926.

[23] This and the following quotations are taken from the Explanatory Memorandum to Mrs White's Bill: the Bill itself did not mention breakdown as a ground for divorce or otherwise.

under the existing matrimonial offence provisions). This was to be achieved by adding seven years' separation to the existing grounds for divorce; but divorce was only to be granted on the separation ground if the court was satisfied, first, that there was no reasonable prospect of cohabitation being resumed; and secondly, that a petitioning husband had made adequate provision for his family's maintenance.

Everyone who spoke on the Bill conceded that the existing law, particularly by denying the freedom to remarry to those whose marriages were long functionally dead, was capable of causing considerable hardship and unhappiness. But opponents of change claimed that in relieving this unhappiness the Bill would weaken the institution of marriage and thereby produce much more unhappiness in the future.[24]

The Labour Government accepted that the problem of the stable illicit union was a real one. But the Attorney-General[25] suggested that there were many other problems with the marriage laws, that it would be wrong to select one of them and deal with it in isolation, and that the right course would be to set up a Royal Commission to make a comprehensive study of the marriage laws.[26]

Although the House of Commons gave a second reading to the White Bill by 131 votes to 60,[27] Mrs White eventually acceded to Government pressure[28] and withdrew her Bill on terms that the Government would set up the Royal Commission it had proposed. In reality, as Lord Chancellor Jowitt told Archbishop Fisher,[29] he had agreed to the Royal Commission 'in the hope of avoiding [the White Bill] which had given rise to it'.[30]

---

[24] A particularly clear statement of this point of view is given by the Hon. R. F. Wood, Conservative MP for Bridlington, *Official Report* (HC) 9 Mar. 1951, vol. 485, col. 941.

[25] Sir Hartley Shawcross. In the light of subsequent developments it is interesting to note that the Government had been concerned that the White Bill might lead to demands for divorce by consent and repudiation of the innocent; and Shawcross assured the House of Commons that he (and as he thought the majority of people) would reject divorce by consent 'and still more reject the idea that one should be able to obtain a divorce unilaterally by filling in a form and presenting it at the Food Office or wherever it may be': *Official Report* (HC) 9 Mar. 1951, vol. 485, col. 1008.

[26] The Lord Chancellor's officials had warned him that the Bill had a 'good deal of support among all parties': PRO LCO2/4854, Dobson to Jowitt, 5 Mar. 1951. The Legislation Committee on 7 Mar. agreed to advise Cabinet that the choice lay between strict neutrality or seeking to secure the rejection or withdrawal of the Bill by promising a Royal Commission; and the following day the Cabinet—whilst accepting that the choice of members would be difficult and that a Commission would be unlikely to produce an agreed report—decided on a Royal Commission. In part this decision was influenced by fears that if the Bill went forward it would be difficult to maintain a requirement for a period of separation as long as seven years, whilst the protection the White Bill gave to the 'innocent' against the risks of being divorced (as to which see below) could be eroded.

[27] *Official Report* (HC) 9 Mar. 1951, vol. 485, col. 1018. The House by a narrow majority (102–99) in effect rejected the Attorney-General's advice not to take the Bill to a division: see the exchanges at cols. 1016–18.   [28] See B. H. Lee, *Divorce Law Reform in England* (1974) pp. 26–7.

[29] Then Archbishop of Canterbury.

[30] Jowitt to Fisher, PRO LCO2/6131, 15 Mar. 1951.

THE BACKGROUND—(II) THE MORTON ROYAL COMMISSION

The Royal Commission, established[31] as one of the last acts of the Attlee Labour Government[32] in September 1951 under the chairmanship of Lord Morton of Henryton was thus a temporising measure of a once traditional kind;[33] and its Report—the fruit of four years' deliberation[34]—certainly did not satisfy the hopes of those who had seen a Royal Commission as the only chance of getting a real reform of the divorce laws,[35] much less the expressed wish of Archbishop Fisher that a full inquiry would lead to a settlement lasting fifty years.[36]

On the main issue of the ground for divorce,[37] the Commission was hopelessly divided. On only one proposition was there any broad agreement. All save

---

[31] Its terms of reference (as might have been anticipated from the Attorney's speech on the White Bill) were wide, including not only divorce and matrimonial causes, the domestic jurisdiction of magistrates, and the law governing the prohibited degrees for marriage but also the law relating to property rights of husband and wife both during marriage and after its termination 'having in mind the need to promote and maintain healthy and happy married life and to safeguard the interests and well-being of children'. The draft terms of reference had originally contained a reference to the desirability of increasing public regard for the sanctity of marriage; but this was eventually removed, whether because of the view of D. Dobson that the phrase was 'somewhat propagandist' since the truth was that no Royal Commission could really do anything about it; or because of Sir Frank Soskice AG's view that the reference's suggested bias would be seized upon by those, particularly in the Labour Party, 'who feel that there should be rather more freedom of approach': Soskice to Jowitt, 3 May 1951: PRO LCO2/6131.

[32] The Government was defeated at a General Election on 25 Oct. 1951. The Conservative Party held power for the next thirteen years. The imminence of an Election—and the certainty that Mrs White's Bill could not be got onto the statute book before it took place—may have been a factor influencing its backers to agree to withdrawal in exchange for the appointment of a Royal Commission: see the incisive comments of Earl Winterton: *Official Report* (HC) 9 Mar. 1951, vol. 485, col. 1006.

[33] As with Sir Alan Herbert's imaginary *Royal Commission on Kissing* which:

> . . . collected evidence, but carefully dismissed
> The opinion of anyone who actually kissed;
> We summoned social workers from the cities of the North,
> Good magistrates from Monmouth, Nonconformists from the Forth;
> We summoned all the Bishops who were over sixty-one
> And asked if they were kissed and, if they were, how it was done.
> They answered in the negative and said there was abundant
> Support for the opinion that the practice was redundant—
> And that took a long, long, time.

(*Punch* (1934) vol. 186, p. 708, as quoted in O. R. McGregor, *Divorce in England, A Centenary Study* (1957) p. 199.)

[34] The Report was signed on 20 Dec. 1955, but not published until Mar. 1956.

[35] Earl Winterton, *Official Report* (HC) 9 Mar. 1951, vol. 485, col. 1007. Equally the Attorney-General's hope that appointing a Royal Commission would 'arouse least bitterness of religious or partisan conflict' (op. cit. col. 1003) was not fulfilled.

[36] Fisher to Jowitt, PRO LCO2/6131, 11 Mar. 1951.

[37] Critics of the Commission tend to ignore its detailed examination of matrimonial law and the extensive changes which followed its recommendations. These included: (a) the Maintenance Agreements Act 1957, empowering the court to vary maintenance agreements; (b) the Matrimonial Causes (Property and Maintenance) Act 1958 (extending the court's powers to make financial orders, including orders for payments out of a deceased husband's estate); (c) the Matrimonial Proceedings

one[38] of the Commissioners agreed that the existing (and much criticised) law based on the doctrine of the matrimonial offence should be retained. Nine of the nineteen signatories went further and took an even more conservative view: they rejected the introduction of the doctrine of breakdown of marriage in any form. For this group such a doctrine would inevitably entail recognition of divorce by consent—a change 'disastrous to the nation' encouraging people to 'abandon their marriages on the flimsiest provocation'[39]—whilst divorce simply on the basis of a period of separation 'would have even more damaging consequences for the institution of marriage . . . it would mean that either spouse would be free to terminate the marriage at pleasure . . . [and] people would enter marriage knowing that no matter what they did or how their partners felt, they could always get free'.[40] For these nine members, the proper function of the law was to give relief where a wrong had been done, not to provide a dignified and honourable means of release from a broken marriage.[41] The matrimonial offence doctrine might indeed be artificial in its application to some cases, but it none the less provided a 'clear and intelligible principle';[42] and the 'external buttress of a system of law' specifying the circumstances in which individuals had the right to seek the dissolution of marriage helped them to strengthen their good impulses and weaken the bad.[43]

Another nine Commissioners did take a more positive view of reform. This group did not accept that divorce should only be available on proof of a matrimonial offence;[44] and recommended making divorce available when a marriage

(Children) Act 1958 (requiring parties to give information about the post-divorce arrangements proposed to be made for the children); (d) the Divorce (Insanity and Desertion) Act 1958 (relaxing the conditions under which divorce could be obtained against a spouse suffering from mental illness); (e) the Legitimacy Act 1959 (permitting the children of void marriages to be treated as legitimate); (f) the Marriage (Enabling) Act 1960 (permitting a divorced man or woman to marry relatives of his or her former spouse); (g) the Matrimonial Proceedings (Magistrates' Courts) Act 1960 (changes in the domestic jurisdiction of magistrates: see also the *Report of the Departmental Committee on Matrimonial Proceedings in Magistrates' Courts* (1959) Cmnd. 638); (h) the Matrimonial Causes Act 1963 which amended the law in an attempt to facilitate reconciliation; and also gave the court power to order a lump sum payment. (This last reform, recommended by the Morton Commission (see para. 516), deserves to be noted since it was the precursor of the extensive powers of the court to reallocate capital on divorce now embodied in Matrimonial Causes Act 1973.) Moreover, the Morton Report for the first time highlighted the unsatisfactory position of divorced spouses in respect of pensions and this led to improvements in the conditions governing eligibility for the state retirement and widow's pensions: see the statement by the Minister of Pensions HP (56) 17th Meeting, 22 Oct. 1956, PRO LCO2/ 6139. Finally, the Commission's Report also gave further support to state provision of reconciliation and marital guidance: ibid. and the speeches in the House of Lords debate: *Official Report* (HL) 24 Oct. 1956, vol. 199, col. 971.

[38] Lord Walker: *Report of the Royal Commission on Marriage and Divorce* (Chairman: Lord Morton of Henryton) (1956, Cmd. 9678) para. 65.   [39] Op. cit. para. 69(viii).
[40] Para. 69(xiii).   [41] Para. 69(xiii).   [42] Para. 69(xxxvi).   [43] Para. 69(xxxvii).
[44] This group recognised that the existing law of divorce in practice allowed divorce by consent: 'nobody who is ready to provide a ground of divorce, who is careful to avoid any suggestion of connivance or collusion [at the time bars to the dissolution of marriage] and who has a co-operative spouse, has any difficulty in securing a dissolution of the marriage'. The 'distasteful expedient' of committing adultery (and the fact that a consensual separation could easily be presented as desertion) weighted the law 'in favour of the least scrupulous, the least honourable and the least sensitive': para. 70(v).

had broken down irretrievably as demonstrated by the fact that the spouses had lived apart for seven years or more. But five of this group would have refused divorce for separation if either party objected;[45] and even the four prepared to accept separation divorce against the will of one spouse would have insisted on an applicant in such a case demonstrating that the separation was attributable to 'unreasonable conduct of the other spouse'. Only one member of the Commission, the Scottish judge Lord Walker, was prepared to take his stand on the ground of principle that the law should favour the dissolution of marriages which had indeed broken down, irrespective of the 'guilt' or 'innocence' of the petitioner; and that divorce should be available to a spouse who had lived apart from the other for at least three years and could establish that the facts and circumstances were such as to make it improbable that an ordinary husband and wife would ever resume cohabitation.[46]

THE BACKGROUND—(III) THE RESPONSE TO THE ROYAL COMMISSION

Although the (Conservative) Government was sensitive[47] to charges that Royal Commissions were a 'recognised and timely method of shelving inconvenient questions'[48] no one, in the light of the divergent views put forward in the Morton Report, could 'possibly expect' any government to introduce legislation permitting divorce (even by consent) after a separation of seven years[49] and any kind of official[50] support for legislation permitting a 'man who had gone off leaving

---

[45] Para. 70(viii).

[46] 'Statement of his Views by Lord Walker': *Report of the Royal Commission on Marriage and Divorce* (Chairman: Lord Morton of Henryton) (1956, Cmd. 9678) pp. 340–1, paras. 4, 7. Contrary to what is sometimes suggested, Lord Walker did not favour a permissive approach to the divorce law; and it seems clear that he would have insisted on proper evidence being available about the irretrievable nature of the alleged breakdown. His support for abolition of the matrimonial offence based divorce law was founded on the belief that lax interpretation had led to its becoming a 'technical cause of action without a real cause for complaint'; and he considered that if (contrary to his own preference) the matrimonial offence basis were to be retained, it should be adhered to 'as closely as may be' without the addition of any separation ground.

[47] See Dennis Dobson's Minute to Sir George Coldstream, 16 Mar. 1956, PRO LCO2/6139; and the Lord Chancellor's Memorandum to the Home Affairs Committee HP(56) 109. The Government's attitude was that it would take all possible steps by means of administrative action, changes in the Rules of Court, and Private Member's Bills (for which drafting assistance might be made available) on those many unanimous recommendations of the Commission which they accepted: ibid.

[48] As Lord Silkin was predictably to claim in the House of Lords debate on the Commission's Report: *Official Report* (HL) 24 Oct. 1956, vol. 199, col. 972.

[49] See the Lord Chancellor's speech in the debate on the Report initiated by Lord Silkin: *Official Report* (HL) 24 Oct. 1956, vol. 199, col. 1058.

[50] For the next forty years, the promotion of legislation on the ground for divorce was exclusively a matter for the private member. The first post-Morton initiative appears to have been taken by the Divorce Law Reform Union which in 1960 arranged for the lobbying of MPs in support of a proposed Matrimonial Causes (Breakdown of Marriage) Bill allowing divorce for breakdown in cases in which the court considered it to be fair and reasonable to do so but also giving the courts power

a guiltless wife for seven years [to] come back and divorce her against her will'[51] seemed even less likely.

Not surprisingly, this setback was a bitter disappointment; and the criticisms made of the Morton Report by Professor O. R. McGregor[52] have been influential in creating an enduring and strongly unfavourable perception of the Morton Commission. In McGregor's view, the Morton Report contributed 'nothing to our knowledge'; and had proved to be a 'device for obfuscating a socially urgent but politically inconvenient issue'.[53] It was (McGregor conceded) a 'matter of opinion' whether the Morton Commission was 'intellectually the worst Royal Commission of the twentieth century' (although since he thought there could be 'no dispute that [it] is the most unreadable and confused'[54] it would seem the competition for the wooden spoon was, in McGregor's view, not severe).

This is not the place for a detailed examination of McGregor's polemic;[55] but subsequent events suggest that at least one of McGregor's criticisms had touched a sensitive nerve. McGregor claimed that Lord Morton and his colleagues were 'hostile to the social sciences', that as a result of their ignorance of evidence[56] which social scientists could have provided—extending, apparently, to

to apportion responsibility for the breakdown which would then be taken into account in assessing maintenance etc. Lord Chancellor Kilmuir (on the advice of his officials—of whom one, J. W. Bourne, subsequently Permanent Secretary, shared the view that the Morton Commission had 'missed a golden opportunity' to put the law on a more logical footing by substituting the breakdown of marriage principle for that of the matrimonial offence) repeated the categorical statement that no government could be expected to introduce legislation in the face of the division of opinion evidenced by the Morton Commission's Report which (it was thought) reflected a similar division of opinion both in Parliament and in the country at large. Kilmuir refused to commit the Government in advance to any course of action should such a Bill be introduced, remarking that the subject 'bristles with difficulties and would require the most careful consideration': Kilmuir to Brooke, 21 Dec. 1960, PRO LCO2/6157. The same source reveals that the Mothers' Union was actively lobbying MPs against any Bill on this subject; and Bourne stated that the 'small trickle of letters' received since 1956 confirmed that there remained a 'wide cleavage of opinion'. Kilmuir does not appear to have responded favourably to a letter from a Conservative peer and officer of the Divorce Law Reform Union attaching a draft of a Bill prepared by the Union and said in its Explanatory Memorandum to give *equitable* jurisdiction to the courts to dissolve a marriage whilst leaving untouched the existing *legal* grounds for divorce.

[51] Lord Morton claimed that not a single member of the Commission had supported such legislation (*Official Report* (HL) 24 Oct. 1956, vol. 199, col. 983) but it appears that Lord Walker would have been prepared to allow divorce in such circumstances. Where he differed from the White proposals was in favouring breakdown established by separation as the *sole* ground for divorce.

[52] *Divorce in England, A Centenary Study*, 1957.   [53] Op. cit. p. 193.   [54] Ibid.

[55] McGregor was a distinguished social historian, and *Divorce in England* contains much statistical, demographic and historical material of great value. But it does not wholly live up to McGregor's insistence on the need to distinguish carefully between matters of fact and matters of opinion.

[56] McGregor pointed out that a research secretariat could have provided the Commission with (a) an analysis of statistical data with suggestions for improvement; (b) empirical investigations designed to test witnesses' assertions about attitudes to marriage and other matters; (c) an analysis of divorce petitions 'in order to make a study of the changing incidence of divorce by social class during the last half-century'; (d) provision of 'socially relevant information' about the use of magistrates' separation and maintenance orders; (e) a factual study of the consequences of their parents' divorces for a representative sample of children: op. cit. p. 187.

'actual knowledge of the types of divorce law most likely to promote marital and familial stability'[57]—the Commission was 'unable to penetrate to the heart of the problems set before them'.[58] The view that the assistance of social scientists was essential to inquiries became part of the conventional orthodoxy;[59] and, as we shall see, considerable efforts were made to secure a social science input for the group established seven years later by the Archbishop of Canterbury.

McGregor also seems to have regarded as a weakness[60] the fact that the Morton Committee—in contrast to the 1912 Gorrell Commission (whose chairman was known to have strong views in favour of divorce law reform, but whose membership also included some known to take a strongly conservative view)—did not include either a representative[61] of the Church[62] on the one hand or any active proponent of reform on the other. It is certainly true that the Government devoted considerable effort[63]

---

[57] Op. cit. p. 192.   [58] Op. cit. p. 194.

[59] For criticism of this orthodoxy see R. Deech, 'Divorce Law and Empirical Studies' (1990) 106 LQR 229.

[60] 'Mr Attlee's Government . . . for reasons of expediency, selected as members men and women who were not publicly committed to either "abolitionist" or "institutionalist" views': op. cit. p. 193. McGregor also claimed that the 'only apparent principle' in the choice of members of the Commission 'appears to have been the importance of securing a preponderance of lawyers': op. cit. p. 179; and it is true that eight of the nineteen signatories were legally qualified, viz. Morton (Lord of Appeal), Keith (appointed Lord of Appeal, 1955), Holroyd Pearce (High Court judge—Divorce Division to 1953, thereafter Queen's Bench), Walker (Scottish Judge), Young (Sheriff), Jones-Roberts (woman barrister), Maddocks (Stipendiary Magistrate) and Lawrence (QC, subsequently High Court Judge). This is all the more striking since at the outset Jowitt had thought it better not to have a judge on the Commission: LCO2/6131, note by D. Dobson, 16 Mar. 1951.

[61] A matter which McGregor attributes to the Church of England being sharply divided in its views: op. cit. p. 179; and it is true that the Modern Churchman's Union (favourably disposed to reform) specifically (but unsuccessfully) sought representation because the opinions of its members would not adequately be reflected by the Anglican hierarchy. The records confirm that Lord Chancellor Jowitt did favour choosing members without preconceived views, 'tho' he realises it may be impossible to avoid having a churchman' (note by D. Dobson, PRO LCO2/6131, 16 Mar. 1951); but there was substantial disagreement between ministerial colleagues about whether the churches should be represented or merely witnesses.

[62] Jowitt had asked Archbishop Fisher for the names of suitable churchmen. Jowitt's suggestion that he and the Archbishop should meet 'quite privately' from time to time was apparently vetoed by his ministerial colleagues (see Jowitt to Fisher, 28 May 1951, PRO LCO2/1362) and would in any event have been frustrated by the defeat of the Labour Government in the 1951 General Election.

[63] The Cabinet adjourned its first discussion of the composition of the Commission, the suggestion having been made that on a topic of this kind there might be a case for 'jury of ordinary men and women with no specialised or professional angle on the problem': CM (51) 33rd conclusions, 3 May 1951. In an undated pencilled note (PRO LCO2/6132) Jowitt minuted Dobson that the list he had put forward had been 'very badly received' as consisting exclusively of 'bourgeois nonentities'. Officials plaintively recorded that the Cabinet considered the 'common man and woman' should be appointed, but 'how the common man is to be selected I do not know': Dobson to R. M. J. Harris, 4 May 1951, PRO LCO2/6132. The Lord Chancellor was punctilious in inviting those who wrote to him about divorce reform to suggest the names of people considered suitable for membership; and the list of persons considered for membership eventually ran to ten foolscap pages (and included no less than three Heads or former Heads of Boys' Public Schools). It is certainly true that (in McGregor's words, op. cit. p. 179 'in social composition [the Commission] was heavily biased towards upper- and middle-class outlooks'). Ministers were invited to put forward names—the Attorney-General suggested the novelist and Labour publicist J. B. Priestley (but he was rejected perhaps because Sir

to achieving[64] a balanced and impartial membership;[65] but if this was an error it was one which was not repeated. As we shall see, there was no nonsense about impartiality as a criterion in choosing sources of advice in the years leading up to the 1969 reforms.

Whatever may be thought about McGregor's triumphalist beliefs in the potential of social science research for policy making, in one respect he can be shown to have been plainly wrong. He asserted that it was 'a safe prediction that divorce reform will take a long, long time'; but in fact, little more than a decade later, the Divorce Reform Act swept the concept of the indissoluble marriage into history.

THE BACKGROUND—(IV) MR LEO ABSE'S MATRIMONIAL CAUSES
AND RECONCILIATION BILL 1962–3

Six years after the Morton Report divorce reform was given another chance. A Bill providing for divorce on the ground of seven years' separation[66] was

John Maud, then Permanent Secretary at the Ministry of Education, considered he was 'not good on committees'), the actress Celia Johnson (possibly because of her sensitive portrayal in the 1945 film *Brief Encounter* of a middle-class housewife seized by romantic passion for a Doctor played by Trevor Howard) and John Fulton (the philosopher Principal of University College Swansea, subsequently Vice-Chancellor of the University of Wales and Chairman of the Committee on the Civil Service, 1966–8). The Minister of Defence, Emmanuel Shinwell, doubted the wisdom of having 'too many women on the Commission': 11 May 1951. None of those mentioned above was eventually appointed.

[64] As Lord Chancellor Jowitt had written (PRO LCO2/6131) to the prominent divorce practitioner W. Latey QC who had written volunteering his services as a member of the Commission 'the dilemma between getting people who have in general settled views and people completely ignorant of the whole thing with neither views nor knowledge is a very difficult one. All one can say is whatever trouble we take we are tolerably certain of satisfying no one and annoying most.'

[65] The evidence from the records suggest a considerable degree of amateurishness in identifying possible members; and this nearly led to disaster in the choice of chairman. The Chair was offered to Lord Eustace Percy—seventh son of the seventh Duke of Northumberland, Unionist MP 1921–37, President of the Board of Education 1924–9, and at the time Rector of King's College Newcastle. In his reply expressing delight at the offer Percy revealed that he held 'the strictest views about the indissolubility of marriage and also about the evil of dissociating religious principle from the marriage law of England': LCO2/6131, 5 Apr. 1951; and indeed his deep religious convictions seem to have been widely known. Not surprisingly, Percy's name disappeared from consideration, and the name of Fergus Morton (an eminent Chancery Judge, appointed Lord of Appeal in Ordinary in 1947, known to the Lord Chancellor's Department as a 'safe' Chairman of the Committee on the Law of Intestate Succession, 1951) emerged instead. On 2 June, after some initial hesitation caused in part by concern about his health, Morton accepted with enthusiasm the prospect of a 'job which is so vitally important': PRO LCO2/6131. Other names put forward for the Chair had included Lord Beveridge ('too old'), the Marquess of Reading (long-standing interest in family matters did not outweigh the fact that he was 'not a Christian') and a woman medical consultant (because there were doubts about her being involved in a 'possible irregular relationship').

[66] Subject to the requirement that in defended cases the petitioner would have to satisfy the court the separation was 'in part due to unreasonable conduct of the respondent'; and subject also to safeguards intended to protect the financial position of wife and children: Bill 19, presented by Mr Leo Abse and others, as ordered to be printed 21 Nov. 1962, cl. 2.

brought forward by Mr Leo Abse MP.[67] The House of Commons gave the Bill a second reading[68] and it passed through[69] its Committee stage.[70] But opponents of separation divorce let it be known that any Bill containing such a provision would be 'talked out';[71] and, faced with this 'formidable opposition',[72] Abse withdrew the clause adding separation to the grounds for divorce in exchange for an agreement[73] that the other provisions in the Bill (designed to remove obstacles to reconciliation attempts[74]) would reach the statute book.[75] An attempt in the House of Lords to reinstate the separation divorce provisions also failed.[76]

THE CHURCH MILITANT

A significant factor in this apparent further reverse for the cause of reform was the—now much more sophisticated—opposition of the Church, organised behind

[67] (b. 1917), at the time Labour MP for Pontypool. A solicitor, he used his knowledge of the law and his mastery of parliamentary procedures to bring about many legislative reforms on homosexuality, illegitimacy, and adoption, and he was the moving force behind the parliamentary proceedings eventually leading to the enactment of the Divorce Reform Act 1969. His autobiography —*Private Member* (1973)—gives an invaluable and detailed (if not always objective) account of the background to reform. [68] *Official Report* (HC) 8 Feb. 1963, vol. 671, col. 806.

[69] Opponents of the Bill—in a move said by Abse to be unprecedented—sought (unsuccessfully) to prevent the Bill being reported: Standing Committee C, *Official Report*, 27 Mar. 1963; L. Abse, *Private Member* (1973) pp. 164–6.

[70] Standing Committee C, *Official Report*, 6, 13, 20 and 27 Mar. 1963. The separation provision which emerged from the Committee was closely modelled on Australian and New Zealand precedents; and the position of a spouse unwilling to be divorced was protected by requiring the court to dismiss a petition in cases in which it would be 'harsh and oppressive to the respondent or contrary to the public interest' to dissolve the marriage (rather than requiring the petitioner to establish that the respondent's conduct was in part responsible for the separation: cf. n. 66 above).

[71] A note by the Archbishop of Canterbury's Lay Secretary, Robert Beloe, records that opponents of separation divorce had met and agreed to put down 'a great many amendments' to ensure this outcome: *Ramsey Papers*, vol. 43, 28 Mar. 1963, and see also Beloe's 'Note on a meeting with Straubenzee on 9 April'—the 'plan was to prevent the Bill reaching the end of the Report stage . . . unless Abse withdrew the offending clause'.

[72] Mr Leo Abse, *Official Report* (HC) 3 May 1963, vol. 676, col. 1557. In a bitter speech, Abse accepted that he had had 'no alternative but to yield to' duress: col. 1562.

[73] According to a file note by Beloe, Abse had negotiated this with W. R. van Straubenzee MP, one of the main opponents of separation divorce and a prominent Anglican layman: *Ramsey Papers* vol. 43, 2 May 1963; and see *Official Report* (HC) 3 May 1963, vol. 676, col. 1564. But it appears that Dr Jeremy Bray (b. 1930, at the time Labour MP for Middlesbrough West) acted as an intermediary: see L. Abse, *Private Member* (1973) p. 170. Straubenzee's 'immense amount of detailed staff work' in achieving the 'careful co-ordination and organisation' essential to defeating the separation provision was acknowledged in a letter (see *Ramsey Papers*, vol. 43, 9 May 1963) to Beloe from David James MBE DSC MP a prominent Roman Catholic layman and director of the English Publishers to the Holy See.

[74] These provisions (based to greater or lesser extent on the Morton Commission's recommendations) converted collusion into a discretionary rather than an absolute bar to divorce and restricted the application of the bar of condonation in cases of attempted reconciliation. They became law in the Matrimonial Causes Act 1963, ss. 1–4.

[75] Abse's detailed account of the manoeuvres is invaluable: L. Abse, *Private Member* (1973) pp. 162–71.

[76] Lord Silkin's amendment to this end was defeated on a Division by 52 votes to 31 in the House of Lords: *Official Report* (HL) 21 June 1963, vol. 250, col. 1578: see below p. 46.

the scenes with great efficiency by the first holder[77] of the post of Lay Secretary to the Archbishop of Canterbury, Robert Beloe. Beloe—a distinguished educationalist[78] and in that capacity a member of the Morton Commission[79]—had special responsibility for organising episcopal representation in the House of Lords[80] and moved easily and confidently between Lambeth Palace, the Palace of Westminster and Whitehall.[81] It is true that the contents of the Abse Bill at first took Beloe by surprise; but intelligence—on such matters as the religious affiliations and marital status of Cabinet Ministers[82]—was rapidly gathered and put efficiently to use. During the passage of the Abse Bill through the Commons, Beloe took an active part in the efforts to organise MPs opposed to separation divorce.[83] He scrutinised the list of MPs nominated to serve on the Standing Committee considering the Bill (and he appears to have been successful in getting one change made[84]).

[77] He had been appointed in 1959.

[78] Beloe (the Wykehamist son of a clergyman public school Head, brother of an Admiral, and for a time an Assistant Master at Eton) had become an Educational Administrator (latterly Chief Education Officer for Surrey). As H. G. Judge puts it in the *Dictionary of National Biography*, he represented the high water mark of the influence of enlightened administrators working amicably with elected councillors, and was a central member of that significant group of chief education officers responsible for putting into effect the provisions of the Butler 1944 Education Act and personally committed to a broad extension of the advantages enjoyed by those, like himself, who came from privileged backgrounds. He served on numerous government and Church committees.

[79] He was one of the 'hardline' nine members who favoured retention of the matrimonial offence and were opposed to the introduction of marital breakdown as a ground for divorce: see *Report of the Royal Commission on Marriage and Divorce* (Chairman: Lord Morton of Henryton) (1956, Cmd. 9678) p. 14, footnote.

[80] At the time of the presentation of the Abse Bill, Beloe had no comparable intelligence network in the House of Commons: Beloe to Guillum Scott, 15 Feb. 1963, *Ramsey Papers*, vol. 43; and see generally E. Carpenter, *Archbishop Fisher—His Life and Times* (1991) pp. 190–1; O. Chadwick, *Michael Ramsey, A Life* (1990) pp. 116 ff. and p. 190.

[81] Beloe's skills in negotiation are reflected in the subsequent events; whilst some indication of his ability to make use of his personal knowledge of those with influence is evidenced in his note briefing Archbishop Ramsey about Lord Chancellor Dilhorne. Beloe recorded that Dilhorne was a low church Anglican, and was 'not thought to be very intelligent but [was none the less] a politician of experience' who (as his officials had told Beloe) was 'contrary to general belief, extremely interested in Reform of the law': *Ramsey Papers*, vol. 43, 21 May 1963. Beloe apparently drew on assessments made by friends married to sisters of Lady Dilhorne, a daughter of the Earl of Crawford and Balcarres.   [82] *Ramsey Papers*, note by Beloe dated 25 Feb. 1963.

[83] '. . . a secret all-party cabal of church and chapel members had been formed to kill the Bill. On the Tory side it was led by van Straubenzee . . . who became the voice of the bishops; and from the Labour Benches, Eric Fletcher . . . a low churchman who co-ordinated opposition on the opposition benches. Both Straubenzee and Fletcher were highly intelligent men, the one incredibly pompous and the other infinitely dreary': L. Abse, *Private Member* (1973) p. 163.

[84] But Beloe's hopes that Eric Fletcher MP (a long-standing Labour opponent of divorce reform, who has given an account of his career and attitudes in *Random Reminiscences* (1986)) would be put onto the Committee were not fulfilled—according to Abse by reason of Fletcher's own clumsiness in coping with the different strands of opinion within the Labour Party on the subject of divorce: see L. Abse, *Private Member* (1973) pp. 163–5. Beloe did have what he described as a 'most valuable meeting' with Fletcher who confirmed that most of the party's intellectuals (such as Michael Foot, who made an incisive intervention in the Commons debate, calling for a

> duty on hypocrisy,
> A tax on humbug, an excise
> On solemn plausibilities

Finally, he masterminded the publication of a firm statement[85] of the Churches'[86] opposition to separation divorce.[87]

But Beloe really came into his element when the Abse Bill got to the House of Lords and Lord Silkin and others made a determined attempt to reinstate the clause permitting separation divorce. Beloe's briefing paper for the Archbishop was prophetically headed 'How to secure rejection of Mr Abse's[88] clause';[89] and to that end he skilfully organised opposition.[90] Ramsey made a speech in the debate[91]

—*Official Report* (HC) 3 May 1976, vol. 676, col. 1576) strongly favoured reform, but on the other hand there were MPs who were Roman Catholics (or who had Catholic constituencies) and also— so Fletcher told Beloe—'there were many people in the Labour Party of the rather inarticulate kind . . . representing Trade Union constituencies . . . [who] were disturbed' by proposals for reform in this area: *Ramsey Papers*, vol. 43, 22 Mar. 1963. It appears that Harold Wilson, Leader of the Labour Party, had 'possibly in order to quieten the outburst' by Labour reformers committed the Shadow Cabinet to consider the whole principle of separation divorce: *Ramsey Papers*, vol. 43, note by Beloe 8 May 1963.

[85] By the Archbishops of Canterbury, York and Wales, the Moderator and General Secretary of the Free Church Federal Council and the Roman Catholic Archbishop of Birmingham. The state- ment (issued on 3 Apr. 1963) declared that the provisions of the Abse Bill would cause injustice to the innocent and introduce into the law the 'dangerous new principle' that a marriage could be terminated by the desire of the parties and thus 'undermine the basic understanding of marriage as a lifelong union'. Beloe was unsuccessful in getting Jewish support for this proposition since (it was pointed out) Judaism was not opposed to the principle of consensual divorce.

[86] Abse records that he was angered when a *Times* journalist told him this was the 'first occasion in the ecclesiastical history of Britain that, on a matter of doctrine, all the churches had combined' and riposted that it had 'taken a Jew to found the Christian churches and evidently took another to unite them . . . This was a time to stand up and fight': L. Abse, *Private Member* (1973) p. 159.

[87] Beloe had been told that the Executive of the 1922 Committee (i.e. Conservative backbenchers) considered a 'forthright statement of the Archbishop's views' would be of great help: Arbuthnot to Beloe, 15 Mar. 1963, *Ramsey Papers*, vol. 43. There had at the outset been criticism of what Sir Peter Agnew MP (a Church Commissioner and long-standing member of the Church Assembly) had described in the Commons (see *Official Report* (HC) 8 Feb. 1963, vol. 671, col. 874) as the Church of England's failure to take a 'strong or indeed any' line on the separation divorce issue; and Agnew was able effectively to defend himself against Archbishop Ramsey's letter of rebuke by quoting a statement made by the Secretary of the Church's Board for Social Responsibility.

[88] The amendment which Lord Silkin moved was modelled on the Australian separation ground (see *Official Report* (HL) 21 June 1963, vol. 250, col. 1528) and had apparently been settled by Parliamentary Counsel: note by Beloe dated 21 May 1963, *Ramsey Papers*, vol. 43.

[89] The Archbishop was advised by Beloe not to appear as a 'whipper up of opposition, but on the other hand there must be a good, though not excessive, show of Bishops'. As already noted, the separation divorce provision was defeated on a division. Beloe had obtained an assurance of assist- ance from the Roman Catholic peers, Monsignor Derrick Worlock (then Private Secretary to the Archbishop of Westminster) writing to Beloe on 31 May 1963 that 'our peers will be glad to help on the combined tactics which were so successful when the Bill was in the Commons'. The defeat on 21 June 1963 of the attempt to reinstate the separation divorce provision evoked modest satis- faction at Lambeth that 'a rather anxious matter' had been concluded so satisfactorily': *Ramsey Papers*, vol. 43.

[90] For example, some Anglican peers sympathetic to separation divorce (such as Lord Stonham: see his letter of 14 June 1963 to the Bishop of London in *Ramsey Papers*, vol. 43) were persuaded not to support the Abse Bill.

[91] *Official Report* (HL) 21 June 1963, vol. 250, col. 1543. Ramsey claimed (i) that the notion of there being an 'honourable respectable way of ending a marriage' constituted a serious threat to the concept of marriage as a lifelong union; (ii) that it was improbable that seven year separation divorce would reduce the number of illicit unions; and (iii) that legitimising children of such unions would

uncompromisingly rejecting the proposed addition of seven years' separation[92] to the existing grounds for divorce, and the Lords defeated the proposal on a division.

THE SEARCH FOR A BETTER WAY

Beloe appreciated that this could not be the end of the matter. He had been warned by the Permanent Under-Secretary at the Home Office that a Bill providing for separation divorce was almost certain to be introduced by a private member the following session;[93] and he was concerned that the Conservative Party[94] faced with the need to modernise its image in the run-up to a General Election[95] might see divorce reform as one means of doing so.[96] He was also conscious that the Church had acquired the reputation[97] of being hostile to any change in what almost

---

be done at the expense of the father's first union and the children of the first union. Ramsey's biographer (O. Chadwick, *Michael Ramsey, A Life* (1990) p. 150–3) believes the speech to have been important in the rejection of the Bill.

[92] The argument that separation divorce would be unfair to women was vigorously put by Lady Summerskill who claimed the Bill was 'a husband's Bill, drafted by a man who . . . has failed to recognise that marriage has different value for a man and a woman, values which are determined by the fundamental difference in sex'. Lady Summerskill said she wanted to protect 'the little earthly paradise, the home, the source of most women's greatest happiness, which she has created for her children': *Official Report* (HL) 22 May 1963, vol. 250, col. 397. Lord Hodson (a Law Lord who had practised in and been a judge in the divorce court) also strongly criticised the economic impact of separation divorce on married women: see at col. 402.

[93] Note, 2 May 1963, *Ramsey Papers*, vol. 43.

[94] Lord Chancellor Dilhorne was (as he had put it in the House of Lords debate: *Official Report* (HL) 21 June 1963, vol. 250, col. 1566) strongly opposed to grafting onto the existing law a proposition based on breakdown; and he had expressed his concern that the Abse provision be defeated to Archbishop Ramsey: Canterbury to York, 27 Mar. 1963, *Ramsey Papers*, vol. 43. But, as he also indicated in that speech (and much more vigorously in private) he did favour 'another system where divorce would . . . be dependent upon the fact of the breakdown of the marriage'.

[95] According to Straubenzee, the Government Chief Whip had been exposed to considerable pressure to give help to the Bill. However, Straubenzee correctly predicted that the Government would not do so: *Ramsey Papers*, vol. 43, note by Beloe dated 8 Apr. 1963.

[96] The 'grouse moor' image of the Conservative Party under Harold Macmillan had become a focus of attention for the burgeoning satire industry (in which such figures as Peter Cook, David Frost, Jonathan Miller and Dudley Moore were prominent) and the need to modernise was all the greater after the Earl of Home 'emerged' as Leader of the Party in October 1963. The view that the Party's traditional leaders were out of touch with modern attitudes may also have been reinforced by the so-called Profumo scandal: see n. 9 above.

[97] The Home Secretary, Henry Brooke, had bluntly warned Beloe of this at a meeting on 7 Oct. 1963: *Ramsey Papers*, vol. 43. Supporters of divorce reform had been active in publicising their claim: see in particular L. Abse, *Private Member* (1973) pp. 169–70 ('I knew that after the Churches had acted I could not, under a Tory government, put my Bill through Parliament . . . It was to the country not to Parliament I was speaking; and although I knew it would take some years before the walls finally fell, this assault had to be fierce if the foundations were to be irrevocably weakened.')

everyone[98] agreed to be an unsatisfactory law and of not being prepared to face reality in its approach to social questions,[99] while the way in which Abse had been forced to drop the separation divorce provision 'had given rise to a great deal of anti-clerical feeling'.[100] Against this background, the Church clearly needed to take some action; and the links and understandings established[101] by Beloe during the progress of the Abse Bill became of crucial importance in apparently restoring the Church to its position of influence over policy.

THE ARCHBISHOP OF CANTERBURY'S GROUP

The Church's Board for Social Responsibility had in fact already initiated 'conversations' about the possibility of some alternative basis for divorce, but progress had been slow.[102] This led Beloe to float, at a meeting with senior officials[103] from the Home Office and Lord Chancellor's Department, the notion that the Archbishop might set on foot a somewhat more formal investigation into marriage and its dissolution; and the suggestion that the Archbishop's mediation might be aimed at the possibility of 'substituting for all other grounds the ground that a marriage had come to an end' emerged.[104] Evidently this was favourably received;[105] and in June the Archbishop announced—albeit in a somewhat low

[98] Including the Archbishop who, in the House of Lords debate on *Putting Asunder* (*Official Report* (HL) 23 Nov. 1966, vol. 278, col. 254), said he had been 'terribly aware of the weaknesses and evils' of the present law.

[99] This point was subsequently put very forcefully by Professor J. N. D. Anderson in successfully urging the Church Assembly to accept irretrievable breakdown as the sole ground for divorce: 'I am convinced that changes in our law of divorce will come. There is a mounting pressure in many different areas and among many different groups. In the past, the Bishops . . . have stood . . . rather like Canute trying to prevent the tide coming in . . . [W]e should realise that we have a responsibility to the nation not merely to say "No" and then accept whatever law comes, but to make constructive and suitable suggestions': *Church Assembly Report of Proceedings*, vol. 47, p. 239.

[100] Note by Beloe, 21 May 1963, *Ramsey Papers*, vol. 43.

[101] A meeting was arranged for the Lord Chancellor, Home Secretary, Solicitor General and Beloe on 29 Apr. 1963 (i.e. after the Commons Second Reading and Committee stages which had left the Abse Bill unscathed, but before the crucial Report stage on 3 May); and on 2 May Beloe recorded that Sir Charles Cunningham (Permanent Under-Secretary of State at the Home Office) would like the Archbishop to expedite the Board for Social Responsibility's discussions (as to which see below): *Ramsey Papers*, vol. 43.

[102] It had been envisaged that the task might occupy three years; and it is not surprising that no conclusion had been reached after a year.

[103] Sir Charles Cunningham, the Permanent Under-Secretary of State, and R. J. Guppy, the Assistant Under-Secretary of State, from the Home Office and Denis Dobson, Deputy Permanent Secretary in the Lord Chancellor's Department.

[104] *Ramsey Papers*, vol. 43, folio 5, Beloe's note of meeting on 21 May 1963.

[105] On 9 May 1963 the Reverend G. R. Dunstan (see n. 116 below) who had chaired the earlier informal conversations told Professor J. N. D. Anderson that it was likely the discussions would 'begin again on a higher and more formal level, *on the instance of the Archbishop of Canterbury himself*' (italics supplied): Dunstan to Beloe, *Ramsey Papers*, vol. 43.

key way[106]—that he had asked 'some fellow churchmen' to seek to find a 'principle at law of breakdown of marriage . . . free from any trace of the idea of consent, which conserved the point that offences and not only wishes are the basis of breakdown, and which was protected by a far more thorough insistence on reconciliation procedure first'.

It is difficult to believe that this announcement brought much cheer to the supporters of divorce reform[107] faced as they were with yet another failure to carry legislation through Parliament, or indeed whether the civil servants[108] who had become involved had any real expectation that the Archbishop's initiative would bear fruit;[109] but in the event it proved to be of decisive importance in preparing the ground for the 1969 Reforms.

A GROUP OF CHURCHMEN OR A MINI-COMMISSION?

The composition of what came to be called[110] the Archbishop's Group (chaired by Robert Mortimer, Bishop of Exeter[111]) was somewhat different from the 'group of

---

[106] '[I]f it were possible to find a principle . . . then I would wish to consider it': *Official Report* (HL) 21 June 1963, vol. 250, col. 1547. The unenthusiastic tone no doubt reflects Ramsey's belief that it was 'very doubtful whether [the group he planned to appoint] would be able to produce anything constructive': Canterbury to York, 6 June 1963, *Ramsey Papers*, vol. 63. The papers reveal a number of instances of Ramsey distancing himself from the work of the Group, and eventually Ramsey and Anderson publicly disagreed about whether the 1969 Divorce Reform legislation did give effect to the principles stated by the Group.

[107] Leo Abse, however, records his belief that there was 'a need for a hiatus. I had played my part as a catalyst. Soon the historical forces would erupt and the enemy would be overwhelmed': L. Abse, *Private Member* (1973) p. 171.

[108] It may be that Ministers were more hopeful. Lord Chancellor Dilhorne subsequently wrote to the Archbishop expressing gratitude for his initiative and referring to the 'desirability of getting away from the present concept of matrimonial offence': Dilhorne to Ramsey, 16 Dec. 1963, *Ramsey Papers*, vol. 43. Beloe had already noted (on 19 Mar. 1963) the preference expressed by Dilhorne at a meeting with Ramsey for 'his own more radical proposal', i.e. a judge considering the 'matter as a whole' and to make a finding as to 'whether or not the marriage had broken down'. Subsequently, in evidence to the Archbishop's Group, Dilhorne expressed himself as favouring divorce for breakdown 'with the least possible fuss': *Minutes of the Archbishop's Group on the reform of Divorce*, Lambeth Palace MS 3460, 30 July 1965, p. 100.

[109] Denis Dobson, in an 'interesting talk' recorded by Beloe on 25 Feb. 1963 (*Ramsey Papers*, vol. 43) doubted whether adjudication on breakdown could be possible; and warned against putting 'more power in the hands of the judiciary . . . What was needed was to define the circumstances in which a judge must give a decree . . .'. It is interesting to note that Scarman J in giving formal evidence on 19 Feb. 1965 to the Group eventually set up by the Archbishop of Canterbury expressed strong disapproval of the 'modern method of law reform' whereby an increasing amount is left to the discretion of the judiciary and urged that discretion should only be a 'safety valve'. (*Minutes of the Archbishop's Group on the reform of Divorce*, Lambeth Palace MS 3460, pp. 60–4.)

[110] The first use of this description seems to be in Ramsey's letter of 6 June 1963 to the Archbishop of York telling him of his intention: Ramsey Papers, vol. 43.

[111] Described by Chadwick (op. cit. n. 91 above, p. 151) as the 'learned moral theologian among the bishops' and 'a conservative', Mortimer (1902–76) had been University Lecturer in Early Canon Law and Regius Professor of Moral and Pastoral Theology at Oxford. He had edited and substantially revised T. A. Lacey's *Marriage in Church and State* (1947)—a text first published in 1912—before being consecrated Bishop of Exeter in 1949.

churchmen' originally envisaged by Ramsey, in part because both the Home Secretary[112] and the Lord Chancellor[113] took an active part[114] in suggesting who should (and who should not[115]) be asked to serve.[116] It is true that membership was confined to those thought to be Christians, but no requirement of religious

[112] Henry Brooke. Names were discussed at a meeting between Beloe, Brooke, the Joint Under-Secretary C. M. Woodhouse, and Guppy on 26 Aug. 1963; and the Home Office was responsible for suggesting the names of two of those who served on the group—Viscount Colville of Culross (a lawyer, subsequently junior Home Office Minister, and since 1993 a Circuit Judge) and E. Short, MP (Labour) for Newcastle upon Tyne Central (who resigned on appointment as Labour Chief Whip in November 1964). In the end Beloe was able to tell Bishop Mortimer that the Home Office thought the composition of the Group was 'all right, or unobjectionable'.

[113] Beloe had consulted Dobson about the names he had in mind on 19 Aug. 1963: *Ramsey Papers*, vol. 43; and Dobson replied from his holiday hotel commenting in detail on membership and on the terms of the draft letter of invitation to be sent by the Archbishop. Lord Chancellor Dilhorne subsequently resolved doubts about whether a judge should be invited to join the group: 'I would like a judge to sit on your Committee and I think Phillimore would be the most suitable': Dilhorne to Ramsey, 16 Dec. 1963. (Sir Henry Phillimore—member of a family of distinguished ecclesiastical lawyers, a judge of the Probate, Divorce and Admiralty Division from 1959 to 1962 and at the time a judge of the Queen's Bench Division—was duly appointed.)

[114] However, the major source of suggestions for possible members was Professor J. N. D. Anderson (1908–94), Professor of Oriental Laws in the University of London and leader of the Evangelical wing of the Church of England: see D. McClean (1995) 90 *Proceedings of the British Academy* 251, 257. (It was the latter rather than the former qualification which accounted for Anderson's involvement; and Beloe had tactfully to disabuse the Home Secretary and his officials that Anderson's role was primarily to advise on Islam—a matter which had evidently caused some concern.) For Anderson's role as a member in the Group's work, see p. 51, below.

[115] The Lord Chancellor's office (see *Ramsey Papers*, vol. 62, Beloe to Mortimer 25 Mar. 1964) advised against the appointment of Mr William Latey QC (who had also volunteered to serve on the Morton Royal Commission: see n. 64 above). The Home Office had reservations about the suitability of Lord Devlin (then a Lord of Appeal in Ordinary) for membership. In the event Devlin was invited to join the group, evidently because it was thought politic to have a Roman Catholic on the Committee. (It is also possible that Archbishop Ramsey's recollection of Devlin as a Cambridge undergraduate and as President of the Union outstripping 'all rivals in the art of the advocate' (R. F. V. Heuston (1993) 84 *Proceedings of the British Academy* 247, 248) contributed to the decision.) But (as *Putting Asunder* states) Devlin's 'public duties prevented his coming to more than one meeting' although he received the papers and commented on the draft Report; and it is to be noticed that Devlin, noting that he had not been able to take part in the Group's detailed discussions, distanced himself from the recommendations eventually made by the Archbishop's Group for procedural change to enable the court to satisfy itself that there had indeed been an irretrievable breakdown: *Putting Asunder* p. 63, footnote. In Mar. 1963, in the Earl Grey Memorial Lecture at Durham University (*The Enforcement of Morals* (1965) Ch. IV, particularly at p. 75 ff), Devlin argued that the State's interest in divorce was primarily concerned with whether the parties should be allowed to remarry, and he apparently favoured an inquiry into whether the public interest would, in any particular case, be injured by a fresh marriage—a suggestion not pursued by anyone else and unlikely to have been regarded as practicable by court administration officials.

[116] In the event, in addition to those already mentioned, the following accepted the Archbishop's invitation issued in Jan. 1964: (1) G. B. Bentley (b. 1909), Canon of Windsor. Although invited to serve when the seventy-year-old Professor of Moral and Pastoral Theology at Oxford (V. A. Demant) declined, Bentley amply justified Demant's recommendation that he be invited to serve and played a large part in the Group's work bearing the main responsibility for drafting the group's Report. (His colleagues, in recognition of this, gave him a specially bound copy of the Report, but Archbishop Ramsey—concerned that he might thereby become associated with the Report's recommendations—refused to allow the presentation copy to be embossed with the Arms of the Province of Canterbury.) (2) the Reverend G. R. Dunstan, Minor Canon of Westminster Abbey and heavily involved in the work of the Board for Social Responsibility (subsequently F. D. Maurice Professor of Moral and

observance was imposed;[117] and the selection process came to resemble that traditionally conducted in Whitehall trawls of the 'great and the good', with 'slots' being allocated to particular professions (for example, child psychiatry) and interests (for example, marriage guidance). There was one particular problem: criticism about the lack of social science expertise in the Morton Commission[118] made it seem imperative that a 'sociologist' be a member of the Archbishop's Group; but considerable difficulty was experienced in identifying a sociologist who could be described as a Christian, even in the broadest interpretation of the word.[119] Eventually Professor Donald MacRae[120] accepted an invitation to join the group.[121]

Invitations to join the group were ultimately sent out in January 1964; and the members held their first meeting at the Institute of Advanced Legal Studies[122] on 26 May 1964. It had been decided (after some discussion) to make public the existence and remit of the Group.[123]

SETTLING THE GROUP'S REPORT, 'PUTTING ASUNDER'

Ramsey's letter of invitation to join the Group had made clear the dilemma the Church faced:[124]

Social Theology, King's College, London). (3) Quentin Edwards (b. 1925), barrister (subsequently a Circuit Judge and Chancellor of Blackburn and Chichester). (4) Lady Helen Oppenheimer (b. 1926), writer on moral and philosophical theology and subsequently Lecturer in Ethics, Cuddesdon Theological College. (5) Dr Desmond Pond (1919–86), Consultant Psychiatrist (subsequently Sir Desmond Pond, Chief Scientist DHSS). (6) Joan Rubinstein, a practising Methodist, solicitor and partner in a London firm with a substantial divorce practice: see Beloe to Dobson 2 Sept. 1963, *Ramsey Papers* vol. 43.

[117] It was for this reason that it was decided not to invite the eminent Jewish lawyer, Professor Otto Kahn-Freund to be a member of the group.

[118] Made by McGregor, Lord Chorley and others: see p. 40 above.

[119] The Warden of All Souls College Oxford was prepared to ascertain whether one distinguished sociologist had religious beliefs 'without the patient being aware' that the enquiry was being made (see Beloe to Sparrow, 3 Dec. 1963, *Ramsey Papers*, vol. 43). O. R. McGregor was rejected as being 'rather too irritating for the sort of calm exchange . . . needed' but in any event (as any reader of *Divorce in England* could testify) he was outspokenly hostile to what he evidently regarded as the pretensions of the Church in relation to family law and otherwise.

[120] (1921–97), Martin White Professor of Sociology in the University of London.

[121] As will be seen, this appointment gave rise to problems: see p. 55 below.

[122] Of which J. N. D. Anderson (n. 114 above) was the Director.

[123] A Press Release was issued on 9 Apr. 1964. The Group's formal terms of reference, settled after lengthy discussion (with the Home Office and Lord Chancellor's Department amongst others) were: 'to review the law of England concerning divorce and, recognising that there is a difference in the attitudes of the Church and State towards the further marriage of a divorced person whose former partner is living, to consider whether the inclusion of any new principle or procedure in the law of the State would be likely to operate (1) more justly and with greater assistance to the stability of marriage and the happiness of all concerned including children than at present; and (2) in such a way as to do nothing to undermine the approach of couples to marriage as a lifelong covenant': *Putting Asunder* (1966) p. ix.

[124] In his letter of invitation to serve on the Group drafted in Jan. 1964, *Ramsey Papers*, vol. 62, folio 21; and see Ramsey to Bentley, 17 Jan. 1964, *Minutes of the Archbishop's Group on the reform of Divorce*, Lambeth Palace MS 3460, 26 May 1964, p. i.

He and other church leaders were opposed to seven years' separation as a ground for divorce since if it did not also require consent this would cause great injustice whilst if it did 'it would undermine the nature of the marriage contract as a life-long intention'. For those reasons it had been right to reject the Abse proposal. But the law remained unsatisfactory 'not least because there is often recourse to a fictitious planning of matrimonial offences in order to obtain a divorce'.

How was the Group to resolve the dilemma? At the outset, Mortimer made it clear that the ultimate objective was to try to put forward proposals 'which would be acceptable to "humanists" and Christians alike'.[125] The numerous letters he had received touched on (1) the desire of one party to a marriage to be free to legitimise a new union and its issue and the reluctance of the other party to permit this; (2) the general ignorance of and impatience with legal procedures, particularly those which submit an undefending spouse to hearing unexpectedly the material facts alleged against him without opportunity to reply;[126] (3) the difficulty of obtaining payment of maintenance without burdensome and costly visits to court; (4) the fear that divorce for separation might endanger 'general acceptance of marriage as a life long contract'.

The Group met on eighteen occasions between May 1964 and March 1966,[127] and considered an impressive body of evidence from some distinguished and expert witnesses.[128] It did not take long for it to reach a consensus.[129] The law as it stood was universally agreed to be unsatisfactory;[130] and there was a strong prima-facie case for the substitution of irretrievable breakdown as the sole ground for divorce, replacing the matrimonial offence. The court would have power to

---

[125] *Minutes of the Archbishop's Group on the reform of Divorce*, Lambeth Palace MS 3460, 26 May 1964, p. 2.

[126] In the House of Lords debate on *Putting Asunder* (*Official Report* (HL) 23 Nov. 1966, vol. 278, col. 241) Mortimer said that if often happened that the so-called guilty party, foolishly attending the hearing, was 'appalled by the terms in which counsel have represented the matrimonial offence . . . He or she is even more appalled when the other party . . . is called into the witness-box and agrees that, indeed, the conduct was so, and that he or she is now so aggrieved that the divorce is abundantly justified. It is then, very often, that bitterness is created between the parties.'

[127] Its Report was presented to the Archbishop at a dinner in the House of Lords on 29 Mar. 1966: *Minutes of the Archbishop's Group on the reform of Divorce*, Lambeth Palace MS 3460, 26 Feb. 1966, p. 161. The Archbishop sent a typescript to the Lord Chancellor on 7 Apr. 1966: Ramsey to Gardiner, *Ramsey Papers*, vol. 102.

[128] Including Simon, P, and Scarman and Ormrod JJ. Professor J. N. D. Anderson also had a meeting (reported by him to the Group on 28 Jan. 1996: see *Minutes of the Archbishop's Group on the reform of Divorce*, Lambeth Palace MS 3460) with Scarman and Professor L. C. B. Gower in their capacity as members of the newly established Law Commission: see further below p. 57.

[129] *Minutes of the Archbishop's Group on the reform of Divorce*, Lambeth Palace MS 3460, Third Meeting, 5 Nov. 1964. So strong was the pro-reform sentiment that A. J. Irvine MP QC (who had been appointed to the Commission in Mar. 1965 in the place of E. W. Short) felt obliged to resign to avoid having to take any part in the drafting of propositions with which he was out of sympathy: Irvine to Beloe, *Ramsey Papers*, vol. 82, 17 Nov. 1965.)

[130] Mortimer in the House of Lords debate on *Putting Asunder*: *Official Report* (HL) 23 Nov. 1966, vol. 278, col. 242.

dissolve marriage if 'having regard to the interests of society as well as of those immediately affected by its decision, it judged it wrong to maintain the legal existence of a relationship that was beyond all probability of existing again in fact'.[131] This would involve the court giving a judgment on the state of the marriage; and its decree would no longer be 'against' the respondent but rather 'against' further legal recognition of the marriage.[132]

The Group remained adamantly opposed to divorce by consent: which (as Bishop Mortimer was to say[133]) was open to the 'grave, indeed overwhelming objection' that it would reduce marriage to a purely private contract and would ignore the interest of the community'.[134] Hence, it was to be for the court, representing the community, to decide whether the marriage had indeed irretrievably broken down;[135] and, although the agreement of the parties in wanting a divorce would not be a bar (and might even count in favour of a decree) in no case would such an agreement of itself suffice to effect divorce.[136] It was, for the Archbishop's Group, essential that the court should always examine[137] the issue of breakdown according to the evidence;[138] and it made it clear that its recommendation for amendment of the substantive law was conditional upon procedural changes to enable the court to conduct the inquest it believed to be necessary[139] into the alleged fact and causes of the death of the marriage relationship and to 'get to grips with

---

[131] *Putting Asunder, A Divorce Law for Contemporary Society* (1966) para. 56.

[132] *Putting Asunder, A Divorce Law for Contemporary Society* (1966) p. 52.

[133] House of Lords debate on *Putting Asunder* (*Official Report* (HL) 23 Nov. 1966, vol. 278, col. 243).

[134] It should also be noted that Lord Walker had denied that to allow divorce founded on seven years' separation (as advocated by Mrs Eirene White) would constitute acceptance of divorce by consent: see 'Statement of his Views by Lord Walker': *Report of the Royal Commission on Marriage and Divorce* (Chairman: Lord Morton of Henryton) (1956, Cmd. 9678) p. 340, para. 7.

[135] i.e. '. . . declare defunct *de jure* what . . . is already defunct *de facto*': *Putting Asunder, A Divorce Law for Contemporary Society* (1966) para. 54. The Group eventually decided not to append a draft Bill to its Report, but had agreed in principle on a clause defining the criterion as there being 'no reasonable probability of such a reconciliation as would enable the spouses to live together for their mutual support and comfort as husband and wife': *Minutes of the Archbishop's Group on the reform of Divorce*, Lambeth Palace MS 3460, 9 Apr. 1965, p. 74.

[136] *Putting Asunder, A Divorce Law for Contemporary Society* (1966) para. 59(a). The Group had agreed as early as its second meeting that divorce based on consent would undermine the natural meaning of the words used in the marriage ceremony and was quite different from the concept of divorce for breakdown: *Minutes of the Archbishop's Group on the reform of Divorce*, Lambeth Palace MS 3460, 28 July 1964.

[137] Possibly aided by counsel representing the public interest and by forensic social workers who would investigate matters about which the court needed to be informed: *Putting Asunder*, para. 89.

[138] *Putting Asunder, A Divorce Law for Contemporary Society* (1966) para. 59.

[139] 'It would have to be made possible for the court . . . to inquire effectively into what attempts at reconciliation had been made, into the feasibility of further attempts, into the acts, events, and circumstances, alleged to have destroyed the marriage, into the truth of statements made (especially in uncontested cases), and into all matters bearing upon the determination of public interest': *Putting Asunder*, para. 84. Professor O. Kahn-Freund (who was invited to comment on a draft of the Group's Report) considered that the procedure in divorce cases should be 'judicial but non-litigious' on the pattern of adoption cases: *Minutes of the Archbishop's Group on the reform of Divorce*, Lambeth Palace MS 3460, 29 Jan. 1966, p. 151.

the realities of the matrimonial relationship' instead of having—as it thought was the case under the offence based law—to 'concentrate on superficialities'.[140]

The Group refused to accept that any of the well-rehearsed objections to the breakdown principle outweighed its advantages. No doubt (the Group accepted[141]) critics would point to the economic deprivation caused by divorce; but the solution to that lay primarily in reforms of the law of property, pensions (a topic much discussed) and insurance.[142] The Group was correct in its prophesy—indeed, the problem of pensions after divorce remains a source of difficulty more than thirty years later—but it did not see it as part of its remit to prescribe detailed remedies for these problems.

What of the objection that breakdown divorce would allow the guilty to take advantage of their own wrong? The Group thought that the court's judgment could and should be seen[143] as the recognition of a state of affairs and a consequent redefinition of status (rather than as a verdict of guilty after a law suit), and for that reason the maxim would have no general application.[144] But even so, the Group accepted[145] the need for a safeguard—in the form of an absolute bar on divorce—in cases in which to grant a divorce would be outweighed by other considerations of fundamental importance such as the public interest in justice and in protecting the institution of marriage.[146]

On one matter in particular the Group was adamant: the doctrine of breakdown was an *alternative* to divorce founded on the matrimonial offence—the lesser[147] of two evils. On no account should breakdown be introduced into the existing law in the form of an additional ground[148] for divorce.[149] Indeed, the Group

---

[140] *Putting Asunder*, para. 69(b).

[141] See *Minutes of the Archbishop's Group on the reform of Divorce*, Lambeth Palace MS 3460, 23 Oct. 1965, p. 119.

[142] In evidence to the Archbishop's Group, Ormrod J said there were very few cases in which refusal to divorce was founded on spite. In his career at the Bar he had in the end 'never failed to get a divorce out of' those solely motivated by spite. In 'the vast majority of cases, the spouses who refuse to divorce their partners are wives who are determined not to lose their pension rights . . . or who are averse to divorce on religious grounds'.

[143] Analogies were drawn with the law of nullity long accepted by the Church in which findings that factors inconsistent with a marital relationship existed would support a decision that the marriage had never in truth come into existence: see *Putting Asunder*, p. 52.

[144] *Putting Asunder, A Divorce Law for Contemporary Society* (1966) p. 52.

[145] *Putting Asunder, A Divorce Law for Contemporary Society* (1966) p. 53.

[146] *Putting Asunder, A Divorce Law for Contemporary Society* (1966) p. 53.

[147] Albeit 'by a very considerable way': *Putting Asunder*, para. 68.

[148] The Minutes of the Group's penultimate meeting record that the Group felt 'most strongly' that if the proposal for divorce founded exclusively on breakdown were rejected, the existing ground for divorce should be preserved: *Minutes of the Archbishop's Group on the reform of Divorce*, Lambeth Palace MS 3460, 28 Feb. 1966, p. 166. A whole section of *Putting Asunder* (pp. 57–9) is devoted to an exposition of 'WHY THE PRINCIPLE OF BREAKDOWN MUST NOT BE INTRODUCED INTO A LAW BASED ON THE MATRIMONIAL OFFENCE'.

[149] In the House of Lords debate on *Putting Asunder* (*Official Report* (HL) 23 Nov. 1966, vol. 278, col. 245) Bishop Mortimer said that to follow the precedent of the Abse Bill would be to leave the matrimonial offence as the main ground of divorce (not least because people would prefer a speedy way of securing divorce once they had decided the marriage was over) and this would accordingly do nothing to remove the unsatisfactory features of the law.

thought that rather than 'to inject into [the offence based law] a small but virulent dose of incompatible principle'[150] it would be better to keep the law based firmly on the matrimonial offence and to consider how the administration[151] of the law could be improved.

All these points were incorporated into the Group's Report, *Putting Asunder*, eventually published (to the accompaniment of much, generally favourable,[152] radio, television and other press publicity[153]) on 29 July 1966.

QUO WARRANTO?

The Established Church had traditionally opposed any further erosion of the 'great principle' proclaimed by Christ holding marriage to be a 'life-long obligation terminable only by death with all the sacrifice which such an obligation imposed';[154] but as long ago as 1937[155] the Church had come to accept that it

---

[150] *Putting Asunder*, para. 69.

[151] The Group noted the decisions of the House of Lords (*Gollins* v. *Gollins* [1964] AC 644 and *Williams* v. *Williams* [1964] AC 698) emphasising the 'principle of the intolerable situation' (i.e. the emergence through the respondent's conduct of a situation the petitioner should not be called upon to endure) as the essence of the matrimonial offence of cruelty, and was evidently concerned that 'if allowed to get out of hand' this might 'transform the doctrine of the matrimonial offence out of all recognition' and turn it 'into something that was neither fish, flesh, nor fowl, but solely a red herring' (*Putting Asunder*, paras. 50, 69).

[152] For example, *The Times*'s leading article on 29 July 1966 declared that it 'is doubtful whether there has been published in recent times a more persuasive, thoughtful or constructive plea on behalf of the breakdown of marriage doctrine or a more effective condemnation of the present method of divorce'.

[153] Originally it had been thought that it might be best if the Group's work were kept confidential; and Ramsey seems to have remained doubtful about the wisdom of publication: see n. 181 below. But in the event Beloe was able to organise lists of speakers prepared to discuss the Report on publication and there was extensive radio, television and other media coverage: Beloe to Hornby, 20 May 1966, *Ramsey Papers*, vol. 102; and note folio 221 commenting that the 'advantages of giving broadcasting organisations ample advance warning and full details of important Church publications have again been demonstrated'. *The Times* and other broadsheet newspapers published favourable comments on the Report on 29 July; as did the *Observer* on 31 July. Ramsey told Mortimer he was sorry that the *Church Times* (which had expressed disquiet—subsequently demonstrated to have been well-founded—that public opinion might misunderstand the message the Church was seeking to give about its teaching on marriage) had 'reacted so stupidly' in contrast to 'the intelligent press': Ramsey to Mortimer 14 Aug. 1966, *Ramsey Papers*, vol. 102.

[154] Royal Commission on Divorce and Matrimonial Causes (1912) Cd. 6478, Minority Report by the Archbishop of York, Sir William Anson and Sir Lewis Dibdin, pp. 186–8.

[155] This was the view recorded by Cosmo Gordon Lang, signatory (as Archbishop of York) of the 1912 Royal Commission Minority Report quoted above, and Archbishop of Canterbury at the time of the enactment of the Matrimonial Causes Act 1937: see J. G. Lockhart, *Cosmo Gordon Lang* (1949) p. 235. Lang remained a firm exponent of the traditional Anglican doctrine of marriage, and in a broadcast on 13 Dec. 1936 bitterly criticised the action of King Edward VIII in abdicating and thereby surrendering his trust for no better reason than a 'craving for private happiness' sought 'in a manner inconsistent with the Christian principles of marriage, and within a social circle whose standards and way of life are alien to all the best instincts and traditions of his people': op. cit. p. 405. On the relationship between the abdication crisis and divorce reform, see G. I. T. Machin, 'Marriage and the Churches in the 1930s: Royal Abdication and Divorce Reform, 1936–7' (1991) 42 *Journal of Ecclesiastical History*, 68.

was no longer possible to impose 'the full Christian standard by law on a largely non-Christian population'.[156] On that basis, *Putting Asunder* at the outset drew a distinction to which it attached great importance.[157] How 'the doctrine of Christ concerning marriage should be interpreted and applied within the Christian Church is one question: what the Church ought to say and do about secular laws of marriage and divorce is another question altogether . . . Our own terms of reference make it abundantly clear that our business is with the second question only.' Hence (as the *Observer* newspaper put it[158]) the Report was not in any sense 'another theological tract written by theologians for the Church's communicants'.

But if *Putting Asunder* did not (and did not purport to) derive its authority from religious principles, what precisely was the basis of the Group's authority? One possibility could have been to analyse the social science evidence (which, as we have seen,[159] critics claimed the Morton Commission had ignored); and certainly great care had been taken to ensure that a sociologist should be a member of the Committee. But in fact *Putting Asunder* contains less by way of hard data about the divorce process and its consequences[160] than did the Morton Commission's Report, whilst the contribution made by the sociologist member[161]

---

[156] The same principle was stated by Archbishop Ramsey in 1963: see *Official Report* (HL) 21 June 1963, vol. 250, col. 1544.

[157] *Putting Asunder, A Divorce Law for Contemporary Society* (1966) paras. 6 and 7. 'This', the Report asserted, 'can hardly be repeated too often.'   [158] Leading Article, 31 July 1966.

[159] See p. 40 above.

[160] The Group noted at its first meeting the difficulty of offering convincing sociological information about such matters as attitudes to permanency—albeit it was also recorded that 'the introduction of the doctrine of frustration into the law of contract had not noticeably altered the legal prescription of the sanctity of contract': *Minutes of the Archbishop's Group on the reform of Divorce*, Lambeth Palace MS 3460, p. 5.

[161] The Group decided to establish specialist subcommittees to advise on theological, legal and sociological aspects of the inquiry, and Professor MacRae was reported on 15 Feb. 1966 to have promised to submit a memorandum based on his specialised knowledge 'within a few days': *Minutes of the Archbishop's Group on the reform of Divorce*, Lambeth Palace MS 3460, pp. 12, 160. But it appears that MacRae never produced a memorandum; and his tardiness in submitting the draft Appendix (eventually printed under his own name as Appendix F to *Putting Asunder* with a disclaimer stating that MacRae 'had been unable to complete [it] in time for adoption by the Group') caused immense problems to his colleagues. Dunstan wrote despairingly to Mortimer on 17 May 1966 (after delivery of the body of the Report to the Archbishop and at a time when the publishers were pressing for copy) explaining that—notwithstanding his having telephoned MacRae seven times a day and even offering the services of Dunstan's secretary to fetch MacRae's manuscript and type it out for his revision— nothing was to hand. Dunstan suggested—'remembering as we do that the sociologists led the attack on the Report of the Morton Commission, on the ground that no consideration was given to sociological data'—that it was essential that 'somewhere there be recorded in our report a statement to the effect that Professor MacRae was appointed a member of our Commission, that he attended X meetings of the full group and one meeting of the Social Sub-Committee; that he was consulted by the Social Sub-Committee throughout its deliberations and that the progress of the whole group's thinking was reported to him throughout its course; that it was the group's intention to include a chapter upon the sociological considerations in its report, but that unfortunately Professor MacRae could not write this in time'.

to *Putting Asunder*[162] and the thinking which led up to it appears[163] to have been minimal.[164] It is difficult to avoid the conclusion that *Putting Asunder* has no more authority than any other well-argued statement of opinion made by an unrepresentative body even more 'heavily biased towards upper- and middle-class outlooks'[165] than had been the Morton Commission. It is true[166] that the policy of appointing the 'common man and woman' to the Morton Commission was difficult to implement; but at least an effort was made to that end and the Commission did have some members drawn from working-class backgrounds.[167] In contrast, no comparable attempt was made to select working-class members for the Archbishop's Group which was exclusively composed of, generally liberally minded, members of the intelligentsia and professional classes, selected in part on the recommendation of Ministers and Civil Servants anxious (whilst not revealing their own involvement) to bring about a solution to what had become, politically and administratively, an embarrassing problem.

---

[162] MacRae's Appendix F runs to eight pages of A5 paper, mostly pitched at a high level of generality. Amongst other propositions soon to be falsified MacRae claimed that the popularity of marriage was increasing, the social stability of families growing 'as the role of the husband and father in the life and work of the home steadily increases in all classes' and that 'every relevant social investigation' seemed further to validate 'the enormous strength and growing solidity of marriage as an institution': para. 3.

[163] MacRae did make the perceptive remark that lawyers tend to believe that the law is widely known and understood; and he commented that lawyers 'believe frequently that the law is also a kind of moral propaganda which persuades behaviour in all areas of life': *Putting Asunder*, Appendix F, para. 10. This view has certainly been held by some of those arguing for a restrictive divorce law (for example, Lord Chancellor Kilmuir thought that facilitating divorce would 'put at the backs of people's minds . . . the idea that marriage has a voluntary break clause' and to do so would change the character of marriage 'in a way which would do immense harm': *Official Report* (HL) 24 Oct. 1956, vol. 199, col. 1057); but how far is it well founded? The best that MacRae could do was to say that this and other similar beliefs 'are in some degree false, though each also embodies some social truth'; and to speculate that it was reasonable to assume the law had 'far less effect on behaviour than lawyers appear to think'. Although discussion of Lord Devlin's view that the law might properly penalise immorality was also stimulated by the publication in 1963 of H. L. A. Hart's *Law, Liberty and Morality* (strongly criticising Devlin's view) this discussion seems to have been largely confined to the proper role of the criminal law and has not extended to a discussion of the role of legal institutions such as marriage.

[164] In fairness to MacRae's memory it should be said that on two occasions he offered his resignation by reason of his inability to contribute sufficiently to the Commission's work, but these offers were rejected, members considering that 'it would be a great pity if he were to resign, as his availability to the Commission and his signature to its Report would be most valuable': *Minutes of the Archbishop's Group on the reform of Divorce*, Lambeth Palace MS 3460, 20 Nov. 1965, p. 125. As his obituarist in *The Times* (2 Jan. 1998) notes, MacRae was 'inhibited by perfectionism and diverted by excess of gifts . . . It is to be suspected that he had come to conclusions about social life which were too bleak and contrary to be articulated. For him, the trouble was that the great banalities were after all mostly true, and for the rest it was the wise man's part to leave the unsayable unsaid'.

[165] One of the criticisms of the Morton Report made by Professor O. R. McGregor, *Divorce in England, A Centenary Study* (1957) p. 179.   [166] See p. 41 above.

[167] Sir Frederick Burrows had served in the ranks throughout World War I and had been President of the National Union of Railwaymen; Mrs Mabel Ridehalgh had been President and General Secretary of the Women's Co-Operative Guild.

THE LAW COMMISSION AND THE ARCHBISHOP'S GROUP

The Archbishop's Group was not the only officially sponsored body interested in divorce law reform. The *First Programme*[168] of the newly created Law Commission[169]—published little more than a month after the Law Commissions Act 1965 had received the royal assent[170]—committed it to a preliminary examination of Matrimonial Law, having regard to the variety of views expressed in and following the Report of the Morton Commission; and individual Commissioners had a strong interest in the subject. Indeed, Sir Leslie Scarman, the Commission's Chairman, had both publicly[171] and privately[172] expressed himself as sympathetic to reform; whilst the evidence given to the Morton Commission[173] by Professor L. C. B. Gower—at one time a committee member of the Divorce Law Reform Union—had not only made pellucidly clear his belief in the need for reform[174] but had attracted considerable public attention.[175] A third[176] Law Commissioner[177] had edited the influential Manifesto, *Law Reform NOW.*[178]

In those circumstances, the Law Commission was inevitably interested in the work on which the Archbishop's Group had embarked; and on 7 March 1966 Scarman wrote to the Archbishop[179] noting the Commissioners' 'close and fruitful' consultation with Anderson, their concern 'if humanly possible' to submit the

---

[168] (1965) Law Com. No. 1.

[169] The Commission was established to undertake the reform and modernisation of the law: see Ch. 1 above.   [170] On 15 June 1965.

[171] In a lecture delivered in Mar. 1966: *Family Law and Law Reform* (Bristol, 1966).

[172] In evidence given to the Archbishop's Group on 19 Feb. 1965 Scarman had said that breakdown as a ground for divorce was 'both sensible and viable' (although, unlike the Group, he favoured the retention of the matrimonial offence as an alternative ground for divorce): *Minutes of the Archbishop's Group on the reform of Divorce*, Lambeth Palace MS 3460, pp. 60–4.

[173] *Minutes of Evidence* First Day 20 May 1952.

[174] To allow divorce based on consent would 'in the main . . . merely allow the parties to do openly what they now do clandestinely. To allow divorce based on (say) seven years' separation, would . . . be a slight extension of the present grounds but one which seems to me to be unobjectionable and essential if blackmail . . . is to be avoided.' Gower considered that to talk about preserving the sanctity of marriage where the parties had been irreconcilably separated for seven years was 'casuistry': *Royal Commission on Marriage and Divorce, Minutes of Evidence*, Paper No. 3 and First Day 20 May 1952.

[175] Gower's exposure of the realities of the divorce process under the matrimonial offence doctrine was widely reported in the Press (see e.g. *The Times*, 21 May 1952 under the headline 'Bogus Cases') whilst this and his courageous admission that he had personally drafted a letter intended to convert what was in truth a wholly consensual separation into desertion clearly antagonised the Royal Commission's chairman Lord Morton and his judicial colleague Pearce J (who no doubt found Gower's dismissal of the Bar Council's evidence as 'arrant nonsense' inflammatory). For a strong criticism of the Commissioners' reaction to Gower's evidence, see O. R. McGregor, *Divorce in England, A Centenary Study* (1957) pp. 134 ff.   [176] There were in all five Commissioners.

[177] Andrew Martin QC.

[178] 1963. The chapter on *Family Law*, by O. M. Stone and A. Gerard, had favoured five years' separation as a ground on which a divorce petition could be presented (although if there were children the court was to have a discretion, 'the sincerity of the efforts at reconciliation made by the petitioner being the touchstone of the matter').

[179] Scarman to Ramsey, 7 Mar. 1966, *Ramsey Papers*, vol. 102.

Commission's Report on its programmed family law work in the course of the year, and their anxiety 'not to commit [themselves] to any view before we have had the opportunity of reading the report of your Commission'. In fact, Scarman already knew perfectly well what *Putting Asunder* was going to say—indeed, Anderson had reported to his colleagues Scarman's assessment of the then unpublished draft as 'an admirable document'.[180]

Ramsey agreed to let Scarman see the typescript of the draft Report in confidence;[181] and it seems reasonable to suppose[182] that the Law Commissioners, with advance knowledge of the contents of *Putting Asunder*, had appreciated the tactical advantage of being able—rather than avowedly giving their own views on divorce reform (which would not have come as any surprise to those aware of the composition of the Commission and the recorded views of a majority[183] of the Commissioners)—to present the Commission's own Report as no more than comments by expert technicians on the practicalities of implementing what the Archbishop's Group proposed. Certainly the Commission's *First Annual Report* did nothing to reduce expectations[184] that the Archbishop's Group's Report would provide the catalysis for divorce reform[185] and the significance of

---

[180] *Minutes of the Archbishop's Group on the reform of Divorce*, Lambeth Palace MS 3460, 28 Jan. 1966, p. 150.

[181] Ramsey made it clear that he had not decided whether or not the Report should be published: Ramsey to Scarman, 8 Mar. 1966, *Ramsey Papers,* vol. 102; and see further n. 188 below. Curiously Beloe was already in discussion with the SPCK about the arrangements for publication of the Report: see e.g. Beloe to Davey 7 Feb. 1966. In fact the Group had already authorised Professor J. N. D. Anderson to show Scarman and Gower a draft of the Group's Report: see below.

[182] The main Law Commission's files dealing with its Review of divorce law down to the publication of the 'concordat' with the Archbishop's Group (i.e. down to and including file No. 56/70/01 Part 2) in June 1967 have been destroyed. Some information is available in the Minutes of Commissioners' Meetings (PRO BC3/1 and 2); but the main source for the Law Commission's activities appears to be the *Ramsey Papers*, vol. 117.

[183] The extent to which the two Commissioners (Neil Lawson QC and N. S. Marsh) who had not already publicly taken a position on the subject took an active part in settling the Commission's policy is not clear. On the one hand, the tradition that the Commission is a collegiate body all of whose members are fully involved in all its publications was already well established and Minutes record discussions on policy at Commissioners' Meetings on 20 Sept. and 10 Dec. 1966: see p. 60 below; but on the other the Report was evidently produced in a very short time and Scarman's recorded statement that 'the Commissioners would have a chance of seeing [*sic*] the preliminary paper' and that it was 'essential that [the Report be] sent out with the authority of all the Commissioners' does not suggest a great deal of involvement, especially since it was made at the beginning of the Long Vacation: (*Minutes of Commissioners' Meeting* PRO BC3/2) 19 Aug. 1966.

[184] The Commission's *First Annual Report 1965–66* (1966), para. 78, reported the Commission's decision to 'make no attempt to formulate views on . . . the grounds for divorce . . . until after the publication of' the Archbishop's Group's Report. 'This Report will be of great value as an indication of the present state of an important and responsible section of public opinion. In the meantime we are collecting and studying the available legal, sociological, and comparative material . . .'

[185] These expectations may have been reinforced by Scarman's reported press statements about a seminar organised by the Law Commission at All Souls College Oxford on 8–9 July 1966 (i.e. some weeks before the publication of *Putting Asunder* on 29 July). The seminar was attended by Mortimer, members of the judiciary, lawyers (practising and academic), marriage guidance workers, McGregor and another sociologist, and Miss Lucy Faithfull (then Children's Officer for Oxfordshire). Apparently it had not been possible to invite all those who wished to attend: Minutes

Putting Asunder was inevitably heightened by the action of the Lord Chancellor[186] —himself a committed advocate of divorce reform—immediately making a formal reference of the document to the Commission for its advice.[187] In this way, what had originally been intended by the Church as a low-key contribution to the debate[188] was officially moved to the centre of the stage; and it was the Church which appeared—for the first time—itself to be advocating the reforms which it had long opposed.

No doubt at the time the members of the Group who had laboured over many months to produce *Putting Asunder* were gratified by the appreciation of their efforts; but, as we shall see, in retrospect Anderson's expressed concern that 'the Law Commission might use the Report for its own purposes but not in the way intended by the Group. It might adopt the Group's support for breakdown of marriage but merely add that ground onto a list of matrimonial offences'[189] seems to have been justified.

of Commissioners' Meeting, 12 July 1966, BC3/3, paras. 52–3. The Commission had prepared a nine-page document dated 29 June 1966 as the basis for discussion; and it, along with the very full note of the seminar proceedings, is amongst the few relevant Law Commission records not to have been destroyed: see PRO BC3/592. Opinion at the seminar seems to have been (i) overwhelmingly critical of the existing law; (ii) sympathetic to breakdown as the ground for divorce in its place; but (iii) concerned as to whether or not breakdown would be justiciable, the potential hardship to the rejected wife, and whether damage to children could be minimised by having different rules for divorce in cases in which the spouses were childless. The Commission's paper had drawn attention to the cost of carrying out an inquiry into breakdown (and the questionable social value of doing so) but it is not clear whether the opinion expressed by Sir Jocelyn Simon, P that Mortimer was 'hopelessly embarrassed by the case of the woman who had substantially performed her matrimonial obligations and would be deprived of her rights on widowhood by any form of divorce by compulsion' and that he had not been able to say more than that 'such a case must be provided for' is a fair reflection of the discussion. (As already noted—see text to n. 141 above—*Putting Asunder* itself is unspecific on the subject.) Simon (in what Scarman described as a 'profoundly important' letter) also put forward again the case for distinguishing between cases in which there were children of the marriage and others: see Simon to Scarman, 15 July 1966, and Scarman's acknowledgement 18 July 1966: PRO BC3/592.

[186] Formerly Gerald Gardiner QC, co-editor with Martin of *Law Reform NOW* and a long-standing member of the Divorce Law Reform Union: B. H. Lee, *Divorce Law Reform in England* (1974) p. 62.

[187] *Reform of the Grounds of Divorce, The Field of Choice, Report on a Reference under section 3(1)(e) of the Law Commissions Act 1965* (1966), Cmnd. 3123, Law Com. No. 15 (subsequently referred to as *The Field of Choice*) para. 1. The Law Commission would, of course, have been able to take such account as it wished of *The Field of Choice* and simply worked to complete its programmed work on divorce; but that would inevitably have involved delay whilst consultation was carried out, and would almost certainly have involved the Commission in abandoning the role it was able to adopt under the reference as a mere purveyor of technical advice about procedural practicability.

[188] See *Ramsey Papers*, vol. 62, Beloe to Hornby (Church Information Office) 27 Jan. 1964: 'My own feeling was in favour of silence' but (i) the Home Secretary had told him personally 'that he thought it would do the Church good for it to be known that there was a feeling of compassion towards this problem. The Church had, in his view, been merely in opposition for too long'; and (ii) the existence of the Group was almost certain to become known in some way or other 'and then there might be in say the Daily Express a tremendous news story'. But in the event publication of the Report was surrounded by much publicity and attracted a great deal of comment: see n. 153 above.

[189] *Minutes of the Archbishop's Group on the reform of Divorce*, Lambeth Palace MS 3460, Fourteenth Meeting 28 and 29 Jan. 1966, pp. 149–52. Scarman had in evidence to the Group indicated his preference for the retention of the matrimonial offence as an alternative: see n. 172 above.

THE FIELD OF CHOICE: THE LAW COMMISSION'S
'PURELY LEGAL' ADVICE

The publicity aroused by the publication of *Putting Asunder* revived interest in promoting legislation; and the Archbishop had to deter two senior Conservatives from seeking to introduce legislation 'before public opinion had had an opportunity' fully to absorb the proposals and their implication.[190] In the event, a House of Lords debate was scheduled for November 1966; and the Lord Chancellor asked the Law Commission to advance the publication[191] of the Commission's Report[192] so that it would be available for discussion in the debate.

The Report, *Reform of the Grounds of Divorce, The Field of Choice*,[193] was published on 9 November 1966,[194] and is often referred to as a blueprint for the 1969 Divorce Reform Act. In fact the *Field of Choice* purports to have a much more limited objective:[195]

It is not [said the Commission] . . . for us but for Parliament to settle such controversial social issues as the advisability of extending the present grounds of divorce. Our

---

[190] Beloe to Duncan Sandys (who had apparently seen a copy of the Report), 13 May 1966, *Ramsey Papers*, vol. 102. After publication, the former Lord Chancellor, Lord Dilhorne (for whose role see pp. 49 above), intimated that he liked the Report 'very much' whilst having some doubts about its practicality. Dilhorne offered to move a motion in the House of Lords approving *Putting Asunder* and thereafter to introduce a Bill to give effect to the proposals; but Ramsey replied that he would be 'a bit chary of inviting approval for fear of riding for a fall' (Ramsey to Dilhorne, 14 Aug. 1966) and in the event a motion was moved by Mortimer simply calling attention to the matter and moving for papers: *Official Report* (HL) 23 Nov. 1966, vol. 278, col. 241.

[191] On any basis—and even making allowances for the fact that the topic did not come as a novelty to some of those involved—the speed with which the Commissioners and their staff prepared *The Field of Choice* is remarkable: on 19 Aug. 1966 (*Minutes of Commissioners' Meeting* PRO BC3/2) Scarman referred to the 'urgent priority of Family Law' in the Commission's activities, and it appears that at that time the Family Law team had not got beyond preparing a 'preliminary paper' on the ground for divorce. Yet the Commission's Report was ready for publication only two months later.

[192] PRO BC3/2 Minutes of Commissioners' Meeting 20 Sept. 1966. At this meeting the Commissioners had settled the policy to be embodied in the Report *The Field of Choice*—the draft was apparently produced by J. M. Cartwright Sharp, then an assistant solicitor on the Commission's staff (and subsequently Secretary to the Law Commission 1968–78). It was decided—Gower only reluctantly agreeing—not to put forward divorce by consent (even in cases where there were no children); and it was agreed that a longer period of separation should be required in cases in which one spouse did not consent to divorce because the single short period 'would not be acceptable to public opinion': para. 13.

[193] Cmnd. 3123, Law Com. No. 15 (subsequently referred to as *The Field of Choice*).

[194] Curiously enough, on 25 Oct. 1966 (two weeks before publication of *The Field of Choice*, the House of Commons ordered that Leo Abse's Matrimonial Causes Bill, Bill No. 112 (said in its Explanatory Memorandum to 'give effect to the Law Commissioners' proposal that there should be as an additional ground of divorce a period of separation irrespective of which party was at fault, thereby affording a place in the law for the application of the breakdown principle') be printed. It appears that the Commission's Report was (inaccurately) leaked to the press: *Official Report* (HL) 23 Nov. 1966, vol. 278, col. 253.

[195] The Commissioners decided that the 'form of the paper would be factual and not recommendatory, excluding value judgments in so far as that was possible': Minutes of Commissioners' Meeting 20 Sept. 1966, PRO BC3/2.

function in advising . . . must be to assist the Legislature and the general public in considering these questions by pointing out the implications of various possible courses of action. Perhaps the most useful service that we can perform at this stage is to mark out the boundaries of the field of choice . . . We have . . . tried to restrict this Report to a consideration of what appears from a lawyer's point of view to be practicable . . .[196]

The Commission's Press Release was even more modest: the Commission was a 'purely legal body';[197] and it had therefore considered the Archbishop's Group's proposals purely 'from the point of view of what would be feasible as a matter of legal administration'. Both then and subsequently the Commission sought in public[198] to adopt a stance of neutrality between the various groups.[199] But the reality is that the Commissioners concerned were determined to achieve reform of the divorce laws. They evidently laid their plans carefully, and used their considerable political skills[200] to achieve this objective. Politics, of course, involves accepting that although every statement must be true it is not always necessary to tell the whole truth.

Consistently with this approach, the Commission rejected[201] the *Putting Asunder* proposal for Breakdown with Inquest—notwithstanding its 'undoubted attractions and our sympathy with the principles' underlying the Archbishop's Group's Report—'because of purely practical difficulties'[202] in making the scheme

---

[196] *The Field of Choice*, paras. 2, 3.

[197] However, *The Field of Choice* did contain a significant amount of demographic material and did not hesitate to make predictions about future trends. As one of those involved in the drafting of that Report (see n. 224 below) has subsequently put it, however, 'every prediction made then, on the basis of the figures used, turned out to be not just marginally wrong, but very far off the mark indeed. This is a reflection not on the accuracy of the figures used but rather on the extrapolations made from them': R. Deech, 'Divorce Law and Empirical Studies' (1990) 106 LQR 229, 231.

[198] Those working in the Commission seem to have had no doubt about the Commissioners' strong personal preferences.

[199] Minutes of Commissioners' Meeting 20 Sept. 1966, PRO BC3/2, p. 2.

[200] As Leo Abse has noted, the Commission's then Chairman (Sir Leslie Scarman) is 'not only a great and courageous lawyer; he . . . is the most formidable non-political politician in the land. His most extraordinary achievement is that he almost succeeded in concealing his talents, and those of the men surrounding him . . . so that . . . politicians and . . . Lord Chancellors can now deceive themselves into believing that the Law Commission is an anonymous body composed of servile civil servants.': L. Abse, *Private Member* (1973) p. 173. For further evidence of Commissioners' minimising the nature and extent of their commitment to reform, see nn. 208, 228 and 252 below.

[201] *Putting Asunder*, para. 70.

[202] Two main questions emerge from the discussion in *The Field of Choice*, paras. 56–70. First, was the issue of breakdown intrinsically justiciable or would it inevitably involve an unacceptably wide judicial discretion leading to 'varying and unpredictable conclusions'. Secondly, would acceptance of the Archbishop's Group's proposals mean that cases would take longer and cost more by reason of the need for far more judges, courthouses and court officials? As to the first, the Commission did not refer to the fact that the President of the Probate, Divorce and Admiralty Division had accepted the practicability of the breakdown test. As to the second, the Commission gave no detailed consideration to techniques for minimising additional cost (such as relying on presumptions and the burden of proof). See generally the remarks of Lord Dilhorne (who, as a former Lord Chancellor, was as well qualified as Gardiner to speak with authority on matters of judicial administration) at n. 216 below.

work.[203] Instead, the Commission put forward a modification of the 'breakdown' scheme. Rather than requiring the court to carry out a detailed examination of the alleged fact and causes of the breakdown—a process necessarily 'elaborate, time-consuming and expensive'[204]—there would be 'an easier procedure'— 'breakdown without inquest'—under which the court, on proof of a period of separation, would presume that the marriage had broken down. This, so the Commission claimed, would 'give effect to the underlying principles'[205] underlying the *Putting Asunder* approach.[206] However, the Commission thought that this could only be acceptable if the requisite period of separation were no longer than six months; for otherwise 'intolerable hardship' would be caused to innocent parties currently able to obtain an offence-founded divorce on the grounds of the other's 'outrageous conduct'.[207] If (said the Commission) so short a period were not acceptable, breakdown could only be adopted as an *alternative* to the other grounds for divorce. In either event, safeguards (for example, to protect the respondent spouse and children) would need to be introduced.

This reasoning is not wholly convincing. Divorce is a procedure whereby the parties are freed to remarry; and there seems no overwhelming case for giving even those who have been the victims of outrageous conduct such a right after a waiting period as short as six months. The Commission made it appear that divorce was a means of *protecting* the victim of outrageous conduct: but it would be perfectly possible to provide such protection by means of the traditional remedy of judicial separation; and it would be equally possible to do so by providing avowedly protective remedies of the kind now found in Part IV of the Family Law Act 1996 (itself in part based on provisions protecting a spouse's right to occupy the family home contained in the Matrimonial Homes Act 1967, then being drafted by the Commission's draftsmen). Nevertheless, the Commission seems to have successfully conveyed the impression that the *Field of Choice* was a dispassionate analysis by a group of disinterested legal technicians (rather than a skilfully drafted statement of the case for reform by a group

---

[203] Similarly, the Scottish Law Commission (to which the issue of the ground for divorce was referred in Dec. 1966) regarded an enquiry into breakdown as not serving any useful purpose; and it favoured (i) retention of the then existing offences (subject to minor modification); (ii) divorce on the ground of irretrievable breakdown founded on the fact that the parties had been separated for specified periods: see *Divorce, The Grounds Considered* (Cmnd. 3256) (1967). In the event, the Divorce (Scotland) Act 1976 closely followed the English Divorce Reform Act 1969: see generally E. M. Clive, *The Law of Husband and Wife in Scotland* (3rd edn. 1992) Ch. 20. The different approaches of the two Commissions were discussed at a meeting in Edinburgh in Feb. 1967 (Scarman, Gower and Cartwright Sharp representing the English body); and the Scots refused to modify the views expressed in their paper (then in draft). There was thought to be 'very little difference of approach in principle' between the two, and that the differences were 'minor ones of procedure which have their origins in the historical traditions of the two countries': Minutes of Commissioners' Meeting, 28 Feb. 1967, PRO BC3/3, para. 12. Discussion on drafting a Bill for Scotland revealed (according to the *Minutes of Commissioners' Meeting* 7 Nov. 1967 BC3/3) that, although the Scottish Bill would be based on irretrievable breakdown, 'there would still be major differences which would not be resolved but it was hoped that the differences in presentation between the two Bills would make these differences less apparent'.   [204] *The Field of Choice*, para. 71.
[205] Ibid.   [206] *The Field of Choice*, para. 70.   [207] *Putting Asunder*, paras. 75–6.

heavily dominated by enthusiasts for that cause). Lord Chancellor Gardiner (who never made any secret of his own personal preferences[208]) felt able to say[209] blandly that *The Field of Choice* 'recommends nothing'.

THE EMERGENCE OF CONSENSUS?

The Field of Choice was well received by the press[210] and commentators;[211] but the fact that there was 'some dispute' about the practicability of the *Putting Asunder* inquest proposals was highlighted[212] when divorce reform was debated in the House of Lords in November 1966.[213] On the one hand, Lord Chancellor Gardiner, speaking as 'the person who knows better than anyone else in the country which is right about this',[214] claimed that the inquest proposals were 'quite impracticable in practice within any measurable distance of time';[215] on the other, Lord Dilhorne (Gardiner's predecessor as Lord Chancellor) expressed astonishment at the basis upon which Gardiner had based this conclusion and doubted whether the Law Commission was any better qualified to express a view on the practical aspects of the *Putting Asunder* proposals than the members of the Archbishop's Group themselves.[216]

---

[208] At the Law Commissioners' Meeting on 11 Apr. 1967 (PRO BC3/3) Scarman read out extracts from a letter written by Gardiner to Abse ('I am, as you know, anxious to see a complete overhaul of the divorce law in this Parliament') as indicating that 'the Commission would have to proceed with some urgency'; and Scarman also noted that the parliamentary progress of the Matrimonial Homes Bill (which was drafted in the Commission) was of 'major importance in considering the Divorce time table'. Neither of these remarks seems easy to reconcile with the Olympian aloofness and impartiality effected by the Commission in its published work on divorce.

[209] Speech at the Annual Conference of the National Marriage Guidance Council, 5 May 1967: PRO BC3/377.

[210] '. . . several newspapers assessed *The Field of Choice* as the most brilliantly written document on divorce ever published in England': B. H. Lee, *Divorce Law Reform in England* (1974) p. 73.

[211] See e.g. O. Kahn-Freund (1967) 30 MLR 180 (agreeing with the Law Commission that to carry out an inquest in each case would be not only 'humanly and socially undesirable' but also procedurally impracticable); and see also to the same effect J. C. Hall [1966] CLJ 184. Sir Brian MacKenna (a judge of the Queen's Bench Division) in a searching analysis of the reform proposals urged the case for easier divorce in cases in which both parties were agreed: 'Divorce by Consent and Divorce for Breakdown of Marriage' (1967) 30 MLR 121.

[212] Only two speakers (Lord Hodson, a former divorce judge and subsequently Lord of Appeal in Ordinary, who was opposed in principle to what he called 'compulsory divorce' of an innocent spouse) and Lady Summerskill (who claimed that breakdown divorce as proposed in *Putting Asunder* would amount to a rejection of a lifelong marriage and the substitution of trial marriage, to the great prejudice of married women) opposed the principle of reform; whilst Lord Reid (also a Lord of Appeal in Ordinary) opposed any reform which would allow the blameless deserted wife to be divorced against her will. [213] *Official Report* (HL) 23 Nov. 1966, vol. 278, col. 241.

[214] At col. 257.

[215] At cols. 260–1 (where Gardiner claimed that the *Putting Asunder* proposals would require the appointment of 110 additional High Court judges).

[216] Dilhorne poured scorn on the notion that elaborate inquiry would have to be made in every case. ('I wonder . . . what happens if [Lady Summerskill] takes her car when it has broken down to a garage . . . Does she take up the time of the garage proprietor in telling him the whole history of the car since it came from the factory? It really is ridiculous to suggest that in endeavouring to prove or establish the fact that the marriage has broken down at the time the petition is lodged the wife will have to go right through the whole history of the married life and produce her love letters to show that at the particular time that marriage has come to an end'.)

But Dilhorne[217] forcefully urged that there was general agreement about the serious defects of the existing law, that it would be wrong simply to quarrel about who was right and who wrong; rather, an attempt should be made to find ways of making the breakdown principle work satisfactorily. Other speakers also questioned whether the difference between the Law Commission's 'breakdown without inquest' basis for divorce and the *Putting Asunder* proposals was an 'absolute, unbridgeable difference'.[218] In fact, as the Bishop of Exeter revealed at the end of the debate,[219] he[220] had arranged to meet the Law Commission[221] the following day; and he was personally 'quite convinced' that the gap between divorce with inquest and divorce without inquest was not wide 'and that in fact we could come to an agreement about a practicable method of working a divorce law which was based wholly on the principle of the breakdown of marriage'.

Mortimer subsequently reported to the Archbishop that a 'very interesting discussion took place' at the meeting, and the Law Commission agreed to 'attempt to reformulate their conclusions in such a way as to base divorce on the breakdown of marriage without giving complete discretion to the individual judge'.[222]

The Commission accordingly produced a Paper,[223] which was discussed at a meeting[224] with Representatives[225] of the Archbishop's Group on 17 February 1966.[226] Mortimer insisted that any presumption of breakdown arising from the various 'fact' situations enumerated by the Commission[227] should be capable of

---

[217] At cols. 302–3.   [218] Per Lord Derwent, col. 269.

[219] *Official Report* (HL) 23 Nov. 1966, vol. 278, col. 347.

[220] And one other member of the Group (in fact Canon Bentley): Cartwright Sharp to Beloe, 29 Mar. 1967, *Ramsey Papers*, vol. 117.

[221] The Chairman (Scarman J) and one other Commissioner (in fact Gower).

[222] *Ramsey Papers*, vol. 102, Mortimer to Ramsey, 29 Nov. 1966. Scarman warned his fellow Commissioners that these 'discussions must be considered confidential' notwithstanding that it was a public fact that attempts to iron out the differences were being made: *Minutes of Commissioners' Meeting*, 22 Nov. 1966, para. 13.

[223] 'Reform of Grounds of Divorce—Basis for Discussion between the Archbishop's Group and the Law Commission'. No copy of this document appears to have survived, but a draft prepared by Cartwright Sharp on 10 Dec. 1966 was, together with a covering letter to Mortimer, copied to the Lord Chancellor: *Minutes of Commissioners' Meeting*, 14 Dec. 1966, PRO BC3/2, para. 2. The Minutes also record the Commissioners' determination that there should be no 'papering over the cracks' in any difference of principle between the Law Commission and the Church. If no true agreement were reached, it would be better, to stop negotiations': para. 1(a).

[224] A photostat of the Minutes appears in the *Ramsey Papers*, vol. 117; the Law Commission's file has been destroyed. The Commission's representatives at the meeting were Scarman and Gower, H. Boggis-Rolfe (then Secretary to the Commission), J. M. Cartwright Sharp (see n. 223 above) and Miss Ruth Fraenkel (then a Legal Assistant to the Commission; subsequently, as Mrs Ruth Deech, Principal of St Anne's College Oxford).

[225] i.e. Mortimer, Bentley, Anderson and Miss Joan Rubinstein.

[226] According to private information given to the author, this meeting was very carefully planned by the Law Commission, and Gower devoted much effort to convincing Mortimer and his colleagues of the difficulties and expense necessarily involved in any inquiry of the kind envisaged by the Archbishop's Group.

[227] i.e. adultery, behaviour, desertion, living apart. There was considerable discussion on the drafting of these provisions: for example, Mortimer wanted the 'fact' of adultery to be formulated in a way which would allow the judge to decide whether there was a likelihood of *the particular couple* involved coming together again; whilst the 'behaviour' fact was not to be so widely drawn as 'to cover cases where the marriage had broken down because of incompatibility' which would have to

being rebutted in order to avoid any suggestion that the matrimonial offence was to be preserved under another name; and he repeatedly emphasised the need to ensure the effectiveness of the various safeguards[228] proposed by the Group. However, the two sides agreed that 'there appeared to be no difference in principle between the Group and the Commission'; and the Commission redrafted its paper to reflect those discussions.

In the meantime, opinion was being prepared for a breakthrough. The Lord Chancellor announced[229] that the gap between the two bodies was being narrowed; and the Church Assembly on 16 February 1967[230]—after an important debate in the course of which Professor J. N. D. Anderson warned of the mounting and increasingly broadly based demand for reform which he thought it would be disastrous for the Church to ignore[231]—resolved to welcome *Putting Asunder*[232]

be brought as separation cases. Importance was also attached to the need for the consent requisite to divorce founded on the shorter 'living apart' fact to be free and informed; and (the Minutes record) it 'was agreed that the court should be enabled to call on welfare officers to check the genuineness of consent . . .'.

[228] Including the financial consequences of divorce, particularly for the 'innocent' wife. In this context, it is often forgotten that the problem of pensions—still far from resolved thirty years later—was a very live issue at the time; and indeed the Minutes record Mortimer as wishing 'that provision for divorced wives' pensions could be made a precondition. Mr Gower explained that a direct solution to the pensions problem seemed almost impossible but financial relief could be improved and rights in the matrimonial home could be safeguarded with less difficulty and this would greatly alleviate the position. Complete reform of matrimonial property law would be a lengthy, controversial undertaking, but for most people the home formed the bulk of their assets . . .' The *Minutes of Commissioners' Meetings* 9 Mar. 1967 put the objectives of the Commission's review of these matters with engaging frankness: the 'Law Commission's aim is to achieve liberalization of the grounds of divorce on the strength of the reforms advocated in its [projected working paper on financial relief] without the need to wait for an overhaul of matrimonial property'. This tactic was successful: the implementation of the divorce reforms was deferred until legislation dealing with financial matters was on the statute book and no comprehensive reform of family property has ever been carried out: see Cretney and Masson, *Principles of Family Law* (6th edn. 1997, pp. 424–5; and Ch. 9).

[229] In the House of Lords debate on the Bill for the Matrimonial Causes Act 1967 (which conferred jurisdiction in undefended divorce cases on the county court): see *Official Report* (HL) 14 Feb. 1967, vol. 280, cols. 176–7 and 202. The Church had been consistently opposed to any move which might be interpreted as diminishing the importance of divorce; and Gardiner had gone to considerable lengths to allay the Archbishop's expressed fears about the move.

[230] See the verbatim *Church Assembly Report of Proceedings*, vol. 47.

[231] Anderson forcefully expressed the fear that 'a period of separation' would be 'tacked on' to the matrimonial offence as an additional ground for divorce; and that this would be 'the worst of the present and an ease of divorce which does not exist today'. He also presciently expressed his fear that 'we might get a law which accepts a breakdown of marriage as a fundamental ground, but which accepts the matrimonial offence so blindly as *prima facie* evidence of divorce that in effect we are having the matrimonial offence plus separation': *Church Assembly Record of Proceedings*, 16 Feb. 1967, vol. 47 at pp. 241–2. Another academic lawyer—Professor Arthur Phillips of Southampton University—could not see any prospect of the *Putting Asunder* proposals being accepted, but thought the reforms which were certain to come would involve adding separation to the offence ground or 'some sort of compromise which would fail to secure the safeguards' proposed in *Putting Asunder*: see at p. 245.

[232] Archbishop Ramsey commended the *Putting Asunder* proposals on the basis that, far from making divorce easier to obtain, they would save some marriages at present dissolved; whilst they would 'get rid of some of the most loathsome features of the operation of the present divorce law': *Church Assembly Record of Proceedings* 16 Feb. 1967, vol. 47, p. 249.

and accepted that the 'fact that a marriage appears to have broken down should be the sole grounds of civil divorce'.[233]

Eventually on 2 June 1967[234] the terms of the agreement[235] between the Archbishop's Group and the Law Commission were finalised and in due course published: irretrievable breakdown was to be the sole ground for divorce, but there should be no detailed inquest. Rather, breakdown was to be inferred, either from one of several specified facts askin to the traditional matrimonial offences or from the fact that the parties had lived apart for two years if the respondent consented to divorce or for five years if there were no consent.[236] Mortimer had insisted[237] on one alteration to what had been intended as the final draft—'namely that the power to refuse a Decree where the Court thinks that in the circumstances it would be wrong to do so, shall be mandatory and not permissive.' This amendment was duly made[238] (whereas various other requests by the Group were not accepted by the Commission).[239]

---

[233] Ramsey had made a speech supporting the adoption of those principles, whilst underlining his rooted objection to divorce by consent. Consistently with his policy of allowing the proposals to be maturely considered before seeking a decision on them, Ramsey had sought to defer the Assembly's debate for three months, and had in the interval convened informal meetings of laymen to discuss the proposals: *Ramsey Papers*, vol. 102, 13 Dec. 1966.

[234] Scarman to Gardiner, 24 July 1967, PRO BC3/377.

[235] Mortimer reported to Ramsey on 17 May 1967, reporting that the two bodies were 'on the verge of agreement' and that the Commission's proposals and the accompanying notes constituted 'the most satisfactory compromise attainable': *Ramsey Papers*, vol. 117. Replying on 22 May, Ramsey welcomed the 'possibility of agreement' but warned that 'it is of the utmost importance that breakdown should be not an additional ground but a substitute for all existing grounds'.

[236] The conclusion of the negotiations was announced in the Law Commission's *Second Annual Report* published on 26 July 1967; and the terms of the concordat were attached to a 'press-handout' distributed on that day. However, as a result of selection and condensation, the proposals were apparently in some instances misstated; and at the request of the Law Commission the full text of the agreement was published in the *New Law Journal* on 3 Aug. 1967. It was subsequently reproduced as an appendix to the Law Commission's *Third Annual Report* (1968, Law Com. No. 12). It appears that originally Gardiner—perhaps influenced by the risk of embarrassment to the Government if the Commission were to appear to be 'too closely associated with definite proposals for reform which had not yet been considered by Parliament' (Dobson to Scarman, 4 July 1967 PRO BC3/377)—was opposed to publication, but Scarman (conscious of the risk that the Commission would appear to be acting secretively) strongly urged the case for publication and it appears that this was conceded at a meeting (of which no record seems to have survived) between the two on 25 July: Scarman to Gardiner 24 July 1967 PRO BC3/377.

[237] And had reinforced this in an informal letter emphasising the importance the Group attached to this.

[238] The concordat (para. 7(b)) provided that the court should be required to refuse a divorce if satisfied that, 'having regard to the conduct and interests of the parties and the interests of the children and other persons affected, it would be wrong to dissolve the marriage, notwithstanding the public interest in dissolving marriages which have irretrievably broken down. However, the explanatory note to this provision warned that this was 'not intended to make the grant of a divorce discretionary' (since to do so would be 'to introduce an impossibly wide area of uncertainty and would inevitably lead to wide variations of practice'). Rather, the provision was intended as a ' "long stop", requiring the court to refuse a divorce in defended cases if the overall justice of the case, including in particular the interests of the respondent and the children, appears to demand it. Where the interests of the respondent and the children can be properly protected, we do not intend that the court should refuse to dissolve the marriage on the ground that to penalize a petitioner who has shown a contempt for the sanctity of marriage in some way upholds the sanctity of marriage.'

[239] 'Our agreement is accompanied by a strong request that the period of desertion should remain at three years and not be reduced to two.' This was because the Archbishop (whom Mortimer

Not surprisingly, news of the agreement was seen[240] in the press[241] as clearing the way[242] for what the *Daily Mirror* described as 'a practical and feasible Bill to reform Britain's divorce laws'; but the *Mirror* was in fact quite wrong to claim that 'the pacemaking Archbishop' had been converted into a 'powerful ally' of Leo Abse and his fellow campaigners. On the contrary, Ramsey had consistently distanced himself from the concordat,[243] refusing to have the document embodying it formally submitted to him;[244] and the Law Commission was firmly told by Beloe that the Archbishop had not given his approval to the concordat and that if the Commission were asked whether the Archbishop approved and agreed with it 'the answer should be that he did not agree with everything in it'. Ramsey evidently saw that the concordat departed in important respects from what *Putting Asunder* had proposed; and he wanted (as Beloe recorded) to be 'free to criticise and seek for amendment of some of the propositions' in the concordat.[245]

had consulted) thought 'that a great deal of Church opinion will be needlessly antagonised by the reduction of the period of desertion from three years to two. The Archbishop thinks it will be difficult for him to counter opposition to the proposals, made on the ground that their effect, if not indeed their intention, is to make divorce easier ... to reduce [the period] to two is, perhaps, to ask for unnecessary trouble': Mortimer to Scarman, 25 May 1967, *Ramsey Papers*, vol. 107. In his informal letter Mortimer also reported that he himself was in full agreement with the Archbishop's expressed hope that legislation would be introduced by the Government and not left to a private member. 'The Archbishop thinks ... that this is very important.' In the event it was not to be: see below, p. 68.

[240] Even more so in the light of a full analysis of the proposals by the Methodist Department of Christian Citizenship presented to the Methodist Conference in July 1967 and recommending the Commission's proposals for breakdown without inquest. Scarman immediately forwarded a copy of this Report (which had been prepared with the benefit of help from the Commission about 'matters of practicality' and assistance from Miss Rubinstein, a member of the Archbishop's Group) to the Lord Chancellor, urging that it was 'awfully important ... because of the importance of methodist opinion in this country', and suggesting that the Methodists had hit on a solution which 'closely resembled' that which Gardiner had put to the National Marriage Guidance Conference: see n. 209, above.

[241] See, for example, the story in the *Daily Express* 13 July 1967 where, under the heading, 'Divorce: Let's wipe out this hypocrisy' Alix Palmer concluded 'For heaven's sake, let's stop wasting our time with petty reforms [a reference to the President's scheme for reconciliation in cases of divorce petitions presented within three years of the marriage] and get on with the big stuff.' The only critical comment seems to have come from the *Justice of the Peace and Local Government Review* which in its number of 2 Sept. suggested there was some lack of clarity about the right of the 'guilty' party to petition and on the extent of the court's discretion to withhold divorce.

[242] See n. 210 above.

[243] He had indeed been careful not at the outset to endorse *Putting Asunder*, telling the Publisher (see *Ramsey Papers*, vol. 102, Ramsey to Davey 25 May 1966) that he had 'to take great care about the words' used in the Preface to *Putting Asunder* (which (i) warned that if there were to be legislation as proposed in the Report the 'Churches would still maintain their own pastoral discipline'; and (ii) concluded with the less than enthusiastic commendation that he hoped the Report would 'lead to a full discussion of the issues which it raises').

[244] So Ramsey put it to Mortimer at a meeting at Lambeth on 24 May 1967. Ramsey wanted to preserve his freedom to 'make such public comment as in due course he may think fit'; and considered that since the document would 'not have been produced by a body appointed by me' a formal presentation could put him 'in a wrong position' and that 'awkward questions might be asked about my place in the matter': Ramsey to Mortimer, 22 May 1967, *Ramsey Papers*, vol. 117.

[245] Leo Abse claims that Ramsey—a 'wily prelate ... following the principles of Machiavelli'— was anxious to keep his options open: L. Abse, *Private Member* (1973) p. 182.

Some perceptive commentators[246] did draw attention to the extent to which the concordat represented a victory for the Law Commission over the Archbishop's Group (particularly in the retention of the matrimonial offences as 'facts' from which the court would infer breakdown, and the gradual erosion of the public interest bar to which the Group had attached importance); whilst even the Divorce Law Reform Union[247] expressed a preference for the simplicity of the Abse Bill as against the complexity of the compromise.[248]

But all this was too late to influence events. On 12 October the Cabinet[249] accepted Gardiner's advice[250] that a Bill to give effect to the concordat should be drafted by Parliamentary Counsel in the Law Commission and handed to a private member.[251] The Government was to remain neutral on the merits of the Bill but would consider making government time available for the Bill 'in the light of the degree of support shown for it on Second Reading'. The Law Commission settled Instructions to Parliamentary Counsel,[252] and on 29 November the House of Commons ordered the Divorce Reform Bill presented by Mr William Wilson MP[253] to be printed.[254] Although there was inadequate parliamentary time for the Wilson Bill to get onto the statute book the Bill was taken over by another private member, Mr Alec Jones, and received the Royal Assent on 22 October 1969.

The Parliamentary Debates and the activities of the press and pressure groups have been analysed in detail by Professor B. H. Lee in his *Divorce Law Reform in England* (1974); and it would serve no useful purpose to seek to summarise

---

[246] Notably L. N. Brown, in the *New Law Journal*, 21 Sept. 1967.

[247] Which had been campaigning for divorce reform since its foundation in 1906: see the account in B. H. Lee, *Divorce Law Reform in England* (1974) Ch. 5.

[248] PRO BC3/367, 17 Aug. 1967.   [249] PRO CAB 128/42, CC(7) 59th Conclusions.

[250] Scarman had met the Lord Chancellor to discuss the 'proposed private member's bill on the grounds of divorce': *Minutes of Commissioners' Meeting*, 17 Oct. 1967, PRO BC3/3.

[251] It appears that Gardiner had already seen Abse on 20 Nov. (see B. H. Lee, *Divorce Law Reform in England* (1974)) but no official record of this discussion has been traced.

[252] In addition to the formulation of the bars to divorce (as to which see below) there appears to have been some disagreement about the wording of the 'living apart' fact, Scarman pointing out that not all separations evidenced breakdown: Memorandum dated 26 Oct., PRO BC3/377. Eventually the Court of Appeal interpreted the relevant provision of the Divorce Reform Act 1969 in the sense which Scarman would have favoured: *Santos* v. *Santos* [1972] Fam. 247, CA (discussed at length in S. M. Cretney, *Principles of Family Law* (4th edn. 1984) pp. 154 ff.). The statement in the Law Commission's *Third Annual Report 1967–1968* (July 1968) para. 51 that the 'Commission gave assistance so as to ensure that the Bill as introduced should accord with the understanding which we reached with the Archbishop's Group' seems to understate the Commission's role. In contrast, when *The Times*'s commentator criticised the drafting of the Bill (which he attributed to its not having been drafted by Parliamentary Counsel) the Secretary to the Law Commission confirmed that 'although the Law Commission do not give advice on controversial social issues, they have given technical and legal assistance at all stages and on all amendments tabled . . .': *The Times* 23 June 1969.

[253] MP (Labour) for Coventry South since 1964, and a solicitor by profession. See further, Lee op. cit. pp. 90–1. In reality Leo Abse was the power behind the scene in organising the passage of the Bill through Parliament.

[254] See Bill 18; and note the account in Lee op. cit. p. 94. No departmental records about the passage of the Bill are yet available.

his account.[255] In essence, the Divorce Reform Act 1969 was the Bill which emerged from the Law Commission and was intended to give effect to the concordat. For present purposes, it is only necessary to point out that, whilst Bishop Mortimer remained convinced that the legislation gave effect to the agreed principle of breakdown (and even acted as Teller for those supporting the Bill on its Second Reading in the House of Lords), Ramsey regarded the Bill as containing 'blemishes' such as made it impossible for him to support it.[256]

CONCLUSION

As has long been recognised, the publication of *Putting Asunder* played an important part in facilitating the reform of the divorce law effected by the Divorce Reform Act 1969—not least influencing what has been described[257] as the 'quite remarkable' consensus on the broad lines of reform—and *Putting Asunder* certainly had a decisive influence on the form which the legislation took. But how far did that Act truly give effect to the principles upon which the Archbishop's Group founded their support for reform?

First, the Group was adamant that irretrievable breakdown should be the only ground for divorce; and it is true that the Divorce Reform Act 1969 provided[258] that the sole ground upon which a petition could be based was that the marriage had broken down irretrievably.[259] But it soon became clear that this ringing assertion was little more than verbiage. However clear it might be that the marriage had broken down, the court could not dissolve it unless the petitioner could

---

[255] Reference should also be made to the perceptive discussion in P. G. Richards, *Parliament and Conscience* (1970) p. 140, Ch. 7. The Law Commission's files on the Bill (including Notes on Clauses) have apparently been preserved at the Public Record Office under reference BC3 3/8–83; and may throw further light on the legislation when they become open to inspection under the thirty-year rule.

[256] 'The existing law is bad, and I would gladly see it replaced . . . by a law based upon breakdown . . . I hope that many noble Lords, like myself, not wanting to be hostile to the Bill, will be with me in trying to get these specific blemishes corrected. I cannot vote for the Bill as it stands, as the things which I have criticised are, for me, matters of justice and principle.' *Official Report* (HL) 30 June 1969, vol. 303, col. 342. The three 'blemishes' Ramsey identified were (i) the short period of separation (two years) required for divorce; (ii) the adequacy of the court's power to withhold divorce (under what became Matrimonial Causes Act 1973, s. 10) on the grounds that adequate financial provision had not been made; and (iii) that the power of the court (under what became Matrimonial Causes Act 1973, s. 5) to withhold divorce when it would be wrong in all the circumstances to do so did not correspond effectively to the 'safeguard for justice for which the authors of *Putting Asunder* pleaded'.

[257] By P. G. Richards, *Parliament and Conscience* (1970) p. 140. Ch. 7 of this work provides an admirably perceptive and well-informed account of the background to divorce reform.

[258] S. 1.

[259] Mortimer continued to believe that 'the great merit of [the Divorce Reform Bill] lies in its first clause, which clearly established' the principle that the true ground for divorce is the breakdown of marriage: *Official Report* (HL) 30 June 1969, vol. 303, col. 377. In fact in the consolidating Matrimonial Causes Act 1973 the draftsman removed the ringing assertion to which Mortimer referred (presumably on the ground that it had no legal function) and substituted the provision that a divorce petition may be presented 'on the ground that the marriage has broken down irretrievably'.

establish adultery, behaviour, desertion, or a period of living apart; and if any of those 'facts' could be established the court was bound to dissolve the marriage unless the respondent could discharge the almost impossible task of satisfying the court that the marriage had *not* broken down. There is no reported instance of a respondent succeeding in so doing;[260] and Mortimer's assumption that the evidence of breakdown would be rebuttable rather than conclusive[261] has been demonstrably falsified. The reality is that the effective ground for divorce under the 1969 Act was not breakdown at all but rather the three matrimonial offences referred to above and separation for the prescribed period: Anderson's gloomy prophesy turned out to have been well founded.[262] The 'remarkable consensus'[263] was obtained by concealing the truth.

Moreover, experience soon showed that the divorcing population wanted the speedy divorce which could be obtained on the basis of an allegation of adultery or behaviour, and more than three-quarters of all divorces were granted in that way.[264] This tendency was reinforced in 1977 when court hearings of divorce petitions were effectively abandoned.[265] Far from burying the matrimonial offence, the reforming legislation ensured that it not only survived but flourished.

Secondly, the Group was adamant that there should be no divorce by consent. The parties might indeed consent to the dissolution of their marriage but this was only to be brought about by court order after appropriate inquiry. Divorce was not only to remain the act of the court, rather than that of the parties; but it was central to the Group's thinking that the Court should first satisfy itself by inquiry that the marriage had truly broken down and (as Mortimer put it in the final debates[266]) 'the courts must take seriously their duty to enquire into all the facts alleged and to be quite sure that they are satisfied that the marriage has irretrievably broken down'. But in fact the court hearings under the Divorce Reform Act were rarely more than a perfunctory formality;[267] and even the formality was effectively abolished in 1977.[268] Yet again, the legislation failed to give effect to the policy on which *Putting Asunder* had been founded. Those responsible for formulating the concordat must have known[269] that there would in practice rarely

---

[260] See for an explanation of the case law, S. M. Cretney and J. M. Masson, *Principles of Family Law* (5th edn. 1990) p. 98.　　　　[261] *Official Report* (HL) 30 June 1969, vol. 303, col. 379.

[262] i.e. that breakdown of marriage would merely be added to a list of matrimonial offences: see p. 71 above.　　　　[263] See above.

[264] Op. cit. pp. 172–3.

[265] When the so-called 'special procedure' was extended to all undefended divorce petitions. For the reasons why almost all petitions are undefended see S. M. Cretney and J. M. Masson, *Principles of Family Law* (6th edn. 1997) pp. 313–16.

[266] *Official Report* (HL) 30 June 1969, vol. 303, col. 379.

[267] Research carried out in 1973 by E. Elston, J. Fuller and M. Murch cast serious doubt on whether hearings of undefended divorce petitions commanded the confidence and respect of the parties or served any other useful purpose: see (1975) 38 MLR 609. This research was influential in the decision to adopt the 'special procedure': see Sir George Baker, P (1977) 74 LS Gaz. 232.

[268] Ibid.

[269] Private information given to the author confirms that Gower in particular was well aware of this.

if ever be any inquiry into breakdown; but, unsurprisingly, they chose not to disabuse Mortimer and his colleagues of their belief that the court would carry out
an inquest, at least in cases of doubt.

Finally, the Group consistently insisted on the need for safeguards—both of
the interests of vulnerable members of the family and of the public interest in
upholding the institution of marriage. So far as economic safeguards are concerned, the one matter on which most attention was focused in the 1960s was
the divorced wife's loss of pension expectations; and that remains a problem to
this day.[270] So far as safeguards for the public interest are concerned, successive
versions of the Bill leading to the 1969 Act gradually whittled away any realistic
bar founded on public policy, and it is only in the wholly exceptional case where
a spouse can show that the dissolution of the marriage will cause 'grave financial
or other hardship'[271] to him or her that the court has a discretion to withhold a
decree. This provision—self-evidently much narrower than that embodied in the
Archbishop's Group/Law Commission concordat—has been restrictively interpreted by the courts and has only rarely been applied.[272]

In all these respects, therefore, those members of the Archbishop's Group who
continued to believe that the Divorce Reform Act 1969 gave effect to the policies elaborated in *Putting Asunder* were mistaken. But this is not surprising. They
were, after all, repeatedly told—as was the public—that the Law Commission
was simply giving objective and disinterested advice on technical matters—a
proposition which in retrospect seems so implausible that it is astonishing that
it was ever taken seriously. Again, it would not be fair to criticise the Group for
all the—now widely admitted—defects of the reformed law. Indeed it seems
inevitable that reform would have come—if for no other reason than that for many
years there had been a majority in the House of Commons favouring reform to
remove the hardships caused to many by the existing law, and this majority had
been steadily growing.[273] In retrospect, therefore, the most seriously damaging
consequence of *Putting Asunder* may have been that the need to appear to give
effect to the principle that irretrievable breakdown should be the sole ground for
divorce (as so eloquently advocated in that Report) whilst in truth scarcely doing
so at all has played some part in making the law 'confusing and misleading'.[274]
As the Law Commission put it when it returned to reform of the Ground for
Divorce in 1990:[275] this 'can only lead to . . . lack of respect for the law' and
indeed to the fact that 'some would call it downright dishonest'.

Possibly the values which the Church wished to uphold would have been
better promoted if the reformers in the fifties and sixties had persisted in the stark

---

[270] See S. M. Cretney and J. M. Masson, *Principles of Family Law* (6th edn. 1997) pp. 490–7.

[271] Matrimonial Causes Act 1973, s. 5.

[272] S. M. Cretney and J. M. Masson, *Principles of Family Law* (5th edn. 1990) pp. 137–8.

[273] For a detailed examination of voting see Lee, op. cit. n. 247 above.

[274] For a recent example (demonstrating that the judiciary may sometimes also be confused) see
Butterworth v. *Butterworth* [1997] 2 FLR 336.

[275] *Family Law: The Ground for divorce* (Law Com. No. 192, 1990) para. 2.8.

simplicity of adding seven years' separation to the grounds for divorce; and indeed if the Church had not felt it necessary to oppose that reform so vigorously and effectively. Pursuit of an unattainable best may, in this case, have defeated what would at least have been tolerable and comprehensible. The 1969 Act certainly failed to remove the humbug and hypocrisy which all the reformers regarded as the main characteristic of the old law; but perhaps it is questionable whether any law dealing with such a powerfully emotive subject can be expected to do so.

3*

The Forfeiture Act 1982: A Case Study of the Private Member's Bill as an Instrument of Law Reform

INTRODUCTION

In a civilised society legislation should surely be based on rationality. Where what is in issue is choice between competing moral principles it seems reasonable to expect a full discussion of those principles so that the choice may be an informed one. And one would certainly expect that the policy finally adopted should be expressed in technically apt language so that doubt about its meaning is minimised.

In many ways, this country is fortunate in such matters. As shown in the first two chapters of this book, the work of the Law Commissions provides material for an informed legislative debate, as do the deliberations of bodies such as the Warnock Committee of Enquiry into Human Fertilisation and Embryology.[1] Even if there remains a division of opinion, the lengthy bicameral parliamentary process might be expected to permit lively discussion of the opposing points of view. Finally, the drafting of primary legislation is entrusted to highly competent experts who—unfashionable though it may be to say so—often create legislative structures of considerable intellectual distinction.[2]

But sometimes, for one reason or another, neither the resources of central government nor those of any official agency are available to tackle a problem believed by some to require investigation and remedy; and in such cases the Private Member's Bill may be used[3] in an attempt to deal with the issue—either definitively, by the immediate enactment of legislation, or at least by arousing interest in the

* The paper on which this Chapter is based was first published in (1990) 10 OJLS 289. Colleagues at Bristol University (Gwynn Davis, David Feldman, Roger Kerridge, Elizabeth Roberts and Christine Willmore) and Mr Leo Abse, Mr Paul Matthews and Professor Gavin Drewry gave helpful comments on drafts. Research assistance was supported by funding from the Bristol University Law Faculty Research Fund. ¹ Cmnd. 9314 (1984).

[2] The Children Act 1989 provides an outstanding example.

[3] Sometimes, of course, the Private Member's Bill is used by Government in order to get onto the statute book legislation which it supports but which (either for convenience or because it does not wish to appear to be too closely associated with the policy) it does not want to adopt itself: see, for example, the Intestates' Estates Act 1952 (discussed in Ch. 10), and the Summary Procedure (Domestic Proceedings) Act 1937 (discussed in Ch. 5). The Divorce Reform Act 1969 is an example of a Private Member's Bill on which the Government preserved a policy of neutrality but for which it provided full technical support (including assistance with drafting): see Ch. 2 above.

subject and thereby securing for it a place on a more official and well-resourced agenda.

The Forfeiture Act 1982 provides an example of this process. It originated in concern about a rule of law which seemed to have the effect that a woman who, under the grossest provocation, killed her husband would be disqualified from the social security benefits to which a widow would normally be entitled and would forfeit all right to succeed to his estate and to his interest in the family home. This draconian rule would—it seemed—be applied even if the woman's moral culpability were such that, in criminal proceedings, she had been held not to deserve any punishment at all.

It has now become possible to piece together, from published and other sources,[4] the story of how an Act which its sponsors never expected to see enacted, and which was undeniably technically defective, came to get onto the statute book. It will be seen that this was achieved largely by discouraging parliamentary and other public discussion and by concealing the potentially controversial nature of the change intended to be effected. The story raises issues about law reform procedures, about the parliamentary process, and about the respective roles of the judiciary and the legislature, which in themselves justify an attempt to place the facts on record.

THE BACKGROUND

The notion that a person should not be entitled to profit from his own wrong, and that in particular a criminal should not benefit from his crime,[5] can fairly be described as a general and fundamental principle of justice, embodied in one form or another[6]

---

[4] The most revealing published account is to be found in an interview with Leo Abse MP who was effectively the Act's sponsor: see 'The Great Backbencher' (1987) *The Law Magazine* 12 June, 30. R. T. Oerton, *A Lament for the Law Commission* (1987) gives, at p. 76, some interesting information about the handling of the issue by the Law Commission and Lord Chancellor's Department when it was raised with the Law Commission in 1975. This Chapter also draws on the author's personal knowledge.   [5] *Re H (deceased)* [1990] 1 FLR 441, 442, per Peter Gibson J.

[6] *Nullus commodum capere potest de injuria sua propria*: Coke on Littleton 148 b. The principle is also reflected in the maxim *ex turpi causa non oritur actio*: see *Beresford* v. *Royal Insurance Co. Ltd.* [1937] 2 KB 197, 219, per Lord Wright MR (and, in Scotland, *Burns* v. *Secretary of State*, 1985 SLT 351); and in the equitable doctrine that he who comes to equity must come with clean hands. See also *A-G* v. *Guardian Newspapers and Others (No. 2)* [1990] AC 109 (*Sunday Times* newspaper not to be permitted to profit from its wrongdoing in publishing in breach of confidence extracts from Mr Peter Wright's memoirs). But there was and is considerable doubt as to the precise scope of the principle: thus in *Beresford* Lord Wright MR (in the Court of Appeal [1937] 2 KB 197, 219) noted that the maxim *ex turpi causa non oritur actio* 'notwithstanding the dignity of a learned language, is like most maxims, lacking in precise definition'. Lord Wright's view was that there was no moral justification to apply the maxim to the many modern statutory offences. For an example of the difficulties still faced by the courts see *Whiston* v. *Whiston* [1995] Fam. 198, CA, and compare *J* v. *S-T (Formerly J)(Transsexual: Ancillary Relief)* [1997] 1 FLR 402, CA (in which the Court ruled that a person who knew that the marriage would be void on the ground that the parties were not respectively male and female should not receive any financial relief in the subsequent nullity pro-

in most if not all legal systems.[7] Its application to cases of homicide seems intuitively to follow: a man shall not slay his benefactor and thereby take his bounty.[8] Hence, sixteen-year-old Elmer Palmer (who, hoping for financial gain, wickedly and intentionally poisoned his grandfather) could not be allowed to inherit under the grandfather's will;[9] nor could the estate of Dr Hawley Harvey Crippen benefit as a consequence of his felonious killing of Mrs Cunigunda Crippen.[10] Although the precise limits to the application of this principle in homicide cases had never been fully worked out by the English courts,[11] the Member of Parliament[12] who claimed in 1982 that it was simple and readily understood by the community and one by which most citizens would wish to abide no doubt expressed a widespread instinctive reaction. But it is possible that this silent majority would begin to have doubts about a universal and inflexible application of the principle if the reality of many domestic killings were more widely understood.

The vision of the home as a place of peace and tranquillity from which the world and its concerns could and should be excluded remains powerful even if few would today wish to use Ruskin's imagery of a 'place of Peace; the shelter,

ceedings. Ward LJ took the view that a person who made a false declaration for the purpose of procuring a marriage should be debarred *in limine* from asserting a claim to financial relief in the proceedings; but the majority (Potter LJ and Sir Brian Neill) would have favoured a more restrictive application of the public policy rule. Note also that in *Tinsley* v. *Milligan* [1994] 1 AC 340 the House of Lords was divided in deciding how far the equitable 'clean hands' doctrine overrode the common law rule that a plaintiff was not debarred from asserting the title acquired under an illegal transaction provided proof of title did not involve disclosure of the illegality, the majority taking the view that the common law rule now applied generally.

[7] For a case in which a claimant appears to have been deprived of a widow's pension under the law of the Federal German Republic because she had been convicted of manslaughter ('totschlag'), see *R(G) 1/88*; below p. 89.   [8] *Hall* v. *Knight and Baxter* [1914] P 1, 7, per Hamilton LJ.

[9] *Riggs* v. *Palmer* (1889) 22 NE 188, New York Court of Appeal. This case has been highlighted in the writings of Professor R. M. Dworkin (see e.g. *Law's Empire* (1986) p. 15) as an illustration of differing approaches to statutory construction by the majority and by Gray J who, taking a strict constructionist approach, dissented on the basis that a court is bound by the clear and rigid rules of the succession laws established by legislation. Subsequently, some American courts have preferred to view the decision as one justifiable by the classical technique whereby a court of equity prevents a person from asserting a valid legal claim if to do so would be inequitable: see e.g. *Ellerson* v. *Westcott* (1896) 42 NE 53, New York Court of Appeal.

[10] *In the Estate of Cunigunda (otherwise Cora) Crippen, deceased* [1911] P 108. (The actual decision was restricted to the question of entitlement to take a grant of administration.)

[11] For a full consideration of the rule, see A. J. Oakley, *Constructive Trusts* (2nd edn. 1987). See also T. G. Youdan, *Acquisition of Property by Killing* (1973) 89 LQR 235; T. K. Earnshaw and P. J. Pace, 'Let the Hand Receiving it be Ever so Chaste' (1974) 37 MLR 481. A full historical perspective is to be found in the learned argument of counsel (L. Blom-Cooper QC) in *R* v. *Cuthbertson* [1981] AC 470. The most extensive analyses of the broad principle in English judicial decisions prior to the enactment of the Forfeiture Act 1982 are to be found in *Grey* v. *Barr* [1971] 2 QB 554, CA; *Beresford* v. *Royal Insurance Co. Ltd.* [1938] AC 586, HL. (In that case A. T. Denning was Junior Counsel seeking to enforce a life policy notwithstanding that the assured had killed himself whilst sane; and some interesting light is cast on the case in Denning, *The Family Story* (1981) 100. Lord Denning believes that the case would now be decided differently because suicide has ceased to be a crime.) For a discussion of this and other related issues, see M. P. Furmston, 'The Analysis of Illegal Contracts' (1966) 16 Univ. of Toronto LJ 267.

[12] Mr Alan Beith, Standing Committee C, 17 Mar. 1982, col. 10.

not only from all injury, but from all terror, doubt and division . . . a vestal temple, a temple of the hearth watched over by Household Gods'.[13] Indeed, many modern feminist writers[14] are strongly critical of the ideology of domestic privacy precisely because it may so often permit the abuse of power within the family. There can certainly be no dispute that in reality home and family are all too often associated with violence—and indeed with violent death. Thus, the criminal statistics revealed that a third of all recorded homicides were committed by a cohabitant, lover, or member of the victim's family.[15] These figures do not differentiate between premeditated killing (of the Crippen type), and killings which are themselves a response to violence. But there seems little doubt that a significant number fall into the latter category; and some indication of the type (if not the extent) of the problem can be found in studies carried out in the United States of women who enter pleas of self-defence to charges of killing their partners.[16]

Some of these cases reveal appalling histories of systematic abuse. For example, one woman tried on a charge of murdering her husband had over the years been hospitalised seven times as a result of beatings with a dog-chain, pistol-whipping, and gunshot injuries; and many had been subjected to sexual abuse such as forced participation in bondage and bestiality.[17] In the light of the data collected in these studies, it is not surprising to find it argued in the United States that battered women who finally kill their husbands are often doubly victimised, first, by the men who have abused them; and then, secondly, by the legal system itself. This is because of legal doctrine which restricts the definition of self-defence, and thereby—so it is said—imposes an unrealistic standard of accountability which is in turn exacerbated by harsh sentencing practices.[18]

In contrast, English criminal law can claim that the need to assert the principle that killing people is wrong is, where appropriate—and especially in the domestic context—tempered by humanity. There have, over the years, been significant changes in the criminal law of homicide reflecting 'public appreciation of the different degrees of culpability that attend conduct that used to be designated as murder'.[19] The result of a much more sophisticated approach to this issue has been to introduce considerable flexibility into the law. In particular, the

---

[13]   J. Ruskin, 'Of Queens Gardens', *Sesame and Lilies* (1865).

[14]   See e.g. K. O'Donovan, *Sexual Divisions in Law* (1985). In this context it is noteworthy that the wife in *Re K* [1985] Ch. 85 (the facts of which are summarised below) was said to have a very high level of respectability, and (according to a probation officer) felt that what went on within closed doors in the house was something that, traditionally, she ought to keep between herself and her husband.

[15]   *Criminal Statistics 1986*, para. 4.5. The statistics also showed that a far higher proportion of female victims compared with male victims are killed by a spouse, cohabitant, or former partner: *Criminal Statistics 1988*, para. 4.5.

[16]   C. P. Ewing, *Battered Women Who Kill, Psychological Self-Defense as Legal Justification* (Lexington, 1987).

[17]   C. P. Ewing, *Battered Women Who Kill, Psychological Self-Defense as Legal Justification*, pp. 27–37.   [18]   In particular, minimum custodial sentences are sometimes prescribed.

[19]   Per Phillips LJ, *Dunbar* v. *Plant* [1998] 1 FLR 157, 175, CA.

availability of the defence of diminished responsibility[20] has had an important impact: in the year in which the Forfeiture Act was passed, more than half of those with no previous convictions found guilty of killing a family member were convicted of manslaughter by reason of diminished responsibility;[21] and non-custodial sentences may be imposed in such cases.[22]

But English *civil* law had not kept pace with the greater sophistication of these humane developments in the criminal law. In *Re Giles, dec'd.*,[23] for example, a defendant with a history of mental illness[24] struck her husband a single blow on the head with a domestic chamber pot. He died (apparently unexpectedly) as a direct result of the blow: the widow was charged with murder. Although her plea of guilty to manslaughter through diminished responsibility was accepted, and a hospital order made,[25] it was subsequently held that she was excluded from all benefit under the deceased's will or intestacy; and that accordingly the defendant's stepson was entitled to the matrimonial home and other property. The judge considered that a conviction for manslaughter required the application of the principle of public policy whereby the courts will not recognise a benefit accruing to a criminal from the crime.[26] The question whether a person guilty of culpable homicide deserved punishment or not was (in this view) irrelevant,[27] as was the presence or absence of extenuating circumstances: there was to be no sentimental speculation as to the motives and degree of moral guilt of a person who has been justly convicted.[28]

There were powerful arguments for thinking this view to have been wrong and that a conviction for manslaughter—a crime which varies infinitely in its seriousness[29]—should not invariably have attracted the operation of the common law rule;[30]

---

[20] Homicide Act 1957, s. 2, provides that a person shall be convicted of manslaughter rather than murder if he was suffering from such abnormality of mind as substantially impaired his mental responsibility for his acts and omissions. It has been suggested that in recent years there has been a return towards convicting of murder persons guilty of the more serious homicides: *Criminal Statistics 1988*, para. 4.9.   [21] Fifty-three out of a total of 100: see *Criminal Statistics 1986*, Table 4.13.
[22] Ibid. Table 4.8.   [23] [1972] Ch. 545.
[24] In 1958 the defendant had been convicted of murdering her son and committed to Broadmoor. In 1961 she was discharged into the care of her husband, whose will was made in 1967: see [1972] Ch. 544, 549.
[25] The judge described the case as a tragic one ([1972] Ch. 544, 553) and the defendant was committed to Broadmoor Hospital, the court restricting her discharge without limit of time. In view of the previous history (and the possible prognosis) the injustice of an application of the forfeiture rule may have been less obvious than in some of the cases referred to below.
[26] Per Lord Atkin, *Beresford* v. *Royal Insurance Co. Ltd.* [1938] AC 586, 599.
[27] *Re Giles, dec'd.* [1972] Ch. 544, 552, per Pennycuick V-C. In *Dunbar* v. *Plant* the Court of Appeal held that the rule applied to a person convicted of aiding and abetting suicide, contrary to the provisions of the Suicide Act 1961; and it appears to have been the Court's view that the rule applied at common law to all cases of manslaughter.
[28] *In the Estate of Hall* (1914) P 1, 7, per Hamilton LJ, cited (apparently with approval) in *Re Giles, dec'd.* [1972] Ch. 544, 552, per Pennycuick V-C.
[29] *Gray* v. *Barr* [1971] 2 QB 554, 581, per Salmon LJ.
[30] This view, which could have been supported by reference to dicta in *Gray* v. *Barr* [1971] 2 QB 554, and in *R* v. *National Insurance Commissioner, ex parte O'Connor* [1981] 1 QB 758, was accepted by Peter Gibson J in *Re H (deceased)* [1990] 1 FLR 441 and it seems that it was influential in the

and it may perhaps be that the judges would over the years have taken a different view of the circumstances in which the rule would be applied.[31] But that is
prophesy: the fact is that in 1982 there was not a single reported case in which
any English court, faced with a conviction for an offence of culpable homicide,
had allowed the killer to take a personal benefit which depended on proof of the
death.[32] Indeed in 1980 the Divisional Court had held in *R* v. *Chief National
Insurance Commissioner, ex parte Connor*[33] that a widow placed on probation
for manslaughter not only forfeited all interests in property of the traditional kind
(such as the family home[34] and its contents) but also her entitlements to the new
property rights created by social security legislation. It seems difficult to deny
that the common law forfeiture rule produced 'grossly unjust consequences' not
only for the perpetrator of the homicide but also others taking through that person;[35] and that the absolute rule, 'whilst apparently defensive of human life', paid
no regard to the 'virtually infinite variety of circumstances in which a homicide
may occur' and the mitigating factors which 'sometimes exist, especially in a
domestic situation'.[36]

The rigidity of the rule seemed strikingly at odds, not only with the greater
sophistication of the criminal law,[37] but in particular with developments taking
place in the 1970s in the law governing family relations. Thus, the right of a
wife to live in the family home was no longer automatically terminated if she
committed adultery; but instead the court was by statute given a discretion to

drafting of the Forfeiture Act 1982: see the remarks of the Solicitor-General, Hansard (HC) vol. 23,
col. 1096. But in *Dunbar* v. *Plant* [1998] 1 FLR 157 the Court of Appeal considered that the
common law forfeiture rule did apply on the facts of *Re H (deceased)*.

[31] See *Dunbar* v. *Plant* [1998] 1 FLR 157, per Phillips LJ at 179.

[32] This appears to be the crucial question: R (P) 2/88. The courts were nevertheless able on public policy grounds to hold that persons convicted of what is often called 'motor manslaughter' were
entitled to rely on their third party insurance policies to indemnify them in respect of death or injury
to others: see *Marles* v. *Philip Trant & Sons Ltd.* [1954] 1 QB 29, CA; *Gray* v. *Barr, Prudential
Assurance Co. (Third Party)* [1971] 2 QB 554; and the discussion in *Dunbar* v. *Plant* [1998] 1 FLR
157, 176, CA, per Phillips LJ.

[33] [1981] 1 QB 758. Husband 'met his death . . . by reason of the fact that a knife held in the hand
of the applicant had penetrated his chest, inflicting a wound on the periphery of his heart which caused
him to die very shortly thereafter'. Widow acquitted of murder, but convicted of manslaughter; and
placed on probation for two years. Held: since she had intentionally used the knife on her husband,
and that what she did caused his death, she forfeited her entitlement to widow's allowance.

[34] See e.g. *Re Royse, dec'd.* [1985] FLR 196, CA, where the widow was discharged from hospital
after less than two years and returned to the matrimonial home (to which she would have been entitled
under the deceased's will). Held: his brother and sister were, by reason of the operation of the forfeiture rule, entitled to the husband's estate, including the home.

[35] See e.g. *Re S (Deceased)(Forfeiture Rule)* [1996] 1 FLR 910, Rattee J, where a man killed his
wife. It appeared that in consequence of the common law forfeiture rule no claim under a life policy effected on the wife's life could be enforced. Under provisions of the Forfeiture Act 1982, however, the Court was able to modify the effect of the rule so that the couple's seven-year-old child
could benefit under the policy. [36] Per Kirby J, *Troja* v. *Troja* [1994] NSWLR 269.

[37] See above p. 77; and note that in *Dunbar* v. *Plant* [1998] 1 FLR 157, 175, CA, Phillips LJ
regarded the 'changes in attitude reflected by the statutory graduation of offences of unlawful killing'
as one of the factors which led to 'justifiable dissatisfaction with the application of the forfeiture
rule indiscriminately in every case of unlawful killing'.

make such order regulating the parties' rights to occupy the house as it considered just and reasonable having regard to all the circumstances of the case, of which conduct would be one, but only one.[38] Again, the divorce court was given extensive powers over spouses' property; and—so it was held in *Wachtel* v. *Wachtel*[39]— matrimonial misconduct would only be allowed to be a decisive factor in terminating financial support obligations after the divorce if the conduct in question were both obvious and gross, so much so that to order one party to support another would be repugnant to anyone's sense of justice.[40]

THE PROBLEM RAISED: THE 1975 INHERITANCE LEGISLATION

An opportunity arose to consider this inconsistency between the trend towards flexibility in family law and the all-or-nothing nature of the forfeiture rule in the course of the Law Commission's review of the scope and extent of the legislation allowing the court to override the terms of a will or the statutory code governing intestate succession and to order that reasonable provision be made for a deceased's dependants. The draft Bill annexed to the Commission's Report[41] empowered the court, on the application of certain defined categories of dependant,[42] to make orders if satisfied that the 'disposition of the deceased's estate effected by his will or the law relating to intestacy, or the combination of his will and that law, is not such as to make reasonable financial provision for the applicant'.[43] Were these words wide enough to permit a widow who had unintentionally killed her husband—possibly after suffering many years of violent attacks and in the result been deprived of all benefit under his will by the operation of the forfeiture rule—to apply to the court for the financial provision which would, having regard to all the circumstances, be reasonable? The difficulty appeared to be that it would not be the disposition of the deceased's estate effected by his will or intestacy which brought about the lack of reasonable (or indeed any) financial

[38] Cf. *National Provincial Bank* v. *Ainsworth* [1965] AC 1175, and the legislation consolidated in the Matrimonial Homes Act 1983.

[39] [1973] Fam. 72. At one time, a wife adjudged to be the guilty party in divorce proceedings would be deprived of all support from her husband, save perhaps a 'compassionate allowance' so as to prevent her being forced into the streets to starve: *Robertson* v. *Robertson* (1883) 8 PD 94, 95, per Jessel MR, *arguendo*.

[40] See per Lord Denning MR, *Wachtel* v. *Wachtel* [1973] Fam. 72, 89–90. Possibly the most striking recent case in which conduct has been held to justify terminating support is *Evans* v. *Evans* [1989] 1 FLR 351, CA (wife convicted of inciting others to murder former husband).

[41] *Family Provision on Death*, Law Com. No. 61 (1974).

[42] See now Inheritance (Provision for Family and Dependants) Act 1975, s. 1(1), as amended. It has been said that the Act is concerned, wherever reasonably possible, to remedy the injustice of one, who has been put by a deceased person in a position of dependency upon him, being deprived of any financial support, either by accident or design of the deceased after his death: *Jelley* v. *Illiffe and Others* [1981] Fam. 128, 137–8, per Stephenson LJ; and see the analysis by R. D. Oughton, *Tyler's Family Provision* (3rd edn. 1997) at p. 45.

[43] Inheritance (Provision for Family and Dependants) Act 1975, s. 2(1).

provision, but rather the application of the forfeiture rule to those dispositions.[44] Would it be appropriate to consider amending the draft Bill to cover such cases?

Such was the suggestion made by a law teacher[45] to the Law Commission during the passage through Parliament of the 1975 legislation. In due course he received a courteous reply, thanking him for his interest but explaining that it would not be opportune to seek to modify the rule in the Bill which had by then made substantial progress through Parliament. No doubt the teacher assumed that this was a stock response, despatched as a matter of routine to those interfering in matters which were not properly their concern. If so, he would have been mistaken. The Law Commission has a general statutory duty to keep the whole of the law under review, and a specific statutory duty to consider proposals for reform which are made to it;[46] and the issue was, in fact, carefully and fully analysed by a gifted and experienced member of the Commission's legal staff.[47] But it was in the end decided—for a variety of reasons, some of principle and some of expediency—that no attempt should be made to introduce amendments at that late stage in the passage of the Inheritance Bill; and there the matter, for the time being, rested.

In 1978, the present writer became a Law Commissioner; and the possibility of reviewing the operation of the forfeiture rule was discussed by him with his colleagues. At that time, however, the Commission was concerned about its ability to meet existing commitments; and the resources needed to investigate a topic which could only with difficulty be isolated from other applications of the maxim *ex turpi causa non oritur actio* would have been formidable. Moreover, the forfeiture rule seemed to affect only a very few people each year; and there was some ground to hope[48] that the courts might come to adopt a less rigid application of the rule. Accordingly, once again, the decision was taken to defer any action—in reality, not because the issue was thought to be undeserving of consideration, but because the institutional framework available was not at the time able to accommodate it.

---

[44] Subsequently this interpretation was adopted by the Court of Appeal: see *Re Royse, dec'd.* [1985] FLR 196, per Slade LJ, at 202. ('It is not a consequence of the will, or of the law relating to intestacy, that the appellant is precluded from receiving the provision made for her [by the deceased's will]. Unhappily, it is a consequence of her own act, coupled with the forfeiture rule.')

[45] In fact, the author of this paper.   [46] Law Commissions Act 1965, s. 3(1)(a).

[47] The former civil servant concerned subsequently published a book about his involvement with the Law Commission, which vividly conveys some of the pressures which can affect those engaged in the institutionalised process of formal law reform: R. T. Oerton, *A Lament for the Law Commission* (1987). Of this particular episode he writes [at p. 76]: 'Another painful memory is of making a sustained effort to have something included in the Inheritance (Provision for Family and Dependants) Act 1975 to modify the forfeiture rule. This attempt, too, was repulsed by the Lord Chancellor's Department and I had to wait eight years before the Forfeiture Act 1982 did the job.'

[48] Founded on dicta in *Gray* v. *Barr* [1971] 2 QB 554, 581, CA, per Salmon LJ; and in *R* v. *National Insurance Commissioner, ex parte O'Connor* [1981] 1 QB 758; and note *Dunbar* v. *Plant* [1998] 1 FLR 157, per Phillips LJ at 179. There seems to have been some confusion amongst the Government's legal team as to the scope of the discretion which the Solicitor-General assured the House of Commons did exist: compare *Hansard* (HC) 14 May 1982, vol. 23, col. 1095 with col. 1097.

Was there an alternative, or was the issue to remain forever pigeon-holed? Perhaps the most striking paradox in the whole story is that the Law Commissioners were, reasonably enough, concerned about the difficulty of confining the discussions within manageable bounds. But the result was that in the end the issue was dealt with by a procedure whose effectiveness depended on there being almost no discussion at all.

HOW THE FORFEITURE ACT 1982 CAME TO BE ENACTED

Many members of both Houses of Parliament have an interest in law reform; but in recent years few can have had such effective enthusiasm for law reform affecting social issues as Leo Abse, at that time the MP for Pontypool. Abse had been a dominant force in the enactment of the Sexual Offences Act 1967 (which decriminalised much homosexual behaviour) and—as seen in Chapter 2—in the reform movement culminating in the Divorce Reform Act 1969.[49] Abse made it his business to keep in touch with law reform activities and was well aware of the value of the Parliamentary Debate as a way of drawing an issue to public attention. Indeed he sometimes employed it as a preliminary to bringing forward legislation.[50] He came to know about, and to be interested in, the problem of the forfeiture rule.

In 1981, Abse was approached by a fellow MP who had drawn a low place in the annual ballot for Private Member's Bills. Abse suggested that this Member introduce a Bill empowering the courts to grant relief from the application of the forfeiture rule. It is vital to an understanding of subsequent events to note that neither Abse, nor the Bill's nominal sponsor,[51] expected the Bill to make progress. The intention was simply to highlight the issue and thereby advance the prospect of future reform, no doubt after further investigation either by a law reform agency or a full consideration within the government machine.[52] How then

---

[49] Ch. 2 above; and see generally Abse's autobiographical account: L. Abse, *Private Member* (1973).

[50] Thus it was his initiative which led to the reform of illegitimacy law being raised in the Commons in 1979; see Hansard HC vol. 963, col. 807; and the Law Commission's subsequent Report was able to refer to the speeches made in that debate as evidence of the demand for reform: see Law Com. No. 118, 1982, para. 1.3. Apart from the balloted private bill procedure, MPs could procure a debate by introducing a Bill under the ten-minute rule, or under Standing Order 37: see generally D. Marsh and M. Read, *Private Members' Bills*, Cambridge, 1988; J. A. G. Griffith and M. T. Ryle with M. A. J. Wheeler-Booth, *Parliament: Functions, Practice and Procedures* (1989) Ch. 10.

[51] Mr W. Homewood, MP for Kettering.

[52] (1987) *The Law Magazine* 12 June, 30 states that Abse told Homewood: 'Look if you want to get a bit of publicity and show what a good fellow you are, I'll draw a bill and we'll have a press conference and we'll get it out so there'll be some local publicity. I drew up a rough and ready bill, practically on the back of a cigarette packet. It was more than rough-hewn, it was a terrible bill.' Clause 1 of the Bill (No. 24 of 1981–2) in fact ordered to be printed would have amended the Inheritance (Provision for Family and Dependants) Act 1975 so as to give any person found wrongfully to have caused death the right to apply to the court, and to empower the court if satisfied that it would in all the circumstances be inequitable for the applicant to forfeit all benefit to which he would have been entitled under the deceased's will or intestacy to grant him such relief as the court, having regard

did it come about that the Forfeiture Act in fact became law? The answer to that question depends on an understanding of the simple truth, confirmed by research,[53] that it is opposition which destroys the chances of a Private Member's Bill becoming law;[54] and that it is often the success of a Bill's promoters in avoiding controversy (rather than—as is often thought—the place obtained by the sponsor in the Ballot)[55] which largely determines whether or not a Bill reaches the statute book. Indeed, the Parliamentary Session 1981–2 provides a striking illustration of this fact: on the one hand, the Dogs (Miscellaneous Provisions) Bill (which would have provided for the establishment of a national dog warden service) was drawn fifth in the ballot, but aroused predictably strong feelings, and did not make progress; but in contrast, the Forfeiture Bill (drawn thirteenth) was successful.[56] The explanation lies largely in the skill of the Bill's sponsors, first, in arranging the timetable for the Bill's passage to maximise the prospects of time being available for the necessary debate; but, more important, in their skill

to all the circumstances including the conduct of the applicant and the deceased and the financial resources and financial needs of the applicant and any other person affected, considers to be just.

Clause 2 of the Bill, intended to reverse the effect of *R* v. *National Insurance Commissioner, ex parte O'Connor* [1981] 1 QB 758, provided that where a woman had been held not to be entitled to certain social security benefits by reason only of her having become a widow by her own unlawful act she might apply to the court for such relief as the court, having regard to all the circumstances, considered just.

[53] D. Marsh and M. Read, *British Private Members' Balloted Bills: A Lottery with Few Winners, Small Prizes, but High Administrative Costs* (1985—Essex Papers in Politics and Government, No. 21) constitutes a preliminary study leading to the same authors' comprehensive *Private Members' Bills* (Cambridge, 1985). For other studies, see P. Bromhead, *Private Members' Bills* (1965); P. G. Richards *Honourable Members: A Study of the British Backbencher* (2nd edn. 1964); P. G. Richards, *Parliament and Conscience* (1970); J. A. G. Griffith and M. T. Ryle with M. A. J. Wheeler-Booth, *Parliament: Functions, Practice and Procedures* (1989) Ch. 10. There is also a valuable brief discussion, particularly focusing on the actual and prospective role of the Private Member's Bill, in G. Drewry, 'The Legislative Implementation of Law Reform Proposals' in G. Zellick (ed.), *The Law Commission and Law Reform* (1988), particularly at 32–6. For the role of the House of Lords— both in Bills coming from the Commons and in Bills introduced by peers (of which comparatively few get onto the statute book because of opposition or lack of time in the Commons)—see D. Shell, *The House of Lords* (1988) Table 5.4.

[54] See the analysis in Marsh and Read, *Private Members' Bills* (1988): in particular, a vote taken on Second or Third Reading indicates opposition, and since 1945 only ten Bills on which such a vote had been taken have become law: p. 14. The only exception to this general rule is where a Bill enjoys government support (as distinct from mere benign neutrality): G. Drewry, 'The Legislative Implementation of Law Reform Proposals' in G. Zellick (ed.), *The Law Commission and Law Reform* (1988), at p. 33.

[55] However, only the first six Bills are guaranteed a Second Reading debate; and, since 1971, the sponsors of the first ten balloted Bills have been entitled to draw a small sum from public funds to assist with drafting expenses. But if there is little debate on a Bill which has priority, there will be time for debate on others; and the sponsors of the Forfeiture Bill were adept in timetabling the Bill so as to exploit this opportunity.

[56] See I. Burton and G. Drewry, *Parliamentary Affairs: Public Legislation: A Survey of the Sessions 1981/2*. The Bill received a Second Reading 'on the nod'; and the first substantive debate took place in Standing Committee C. It appears that there had not been any time for a preliminary discussion between the Government and the Bill's promoters: see Standing Committee C *Official Report* 17 Mar. 1982, col. 4, and the explanation given by Mr Peter Archer of his failure to make contact with the Solicitor-General.

in minimising the Bill's potentially highly controversial nature. The fact that the Bill could be presented as involving largely technical problems of legal doctrine was helpful in achieving the success of this strategy;[57] and minimised the possibility of the Bill being talked out or defeated. Moreover, the Government was persuaded to remain neutral on the issue of principle, and indeed to offer drafting assistance in putting the Bill into what was thought to be an acceptable legislative form.[58] Once it became apparent that there was some possibility of getting the Bill through, the overriding need to avoid arousing opposition accounts for the way the issues were presented in the Parliamentary Debates (which took up only three and a half hours in the Commons).[59] As Leo Abse put it: 'if they'd woken up to what they were doing, they'd have killed it'.[60] No doubt this consideration explains why the sponsors accepted an amendment to prohibit any modification of the forfeiture rule in cases of murder, notwithstanding the fact that there may well be murder cases—some instances of so-called mercy killing, for example—in which the forfeiture rule might operate harshly and unjustly.

Again, it was important to avoid antagonising the Government and the officials (who were responsible for producing the Bill in the form in which it received the Royal Assent) to give the impression that the drafting and other problems which they faced required more extensive deliberation than would be possible in the time available. In particular, the history of the Law Commission's earlier involvement was known to the sponsors (and presumably to others favouring legislation) and this factor no doubt accounts for the silence which greeted repeated suggestions that the Bill be referred to the Commission.[61]

Similar considerations no doubt explain the failure of any of those concerned to raise publicly any points about the detailed drafting of the legislation[62]

---

[57] Leo Abse is reported as saying that the Lord Chancellor's staff were intrigued by what they saw. Indeed, so absorbed did they become in the technical problems of the Bill that they devoted themselves entirely to trying to fix them, rather than worrying about its significance: (1987) *The Law Magazine* 12 June, 30.   [58] See Hansard HL, vol. 431, col. 716, per Lord Hailsham.

[59] I. Burton and G. Drewry, *Parliamentary Affairs: Public Legislation: A Survey of the Sessions 1981/2*. A further factor relevant to a Bill's prospects may be whether Members (who have heavy constituency and other duties) are sufficiently interested in a measure to be present in the House and Chamber. In some cases the promoters of a Bill may encourage those known to be hostile to recognise that their time could be more profitably spent elsewhere on the Friday in question.

[60] (1987) *The Law Magazine* 12 June, 30.

[61] Mr Douglas Hogg, for example, made the suggestion of a reference to the Law Commission on a number of occasions: see e.g. Hansard HC 14 May 1982, vol. 23, cols. 1104, 1110. In reply Mr Peter Archer (a former Solicitor-General, with great experience of the law reform process) observed that he was a 'great believer' in using the Law Commission 'which has done great service. But where there is a specific, fairly narrow and clearly defined problem on which it is possible to form a view, the House should be able to form a view without the kind of consideration that it is normal for the Law Commission to give': Hansard HC 14 May 1982, vol. 23, col. 1104.

[62] In *Re K (deceased)* [1985] Ch. 85, Vinelott J stated that the Bill 'was, I understand, a private member's bill and may not have been drafted by parliamentary counsel. It is not couched in technical language but in language intended to be understood by persons other than lawyers specialising in property and trust matters.' As stated above, the Bill was (in the form in which it was enacted) drafted by Parliamentary Counsel.

notwithstanding the fact that no part of the Act—which duly received the Royal Assent on 13 July 1982[63]—remotely resembles any part of the Bill which had originally been introduced and debated.

TACTICAL SUCCESS—LEGISLATIVE DISASTER?

To get a major Bill onto the statute book is a great political achievement for a backbencher;[64] and those concerned to remedy a significant injustice might congratulate themselves on a brilliant tactical success. The Bill would, it seemed, provide a remedy for injustice; and there was no reason to question the Lord Chancellor's assurance that any technical defects would have been removed from the Bill.[65] But the more enquiring and sceptical would perhaps remember Leo Abse's perceptive autobiographical comment[66] that advocates should often be more perturbed by their successes than by their failures. Leaving on one side the issues of principle—is it really desirable that law reform should be achieved by sleight of hand and by avoiding public discussion?—was there perhaps substance in the Solicitor-General's warning that easy it is to get in a muddle, with the best of intentions, and to end up with an even less clear law than existed before?[67]

Certainly little enthusiasm for the Act was expressed by writers in the academic and professional legal press.[68] A commentator in the *Modern Law Review*, indeed, concluded that the reformer and the draftsmen together had simply introduced needless statutory distinctions and complexities to the law,[69] and that the common law rule was sufficiently flexible to meet the justice of the case. Another writer, in a particularly impressive piece of legal analysis,[70] described the Act as a 'legislative disaster which failed to solve the mischief against which it was directed and would ultimately disappoint those whom it was designed to help'.

How justified are such criticisms? It is necessary first to look briefly at the terms of the Act. It identifies the 'forfeiture rule',[71] and confers on a court the power to make an order modifying the effect of that rule.[72] But it is also

[63] The Act (apart from the provision dealing with social security benefits) came into force on 13 Oct. 1982: s. 7(2).   [64] P. G. Richards, *Parliament and Conscience* (1970) p. 34.
[65] Hansard (HL) 17 June 1982, vol. 431, col. 716.   [66] *Private Member*, p. 37.
[67] See Official Report, Standing Committee C, 17 Mar. 1982, col. 8.
[68] See P. H. Kenny (1983) 46 MLR 66; P. H. Kenny (1982) 132 New LJ 897; P. Matthews, 'Property, Pensions and Double Punishment: the Forfeiture Act 1982' [1983] JSWL 141.
[69] P. H. Kenny (1983) 46 MLR 66, 72.
[70] P. Matthews, 'Property, Pensions and Double Punishment: the Forfeiture Act 1982' [1983] JSWL 141.   [71] S. 1.
[72] S. 2(1). The Act thus envisages a two-stage process in which the court first decides whether the forfeiture rule applies—i.e. whether the moral guilt involved in the commission of the offence requires the person concerned to be exposed to the sanction of forfeiture; and if, but only if, it does so decide, it proceeds to consider whether 'the justice of the case' none the less requires the effect of the rule to be modified. This may be thought to be logically difficult to defend; and until Vinelott J's decision in *Re K (deceased)* [1986] Ch. 180 there was doubt about whether a power to 'modify'

provided[73] that the court shall not make an order modifying the effect of the rule unless 'it is satisfied that, having regard to the conduct of the offender and of the deceased and to such other circumstances as appear to the court to be material, the justice of the case requires the effect of the rule to be modified in that case'. Moreover, the court is not to make such an order in any case where a person 'stands convicted' of an offence of which unlawful killing is an element unless proceedings for the purpose are brought within three months beginning with the date of his conviction;[74] while nothing in the Act is to affect the application of the forfeiture rule in the case of a person who 'stands convicted' of murder.[75] The Act also contained a complex provision[76] dealing with certain specified social security benefits: the question whether a person would be precluded by the operation of the forfeiture rule from receiving the whole or part of the benefit was to be determined by a Social Security Commissioner; and the Secretary of State was empowered to make regulations for carrying the provision into effect. Against this background, some of the criticisms made of the legislation can be examined.

WAS THE FORFEITURE ACT NECESSARY?

The most fundamental is that the enactment of the Forfeiture Act was unnecessary because the common law was sufficiently flexible to achieve substantial justice.[77]

It is true that this view derives some support from dicta in subsequent case law;[78] but the case law also demonstrates the real and substantial injustice which application of the common law rule as it existed in 1982 would have caused. For example,[79] in *Re K (deceased)*[80] the applicant widow had been subjected to violent physical attacks by her husband throughout the greater part of her eighteen years' marriage. The last of many quarrels occurred in September 1982. The husband began to lose his self-control. The wife, knowing from experience how easily the situation could slip into serious violence against her, picked up a 12-bore shotgun which the husband kept loaded for the purpose of shooting rabbits. She pointed it at him in the hope of deterring him. In order to attract his

could extend to exclude the application of the rule altogether: see the Scottish decision in *Cross, Petitioner*, 1987 SLT 384 (OH). There may be something to be said in favour of the single-stage relieving process provided for in the Bill as originally introduced.

[73] S. 2(2).
[74] S. 2(3). It may be that this provision explains the absence of any application by the plaintiff in *Jones* v. *Roberts* [1995] 2 FLR 442, HH Judge Kolbert. See further at p. 86 below.
[75] S. 5.   [76] S. 4.   [77] See Kenny, op. cit. n. 69 above.   [78] See below.
[79] Note also the Australian case of *Troja* v. *Troja* (1994) 33 NSWLR 269. The New South Wales Court of Appeal held that the common law forfeiture rule applied to deprive a depressive wife, who had intentionally killed her husband because she wanted to stop the abuse to which he had subjected her over a prolonged period, of the interest he had left her under his will.
[80] [1985] Ch. 85 (Vinelott J); [1986] Ch. 180, CA.

attention and make sure he would see she had the gun, she released the safety catch. The gun went off accidentally. The husband was killed, and his widow was charged with murder. Her plea of guilty to manslaughter was accepted, and she was put on probation for two years.

Vinelott J, in a careful and thorough judgment (to which the Court of Appeal paid tribute),[81] concluded that the forfeiture rule did apply to manslaughter cases in which a person had been guilty of deliberate, intentional and unlawful violence; and that since the applicant was guilty of such violence the common law rule applied.[82] Accordingly, had it not been for the provision of the Forfeiture Act, which empowered the court to modify the effect of the rule, the widow—who had few assets of her own, and was apparently in receipt of supplementary benefit—would have been debarred from succeeding to her husband's share of the family home or to any part of his estate.

In *Jones* v. *Roberts*[83] the plaintiff was a paranoid schizophrenic who believed he was being persecuted by the IRA and the KGB and that his parents, 'controlled' by the Romanian Secret Service, were trying to poison him. He killed them both with a hammer. The prosecution accepted a plea of manslaughter on the ground of diminished responsibility, and a hospital order was made. In subsequent proceedings to determine the devolution of the father's estate the judge, believing the law as it stood on the authorities to be 'overwhelming', held that the forfeiture rule prevented the plaintiff from taking any interest in the estate which thus passed on the father's intestacy to more remote relatives. No application was apparently made by the plaintiff under the Forfeiture Act.[84]

Finally, in *Dunbar* v. *Plant*,[85] a young man and woman, concerned that she would be imprisoned for misappropriating her employers' funds, agreed to commit suicide. After a number of attempts, the man died but his lover survived. Since the woman had committed[86] the offence of aiding and abetting suicide the Court of Appeal held that the application of the forfeiture rule would have involved her forfeiting her right to take the interest to which she would otherwise have been entitled in (1) the couple's intended matrimonial home held in their joint names; (2) the endowment policy charged to the lender by way of collateral

---

[81] See per Ackner LJ at [1986] Ch. 186, and per Griffiths LJ at 196.

[82] This was the test formulated, obiter, by Geoffrey Lane J in *Gray* v. *Barr, Prudential Assurance Co. (Third Party)* [1970] 2 QB 626, 640; and referred to approvingly by the Court of Appeal in that case: see [1971] 2 QB 554, 568, CA, per Salmon LJ. But in *Dunbar* v. *Plant* [1998] 1 FLR 157 the Court of Appeal rejected the view—also applied by Peter Gibson J in *Re H (deceased)* [1990] 1 FLR 441—that the forfeiture rule only applied to cases in which violence had been used or threatened. Accordingly, as the authorities now stand, it appears that the forfeiture rule applies to all cases of manslaughter (except motor insurance cases, which are subject to different considerations of public policy).   [83] [1995] 2 FLR 422, HH Judge Kolbert.

[84] This may have been because of the requirement imposed by s. 2(3) of the Act that an application for relief must be made within three months of the conviction; or possibly because those entitled on intestacy had agreed to settle one-third of their entitlement on trust for the plaintiff's benefit and that in the circumstances an application for relief would have been unlikely to have succeeded.

[85] [1998] 1 FLR 157, CA.   [86] So the Court held. There was no prosecution.

security; and (3) the £31,801 proceeds of an insurance policy on the deceased's life written in trust for the woman. The Court held that the common law forfeiture rule applied, but that the Forfeiture Act gave the court a discretion (which on the facts it was prepared to exercise) to modify the effect of the rule. The judgment of the majority includes an assertion[87] that 'but for the intervention of the legislature' in the 1982 Act 'the judges would themselves have modified the rule'. However, the same judgment rejects judicial attempts made since the Forfeiture Act to modify the scope of the rule.[88] The 'appropriate course where the application of the rule appears to conflict with the ends of justice is [said Phillips LJ] to exercise the powers given by the Forfeiture Act'.[89]

As a result of the enactment of the Act, therefore, the court now unquestionably has power to modify the application of a rule which, as these cases demonstrate, could cause serious hardship and injustice. Perhaps the most dramatic illustration of this is provided by the facts of *Re K (deceased)*[90] set out above: what court, on those facts, would consider a fine of almost half a million pounds to be an appropriate response to the widow's culpability? It may be true that faced with such injustice the courts would themselves have developed modifications of the rule, and might even have gone so far as to decline to apply it 'where the facts indicated such a low degree of culpability, or such a high degree of mitigation, that the sanction of forfeiture, far from giving effect to the public interest would have been contrary to it'.[91] But this is speculation; and it also needs to be remembered that any such judicial modification would only have been effected at the cost of litigation, the outcome of which might have been far from certain.[92]

RULE, DISCRETION, OR PALM-TREE JUSTICE?

The Act[93] provides that if the common law forfeiture rule 'has precluded a person ... who has unlawfully killed another from acquiring any' of certain specified interests in property, the court may make an order 'modifying the effect'

---

[87] Per Phillips LJ at 179 (Hirst LJ concurring at 182).

[88] See per Phillips LJ at 180 (pointing out that violence may be used or threatened in cases of diminished responsibility or provocation, but that the mitigating features in such cases may make the application of the forfeiture rule particularly harsh); and note Mummery LJ at 168–9 also rejected attempts to restrict the application of the common law rule to cases in which violence has been used or threatened not least because such a rule might exclude cases of poisoning.

[89] Note also that in *Troja* v. *Troja* (1994) 33 NSWLR 269 the majority of the New South Wales Court of Appeal rejected a submission that it could properly impose a constructive trust in favour of the wife, preferring the view that the creation of such a broad adjustive discretion required legislative intervention (as seen in this country with the 1982 Act).

[90] [1985] Ch. 85 (Vinelott J); [1986] Ch. 180, CA.

[91] As suggested by Phillips LJ, *Dunbar* v. *Plant* [1998] 1 FLR 157, 179.

[92] In this context, it has also to be remembered that circuit judges (who would no doubt be responsible for hearing cases involving comparatively small estates) may well be less confident about seeking to develop what appears to be settled case law than would be some judges with a higher position in the judicial hierarchy.   [93] S. 2(3).

of the rule; but the court is not to make such an order 'in any case unless it is satisfied that, having regard to the conduct of the offender and of the deceased and to such other circumstances as appear to the court to be material, the justice of the case requires the effect of the rule to be so modified . . .'; and it has been said[94] that since this gives 'absolutely no guidance' as to the principles to be applied the result is likely to be an inconsistency in judicial decisions, and difficulty for those required to advise on the devolution of property.

This argument is not easy to refute. In *Dunbar* v. *Plant*[95] (the facts of which have been summarised above) the trial judge held that in exercising his discretion under the Act he took account of the fact that the deceased would have wished his intended wife to take all his property; but he considered that this was not the only relevant matter. He believed that he also had to do 'justice between the parties'; and that the deceased's parents (who would have taken all his property if the application of the forfeiture rule were not modified) should not be entirely excluded from the 'unwelcome windfall' brought about by their son's sudden death.[96] The Court of Appeal unanimously accepted that the judge had been right to modify the application of the forfeiture rule; and they unanimously held that the judge had been wrong to regard his task as being to 'do justice between the parties' (as distinct from doing what 'the justice of the case' required). However, they disagreed about whether the judge's decision should be upheld. For the minority,[97] the judge had been entitled to make the order he had (rather than one more generous to the survivor); and it was also right to take account of the fact that the survivor's conduct had been unlawful, and justice also required the wishes of the deceased's father and family to be taken into account. But the majority[98] considered that 'the first and paramount consideration . . . must be whether the culpability' attending the survivor's criminal conduct was such as to justify the application of the forfeiture rule at all; and that her irrational and tragic action was not such as to justify any departure from the principle that full relief should be given in those cases where one party to a suicide pact survived. In essence, therefore, the Act entitles and requires the court to form a view on the degree of moral culpability attending a killing.[99] So the court is faced with the task of deciding what degree of turpitude justifies the court in debarring a claimant from the rights he or she would otherwise have.[100]

[94] By P. H. Kenny (1983) 46 MLR 66, 72.   [95] [1998] 1 FLR 157, CA.

[96] The judge's order modified the application of the rule so as to allocate the proceeds of sale of the jointly owned home and the policy effected to support the mortgage on it to the survivor; but to deny her the £31,801 proceeds of an insurance policy on the deceased's life. However, he also made an order for costs which in the events which had happened would have meant that she derived no benefit from the modification of the rule.   [97] Mummery LJ.

[98] Phillips LJ, with whom Hirst LJ concurred.

[99] *Re K (Deceased)* [1986] Fam. 180, Vinelott J; see above. The Court of Appeal refused to interfere: see p. 85 above.

[100] See the striking example of the difficulty which confronted the courts in *Whiston* v. *Whiston* [1995] Fam. 198, CA, and *J* v. *S-T (Formerly J) (Transsexual: Ancillary Relief)* [1997] 1 FLR 402, CA.

There can be no dispute that such assessments will often be difficult,[101] both for the courts and for the parties' advisers;[102] and that there will inevitably be a substantial measure of palm-tree justice in some court decisions. But the problem to which no really convincing answer has been given is: what alternative would produce more predictable and principled results?[103] It has been well said[104] that 'the objectives of the law . . . should be to ensure, first of all, that no conceivable encouragement is provided to the commission of crime, secondly, that a result is reached in each case which appears, as far as possible, to be humane and intuitively just, and, thirdly, that the relevant principles are not avoidably uncertain in their operation'. Regrettably, however, the last two of these principles may often conflict.

The fundamental question, therefore, remains unanswered (and indeed unanswerable): is palm-tree justice worse than no justice at all? The Act was certainly defective as it was originally[105] enacted;[106] and what took place during the parliamentary proceedings amply demonstrates the technical and procedural imperfections of the Private Member's Bill as a means of promoting law reform

---

[101] See e.g. the decision of a Social Security Commissioner in *R(G) 1/88* (woman who had been drinking with her husband became enraged by his verbal abuse and stabbed him—convicted of manslaughter by a German court, and served a sentence of imprisonment—full account taken of fact that claimant had had no intention of killing husband she loved and that she was deeply contrite about having done so; but offence was a grave one, right that she should forfeit entitlement to widow's benefit for five years after offence). The Act, as originally enacted, did not effectively provide for modification of the forfeiture rule in its application to social security benefits, but the necessary amendments were made by the Social Security Act 1986.

[102] The application of the rules determining liability for the legal costs involved—which penalise those who reject settlement offers equalling or exceeding the amount eventually awarded by the court—make it all the more important to make a correct estimate of the likely outcome. It was (see per Phillips LJ at 172) the impact of this so-called *Calderbank* principle which meant that the modification ordered by the first instance judge in *Dunbar* v. *Plant* (above) did not benefit the survivor; and it is tempting (if impermissible) to speculate as to whether this aspect of the case weighed heavily with the majority in the Court of Appeal.

[103] It is tempting to suggest that the introduction of fuller guidance about the factors to be taken into account—perhaps on the pattern of the Inheritance (Provision for Family and Dependants) Act 1975 or the Matrimonial Causes Act 1973—would go some way to meet critics' views; and it has been held that the court may in any event take account of the matters referred to in the 1975 Act (see *Re K (Deceased)* [1986] Fam. 180, Vinelott J, where the fact that the deceased was under no duty to provide for others was a factor). It is even more tempting to argue that the forfeiture rule represents an archaic survival in a developed system of justice, that it should be allowed to join the deodand and escheat *propter delictum tenentis* in the textbooks of legal history, and that the policy of ensuring that a person who kills for gain should, like any other criminal, not be allowed to profit at another person's expense from the fruits of a conscious and deliberate crime would best be achieved by following the example of recent legislation giving the courts power to order a forfeiture as part of the sentencing process. But (as in *Dunbar* v. *Plant*) there may not be a criminal trial and the legislation has not proved entirely straightforward.   [104] By R. A. Buckley (1995) 111 LQR 196, 198.

[105] Once the Act was on the statute book, drafting errors could be dealt with uncontroversially by amending legislation given that Parliament had accepted the principle: see n. 101 above (social security entitlements).

[106] Not least in failing to make provision for social security benefits: see above, n. 101. For a general (and penetrating) critique, see P. Matthews, 'Property, Pensions and Double Punishment: the Forfeiture Act 1982' [1983] JSWL 141.

as well as the pressure to minimise public discussion and to discourage even informed controversy which the realities of parliamentary life place on those who seek change. The Forfeiture Act 1982 is not perfect legislation; and in a perfect world, things would certainly not happen in the way that they did. However, the Act does provide a crude but workable solution to a problem which was not statistically great, but which had a potentially devastating impact in some cases. Its enactment has enabled a number of cases where grave injustice might otherwise have been done to be resolved. Those responsible for bringing the legislation before Parliament can claim that their efforts have enabled the principle that criminal killing should not necessarily entail forfeiture and that there should be some proportionate relationship between the degree of moral guilt and the penalty which the perpetrator suffers to be shown to be acceptable and indeed workable. Practical law reformers and politicians have to accept the simple truth embodied in the saying that half a loaf is better than no bread. Rationality is indeed an excellent thing; but its pursuit should not be allowed to inhibit those who have the skill and experience to make use of admittedly imperfect parliamentary machinery in order to remove one source of injustice from the laws of the United Kingdom.

4*

'Disgusted, Buckingham Palace . . .': Divorce, Indecency and the Press, 1926

INTRODUCTION

As we have seen in Chapter Two, the matrimonial offence based divorce law caused a good deal of hardship and injustice. But the bitterness, distress and humiliation[1] so often associated with divorce was not entirely attributable to the substantive law. Press publicity—often perhaps just the fear of publicity—was distressing; whilst the adversarial tradition of court proceedings in which one party had to prove the guilt of the other (although occasionally cathartic) made matters worse for husbands and wives sucked (often uncomprehendingly) into litigation. The following chapters of this book deal with some of these aspects of divorce. This Chapter deals with the circumstances which led to statutory restrictions being put on press reporting of divorce cases; whilst Chapters 8 and 9 continue to explore the theme of humanising the process of divorce.

THE KING 'DISGUSTED'

At the end of the twentieth century, divorce in England has become a routine matter of filling in forms;[2] but at one time it could be a matter of high drama. Thus it was on 8 July 1922 when Sir Henry Duke,[3] President of the Probate, Divorce and Admiralty Division (sitting with a jury), began the hearing of a divorce petition brought by the Hon. John Hugo Russell, son and heir of the third Baron

---

* The material in this Chapter was first published as an article, under the title '"Disgusted, Buckingham Palace . . ." The Judicial Proceedings (Regulation of Reports) Act 1926' in [1997] CFLQ 43. The author is grateful to Sir Michael Wheeler-Booth KCB, sometime Clerk of the Parliaments, for helpful comments.

[1] *Reform of the Grounds of Divorce: The Field of Choice* (Law Com. No. 6, 1966) paras. 23–8.

[2] See S. M. Cretney and J. M. Masson, *Principles of Family Law* (6th edn. 1997) pp. 314–15.

[3] (1855–1939). The son of a clerk, Duke took up journalism on leaving school but was subsequently able to qualify as a barrister. Sir Claud Schuster (Permanent Secretary to the Lord Chancellor) recorded that 'direct and vehement pressure was needed to induce him to accept' appointment as President of the Probate, Divorce and Admiralty Division in 1919 which took him away from work which he enjoyed and compelled him to devote himself to 'an extremely laborious and, in many respects, repulsive occupation': Memorandum to the *Business of the Courts Committee*, 22 Mar. 1933. Duke was raised to the peerage as Baron Merrivale in 1925.

Ampthill,[4] on the grounds of his wife Christabel's adultery. The eminence of the advocates—the petitioner was represented by three leading counsel (including two future Lords Chancellor[5]), the respondent by leading counsel shortly to become Attorney-General[6]—and the social standing of the parties was sufficient indication that the stage was set for a fashionable law suit. Day by day (reported the *News of the World*[7]) 'fashionable women and blasé young men have clamoured for admission to the court as though it were some place of entertainment'; and the wife admitted she had written letters saying she was 'relishing the fray' and suggesting her friends come down to reserved stalls and boxes. But the extensive press publicity[8] was not universally welcomed. On the fourth day of the hearing, King George V caused his Private Secretary to write to the Lord Chancellor:[9]

. . . the King is disgusted at the publication of the gross, scandalous details of the Russell divorce case. His Majesty doubts whether there is any similar instance of so repulsive an exposure of those intimate relations between man and woman which hitherto through the recognition of the unwritten code of decency indeed of civilisation have been regarded as sacred and out of range of public eye or ear. The pages of the most extravagant French novel would hesitate to describe what has now been placed at the disposal of every boy or girl reader of the daily newspapers.

But the view from the Lord Chancellor's office was different. Certainly, the 'natural instincts of healthy minded people' would favour trial in camera for such cases; but there were 'very weighty' considerations pointing against such a solution, and these had 'commended themselves practically to all those who have long experience in the matter'.[10] No legislative action, it appeared, was in contemplation.

But the Monarch did not give up his belief that sexual scandal should be kept out of the press. Three years later, another missive was despatched from Buckingham Palace to the House of Lords:[11]

---

[4] As Lord Russell of Killowen had to point out in *The Ampthill Peerage* [1977] AC 547 the surname 'Russell' is not uncommon; and the reader may find it helpful to be reminded there are three distinct peerages held by different branches of the great Whig family conveniently described as the Bedford Russells, viz., (i) the Dukedom of Bedford, created in 1694; (ii) the Earldom of Russell of Kingston Russell granted in 1861 to the former Prime Minister Lord John Russell. (This peerage descended to the philosopher Bertrand Russell, the third Earl Russell; and it is now held by the third Earl's son, Professor of British History at King's College London and spokesman on social security matters in the House of Lords for the Liberal Democrat party); and (iii) the Ampthill Peerage, a barony granted in 1881 to Lord Odo Russell (a distinguished diplomat and brother of the then Duke of Bedford).

[5] Sir John Simon KC (Lord Chancellor 1940–5 (formerly Attorney-General 1913–15 and Home Secretary 1915–16; and subsequently Foreign Secretary 1931–5, Home Secretary 1935–7, and Chancellor of the Exchequer 1937–40)) and Sir Douglas Hogg KC (Lord Chancellor 1928–9 and 1935–8 (Attorney-General 1922–4, 1924–8; Secretary of State for War 1931–5)).

[6] Patrick Hastings KC (Attorney-General in the first Labour Government, 1924).

[7] On 16 July 1922.

[8] The case is reported in The Times Law Reports on 8, 12, 14, 15, 19, 20, 21, and 22 July 1922.

[9] Stamfordham to Birkenhead, 15 July 1922: PRO LCO2/775.

[10] Schuster to Stamfordham, 19 July 1922: PRO LCO2/775.

[11] Stamfordham to Cave, 6 Mar. 1925: PRO LCO2/775.

The King feels sure that you will share his feelings of disgust and shame at the daily published discreditable and nauseating evidence in the Dennistoun case. His Majesty asks you whether it would not have been possible to prevent the case coming into Court, either by a refusal of the Judge to try it, or by the joint insistence of the respective Counsels to come to an arrangement, especially when, apparently, the question at issue was one of minor importance.

The King deplores the disastrous and far reaching effects throughout all classes and on all ranks of the Army of the wholesale press advertisement of this disgraceful story.[12]

On this occasion a less discouraging reply was sent to the Palace; and the following year the Judicial Proceedings (Regulation of Reports) Act 1926—one of the rare examples of peace-time legislation specifically restricting the freedom of the press to publish material lawfully in a reporter's possession—received the Royal Assent. It is true that the Act is rarely[13] invoked; but the issue of how far family proceedings should be protected from publicity is an important (and topical[14]) one, whilst the background to the *Russell* case offers some revealing insights

---

[12] It is not surprising that the King should have been disturbed by the publicity given to the case of *Dennistoun* v. *Dennistoun* (1925) 69 Sol. J 476—an action for breach of contract brought by a divorced woman against her former husband (a retired officer in the Grenadier Guards, and at the time the husband of Almina Lady Carnarvon) heard before McCardie J and a jury over sixteen days in 1925. It appeared from the evidence as reported in *The Times*, 4–27 Mar. 1925 that Mrs Dennistoun had, with her husband's connivance, become the long-standing mistress of General Sir John Cowans GCMG GCB. As Sir Edward Marshall Hall KC (who appeared with Norman Birkett KC for the defendant) put it: the allegation was that 'the General bought her and the price he paid was that he obtained preferment in the Army for her husband'. General Cowans—said to be an administrative genius who served with remarkable success as Quartermaster General of the Army throughout World War I and in that capacity was responsible for the supplies needed for nearly half a million military personnel (not to mention 895,770 animals)—had died in 1921. The General's memorialist in the *Dictionary of National Biography* states that 'his recommendations for appointments were criticized, and not without reason; but there is no doubt that the chief secret of his success lay in his power of selecting the best men to serve him in the really responsible positions'.

[13] But two cases are important exceptions. In *Argyll (Duchess of)* v. *Duke of Argyll* [1967] Ch. 302 it was held that the Act could be invoked by a party to divorce proceedings to obtain an injunction against the disclosure of matters revealed in the course of divorce proceedings. In *Moynihan* v. *Moynihan (Nos. 1 and 2)* [1997] 1 FLR 52 it was held that the Act prevented the press from publishing full and contemporaneous reports of the Queen's Proctor's application to set aside a divorce decree granted six years earlier to the (subsequently deceased) third Lord Moynihan. Although *The Times* reported that the *Moynihan* case 'promised an insight into the antics' of the third Baron who (the paper reported on 16 July 1996) had 'lived life to the full, building up a three million pound fortune from the sex industry and earning himself the nickname of the Ermine Pimpernel' in reality it seems that the case did not produce what are sometimes described as salacious details. Moreover, neither the Queen's Proctor nor anyone else involved resisted the unrestricted reporting of the proceedings; but this was held to be irrelevant: the 1926 Act was mandatory in effect and it applied because the divorce proceedings instituted by the petitioner were still 'continuing'.

[14] There have been three significant developments. First, a *Review of Access to and Reporting of Family Proceedings* (Lord Chancellor's Department, 1993) was carried out by the Government's Family Law and Administration Working Party (following a recommendation made by the Calcutt Committee on *Privacy and Related Matters* Cm. 1102 (1990). The Working Party's terms of reference were to 'identify anomalies and shortcomings within the present system and to make recommendations for reform. In particular it shall:—

(a) have regard to the underlying principles of open justice, the need to promote the welfare of children and respect for the privacy of individual family members;

into the extent to which the judicial process is apt for resolving issues of family breakdown. In this Chapter, therefore, we examine the events leading up to the 1926 Act, the circumstances surrounding its enactment, and its effect over the seventy years that it has been on the statute book.

BACKGROUND TO THE 1926 ACT: A LONG-STANDING PROBLEM

George V's protests in fact echoed[15] those made sixty years earlier by his grand-mother, Queen Victoria. Before the creation of the Divorce Court in 1857 evidence in the Ecclesiastical Courts had been taken in private before an examiner, and proceedings for private Acts of Parliament were not sufficiently frequent to give rise to any large-scale problem.[16] But the Matrimonial Causes Act 1857 required witnesses in the Divorce Court to be examined orally in open court;[17] and the court became a 'place of resort . . . of characters of the worst description'. Crowds congregated there for the purpose of hearing details which could

(b) identify existing inconsistencies and anomalies in the law and practice of access to and reporting of family proceedings;
(c) in the light of (a) and (b) consider whether there should be a consistent code, what this code should contain and whether any special rules are necessary in respect of any particular type of proceeding or any particular matter; and
(d) consider a means of ensuring the effective operation of this code at all levels.'

Secondly, case law has drawn attention to the problem: see e.g. *Re PB (Hearings in Open Court)* [1996] 2 FLR 765, CA (unsuccessful appeal by father of five-year-old boy against judge's refusal to order hearing of residence order application in open court); and *Forbes* v. *Smith* [1998] 1 FLR 835 (status of judgment given in chambers); and it is understood that a 'Campaign for Open Justice' has been started by the organisation Families Need Fathers. Finally, a number of judges speaking extrajudicially have expressed concern at the secrecy which now surrounds many family proceedings. In particular, Wall J has stated that the most cogent of the many arguments in favour of applying the principle of open justice in the family jurisdiction are (1) to permit 'informed and proper public scrutiny of the administration of justice; (2) to facilitate informed public knowledge, understanding and discussion of the important social, medical and ethical issues which are litigated in the family justice system; and (3) . . . to facilitate the dissemination of information useful to other professions and organisations in the multi-disciplinary working of family law': [1995] Fam. Law 136 (and see also Booth J's comments at the Annual Conference of the Family Law Bar Association, 1987: (1987) New LJ 444).

[15] Both in language and content: see Queen Victoria's letter to Lord Chancellor Campbell, 26 Dec. 1859, as quoted in the *Report of the Royal Commission on Divorce and Matrimonial Causes* (1912, Cd. 6478, BPP 1912–13 vols. 18–20) para. 477—'The Queen wishes to ask the Lord Chancellor whether no steps can be take to prevent the present publicity of the proceedings before the new Divorce Court. These cases, which must necessarily increase when the new law becomes more and more known, fill almost daily a large portion of the newspapers, and are of so scandalous a character that it makes it almost impossible for a paper to be trusted in the hands of a young lady or boy. None of the worst French novels from which careful parents would try to protect their children can be as bad as what is daily brought and laid upon the breakfast-table of every educated family in England, and its effect must be most pernicious to the public morals of the country.'

[16] *Report of the Royal Commission on Divorce and Matrimonial Causes* (1912, Cd. 6478, BPP 1912–13 vols. 18–20) para. 471. The same could not be said of actions for damages in the common law courts for criminal conversation (i.e. adultery): see op. cit. para. 472, and L. Stone, *Road to Divorce* (1990) particularly Ch. 9, 'Publicity and the Press'.   [17] MCA 1857, s. 46.

only give gratification to depraved and diseased minds;[18] and the press increasingly printed lurid accounts of the more sensational cases.

Eight attempts were made between 1857 and 1900[19] to legislate against the publication of evidence, but all were unsuccessful. Matters seemed to get progressively worse with the growth of the popular press in the last quarter of the nineteenth century;[20] and in 1912 the *Royal Commission on Divorce and Matrimonial Causes*[21] reported that a mass of details 'more suggestive than actually indecent'[22] was daily placed before the public. Although the more reputable journals showed a measure of restraint[23] there was a class of paper—'chiefly weekly penny papers which have mainly a working class circulation'[24]—which habitually gave 'great prominence' to the details of cases. The Commission[25] was 'greatly impressed by the evidence . . . as to the corrupting and demoralising consequences' flowing from this excessive publicity; and it concluded that the evils[26]

---

[18] Sir Richard Bethell A-G speaking in support of a provision in the Bill for the Matrimonial Causes Act 1859 which would have given the court a discretionary power to sit in camera: *Hansard*, 11 Aug. 1859, vol. 155, col. 1370. The House of Commons struck the clause out of the Bill: ibid.

[19] The details are set out in the *Report of the Royal Commission on Divorce and Matrimonial Causes* (1912, Cd. 6478, BPP 1912–13 vols. 18–20) para. 478.

[20] The Education Act 1870 made elementary education universal and obligatory.

[21] Cd. 6478, para. 474.

[22] Publication of 'indecent' matter was technically an offence at common law, being excepted from the protection given by the Law of Libel Amendment Act 1888 s. 3 to fair and accurate accounts of legal proceedings. The Royal Commission did not think that most coverage of matrimonial cases could properly be described as 'indecent' (since this required evidence of a tendency to deprave and corrupt readers); but considered that excessive prominence given to sexual relations tended 'both to bring marriage into disrespect, and to create a demand for reading of this character': para. 499. The Royal Commission quoted at para. 487 the evidence of the Lord Chief Justice of England that infinite harm was done, particularly to boys and girls between the ages of 14 and 18, by headlined accounts of 'the ladysmaid's evidence' and 'the housemaid's evidence' followed by 'a detailed account of question and answer; of the servant going to the room and saying what she sees and incidents which the prurient mind fastens on'. The mischief was done, 'not by the indecency . . . but by the suggestion': ideas were put into the minds of the young and vulnerable.

[23] The Royal Commission commissioned research into press coverage of divorce and matrimonial cases which showed considerable variation in the extent of coverage. In the first two law terms of 1910 the *Morning Post* gave 39 columns, *The Times* 105, and the *Daily Telegraph* 165. But the real offenders seem to have been the Sunday Papers (led by the Manchester-based *Umpire* with no less than 238 columns as against 128 in its nearest rival, the *People*) and the London Evening Papers (led by the *Evening Standard* with 171 columns): see Cd. 6478, col. 475.

[24] Op. cit. para. 493.

[25] The Commission's recommendations on publicity represented the practically unanimous view of the whole Commission after 'the most careful and constant attention' had been given to the 'vast amount of evidence on the subject': see per the Archbishop of York, *Hansard* (5th series) (HL) 4 May 1920, vol. 40, col. 91.

[26] *Report of the Royal Commission on Divorce and Matrimonial Causes* (1912, Cd. 6478, BPP 1912–13 vols. 18–20) para. 494. In addition to the deleterious effects of publication (especially on 'young persons of both sexes of the poorer classes') the Royal Commission accepted evidence that fear of publication had detrimental effects, firstly on the administration of justice (e.g. by deterring nervous persons from going into the witness box to support their cases and providing opportunities for blackmail: see para. 488) and, secondly, on the welfare of 'innocent children' who were given 'the opportunity of reading the miserable details of their parents lives which . . . might never be brought before them unless by the public newspapers': para. 489.

were 'real and serious' and such as to outweigh any advantage[27] flowing from unrestricted publication.

But the Commission found it much more difficult to find an acceptable remedy.[28] The English view—in contrast perhaps to that of countries taking a more lenient view of matrimonial offences and regarding 'the dissolution of marriage as a private affair of the parties concerned, in which the public has no interest, and the characters of the litigants are not at stake'[29]—was that 'divorce is a grave matter, which concerns the public as well as the parties, and . . . the characters and the future prospects of the litigants are seriously at stake'.[30] In this view, there was a presumption in favour of publicity for divorce as for other proceedings; and the Commission accordingly concluded that hearings should continue to be in open court, without any general prohibition of publication. But the public interest required the imposition of a prohibition on publishing material 'deleterious to public morals';[31] and the appropriate balance could best be struck by prohibiting publication of any report of a case until its conclusion; and by giving judges (firstly) an express statutory power to close the court if the interests of decency, morality, humanity or justice so required, and (secondly) power to prohibit the reporting or publication of any portions of the evidence and other material considered 'unsuitable for publication in the interests of decency or morality'. Publication of photographs or other pictures of parties, witnesses and others should also be prohibited.[32]

The Commission concluded this Part of its Report by expressing the hope that the press would 'do their utmost of their own free will to check what they have acknowledged to be a serious evil',[33] and expressed its confidence 'that the attention which has been drawn to this subject will strengthen the hands of those who desire to raise the standard in this matter, and help them to exert their influence on the side of moderation'.[34] But the Commission thought it prudent to threaten that if the recommended provisions failed to produce the effect anticipated, 'it may be necessary for the Legislature to strengthen the law further in the direction of prohibiting reports which are deleterious to public morals'.[35]

THE ROYAL COMMISSION'S RECOMMENDATION PIGEON-HOLED?

The Royal Commission's apparent confidence that its recommendations about press reporting would command support was soon shown to be misplaced. First, within a year the House of Lords in its judicial capacity had resoundingly asserted, as 'an almost priceless inheritance',[36] the principle that publicity in the

---

[27] In particular, that fear of public exposure was a deterrent to the commission of acts of immorality: para. 486.   [28] Op. cit. para. 494.

[29] Op. cit. para. 518.   [30] Ibid.   [31] Op. cit. paras. 502(4), 506.

[32] *Report of the Royal Commission on Divorce and Matrimonial Causes* (1912, Cd. 6478, BPP 1912–13 vols. 18–20) paras. 507–20, and Summary, para. 528.   [33] Para. 518.

[34] Ibid.   [35] Op. cit. para. 519.

[36] *Scott* v. *Scott* [1913] AC 417, 447, per Lord Loreburn.

administration of justice was a sure guarantee of liberty. To create exceptions to that principle would signify not only an encroachment upon and suppression of private rights but the undermining of constitutional security.[37] It was for this reason that the Divorce Court had to be denied any power (whether or not the parties wished it to do so) to hear a nullity suit in camera in the interests of public decency. Secondly, the one precedent for holding trials in camera seemed increasingly a distinctly unhappy one. The Punishment of Incest Act 1908 contained a provision that all proceedings under that Act were to take place in camera; but it appeared that the judges who had most experience in trying cases under that Act had 'again and again represented to the Lord Chancellor that this provision was a hindrance to the ends of justice'.[38] Thirdly, debates in the House of Lords in 1920[39] revealed strong opposition to measures such as those proposed by the Royal Commission[40] which would restrict the freedom of the press in divorce cases and, indeed, to any whittling away of the principle that justice should be done in open court. It would be impossible to improve on the statement of the case made by the Lord Chancellor's Permanent Secretary, Sir Claud Schuster:[41]

... it is necessary not only that justice should be done, but that there should be a universal confidence that justice has been done impartially. Nothing could be worse than that there should exist among the mass of population any suspicion of the integrity of Judges or juries, but this is a matter upon which people will only be convinced if they have the proofs. The minds of men are so framed that they inevitably associate secrecy with the idea that there is something wrong. Nor is this all: the charges which opposing parties make against one another in the Divorce Court are of their very nature unpleasant in themselves. If these unpleasant facts are hidden from the public, there will be a disposition to believe that there is worse behind. Even those who have had long experience of this class of case remain perhaps to the end of their lives still ready to meet new and surprising revelations of the eccentricities and the depravities which are from time to time laid bare, and between a case which arises from some normal, though regrettable, development on the one hand, and one which displays all the perversities of which human nature is capable on the other, there remain infinite gradations. If all these cases of whatever nature are tried in camera, the public will assume that they are all of the worst type. If some only are selected for the purpose, it will be assumed that the parties to those cases are of

---

[37] *Scott* v. *Scott* [1913] AC 417, 476, per Lord Shaw of Dunfermline.

[38] Schuster to Stamfordham, 19 July 1922: PRO LCO2/775. The *Select Committee on the Matrimonial Causes (Regulation of Reports) Bill* noted the belief that young people did not know that incest was a crime: *Minutes of Evidence*, 10 July 1923 (1923) HC 118, BPP 1923, vii, q. 768, p. 73; and the rule requiring incest prosecutions to be conducted in camera was repealed by s. 5, Criminal Law Amendment Act 1922.

[39] Lord Buckmaster attempted to get parliamentary approval to the Majority Report of the Royal Commission on the ground for divorce, and although he was unsuccessful—the recommendations only became law in 1937—there was a detailed debate on the Commission's Report: see *Hansard* (5th series) (HL) 4 May 1920.

[40] Clause 32 of the Bill introduced by Lord Buckmaster would have given the courts powers to direct that hearings should take place in camera and to direct that evidence should be withheld from publication. There was a general prohibition on publication of any material relating to proceedings under the Matrimonial Causes Act 'until the conclusion of the proceedings'.

[41] Schuster to Stamfordham, 19 July 1922: PRO LCO2/775.

peculiar atrocity, and it will be impossible from the very fact of the secrecy to distinguish between the two sides. Both will be overwhelmed with a kind of anonymous obloquy. Furthermore, in either case there will arise a cloud of gossip and calumny from which neither party, however innocent, will be free for the remainder of his or her life.

The instinct for publicity, which is so strong in all democracies, and particularly in England, often produces unfortunate results. They are too obvious to need comment. Yet, on the other hand, with all its disadvantages it is a sound and healthy instinct. The greatest function of government is to maintain the purity of the administration of justice: that purity cannot be maintained without public confidence; and long years of experience show that public confidence can only be maintained if justice is administered, wherever possible, before the public eye.

That magisterial statement was despatched to the Palace as the 1922 *Russell* trial moved to its unsatisfactory end, with the jury disagreeing on the vital question of whether the petitioner had made out his charge of adultery against his wife. There was a retrial—with further lengthy reporting of marital intimacies—and the case seems to have been instrumental in changing the balance of opinion: something, it seemed, had to be done. To understand why the *Russell* case had such an impact it is necessary to give a brief account of the facts, and of the way in which the press reported them.

THE IMPACT OF THE RUSSELL DIVORCE: A 'PAINFUL AND DELICATE CASE'[42]

In spite of Sir John Simon's[43] cross-examination on what precisely had taken place in a wagon-lit between Paris and Calais and whether the wife had indeed danced cheek to cheek with the co-respondents, the jury seemed to have little difficulty in deciding that the husband had failed—notwithstanding the expenditure of many thousands of pounds[44] on private detectives—to prove that the wife had committed adultery with any of the three men he had named;[45] and a lawyer could summarise what was left of his case in a few words: the wife 'was delivered of a child which the husband said was not and could not be his, because he had had no connection with her at any time which could have produced conception at the time conception in fact took place'.[46] But of course this bleak

---

[42] The description which the *Evening Standard*'s headline writer attributed to Sir John Simon KC.

[43] For Simon's remarkable career as a Minister of the Crown see n. 5 above. Renowned as the most powerful advocate of his day, he held the (even then) unfashionable view that an advocate should not specialise in any one field of law, and apparently made a point of appearing once a year in the Divorce Court: see D. Dutton, *Simon, A Political Biography of Sir John Simon* (1992) p. 9.

[44] In 1998 values.

[45] The husband (educated at Osborne and Dartmouth) had served in the Royal Navy (latterly as a submarine officer) throughout World War I. One of the co-respondents was a former shipmate of the husband's, and fiancé of the wife's.

[46] Per Lord Sterndale MR, *Russell* v. *Russell* [1924] P. 1, 8. This became the sole issue in the trial once it was accepted there was no other sufficient evidence of adultery.

summary conceals both the excitement engendered by glimpses into the lives of the privileged and the wealth of salacious detail in which, not surprisingly, the press revelled.[47] There were vivid pen portraits of those involved—the *News of the World*, for example, recounting that the wife wore a 'black satin dress with boat-shaped neck cut on long loose lines that suggested excellent taste . . . Her ribbon edged black hat hid most of her hair . . . and its broad rim cast shadows across her pale girlish face.' This was the woman who, the day before the wedding, was said to have made her husband promise that there should be no children. There were detailed accounts of the parties' life—in the same house but mostly in separate rooms—and of the wife's enthusiasm (not shared by her husband) for ballroom dancing. There was the clairvoyant[48] whose skills in detecting the 'vibration of the wife's hormones'[49] enabled her to reveal to an astonished client that she was (unknowingly) five and a half months' pregnant. There was the husband's habit of dressing in women's clothes. Above all, there was the mystery of the child's conception. Perhaps this had occurred while the husband was sleepwalking? But the medical evidence established that the wife had never had complete intercourse with any man, so perhaps the 'hunnish practices'[50] in which the couple had indulged were responsible? The husband's explanation was simpler: the wife had committed adultery if not with one of the co-respondents then with someone else—perhaps one of the thirty or more she claimed had been in love with her.[51]

[47] However, the more popular press displayed a measure of reticence about reporting medical evidence. Even at the second trial (which was reported much more fully than the first) the *Evening Standard* referred to *fecundatio ab extra* as 'a certain event' taking place. A typical *Standard* headline was 'MORE ABOUT BATH INCIDENT, POWDER AND HAIRPINS' referring to the evidence that the wife had taken a bath in the co-respondent's flat (a matter which was thought to be evidence of adulterous tendencies).

[48] Mrs Naismith, who informed the court that she was not a fortune teller but a psychological expert and that she had passed examinations conducted by a doctor.

[49] The witness was unable to tell Sir John Simon whether the word 'hormone' was derived from Latin or Greek; but it is not easy to tell what effect this failure had on the jury.

[50] A term apparently used by the parties. Lord Dunedin subsequently put the matter bluntly (much more so than any of the newspaper reports): the wife 'conceived and had a child without penetration having ever been effected by any man; she was fecundated ab extra; she had denied intercourse of any sort with any man not her husband; she had admitted that her husband had never effected penetration, but she had said, and he had admitted, that he had been in use to lie between her legs with the male organ in more or less proximity to the orifice of the vagina, and to proceed to emission; but he . . . specifically denied that there had been these practices during the relevant period, though he admitted that he was in bed with her on at least two nights during the same. The jury . . . came to the conclusion that she had been fecundated ab extra by another man unknown, and fecundation ab extra is, I doubt not, adultery': *Russell* v. *Russell* [1924] AC 687, 721, per Lord Dunedin. (It may be noted that, thirty years later, the Court of Appeal held that penetration *was* a necessary element of adultery: *Dennis* v. *Dennis* [1955] P. 33, CA. Lord Dunedin's dictum was not cited and the Court of Appeal distinguished Lord Birkenhead's similarly unequivocal view in the earlier case of *Rutherford* v. *Richardson* [1923] AC 1, 11, in a somewhat unconvincing way. But if the Court of Appeal was right in 1955, there had been no evidence of adultery against Mrs Russell, and the issue should never have been left to the jury.)

[51] The wife told the court that she was not in love with her husband; and she had married him because it would 'be nice to be no longer pestered by men to marry them. I thought it would be peaceful . . .'.

The wife's own counsel described his client[52] as 'a remarkable, perhaps an unhappy, product of modern education';[53] and she had complained that her husband never stood up for himself.[54] For eight days the most private and embarrassing marital intimacies were 'extensively regaled to a salacious public';[55] and the eleven-day retrial in the spring of 1923[56] attracted even more extended and prominent[57] press coverage.[58] On this occasion, the jury—perhaps swayed by Marshall Hall's[59] emotional plea[60] that they should give the husband[61] his

[52] By any standards the assessment of her as 'remarkable' seems justified. According to her leading counsel's biographer, she emerged completely unshaken from a searching cross-examination by Sir John Simon and 'gave her evidence with all the fire and determination of a woman who felt that she had been wrongly accused of a matrimonial offence': H. Montgomery Hyde, *Sir Patrick Hastings: His Life and Cases* (1960) p. 90. She made a similar impression on her opponent's counsel: E. Marjoribanks, *The Life of Sir Edward Marshall Hall* (1929) pp. 426–8) writes of this 'clever, brilliant woman . . . whose nerve never gave way and must be like steel', standing up to four hours' ruthless cross-examination by Marshall Hall, perhaps 'the most remarkable court duel of Marshall's whole life'.

[53] The wife admitted that she had been brought up in Bohemian and free and easy circles in Paris. But she had been a highly-paid manager in control of 2,000 workers at Woolwich Arsenal during World War I, and was determined to be independent of her husband and his family. The contemporary press provides other instances of the judiciary making it clear that they (no doubt in common with others of their class and generation) found it difficult to come to terms with the changes in social convention following World War I: on 26 July 1922, for example, the *Evening Standard* reported Horridge J (granting a decree against a wife who had denied adultery) as commenting that it was 'pitiable the way women went about nowadays with men not their husbands'.

[54] She was, counsel observed, just the sort of woman 'who wanted to marry a man. Instead, she married the petitioner . . . asking for what he ought to have taken, beseeching where he ought to command'. Could not the jury (counsel asked rhetorically) imagine her thinking, 'Is this a man or a jelly who behaves like this? . . .' If only he had 'taken her and said, "You have married a man, and not a mouse" . . . she might have respected him . . .'. The view, apparently prevalent even in the upper reaches of society, that force was an acceptable incident of marital relations is also supported by evidence that the husband's mother—Lady Ampthill, a Lady in Waiting to the Queen—suggested to the wife's mother that it would be better if her son beat his wife and locked her up.

[55] *The Ampthill Peerage* [1977] AC 547, 575, per Lord Simon of Glaisdale.

[56] *Russell* v. *Russell and Mayer* (1923) *The Times*, 1, 2, 3, 7, 8, 9, 10, 14, 15, 16, 17 Mar.

[57] This may have had something to do with pressure from other news stories in 1922. The civil war in the twenty-six counties of the South of Ireland between those in favour of the Treaty creating the Irish Free State and their Republican opponents was in full spate at the time of the first trial; whilst there was also competing society interest in the wedding of Lord Louis Mountbatten and the heiress Edwina Ashley.

[58] The reports of the first trial never made the front page of the *Evening Standard*, for example, whereas the second trial was front page news on almost every day (and often the lead story).

[59] Neither Sir John Simon nor Sir Douglas Hogg (who had become Attorney-General in Oct. 1922) was available at the retrial; and Marshall Hall (the most fashionable advocate but not the greatest lawyer of his day) was finally persuaded to take the brief: E. Marjoribanks, *The Life of Sir Edward Marshall Hall* (1929) pp. 426–7.

[60] 'I ask you to find a verdict in favour of John Russell, and free him from the tie which he once hoped would be a tie of love, but which is now a rusty chain that burns into his soul': E. Marjoribanks, *The Life of Sir Edward Marshall Hall* (1929) p. 428.

[61] Patrick Hastings KC for the wife accepted in his closing speech that the husband had given his evidence 'like an English gentleman', suggested that there were still prospects for reconciliation between the parties, and made an emotional speech about the 'little chap' who would be rendered fatherless by a verdict against the wife. Hastings' biographer, H. Montgomery Hyde, confirms that the husband made a favourable impression on the jury: he 'gave his evidence admirably' and was 'simple, manly, and quite obviously speaking what he believed to be the truth': *Sir Patrick Hastings: His Life and Cases* (1960) p. 90.

freedom—found the wife guilty of adultery with an unknown man; and Hill J pronounced a decree nisi.

But this was by no means the end of the family's troubles: the wife appealed, and eventually the House of Lords held that the husband's evidence denying that he had had any kind of sexual relations with the wife should not have been admitted.[62] The presumption[63] that he was the father of his wife's child had not therefore been rebutted. There was no other evidence that she had committed adultery; the decree nisi obtained by the husband was accordingly rescinded; and in 1926 the High Court made a declaration that Christabel's child was the legitimate child of the marriage.[64]

As Lord Simon of Glaisdale put it:[65] 'if ever there was a family, seemingly blessed by fortune, where the birth of a child was attended by an evil spirit bearing a baneful gift liable to frustrate all the blessings, it was the . . . Russells. Its curse was litigation.' Apart from the costs[66]—which evidently made it necessary for the Ampthill family to raise money on their estates—there was the almost unbelievable human misery. John Russell had to wait another fourteen years to get his freedom[67] to remarry. Throughout his life[68] he refused to recognise Christabel's child Geoffrey as his lawful son and heir, and declined to meet him or have any contact with him or to provide any financial support for him except

---

[62] The Court of Appeal had dismissed her appeal: the Evidence (Further Amendment) Act 1869 made spouses competent to give evidence in proceedings instituted in consequence of adultery, and they could accordingly give evidence on any matter relevant to that issue: *Russell* v. *Russell* [1924] P. 1. The House of Lords, by a bare majority, held that the Court of Appeal had been wrong. Evidence by a party to a marriage was (so it had been conceded) inadmissible in proceedings in which the *direct* consequence could be to bastardise a child born during the marriage, and the same rule (so the majority held) must apply to divorce proceedings notwithstanding the fact that the legitimacy of the child was not *directly* in issue in such a case: *Russell* v. *Russell* [1924] AC 687.

[63] At each of the two trials, the child had been produced for inspection by the jury in support of Christabel's belief that there was a physical resemblance to the husband (who, when in the witness box, was invited by the wife's counsel to move his head so that his ears—the formation of which was evidently thought to be strikingly similar to that of the child—were clearly visible to the jury). In rebuttal, Lady Ampthill was recalled to say that there was 'no resemblance at all' between the husband and Christabel's child. The press published a number of photographs of the child, including a photograph of his being taken into court by a nurse; and summed up the impression of most onlookers that he was a 'happy looking child'.

[64] *Russell (GDE) (By his guardian)* v. *The Attorney-General* (1926) *The Times*, 29 July, Swift J.

[65] In *The Ampthill Peerage* [1977] AC 547, 575, HL.

[66] Those of the first trial alone apparently amounted to some £10,700 (approximately £290,000 in 1998 currency values).

[67] *Baroness Ampthill* v. *Baron Ampthill* (1935) *The Times* 26 Nov., Bucknill J. The husband did not contest the wife's petition on the ground of his adultery with a woman named Doris Jones at a hotel in London in 1931; and the wife was awarded a decree nisi, costs, and custody of the child Geoffrey. Norman Birkett KC led Quintin Hogg (the son of Sir Douglas Hogg KC who had unsuccessfully appeared for the husband at the first trial) for the wife.

[68] The husband had succeeded to the peerage in 1935. He remarried in 1937 but there were no children of that marriage. A year after his second wife's death in 1948 he again remarried, and by his third marriage had a daughter and a son, John Hugo Trenchard Russell born on 13 Oct. 1950. J. H. T. Russell's claim to be entitled to succeed to the Ampthill Peerage as his father's only legitimate son was rejected by the Committee of Privileges: *The Ampthill Peerage* [1977] AC 547; see further n. 70 below.

in so far as he was legally compelled[69] to do so. The question of Geoffrey's legitimacy was only resolved by decision of the Committee for Privileges in his favour
in 1976.[70]

The desperate struggle between 'a great English family fighting to the last for
the honour of its name, and . . . a woman doing battle for her own honour and
that of the little child whose mysterious birth'[71] had been its focus was thus at
last over. The long years of litigation must have been an appalling experience[72]
for all those involved. But what is significant for present purposes is that the
Russell divorce seems to have been one of those few *causes célèbres* which directly
prompted an important change in the law. In fact, both the facts and the press
coverage of the case were completely out of the ordinary: a typical press report
of a routine divorce—one not involving the aristocracy or the clergy[73]—merely
recited the wife giving evidence that she recognised the signature in a hotel register as being in her husband's hand, and the evidence of a hotel clerk that the
husband had stayed at the hotel overnight with a woman who was not the wife.[74]
But the coverage of the *Russell* case evidently struck sensitive nerves, and seems

[69] It appears that in Oct. 1933 the wife petitioned for a decree of Restitution of Conjugal Rights,
but this petition was withdrawn on a deed of separation being made: *Baroness Ampthill* v. *Baron
Ampthill* (1935) *The Times* 26 Nov.

[70] On 27 Apr. 1976 the Committee for Privileges reported that Geoffrey had made out his title to
the barony of Ampthill in accordance with the terms of the letters patent which limited the peerage
to the heirs male of the body of the first Lord Ampthill. The Committee regarded Geoffrey's claim
to be the legitimate child of the third Baron as concluded (in the absence of fraud or collusion) by
the Declaration of Legitimacy made fifty years earlier in *Russell GDE (By his Guardian)* v. *The
Attorney-General* (1926) *The Times* 29 July. Under the Legitimacy Declaration Act 1858 the declaration was 'binding to all Intents and Purposes on Her Majesty and on all persons whomsoever'; and
the Committee did not accept that Christabel's alleged refusal to submit a blood sample for testing
could be evidence of such fraud—'conscious and deliberate wrongdoing': per Lord Wilberforce
at 571—or collusion as under the statute alone justified reopening the issue. (It appears from the
transcript of the hearing before the Committee that in fact Christabel did provide a sample, but this
evidence was not made available before the hearing, and was evidently not considered by those
concerned, notwithstanding the claimant John's offer to withdraw if tests did not rule out the *possibility* of the third baron being Geoffrey's father): see *Report from the Committee for Privileges*
(HL 1975–6, 147–1, BPP 1975–6, vol. 9, particularly at pp. 109, 119.

[71] In the words of E. Marjoribanks, *The Life of Sir Edward Marshall Hall* (1929) p. 429.

[72] Geoffrey has, however, had a long and successful career, serving in the Irish Guards in World
War II and subsequently pursuing an active career as a director of companies. He took his seat in the
House of Lords as the fourth Baron Ampthill, and served as a Chairman of Select Committees and Lord
Chairman of Committees. He was appointed CBE in 1986 and called to the Privy Council in 1995.

[73] 'Bishop in the Witness Box—A Lady's Hallucinations—Blind Clergyman's Unsuccessful
Petition for Divorce' is one example of this genre taken from the avowedly sensational *Umpire* on
18 July 1909. Such stories are unlikely to appear today, any more than are the small advertisements
carried in the same paper from dealers in used false teeth.

[74] A typical report in *The Times* is that of *Cruise* v. *Cruise and Gaunt* (1926) *The Times* 30 July,
in which Sir R. R. Cruise, an eminent Wimpole Street Ophthalmic Surgeon, obtained an undefended
divorce against his wife on the basis of hotel evidence (from Canada) of her adultery and his own
statement that the co-respondent had told him 'I am getting too fond of your wife, and I intend to
leave the country.' Even when the aristocracy were involved the typical report (even in the popular
press) was confined to the material given in the text (which is taken from the *Evening Standard*'s
report on 22 July 1922 under the heading 'Divorce for a Countess' of an undefended divorce action
against the Earl of Eglington).

to have had a decisive impact[75] in convincing responsible opinion that something had to be done.[76]

THE PRESSURE MOUNTS . . .

Within days of the ending of the first *Russell* trial a Parliamentary Question to the Home Secretary[77] produced a bland reply, but also a measure of action[78] behind the scenes. Again, within days of the ending of the second *Russell* trial a question by Lord Balfour of Burleigh led to a debate in the House of Lords. There was much talk of the baneful influence of press reporting[79] and of the need to restrain indecorous reporting;[80] but, as Lord Balfour himself accepted, quite how this was to be done was not easy to decide. There were those who would take the extreme course of prohibiting publication of anything concerning divorce cases except the result;[81] but Lord Chancellor Cave counselled caution. Cave thought the best solution would be for the press to accept voluntary

[75] 'Parliament was apparently so disturbed as in consequence to pass the Judicial Proceedings (Regulation of Reports) Act 1926' per Lord Simon of Glaisdale, *The Ampthill Peerage* [1974] AC 547, 575, HL. For contemporary evidence of the link see the *Special Report of the Select Committee on the Matrimonial Causes (Regulation of Proceedings) Bill* (HC 118, BPP 1923, vii) para. 2; and see in the *Minutes of Evidence* particularly the remarks of Sir Henry Duke (apparently agreeing that the 'present agitation' was 'very largely due' to the publicity surrounding the *Russell* case (p. 9, q. 80)) and note particularly the examination of Sir Ellis Hume-Williams KC (counsel for one of the co-respondents in the first trial and a consistent opponent of any restriction on publicity) at p. 62.

[76] The so-called rule in *Russell* v. *Russell* (i.e. that neither spouse could give evidence tending to show that he or she did not have marital intercourse if such evidence would tend to bastardise a child prima facie born in wedlock) caused expense, particularly in many war-time divorce cases where the birth of a child of whom the husband could not be the father had to be proved by reference to military records or other third party evidence of his absence beyond the seas. It was strongly criticised by the (Denning) *Committee on Procedure in Matrimonial Causes* (Final Report, Cmd. 7024, 1947) and was abolished by the Law Reform (Miscellaneous Provisions) Act 1949. Subsequently, the Civil Evidence Act 1968 made spouses compellable witnesses on the question whether or not marital intercourse had taken place between them; and provided that witnesses in proceedings instituted in consequence of adultery were no longer excused from answering questions which tended to show that they had been guilty of adultery.

[77] Edward Shortt (1862–1935) Liberal MP and barrister.

[78] To the extent that the Home Office wrote to the Lord Chancellor's Permanent Secretary: 'The Home Secretary is aware of the objections on general grounds to conferring statutory power upon Judges to close the Courts, but it has been represented to him that recently the newspapers have taken exceptional licence in the publication of objectionable details . . .': Maxwell to Schuster, 22 July 1922, PRO LCO2/775. Schuster's views at this stage have been set out above.

[79] Apparently the consequences were aggravated by what the liberal Herbert Hensley Henson (1863–1947), Bishop of Durham, described as the 'almost complete breakdown of domestic discipline', whilst the Earl of Meath spoke with nostalgia for his young days when there was 'family control amongst all classes. No young girl was permitted to read any of these horrible papers . . .': *Official Report* (HL) 24 Apr. 1923, vol. 53, col. 856.

[80] Notably by the Bishop of Durham, who spoke eloquently of being haunted and depressed by the 'rapid, the tragic decline of sexual morality amongst the people': *Hansard* (HL) 5th Series, 24 Apr. 1923, vol. 53, cols. 854–5.

[81] This was the view eventually taken by the ardent divorce reformer Lord Buckmaster (1861–1934) *Hansard* (HL) 5th series, 24 Apr. 1923, vol. 53 col. 852, apparently retreating from his earlier view that the best way to control the newspapers was to trust them: *Hansard* (HL) 5th series, 4 May 1920, vol. 40, col. 102.

restraint.[82] But it would also be sensible for a private member to introduce a Bill into the House of Commons in order to ascertain the strength of feeling there on the matter.[83] As Cave knew,[84] Sir Evelyn Cecil[85] was preparing to do precisely that.

THE MOVE TO LEGISLATION—AND COMPROMISE

The method which Cecil adopted, however, did not seem particularly apt to assess feeling amongst Members of Parliament generally. A Bill—the Matrimonial Causes (Regulation of Reports) Bill—was drafted; but instead of the full Second Reading debate on the floor of the House which might have been expected, the Bill was given a Second Reading 'on the nod' and referred to a Select Committee.

The eleven members of the Select Committee held ten sittings and interviewed eleven witnesses. The Committee heard some powerful evidence that publicity for divorce cases had positively beneficial effects: the President of the Probate, Divorce and Admiralty Division[86] told the Committee that adulterers and others had a 'very wholesome horror of the public opprobrium' to which they were exposed.[87] He thought that the 'sense of shame and of repugnance at the public consequences' of their conduct[88] was 'a most wholesome state of affairs'.[89] And the Committee accepted[90] that publicity was a tradition and principle of British

---

[82] Although Cave had to admit that efforts had 'been made in that direction but hitherto without result': col. 864.   [83] *Official Report* (HL) 24 Apr. 1923, vol. 53, col. 864.

[84] The Lord Chancellor (accompanied by the Home Secretary W. C. Bridgeman and the Director of Public Prosecutions Sir A. Bodkin) had received a delegation led by Sir Evelyn Cecil on 7 Mar. 1923. An agreed statement had appeared in *The Times* on 7 Mar.

[85] Conservative MP (since 1918 for Birmingham, Aston), barrister, director of railway and investment companies, and author of *inter alia* a work on primogeniture.

[86] Sir Henry Duke: see n. 3 above.

[87] But the Committee also had to accept that in some cases publicity had the opposite effect: offenders were 'written up into heroes to be snap-shotted' and 'placed on a kind of national pedestal': *Report of the Select Committee on the Matrimonial Causes (Regulation of Reports) Bill* (1923) HC 118, BPP 1923, vii, para. 4.

[88] In 1996 it is difficult to understand the stigma which, within living memory, flowed from having 'gone through the divorce court'. At the time of the *Russell* trial the press contained stories of an Australian prima donna who was barred from singing at the Three Choirs Festival at Hereford because she had been named in (Australian) divorce proceedings; whilst a striking, and more recent reminder of attitudes is provided by the reaction to complaints made in 1947 by two High Court judges who had not received the invitations to Royal Garden Parties routinely extended to their brethren. The Lord Chamberlain explained that the 'guilty party' in a divorce case (and anyone else who had asked for the exercise of the court's discretion in respect of their own adultery) would not be invited to any court function (Clarendon to Jowitt, 18 July 1947). The Lord Chancellor had been unaware that the judges in question had been divorced (plaintively noting that there 'was nothing in *Who's Who* to indicate it'); and minuted that divorce was a matter which would have counted against judicial appointment. It appears that thereafter Jowitt made a practice of asking those under consideration, 'Is there anything about your private life which you think you ought to tell me?' See PRO LCO2/4618, and R. Stevens, *The Independence of the Judiciary* (1993) p. 88.

[89] *Select Committee on the Matrimonial Causes (Regulation of Reports) Bill, Minutes of Evidence*, 26 June 1923 (1923) HC 118, BPP 1923, vii, q. 8, p. 2.

[90] *Report of the Select Committee on the Matrimonial Causes (Regulation of Reports) Bill* (1923) HC 118, BPP 1923, vii, para. 4.

justice, and that there was a particular need for a measure of publicity in divorce cases not only to act as a deterrent but also publicly to vindicate the innocent.[91] But this conclusion was not inconsistent with the view that 'polluting details elaborated for purposes of profit'[92] should be suppressed, all the more so since constant reporting unnecessarily encouraged 'familiarity with what ought to be avoided' and in consequence took away 'half the horror of it'.[93]

What was to be done? The best solution—the Committee agreed—would be voluntary restraint on the part of the press; but the Committee accepted that the Royal Commission's pleas for such restraint had fallen on deaf ears. Competition between newspapers led inevitably to wide-scale and selective[94] reporting, and what a journalist witness described as 'painstaking elaboration of nauseous details' decked out with 'alluring headlines'. The Committee concluded, with regret, that it had become impossible for the press to agree on measures necessary to eliminate 'objectionable and unnecessary details from divorce and similar reports';[95] and that 'the recent Russell case, and others not always in the divorce court, are standing proofs . . . that the existing law is insufficient'.[96]

Legislation was accordingly inevitable. One solution—giving judges a discretion to prohibit publication of matter believed to be injurious to public morals —found favour in some quarters, but the Committee thought this solution impracticable[97] and that the exercise of such a power would prove 'precarious and spasmodic'.[98] Against this background, the Committee then turned to examine the draft Bill[99] in some detail, and proposed important amendments to it: in

---

[91] Little consideration was given to the effect of publicity on the parties and their families; but cf. Lord Buckmaster's view that there was no legitimate interest in the proceedings of the Divorce Court: 'If there is any matter which is a private and domestic concern it is a quarrel between a man and his wife, and the Divorce Court is merely there for the purpose of saying whether that quarrel is of such a character as entitles one of the parties to be freed' (*Hansard* (HL) 5th series, 24 Apr. 1923, vol. 53, col. 853).

[92] *Report of the Select Committee on the Matrimonial Causes (Regulation of Reports) Bill* (1923) HC 118, BPP 1923, vii, para. 4.

[93] *Report of the Select Committee on the Matrimonial Causes (Regulation of Reports) Bill* (1923) HC 118, BPP 1923, vii, para. 2. There is a curious echo of this in the view of the former Chief Rabbi, Lord Jacobovits who, in the debates on the Bill for the Family Law Act 1996 (*Official Report* (HL) 29 Feb. 1966, col. 1658) referred to the 'shudder effect' of divorce in traditional Orthodox communities.

[94] As Sir Henry Duke, P said (no doubt with feeling) 99 per cent of the evidence in divorce cases was 'not only not indecent but could be stigmatised as dull': *Select Committee on the Matrimonial Causes (Regulation of Reports) Bill, Minutes of Evidence,* 26 June 1923 (1923) HC 118, BPP 1923, vii, q. 72, p. 8.

[95] *Special Report of the Select Committee on the Matrimonial Causes (Regulation of Reports) Bill* (1923) HC 118, BPP 1923, vii, para. 2. The press did not speak with one voice on the desirability or otherwise of legislation (see the speech by Sir Evelyn Cecil on the Second Reading of the Bill for the Judicial Proceedings (Regulation of Reports) Act 1926, *Hansard* (5th series) (HC) 16 Apr. 1926, cols. 750–5). [96] Para. 2.

[97] Sir Henry Duke had, in evidence to the Committee, strongly resisted such a solution: *Select Committee on the Matrimonial Causes (Regulation of Reports) Bill, Minutes of Evidence,* 26 June 1923 (1923) HC 118, BPP 1923, vii. [98] Para. 3.

[99] The Bill (Bill No. 136) which had been introduced and given a Second Reading was described in its long title as a Bill 'to regulate the publication of reports of certain judicial proceedings in such manner as to prevent injury to public morals'; and that long title survives in the Judicial Proceedings (Regulation of Reports) Act 1926. The underlying scheme of the Bill has also survived: it is made unlawful to publish any save certain specified particulars of matrimonial proceedings.

particular it considered that the prohibition on the publication of 'indecent matter, or medical, surgical or physiological details being matter or details the publication of which would be calculated to injure public morals or otherwise be to the public mischief'[100] should be extended[101] to cover the report of *all* judicial proceedings (rather than being confined[102] to divorce, nullity and judicial separation).[103] But the Committee, taking the view that it was often the cumulative effect of evidence and statements not obscene in themselves[104] which did the mischief[105] agreed that there should also be special restrictions on the reporting of divorce and other matrimonial cases. The Committee wished to take a *via media* between, on the one hand, holding hearings in private—which it believed would be 'contrary to British sentiment'—and, on the other hand, allowing the right to publish full reports as under the existing law.[106] The solution proposed was to allow[107] publication of the judge's summing up (if any) and any observations made by the judge in giving judgment,[108] to allow publication of the parties' 'addresses and occupations' (as well as their names),[109] the grounds on which the proceedings were brought and resisted,[110] and submissions and decisions on points of law.[111] The

---

[100] Clause 1(1)(b) of the Bill as read a second time.

[101] In consequence of this amendment the short title of the Bill was changed from *Matrimonial Causes* (Regulation of Reports) to *Judicial Proceedings* (Regulation of Reports). Subject to minor amendment, the Committee's recommended version is now s. 1(1)(a) of the 1926 Act.

[102] As in the Bill originally presented.

[103] The Committee accepted that such a provision added little to the substance of the existing law (see n. 22 above), but believed that an express statutory provision would have the advantage of 'giving more or less specific instructions to a news editor what is to be blue-pencilled out'; whilst the decision to recommend that the offence be triable summarily would make the prohibition more readily enforceable: para. 6. Sir Henry Duke, P had also expressed his preference for summary trial: 'I would not like to dignify people who are guilty of these acts of indecency by characterising their conduct as contempt of court. It is a low and filthy offence which is committed': *Select Committee on the Matrimonial Causes (Regulation of Reports) Bill, Minutes of Evidence*, 26 June 1923 (1923) HC 118, BPP 1923, vii, q. 41, p. 6.

[104] Sir John Simon put this point with his customary clarity in the Second Reading debate on the Bill for the Judicial Proceedings (Regulation of Reports) Act 1926, *Official Report* (HC) 16 Apr. 1926, vol. 194, col. 806: the mischief lay in 'selling columns and columns of carefully and elaborately extracted evidence from chamber maids and ladies' maids and all the wretched miserable business of the divorce court'. The fact that the motive for this activity was that 'this particular kind of publication is calculated apparently to lead to very great profit and very large circulation for a particular class of proprietor . . .' aggravated the evil.

[105] *Report of the Select Committee on the Matrimonial Causes (Regulation of Reports) Bill* (1923) HC 118, BPP 1923, vii, para.12.   [106] Para. 9.

[107] Subject to the overriding prohibition on publication of indecent matter: see now Judicial Proceedings (Regulation of Reports) Act 1926, s. 1(1)(a), and s. 1(1)(b), proviso.

[108] The Bill given a Second Reading would have allowed publication of only the findings of the jury (if any) and the judgment of the court: cl. 1(1)(a)(iv).

[109] This extension was apparently intended to meet the King's Proctor's concern that the absence of addresses would reduce the likelihood of neighbours and others informing him of grounds for intervention: *Special Report* para. 8; and *Minutes of Evidence* 5 July 1923.

[110] The legislation eventually extended this to permit a concise statement of the charges, defences and counter-charges in support of which evidence has been given: see Judicial Proceedings (Regulation of Reports) Act 1926, s. 1(1)(b)(ii). The restriction to matters in support of which evidence has been given may mean that matters alleged in the pleadings but not pursued are protected from publication: *Argyll (Duchess of)* v. *Duke of Argyll* [1967] Ch. 302.

[111] See now Judicial Proceedings (Regulation of Reports) Act 1926, s. 1(1)(b)(iii).

Select Committee concluded with an eloquent assertion of the case for imposing restrictions on the publication of evidence and statements:

The pernicious transformation of sordid stories into epics for profit cannot really be restrained in any other way. The flaunting of immorality before readers of all ages and positions must be injurious to public morals, and making light of such conduct challenges the whole structure of family life on which society is founded . . . If it be maintained that limiting publication hampers the chances of justice, the whole matter becomes a question of balancing the advantage of unrestricted publication to secure justice as against the disadvantage of publication in lowering the standard of national character. Your Committee think that if a choice has to be made, the high standard of national character must be chosen.[112]

Sir Evelyn Cecil lobbied enthusiastically for the Government to take up the Select Committee's recommendations,[113] but Lord Chancellor Cave was not able to take effective action;[114] and no progress was made with the Bill in 1924 (when the minority Labour Government had to face more pressing problems).

THE CABINET ACTS

A wholly different attitude is manifest in 1925. The Bill, as amended by the Select Committee, was reintroduced into the Commons by Sir Evelyn Cecil. In March (shortly after the King's letter to Cave about reporting of the *Dennistoun* case[115]) the Home Secretary, Sir William Joynson-Hicks,[116] asked the Cabinet to take a view on what he described as 'a short but highly controversial bill'.[117] He reported[118] that:

. . . the Bill is supported by social workers but opposed by the press and the trades connected therewith on the grounds that it is a slur on the great majority of British newspapers, that it is an unwise interference with the liberty of the press, that to suppress reports on cases dealing with white slave traffic, cocaine and other matters in connection with which sex questions arise will play into the hands of guilty persons by keeping their misdoings out of the press . . .[119]

---

[112] Para 12.   [113] See Cecil to Cave, 7 Sept. 1923: PRO LCO2/775.

[114] At this stage, the Home Office seems to have demonstrated a greater commitment to legislation: Maxwell to Schuster, 15 Aug. 1923.

[115] See n. 12 above. One of the curious paradoxes of this episode is that the *Dennistoun* case was not a matrimonial case nor did it involve the reporting of any material which could on even the widest definition be categorised as obscene. What made the case shocking and notorious were the allegations of scandalous conduct; and the only possible public interest infringed by reporting of the case seems to be military pride and perhaps morale in the armed forces. The right to publish would therefore be totally unaffected by legislation such as the Judicial Proceedings (Regulation of Reports) Act, and indeed by any other legislation which a democratic parliament could conceivably enact in peacetime. It is perhaps unfortunate that Lord Chancellor Cave's reply to the royal complaint clearly implies (although it does not state) that the legislation which Sir Evelyn Cecil intended to bring forward could be relevant to the matter.

[116] (1865–1932); solicitor and founder of the firm of Joynson-Hicks & Co; Home Secretary 1924–9.

[117] *Memorandum by the Home Secretary* CP 163 (1925) 17 Mar. 1925.   [118] Ibid.

[119] Less than two weeks earlier, Lord Chancellor Cave had written to the Palace that there would be considerable opposition to the Bill from the associations representing the press. He concluded

The Conservative Government took a, perhaps unexpectedly, firm line; and it may be that the Monarch's acknowledged constitutional right[120] to encourage action by Ministers[121] was of some significance in this context.[122] The Cabinet agreed:

That the Government should do all in their power, individually and collectively, to encourage the support already existing in the House of Commons, with a view, if possible, to a strongly-supported petition from Members to the Home Secretary: [and]

That the Home Secretary should see representatives of the Press, with a view to careful consideration of the objections taken in some quarters to the Bill, but that he should make clear to them the strength of the feeling in the House of Commons and in the country in favour of some action of the kind suggested in the Bill[123]

Further pressure was applied by Lord Darling's[124] action in introducing a Bill giving effect to the Select Committee's recommendations in the House of Lords. Although the Cabinet[125] could not make time to give the Bill special facilities in the House of Commons the Home Secretary applied himself vigorously to negotiations with press interests, speaking to them 'in plain Anglo-Saxon' and telling them they had got to 'agree to something'.[126] But once again, the Bill failed for lack of parliamentary time; and Joynson-Hicks's suggestion that the Government should promote its own legislation was not pursued.

THE JUDICIAL PROCEEDINGS (REGULATION OF REPORTS) ACT ON THE STATUTE BOOK

In 1926 a private member[127] who had drawn a favourable place in the ballot introduced the Bill; Joynson-Hicks made a powerful speech in the House of

---

that if 'further action should be taken, I should certainly be disposed to ask the Cabinet either to support the Bill or to make some proposal on their own behalf, but I do not know what view they would take of the matter': Cave to Stamfordham, 6 Mar. 1925, PRO LCO2/775.

[120] W. Bagehot, *The English Constitution* (Fontana edn. with introduction by R. H. S. Crossman, 1963) p. 110.

[121] See generally on the Monarch's influence V. Bogdanor, *The Monarchy and the Constitution* (1995) Ch. 3; and in particular Lord Esher's *Memorandum* of Sept. 1913, quoted at p. 70.

[122] The constitutional proprieties were, however, observed. Although Queen Victoria's published views (see n. 15 above) were referred to in debate, only the most discreet allusion was made to George V's interest: 'attention has been called to the matter not only by Queen Victoria but by other members of our Royal House . . .': per Viscount Cave, *Official Report* (HL) 16 July 1925, vol. 62, col. 142.

[123] Conclusion 3, paras. (b) and (c). The Cabinet minutes record the view that the objections made by Sir J Gilmour, Secretary for Scotland (that the general prohibition on publication of indecent material would be unworkable 'because it did not sufficiently inform the lieges what they may do or not do', whilst the question whether something was 'calculated to injure public morals or otherwise be to the public mischief' was merely a matter of opinion), could be met by amendment, but in fact no relevant amendment was ever brought forward.

[124] (1849–1936). Conservative MP 1888–97, when appointed to the bench.

[125] At its meeting on 16 July 1925.

[126] Joynson-Hicks to Cave, 5 Aug. 1925: PRO LCO2/775.   [127] Major Kindersley.

Commons,[128] and the Bill was given a Second Reading on a division by 222 votes to 3. Although tactical[129] and other difficulties still lay ahead[130] the pressure had now become irresistible. In the end, even the newspaper proprietors[131] had to accept that, whilst 'everything in politics is a choice of evils . . . the balance of evil is in favour of passing this Bill'. On 15 December 1926, nearly fifteen years after the Royal Commission had recommended action, the Judicial Proceedings (Regulation of Reports) Act received Royal Assent. Thenceforth it was not lawful[132] to print or publish,[133] or cause or procure to be printed or published:[134]

[128] *Official Report* (HC) 16 Apr. 1926, vol. 194, col. 790. Joynson-Hicks was careful to assert the 'inalienable right' for citizens to have their case heard in open Court, and that 'if anybody chooses to go to Court and hear these cases the right of the English public must not be interfered with', but was convinced by 'that great solid force of public opinion which stands for solidity, and for well-being in the Government and the future prosperity of our country' that a restriction on reporting was essential. The Government would 'do their utmost' to find time for the further stages of the Bill: see cols. 792–4.

[129] In particular, the newspaper proprietors evidently played a skilful game suggesting that all matrimonial cases should be heard in camera. No doubt the proprietors were aware of the fact (as Joynson-Hicks put it to Cave on 12 Feb. 1926: PRO LCO2/775) that 'in legal circles the proposal for hearing cases in camera would not be accepted'.

[130] Joynson-Hicks had envisaged that there could be serious difficulties in the Committee stage in the House of Commons; and in fact the Bill was considered by Standing Committee A between Apr. and July 1926. Although few amendments of substance were in the event made, the Bill was only brought to the Lords on 14 Dec. 1926, the last day of the session. Standing Orders were suspended (against some protest) and the Bill was allowed to go through all its stages in one day: *Official Report* (HL) 14 Dec. 1926, vol. 65, col. 1591.

[131] Per Viscount Burnham (1862–1933) then owner of the *Daily Telegraph*: *Official Report* (HL) 14 Dec. 1926, vol. 65, col. 1595.

[132] Contravention of the provisions of the Act exposes the offender, on summary conviction, to imprisonment for a term not exceeding four months, or to a fine not exceeding level 5 on the standard scale, or to both such imprisonment and fine: Judicial Proceedings (Regulation of Reports) Act 1926, s. 1(2) (as amended by Criminal Justice Act 1982, s. 46(1)). No prosecution is to be started in England and Wales without the sanction of the Attorney-General: s. 1(3).

[133] The Judicial Proceedings (Regulation of Reports) Act 1926, s. 1(4) provides that nothing in the provision under consideration applies to 'the printing of any pleading, transcript or evidence or other document for use in connection with any judicial proceedings or the communication thereof to persons concerned in the proceedings, or to the printing or publishing of any notice or report in pursuance of the directions of the court'. S. 1(4) of the Act also contains a carefully but restrictively drafted provision allowing publication of any matter (whether indecent or not) 'in any separate volume of part of any bona fide series of law reports which does not form part of any other publication and consists solely of reports of proceedings in courts of law . . .'. (It will be noted that this provision does not extend to Law Reports published even in such reputable newspapers as *The Times*; but in practice such reports are normally confined to extracts from the judgment, and reporting of such material is permitted without restriction under s. 1(1)(b)(iii) and (iv).) S. 1(4) also disapplies the statutory restrictions from 'any publication of a technical character bona fide intended for circulation among members of the legal or medical professions'; but it has been pointed out that it is not clear whether publication in journals not confined to these two named professions is protected: *Review of Access to and Reporting of Family Proceedings* (Lord Chancellor's Department, 1993) para. 2. 32.

[134] But 'no person, other than a proprietor, editor, master printer or publisher' is liable to be convicted of an offence under the Act: Judicial Proceedings (Regulation of Reports) Act 1926, s. 1(2), proviso—introduced to protect newspaper vendors and others from prosecution. The proviso does not affect the principle that publication is unlawful, and accordingly it has been held that an injunction could be obtained against a party or other person in possession of material about matrimonial proceedings even though there would be a defence to a prosecution: see *Argyll (Duchess of)* v. *Duke*

(a) in relation to any judicial proceedings any indecent matter or indecent medical, surgical or physiological details being matters or details the publication of which would be calculated to injure public morals;

(b) in relation to any[135] judicial proceedings for dissolution of marriage, for nullity of marriage, or for judicial separation, any particulars other than the following, that is to say:

(i) the names, addresses and occupations of the parties and witnesses;

(ii) a concise statement of the charges, defences and counter-charges in support of which evidence has been given;[136]

(iii) submissions on any point of law arising in the course of the proceedings, and the decision of the court thereon;

(iv) the summing-up of the judge and the finding of the jury (if any) and the judgment of the court and observations made by the judge in giving judgment.[137]

THE 1926 ACT IN RETROSPECT

What, then, has been the effect of the 1926 Act? First, it is clear that the prohibition on publication of indecent matter[138] added little to the law and has, in the context of press reporting,[139] been effectively a dead letter.[140]

of Argyll [1967] Ch. 302 (but note that doubt has been expressed as to whether that decision is consistent with the general principle that public rights can only be enforced by the Attorney-General: *Review of Access to and Reporting of Family Proceedings* (Lord Chancellor's Department, 1993) para. 2.118–2.120, citing *Gouriet* v. *Union of Post Office Workers* [1978] AC 435).

[135] Family Law Act 1996, Sch. 8, para. 2, will, from a date to be appointed, insert the words 'any proceedings under Part II of the Family Law Act 1996 or otherwise in relation to': see further below p. 113. The Domestic and Appellate Proceedings (Restriction of Publicity) Act 1968 (as to which see further n. 147 below) extends the restricted class to proceedings under Matrimonial Causes Act 1973, s. 27 (failure to provide maintenance) and Part III Family Law Act 1986 (declarations of status). The Magistrates' Courts Act 1980 s. 71 includes a similar prohibition in respect of family proceedings in magistrates' courts; and there are numerous statutory provisions relating to the publication of material relating to children: see generally the summary in *Review of Access to and Reporting of Family Proceedings* (Lord Chancellor's Department, 1993).

[136] For the significance of this see *Argyll (Duchess of)* v. *Duke of Argyll* [1967] Ch. 302, n. 13 above.

[137] Nothing in this subsection (i.e. permitting publication of the specified material) is to be held to permit the publication of indecent material contrary to Judicial Proceedings (Regulation of Reports) Act 1926, s. 1(1)(a), above): see s. 1(1)(b) proviso.

[138] S. 1(1)(a). The impact of this provision may not be widely understood. *The Times* stated incorrectly on 16 July 1996 that the Act empowers the court 'to impose restrictions on what may be reported of "indecent matter"'.

[139] The *Review of Access to and Reporting of Family Proceedings* (Lord Chancellor's Department, 1993) para. 3.21 draws attention to reports of circulation amongst paedophiles of written statements of children's testimony in cases of sexual abuse; but the existence of a summary offence punishable by a maximum of four months' imprisonment seems of limited relevance to such practices.

[140] Publication of such matter would be an offence under the Obscene Publications Act 1959 (s. 1 of which embodies the common law criterion of whether the matter is calculated to 'deprave and corrupt') and the fact that the publication was a report of court proceedings would not be a defence; the Law of Libel (Amendment) Act 1888 s. 3 remains in force and has been extended to broadcasts by Broadcasting Act 1990, Sch. 20, para. 2.

Secondly, although the 1926 Act prevented the daily press from giving detailed verbatim accounts[141] of sensational divorce cases, the direct[142] effect of the restrictions on reporting divorce cases was never great; and the press proved well able to make copy, even in undefended cases, from the materials which the 1926 Act allowed to be published.[143] In contested divorce cases[144] judges would almost necessarily refer in detail to the allegations and the evidence in giving judgment;[145] whilst some judges did not resist the temptation to make assessments and comments which, sometimes unnecessarily,[146] must have caused distress to those concerned. As the Law Commission put it in 1966:[147]

[141] In any event, this style of reporting was gradually going out of fashion as the popular press increasingly relied on photographs and general accounts rather than direct quotation from participants.

[142] The Act may have had indirect effects in other ways. For example, Parkis (the fictional enquiry agent not unsympathetically portrayed in Graham Greene's *The End of the Affair* (1951)) makes a practice of spending his leisure hours in the *British Museum* reading the *Times Law Reports*; and says 'Today I'm on the Russell case. They give a kind of background to one's work, sir. Open up vistas. They take one away from the daily petty detail. I knew one of the witnesses in the case, sir. We were in the same office once. Well, he's gone down to history as I never shall now . . . The law that forbade the evidence in divorce cases being published was a blow to men of my calling. The judge, sir, never mentions us by name, and he's very often prejudiced against the profession.' (Book 4, Ch. 2.)

[143] In 1938—the year after the 1937 reforms to the ground for divorce—the *News of the World* routinely published several columns of accounts of undefended divorces giving details of the 'charges made'. A possibly unusually banal example reported on 27 Nov. 1938 recorded that the co-respondent came to the matrimonial home to change the accumulator on the wireless. The husband alleged that the wife said she loved the co-respondent; and she had lived with him at various addresses in Clapham and elsewhere. A decree was granted.

[144] Including claims for damages for adultery, not abolished until 1970: Law Reform (Miscellaneous Provisions) Act 1970. The 1970 Act also abolished the action for breach of promise of marriage, and probably did significantly more than the 1926 Act to reduce press coverage of dysfunctional family relationships.

[145] See e.g. *Mason* v. *Mason* (1980) Fam. Law 143, CA—wife's refusal to permit sexual intercourse more than once weekly—widely reported under headlines such as 'once a week is enough, say Law Chiefs'. The 1926 Act did not prevent reporters from three newspapers seeking to interview the wives of the three Lords Justice concerned in an attempt to ascertain whether they agreed with the views thus attributed to their husbands: see *Official Report* (HL) vol. 416, col. 409, per Lord Hailsham of Saint Marylebone. The Contempt of Court Act 1981 Sch. 1, para. 15 provides that appellate proceedings are 'active' for the purposes of the strict liability rule from the date of giving notice of appeal or making an application for leave; and these provisions are based on a different view from that of Lord Parker CJ (*R* v. *Duffy, ex p. Nash* [1960] 2 QB 188, 194) about the possible susceptibility of appellate judges to improper approaches.

[146] See, e.g., the *Daily Express*, 25 Jan. 1969, where the judge described the wife as a 'well-dressed well preserved woman, stupid in many ways but not uncultured'. Note also the report in *The Times*, 17 Oct. 1981, in which the judge referred to the wife's attempts to gain sexual gratification from 'members of the labouring classes' and to her distaste at having intercourse with one lorry-driver's mate on the grounds that he had an unpleasant body odour.

[147] *Report on the Powers of Appeal Courts to Sit in Private, and The Restrictions upon Publicity in Domestic Proceedings* (1966), Law Com. No. 6, para. 17. This report was prompted by the decision in *B (otherwise P)* v. *Attorney-General* [1967] P. 119 (no power to hear application for declaration of legitimacy in camera); and the Lord Chancellor referred to the Commission the desirability of the Court of Appeal having the same power to sit in private or in chambers as had been enjoyed by the court from whose decision the appeal was brought: see para. 1. Effect was given to the Commission's recommendations by the Domestic and Appellate Proceedings (Restriction of Publicity) Act 1968 (which gave the Court of Appeal the right to sit in private in certain cases, and extended the protection of the 1926 Act to a number of other proceedings: see n. 135 above).

The prohibition on publishing the evidence in divorce and similar cases, though it pro-
tects the public from being titillated by morning and evening accounts of the salacious
details brought out in evidence, does not prevent it from learning those details in due
course if the judge thinks it necessary or desirable to review the evidence in full in his
judgment or summing up . . . What is more serious is that the parties and, more especially,
their innocent children whose identity is frequently revealed as a result of the details which
can be published, suffer the disturbing experience of having the most intimate details of
the family life exposed. While it may be said that the parties have only themselves to
blame, no such argument can apply to the children whose privacy the law takes pains to
protect in other cases.[148]

Thirdly, the limited restrictions imposed by the 1926 Act did nothing to prevent
the press from pursuing those involved in sensational matrimonial and other cases
in attempts to get interviews or even from photographing those involved as they
left court.[149] Nowadays, criticism of such practices is widespread; but it is based
on a much more general concern for privacy no longer related primarily to divorce
or similar cases.[150] By the end of World War II the reporting of divorce cases[151]

---

[148] See also *Moynihan* v. *Moynihan* (*Nos. 1 and 2*) [1997] 1 FLR 52, 62, per Sir Stephen Brown,
P: in practical terms the effect of the 1926 Act 'has been that in defended divorce suits, although
the hearing was and is in open court, the actual evidence given in the course of the suit could not
be reported although the statement of the charges, defences and countercharges in support of which
evidence was given could be published, but not the actual details of evidence. That meant that effectively the nature of the charges would be published and finally the judgment of the court, which
could be published of course without editing in any sense so that the full matter might be revealed
in the course of the judgment.' As the President remarked, there would on the facts of the case before
him 'appear to be ample scope in the context of the [permitted material] for clear and full details of
the proceedings to be given, though not necessarily a line by line account of what a particular witness says at any particular time'.

[149] The practice of reproducing photographs or sketches of litigants and witnesses was strongly
condemned in evidence to the 1912 Royal Commission; and s. 41, Criminal Justice Act 1925, pro-
hibits the taking of photographs within court precincts and the making or attempting to make 'with
a view to publication' any portrait or sketch of any party, witness, judge, etc. in any court. Scenes
on the steps of the Royal Courts of Justice suggest that prosecuting authorities must take a narrow
view of the term 'precincts'; whilst no sensational trial is now complete without sketches of those
involved being reproduced in the press. It must be assumed that the artists have not only considerable artistic skill but are also endowed with exceptional memories: see generally Borrie and Lowe,
The Law of Contempt (3rd. edn. 1996 by N. V. Lowe and B. Sufrin) p. 24.

[150] The Calcutt Committee on *Privacy and Related Matters* Cm. 1102 (1990) received no evidence on the reporting of divorce and similar matters and accordingly made no comment on this
subject. The Committee accepted that the question of what remained essentially a matter for the private domain was best dealt with by press agreement on appropriate standards accompanied by appropriate procedures for self-regulation; and it accordingly rejected the statutory creation of a tort of
infringement of privacy. But in 1993 Sir David Calcutt's *Review of Press Self-Regulation* (Cm. 2135,
1993) found that the press had not taken the 'one final chance' offered by the 1990 inquiry and that
the Press Complaints Commission had not proved itself to be an effective regulator of the press. Sir
David accordingly recommended that a statutory tribunal be established to deal with complaints of
infringement of privacy etc.; and he also recommended the creation of a number of criminal offences
designed to penalise practices such as 'door-stepping'.

[151] In 1949 the *Royal Commission on the Press* (Cmd. 7700 (1949)) investigated the amount of
press coverage given to news of 'sex interest' (noting, however, at para. 488 that 'whether or not the
reader finds any sex interest in a particular picture or news item' depends on subjective assessment
and is in any event heavily influenced by the context in which the material appears). The Royal

had ceased to be the focus of any special public concern.[152] The press remained capable of finding ample evidence of the follies and tragedies[153] of human life in other aspects of the legal system (as evidenced by reports of actions for breach of promise of marriage, enticement, and even in publication of the details of wills).

For all these reasons, the provisions of the 1926 Act seemed to have become largely irrelevant—albeit, as the *Moynihan*[154] case exemplifies, an occasionally troublesome irrelevance. But the most important reason why the Act ceased to serve any useful purpose is because of the dramatic changes which have taken place over the past seventy years in the law's approach to divorce and other matrimonial causes. The view, almost[155] universally accepted in 1926, that the public had a legitimate interest in the trial of matters affecting the status of the marriage and the family, has come to be gradually (albeit with little or no public discussion) supplanted by the view that family matters are essentially private and that this privacy is to be respected by the legal system. The vast majority of divorce cases are dealt with in private under the so-called 'special procedure';[156] and although it is true that until the coming into force of Part II of the Family Law Act 1996 there remains the remote possibility of a defended[157] petition being heard in open court, the introduction of divorce as 'a process over time' under the Family Law Act 1996 makes it inconceivable that there should be any public hearing of the essentially administrative procedures which will lead to a marriage being dissolved on the ground that it has irretrievably broken down. It is also true that there remains scope not only for applications in the course of the proceedings,[158]

Commission noted the increased press coverage of 'law police and accident cases', and (at para. 490) condemned the 'degradation of public taste which results from the gratification of morbid curiosity' in such matters. But the subject of divorce is not even mentioned in the index to the Commission's Report.

[152] Subsequent inquiries into Press standards shared the view that reporting of matrimonial cases did not justify special treatment.

[153] A particularly painful genre used to be the reporting of coroners' inquests into suicides: until comparatively recently it was the practice to publish a full account of the notes often left by the deceased and lengthy accounts of the family circumstances and the events surrounding the death.

[154] See n. 13 above.

[155] Cf. the view of Lord Buckmaster, n. 91 above.

[156] By way of exception to the general rule that filed documents are not open to inspection, the Family Proceedings Rules 1991 confers a general right, exercisable within fourteen days of the pronouncement of a decree *nisi* under the special procedure, to inspect the District Judge's certificate and the evidence filed in support of the petition: see Family Proceedings Rules 1991, SI 1247, r. 2.36(4). The purpose of this Rule is presumably to give an opportunity to exercise the right of intervention in divorce proceedings to show cause why a decree should not be made absolute (perhaps, e.g., on the ground that contrary to the affidavit evidence the parties are not living apart): see Matrimonial Causes Act 1973, s. 9; Family Proceedings Rules 1991, SI 1247, r. 2.47. It was presumably under this Rule that journalists obtained copies of the affidavit sworn by the Prince of Wales in his 1996 divorce suit; but it would appear that *publication* of this evidence may have infringed the provisions of the Judicial Proceedings (Regulation of Reports) Act 1926.

[157] Undefended cases which have not been entered in the special procedure list (Family Proceedings Rules 1991, r. 2.24(3)) will also be heard in open court: see r. 2.28(1).

[158] For example, applications for financial orders (which should be resolved before dissolution) or applications for an order preventing divorce under Family Law Act 1996 s. 10 on the ground that dissolution would cause substantial hardship.

but for applications thereafter.[159] However, it seems certain that such proceedings will take place in private; and the decision whether to permit reporting or other publication of what transpires in proceedings taking place in private is currently governed by other statutory provisions.[160] For all practical purposes, on the coming into force of Part II of the Family Law Act 1996 the effect of the 1926 Act will have become well and truly spent.

THE FUTURE: BROADER ISSUES TO BE FACED?

It does not, however, follow that the question of how far family proceedings should be protected from publicity has been satisfactorily concluded. In recent years it has come to be seen that the view, expressed by the Finer Committee in 1974,[161] that such proceedings should take place in private unless the public interest 'decisively demanded that they be heard in open court' begs a number of questions. But what precisely does the public interest require? And how far does the decision on whether or not proceedings should take place in private conclude the question of whether or not information about what has occurred is to be allowed to be published? These are indeed difficult issues; but they need to be faced. The *Russell* case may exemplify the principle that sensational cases make bad law; and there must always be a risk that campaigns by perhaps narrowly-focused pressure groups will once again produce a hasty and unsatisfactory legislative response.

[159] Paradoxically the Family Law Act 1996 prevents the 1926 Act from applying in circumstances in which it might be thought to have some possible utility. (i) the 1926 Act only applies to 'proceedings', and divorce proceedings do not start until a statement of marital breakdown is filed: Family Law Act 1996, s. 20(1). It follows that attendance at an information meeting (and what takes place at such a meeting) is not protected by the 1926 Act (nor, so far as the author is aware, by any other statutory provision, although if the meeting takes place on court premises the taking of photographs and the making of sketches for publication would be prohibited by s. 4 Criminal Justice Act 1925). (ii) The 1996 Act provides that marital proceedings come to an end on the making of a divorce order (s. 20(6)(b)) thereby dramatically altering the position under the law formerly in force under which the suit continued perhaps for many years. The effect appears to be that financial applications which are heard after the divorce order (and in particular applications under the Matrimonial Causes Act 1973 to vary a financial order) will no longer qualify as proceedings to which the 1926 Act applies. No doubt such applications will be heard in private: see below.

[160] Notably the provisions of s. 12, Administration of Justice Act 1960: for a full and lucid account of the law governing the reporting of court proceedings, see Borrie and Lowe, *The Law of Contempt* (3rd. edn. 1996 by N. V. Lowe and B. Sufrin) Ch. 8.

[161] *Report of the Committee on One-Parent Families* (1974) Cmnd. 5629, para. 4.408.

5*

Marriage Saving and the
Early Days of Conciliation:
The Role of Claud Mullins

INTRODUCTION

The Judicial Proceedings (Regulation of Reports) Act 1926 may have done something to reduce fear of press publicity amongst those involved in divorce proceedings; but it did nothing to change the distressing nature of court proceedings. Moreover, the Act did not apply to proceedings in the magistrates' courts for separation or maintenance orders[1]—before the creation of the legal aid scheme in 1949, the only form of redress readily available to wage earners and others of modest means. In the 1930s pressure began to build up to improve the legal system's response to the problem of marriage breakdown amongst the working classes; and the Summary Procedure (Domestic Proceedings) Act 1937 can in retrospect be seen as a decisive breakthrough—not only in relation to the procedures in the magistrates' courts but by highlighting the case for making 'conciliation' generally available in family cases[2] as a means of resolving the questions which have to be settled.

The case for 'conciliation' had been pursued with particular vigour by one of the Metropolitan Police Magistrates, Claud Mullins; and Mullins's contribution to law reform in this area deserves more attention than it has received from lawyers[3] in the past. This Chapter therefore seeks to give an account of the background to, and the significance of, the 1937 Act and to place on record the part played in the story by a very remarkable individual.

* The material in this Chapter was first published as an article, under the title 'Marriage saving and the early days of conciliation: the role of Claud Mullins', in [1998] CFLQ 161. Two of Mullins's three children—the writer and art historian Edwin Mullins and the psychiatrist and historian Dr Ann Dally—kindly read the typescript of that article.

[1] Under Summary Jurisdiction (Married Women) Act 1895, as amended. An excellent historical account of the magistrates' matrimonial jurisdiction is given in O. R. McGregor, L. Blom-Cooper and C. Gibson, *Separated Spouses* (1970).

[2] J. R. Rathbone MP, seconding the Motion for the Second Reading of the Summary Procedure (Matrimonial Matters) Bill, said that the declared objective of the legislation was to 'provide machinery for conciliation' *Hansard (5th series)* (HC) 5 Feb. 1937, col. 1947.

[3] Mullins's career has, however, been explored by G. Behlmer, 'Summary Justice and Working-Class Marriage in England, 1870–1940' (1994) *Law and History Review*, vol. 12, 229, 264–75; and the material gleaned from the local press about the operation of the South West London Police Court is particularly valuable.

THE FAMILY PROBLEMS OF THE WAGE-EARNING CLASSES

In the period between the two World Wars magistrates' courts made some 10,000 matrimonial orders each year. In contrast, the divorce court dealt with only half that number of cases. But simple comparison of the number of orders made by the magistrates and the divorce court[4] in fact seriously understates the role of the magistrates' courts in dealing with marital problems. Magistrates could only make an order if a summons had first been issued; and those approaching the courts found that the application for a summons was not a formality. As Sir Chartres Biron[5] explained to a Parliamentary Select Committee in 1922:

[I]t was always my object . . . to keep people out of court if possible. You cannot expect an ideal home in Hoxton any more than perhaps you can in Mayfair, but you want to get the thing on a reasonable basis, and what we always tried to do was to get together the people if possible. Before granting any summons I always went very carefully into the cases and a great many were obviously frivolous applications . . . The whole object in all these matters dealing with women and children and husbands was at all costs, even at some sacrifice of the individual, to keep the homes together, because we were always firmly persuaded that it was very much better for people to live together even under circumstances of some discomfort and with occasional outbreaks . . .[6]

It seems often to have required a certain persistence to get an application for a summons heard by a magistrate. Since early in the twentieth century the missionaries and probation officers[7] located in many metropolitan police and other magistrates' courts had routinely[8] interviewed those who indicated that they wanted (or might want) a summons issued; and experience (so the Lord Chancellor told

---

[4] For statistical data, see the *Report of the Committee on Social Services in Magistrates' Courts* (Chairman: S. W. Harris) (1936) Cmd. 5122 (subsequently referred to as 'the Harris Report') para. 6 and App. 2.

[5] Chief Magistrate, Bow Street, 1920–33. Sir Chartres Biron (1868–1920), son of a QC, was educated at Eton and Trinity College Cambridge. A member of Brooks's, the Garrick, the Beefsteak, Princes and the Royal Yacht Squadron, he recorded his recreation as travel but also had some taste for letters and wrote a collection of essays (*Pious Opinions*, 1923) on literary subjects (including a sympathetic piece on 'Dickens and the Law'). His autobiography (*Without Prejudice*, 1936) does not shrink from pungent observations on the legal system: for example, although he thought the juvenile courts created under the Children Act 1908 had 'thoroughly justified their existence' he also recorded his view that they had become the 'happy hunting ground of all the cranks, male and female. Psychoanalysts, psychiatrists, Christian scientists, all got to work, and it was not too easy to keep them in order.' (P. 259.)

[6] *Joint Select Committee on the Guardianship of Infants Bill*, Minutes of Evidence, 19 July 1922, q. 9.

[7] The work of the voluntary missionaries was, after the coming into force of the Probation of Offenders Act 1907, gradually replaced by professional probation officers: see generally the Harris Report, paras. 133–80.

[8] In 1936 the Harris Report found that 'conciliation' was attempted in 71 per cent of cases coming to County Borough courts, 69 per cent of those coming to the Metropolitan Courts, and 51 per cent of those coming to country petty sessions: see para. 11.

the House of Lords in 1934[9]) confirmed that it was 'often possible for a mediator of experience to remove misunderstandings, to show how difficulties may be overcome and to bring about a permanent reconciliation'.[10] Indeed, on one view, the work of the police court missionary led the urban poor to realise that the magistrates' court was a 'place where they could seek advice and even help in trouble';[11] and historical research[12] gives some support for the view that at the beginning of the twentieth century the major city courts did play a part as centres of advice and charity[13] for the working class.

A ROSEATE VIEW?

How far did this roseate view of the role of the magistrates' courts reflect reality? Was it the courts' function to provide advice and assistance or to seek to 'save' marriages? If so, how should these services be provided?[14] Did the emphasis placed on marriage saving by court missionaries and probation officers risk denying the weak and vulnerable the legal remedies the law provided for them? In any event, was the way in which the magistrates' courts—with their dominant function of policing the community by the administration of the criminal law—dealt with the family problems of the poor really (as Biron and others

---

[9] *Hansard (5th series)* (HL) 15 May 1934, vol. 92, col. 382 (Lord Sankey). The Harris Report subsequently found that as many as 'two-thirds of the attempts to effect a reconciliation appear to be successful': Harris Report, para. 13. Even if the case got as far as a formal hearing by the bench it appears that there was a considerable likelihood that no order would be made: see Harris Report, p. 155 (order made in only 914 of the 1,766 cases heard by the courts surveyed). Behlmer (op. cit. n. 3 above, p. 238) infers that 'for every person who actually saw a marital complaint through to trial, perhaps three more sought relief of some kind without invoking the formal machinery of justice'; and concludes (op. cit. p. 270) that the conciliators sought to persuade applicants for separation orders that they should cease legal action; and that 'the overriding concern of legal reformers was not with guaranteeing due process to spouses at odds but rather with regularizing the domestic work of police courts. If legislation could create a universal "atmosphere of understanding" in which to "adjust" marriages, then one root cause of family disintegration might be removed.'

[10] Sir Chartres Biron recorded that the police court missionaries' intervention led to reconciliation in 50 per cent of the cases in the London courts and that this, to his mind satisfactory, result was largely due to the missionaries' tact and discretion: *Without Prejudice* (1936) pp. 246–7.

[11] Ibid.

[12] See J. Davis, 'A Poor Man's System of Justice: the London Police Courts in the Second Half of the Nineteenth Century', *Historical Journal* 27 (1984) 309, at 321. Although a number of factors (including the emergence of alternative sources of advice and problem resolution) tended progressively to reduce reliance on the courts for these purposes, the continuing importance of the magistrates' role in pre-World War II working-class communities is emphasised by Behlmer: see op. cit. n. 3 above, at p. 238.

[13] The London courts had financial resources; and in a letter to *The Times* (6 Jan. 1939) Biron claimed that 'with the assistance of the poor box the work done out of court was almost as important as the legal routine'.

[14] The Home Office file dealing with conciliation (PRO HO45/15719) opens with a letter dated 15 Apr. 1919 from an East End charitable organisation urging the establishment of Domestic Courts in which the magistrate would give 'invaluable advice to poor married people who cannot get on together, or who would get on if they had the advantage of wise trained advice and guidance'.

seemed to believe) the best that could be devised? Not everyone thought so. As Claud Mullins was to put it:

Cases sometimes involving the inmost secrets of married life 'were dealt with in precisely the same way as the other work of the court. The wife . . . stood in the witness box, like a policeman prosecuting a criminal. The husband stood in front of the dock, like a motorist accused of having driven contrary to law. Later the husband, like the motorist, came into the witness box to tell his story . . . There was no restriction on the attendance of the public, so that gossiping neighbours could come and hear the cases; and there was no restriction on reports in the newspapers . . . In addition to all this, the parties had to be invited to cross-examine each other, a procedure that sometimes threatened to develop into a brawl . . .'[15]

Hence, perhaps to some extent influenced by the development of separate domestic courts in the United States and elsewhere,[16] pressure for improvement in facilities for dealing with family problems amongst the poorer classes in society began to build up after World War I;[17] and in 1928 Henry Snell MP[18] put down a question referring to dissatisfaction with the system of investigation of matrimonial cases in the police courts. Would the Government consider the advisability of establishing special courts to deal with such cases?

THE CAMPAIGN FOR REFORM 1928–1937

The Government's response to the question was discouraging, and the Courts of Domestic Relations Bill which Snell subsequently introduced was permanently blocked. But the policies to which Snell's Bill sought to give effect—the domestic jurisdiction of magistrates to be separated from the criminal jurisdiction; the public not to be admitted to domestic proceedings hearings; probation officers to be available—were essentially what became law in 1937 and the substantive provisions of that Act remain largely unchanged sixty years later. The striking fact that what had seemed so unacceptable should within ten years find its place on the statute book[19] is a remarkable example of the impact which determined individuals may

---

[15] *Marriage Failures and the Children*, by Claud Mullins (1954) p. 15 (in part a quotation from the same author's *Wife v. Husband in the Courts* (1935)).

[16] See on this Behlmer, op. cit. n. 3 above at pp. 260–1. The American experience continued for some years to be invoked by supporters of reform of court structures: see L. N. Brown, 'The Legal Background to the Family Court' (1966) *British Journal of Criminology* 139. The example of the juvenile courts established by the Children Act 1908 was also influential.

[17] Note that the Home Office file on the subject starts in 1919: see n. 14 above.

[18] (Labour) for East Woolwich.

[19] And although in form a Private Member's Bill the Summary Procedure (Domestic Proceedings) Act 1937 was in substance a government Bill: in 1937 Mr Maurice Petherick drew a favourable place in the ballot for Private Members' Bills and asked the Home Office if they had a suitable Bill for him to introduce. He was handed a draft of the Bill for the 1937 Act produced by George Coldstream (then one of the Parliamentary Counsel but subsequently Permanent Secretary in the Lord Chancellor's Office) and the Government continued effectively to have the carriage of the legislation: see Home Office to Treasury 9 Nov. 1936, PRO file HO45/15719; and (for the Instructions to Parliamentary Counsel) HO45/17152/695967.

have on law reform; and the outcome of the campaign which they fought cruci-
ally influenced the future development of English family law. But—apparently
unnoticed at the time or indeed subsequently—the development was in reality
in the opposite direction to that which the campaigners themselves wished.

AN IMPROBABLE ALLIANCE

Four very different men can claim at least some of the credit for what appeared
to be a successful campaign for reform. First, there is Henry Snell, the illegitimate child[20] who, abandoning school at the age of eight to work as a farmer's lad,
became an MP, Chairman of the London County Council, and finally (during
World War II) Deputy Leader of the House of Lords.[21] Secondly, there is the
young hereditary peer, Lord Listowel;[22] and thirdly, playing a vital role behind
the scenes with his sympathetic concern for humanising court procedures,
the Home Office official Sidney Harris.[23] Finally, there is the controversial

[20] But he was not brought up in a one-parent family: his mother married an agricultural labourer
and the young Snell had a family upbringing in their cottage: see the memoir by H. B. Grimsditch,
Dictionary of National Biography 1941–50 (1959).

[21] Snell wrote many books on social, moral and political matters, and his autobiography (*Men,
Movements and Myself*, 1936) movingly evokes life amongst the agricultural and urban poor at the
beginning of the twentieth century. Snell's *Dictionary of National Biography* memorialist (see n. 20
above) states that his 'unremitting pre-occupation with ethics and sociology, unrelieved by any
winning weaknesses, often made him seem bleak to more human mortals' whilst his entry in *Who's
Who* asserted that he had no hobbies. His main intellectual interest was in the Ethical Movement on
which he wrote extensively; and whilst this passionate secularist would no doubt have been satisfied
that his funeral service (at which C. R. Attlee—Prime Minister 1945–51—gave the address) was
conducted by the Chairman of the Ethical Union, he would presumably not have wished to be
commemorated at a Memorial Service conducted by the Dean and held in Westminster Abbey on
28 Apr. 1944.

[22] William ('Billy') Hare (1906–97) became the fifth Earl of Listowel (in the peerage of Ireland)
and the sixth Baron Hare (in the peerage of the United Kingdom) on his father's death in 1931. In
an attempt to shield his son from left-wing influences, Listowel's father had removed him from Balliol
College Oxford and sent him to Magdalene College Cambridge. Listowel none the less remained a
lifelong socialist and advocate of progressive causes, serving as a Minister throughout the post-World
War II Attlee administration (briefly from Apr. 1947 to Jan. 1948 in the Cabinet as the last Secretary
of State at the India Office). Subsequently, on Dr Kwame Nkrumah's personal request, Listowel served
as Governor-General (1957–60) of the newly independent Ghana: see further *The Times*, 13 Mar.
1997. Evidently in the thirties rather unpopular with the more traditional members of the House of
Lords—the late Sir Isaiah Berlin told the author that Listowel was regarded as 'very left' by his contemporaries—it was thought prudent to find another peer 'more acceptable to the House generally'
to pilot the Bill for the Summary Procedure (Domestic Proceedings) Act 1937 through the House of
Lords. However, Listowel played a leading part in exercising pressure on the Government: *Hansard
(5th series)* (HL) 25 July 1934, vol. 93, col. 1055; *Hansard (5th series)* (HL) 29 Apr. 1936,
vol. 100, col. 632 (implementation of the Harris Report).

[23] Sir Sidney Harris (1876–1962) served for forty-eight years in the Home Office, acted as Secretary
to the Tomlin Committee on Adoption in 1924, and was Chairman of the Committee on the Social
Services in the Courts of Summary Jurisdiction in 1936. After his retirement from the civil service
he chaired the British Board of Film Censors, but for the development of the family justice system
his role as Chairman of the Departmental Committee on Grants for the Development of Marriage

Metropolitan Police Magistrate, Claud Mullins. Considerations of space preclude anything more than the footnote accounts given above of the careers of Snell, Harris and Listowel; but Mullins's career deserves more extended treatment, not only because of its human interest and the light which it throws on the tensions which can exist within the judicial system, but also because Mullins's extensive writings raised important questions about the proper role of the legal system—in particular, about the relationship between, on the one hand, the courts' basic role in adjudicating on disputes in accordance with established legal norms, and, on the other, the extent and nature of their involvement in the provision of guidance, counselling and other forms of assistance to those with problems in their personal relationships.

CLAUD MULLINS AND THE PLACE OF SOCIAL WORK IN THE COURTS

Claud Mullins[24] had what at the time was an unusual background for one of the Metropolitan Police Magistrates.[25] The son of a gifted but only modestly successful sculptor, his father's premature death was a factor leading to Mullins leaving Mill Hill at sixteen and taking employment as a clerk in the LCC. He was eventually called to the Bar but his practice was never large. Becoming less and less convinced that English law and procedure satisfied public demands, he did not hesitate to publicise his views in books,[26] articles and lectures: he was (he said) a law reformer before he was a magistrate.[27]

Guidance is more significant, since the Committee's Report (Cmd. 7566, 1948) led to the provision of government funding for a number of marriage guidance organisations: see further Ch. 6 below. From 1919 to 1934 he was in charge of the Children's Branch of the Home Office and—as will be seen in Ch. 9 below—was between 1944 and 1947 passionately (and, in the result, successfully) concerned to preserve the Home Office's departmental responsibility for children deprived of a normal home life. Described by John Watson JP as 'sweet and unwarlike' and by *The Times* (10 July 1962) as 'of a somewhat shy and retiring nature'—a colleague wrote that he would bid you good morning and then wonder if he had gone too far: C. P. Hill, *The Times* 27 July 1962—his personality may explain why he failed to reach the heights to be expected of his abilities, but 'no one in his generation better upheld the best traditions of the civil service' whilst the modern observer must note with admiration the effectiveness of his concern for securing the public good in general and the welfare of children in particular.

²⁴ 1887–1968.

²⁵ Such magistrates were qualified lawyers appointed under the Metropolitan Police Courts Act 1839 to serve in the Metropolitan Police area. Stipendiary magistrates could be, and occasionally were, appointed to serve elsewhere in the country (Stipendiary Magistrates Act 1863) but the tradition for long prevailed that, outside London, the bench should consist of lay justices. The Metropolitan Police Magistrates had, as will emerge, a distinctive and proud identity.

²⁶ The books by Mullins most relevant to the subject matter of this Chapter are *Wife v. Husband in the Courts* (1935), and *Marriage Failures and the Children* (1954). Two autobiographical works —*Fifteen Years' Hard Labour* (1948) and *One Man's Furrow* (1963)—are revealing. He also wrote extensively on criminological and penological subjects (notably *The Sentence on the Guilty* (1957)), whilst his books for youthful readers demonstrate his concern for a wider understanding of the principles of the legal system.

²⁷ Mullins had, before his appointment to the bench, published *In Quest of Justice* (1931) and this—together with the numerous articles written for the quality press—served to give him a reputation for what the *Daily Mail* (30 June 1931) described as 'broadminded views on law reform'. Mullins

Although Mullins had hoped to be appointed a County Court judge, he expressed delight when in 1931 he was offered appointment as a Metropolitan Police Magistrate. But he soon became disillusioned. In part this was because he wished to take his duties more seriously, or perhaps earnestly, than did his colleagues. The ink was scarcely dry on his warrant of appointment before he sought an interview with the Permanent Under-Secretary of State at the Home Office to complain that the Metropolitan Police Magistrates were underworked.[28] (Sir John Anderson advised him that it would be unwise to advertise the fact.) A particular source of tension was his colleagues'[29] apparent lack of interest in social problems; and although Mullins was able informally to make some procedural improvements[30] in the 'shocking' system for dealing with domestic cases, the scope for initiatives unsupported by legislation was limited. In particular, legislation would be necessary to control the publication of what Mullins described[31] as 'flashy stories . . . given prominence in many of the cheaper newspapers'[32] which

subsequently complained that the permanent Under-Secretary of State at the Home Office (Sir John Anderson) had given him to understand that keenness for legal reform was not a drawback to his appointment: Mullins to Sir John Simon, 27 Feb. 1936, PRO HO45/21034.

[28] By convention, for much of the year the Metropolitan Police Magistrates only sat for three days each week; and Mullins thought difficulties were 'inevitable when a young and energetic man joined a body which was steeped in a tradition of 3 days a week and no interest in social problems': Mullins to Maxwell, 28 Oct. 1936, PRO HO45/17152.

[29] Mullins's relationship with the Chief Magistrate Sir Chartres Biron (see n. 5 above) was particularly unharmonious. Shortly after appointment to the bench, Mullins wrote in his diary that he had 'never heard such deep-dyed Toryism in my life . . . Biron's idea of a magistrate is one who does his three days a week and plays the rest of the time' and Mullins recorded that at both ends of his life Biron 'had a strong distaste for work': C. Mullins, *Fifteen Years' Hard Labour* (1948) pp. 163, 168. And although Mullins's published assessment of Sir Rollo Graham-Campbell (Chief Magistrate 1933–40) was somewhat more charitable it was hardly favourable: 'Eton all through, with all its excellent qualities and its limitations . . . courtesy personified . . . deeply religious . . . hard working even to the detriment of his own health . . . [but] completely out of touch with modern movements . . . doubtful if [he] realised the necessity for any reforms in the courts: . . . this lovable old man really belonged to the world of aspidistras, heavy curtains and red-papered dining rooms . . .': C. Mullins, *Fifteen Years' Hard Labour*, pp. 171–2. Mullins's failure to establish a satisfactory relationship with his colleagues eventually led to something close to a constitutional crisis: see further below.

[30] Particularly after Oct. 1934 when he was transferred to the South-Western Police Court in Balham High Road. This court had an established tradition for its progressive approach to domestic cases: see the detailed account by G. Behlmer, 'Summary Justice and Working-Class Marriage in England, 1870–1940' (1994) *Law and History Review*, vol. 12, 229, 264–5. Mullins deliberately held what he described as his Domestic Court in a small room, with no dais, and the parties seated at a table: *Fifteen Years' Hard Labour* (1948) pp. 136–7. But his conduct has been seen by some as not only taking 'huge liberties with accepted police court procedure' but as fundamentally 'coercive by most contemporary standards save his own'. In this view, Mullins and others who thought like him were primarily concerned to preserve working-class marriages and thereby to deal with domestic disharmony in a way which 'offered urban elites hope': see Behlmer, op. cit. above, particularly at pp. 266–71.   [31] *Marriage Failures and the Children* (1954) p. 16.

[32] Many would agree that press reporting as recorded by the Harris Report—'Treated like a Lodger', 'Husband denounces Wife as Adventuress'—was at best distasteful; and see generally C. Mullins, *Fifteen Years' Hard Labour* (1948) Ch. 10. But one scholar believes that Mullins regarded such reporting as 'morally wrong . . . because the public's right to know about the inhumanity still possible in English homes did not match society's need to resuscitate marriage among its labouring majority': G. Behlmer, op. cit. n. 3 above, p. 268. It is certainly true that towards the end of his career on the bench Mullins became obsessional about press reporting, particularly after wide publicity was given to the fact that his wife had been prosecuted for a motoring offence.

often effectively destroyed any prospect of achieving a reconciliation.[33] But Mullins's diagnosis of what was required went far beyond these narrowly legalistic measures: he believed the underlying problem to be the courts' insistence on seeing matrimonial disputes 'solely as matters of law'.[34] To effect a cure for the ills Mullins believed to infect the family justice system could only be achieved by making available some 'form of social help' for those involved.[35]

Mullins's view that such help might extend to advice from 'sex experts'[36] and his belief that magistrates needed training in the causes of marital disharmony[37] was unlikely to appeal to those who shared Sir Chartres Biron's contempt for 'social workers' and other 'do-gooders';[38] but Mullins was not alone in believing that the functions of the courts needed radical redefinition. As he recorded:

Through Lord Snell, Lord Listowel, then not widely known save in the world of art and aesthetics, approached me. He was keen to work for legal reform so I suggested that he should introduce a Bill . . . We worked out our policy together, and then I drafted a Bill . . .[39]

Listowel duly introduced this Bill—the Summary Jurisdiction (Domestic Procedure) Bill—into the House of Lords in 1934. Press comment was favourable, and even enthusiastic;[40] but in reality the Second Reading debate was not quite the success—at least in the short term—that Mullins was subsequently to claim. To understand why this should have been so, it is necessary to outline the 1934 Bill's main provisions.

THE LISTOWEL/MULLINS 1934 SUMMARY JURISDICTION (DOMESTIC PROCEDURE) BILL

The Listowel Bill was intended to change the court's function 'from one of litigation to one of investigation and reconciliation';[41] and to that end it would have

---

[33] C. Mullins, *Wife v. Husband in the Courts* (1935), p. 29; *Fifteen Years' Hard Labour* (1948) p. 129.　　　　　　　　　　　　　　　　[34] *Marriage Failures and the Children* (1954), p. 16.

[35] *Marriage Failures and the Children* (1954), p. 11.

[36] See C. Mullins, *One Man's Furrow* (1963) pp. 104–8; and for other references Behlmer op. cit. n. 3 above, pp. 264–5. Mullins's publicly expressed views on birth control were subsequently to involve him in serious trouble: see below.

[37] C. Mullins, Memorandum on Home Office file PRO HO45/21034 'for private circulation only' commenting on the *Report of the Committee on Social Services in Magistrates' Courts* (1936) Cmd. 5122.

[38] See n. 5 above. In fairness to Biron's memory it should be said that he was, as already indicated, a strong supporter of the work of the police court missionaries in their dealings with marital problems.

[39] *Fifteen Years' Hard Labour* (1948) p. 138. Mullins characteristically did not seek to conceal his involvement: his book *Wife v. Husband in the Courts* (1935) is dedicated to the Earl of Listowel 'whose speech in the House of Lords on May 15 1934 when introducing the Summary Jurisdiction (Domestic Procedure) Bill (drafted by the author) directed the attention of public opinion to the urgency of the matters discussed in this book'.

[40] Mullins wrote that 'We had got our publicity, which proved to be vast. We had a very good Press indeed, despite our clause to clip the wings of certain newspapers': *Fifteen Years' Hard Labour* (1948) p. 138; and for references to press comment see Behlmer, op. cit. n. 3 above, p. 263, fn. 142.

[41] *Hansard (5th Series)* (HL) 15 May 1934, vol. 92, col. 365.

allowed magistrates to conduct cases according to a special 'domestic procedure' in which the laws of evidence would not apply,[42] there would be no right of cross-examination,[43] and statements to the court would not (unless the court directed otherwise) be made under oath.[44] But the most remarkable provision of the Bill[45] was that allowing husband or wife to apply for a 'conciliation summons' which the court could grant if the family's circumstances threatened to give rise to an application for a separation, maintenance, or custody order or even if the circumstances were 'detrimental to the happiness of the parties'. The court was then to investigate the matter, and 'advise or admonish' the parties.[46] Finally, the court was not to exercise its statutory jurisdiction to make a separation, financial, or custody order unless it had 'failed to achieve a reconciliation' or was satisfied that reconciliation was impossible.[47] It is clear, therefore, that the court was—in accordance with Mullins's deeply held belief—itself to be deeply involved in the conciliation process; and it was clear that the court was to go far beyond its traditional role of applying ascertainable legal rules and instead to act as a general purveyor of advice and therapy.

Not surprisingly the Bill was severely criticised (in sometimes extreme language) by the lawyers and officials responsible for the administration of the legal system. Lord Merrivale[48] (the recently retired former President of the Divorce Division), for example, not only described the procedure envisaged by the Bill as a 'burlesque'[49] but put down an amendment asserting that the Bill subverted 'the established principles and methods of administration of justice'.[50] The complaint was essentially (in the Lord Chancellor's words)[51] that the Bill would allow the court itself to investigate the parties' private lives and give advice, and that it would thus:

---

[42] Clause 4(5).   [43] Clause 4(5)(b).   [44] Clause 4(4).

[45] Clause 5.   [46] Clause 6.   [47] Clause 6.

[48] Formerly Sir Henry Duke: see Ch. 4 n. 3 above. Merrivale's view is the more impressive since he was strongly in favour of improving the magistrates' procedure and of encouraging settlement, and subsequently introduced his own Matrimonial Causes (Amended Procedure) Bill (HL Bill No. 7, 1934–5) into the House of Lords. The Merrivale Bill (which passed all its stages in the House of Lords) provided for proceedings to be started by a deposition, required the court to consider 'whether it will be well to hear the parties in private with a view to settlement by mutual consent of the matters in question', permitted it to hear the views of any person with knowledge of the parties' relationship, and empowered the court to make consent orders.

[49] *Hansard (5th series)* (HL) 15 May 1934, vol. 92, col. 371.

[50] *Hansard (5th series)* (HL) 15 May 1934, vol. 92, col. 366. Similarly critical comments were made inside the government machine (Sir Claud Schuster, Permanent Secretary in the Lord Chancellor's office describing the Bill to a Home Office colleague on 19 Apr. 1934, PRO file HO45/15719, as 'ridiculous'); whilst Mullins's magisterial brethren were strongly opposed to the Bill, and informed the Home Secretary that it was 'objectionable in many respects and would wholly fail to attain the ends it professed to serve': see further below.

[51] Viscount Sankey, *Hansard (5th series)* (HL) 15 May 1934, vol. 92, col. 382. Viscount Sankey's patronising words about the twenty-seven-year-old Listowel (the House 'always welcomes the contributions . . . made by our younger members . . . we are always anxious to know the opinions of those to whom, after we are gone, the destinies of our country may from time to time be entrusted': *Hansard (5th series)* (above), vol. 92, col. 380) may be revealing of his attitude.

confer upon a court of law functions of a non-judicial, advisory and patriarchal character which are difficult to reconcile with the purposes for which a court exists. That in
matrimonial disputes such functions can often be usefully exercised by some unofficial
person or body of persons is admitted, but they are not functions of a court of law . . .

THE HARRIS COMMITTEE ON SOCIAL SERVICES IN
MAGISTRATES' COURTS AND THE 1937 LEGISLATION

In these circumstances, it might be supposed that the whole notion of legislating to improve the magistrates' family jurisdiction had been fatally damaged;
but, as already noted, the Government did act and act comparatively quickly.
There seem to have been several reasons for this. First, although many lawyers
regarded the Listowel Bill as fundamentally flawed, it did not follow that they
were satisfied with the existing situation.[52] Secondly, although the Metropolitan
Police Magistrates had their views, so too did the far larger number of predomin-
antly lay magistrates sitting outside London; and the Magistrates' Association
was receptive to ideas for reform.[53] Thirdly, the Home Office had long been faced
with difficulties about the organisation and (to some extent) the functions of
probation services; and these had now become pressing.[54] Although for some time
government continued to believe that[55] the necessary improvements could be effected
administratively, continuing pressure eventually compelled it to admit that
reform was overdue;[56] and a Committee was set up under the chairmanship of
S. W. Harris.[57]

[52] Note Lord Merrivale's view in the debate on his Matrimonial Causes (Amended Procedure)
Bill 1934: *Hansard (5th Series)* (HL) 7 Nov. 1934, vol. 94, col. 173 that 'our tackle is out of date'.
[53] According to a Home Office briefing note of 10 Mar. 1936, PRO HO45/21034, para. 6, all the
London stipendiary magistrates and indeed all the country stipendiaries with the exception of Sir
Marley Sampson (Stipendiary Magistrate for Swansea) 'cold-shoulder the Magistrates' Association'.
[54] Although the Harris Committee complacently noted that Courts of Summary Jurisdiction had
'built up their own procedure based on the good sense of the Justices of their Clerks and on the
facilities available to them' the fact that there was no statutory or other authority for the employment of probation officers in this work was a significant concern to the Home Office: see the
Memorandum for Parliamentary Counsel (1936) PRO HO45/17152/62567.
[55] *Hansard (5th series)* (HL) 15 May 1934, vol. 93, col. 384.
[56] Per Viscount Sankey LC, *Hansard (5th series)* (HL) 25 July 1934, vol. 93, col. 1058.
[57] For S. W. Harris, see n. 23 above. It had originally been intended that the Harris Committee
should confine itself to the long-standing administrative problem of probation service organisation;
but the Committee's terms of reference were broadened to allow consideration of the procedure and
constitution of summary courts in the exercise of their matrimonial jurisdiction: see *Report of the
Committee on Social Services in Magistrates' Courts* (1936) Cmd. 5122, pp. vi–viii. No doubt by
reason of its original remit the Committee's membership was dominated by persons with an established interest in probation work, and this factor may have had some influence on the report's recommendations about the proper division of function between courts and social services: see below.
The Harris Committee's Report marked an important stage in the development of the probation service as a provider of general social services in the courts (as to which see generally *Probation and
After-Care: its development in England and Wales*, by D. Bochel (1976), particularly Ch. 6) rather
than being exclusively concerned with the supervision of offenders, but that aspect of the
Committee's work is outside the scope of this Chapter.

The Harris Committee's report acknowledged that its remit derived from the debate on the Listowel Bill;[58] and there can be no doubt that the Harris Report led directly to the enactment, with little trouble or amendment,[59] of the Summary Procedure (Domestic Proceedings) Act 1937. Claud Mullins rightly claimed the credit for what had been achieved;[60] but it is more questionable whether the 1937 Act truly gave effect to the policies which he had advocated.[61] That is a matter to which we must return; but on any basis the enactment of the 1937 Act was the high point of his effectiveness as a law reformer.

DECLINE AND FALL OF A REFORMING MAGISTRATE

Mullins's difficulty in establishing a rapport with his professional brethren has already been mentioned; and they were all opposed to the principles which he sought to embody in the 1934 Listowel Bill.[62] But things were to get far worse. The magistrates' smouldering resentment[63] became a matter of official record at a meeting of Metropolitan Police Magistrates on 27 February 1936 when Mullins's colleagues unanimously censured his conduct[64] and demanded that the

---

[58] Harris Report, p. vi; cf. the remarks of Lord Merthyr, *Hansard (5th series)* (HL) 23 June 1937, vol. 105, col. 352.

[59] The only major difficulty was caused by Lord Atkin's insistence that bastardy proceedings should be removed from the scope of the Act. It was decided to give way on this point (see *Hansard (5th Series)* (HL) 13 July 1937, vol. 106, col. 343) because support (in what would necessarily be a free vote) from those Lord Chancellor Hailsham categorised as 'the sentimentalists and socialists' would not be sufficient to secure the passage of the Bill: Hailsham to Hoare, 14 June 1937, PRO file HO45/15719.

[60] Defending himself against criticism from his magisterial colleagues, Mullins claimed that the 'appointment of the Committee and the later widening . . . of its terms of reference were both the direct consequence of' his activities: Mullins to Simon, 6 Apr. 1936, PRO HO45/21034.

[61] Mullins himself told Harris that he was 'immensely pleased' with the report (Mullins to Harris, 6 Apr. 1936, PRO HO45/17152) and sent a memorandum to the Home Office 'for private circulation only' saying that the report was a 'most satisfying document [whose recommendations] go far beyond my most optimistic expectations'. He wanted the Home Office to circulate magistrates about improvements which could be made without legislation, and urged that magistrates be trained in the causes of marital disharmony: 'while nobody wishes to exaggerate sex as a cause of marital disharmony it is a cause and . . . Probation officers are woefully ignorant and shy . . . especially the women.' But Harris reported that he had lunched with Mullins and found him 'in a chastened mood'. Apparently Mullins was confident that Lord Listowel would 'do anything for him' but had become conscious of the fact that Listowel was not persona grata in the House of Lords.

[62] Privately some used strong language: R. A. Powell, the Metropolitan Police Magistrate at Westminster, wrote on 1 May 1934 to a Home Office official complaining that the Bill was 'clearly a propaganda stunt and one that is misleading and mischievous and calculated to bring the stipendiaries' courts into disrepute'. Powell continued that 'it is all the more obnoxious when a Metropolitan magistrate gives this agitation his open support . . . I wish he [Mullins] could be muzzled!'

[63] At a meeting between the Chief Magistrate and Sir John Simon it was admitted that 'some of the other Magistrates had been unfortunate in their behaviour' to Mullins (who had resigned from the Magistrates' Dining Club and ceased to attend the periodical meetings of magistrates): Home Office note dated 22 June 1936, PRO HO45/21034.

[64] The magistrates asserted their 'conviction that it is the duty as it has hitherto been the practice of Metropolitan Magistrates . . . to administer the law without giving public expression by words or writing to their personal opinion on matters of public controversy, to refrain from self-advertisement,

Chief Magistrate make a public statement asserting the duty of the magistracy not to engage in controversy.[65] Mullins had vigorously defended himself and claimed that he hoped the resolution would be passed, thereby furnishing 'irrefutable evidence' for the Home Office and others in authority 'of the hopeless inadequacy and conservatism'[66] of the Metropolitan Police Magistracy. But his outspoken defiance and denunciation of the 'traditions' of the bench and expressed determination of 'going his own way whatever Resolution was passed'—language perhaps surprising for one so closely identified with extolling the virtues of the conciliatory approach to family matters—made it difficult to believe that relationships with his colleagues could ever again be restored to what might be considered appropriate for those professionally engaged in the service of the judicial system.

It is true that the meticulous analysis carried out by Home Office officials into his colleagues' complaints against Mullins concluded that none of the statements made by Mullins to which his colleagues objected 'could reasonably be challenged as being in any way prejudicial to the impartial administration of the law' and that 'the trouble is not with what Mr Mullins says but [his] self-assertive manner'; and they advised firmly[67] against accepting the magistrates' demand that the Chief Magistrate make a public statement on the issues.[68]

Faced with this crisis, the Home Secretary, Sir John Simon, deployed his formidable diplomatic skills in seeking to minimise the harm which had been done.[69]

in keeping with the traditions of the Bar of which they remain members, and to avoid public criticism of their colleagues'.

[65] A colleague's statement that 'he was utterly sick of constantly reading public pronouncements in the Press generally accompanied by a photograph of Mullins, and impliedly slighting to his colleagues' is revealing of the underlying basis of the complaints: Minutes of Magistrates' Meeting at Bow Street, 27 Feb. 1936, and forwarded by the Chief Magistrate to the Home Secretary on that day: PRO HO45/21034.

[66] One of the main arguments used by Mullins in seeking Home Office support against his colleagues was that the recently published Harris Report had endorsed all his proposals for change and 'refuses to endorse the attitude of complacency adopted by my colleagues': Mullins to Simon, 6 Apr. 1936, PRO HO45/21034.

[67] Home Office officials considered the magistrates' demand that the Chief Magistrate make a public pronouncement to be 'most misguided' not least because any 'such pronouncement would . . . lead to a retort from Mullins, and a very considerable body of thoughtful people would . . . sympathise with Mullins rather than his opponents. In any case nothing could be worse for the reputation of the Metropolitan Magistrates than to advertise publicly this rather childish quarrel': Home Office briefing note of 10 Mar. 1936, PRO HO45/21034.

[68] See the briefing note of 10 Mar. 1936, annotated in manuscript: PRO HO45/21034.

[69] Simon's considered statement of the conditions under which magistrates might properly engage in advocacy of reform is worth recording: '(1) Such activities should be entirely separate from the discharge of the Magistrate's work in his Court. In his Court his duty is to administer the existing law according to the established procedure without reflecting any views he may have as to its inadequacy or improvement. After all, a Magistrate is first and foremost a judicial officer and not a legislator or a law reformer. (2) . . . It seems to me to be perfectly legitimate and proper for a Magistrate to interest himself in law reform or in improvements in procedure and to take a public part in advocating these changes so long as he avoids reflections upon colleagues who may take a different view. It is all a question of choosing the right occasion and presenting his views in the right manner. In my opinion he does not expose himself to any rebuke because he is zealous for law reform any more

He saw the Chief Magistrate and then[70] interviewed Mullins (who, not surprisingly, made a great deal of the fact that—as he believed—the Harris Committee had accepted every reform he had advocated). But, regrettably, Simon's efforts to bring peace to the Metropolitan Magistracy[71] were to be no more successful than the efforts he had made (as Foreign Secretary between 1931 and 1935) to preserve lasting peace in Europe.

The opposition of his colleagues would not, of itself, necessarily have impeded Mullins's effectiveness as a law reformer;[72] but unhappily for him there was a further problem: his behaviour on the bench began to attract critical comment. In 1938 the claim by an East London Labour MP[73] that there was 'wide and growing dissatisfaction' about the way Mullins conducted judicial business[74] was greeted with 'Hear, Hears' in the Commons.[75] In 1939 ill-considered remarks,[76]

than any other Magistrate is open to rebuke because he holds the view that things are better left as they are. (3) It goes without saying that anyone in the responsible position of a Magistrate, with colleagues who share a similar responsibility, should discuss and advocate the reforms which appeal to him as far as possible in an impersonal way and give credit to the good intentions of those who might take a different view. But the obligation to give credit to others applies both ways . . .': Simon to Graham-Campbell, PRO HO45/21034, 13 July 1936. (Paragraph (2) of this letter was to rebound on Simon in 1938 when Mullins sought to publicise a selective quotation. On Home Office advice, a secretary firmly rebuffed Mullins on the basis that Simon—by then Chancellor of the Exchequer—had not intended the letter for publication and 'Sir John observes that [the words Mullins intended to use] do not even constitute a complete sentence of what he wrote . . .': Treasury to Mullins, 8 Dec. 1938, PRO HO45/21034.)

[70] On 13 July 1936.

[71] '. . . I feel indebted to all who have come to see me for discussing the matter fairly and temperately. If anything I have said could possibly lead to a forgetting of past differences on both sides and an effort being made under [the leadership of Sir Rollo Graham Campbell] for a new start, in which every effort ought to be made not to ruffle susceptibilities and to believe the best of one another, I should be very happy at such an outcome': Simon to Graham-Campbell (copied to Mullins) 13 July 1936.

[72] Although his efforts to extend the powers of magistrates during the passage of A. P. Herbert's Bill for the Matrimonial Causes Act 1937 by effectively giving them jurisdiction to hear divorce cases caused particular offence to the judiciary and the Lord Chancellor's officials ('a confused mass of muddled thinking by that mischievous creature Mullins': Schuster to Maxwell, 9 Apr. 1937, PRO LCO2/1195). See generally S. Redmayne, 'The Matrimonial Causes Act 1937: A Lesson in the Art of Compromise' (1993) 13 OJLS 183, 193–5.

[73] Seeking unsuccessfully to put down a motion declaring Mullins unfit for office.

[74] In 1942 (when Mullins's conduct was again criticised in the Commons) G. R. Strauss (MP for Lambeth North) wrote an unsolicited letter to the Home Secretary reporting that he often had complaints in his constituency about the 'boorish manner in which [Mullins] treats prisoners and witnesses alike': Strauss to Morrison, 7 Dec. 1942, PRO HO45/21034; and see *Hansard (5th Series)* (HC) 15 Dec. 1942, vol. 385, col. 1786 ('frequent complaints about the remarks which this magistrate makes about people attending the court—witnesses, interpreters and all sorts of people'). Behlmer (op. cit. n. 3 above, at p. 266) records Mullins's 'deep bass voice, curt delivery, and impatience with trifles'; whilst Mullins himself may have revealed more than he intended by admitting that he had the habit of using 'dramatic language' in order to catch 'the attention of delinquents': Mullins to Maxwell, 31 July 1939. [75] *The Times* 18 Nov. 1938.

[76] Mullins said his remarks were an explanation of why he had sentenced a couple convicted of neglecting their seven children ('well fed but living in ragged and indescribably filthy conditions' in a condemned house) to one month's imprisonment rather than the six months indicated by the 'tariff'; and he told the Home Office that 'the public ought to hear how appalling cruelty can be inflicted on young children by the very fact that they are brought into the world in conditions like these'.

predictably widely reported,[77] about birth control[78] prompted official[79] wrath; but it was Mullins's remark—made in the course of a shop-lifting case—that the word 'housekeeper' usually meant 'something immoral' which was the final straw. Although Home Office officials remained loyal,[80] the Home Secretary, Herbert Morrison, refused to support Mullins[81] against the parliamentary criticism.

[77] Mullins repeatedly complained that he was being misreported; but his relationship with the media was ambivalent. He believed (see Mullins to Maxwell, 31 July 1939, PRO HO45/21034; Mullins to Morrison, 4 Dec. 1942) that the reporters in his court had a vendetta against him—indeed, one had been 'overheard to swear vengeance against' him—on account of their wings being clipped by the Domestic Proceedings Act. 'Reporters here [he claimed] used to make a lot of money by "stunting" marriage cases and they hold me responsible for the movement which resulted in the' imposition of reporting restrictions. But Mullins certainly did not resist making full use of publicity for the causes in which he believed. Thus, in 1938 he sought Home Office comment on a suggestion that he give an anonymous broadcast talk about the treatment of shoplifters; and reacted bitterly to the response that 'while the official answer to your letter would be that the Home Office can have no objection to an anonymous address on this subject' it would be better—since Mullins's voice and style were known to so many people, including journalists, and thus in practice anonymity would not be achieved— if Mullins were to 'try and get someone else to put over the wireless the views and information which you rightly want the public to have': Maxwell to Mullins, 21 Dec. 1938, PRO HO45/21034. Mullins said he bowed to the ruling given by Sir Alexander Maxwell (Permanent Under-Secretary of State at the Home Office) 'not because you convince me, but because I do not want any more trouble'. He accused Maxwell (who loyally supported Mullins throughout his magisterial career) of using 'pathetic' arguments; claimed that he was being criticised for refusing simply 'to bask in the sunshine of our glorious past'; and complained that Maxwell had 'a genius for (1) accepting the jam of reform propaganda by a magistrate and at the same time refusing to swallow the powder, and (2) discouraging the reforming magistrate from continuing his work'. Mullins claimed to walk 'humbly in the line of Zola and Pasteur' and that he deserved a 'gesture of support and thanks from the Home Office [which] would silence the unscrupulous critics of me and, what is more important, would quickly produce other reforming magistrates': Mullins to Maxwell, 31 Dec. 1938.

[78] Mullins claimed that there was 'nothing controversial in birth control in the true meaning of the words . . . What is controversial is contraception and I never have said, did not say in the . . . case, and will never say anything about that in court': Mullins to Maxwell, 31 July 1939, PRO HO45/21034. It may be doubted whether this distinction would be readily apparent to those described by Mullins in the same letter as 'too ignorant to know Christian teaching . . .'.

[79] The Lord Chancellor's Permanent Secretary wrote to the Home Office that 'the Lord Chancellor would be glad if you would be good enough to tell the Home Secretary that if he should see fit to rebuke Mullins, he would have the Lord Chancellor's support. The Lord Chancellor considers that observations of this nature made ex cathedra by a person holding a judicial office are gravely detrimental to the administration of justice. They can be made only for the purpose of obtaining publicity for the speaker and are in themselves grossly offensive to a large section of the population, I should explain that the Lord Chancellor would be of the same opinion if the views expressed . . . on this particular subject had been the opposite of those expressed on this occasion': Schuster to Maxwell, 21 July 1938, PRO HO45/21034. It seems doubtful whether the mild rebuke (Maxwell to Mullins, 3 Aug. 1939) administered to Mullins by the Home Office ('The Home Secretary . . . earnestly hopes that on future occasions you will refrain, when dealing with cases in your Court, from general comments which go beyond what is necessary and proper for disposing of the case on which it is your duty to adjudicate') would have satisfied Schuster.

[80] Maxwell minuted Morrison (PRO HO45/21034, 7 Dec. 1942) that, although he had had to 'talk firmly' to Mullins, he did not consider the incident provided a good ground for censuring him; and that on the contrary the right line would be 'to make some excuse and explanation for [Mullins] and to point out how easy it is for press reports to give a misleading impression by methods of selection and compression'.

[81] Morrison minuted Maxwell that he could not 'defend Mr Mullins—rather must I be critical . . . Magistrates must keep a curb on their tongues and understand that the Secretary of State has no obligation to defend them, just as they (or some of them) take the view that they have no need to take a/c of his views on these matters . . .': PRO HO45/21034, 7 Dec. 1942.

Morrison told the Commons[82] that Mullins's remarks were 'most regrettable'; the trouble and misunderstanding caused by the reporting of 'unguarded and inapt comments' should be present to the minds of all magistrates. Serious notice would be taken of 'any departure from the standards which are expected from those who exercise judicial functions'; and Morrison said the publicity given to the matter would serve 'to drive the lesson home'.

At an evidently tense interview,[83] Mullins complained to Morrison that he should not have been 'castigated' by the Home Secretary in Parliament;[84] but Morrison stood firm, and indeed refused Mullins's increasingly hysterical demands for a further meeting. Thereafter relationships between the Home Office and Mullins deteriorated; and the almost paranoid tone of the correspondence makes it—even at this distance of time—distressing to read.

Eventually, after fifteen years' service, Mullins retired from the bench[85] on the grounds of ill health.[86] He lived for a further twenty-one years—devoting much time to writing[87] and lecturing, playing an active part in marriage guidance, and continuing to take a close interest in law reform.[88] Although Mullins may well have been disappointed that his views no longer seemed to inspire the enthusiasm built up in the thirties for reforming the magistrates' domestic jurisdiction, his part in creating the pressure leading to the enactment of the 1937 Act entitles him to a place in the history of the family justice system. But to assess the true significance of that achievement requires us to return to the provisions of the 1937 Act.

[82] *Hansard (5th Series)* (HC) 15 Dec. 1942, vol. 385, col. 1784.

[83] On 29 Dec. 1942. Mullins had unwisely made a public attack on the 'yellow press' for reporting 'foul lies' (see e.g. *Daily Mail* 8 Dec. 1942) and complained to the Home Office that 'these Devils' had incessantly rung him up at home 'and made life a Hell'; and the Home Office note (PRO IIO45/21034) records Morrison as telling Mullins he had 'something of a persecution complex' with regard to the press, and that he had 'asked for trouble' by using 'abusive language about the press'. In response to Mullins's remark that if 'the Home Secretary was not prepared to support him he would find it necessary to take a long period of sick leave' Morrison bluntly told him that if he was unfit to carry on his work it would be his duty to resign. Mullins replied that he had no intention of resigning.

[84] Mullins subsequently wrote, 'I hope to forgive Herbert Morrison before I die but that stage has not been reached': C. Mullins, *Fifteen Years' Hard Labour* (1948) p. 149.

[85] He last sat on 10 Feb. 1947.

[86] Mullins complained that illness had 'haunted' him since 1936; and apparently a tumour affecting the pituitary gland was ultimately diagnosed and successfully treated, with the result that he had 'far better health in [his] sixties and seventies' than he had ever had in his fifties: C. Mullins, *One Man's Furrow* (1963) p. 159. Whatever the causation it is clear that Mullins was unable to follow the advice given him by Maxwell in 1942 to 'take the ups and downs of life more calmly'; but, as Maxwell recognised, it was Mullins's capacity to feel things deeply which gave him such energy and driving force: Maxwell to Mullins, 23 Dec. 1942, PRO HO45/21034.

[87] For a selective bibliography, see n. 26 above.

[88] Mullins gave carefully prepared evidence to the Royal Commission on Marriage and Divorce, Cmd. 9678, 1956, *Minutes of Evidence*, Day 13. He emphasised his conviction that the root of the problem was the concentration on legal rather than social issues; and he regarded the ready availability of Legal Aid for divorce as a serious misuse of resources. 'Social help' should be made available, through the medium of the magistrates' court, before the matter 'passed into the hands of lawyers': C. Mullins, *Marriage Failures and the Children* (1954) p. 30. His views 'struck no chord of sympathy' with the Royal Commission but seem consistent with the policy recently embodied in the Family Law Act 1996: see below.

THE PROVISIONS OF THE SUMMARY PROCEDURE
(DOMESTIC PROCEEDINGS) ACT 1937

The Act provided that the hearing of domestic proceedings be separated from hearings of other types of case;[89] that not more than three justices[90] including both a man and a woman[91] should hear domestic cases; and that the courts' procedures be adapted to enable unrepresented parties to 'tell their story in their own words'[92] (so that, for example, the court should where necessary itself put appropriate questions by way of examination or cross-examination[93]). In a further attempt to adapt the courts to usually unrepresented and often emotional litigants unused to expressing themselves to outsiders, the Act[94] accepted the Harris Committee's recommendation that where conciliation failed the probation officer or other conciliator should draft a statement of the allegations made by the parties, to enable the court itself to inquire into the case.

The Act also provided that only those with a legitimate interest in the case should be present at the hearing,[95] whilst press reporting was restricted along the lines already applying to the hearing of divorce cases.[96]

In all these respects, the Act was (as the Harris Report put it) intended to bring about a 'marked distinction in the atmosphere of the Court when it hears matrimonial cases from that when it hears criminal cases';[97] and thus to meet one of Mullins's declared objectives—providing 'decent conditions . . . for hearing the matrimonial troubles of wage-earners'.

But what of the machinery for 'conciliation' which the Act was claimed by its promoters to provide? It is true, as already noted, that the 1937 Act contained a provision[98]—which experience demonstrated to be of little practical effect[99]

---

[89] Summary Procedure (Domestic Proceedings) Act 1937, s. 2(1) (now Magistrates' Courts Act 1980, s. 69(1)).

[90] Perhaps one of the most significant changes subsequently made to much the same end was the requirement imposed by the Domestic Proceedings and Magistrates' Courts Act 1978, s. 80, that magistrates sitting in domestic cases should be members of a specialist panel: see, further, n. 124 below.

[91] Summary Procedure (Domestic Proceedings) Act 1937, s. 1 (now Magistrates' Courts Act 1980, s. 66(1)). Paradoxically these provisions did not apply to the metropolitan police courts (s. 9(1)); and it was only in 1964 that the Administration of Justice Act made the necessary provision. For a manifestation of the Metropolitan Magistrates' attitude to this change see Watson to Harris, PRO HO45/25034, 8 Dec. 1942.

[92] Harris Report, *Summary of Recommendations*, 15.

[93] Summary Procedure (Domestic Proceedings) Act 1937, s. 6 (now Magistrates' Courts Act 1980, s. 73).   [94] S. 4.

[95] Summary Procedure (Domestic Proceedings) Act 1937, s. 2(2)–(6) (now Magistrates' Courts Act 1980, s. 69(2)–(6)).

[96] Summary Procedure (Domestic Proceedings) Act 1937, s. 3 (now Magistrates' Courts Act 1980, s. 71). For the background to the 1926 Act see Ch. 4 above.   [97] Harris Report, para. 28.

[98] S. 4.

[99] See *Report of the Departmental Committee on the Probation Service* (1962) Cmnd. 1650, paras. 128–9 recommending that any report on conciliation should be limited to a statement whether the attempt had been successful or not; and in 1976 the Law Commission (*Report on Matrimonial*

—apparently intended to enable a conciliator to report the parties' complaints to the court 'not to be used as evidence but as a basis for the court's examination';[100] but with that exception the Act was totally silent on the subject.[101] In part this is because the Home Office considered that conciliation procedures could be introduced without legislation and undertook to draw magistrates' attention to the relevant recommendations of the Harris Report.[102] But in part it is because the Harris Report on which the Act was based rejected much of the philosophy which Mullins and others had so enthusiastically developed.

It is true that the Committee[103] declared that 'some machinery for conciliation [was] an essential part of the administration of the Acts relating to matrimonial disputes'; but its approach was cautious.[104] On one issue, however, it had no hesitation: it emphatically rejected the view—shared by Mullins and Lord Merrivale[105]—that conciliation was a proper function for the court itself to undertake. On the contrary, the line between adjudication and social work had to be preserved. The Committee was strongly hostile not only to procedures such as those envisaged by the 1934 Listowel Bill (which, as already noted, would have had the courts giving advice and assistance to husband and wife) but even to the modified procedures contemplating some degree of judicial involvement put forward by Lord Merrivale.[106] For the Harris Report, the court's true function should be to identify cases in which conciliation[107] might usefully be

Proceedings in Magistrates' Courts (Law Com. No. 77) para. 4.14) endorsed this view: see now Domestic Proceedings and Magistrates' Courts Act 1978, s. 26(2); and note that under the modern divorce law it is accepted that what is said in the course of conciliation is privileged and can only be disclosed in exceptional circumstances: see *Re D (Conciliation: Privilege)* [1993] 1 FLR 932, CA; *Practice Direction: Ancillary Relief Procedure: Pilot Scheme (16 June 1997)* [1997] 2 FLR 304.

[100] See para. 7 of the Home Office *Memorandum to Parliamentary Counsel*, PRO file HO45/17152/695967.

[101] The Home Office resisted suggestions by Mullins that the Bill should provide for the defendant's evidence to be given at an early stage in order to allow the court to understand the whole situation. Even the mild-mannered S. W. Harris (see n. 23 above) expressed himself with unusual force to Mullins on this point: 'we are going to have trouble enough with the Bill as it is. Whether we shall get it through Committee, in view of the opposition which developed . . . , seems very doubtful. To ask for further opposition . . . would be suicidal': PRO file HO45/15719.

[102] See the Home Office Minister's statement *Hansard (5th Series)* (HC) 5 Feb. 1937 vol. 319, col. 1978. Circulars had been issued on 30 July 1936 and 6 Sept. 1937.

[103] Harris Report, para. 13.

[104] Note, for example, the Report's statement that the success of conciliation had 'clearly been substantial and even if it were not so marked as is sometimes claimed, any failure cannot ordinarily be attributed to want of effort' (para. 14) and its acknowledgement (para. 16) of the 'real risk that conciliation may be carried too far' (as, perhaps, was to happen in the case of Mrs Esther Gough: see Ch. 9 below).

[105] And indeed by several subsequent Presidents of the Divorce Division: see text to n. 118 below.

[106] The Merrivale Bill (see n. 48 above) would have allowed 'Justices—and even a single Justice—at a private hearing where formal evidence is not taken to make, with the consent of the parties, orders which under the present law can only be made in public by a Court under strict legal procedure': Harris Report, para. 18.

[107] Which should always be voluntary: anything like forced conciliation might not only appear to be depriving the parties of their legal rights, 'but also may in the end aggravate the situation. Successful conciliation can only be arrived at by the consent and co-operation of both parties': Harris Report, para. 20.

attempted and the person to whom it should be entrusted, and to exercise such general supervision over the process 'as may be consistent with the judicial functions which it may be called upon to exercise at a later stage'.[108] Conciliation was to be primarily a matter for the probation service.

Against this background, it could be argued that in reality the most significant provision of the 1937 Act was that[109] which gave statutory recognition to the role of probation officers in conciliation[110] and other investigatory matters. Paradoxically one of the main effects of the 1937 Act and the events leading up to it seems in retrospect to have been to lay the foundation for the doctrine that conciliation—at least in the 'marriage-saving' sense in which it was then[111] universally used[112]—was not an appropriate function for the courts at all. As the Law Commission was to put it in 1976:[113]

---

[108] Harris Report, para. 18.

[109] S. 7. The Act also empowered probation officers to report to the court about the parties' financial means: s. 5 (see now Magistrates' Courts Act 1980, s. 72).

[110] The Act did not define the duties of probation officers in this respect, but guidance published by the Home Office in 1948 (*Memorandum on the Principles and Practices in the Work of Matrimonial Conciliation in Magistrates' Courts*) produced, for the use of probation officers, by a committee of probation officers and probation inspectors, Dec. 1948 (copy on PRO LCO2/6135, pp. 8–9) gives a very clear picture of what was then seen as the objective of conciliation. The probation officer, having seen the parties separately, should ask himself: 'How did this couple come to marry, what brought them together, and what has since gone wrong?' He should take them through their engagement and early married life. 'Bit by bit the story unfolds and the conciliator tries to see it as both see it. He watches, too, for any sparks of affection that could be rekindled, any common interests that can be revived and at the same time for the mistakes which were made and which should be avoided if the marriage is to be rebuilt. Now diagnosis begins to merge into mediation . . . The conciliator points out where he sees goodwill and constructive factors and also where he sees mistakes . . . Then comes consideration of what can be done. If the causes are agreed, are the couple prepared to try to remedy them and rebuild from the start with the help of the conciliator or a specialist, or do they feel the rift has grown too great? If so' the couple will need to consider the impact of separation for the children, and the 'economics of keeping two homes must also be discussed. Sometimes the realisation of these dilemmas will bring the two back to a fresh consideration of a way out, back to the possibilities of conciliation . . . Conciliation in the true sense of the word can be achieved only where there remains some affection between the two. There is then a desire to make the readjustment necessary to regain the respect and affection of the other, and it is the purpose of the conciliator to show how this can be done . . .'

[111] Thus, the Harris Committee evaluated the success of 'conciliation' procedures by the extent to which the parties did not pursue the legal remedy available from the courts; and the Home Office's description of the probation officer's role (see n. 110 above) strongly supports the view that this is the meaning then given to the word 'conciliation'.

[112] In 1974 the *Report of the Committee on One-Parent Families* (Chairman: Sir M. Finer, 1974, Cmnd. 5629, para. 4.305) drew a sharp distinction between 'reconciliation' ('reuniting persons who are estranged') on the one hand and 'conciliation' ('the process of engendering common sense, reasonableness and agreement in dealing with the consequences of estrangement') on the other. But the eloquent language of the *Finer Report* conceals the reality that this was in fact a *redefinition* of the word 'conciliation' in order to give it the sense which the Committee favoured as the desirable policy objective, i.e. encouraging the victims of family breakdown to wind up their failures with the least possible recrimination, but not encouraging the belief that reconciliations between people who went to court could often be achieved. This redefinition was almost universally adopted until, in the nineties, the synonym 'mediation' came to be favoured in preference to 'conciliation'; and 'mediation' is the term used in the context of the reformed divorce process to be introduced under the Family Law Act 1996.

[113] *Report on Matrimonial Proceedings in Magistrates' Courts* (Law Com. No. 77, 1976) para. 4.12.

The primary function of any court is adjudication and, while that certainly does not exhaust its functions, a careful limit must be set to any functions going beyond adjudication.

This was very far from the view taken by Mullins of the court being itself involved in social work; and although lip-service continued to be given to the notion that the court might have a contribution to make at least in identifying cases in which there was some prospect of reconciliation this increasingly seemed remote from reality.[114] Mullins's dream of the magistrates' court as the central point in a harmonised system of social work and legal provision was apparently dead beyond recall. 'Conciliation' was indeed available in many courts,[115] but it was provided by the probation service, not by the bench. Subsequent official inquiries, from the Denning Committee's Report in 1947[116] to the Finer Report in 1974,[117] accepted the need rigorously to separate the functions of adjudication and welfare provision.

Perhaps they were right to do so. But it is interesting to note that three successive Presidents of the Divorce Division have refused to accept the view[118] that conciliation is not properly a function for the court itself: Lord Merrivale's 1934 Matrimonial Causes (Amended Procedure) Bill[119] envisaged the court mediating between the parties; in 1945 Lord Merriman put forward a scheme to refer undefended divorce cases to Commissions of Conciliation and Enquiry with tribunals including lawyers and social workers;[120] whilst in 1966 Sir Jocelyn Simon

---

[114] The Domestic Proceedings and Magistrates' Courts Act 1978, s. 26, requires the court to consider whether there is any possibility of reconciliation between the parties before deciding whether to exercise its powers to make financial orders; and provides for reference to a probation officer or other person to attempt to effect a reconciliation. However, it appears that few references were made under this provision: see A. Guymer and P. Bywaters, 'Conciliation and Reconciliation in Magistrates' Domestic Courts' in T. Marshall (ed.), *Magistrates' Domestic Courts* (Home Office Research and Planning Unit Paper 28, 1984) pp. 24 ff. The Divorce Reform Act 1969 was described in its long title as 'an Act to facilitate reconciliation in matrimonial causes' but the substantive provisions which it contained to that end seem to have had little practical impact: see S. M. Cretney, *Principles of Family Law* (4th edn. 1984) pp. 188–90.

[115] For a full account of the practice as it had developed after World War II see the (Finer) *Report of the Committee on One-Parent Families* (1974, Cmnd 5629) paras. 4.295–4.314; and note also the discussion of reconciliation and conciliation in the Law Commission's *Report on Matrimonial Proceedings in Magistrates' Courts* (Law Com. No. 77, 1976) paras. 4.9–4.17.

[116] *Committee on Procedure in Matrimonial Causes* (1947, Cmd. 7024): see generally Ch. 6 below.

[117] *Report of the Committee on One-Parent Families* (1974) Cmnd. 5629. The Finer Report rejected out of hand the concept—founded in a 'social work philosophy which regards family breakdown as a phenomenon to be dealt with primarily by diagnosis and treatment'—of the family court as an essentially therapeutic institution concerned to diagnose and cure the underlying cause of family disorder. Whilst the courts should certainly encourage reconciliation, make orders designed to promote the welfare of those affected, and in suitable cases refer questions of reconciliation and welfare to other more appropriate agencies they should not assume responsibility for either reconciliation or welfare.

[118] Others with practical experience of the family justice system have also favoured a different approach: see B. Mortlock (the pseudonym of a distinguished London solicitor), *The Inside of Divorce* (1972) for the case for tribunals discussing 'the particular family matter in a friendly relaxed atmosphere in order to decide how best to effect the reorganisation with the smallest disadvantage to anybody'.   [119] See n. 48 above.

[120] See Ch. 6 below.

expressed the view[121] that adjudication in family matters should be regarded as a social service, supervening on other social services.[122]

Be that as it may, the belief that the court's role is to be restricted to adjudication has become so much part of the orthodox understanding of the legal process that it seems now pointless to question it;[123] but at least it is now universally accepted that there must be a social work input into the family justice system and that the judiciary must be properly trained.[124] Claud Mullins deserves to be remembered as a pioneer of these views even if the structures and methods whereby social work is delivered are not those he originally advocated.

In one other respect Mullins's views seem recently to have enjoyed something of a revival. He was, as we have seen, an enthusiastic proponent of the view that the legal system could and should be used to promote reconciliation;[125] and, after a period in the seventies and eighties when the idea that reconciliation could plausibly be an objective of the legal system became unfashionable, the Family Law Act 1996 marked a return to the view that it is for the legal system to encourage the parties to take all practicable steps (by counselling or otherwise) to save a marriage which may have broken down.[126]

---

[121] In a letter to the then Chairman of the Law Commission, Scarman J: PRO BC3/387, 22 June 1966. Simon was critical of arguments based on the separation of powers (a 'fundamental principle of the American constitution, but . . . certainly not of the British') and thought that 'we are putting our feet into a trap laid by Montesquieu for the French monarchy'.

[122] Sir Jocelyn believed there should be a three-stage process for dealing with marriage breakdown: '(a) marriage guidance to ascertain whether spouses will not . . . ultimately be better off on a reconciliation of those differences; (b) marriage guidance to secure, on a failure of complete reconciliation, the maximum agreement on . . . ancillary matters . . . ; (c) in the face of continued and irreconcilable differences on any of these points, adjudication'. See also *S* v. *S* [1968] P. 185, Sir J. Simon, P, for the public announcement of an experimental scheme and some reference to the division between adjudication and welfare provision; and *Practice Note (Divorce: Conciliation)* [1971] 1 WLR 223.

[123] Although the Family Law Act 1996 seeks to promote reconciliation, Lord Mackay of Clashfern has stated his view of the primary role of courts being to resolve disputes 'where an authoritative judicial decision has something positive to contribute to a family's well being': *Official Report* (HL) 31 Jan. 1991, vol. 925, col. 799.

[124] Magistrates sitting in Family Proceedings Courts are required to undergo an approved syllabus of training. This extends to attachment and the effect of separation and divorce on children, approaches to child rearing in families of varying ethnic origin, signs of emotional, physical and sexual abuse and the treatment of children who have been abused, and the services available to assist families and children in need: *Children Act Advisory Committee, Final Report*, June 1997, Annex B.

[125] Mullins did later come to take a rather broader view of the functions of conciliation, writing that the process 'involves a patient hearing of the married partner or partners in difficulty by someone with wide social experience who has studied marriage problems, the laying of emphasis on the best interests of the children of the marriage, the offering of suggested means of improving the situation, and, where necessary, an explanation of the different remedies provided by law . . . If a wife or husband is really determined, after careful consideration of all the relevant issues, to break up the marriage and to apply for legal relief, conciliation does not stand in the way.' He was also—anticipating the policy adopted in the 1995 *Divorce White Paper*: see now Family Law Act 1996, s. 8, under which people contemplating divorce are to be made to 'face up to the consequences of their actions and make arrangements to meet their responsibilities'—insistent on the need for the parties to understand the consequences of the process being put in motion: see *Marriage Failures and the Children* (1954) p. 26; *Fifteen Years' Hard Labour* (1948) pp. 134–5.

[126] Family Law Act 1996, s. 1(b). But the Act does not involve the courts in the provision of counselling or reconciliation services: see S. M. Cretney and J. M. Masson, *Principles of Family Law* (6th edn. 1997) pp. 328–33.

Finally, although the extent to which magistrates' courts were able effectively to separate domestic proceedings from the criminal work which constitutes so much of their business remains to some extent unclear,[127] the procedural provisions of the 1937 Act restricting publicity and so on laid a solid basis for further reform.[128]

CONCLUSION

All in all, the enactment of the 1937 Act was a significant achievement; and Mullins is entitled to a place in the pantheon—not overcrowded with judges—of 'trouble makers',[129] whose refusal to accept the conventional wisdom has effectively promoted a good deal of social progress.[130] It seems impossible to fault the assessment made by the Permanent Under-Secretary of State at the Home Office[131] on Mullins's retirement:

Although Mr Mullins has from time to time done indiscreet things and landed himself in troubles for which he is himself to blame, something ought to be said in appreciation of his work. With his egoism and assertiveness he has combined a very genuine zeal for improving the work of the Courts and for helping the numerous classes of unfortunate people with whom the Summary courts come into contact. He has written several excellent books on aspects of Court work and contributed numerous articles and speeches

---

[127] The Finer Report gave currency to the view that the criminal atmosphere it associated with the magistrates' courts, and their almost exclusively working-class clientele, evidenced the fact that these courts had been designed to meet the 'special and cruder requirements of the poor': *Finer Report* vol. 2, App. 5, para. 36. There is some more recent empirical evidence that the stigma of criminality has not been wholly eradicated from the magistrates' domestic court: see *The Overlapping Family Jurisdiction of Magistrates' and County Courts*, by M. Murch (with M. Borkowski, R. Copner and M. Griew), University of Bristol (1987).

[128] Progress has also been made in improving the physical amenity of Family Proceedings Courts and thereby diminishing the stigmatisation noted by Mullins and identified by subsequent research. Major rebuilding schemes have taken place; and a conspicuous example of what can be achieved is provided by the opening in 1997 of the refurbished Inner London and City Family Proceedings Court situate in the West End of London and serving the twelve Inner London Boroughs and the City of London. No criminal cases are heard in the seven courtrooms, which were refurbished to provide what the court service described as 'a light and relaxed atmosphere consistent with the informal approach taken in family proceedings'.

[129] The assertion made by Mullins to Maxwell on 28 Oct. 1936 that 'one day . . . the whole Home Office will realise that I am a tactful person' (PRO HO45/24151) would seem to indicate a certain lack of self-awareness on his part.

[130] As the historian A. J. P. Taylor put it in his 1956 Oxford Ford Lectures, *The Trouble makers —dissent over foreign policy 1792–1939* (Hamish Hamilton, 1956), without such people 'we should still be living in caves'.

[131] Maxwell to Chuter Ede (Home Secretary, 1945–51), 3 Feb. 1947, PRO HO45/21034. In 1942 Maxwell had, as noted, supported Mullins, and—conceding that he 'was in no sense a gentleman'— urged that he had 'virtues not possessed by some of his gentlemanly colleagues who seem to have become magistrates for the sake of a quiet and comfortable life': Maxwell to Morrison, 9 Dec. 1942, PRO HO45/21034.

in favour of reforms, such, for example, as reforms in connection with the conduct of domestic proceedings.[132]

Mullins might reasonably claim that 'on balance his influence [had] been for the good'.[133]

---

[132] Ede duly wrote in the terms of Maxwell's draft commenting on the 'spirit of resolution and fortitude which has enabled you to continue your exacting public work' in the face of illness; and expressing 'warm appreciation of the zeal with which you have sought to improve the work of the Courts of Summary Jurisdiction, and of the value of the contributions which you have made to this cause as a writer and speaker': Chuter Ede to Mullins, 5 Feb. 1947, PRO HO45/21034. Mullins would have been less than human had he not contrasted these words with the views expressed by Morrison at their meeting five years earlier: see text to n. 83 above.

[133] *Fifteen Years' Hard Labour* (1948) p. 9.

6*

'Tell me the Old, Old Story':[1]
The Denning Report, Divorce and Reconciliation

INTRODUCTION

As World War II drew to a close in 1945, the legal system faced crisis. On 3 September 1945[2] Lord Jowitt, Lord Chancellor in the recently elected Labour Government,[3] informed the Cabinet that the judicial system was barely able to cope with the number of divorce petitions currently being entered,[4] and that it was likely to collapse under the avalanche of cases expected to be entered for trial in the near future. What was to be done?

The story—culminating in the appointment of the Denning Committee[5] and that Committee's eloquent assertion that 'the reconciliation of estranged parties to marriages is so important that the State itself should do all it can to assist reconciliation'—takes up one of the themes discussed in Chapter 5. As shown in that Chapter, the Summary Procedure (Domestic Proceedings) Act 1937 gave formal recognition to a system under which probation officers were involved in seeking to reconcile married couples. However, there was no counterpart to this in the divorce court. At one time it could be said that there was no scope for reconciliation in the divorce court because the social stigma of divorce meant that only those whose marriages were broken beyond any possibility of repair would

---

* The material in this Chapter was first published as an article under the title ' "Tell me the old, old story"—the Denning Report 50 years on' in [1995] CFLQ 163.

[1] Verse 2 of this hymn (by Arabella C. Hanley, 1834–1911), once popular with the Salvation Army and other religious groups, continues: 'Tell me the story often, for I forget so soon; the early dew of morning has passed away at noon'.

[2] Lord Chancellor's Memorandum to the Cabinet: CP 45, 3 Sept. 1945.

[3] The divorce problem—which continued to cause Jowitt the 'greatest worry and the greatest anxiety': *Official Report* (HL) 13 Nov. 1946, vol. 144, col. 67—had also weighed heavily on Jowitt's predecessor as Lord Chancellor, Lord Simon; and three of the five matters to which Simon drew his successor's attention as needing attention related to divorce and its administration—the other two were apparently trivial personal matters: see 'Memorandum to my Successor', July 1945, LCO2/4197.

[4] 19,000 petitions were filed in 1944, as compared with 8,703 in 1939. However, there was a large backlog of cases—Jowitt estimated as many as 25,000—caused by the collapse of the system of Legal Aid for the Armed Forces and those cases would come into the court system once the problems of personnel (and in particular the shortage of copy-typists, in part accounted for—according to Ernest Bevin, Minister of Labour, Bevin to Simon 23 Mar. 1945, LCO2/4197—by the reluctance of women to deal with the sordid subject matter) had been remedied.

[5] The Committee on Procedure in Matrimonial Causes (1947, Cmd. 7024).

petition. But the huge war-time increase in the number of divorce petitions[6] brought
that belief into question. Something ought to be done. But how could the issue of
reconciliation be best approached? Was reconciliation a matter for the courts or
for other (and if so which) agencies? These issues have a particular relevance in the
light of the emphasis placed by the Family Law Act 1996[7] on the need for the
law to support the institution of marriage, to encourage husband and wife to 'take
all practicable steps, whether by marriage counselling or otherwise, to save the
marriage', and to bring marriages which have broken down irretrievably to an end
'with minimum distress to the parties and to the children' and with 'questions
dealt with in a manner designed to promote as good a continuing relationship
between the parties and any children affected as is possible in the circumstances'.

It is necessary first to explore the background to the appointment of the Denning
Committee; and then to look at its recommendations and the response to them.
Finally, the significance of the Committee's work for the development of Family
Law can be assessed.

BACKGROUND TO THE APPOINTMENT OF THE DENNING COMMITTEE: (I) COPING WITH THE FLOOD

At first, Lord Chancellor Jowitt believed the solution for what he saw as a temporary situation arising from the social disruption associated with the war[8] would
be to confer jurisdiction to deal with undefended divorces on the divorce registrars. But the Law Officers[9] were unimpressed by this proposal[10] and favoured
the more radical course[11] of transferring jurisdiction in divorce from the High

---

⁶ See n. 4 above.   ⁷ S. 1(a), (b) and (c).

⁸ 'If the experience of the last war [when the number of petitions rose to 5,184 in 1919 but had
fallen back to 2,468 by 1922] proves any guide we should be able in two or three years time to cope
with all the divorce cases with our existing judge power': CP 45, para. 5; and see *Official Report*
(HL) 26 Mar. 1946, vol. 140, col. 356. See also Jowitt's letter of 7 Nov. 1946 (LCO2/3951) to Lord
Chief Justice Goddard: 'I hope and believe that this will prove to be largely a temporary problem,
unless it be the fact that the idea of Christian marriage has gone. It is a squalid business . . .'

⁹ A joint memorandum dated 24 Aug. (PRO file LCO2/4197) stated that 'on the principle that
half a loaf is better than no bread we cannot dissent from [words substituted in manuscript for 'we
agree with'] the proposed legislation, but we consider that *at the best* it only meets half the problem [i.e. delay, as distinct from expense which the Law Officers saw as a 'grave social mischief'] and
that it does not solve that in the most satisfactory way'. Shawcross also wrote to Jowitt on 18 Sept.
saying that sooner or later in the lifetime of the present Parliament the problems would have to be
tackled more drastically, and that the solution was the County Court. He urged that outside London
the County Court judges were not unduly pressed (listing an average of eighteen sittings a month,
and very often a sitting was finished by lunch time); and that County Court judges had told him they
wished to have more to do.

¹⁰ Opinion in the Labour Party was far from universally impressed by claims for the preservation
of the High Court jurisdiction as had already emerged in interventions by Home Secretary Herbert
Morrison in the War Cabinet discussions. Shawcross sought to exercise pressure on Jowitt by saying that it was not impossible that 'some of the lawyers may divide the House against the Bill'.

¹¹ The most outspoken advocate of this course had been Sir F. D. MacKinnon, who regarded 'the
actual work' involved in undefended divorce cases—which he had been required to hear as a King's
Bench judge on circuit—'would be degrading to the meanest intellect'. He could not 'conceive why

Court to the County Court; whilst there was also opposition from those concerned that divorce might be seen to being made 'easier'. The Cabinet—notwithstanding the powerful argument that Jowitt's proposal had influential cross-party support[12] and that to adopt it would minimise the risk of becoming 'embroiled at the beginning of our term of office in a controversy about divorce, which in no way concerns the distinctive outlook of our party'—rejected the proposal and decided against any immediate legislation.[13] Instead, an additional divorce judge was to be appointed, and the Prime Minister was to consider the appointment of a ministerial committee to review the position generally with particular reference to the possibility of cheapening and expediting the procedure in divorce cases.[14]

THE BACKGROUND: (II) PART OF A GENERAL REVIEW
OF CIVIL PROCEDURE?

Prime Minister Attlee soon came to feel that the problems of delay and expense were not confined to divorce;[15] and a ministerial committee was established[16] to

these cases cannot be heard in the County Court, and by its Registrar. It would still be hard on that capable official; for in fact they would not tax the powers of the stupidest man who was ever an acting-deputy-Registrar of a County Court': F. D. MacKinnon, *On Circuit 1924–1937* (1940) pp. 112–13.

[12] Jowitt's proposal was in substance identical to that put forward by Jowitt's predecessor Simon (see WP (45) 127, 1 Mar. 1945, LCO2/1497) and approved by the War Cabinet on 12 Mar. 1945. All the divorce judges save one approved the scheme, both the President and Lord Simon had undertaken to support it in the House of Lords, and Simon (when Lord Chancellor) had worked hard to overcome the Archbishop of Canterbury's threat—'If a Bill of this sort is contemplated . . . the Church would certainly wish to oppose it with all its might and to have full time to assemble its forces': Fisher to Simon 24 Mar. 1945—and given a number of assurances to the Archbishop in a long letter dated 12 Apr. 1945. The Archbishop might have been disconcerted to know that one of the Lord Chancellor's senior officials (G. P. Coldstream) had written to the President on 25 Apr. 1945 saying that he hoped they would not feel themselves 'bound too closely by the terms of the Lord Chancellor's letter to the Archbishop'; whilst the unctuous tone of Simon's letter to Fisher—for example, the passage in which he urged Fisher to keep the list of those to be told about the proposal 'narrow and well selected' to avoid 'tendentious articles and hints in unauthorised quarters' and concluding 'I need not tell you, my dear Archbishop, how much I hope that our first contact in the legislative field should exhibit an agreement not unworthy of the ancient traditions of the Woolsack when that awkward piece of furniture was usually occupied by a distinguished Ecclesiastic, though I will not offer the instance of Cardinal Wolsey as the model of how to deal with divorce law! Yours very sincerely . . .' —may provide some clue as to why Simon—a statesman and lawyer of outstanding gifts—was not widely popular or indeed universally trusted.

[13] Jowitt commented to Merriman on 20 Sept. 1945 (LCO2/4197) that the problem was indeed 'thorny and difficult . . . I do not wonder that my colleagues are reluctant to get their hands scratched'. [14] CM (45) 34th Conclusions, LCO2/4197.

[15] 'Although the discussion at Cabinet was mainly directed to the problem of the high cost and long delays involved in divorce proceedings, the wider question of cost in litigation in general was also touched on and since the meeting the Chancellor of the Exchequer [Hugh Dalton] has suggested that this wider question should be made the subject of inquiry. The question of expense must, in turn, lead on to the question of procedure—for complicated procedure contributes very largely to the high cost of litigation . . .': Attlee to Jowitt, 12 Oct. 1945, LCO2/3927.

[16] Under Jowitt's chairmanship. The other members were the Home Secretary (J. Chuter Ede), the Minister of Education (Ellen Wilkinson), the Minister of Health (Aneurin Bevan), the Minister of Town and Country Planning (Lewis Silkin), the Law Officers and the Lord Advocate: see Cabinet Secretary's Note CP(45) 264, 7 Nov. 1945.

consider whether there were grounds for an inquiry into the whole system of administering civil justice with a view to reducing the cost of litigation.[17] But the Lord Chancellor and his officials were clear that 'no other class of civil proceedings presents problems in any way comparable to the urgent problem of divorce';[18] and fortunately the terms of reference allowed the ministerial Committee to make an interim report on the divorce issue. This it set out to do;[19] but it soon became apparent that, in this area, few issues were simple or uncontroversial. At its first meeting, the Committee decided to recommend the abolition of the six-month waiting period between decree nisi and absolute in the interest of reducing delay; but the Committee then found itself faced with a cogently argued paper[20] from the King's Proctor[21] urging that this recommendation be reconsidered.[22] The King's Proctor's view was all the more difficult to resist because the President of the Probate, Divorce and Admiralty Division[23] had already made it clear that he believed the interval between decree nisi and decree absolute gave an opportunity for the 'reconstruction of a broken marriage'.[24] But much the most important development —not only for its influence on the decision to set up the Denning Committee but also, directly and indirectly, for many subsequent developments—was a far-reaching proposal put forward by the President.

THE BACKGROUND: (III) PRESIDENT MERRIMAN'S SCHEME FOR STATUTORY TRIBUNALS OF CONCILIATION AND INQUIRY

On 9 January 1946 Lord Merriman wrote to Jowitt[25] suggesting[26] that Commissions of Conciliation and Inquiry be set up by statute. Undefended divorce

---

[17] The terms of reference are set out in the Cabinet Secretary's Minute of 7 Nov. 1945, CP(45) 264.

[18] Draft Memorandum prepared by G. P. Coldstream for the Committee: LCO2/3927.

[19] In the event, the Committee took no action on other civil litigation; and on 13 Oct. 1946 the Prime Minister directed that the Committee be abolished.   [20] See LCO2/3927, 31 Dec. 1945.

[21] i.e. the Treasury Solicitor, T. S. Barnes.

[22] Barnes considered that in undefended divorce proceedings the whole story was hardly ever before the court, and that the judge could only get at the truth in some cases with the assistance of an independent officer such as the King's Proctor whose duties include preventing abuse of the court's process. But perhaps most telling was his conclusion that abolition would 'arouse considerable opposition from the large number of people who hold the opinion that facilities for divorce should not be made easier and whose opposition may be supported by some of the considerations which I have mentioned' (para. 9).

[23] Lord Merriman: see his letter to Jowitt dated 27 Aug. 1945. For Merriman's controversial personality see text to n. 71 below.

[24] The need to avoid any step which might hinder a reconciliation was also (it has been said) the reason underlying the rule that no order for permanent financial support can be made until decree nisi (*Pounds* v. *Pounds* [1994] 1 FLR 775, 776, per Waite LJ) and no such order takes effect until decree absolute: see now Matrimonial Causes Act 1973, ss. 23(5), 24(3).   [25] LCO2/2971.

[26] Lord Merriman's scheme was—as will appear—developed, with strong encouragement from the Lord Chancellor and others.

cases would be referred to tribunals consisting of a lawyer and welfare worker or probation officer.[27] The tribunal would first consider the possibilities of effecting a reconciliation between the parties. If there were no reconciliation[28] the tribunal would, by consent, deal with financial and custody issues. Eventually, the case would be remitted to the court;[29] and, in the absence of any objection, a decree (including relevant ancillary orders[30]) would be pronounced. The role of lawyers (and the potential of lawyers for engaging in 'unhelpful recrimination'[31]) would thus be greatly reduced.[32] This scheme[33] attracted the unanimous approval of the divorce judges[34] and of the Archbishops[35]—'a fact which was

[27] The question of the qualifications of the lay people to be involved in this way remained troublesome. Although the work of probation officers in the matrimonial jurisdiction of the magistrates' courts was long established (and had, as seen in Ch. 5, been reinforced by the provisions of the Summary Procedure (Domestic Proceedings) Act 1937) the Denning Committee was apparently concerned that 'better class parties would not readily turn to probation officers or a state service' and it considered the employment of 'voluntary workers of superior class': see the note of a discussion between the Assistant Secretary in charge of the Probation Department in the Home Office and T. G. Skyrme (Secretary of the Denning Committee) on PRO file HO45/25202.

[28] Merriman accepted that attempts at reconciliation would be unsuccessful in many, perhaps most, cases; but considered, first, that it was 'the successes that matter, as in the Parable of the Lost Sheep', and secondly, 'that if the scheme as a whole appeals to the public imagination the educative effect of the reconciliatory procedure may be a great, if imponderable gain': see his further letter to Jowitt, 8 Feb. 1946, LCO2/3928.

[29] One of the matters upon which Merriman and others felt strongly was that the dissolution of a marriage should under no circumstances be allowed to become an administrative (as distinct from a judicial) act and he attached importance to the fact that his proposals would avoid this: Merriman to Jowitt, 8 Feb. 1946, LCO2/3928.

[30] There would be no separate ancillary relief proceedings, but a single 'comprehensive but informal' investigation: Merriman to Jowitt, 9 Jan. 1946, LCO2/3927.

[31] Merriman to Jowitt, 8 Feb. 1946, LCO2/3928.

[32] Merriman explained to Jowitt that it was essential that the hearing should be in camera and informal; and although he 'would not preclude' [*sic*] the attendance of legal advisers the tribunal should be able to insist on a private interview with either party or with both: Merriman to Jowitt, 8 Feb. 1946, LCO2/3928.

[33] There was no proposal at this stage to amend the substantive law governing the availability of divorce; and there was strong opposition to any notion that divorce should be available by consent: see, for example, the Hon. Mr Justice Denning, *The Divorce Laws* (1947) p. 6: 'Marriage is not a contract which the parties can mutually agree to rescind. It confers a status in which others besides the parties are interested. The parties to it bring forth children . . . Society itself, for the sake of the children, cannot allow the unity of family life to be broken by the consent of the parties. Hence in this country the fundamental rule that divorce by mutual consent is not allowed.' The opposition to consensual divorce accounted for the considerable concern that opportunities for collusion should not be increased. Merriman took the view that his scheme would tend to promote greater reality in divorce proceedings and reduce collusion: Merriman to Jowitt, 9 Jan. 1946, LCO2/3927. However, the need to be satisfied that the charges in the petition were true created difficulties; but Merriman's robust view was that priority should be given to the 'enormous body of cases in which the facts are plain and in which the Respondent is at least as anxious as the Petitioner for a divorce and, very often, has said so . . .': Merriman to Jowitt, 8 Feb. 1946, LCO2/3927.

[34] Merriman to Jowitt, 17 Jan. 1946, LCO2/3927.

[35] The Archbishop of Canterbury wrote to Jowitt on 19 Apr. 1946 (LCO2/3928) urging that Merriman's scheme 'does something to deal with the social questions involved and would really help to stem the tide of divorce by enabling people primarily interested in reconciliation to meet both parties . . .'. But by then the decision to appoint the Denning Committee had been taken.

very valuable politically'[36]—whilst the Lord Chancellor[37] told Merriman that he personally[38] thought Merriman had 'hit upon a really great idea, which may do very much to reform our marriage laws'. But the Law Officers presented a united and hostile front; and in the end, the Committee on Reform of Legal Procedure agreed not to express any view on the matter but rather to recommend examination by a new committee. This was accepted. On 26 June 1946 the appointment of the Denning[39] Committee[40] was announced.[41] The Committee's terms of reference were:

to examine the present system governing the administration of divorce and nullity of marriage in England and Wales; and, on the assumption that the grounds upon which marriages may now be dissolved remain unchanged,[42] to consider and report upon what procedural reforms ought to be introduced in the general interests of litigants, with special reference to expediting the hearing of suits and reducing costs and to the Courts in which such suits should proceed; and in particular whether any (and if so, what) machinery should be made available for the purpose of attempting a reconciliation between the parties, whether before or after proceedings have been commenced.

---

[36] As Jowitt told his colleagues: Minutes of the Committee on Reform of Legal Procedure, 5 Apr. 1946, RLP(46) 3rd meeting, LCO2/3928.

[37] Jowitt thought the scheme would bring the parties together in private, and that this was the only way in which attempts at reconciliation had any prospect of success: Minutes of the Committee on Reform of Legal Procedure, 4 Feb. 1946, RLP(46) 2nd meeting, LCO2/3927.

[38] 'notwithstanding the fact that I am a lawyer'—it appears that the lawyers on the Committee were doubtful whether Merriman's scheme could be made to work: Jowitt to Merriman 5 Feb. 1946, LCO2/3928.

[39] The Committee on Reform of Legal Procedure had noted the view that since the Committee would have to consider 'social' issues as well as technical subjects such as costs and procedure it would probably be better not to have a legal chairman (see minutes of meeting on 5 Apr. 1946). In the event, although the name of Lord Lindsay, Master of Balliol College Oxford, was considered as chairman it was decided to approach Denning (recently translated from the Divorce to the King's Bench Division). Although Lord Denning has recorded his distaste for divorce work ('sordid in the extreme': *The Due Process of Law* (1980) p. 189) his work there was admired by Jowitt (who told Denning in 1949 that he congratulated himself on realising that 'sitting in the Divorce Court you used to be wasting your sweetness on the desert air': PRO LCO2/4617); whilst Lord Uthwatt had on 28 Apr. 1945 told the Lord Chancellor's Permanent Secretary that Denning was wasted in the Divorce Court notwithstanding the fact that he was the only judge there who gave proper consideration to the children's welfare.

[40] The membership had been considered by the Committee on Legal Procedure which did not want the Committee to be dominated by lawyers. It accepted that someone 'e.g. a working class woman' who could be expected to make a valuable contribution to discussion of the social issues 'would be unable to contribute much if anything' on legal matters; and it appears that two such women were appointed. None of the lawyers (T. Donovan KC MP, John Foster MP, and Ethel Lloyd Lane from the Bar and solicitors Sir Edwin Herbert and Eric Davies) were divorce specialists; but Dr Grace Calver had a substantial psychiatric practice of referrals from the Tavistock Clinic, and this experience led to her being preferred to Mrs Geoffrey Fisher—wife of the Archbishop of Canterbury—who had seven children and was active in the affairs of the Mother's Union.

[41] *Official Report* (HL) vol. 141, col. 1152.

[42] The Committee did in fact note 'for consideration' a number of proposed reforms of the substantive law, not least that separation for seven years might be a ground for divorce: see *Committee on Procedure in Matrimonial Causes* (1947, Cmd. 7024) para. 86(iii).

THE DENNING COMMITTEE AT WORK:
(I) THE FIRST INTERIM REPORT

The Denning Committee[43] wasted no time.[44] Within a fortnight it began to hear evidence[45] and by the end of the month its first Interim Report[46] had been presented[47] and acted[48] on by Government.[49] The six-month period between decree nisi and decree absolute allowed for the King's Proctor to make investigations into collusion and other matters and for him or others to intervene to prevent the marriage being finally terminated was reduced from six months to six weeks; and this decisive action suggested that the Committee was not afraid to propose radical reforms.

THE DENNING COMMITTEE AT WORK:
(II) THE SECOND INTERIM REPORT

The Committee continued to work with remarkable speed; and before the end of 1946—and indeed before the Committee had finished hearing all the

[43] Lord Denning subsequently wrote (in *The Due Process of Law* (1980): 'The Committee was a good one . . . Tom Skyrme [the Secretary] was most efficient. We took no time off from Court. We sat in a committee room in the Lords from 4.30 p.m. to 7 p.m. We worked quickly. No Committee has ever worked so quickly or so well.' The minutes of the Committee's deliberations available in the Public Record Office (file PRO LCO2/3947) are sparse.

[44] No doubt it was aware of the fact that its appointment had been greeted with 'rather heavily diluted enthusiasm' by some (such as the Marquess of Reading: *Official Report* (HL) 26 June 1946, vol. 141, col. 1152) who thought the inevitable result would be unnecessary delay.

[45] The oral evidence (heard, from 78 witnesses, between July and Dec. 1996) was transcribed and is available on PRO file LCO2/3948; and there were 58 written memoranda: see *Final Report of the Committee on Procedure in Matrimonial Causes* (Cmd. 7024, 1947) para. 2 and Appendix. It is also apparent from the correspondence that Denning interviewed a number of solicitors and managing clerks in private; and also consulted the staff of the Divorce Registry: see in particular Coldstream's note to the Law Officers for the debate on 6 May 1947 (below n. 81).

[46] (1946) Cmd. 6881. The Report is not dated, but was presented to Parliament in July.

[47] The Committee explained that the 'evidence already given' had convinced the Committee that the 'need for a reduction [in the period between decree nisi and decree absolute] appears so urgent and plain' that there should be no delay in dealing with it: para. 2. This statement is somewhat surprising, since the Committee only heard evidence from the King's Proctor—who, as we have seen, had reservations about interfering with the existing procedure sufficient to influence the Cabinet Committee to resile from its original view: see text to n. 20 above—on 17 July (i.e. after the Denning Committee had taken its decision). Many proponents of reform thought the two-stage divorce process should be abandoned, but the Denning Committee's Final Report (Cmd. 7024, 1947) paras. 58–64 recommended against so radical a course. The King's Proctor, Barnes, and his successor both subsequently told the *Royal Commission on Marriage and Divorce* (Cmd. 9678, 1956) that the reduced period was insufficient for them to make necessary enquiries; and the question of the length of the period of delay continued to cause problems: see Matrimonial Causes Act 1973, s. 1(5); Matrimonial Causes (Decree Absolute) General Order 1972; *Practice Note* [1972] 1 WLR 1261; *Dryden* v. *Dryden* [1973] Fam. 217.

[48] Coldstream had written to the President on 25 July 1946 saying that it seemed right to accept the recommendation: LCO2/4201, 4202. The departmental file (LCO2/3949) 'Denning Committee—1st Interim Report: Reduction of Period between Decree Nisi and Absolute' is still closed; and this fact excites curiosity if not suspicion.

[49] The Law Society protested that they had not been told what was to happen: see LCO2/4201.

witnesses[50]—it presented another Interim Report,[51] again justifying this piecemeal approach by emphasising the need for 'urgent action'.[52] But the Second Report was a considerable disappointment to those whose expectations of radicalism had been raised.

DIVORCE IN THE COUNTY COURT?

The first part of the Report dealt with the jurisdiction of the courts, and not only set the scene for divorce litigation for twenty years but was responsible for consequential changes[53] which have had a permanent effect on the administration of family law. The Report rejected the case—made increasingly forcefully over the years—for transferring jurisdiction over at least some categories of divorce to the County Court, and insisted[54] that divorce cases should continue to be determined by the 'Superior Courts of the country, assisted by the attendance of the bar'. To allow the County Court to assume jurisdiction[55] in divorce would—so the Committee declared—give insufficient recognition to 'the significance attaching to matrimonial causes of every kind'.[56] But the Committee's investigations made

[50] See n. 45 above.

[51] *Second Interim Report of the Committee on Procedure in Matrimonial Causes*, Cmd. 6945 (1946).

[52] Para. 1.

[53] Not least the decision that the District Registrars should have all the powers of a Registrar of the Divorce Registry: 'The District Registrars have shown themselves quite capable of dealing with applications for alimony pending suit, maintenance and the like, and there is no reason why they should not deal with the other kinds of ancillary relief which under the present system must proceed in London' (para. 11(vii)). Acceptance of this recommendation was the decisive step in the transformation of District Registrars from officers primarily concerned with the routine processing of the preliminary stages of civil litigation into judges (now, in recognition of this, called District Judges) mainly responsible for routine family law business and in particular for the exercise of the wide discretion to make financial orders conferred by the Matrimonial Proceedings and Property Act 1970. See generally W. Barrington Baker and others, *The Matrimonial Jurisdiction of Registrars* (1977) and P. W. J. Bartrip, 'County Court and Superior Court Registrars 1820–1875' in G. Rubin and D. Sugarman (eds.) *Lawyers, Courts and Industrial Society* (1984).

[54] Echoing the language of the *Royal Commission on Divorce and Matrimonial Causes* (1912) Cmd. 6478.

[55] This was a matter on which professional opinion remained irreconcilably divided: Lord Chancellor Simon (see LCO2/4197 Simon to Merriman, 29 Jan. 1945; and to Archbishop Fisher, 12 Feb.—'I shall remain wholly opposed to changes which would encourage the idea that this sort of suit can be dealt with lightly and without the full dignity of the law') had been strongly hostile as was the President; but Lord Chief Justice Goddard favoured the transfer of jurisdiction to deal with undefended divorce to the County Court, as did Sir Hartley Shawcross AG and other influential figures in the Labour Party. Lord Merriman's real objection was to solicitors having the right of audience—apparently, as the Lord Chancellor's Permanent Secretary Sir A. Napier subsequently noted, because he thought solicitors could not be trusted not to condone collusion. However, Napier's comment that Merriman was 'naturally reluctant to express [this view] in public' is unfair given what Merriman had told the House of Lords in a speech on 28 Nov. 1946, *Official Report*, vol. 144, cols. 480–2. It should be noted that Merriman's own professional life had started as a solicitor's articled clerk.

[56] *Second Interim Report of the Committee on Procedure in Matrimonial Causes*, Cmd. 6945 (1946) para. 9. The Committee took the view that if 'there is a careful and dignified proceedings such as obtains in the High Court for the undoing of a marriage, then quite unconsciously the people will have a much more respectful view of the marriage tie and of the marriage status than they would if divorce were effected informally in an inferior court': para. 4.

it clear that the seven High Court judges then in post could not be expected to cope with the existing caseload, much less with any increase.[57] The solution to the problem lay in what Lord Chancellor Gardiner subsequently[58] described as 'the usual brilliant English compromise'. All County Court judges would be appointed[59] Commissioners[60] of the High Court with power to try both defended and undefended divorce cases.[61] This would (so the Committee thought[62]) 'provide a solution for the pressing needs of the moment and also for the demands of the future'.

This recommendation was precisely what the Lord Chancellor's officials had wanted[63]—not least because it dealt with fears that the abolition of Workmen's Compensation Act arbitrations[64] would lead to under-employment of the County Court bench[65]—and it was swiftly implemented.[66]

---

[57] The Committee (see Cmd. 6945, para. 6(ii)) calculated that only one-third of the cases in the London list for the Michaelmas term would in fact be heard; and its demonstration that there were delays in the courts (as distinct from in the preliminary processing of service divorces) was a serious embarrassment to Jowitt, who had publicly committed himself to a contrary view: *Official Report* 26 Mar. 1946, vol. 140, col. 351.

[58] In the debate on the Matrimonial Causes Act 1967, *Official Report* (HL) 14 Feb. 1967, vol. 280, col. 169.

[59] (along with others suitably qualified) as Commissioners under the powers conferred by Supreme Court of Judicature (Consolidation) Act 1925, s. 70.

[60] It appears that this term was thought likely to indicate the special and high status of those so appointed; and it is to be noted that when Parliamentary Counsel (Sir G. Ram) drew the—in the end aborted—Bill to give effect to the War Cabinet's scheme of conferring jurisdiction on Registrars, he sought to 'minimise opposition' by designating those concerned 'commissioners' in case people were 'foolish enough to think that anyone wishing to dispose of a superfluous spouse by consent would only have to register him or her as no longer wanted by the same sort of process as would be applicable if the spouse were dead . . .': Ram to Coldstream 13 Apr. 1945, LCO2/4197.

[61] The *Report of the Royal Commission on Divorce and Matrimonial Causes* (1912, Cmd. 6478) had recommended that a number of County Court judges be so appointed; and it was said that the only difference was that the Denning proposals were 'comprehensive rather than selective': Marquess of Reading, *Official Report* (HL) 28 Nov. 1946, vol. 144, col. 471.

[62] *Second Interim Report of the Committee on Procedure in Matrimonial Causes*, Cmd. 6945 (1946), para. 11(ix).

[63] The device of appointing Commissioners had already been used in an attempt to deal with the backlog of service divorces: see Jowitt's statement, *Official Report* (HL) vol. 140, col. 358.

[64] By National Insurance (Industrial Injuries) Act 1946 s. 89(1).

[65] There had been some 5,000 Workmen's Compensation cases each year. The Denning Committee calculated that each of the fifty-seven County Court judges, by giving twenty days each year to divorce, could deal with 500 cases a year—a total of 28,500: *Second Interim Report of the Committee on Procedure in Matrimonial Causes*, Cmd. 6945 (1946) para. 7(i). But the hope that the transfer of jurisdiction to Commissioners would enable the Lord Chancellor to 'cut down my High Court judges from the present seven sitting in divorce to something like three or four . . .' (Jowitt to Dalton 2 Nov. 1946, PRO LCO2/3950) was not fulfilled.

[66] The Council of County Court judges had resolved on 2 Nov. 1946 to co-operate with the proposals which Jowitt had taken to the Cabinet on 7 Nov. The Government's intention to implement the scheme for divorce commissioners—paid as High Court judges for the days on which they sat in divorce—was announced on 13 Nov. 1946 and put into effect on 1 Jan. 1947: see the debate *Official Report* (HL) 28 Nov. 1946, vol. 144, col. 472. PRO file LCO2/3955 indicates that Coldstream and his staff had to work 'night and day' on implementation, and there is a great deal of correspondence on such matters as textbooks (the Lord Chancellor wished *Rayden on Divorce* to be the 'official textbook' although some difficulty was experienced in supplying sufficient copies) and robes (the Lord

A More Efficient Procedure?

Having settled the issue of the courts in which matrimonial suits should proceed, the Denning Committee went on, in the second part of the Interim Report, to make no less than forty-nine recommendations for procedural reforms which (it believed) would save much delay and expense[67]—all, it might be thought, comparatively[68] uncontroversial. But in fact many were strongly and effectively resisted; and the strength of the resistance was clearly affected by the way in which the Denning Committee handled the issues on which it had to report.

Brilliant Compromise—but Tactical Disaster?

The Committee justified its decision to deal with procedural matters in an Interim Report before turning to the issue of reconciliation procedures by announcing that it had concluded that 'any means for effecting reconciliation must function separately from judicial procedure'.[69] This bland statement did not make explicit what was clearly implicit in it—that the Committee had rejected the Reconciliation Tribunal scheme put forward, and worked out in considerable detail by the President of the Divorce Division.[70] Even worse, the Interim Report did not mention that scheme, much less give any reasons for not recommending its adoption. In the circumstances, it is not surprising that the President should have been 'ruffled'[71] not only by the—apparently summary—rejection of a scheme

Chancellor letting it be known that the judges should wear a black gown and not, in any circumstances, the purple robes of a County Court judge, and that he also wished them to wear a court black coat and waistcoat for which clothing coupons were not to be required). Coldstream reported that the results of the new procedure 'entirely justified the views of the Denning Committee, and incidentally, the confidence of the Lord Chancellor in the County Court Judges and in the County Court administrative system': Coldstream to Shawcross, Apr. 1947, LCO2/3958.

[67] Para. 12. The recommendations ranged from the apparently trivial (for example, that all petitions should be numbered) to those which were subsequently thought to involve major issues of principle (for example, whether a petitioner should be required to swear an affidavit in support of the petition): see n. 79 below.

[68] Archbishop Fisher made the point that greater procedural efficiency meant that divorce would be more rapidly—and thus more readily—available. But he accepted that even a bad law should not be impeded by merely procedural delays: see *Official Report* (HL) 28 Nov. 1946, vol. 144, col. 485, and *Official Report* (HL) 27 Mar. 1947, vol. 146, col. 887. It was said that the long delays sometimes resulted in reconciliation taking place 'from sheer weariness': Marquess of Reading, *Official Report* (HL) 28 Nov. 1946, vol. 144, col. 468.

[69] This was said to justify the decision to deal immediately with questions of courts and procedures, leaving discussion of reconciliation for the final report: Cmd. 6945, para. 3.

[70] See p. 140 above.

[71] Jowitt to Goddard, 7 Nov. 1946, LCO2/3951. As Jowitt put it, Merriman 'has not been treated with that consideration which he might have expected. It is . . . the fact that his own scheme . . . was passed over *sub silentio*, and it is further the fact that in regard to the detailed procedural reforms he was never asked about them.' Jowitt went out of his way in the House of Lords debates to emphasise how unwise it would be to commit the Government to change until he had had the fullest opportunity of discussing the proposals with Merriman 'in view of his great experience and knowledge': *Official Report* (HL) 13 Nov. 1946, vol. 144, col. 66.

which had attracted much support, but also by the fact[72] that the Denning Committee had without any consultation[73] made detailed recommendations about the procedural rules to govern the Division for which the President was responsible.[74]

The President, whilst scrupulously observing the proprieties in public,[75] did not conceal from the Lord Chancellor or the officials his 'bitter hostility'[76] to the Denning proposals. Although Merriman did come to accept that he could no longer press for his own original proposal[77] and was even prepared to concede that the Denning scheme for the appointment of Divorce Commissioners might well be successful 'provided always that the safeguards, particularly the audience of the Bar, are

[72] Merriman began a fifteen-page (single-spaced) letter of detailed comment dated 6 Nov. 1946 (PRO LCO2/3957) with the statement that he took 'serious exception' to the fact that he had not been consulted about a single point, 'more particularly as in this respect the [Denning] Report reads as if this Division had lagged behind other Divisions of the High Court in reforming its procedure. Actually the contrary is the fact . . .' For Coldstream, the situation raised 'extremely awkward' constitutional issues. Who was to advise the Lord Chancellor on the matters in dispute between the President—who was prepared 'grudgingly' to accept only twelve of the Denning recommendations, saying that the others are 'either misconceived or completely impracticable'—and the Denning Committee? 'The lesson to be learned [said Coldstream] is that no such inquiry ought to be allowed to be started unless we are quite sure that it is one which is likely to have the approval of the Head of the Division concerned': Coldstream to Napier, LCO2/3957, 26 Nov. 1946.

[73] Jowitt believed that he had 'calmed Merriman down a bit' (Jowitt to Goddard, 7 Nov. 1946, LCO2/3951); but Coldstream noted that Merriman had said 'what was plain to all of us, that he was near a breakdown'. Notwithstanding the officials' views about Merriman's state of health he died in office aged 81 (see *Ross-Smith* v. *Ross-Smith* [1963] AC 280, 291) having served as President for nearly thirty years.

[74] The Lord Chancellor's officials had had their doubts about Merriman's discharge of this responsibility. In Dec. 1944 Napier minuted the Lord Chancellor that it was 'possible (and even probable) that the President is not aware of this state of affairs' (i.e. the arrears in dealing with service divorces): PRO LCO2/4197; and, after the publication of the Denning Committee's interim reports, Coldstream (PRO LCO2/3951) expressed doubts to Jowitt as to whether the President understood that the motion put down by Lord Reading in Nov. 1946 was 'an attack on the *President's* own past and present administration'. There had also been complaints about the Admiralty work: see PRO file LCO2/3828, *Probate Divorce and Admiralty Division, Suggested Amalgamation with King's Bench Division* (which begins with a letter from the Treasury Solicitor alleging that 'Lloyds will not allow their cases to be tried by the President').

[75] See his speech on 28 Nov. 1946, *Official Report* (HL) vol. 144, col. 477: 'I only wish to say that no one reading [the] Report . . . would realize that there was a complete revision and simplification of the whole procedure and practice of the Division . . . in 1937 and again in 1944. In fact, neither I nor any of the judges—and particularly the two who are most versed in this matter, having spent all their professional lives in the Court—were consulted about any of these procedural recommendations. I therefore propose merely to say that at the moment I am not wholly convinced of the wisdom and efficiency of all of them.'

[76] Jowitt to Goddard, 7 Nov. 1946. Warned by Coldstream (in a 'highly confidential' minute of 24 Oct. 1946, PRO LCO2/3951) about the feelings expressed by Merriman in a post-prandial talk 'lasting about an hour, and occasionally of a somewhat painful character', Jowitt wrote an emollient letter to Merriman—'You and I this week-end are both going to engage on what I confess I find the rather unpleasant task of reading this draft Denning report': PRO LCO2/3950—and had a subsequent 'frank and friendly talk' with him. However, Jowitt made it clear that he was embarrassed (see n. 57 above) by Denning's analysis of the need for more judicial resources; and that he would be 'placed in a position of extreme difficulty' if he were questioned.

[77] See Merriman's dignified and reticent maiden speech in the House of Lords, *Official Report* 28 Nov. 1946 (HL) vol. 144, col. 475; n. 98 below.

strictly maintained',[78] he persisted in his opposition to many of the Denning procedural proposals; and passions were raised about matters which now would scarcely be thought worth discussion.[79] There was great embarrassment.[80] But eventually a means of dealing with these problems[81] was developed; and some—but by no means all—of the procedural changes which Denning had recommended were made.[82] It seems that personal relations between those concerned were permanently soured;[83]

[78] Merriman to Jowitt, 19 Nov. 1946, LCO2/3951.

[79] Such as the Denning proposal that a petitioner (who would still be required to give sworn evidence in open court) should no longer be required to swear an affidavit in support of the petition. There is an extensive correspondence, and on 15 Apr. Denning summarised twenty-five recommendations made by the Committee which he considered had not been fully implemented: LCO2/3959.

[80] Coldstream wrote to the Attorney-General on 6 Feb. 1947 that 'For better or worse the fact is that the story that the President and some of his puisnes on the one hand, and the Denning Committee on the other hand, are at loggerheads has gained currency—I regard that situation myself as something of a disaster, but it is no use trying to shut one's eyes to the facts. It is, I think, a pity that Denning J, and perhaps one or two other members of the Committee have been lobbying Hodson J.' Coldstream noted that although it was very difficult to annoy Hodson J about anything, the judge 'had been intensely irritated by Denning coming to see him and trying to persuade him to advise the President to accept this and that reform': LCO2/3957.

[81] In his minute of 26 Nov. 1946 (quoted at n. 72 above) Coldstream had suggested the Lord Chancellor seek the advice of Hodson J—who had been a divorce judge since 1937 whereas Denning had only been a judge of the Divorce Division for two years and (Coldstream said) 'as the President observed to me last night . . . he seemed to have learned very little'. In fact, in a skilful manoeuvre the President was persuaded to suggest the appointment of a committee under Hodson J; but unfortunately (as Coldstream subsequently remarked) 'the Hodson Committee regarded the consideration of each of the Denning recommendations on their merits as part of their functions'; and, although Jowitt told questioners that the Denning proposals had in the main been accepted, Denning himself pointed out that in fact only half the Committee's recommendations had been implemented. Pressure began to be exercised by the Labour Party's Legal and Judicial Group and by the Haldane Society (in a Memorandum which, according to Coldstream, Jowitt 'characterised as extremely impertinent'). The matter was brought to a head when two members of the Denning Committee—T. Donovan KC and J. G. Foster—initiated a debate in the House of Commons on 6 May 1947 (see *Official Report* (HC) vol. 437, col. 363); but the Attorney-General's defence (all the more remarkable to anyone who knew Shawcross's own preference for much more radical reform) seems to have quelled opposition for the time being. Shawcross's defence was based (i) on the high constitutional principle that it was for Government and Parliament to decide on whether or not to accept the advice of a Committee; (ii) on the perhaps more telling point that implementation of all the Denning proposals would only result in a saving of £4 in costs, and (iii) on the fact that none of the Committee's recommendations had been definitively rejected and that further consideration would be given to those which were outstanding. Coldstream commented to Jowitt that the Attorney-General had perhaps gone 'too far in suggesting that something would happen quickly, but I do not think that the House was in any way misled by this indiscretion': see his minute of 7 May 1947, LCO2/3958; and on 14 Oct. 1947 Coldstream warned Hodson that there was certain to be further parliamentary pressure for action.

[82] Coldstream's assessment (to Shawcross, 6 Feb. 1947, LCO2/3945) was that the 'scope and character of the reforms advocated by Denning are, *prima facie*, extremely attractive, inasmuch as they give the impression that the whole procedure in the Divorce Division is archaic, needlessly expensive and exists solely to provide impediments to the suitor. But I personally have been impressed by the criticisms which both Hodson J and Mr Registrar Pereira—two very fair-minded people with long experience of the Divorce Division—have made of the Denning proposals, and it seems fairly plain that on some at least of these proposals there is much to be said against their acceptance.'

[83] Lord Denning subsequently wrote: Merriman 'felt very strongly . . . He never forgave me. When I happened to go to his room afterwards on another matter, he said to me: "You are a blackguard" . . .': Denning, *The Due Process of Law* (1980) p. 192. Relationships between the Lord Chancellor's Office and Denning also seem to have cooled: there is interesting and revealing correspondence on Denning's Hamlyn Lectures, *Freedom under the Law*: see LCO2/4617 (1949).

and it is difficult to resist the feeling that the high emotions generated by the unhappy controversy about the Denning Committee's Interim Reports greatly weakened the impact[84] in government circles of what had been held out as the most important and constructive aspect of its work[85]—the improved machinery for reconciliation.

THE DENNING COMMITTEE AT WORK: (III) THE FINAL REPORT

Preparation of the Denning Committee's *Final Report*[86] seems not to have been significantly delayed by the furore over the earlier procedural reforms. The Committee dealt with a number of outstanding points on such matters as the rule in *Russell* v. *Russell*;[87] and the Committee made ambitious proposals—never implemented[88]—based on the principle that ancillary relief matters should be decided by the judge who dealt with the main divorce suit.[89] But in the long term its recommendations relating to children and reconciliation were more significant.

(a) The Welfare of Children

The Committee[90] recorded that no subject had caused it greater concern than that of the welfare of children; and found the divorce court's procedures 'but poorly fitted' for giving effect to the statutory requirement[91] requiring that consideration to be given paramount importance. The Committee considered that divorced parents had 'disabled themselves from fulfilling their joint responsibility'; and proposed that there should be court welfare officers who would have access to all petitions and would be empowered to report to the court in any case. The

---

[84] Archbishop Fisher (who was clearly aware of some of the background) tactfully expressed regret that 'what had first come to the public knowledge' were the Committee's proposals for more efficient divorce rather than for improving machinery for reconciliation: *Official Report* (HL) 28 Nov. 1946, vol. 144, col. 485.

[85] Jowitt's description: see *Official Report* (HL) 28 Nov. 1946, vol. 144, col. 506.

[86] Cmd. 7024.

[87] See Ch. 4 above. As already noted the Committee rejected proposals for the abolition of the decree nisi of divorce. Other topics dealt with in Part IV of the Report were: the rule excluding previous findings from being admitted in evidence, security for costs, the procedure for recording decrees, and the rules for jurisdiction in international cases. Official reaction to these proposals is to be found on PRO file LCO2/3964.

[88] Merriman did not accept this principle: see his comments to Jowitt, 20 Feb. 1947, LCO2/3962; and Jowitt accepted that these proposals 'require very careful consideration' and that we 'should certainly hesitate to adopt any proposal at the present time which is likely to slow up the work of the judges': Jowitt to Merriman, 27 Feb. 1947, LCO2/3957. The departmental file on 'Denning Committee, Second and Final Reports, Consideration of outstanding recommendations' LCO2/3964 remains closed.

[89] However, effect was given to some of the other proposals in Part III of the Report—for example, that the restrictions on the amount of maintenance orders made by magistrates should be modified and that the divorce court should itself have statutory power to order maintenance on the ground of neglect to maintain—by legislation over the years. [90] Para. 30.

[91] The requirement embodied in Guardianship of Minors Act 1925, s. 1.

Committee thought that the judge should in all cases deal with the future of the children on the same day as he dealt with the divorce.

The immediate impact of these recommendations may not have been great;[92] but in the long term it can reasonably be claimed that the Denning Committee marked a decisive shift in the approach taken by the law to the legal consequences of divorce in relation to children.[93]

(b) Reconciliation

The Committee's terms of reference (as we have seen) required it to give particular attention to the question whether machinery should be made available for the purpose of attempting reconciliation between the parties[94] and its Final Report appeared to give a clear and positive answer to this question. The 'preservation of the marriage tie' (the Committee declared) 'is of the highest importance in the interests of society' as well as to the parties and their children, and accordingly 'reconciliation should be attempted in every case where there is a prospect of success'.[95] It was indeed 'so important that the State itself should do all it can to assist reconciliation'.[96]

But how was this objective to be achieved? The Committee[97] first summarised Merriman's Commission of Conciliation and Inquiry proposal and (as all concerned knew would be the case[98]) rejected it. The Committee gave two reasons. First, work towards a reconciliation would not start until after proceedings had been started, whereas if reconciliation were to have any prospects of success it had to be attempted 'long before proceedings are begun'.[99] Secondly:

---

[92] Coldstream told Hodson J on 14 Oct. 1947 (file PRO LCO2/3959) that the prospect of the necessary legislation for the appointment of court welfare officers was 'exceedingly remote'; and although the Matrimonial Causes Rules 1947 did give effect to the Committee's recommendation that all divorce petitions contain a statement about the children, this requirement was (according to the *Royal Commission on Marriage and Divorce*, Cmd. 9678, 1956, para. 379) dropped because it was found that it did not achieve its object. The Royal Commission recommended a procedure which was intended to ensure that the court did examine the welfare of the children, and that objective survives (albeit in a modified form) in the provisions of the Matrimonial Causes Act 1973, s. 41, as substituted by Children Act 1989.

[93] The Report was influential in the gradual development of the divorce court welfare service. In 1950, acting on the Committee's recommendations, the Home Office appointed a probation officer as a court welfare officer in the divorce court in London; and (following recommendations of the 1956 *Royal Commission*, Cmd. 9678, Part V) the arrangement was extended in 1957 to all divorce courts, and eventually by the Matrimonial Proceedings (Magistrates' Courts) Act 1967 to magistrates' courts.   [94] See the terms of reference as quoted at p. 142 above.

[95] Cmd. 7024, para. 3.   [96] Para. 28(1).

[97] Committee on Procedure in Matrimonial Causes (1947, Cmd. 7024).

[98] In the House of Lords debate on the Denning Committee's *Second Interim Report* (see *Official Report* (HL) 28 Nov. 1946, vol. 144, col. 479) Lord Merriman had, after giving a brief account of the scheme, stated that he regarded it as 'being ruled out, at least for the time being', in part because any Government would prefer solutions which could be dealt with by administrative measures rather than by legislation, and in part because 'one must realize . . . that when a Committee has been set up and has either rejected a solution or has, as in this case, not even paid it the tribute of a passing reference, it is hopeless to expect that the question will be reopened'.   [99] Para. 25.

... the work of reconciliation is ... necessarily a personal task for those who undertake it, and if it is to appeal to the Englishman's character must be removed as far as possible from any suspicion of official supervision or interference in the private affairs of individuals ... [T]he work of welfare officers as proposed in the [Merriman] scheme would be prejudiced from the outset by their status as members of the Tribunal.[100]

It followed therefore that there was to be a clear distinction between the judicial role[101] on the one hand and the—essentially social work—task of providing treatment (and hopefully cures) for marriages which seemed to have failed on the other. It also seemed to follow that there should be no direct state intervention in the private realm of married life. The State should 'assist' in reconciliation; but the assistance which the State gave should be at one remove from the spouses concerned.

This analysis—effectively following the principles which had been adopted in the 1937 Magistrates' Courts legislation[102]—led the Committee to conclude—after a sympathetic account of work done by probation officers, the welfare services and legal aid sections of the Forces,[103] and of the Marriage Guidance Council, the Family Welfare Association 'and many other voluntary societies and individuals'—that what was required was a

Marriage Welfare Service to afford help and guidance both in preparation for marriage and also in difficulties after marriage. It should be sponsored by the State but should not be a State institution ... It should not be combined with the judicial procedure for divorce but should function quite separately from it.[104]

The judicial system was thus to be adapted to facilitate reconciliation so far as practicable; but the actual provision of services was a matter for others—and above

---

[100] Para. 25.

[101] The Committee in effect accepted the view put forward by the Treasury Solicitor that the Merriman scheme mixed up 'two things. You are having divorce by more or less an administrative machine with a sort of rubber stamp of the Court put upon it' (Minutes of Evidence, 17 July, LCO2/3948). Note also the view put forward in evidence by Sir Hartley Shawcross AG that people with an established legal right to a divorce should not be compelled to submit their private affairs to enquiries by strangers, and that the legal system should not tolerate secret inquisitions at which adultery would have to be disclosed. [102] See Ch. 5 above.

[103] Evidence given by J. B. Latey about the success of the scheme operated (for non-commissioned ranks only) in the Army seems to have been particularly influential. The Committee was given figures suggesting that a quarter of the total number of divorce applications resulted in reconciliation; but it evidently viewed this figure with a measure of scepticism—'. . . there is no record of how many of these reconciliations proved permanent. Nor is it possible to determine how close is the parallel between service and civilian conditions': Cmd. 7024, para. 18. In one respect at least there was a significant difference, in that soldiers who were estranged had to report the matter and were not allowed to stop the compulsory allotment of part of their pay until the prospects of reconciliation had been explored. But Latey's urging of the need to 'get at them early. Co-ordinate the thousands of voluntary social workers into an integrated (but not over-organised) network; publicise its existence so that ... it becomes the habit of the ordinary person to turn to it for help' would have struck a sympathetic chord with those responsible for the proposals in *Looking to the Future* (Cmd. 2799, 1995) relating to compulsory information sessions: see further below. [104] Para. 28(iii).

all for voluntary action.[105] This hardly constituted the detailed blueprint of the machinery for reconciliation for which many had looked;[106] and although there could be little opposition[107] to the Denning Committee's well-intentioned emphasis on promoting reconciliation the real question (as Lord Simon pointed out) was whether this could properly be seen as a matter of governmental or parliamentary action.[108]

THE SIGNIFICANCE OF THE DENNING COMMITTEE

With the benefit of hindsight, it can be seen that the Denning Committee's Reports marked a decisive step in the evolution of the divorce process. In particular, after the acceptance of Denning's recommendation for divorce to be administered in effect by County Court judges dressed up for the day[109] as High Court judges, it could only be a matter of time before the reality came to be recognised; and divorce—admittedly at first[110] only undefended divorce—became a matter for the County Court[111] with the consequence—to many in 1947 unthinkable[112]—that solicitors would have a right of audience. The belief that the legal dissolution of marriage was an occult mystery to be left in the hands of a small priestly caste could not survive for long; and it can be argued that the modern practice of divorce by form filling was the inevitable outcome. Indeed, the divorce process envisaged by the Family Law Act 1996 was foreseen by some fifty years ago:

---

[105] See the remarks of Archbishop Fisher in the debate on the Denning Report's reconciliation procedure recommendations, *Official Report* (HL) 27 Mar. 1947, vol. 146, col. 890; whilst Jowitt declared himself 'absolutely satisfied—good Socialist though I am—that it would be completely disastrous if the State were to try to undertake this task': *Official Report* (HL) 27 Mar. 1947, vol. 146, col. 914.   [106] Notably Archbishop Fisher; see *Official Report* (HL) vol. 144, col. 485.

[107] However, Jowitt seems (notwithstanding his remarks in public suggesting enthusiastic support for the work of marriage guidance: see *Official Report* (HL) vol. 146, col. 920) to have had doubts about the likely effectiveness of marriage guidance work in achieving reconciliation; but recorded that in view of the Denning Report he did not want to 'adopt too luke-warm an attitude' to the work of the National Marriage Guidance Council. He told the Home Secretary that he would therefore not object to grants made to Marriage Guidance organisations being spent on preventive as well as remedial work: Jowitt to Ede, 3 Feb. 1949, HO45/25202.

[108] *Official Report* (HL), 25 Mar. 1947, vol. 146, col. 896.   [109] And paid.

[110] Divorce County Courts were given jurisdiction to hear defended divorces by the Matrimonial and Family Proceedings Act 1984, s. 33.

[111] Matrimonial Causes Act 1967. Lord Denning opposed this extension largely on the ground that it perpetuated the undesirable distinction between defended and undefended cases. He said that in 1947 he had envisaged that within twenty years there would be family courts; and that there should be regional courts presided over by a High Court or County Court judge with lay justices or an assessor, and with the help of a probation or welfare officer. In a curious echo of Lord Merriman's proposal, he urged that such a system would enable the matter to be dealt with 'more on a social than on a legal aspect': *Official Report* (HL) 14 Feb. 1967, vol. 280, col. 202.

[112] Because of the dangers of facilitating collusive divorce: see above. In 1967 Lord Gardiner robustly asserted that the fear of the Bar was simply that they were going to lose a certain amount of work to the solicitors, and that barristers should remember the language they used about demarcation disputes between shipwrights and boilermakers: *Official Report* (HL) 14 Feb. 1967, vol. 280, col. 176.

... we should follow the practice ... of the parties merely making an application ..., and that after a reasonable period for reflection has been allowed a certificate of dissolution of marriage should be automatically issued.[113]

On a more positive note, the Denning Committee can, as already pointed out, claim credit as the inspiration for the creation of the divorce court welfare service. But what of the Denning Committee's eloquent witness to the desirability of promoting reconciliation and marriage welfare as desirable objectives of policy? On one view, it could be argued that the Committee—consistently with the approach adopted in 1937 for the magistrates' courts[114]—defined responsibility for these matters in a way which not only separated them from the legal process but also resulted in the State's contribution to them being restricted to the not overgenerous provision of financial assistance.[115] On this view, although the desirability of reconciliation continued[116] to play a part in the rhetoric of divorce reform, the Denning Committee's Report led inevitably to acceptance of the belief that marriage saving was not an attainable objective of the law. But the 1996 divorce reforms do not accept that approach, and are based firmly on the philosophy that the divorce process can be and is to be tailored to the identification of savable marriages and that it is to give every opportunity to explore reconciliation, the door to which should never be closed.[117] To this end, much effort is being given

---

[113] The Marquess of Reading, *Official Report* (HL) 28 Nov. 1946, vol. 144, col. 470. Lord Reading thought that legislation to this end would be bitterly and successfully opposed.

[114] See Ch. 5 above.

[115] After some interdepartmental manoeuvring, it was accepted that marriage guidance was a matter for the Home Office; and a *Departmental Committee on Grants for the Development of Marriage Guidance* was established under a retired senior Home Office official, Sir Sidney Harris (as to whom see Ch. 5, n. 23, above). The Harris Committee's Report (Cmd. 7566, 1948) recommended that certain agencies should be funded and made a number of other proposals. Relevant papers are to be found in PRO LCO2/3963—'Financial Assistance to enable the Marriage Guidance Council to carry on their work', and on Home Office files HO45/25202. The *Report of the Royal Commission on Marriage and Divorce* (Cmd. 9678, 1956, Part IV) is also relevant. For subsequent developments in relation to marriage counselling and related activities see the Consultation Paper *Marriage Matters* (1979) issued by a Home Office/DHSS Working Party; and note that J. Lewis, D. Clark and D. H. J. Morgan, *'Whom God hath joined together' The Work of Marriage Guidance* (1992) is an indispensable if controversial study of the work of Relate National Marriage Guidance (which received public funding as a direct result of the Denning and Harris Committees' recommendations).

[116] The long titles of the Acts of 1937 and 1969 which reformed the divorce law indicate the apparent appeal of reconciliation as an objective of the law. The Matrimonial Causes Act 1937 was an Act to amend the law relating to divorce 'for the true support of marriage, the protection of children, the removal of hardship, the reduction of illicit unions and unseemly litigation, the relief of conscience among the clergy, and the restoration of due respect for the law' (and s. 1 of the Act sought to deal with the perceived mischief of 'quicky' divorces by imposing a restriction on divorce within three years of marriage); whilst the Divorce Reform Act 1969 was 'an Act ... to facilitate reconciliation in matrimonial causes' (an objective to be attained, for example, by requiring solicitors to certify whether they had discussed reconciliation with clients, a proposal to be compared with the proposal in *Looking to the Future*, para. 7.31, that solicitors be required to certify whether they have informed their clients of the nature and purposes of counselling etc.).

[117] The wording of the text draws on the Preface ('the key aspects of the Government's proposals' and 'the benefits of the proposals') to the *Summary of the Government's Proposals on Mediation and the Ground for Divorce* (Lord Chancellor's Department, Apr. 1995) pp. 2–3. For the implementation

to the creation of marriage support services; and the proposals for a Marriage Welfare service made by the Denning Committee almost fifty years ago seem at last to have become the stuff of practical politics.

The words used in the title to this Chapter were often used ironically by those who lacked the evangelists' faith; and time will tell whether the faith in the scope for reconciliation and marriage saving voiced by the Denning Committee fifty years ago and now the basis for the reformed divorce law is securely founded.

of this philosophy in the Family Law Act 1996, see S. M. Cretney and J. M. Masson, *Principles of Family Law* (6th edn. 1997) pp. 326–33.

7

'What will the Women Want Next?'[1] The Struggle for Power within the Family, 1925–1975

1. INTRODUCTION

The earlier chapters in this book have focused largely on the consequences of marital breakdown; but in fact—notwithstanding the widely voiced pessimism about the future of marriage and even of the family and concern about the plight of single-parent families—the majority of marriages are only terminated by death; and the majority of children live in households formed by their two married parents. The law sometimes seems little concerned about the rights and duties of the members of functioning families; and it is often forgotten that in the nineteenth and twentieth centuries married women have had to struggle, not only to better their property and civic rights, but even to gain equal legal standing as parent of their children.[2] The Guardianship of Infants Act 1925 was the outcome of a prolonged and bitter struggle to achieve that objective; but in fact the 1925 Act still left parental authority over children exclusively in the husband, and it took nearly fifty more years to attain full legal equality. This Chapter explores —with the aid of departmental files now available in the Public Record Office[3] and other material[4]—the background to the 1925 Act, and seeks to explain the

* This Chapter was first published as an article in (1996) 112 LQR 110. The author is grateful to Professor Gillian Douglas, University of Wales Cardiff Law School whose comments on a draft were most helpful.

[1] This rhetorical question was endorsed by a Home Office official on the twenty-seven pages of minutes recording the meeting on 19 Apr. 1929 between the Prime Minister (Stanley Baldwin) and the Chancellor of the Exchequer (Winston Churchill) and a Deputation of Representatives of Women's Organisations organised by the Equal Rights General Election Campaign Committee and the National Union of Societies for Equal Citizenship.

[2] See P. H. Pettit, 'Parental Control and Guardianship' in R. H. Graveson and F. R. Crane, *A Century of Family Law 1857–1957* (1957).

[3] P. Polden, *Guide to the Records of the Lord Chancellor's Department* (1988) is an invaluable introduction to these materials. The files most relevant to the enactment of the 1925 Act from the Lord Chancellor's Office are: LCO1/47 (Guardianship of Infants Act 1886); LCO2/757 (Guardianship of Infants Bill 1920, 1921, 1922, and 1923); LCO2/758 (Guardianship of Infants Bill 1 Jan. 1924–21 Dec. 1924). The main Home Office files on the guardianship legislation are HO45/11566/404730, and HO45/11982/456799 and HO45/12054/474998—these last two files being particularly significant since the Home Office took the lead in the passage of the 1925 Bill through Parliament. Use has already been made of some of these papers by J. Brophy, 'Parental Rights and Children's Welfare: Some Problems of Feminists' Strategy in the 1920s', *International Journal of the Sociology of Law* 1982, 10, 149–68.

[4] Notably the records of the National Union of Societies for Equal Citizenship deposited in the Fawcett Library at London Guildhall University. The collection of British Parliamentary Papers in the Bodleian Library at Oxford have also yielded material not widely available.

concerns of the promoters and their opponents. It also evidences the sometimes ambivalent role played by civil servants in the process of law reform, and provides another illustration of both the advantages and disadvantages of compromise on issues of principle.

The story also furnishes evidence that (contrary to the interpretation subsequently placed on section 1 of the Guardianship of Infants Act 1925 by the House of Lords[5]) it was never intended that this provision should make a child's welfare the *only* consideration in resolving questions about upbringing, and may be seen as a case study in the difficulties of interpreting the 'intention' of the legislature—not least because of the extent of the enquiry necessary if the courts are to be fully informed about the legislative history of the texts they have to interpret.

2. THE BACKGROUND: REVOLUTIONARY CHANGE?

For most English lawyers, 1925 is a date still to be remembered if only because of the remarkable reforms of property law which were then brought to fruition. In contrast, the Guardianship of Infants Act 1925 has today little resonance. Yet it was this Act which first proclaimed[6] the principle[7] that the child's welfare was to be the court's first and paramount consideration in deciding issues relating to a child's upbringing; and for that reason the Guardianship of Infants Act clearly deserves at least a modest place in history as establishing an important but surely uncontroversial principle. At the time, however, the Act was far from uncontroversial; and we find a respected scholar[8] asserting, in the 1928 *Law Quarterly Review*,[9] that the Act's 'revolutionary'[10] provisions[11] subjected the institution of the family—'one of the pivots of the social system'—to 'drastic alteration'. That assertion is all the more surprising to those who know that a provision giving a mother the same legal authority as the father over the child of their marriage had been removed from the Bill originally presented in order to still the opposition

---

[5] See *J* v. *C* [1970] AC 668.   [6] Guardianship of Infants Act 1925, s. 1.

[7] Subsequently adopted as the governing principle by Children Act 1989, s. 1(1).

[8] Edward Jenks FBA (1861–1939). Jenks played an important part in the foundation of the Society of Public Teachers of Law (1909); while his *Digest of English Civil Law* (3rd edn. 1938, in collaboration with W. M. Geldart, Sir W. S. Holdsworth, R. W. Lee, Sir J. Miles and W. Latey) is one of the rare works which might lead the enquirer to think that English law had a coherent and logical structure such as could be expressed along the lines of the German and other European codes.

[9] E. Jenks, 'Recent Changes in Family Law' (1928) 44 LQR 314.

[10] This echoes the language ('revolutionary in character') used by the Attorney-General, Sir Gordon Hewart, in the opinion he gave to Sir Claud Schuster (Permanent Secretary to the Lord Chancellor) in response to Schuster's request for advice about an early draft of reforming guardianship legislation: 3 June 1920, PRO LCO2/757.

[11] Jenks considered that the Guardianship of Infants Act 1925 (along with the Summary Jurisdiction (Married Women) Act 1925, the Legitimacy Act 1926 and the Adoption Act 1926) profoundly affected the legal institution of the family and that they contained provisions which were either unworkable or contrary to public opinion.

of critics (such as Lord Chancellor Cave[12]) who thought that to give the mother legal equality in this respect would be destructive of all domestic felicity.[13] How could anyone have thought that this emasculated measure was capable of having an impact as profound as Jenks thought? And, even more, how could it be that when the equal authority principle which had been unacceptable in 1925 was adopted by the Conservative Government's Guardianship Act in 1973 there was almost universal approval—not to say a rather unseemly competition between the political parties, all seeking credit for the change?[14]

The third part of the Chapter sets out the background to the 1925 Act, analysing both the mischief at which it was aimed and the grounds upon which legislation was opposed. The fourth deals with the struggle—both in Parliament and behind the scenes in Whitehall—which took place between 1920 and 1924. This led to a compromise, as explained in the fifth part of the Chapter. The sixth part deals with the interpretation of some key provisions of the 1925 Act by the courts; and the seventh part gives, by way of a postscript, a brief account of the final legislative acceptance of the claim that husband and wife should have equal parental authority over their children, and of some subsequent developments.

3. THE BACKGROUND TO THE GUARDIANSHIP OF INFANTS ACT 1925: THE GRIEVANCE

The long and sometimes bitter campaign for women's suffrage[15] achieved at any rate partial[16] success in 1918. But what use were women to make of the power conferred by the vote and parliamentary representation? Real equality of liberties,

---

[12] George Cave, Viscount Cave (1856–1928), Unionist Member of Parliament for Kingston Surrey from 1906 until raised to the peerage as a Lord of Appeal in Ordinary, became Lord Chancellor in Bonar Law's administration in Oct. 1922 and held that office until a few days before his death. As will be seen below, he exercised a decisive influence on the form in which the Guardianship of Infants Act was enacted.

[13] Cave to the Home Secretary, W. C. Bridgeman, 22 Jan. 1923 (PRO LCO2/757). Similar language had been used by Parliamentary Counsel in a letter dated 27 June 1922 to Sir E. Blackwell, Permanent Under-Secretary of State at the Home Office, about the Separation and Maintenance Bill—also eventually enacted in 1925—as 'this preposterous Bill which, like many other Bills promoted by the Women's Societies, under the pretence of removing slight inequalities between the sexes, strike at the foundations of domestic felicity': HO45/11936/42906.

[14] See the remarks of Viscount Colville of Culross *Official Report* (HL) 20 Feb. 1973, vol. 339, cols. 19–20; and cf. Baroness Bacon at col. 28.

[15] See R. Strachey, *The Cause, a short history of the women's movement* (1929, reprinted 1978).

[16] The Representation of the People Act 1918 conceded the vote to women, but only to householders aged thirty or more; full equality between the sexes was only attained by the Representation of the People (Equal Franchise) Act 1928. The fact that the female vote was a matter of great concern to politicians is of significance in the discussions on guardianship of children culminating in the enactment of the 1925 Act; and this solicitude no doubt accounts for the willingness of Baldwin and Churchill to receive the delegation in 1929, referred to at n. 1 above. However, the enlarged electorate returned only 261 Conservatives (as against 287 Labour and 59 Liberals); Baldwin resigned, and Ramsay MacDonald formed the United Kingdom's second Labour administration.

status and opportunities between men and women[17] was the ultimate objective. Yet the common law of England denied to a wife any legal right to the custody or care and control of her children;[18] and the concept of a wife as a mere chattel, her identity merged in that of her husband,[19] was thus reinforced by the legal structure governing the most basic of human relationships. It could of course be argued that the husband's exclusive right to custody[20] had been eroded in the course of the nineteenth century;[21] but the law still recognised only one head of the family,[22] and the father had, in that capacity, 'tremendous power'[23] over its members. The truth was that the law denied a married woman[24] the legal status

[17] Rule II of the Constitution of the leading women's group, the National Union of Societies for Equal Citizenship. The history and development of the various women's groups prominent between 1888 and 1934 is clearly set out in a chart in B. Harrison, *Prudent Revolutionaries, Portrait of British Feminists between the Wars* (1987) pp. 4–5.

[18] *Wellesley* v. *Duke of Beaufort* (1827) 2 Russ. 1 (affirmed (1828) 2 Bli. NS 124); *Re Fynn* (1848) 2 de G&Sm. 457; *Re Agar-Ellis* (1883) 24 Ch. D 317; *R* v. *Gyngall* [1893] 2 QB 232. A useful account of the legal position of women at the time is given in E. Reiss, *Rights and Duties of Englishwomen* (1934) Ch. 3, 'Woman as Mother 1837–1933'.

[19] Per Lord Upjohn, *J* v. *C* [1970] AC 668, 720.

[20] This essay does not deal with the relationship between the legal status of a parent and that of a guardian, notwithstanding the fact that at one time the father's dominant position may have been attributed to the common law rule, abolished by Children Act 1989 s. 2(4), whereby a father was the natural guardian of his legitimate child: see generally the Law Commission's *Working Paper No. 91, Guardianship* (1985) para. 2.35, and the illuminating analysis in S. Maidment, 'The Fragmentation of Parental Rights' [1981] CLJ 135. It was no doubt because of the rule that a father was solely entitled to the child's guardianship that the Bills introduced in 1920 and subsequent years would have made mother and father joint guardians of their child; but the essence of the debate was about the *consequences* of that guardianship in terms of parental authority.

[21] See generally P. H. Pettit, 'Parental Control and Guardianship' in *A Century of Family Law 1857–1957* (eds. R. H. Graveson and F. R. Crane, 1957); H. K. Bevan, *Child Law* (2nd edn. 1989) pp. 6–8. The most important developments were: (i) the Custody of Children Act 1839 gave the court power to award custody of a child to the mother (provided she had not been found guilty of adultery) until the child reached the age of seven; (ii) the Custody of Infants Act 1873 gave a general power to award a mother (adulterous or not) custody of a child up to the age of 16 (raised to 21 by the Guardianship of Infants Act 1886); (iii) on divorce, the Matrimonial Causes Act 1857 had conferred power on the court to make custody orders in respect of the parties' children up to the age of 21; whilst the Matrimonial Causes Act 1878 empowered magistrates to make orders in respect of children up to the age of 10. The Guardianship of Infants Act 1886—the outcome of a compromise: see *Hansard's Parliamentary Debates* (3rd Series) 2 Apr. 1886, vol. 304, col. 650—gave the mother the right to be guardian of the infant children after the husband's death although she had to act jointly with any guardian he had appointed. The 1886 Act (s. 5) required the court to 'have regard' to the welfare of the child when deciding a mother's custody application; and the Court of Chancery in the exercise of its inherent jurisdiction over wards of court would attach weight to the children's welfare (although it is difficult to state confidently the practice of the court at the time: see further n. 129 below).

[22] Per Mrs Margaret Wintringham MP (as to whose significant role see p. 168 below) on the Second Reading Debate on the Guardianship of Infants Bill on 4 Apr. 1924: see *Hansard* (HC) vol. 171, col. 2661.

[23] Viscount Haldane (Lord Chancellor in the Labour Government) *Hansard* (HL) 3 June 1924, vol. 57, col. 791.

[24] Parental authority in respect of an *illegitimate* child was (and still is) vested in the mother: *Barnado* v. *McHugh* [1891] AC 388; and see now Children Act 1989, s. 2(2)(b). The paradox that the mother of an illegitimate child did have sole legal authority (and that a divorced wife might have sole legal authority by court order) was highlighted by Mrs Margaret Wintringham in the crucial 1924 parliamentary debates: see *Hansard* (HC) 4 Apr. 1924, vol. 171, col. 2260.

of her children's parent,[25] and the case for reform seemed to many overwhelming. The leading women's group—the National Union of Societies for Equal
Citizenship[26]—put a commitment to legislation giving wives equal rights to the
legal guardianship of their children in the forefront of its programme;[27] and NUSEC
quickly brought equal rights Bills to Parliament.[28] Yet—notwithstanding politicians' concern to capture the women's vote—NUSEC's proposals were from the
outset[29] strenuously opposed, particularly by officials in the Lord Chancellor's
Office, the Home Office, the Ministry of Health and even by Parliamentary Counsel.
In the result, no legislation was enacted until 1925; and, even then (as already
noted), the Guardianship of Infants Act did not achieve the equality which NUSEC
had claimed to be the 'keystone'[30] of its proposals. At the end of the twentieth
century the case for equality may seem self-evident; so why was this emphatically not so seventy years ago? What arguments were so effectively used against
the equality principle?

The Case for Equality between Parents

(i) Legal Status

The main argument in favour of equal authority legislation advanced by NUSEC
was one of principle. Parliament had accepted that men and women were entitled to equal citizenship before the law; and the consistent policy of modern
legislation had been to put man and woman and husband and wife on equal terms
as regards their property and their civic rights. That principle should now be applied
in all matters concerning the control and upbringing of children;[31] not least because
to do so would recognise and raise the status of motherhood. The fact that the

[25] Even though she would be criminally responsible if the child were neglected: see the remarkable case of the mother of twenty children who, unable out of the £2 weekly allowed her by the husband to provide the footwear they needed to attend school, was fined under the education legislation
for failing to secure their attendance: evidence of Miss Chrystal Macmillan, *Joint Select Committee
on the Guardianship of Infants Bill, Minutes of Evidence*, 19 July 1922, p. 17.

[26] Henceforth abbreviated to 'NUSEC'.

[27] NUSEC actively campaigned against other cases of discrimination such as the rule (abolished
by the Matrimonial Causes Act 1923) that a wife could be divorced because she had committed adultery, but a husband could only be divorced if there were also aggravating circumstances.

[28] The first equal parental authority Bills were introduced into the House of Commons during the
post-World War I Coalition administration by the Liberal Member for West Lothian, Sir James Greig
(1859–1934) with the support of Lady Astor (Conservative Member for Plymouth Sutton 1919–45
and the first woman to take her seat in the House of Commons). Greig was able to remind the House
that a pledge to remove 'all existing inequalities of law as between men and women' had been given
by Bonar Law and Lloyd George in the so-called 'coupon' election in Nov. 1918: see *Hansard* (HC)
29 June 1921, vol. 143, col. 1400.

[29] The first letter, dated 31 May 1920, on file PRO LCO2/757 from Sir Claud Schuster to the
Attorney-General characterised the equal authority measures in the first NUSEC equal authority Bill
(introduced in 1920, but never debated) as 'somewhat serious'.

[30] Mrs E. Hubback, Parliamentary Secretary to NUSEC, in a letter to the Attorney-General,
Sir E. Pollock (and, at the time, chairman of a Cabinet Committee established to consider the Bills:
29 Apr. 1922, PRO HO45/11566/14797).

[31] Per Colonel Greig moving the Second Reading of the Guardianship of Infants Bill, *Hansard*
(HC) 6 May 1921, vol. 141, cols. 1394–5.

ordinary married woman was not the legal guardian of her child and had no rights over the child was (according to NUSEC's skilful and adroit Parliamentary Secretary Mrs Eva Hubback[32]) a major factor in explaining the 'extraordinary amount of support' that the campaign for legislation 'had among organised women'.[33] It might be true that in many cases the mother had in practice 'just as much, if not more actual voice in deciding the practical issues with regard to the children as the father has'. But if that were so, recognition of her equal legal status would cause no practical difficulties and would 'have the advantage of bringing actual facts into line with the law'.[34] As Sir John Simon put it, the law should reflect the practice of normal and happy families.[35]

(ii) Abuse of Power

Important though the argument of principle might be, the grievance was not merely theoretical nor was the denial of equal authority to the mother of only symbolic significance. There were (it was said) many cases in which the discrimination against the mother had serious practical consequences:[36]

[32] (1886–1949), Parliamentary Secretary of NUSEC 1919–27, and thereafter Principal of Morley College. To the lawyer, her skill in mastering complex legal issues and securing the confidence— if not always the agreement—of influential civil servants (and in particular that of the Lord Chancellor's Permanent Secretary, Sir Claud Schuster) is remarkable. The Department's continuing respect for her abilities is evidenced by its suggestion (not in the event accepted) that she should serve on the (Denning) Committee on *Procedure in Matrimonial Causes* in 1946. It may (as suggested by M. Pugh, *Women and the Women's Movement in Britain 1914–1959* (1992)) be true that Hubback's writings—and notably *The Population of Britain* (Pelican, 1948) in which she urged that the *bearing and rearing of children* was the finest of all professions for women (p. 283)—reflect a 'highly conventional concern with finding means of encouraging women to have more children'; but it would be impossible to deny her contribution to the development of English family law between the two World Wars. There is an informative memoir by Gillian Sutherland in *Dictionary of National Biography, Missing Persons* (1993) and biographical writings by her daughter, Diana Hopkinson (*Family Inheritance, a Life of Eva Hubback* (1954); *The Incense Tree* (1968)); but the most accessible account is now to be found in Ch. 10 of B. Harrison's *Prudent Revolutionaries, Portraits of British Feminists between the Wars* (1987).

[33] Mrs Eva Hubback in evidence to the Joint Select Committee on the Guardianship of Infants Bill, Minutes of Evidence 19 July 1922, p. 16; and see also to the same effect her letter to the Attorney-General Sir E. M. Pollock, 29 Apr. 1922: PRO HO45/11566/14797.

[34] The Chief Magistrate Sir Chartres Biron (1863–1940) believed from his experience that working-class mothers had no sense of grievance at all about the lack of parental authority: '. . . when people come, especially women, to ask for [summonses under the matrimonial legislation] and when these cases are tried they talk a great deal, and they tell us everything that is in their mind, and in the enormous number of cases I have had I do not remember any case in which a woman made a grievance of that kind': Joint Select Committee on the Guardianship of Infants Bill, Minutes of Evidence 19 July 1922, pp. 2, 8.

[35] *Hansard* (HC) 4 Apr. 1924, vol. 171, col. 2968. Simon said that it would 'have greatly astonished my father to have been told, when I was a small boy, that he had the exclusive right of determining . . . matters and that my mother had nothing to do with them': ibid.

[36] As in the case—recounted by Mrs Hubback—of the 'perfectly sober, respectable woman and broken hearted' whose husband had sent her six-year-old son to live in Canada with an aunt. The mother had no effective redress against an adamant father: see 'Effect of Women's Franchise on Legislation', Hubback papers, NUSEC/X3/3, Fawcett Library, London Guildhall University.

The father may use his power over the children as a means to induce the mother to do what he wishes, by the threat of removing them from her. He can take the children away from her entirely, and entrust them to the custody of a third party without her consent ... The mother may apply to the High Court or to the County Court, but the costs are prohibitive to the poorer classes.[37]

The case for reform seemed overwhelming. As Eleanor Rathbone[38] put it:[39]

It is surely ... a great positive disability that a wife, so long as she nominally lives with her husband, has no legal right to any say or part whatever in the management of their children, nor any remedy ... against being totally separated from them ... [The father's exclusive rights are not even] dissolved by death, since even when he leaves his children entirely unprovided for, he has the power of directing by will the religion and manner in which they are to be brought up and of appointing a guardian who, acting jointly with the wife, must see to it that so far as possible the father's wishes are carried out ... If comparatively few husbands abuse their power in this respect, it is because the sense of justice of the ordinary man refuses to let him take seriously the monstrous legal fiction that a man has a primary right to the sole control of the children whom a woman has borne with great suffering and at the risk of her life and to whose care Nature and custom require her to devote herself as the chief work of the best years of her life.

The Case against Parental Equality

The case for equality of parental authority seems formidable; but opponents relied on a wide range of arguments.

(i) Arguments of Principle

There were a few voices[40] opposed in principle to the notion that a child's mother should have equal authority with the father. In this view, the maintenance of family life required there to be a single head of the family; and since the beginning of civilisation the burden of taking decisions had been given to the father as the stronger and the better able to protect his children. Even in the twentieth century, the man was usually the wage earner, had more experience of the world

---

[37] Summary of the views of those witnesses who supported the principle of conferring equal rights on the mother before the Joint Committee of Lords and Commons to consider the Guardianship of Infants Bill introduced into the House of Lords by Lord Askwith and given a Second Reading on 26 Mar. 1923, taken from a draft Report: PRO LCO2/757.

[38] (1872–1946), President of NUSEC and MP (Independent) for Combined English Universities from 1929 until her death. Perhaps the leading parliamentary proponent of women's interests (note in particular *The Disinherited Family, A Plea for the Endowment of the Family* (1924)) she fought and won her last feminist battle on the issue of paying family allowances to mothers—a matter on which the Ministry of National Insurance had strong views based on 'departmental legalism connected with the law of maintenance'. See generally M. Stocks, *Eleanor Rathbone, a biography* (1949) and B. Harrison, *Prudent Revolutionaries, Portrait of British Feminists between the Wars* (1987) Ch. 4.   [39] *The Disinherited Family* (1924) pp. 91–2.

[40] Notably Lord Banbury of Southam (1850–1936) who consistently opposed the measures promoted by women's organisations both while serving as a Conservative MP (latterly for the City of London) from 1892 to 1924—one of the most 'destructive and uninspiring' members in the view of *The Women's Leader and Common Cause* 4 Jan. 1924—and subsequently in the House of Lords.

and was better educated than the wife. The simple truth was that women were 'not equal, they never will be equal, and you cannot make them equal'.[41] And such views were not confined to reactionary City magnates: the Chief Magistrate[42]— a person with practical experience of dealing with working-class domestic quarrels—shared the belief that to interfere with the father's natural primacy would 'sacrifice entirely the peace of the home and the interests of the children'.

(ii) Divided Authority Bad for Children

Arguments founded explicitly on the supposed natural right of the father could not have been expected to command a great deal of support in a society which had come to accept the principle of equality between men and women. An argument which in contrast evidently did carry weight with middle-of-the-road opinion appealed to the effect which division[43] of parental authority would have on the welfare of the children, and the need for children to be in no doubt where authority lay:

What is at stake . . . is the well-being of the child itself, and any duality of control must militate against that. The mate of a ship may be as good or better seaman than the captain, but he must either take his place and act in his stead, or else remain the second in command. No ship-owner would contemplate giving him equal authority and power. One man alone must dictate the course and prescribe the speed. Divided counsels in bad weather would make for ship-wreck, even though both parties aspired to save the ship. [We] hold no brief against equality in status between man and woman. It is on practical grounds alone [that the proposal is objectionable].[44]

(iii) Resolving Disputes about Exercise of Parental Authority

If equal authority were conceded, there would have to be a procedure for resolving disagreements between parents about their child's upbringing; and there seemed to be no real alternative to providing for the matter in issue being referred to the court. The opponents of equal authority legislation believed this to be unacceptable; but their argument took two rather different forms.

---

[41] Lord Banbury of Southam, *Hansard* (HL) 9 July 1924, vol. 58, col. 368.

[42] Sir Chartres Biron (1863–1940), Joint Select Committee on the Guardianship of Infants Bill, Minutes of Evidence 19 July 1922, pp. 2, 8. Sir Chartres did not hesitate to make confident generalisations even on matters not within his experience on the bench. For example, when confronted with the fact that many American states had equal authority legislation, he replied: there 'is some very odd legislation in the United States of America. I should be very sorry to see it adopted in this country, and all I can say is from my experience of the United States the children are very badly brought up. You never see such ill-behaved children as you do in the United States of America': Joint Select Committee on the Guardianship of Infants Bill, Minutes of Evidence 19 July 1922, p. 8.

[43] Some opponents of equal authority legislation attached such importance to the principle of there being one person who could exercise authority that they would have preferred to constitute the mother sole guardian in place of the father: see Lord Onslow to A. Maxwell (Private Secretary to the Home Secretary) 22 July 1922 (PRO HO45/11566/14797).

[44] Extracted from a draft *Report from the Joint Committee of Lords and Commons to consider the Guardianship of Infants Bill given a second reading on 26 March 1923* prepared by Lord Askwith. In the event, the Committee was unable to agree and no report was ever finalised: see below.

First, there was the view that intervention by a court—and particularly by the magistrates' court[45]—into the private realm[46] of family life was intrinsically undesirable and would inevitably introduce an element of discord into a family which would never thereafter be eradicated.[47] Secondly, there was the argument that the issues involved would not be justiciable. As P. O. Lawrence J put it in evidence to the Joint Select Committee which sat to examine the issues in 1922, a judge would in the end simply have to let his personal inclination determine the outcome;[48] and in this view, no court should be asked to decide questions where no actual right or wrong was involved. A court (said[49] Sir Claud Schuster[50]):

is concerned . . . with the definite ascertainment of the rights of the parties, a party on one side and a party on the other, and if they can ascertain what the right is then the court is inevitably led to its decision. There are no rights here. It is a question of discretion.

[45] See in particular the evidence of Sir Chartres Biron (1863–1947) the Chief Magistrate: Joint Select Committee on the Guardianship of Infants Bill, Minutes of Evidence 19 July 1922, pp. 4–6. The fact that magistrates' courts outside London were usually composed of laymen was also a factor: the Home Secretary (E. Shortt) told the Home Affairs Committee that it would be a 'grave mistake' to entrust questions requiring the nicest discretion and in many cases involving difficult points of law to lay justices with little legal knowledge: see his Memorandum dated 20 Feb. 1922 repeating almost verbatim Biron's letter to the Home Office dated 23 June 1921, PRO HO45/11566/404730.

[46] There was concern that 'fussy people' might be encouraged to interfere 'when their interference was neither required nor useful' (as Sir Chartres Biron put it) by bringing matters before the court; and it is true that the equal authority Bill introduced in 1920 would have allowed applications to be made to the court by any person on behalf of the child. The 1924 Wintringham Bill (possibly in response to criticism by witnesses giving evidence to the Joint Select Committee) would have restricted the right to parents or guardians (cl. 5); whilst eventually the 1925 Act (see ss. 2, 3) restricted the right of access to the spouses during their joint lives. The question of standing in relation to decisions about the upbringing of a child remains difficult; but note the ingenious solution adopted by Children Act 1989 s. 10 (which distinguishes between persons entitled to bring any such issue before the court as of right, those entitled to bring a restricted range of issues before the court as of right, and those who require the court's prior leave to do so).

[47] This view is eloquently put by Lord Onslow (1876–1945) in his letter of 22 July 1922 to A. Maxwell (1880–1963) then Private Secretary to the Home Secretary: HO45/11566/14797. Note also the opposition within the Home Office to legislation strengthening 'the hold married women have over their husbands and so increase the number of men committed to prison for debt', and officials' expressed concern 'whether society will as a whole gain by continuous legislation in favour of one sex against another': see PRO HO45/11936/429604, Sept. 1924.

[48] Joint Select Committee on the Guardianship of Infants Bill, Minutes of Evidence 25 July 1922, p. 65.

[49] Joint Select Committee on the Guardianship of Infants Bill, Minutes of Evidence 25 July 1922, at p. 28; and note the similar objection of the Minister of Health to giving a court the impossible task of resolving a dispute between parents about vaccination: see his memorandum dated 16 Feb. 1922 to the Home Affairs Committee PRO LCO2/757.

[50] (1869–1956), Permanent Secretary and Clerk to the Crown in Chancery (1915–44). Schuster played a central role in the events leading up to the 1925 legislation; and the record of his involvement bears out the assessment (made by R. Stevens, *The Independence of the Judiciary, The View from the Lord Chancellor's Office* (1993)) that he was 'one of the most powerful of the permanent secretaries . . . seen as the *alter ego* of the Lord Chancellor and a moving force in Whitehall'. His successor as Permanent Secretary, Sir A. Napier, wrote in the *Dictionary of National Biography* that Schuster 'had many of the prejudices common amongst Englishmen of his class, and he often gave pungent expression to his dislikes'; and the papers certainly bear out that assessment. But equally they demonstrate his readiness to form close working relationships with those—such as Mrs Hubback—for whom he might not have been expected to have much sympathy.

To take a ridiculous instance, a dispute whether a child is to go to one school, or to another school—how on earth is the Court going to deal with that?[51]

And in addition to these questions of high juristic principle, there was also the practical question of judicial resources: it would (said Schuster[52]) be impossible for the High Court or County Court to take on more judicial work unless additional judges were appointed.

(iv) Divided Authority Incompatible with Sound Public Administration

Much the most influential and effective argument used against making any change in the principle of undivided parental authority was that such legislation would create insuperable difficulties for public authorities in the performance of their legal duties.[53] Sir Claud Schuster was characteristically and typically insistent[54] that the merits of equal authority legislation had nothing to do with him or any other official;[55] but he and his colleagues had a duty to emphasise that it was 'essential from an administrative point of view' that a household should be treated as a single unit and that there should be some person within it to take decisions.[56]

---

[51] It seems that Sir Claud, like his Home Office colleagues (who resisted giving magistrates power to order transfer of tenancies and the division of household furniture between husband and wife on separation: PRO HO45/11936/429604, Sept. 1924), would have found difficulty in understanding the work of the Family Division of the High Court where judges routinely decide issues about the schools children should attend (see *Re P (A Minor) (Education)* [1992] 1 FLR 316, CA), the religion in which they should be brought up (see *Re R (A Minor) (Residence: Religion)* [1993] 2 FLR 163, CA) and the medical treatment which they should (or should not) receive (*Re W (A Minor) (Consent to Medical Treatment)* [1993] 1 FLR 1, CA).

[52] See n. 50, above. Schuster on 24 Mar. 1922 had had to press upon the Solicitor-General (Sir Leslie Scott) 'the very grave difficulties which will arise if the Court . . . is to be imported into every family difference in every household in which perhaps some temporary contest of will or misunderstanding may arise'. Apart from attempting to 'preserve a comparative purity of English law' the Department's main interest in the matter was 'to prevent the County Court or the High Court from having its time occupied in such matters . . .'.

[53] This impression, formed from the departmental records, was shared by NUSEC's Parliamentary Secretary: see *The Government's Guardianship of Infants Bill, 1924*, by Eva M. Hubback published by NUSEC in Sept. 1924, price 1d.

[54] In evidence to the Joint Select Committee on the Guardianship of Infants Bill, Minutes of Evidence 20 July 1922, p. 28.

[55] However, Schuster appears to have been sensitive to the risk that civil servants might appear to have taken an excessively prominent part in opposition to change. In 1923 he asked the Home Office to stimulate 'some private peer . . . to put up an argument against the Bill' (then before the House of Lords) and suggested that the Government spokesman, Lord Onslow, might 'stir up such a peer as Willoughby de Broke or Stuart of Wortley, *so that the House may see that the opposition is not merely official*' (italics supplied): Schuster to Maxwell, 22 Mar. 1923. It appears that Lord Onslow did get up 'a band of stalwarts' and Schuster told Maxwell that the Lord Chancellor hoped that Onslow would 'continue this good work': Schuster to Maxwell, 23 Mar. 1923 PRO LCO2/752.

[56] These views were also reflected in the evidence of Maurice Gwyer (1878–1952), then legal adviser and solicitor to the Ministry of Health (which was particularly perturbed about the impact of equal authority legislation on the administration of the law relating to vaccination—'a subject on which many people feel very strongly indeed'—birth notification and the administration of the Poor Law): Joint Select Committee on the Guardianship of Infants Bill, Minutes of Evidence 25 July 1922; and note the memorandum submitted to the Cabinet's Home Affairs Committee in 1921 by the Minister of Health, Sir Alfred Mond: PRO LCO2/757. Schuster, Gwyer and others would no doubt have seen

Concern for practical difficulties drove Schuster to the view that equal authority legislation was something on which '. . . no compromise is possible because the principle which it embodies is nonsense . . . [I]f two persons have equal rights a deadlock issues whenever there is a difference between them.'[57]

4. THE WAR OF ATTRITION, 1920–1924

In the circumstances, there did not appear to be much scope for compromise between the two rival—and apparently polarised—positions. On the one hand, the officials seemed implacable. On the other, NUSEC had committed itself to the proposition that it was 'absolutely impossible' to give up the principle of equal guardianship including joint rights and responsibilities. But the outcome was in fact a compromise: the Guardianship of Infants Act was introduced as a Government Bill; but it was a Bill which made no concession to the demand for equal parental authority. There are two main strands in the story. The first is the achievement of the women's groups in creating a climate of opinion in which legislation dealing with the wife's legal position in respect of her child came to be thought inevitable. The second is the achievement of Ministers and officials in persuading the women's groups to accept a measure which—although skilfully presented to disguise the fact—denied almost all the matters to which NUSEC had attached importance.

Changing the Climate of Opinion

The political situation in the years between 1920 and 1924 was exceptionally volatile;[58] and this factor contributed to governments' reluctance to offend groups claiming to represent significant numbers of voters.[59] Even those with the

---

their fears confirmed by the ruling that the consent of both parents was necessary to change a child's surname, and that education and health authorities were under a duty to make enquiries before giving effect to a request from one parent: see *Re PC (Change of Surname)* [1997] 2 FLR 730, Holman J.

[57] Schuster's minute dated 1 Mar. 1922 advising the Lord Chancellor on a response to the 1922 Bill, PRO LCO2/752. The draftsman shared Schuster's view, and considered it pointless to attempt a redraft of the Bill which had been introduced unless and until the equal authority and other issues of policy had been settled: H. Godley to the Attorney-General, 23 Mar. 1922, PRO LCO2/752.

[58] There were three general elections in less than two years. The Lloyd George coalition was in power when the first equal authority Bills were introduced in 1920, 1921 and 1922. Lloyd George resigned on 19 Oct. 1922; and a Conservative Government (first under Bonar Law, and then Baldwin) took office after the Nov. 1922 election. Parliament was again dissolved and a general election held in Dec. 1923. A minority Labour Government was formed by Ramsay MacDonald on 22 Jan. 1924 but fell in October. The Conservatives gained a large majority (419 seats out of 615) at the election.

[59] In 1922 Sir Claud Schuster minuted the Lord Chancellor that it was 'desirable to postpone for as long as possible the appearance of opposition to the Bill': see 1 Mar. 1922, PRO LCO2/757. He also stated that the decision of the Home Affairs Committee on 23 Feb. 1922 to allow the NUSEC

firmest views were prepared to change their minds—at least to the extent of accepting that something had to be done which would satisfy the insistent demands made by the women's organisations. The most dramatic example of an apparent readiness to be flexible is furnished by the Conservative Lord Chancellor Cave: on taking office in 1923, he told the Home Secretary[60] that the NUSEC Bill conferring parental authority on both parents 'would not effect any useful purpose and would indeed be mischievous in its effects',[61] but two years later he sat in a Cabinet which took the decision to include guardianship legislation in its programme, and in 1925 he had the carriage of the Bill which became the Guardianship of Infants Act 1925 in the House of Lords. But as we shall see, the flexibility was more apparent than real.

The fluid political situation was skilfully exploited by NUSEC, and particularly by its Parliamentary Secretary, Mrs Eva Hubback. Some years later she gave a vivid account of how she saw the task facing the women's movement in the first years of women's suffrage:

We had to learn a new technique, to enter into questions of law and of policy far more subtle and complicated than in the old suffrage days. We had ourselves to become experts, and to spread abroad our expertise . . . We had to maintain our reputation for disinterestedness, common sense and accuracy in successive Parliaments. We had to discover new ways of moulding public opinion, especially parliamentary opinion. We had to bring along other women's organisations to follow where we had blazed the trail . . .

One of the ways in which NUSEC moulded opinion was by exploiting the possibilities[62] of the Private Member's Bill as a means for securing discussion and

---

equal parental authority Bill to be referred to a Select Committee was influenced by the consideration that it was 'very undesirable to annoy the women who are the main backers of the Bill'. He also noted that some members of the Cabinet were probably vaguely in favour of the Bill: see PRO LCO2/757; and note the minutes by Blackwell, the Permanent Under-Secretary of State, and the Home Secretary (E. Shortt) to like effect: PRO HO45/11566/404730, 20 Feb. 1922.

[60] W. Bridgeman (1864–1935), Conservative Member for North Shropshire 1906–29 (in which year he was raised to the peerage as a Viscount), insisted on the strength of 'the pressure which is sure to be put upon us by Private Members . . . [T]he agitation is sufficiently strong to persuade a large number of Members who have not carefully examined the subject to support the proposal.' Bridgeman thought that 'it would be difficult for the Government to put the Whips on against a Private Member's Bill [in the House of Commons] on this subject'. Bridgeman to Cave, 30 Jan. 1923, PRO LCO2/757. Bridgeman's pragmatic approach to the question carried the day; but it may be noted in passing that in at least one respect Bridgeman was ideologically committed to equality between the sexes—as Home Secretary he took the controversial decision not to recommend the exercise of the prerogative of mercy in the case of Mrs Edith Thompson (convicted of the murder of her husband although the killing was actually effected by her lover) and recorded his view that in this respect the law admitted of no distinction between men and women: P. Williamson, *The Modernisation of Conservative Politics: the diaries and letters of W. Bridgeman* (1988) p. 165.

[61] Cave to Bridgeman, 22 Jan. 1923 (PRO LCO2/757).

[62] Already demonstrated in the 19th century in relation to reform of the law governing married women's property.

publicity, and ultimately for driving Government to take action.[63] This technique was adopted in the campaign which led to the enactment of the Guardianship of Minors Act 1925; and NUSEC ensured that equal authority Bills were repeatedly brought before both Houses of Parliament.[64] NUSEC Bills were examined by Joint Select Committees of both Houses in 1922 and 1923;[65] and by the summer of 1923 it had apparently come to be accepted that there was general support for legislation,[66] and Ministers were faced with the 'very disagreeable' possibility that the Committee would report in favour of the legislation.[67] At the same time (or so officials considered) the detailed examination of the issues led to the women's groups understanding more clearly the strength of the objections to the equal authority Bills they had put forward. The time had come for an official[68] initiative.

[63] This approach is explained in an article 'The Case for the Private Members Bill' in *The Women's Leader and Common Cause* 3 Aug. 1920, p. 210: 'there are certain specific reforms which can command such a strong backing that they can be assured of considerable support from all sections of the House, although they have not attained the definite recognition of the Government. For the introduction of such reforms the Private Member's Bill is an indispensable vehicle which women's organisations which mean business cannot afford to despise.' This use of the Private Member's Bill is also evidenced in divorce reform and other legislation on social issues: see Chs. 2 and 3 above.

[64] A Bill ordered to be printed on 18 May 1920 failed to make progress; but a virtually identical Bill was given a Second Reading on 6 May 1921 and was considered by Standing Committee D in June 1921. In the spring of 1922 Bills were introduced into both Houses, and debated, and a Select Committee of both Houses was set up to examine the matter. The Committee had not reported by the time the Coalition came to an end with Lloyd George's resignation on 19 Oct. 1922. In Mar. 1923, under Bonar Law's Conservative administration, Bills were again introduced and debated.

[65] Both Committees heard a great deal of evidence, but neither reported—the 1922 Committee was still deliberating when the Lloyd George coalition fell, and the 1923 Committee was still deliberating when Parliament was dissolved on 16 Nov. 1923. The decision of the Bonar Law administration in Jan. 1923 to allow the NUSEC Bill to be recommitted to a Select Committee seems, in the light of events, to have been crucial. That decision was taken on the advice of the Home Secretary W. Bridgeman (who told Cave in a manuscript addendum to a letter of 15 Jan. 1923 that although 'there was no very great demand for the measure' a large number of Members were interested in the issue and 'there is no possibility of shelving it and . . . in the circumstances I do not see how the Government could resist a request for a reappointment of the Select Committee'). Bridgeman thought steps should be taken to ensure the Committee was more broadly based than the 1922 Committee, while Cave hoped the Committee might condemn the Bill with praise 'which may be slightly more than faint, and we might then be in a position to prevent its further progress, or at least to refuse any facility of any kind': Cave to Bridgeman, 2 Feb. 1923, PRO LCO2/757.

[66] See the Solicitor-General's Memorandum to the Home Affairs Committee: PRO LCO2/757. Lord Onslow (see n. 68 below) reported a discussion with Mrs Wintringham (see n. 75 below) in which 'she said that all the common sense was on one side, i.e. ours, and all the human sympathy on the other: and I am afraid that with constituents in the background human sympathy may overrule common sense': Onslow to Bridgeman, 5 July 1923, HO45/11190/371349.

[67] See the letter from Lord Onslow to Bridgeman, 5 July 1923, HO45/11190/371349, in which this possibility is given as the reason for seeking a compromise.

[68] The Earl of Onslow (1876–1945) (then Parliamentary Secretary to the Ministry of Health and a member of the Joint Select Committee) seems to have taken responsibility for setting up the interdepartmental meeting from which eventually the compromise emerged. In a letter to Bridgeman, he wrote that in view of the possibility that the majority of 'weak-kneed' members on the Committee would report in favour of the NUSEC Bill 'it would be a good thing to go through the Bill carefully and for me to be able to produce some suggestions which might lead to a compromise . . . I arranged,

5. THE COMPROMISE EMERGES

On 13 July 1923 officials held a meeting at the Home Office;[69] and Parliamentary Counsel produced draft clauses which eventually formed the basis of the compromise embodied in the Guardianship of Infants Act 1925.[70] Sir Claud Schuster then proceeded to negotiate with influential peers.[71] But for a time—in the event a very short time—it must have appeared to NUSEC that no compromise would be necessary; and that their Bill could, unamended, become law. Baldwin unexpectedly called an election; and the outcome was to produce (according to NUSEC's monitoring), for the first time, a majority in the House of Commons 'definitely pledged to social political and economic equality between men and women'.[72] Supporters of the equal authority campaign might reasonably believe the formation of a Labour Administration on 24 January 1924[73] meant that complete victory was at last in sight.[74] Mrs Margaret Wintringham[75]

therefore, with Anderson [Permanent Under-Secretary of State at the Home Office, see n. 108 below] that we should have a confabulation next week. I have not mentioned this, of course, to any members of the Committee . . .': Onslow to Bridgeman, 5 July 1923, HO45/11190/371349. Lord Onslow's autobiography (*Sixty Three Years: An autobiography* (1944) does not mention his involvement in the compromise (or indeed in the legislation).

[69] See the manuscript minute on HO45/11566/404730. The suggestion that 'some general principle in favour of equality' be formulated which would avoid the practical difficulties so forcefully represented by officials appears to have come from Lord Onslow. This suggestion was the inspiration of the 'first and paramount' provision which eventually became s. 1 of the 1925 Act.

[70] See F. J. Liddell to Schuster, LCO2/759, 16 July 1923.

[71] The clauses were (Schuster said) exactly what he had wanted; and he thought that 'it would be quite possible to make a bargain' with the Select Committee then sitting: Schuster to Liddell, 17 July 1923, and 10 October 1923, PRO LCO2/757. The files indicate that Schuster met the Committee's chairman, Lord Wemyss; and he also had meetings with Lord Askwith (1861–1942)—a lawyer and leading industrial arbitrator who was one of the most influential and active supporters of equal authority legislation. Schuster had the advantage of having been told 'quite privately' by the Committee's secretary, C. Davidson, that Wemyss (who Schuster thought to be 'very prickly and jealous of outside interference') did not approve of Askwith seeing Schuster, and thought that any discussions should have taken place between the two peers direct: Davidson to Schuster, 1 Nov. 1923; Schuster to Liddell, 2 Nov. 1923. Wemyss was evidently unaware of the part being played by Lord Onslow.

[72] NUSEC Annual Report, 1924.

[73] No party obtained a clear majority at the election; and the King insisted that Baldwin should meet Parliament. Only when his administration was defeated on a vote on 21 Jan. did the King accept Baldwin's resignation, and invite MacDonald to form an administration.

[74] Labour had consistently supported women's causes: a major part of its 1918 Election Manifesto was given over to an attempt to demonstrate that Labour was *the* women's party, and this claim was subsequently repeated.

[75] A former headmistress and the second woman (and the first Liberal) to take her seat in the House of Commons, being returned at a by-election in 1921 as Member for Louth in place of her deceased husband. She was defeated in the 1924 General Election and never re-entered Parliament. But she was evidently endowed with considerable personal qualities—on her death (aged 76) on 10 Mar. 1955 *The Times* obituary said that she had 'remained until her death the same bright helpful and generous being whose presence so captivated the House of Commons over 30 years ago'—and her influence was considerable: see Mary Stocks, *Eleanor Rathbone* (1949) at p. 142; B. Harrison, *Prudent Revolutionaries, Portraits of British Feminists between the Wars* (1987) at p. 13. Although a committed supporter of the women's movement she was far from the stereotyped militant feminist;

introduced a Guardianship of Minors Bill into the House of Commons;[76] the Prime Minister expressed the Government's willingness to meet the promoters 'with a view to seeing whether agreement can be reached'; and the Government spokesman[77] announced that it was prepared to introduce a Bill into the House of Lords 'embodying the main principles of Mrs Wintringham's bill' forthwith. But appearances were misleading.

The Officials Have Their Way

The Cabinet 'appointed a small informal committee'[78] to examine the matter; but since almost all its members were officials who had committed themselves to the impracticability of equal authority legislation[79] it is not surprising that the Government (although favouring the 'principle of giving equal rights' to parents) was driven to the conclusion that the Wintringham Bill was (like its predecessors) 'open to serious legal and practical objections'.[80]

What then was to be done? The answer was to persuade Mrs Wintringham and her colleagues to accept something in fact very different; and the Bill drafted in 1923[81] was available; and it was this Bill which was put forward by the Committee in the course of lengthy negotiations with Mrs Wintringham and her supporters.[82] The fact that Mrs Wintringham's group eventually agreed to support the Government's Bill,[83] and to refrain from moving hostile amendments to it,[84]

---

and (according to S. Baxter, *The Times* 5 Feb. 1994) she did not utter a word in public during her by-election campaign 'out of respect for her late husband'.

[76] Mrs Wintringham claimed that her Bill took into account the objections which had been made to the original NUSEC Bill; but in fact it included all the principles—equal entitlement to parental authority, obligations on both parties to maintain, jurisdiction in the magistrates' courts—on which opposition had focused.

[77] See the speech by the Home Office Minister, Rhys Davies, on the Second Reading of Mrs Wintringham's Bill: *Hansard* (HC) 4 Apr. 1924, vol. 171, col. 2691.

[78] Chaired by the Solicitor-General, Sir H. H. Slesser (1883–1979). Slesser reappears in this chronicle (in his later capacity as a Lord Justice of Appeal) when it fell to him, in *Re Carroll (No. 2)* [1931] 1 KB 317, to define the scope of the Guardianship of Infants Act 1925, see text to n. 143, below.

[79] The members seem to have been Schuster, Anderson and Gwyer: see the letter from Arthur Henderson to Slesser, 14 Mar. 1924, PRO LCO2/758.

[80] Home Affairs Committee 4 Apr., Conclusion 9(2)(3).   [81] See text to n. 70, above.

[82] The first meeting (at which a draft of the officials' 'compromise' was available) had taken place on 3 Apr. before the Second Reading Debate on the Wintringham Bill; and there were—prompted by Mrs Wintringham: see her letter to Rhys Davies on 8 Apr.: HO45/11982/456799—subsequent meetings on 14 Apr. and on 1 May. See also the detailed account in the Solicitor-General's Memorandum to the Home Affairs Committee dated 6 May 1924, PRO LCO2/758.

[83] They continued to exercise pressure in newspapers and elsewhere about the unsatisfactory nature of the Government's original proposals and urged at least that the provisions of the Bill be widened to give effect to the 'principles of Mrs Wintringham's Bill': see e.g. *The Times*, 17 Apr. 1924.

[84] Home Affairs Committee, 2 May 1924, Conclusion 4. The 'concordat' reached on 1 May involved a number of changes to the officials' original draft—e.g. a mother was given the like power to apply to the court in respect of any matter affecting a child as was possessed by the father; and provisions empowering the mother to appoint a testamentary guardian were inserted: see the annotated Bill on HO45/11982/456799.

is a powerful tribute to the officials' negotiating skills since the Bill did not contain what NUSEC had regarded as the 'essential' provisions giving the mother equal parental authority, and imposing on each parent the duty to maintain their children. Nor did the Bill enable a maintenance order to be enforced unless the parents separated.

What, then, did the Bill do to improve the legal position of mothers? First, it gave each parent the right to appoint a testamentary guardian to act jointly with the surviving parent; and it thus removed a husband's right to control the child's upbringing beyond the grave.[85] Secondly, it gave the mother the same powers as the father to apply to the court in respect of any matter affecting the child; and gave the court power to order maintenance to be paid to a mother in whose favour a custody order was made.[86] Thirdly, it provided that in resolving questions relating to a child's upbringing[87] the court should have regard solely to the child's welfare rather than to any question of parental right. Fourthly, it provided that proceedings could be brought in the magistrates' court (as well as in the High Court and County Court). Finally, it was agreed that the Bill should, unusually,[88] contain a preamble stating that it was expedient that the principle of equality in law between the sexes, as embodied in the Sex Disqualification (Removal) Act 1919 and other legislation, 'should obtain with respect to the guardianship of infants and the rights conferred thereby'.

This resounding statement of general principle no doubt sounded very well; but the reality was that a mother was still to be denied any legal authority over her child during the marriage, and that she could only obtain such authority by court order. In the circumstances, it is not surprising that the Cabinet Committee advised that the Bill represented 'the absolute minimum necessary to secure anything like agreement in the House of Commons . . . and to avoid the danger which might result from a renewal of the agitation for a more radical amendment of the law'.[89] On 15 May 1924 the Cabinet (after 'a long discussion'[90]) agreed. The

[85] Under the Guardianship of Infants Act 1886 the mother had only restricted rights in relation to the appointment of a guardian.

[86] The Bill allowed such orders to be made (albeit not enforced) even if mother and father were still residing together. This proved to be a controversial matter: see text to n. 107, below.

[87] Or the administration of any property belonging to or held in trust for him or the application of the income thereof.

[88] The preamble makes its first appearance in the draft put forward by Parliamentary Counsel and printed on 16 Apr. 1924, i.e. two days after the meeting between Mrs Wintringham's group and the Cabinet Committee held on Monday 14 Apr. The 'Agreed Memorandum by members of the Committee appointed by the Home Secretary on the Guardianship of Infants negotiations' (Annex to CP 287 (24), 6 May) records that the 'promoters attach great importance' to this statement of principle.

[89] Memorandum by the Solicitor-General (CP 287(24)) for the 9 May 1924 Home Affairs Committee meeting.

[90] Most of which seems to have been concerned with the provision referred to in n. 86 above allowing a wife to get a financial order whilst still residing with her husband: Cabinet 32(24) Conclusion 7. See also the minutes of the Home Affairs Committee, 2 May 1924, para. 4 (which records that 'considerable discussion took place') and the Solicitor-General's memorandum: PRO LCO2/758, 6 May 1924.

Lord Chancellor introduced the compromise as a Government Bill and it passed through all its stages[91] in the House of Lords.

But this was not the end of the saga. Potentially disastrously for the supporters of legislation[92] the MacDonald administration fell in October 1924, and the Conservatives were returned to power with a large majority.[93] But the rewards of the long campaign were realised: the Conservative Election Manifesto —no doubt influenced by the desirability of removing a 'difficult question from practical politics'[94]—gave a specific and unequivocal pledge to ensure equal rights to women in the guardianship of children;[95] and the King's speech for the first time incorporated a government commitment[96] to introduce legislation. The Government prudently decided speedily[97] to reintroduce the 1924 compromise with only minor drafting[98] amendments.[99]

[91] Subject to some amendments thought to be non-controversial—including the substitution of the direction that the court should regard the child's welfare as its 'first and paramount' (rather than its 'sole') consideration: see text to n. 133, below.

[92] Including the officials who had evidently become committed to the skilfully formulated compromise: it was 'a great disappointment to me that the turn of events' destroyed the Bill, Schuster wrote to Mrs Hubback on 20 Nov. 1924; but Mrs Hubback's statement that their 'joint labours' had been 'entirely in vain' was falsified by events.

[93] NUSEC's 1924 Annual Report, commenting that 'no brand . . . was this year saved from the burning caused by the General Election', noted that four out of a total of eight women MPs had lost their seats. The new House of Commons would be sadly lacking in many of the friends who had stood the Union in good stead, and the loss of Mrs Wintringham was 'little short of tragedy'. But Mrs Hubback had written to Schuster immediately after the election—and the warmth of their relationship is evidenced by the fact that he sent her both a formal and a (more informative) 'informal' letter about the legislative programme. In her turn, she sent him a formal request for early legislation, under cover of a handwritten note, which she hoped was 'on the lines you thought would be of use': Hubback to Schuster 20 Nov. 1921.

[94] As Lord Wemyss put it.

[95] See Stanley Baldwin's Manifesto as reproduced in F. W. S. Craig, *British General Election Manifestos 1918–1966* (1970).

[96] Immediately after the election, Mrs Hubback wrote to Sir John Anderson to urge that this pledge be met by a specific reference in the King's speech, and she subsequently had a meeting with Anderson: see Hubback to Anderson, 29 Nov. 1924, PRO HO45/11936/429604. George V complained that the speech his Ministers required him to read on 9 Dec. 1924 was 'the longest on record . . . The crown gave me an awful headache. I could not have born it much longer': see H. Nicolson, *King George V, His Life and Reign* (1952) p. 403.

[97] At Schuster's suggestion an interdepartmental meeting on the Bill (and the Legitimacy and Summary Jurisdiction Bills) took place on 17 Dec. 1924; and on 9 Feb. 1925 the Home Affairs Committee took the decision on the basis that the Guardianship and Summary Jurisdiction Bills were desired specially by women and were non-controversial and non-party.

[98] These did not remove some important flaws. In 1928 it was found necessary to make it clear that a father did indeed have a right to apply to the court for a custody order under the Act: Administration of Justice Act 1928, s. 16.

[99] The decision to do so was taken (as the Home Secretary, Sir W. Joynson-Hicks, put it to Lord Chancellor Cave on 20 Dec. 1924) because the compromise Bill represented the 'result of long negotiations and any alteration would undoubtedly lead to a renewal of the argument that arose on the earlier Bills from 1920 onwards': see PRO LCO2/759. The Bill passed through all its stages in the House of Commons without a division, and was given a Second Reading in the House of Lords on 26 May: *Hansard* (HL) vol. 61, col. 521.

Trouble to the End

Notwithstanding the fact that the Home Office Minister[100] described the Bill as absolutely uncontroversial[101] it gave rise to difficulty to the last. In particular,[102] the question of whether the court should have power to make orders whilst husband and wife were living together remained[103] contentious.[104] Amendments were moved, and accepted by the Government, that no order for custody or maintenance should be enforceable,[105] that no liability should accrue whilst mother and father resided together, *and* that any such order should cease to have effect if

[100] G. Locker Lampson (Under-Secretary of State at the Home Office), *Hansard* (HC) 4 Mar. 1925, vol. 181, col. 532.

[101] For reasons about which one can only speculate, the Lord Chancellor 'as a personal matter' asked the Home Secretary to introduce the Bill in the Commons: Schuster to G. R. Buckland, 23 Dec. 1924, PRO HO45/11982/456799.

[102] The birth pangs of the 1925 Act were made more painful by the complexities of legislation dealing with the consents required to the marriage of an infant. The problems which arose under the provision of the Marriage Act 1823 had first been drawn to attention by the Registrar-General, S. P. Vivian, in evidence to the Joint Select Committee on the Guardianship of Infants Bill, Minutes of Evidence 20 July 1922, p. 38. The 1924 compromise Bill sought to deal with these matters by giving a dispensing power to the Registrar (in cases in which the parent or other person concerned could not be found) and to the court—including the magistrates' court—in other cases. Although there was no dispute on the *principle* of these measures, on 18 June the Lord Chancellor unwisely accepted what appeared to be a technical amendment moved by Lord Phillimore about marriage licences granted by the Church; but unfortunately Phillimore had not spoken about the matter to either the Archbishop of Canterbury or to his Vicar-General, Sir Lewis Dibdin. Dibdin first learnt of the matter from *The Times* of 19 June and protested about the 'unusual course' of making a material change in the duties of public officials 'without their being consulted or even informed beforehand': see the Memorandum enclosed with a letter dated 20 June 1925 from the Archbishop to the Lord Chancellor.

[103] In contrast, the NUSEC and Wintringham Bills would have allowed an order to be *enforced* without the wife having to leave; and, as seen above, the 1924 compromise would have allowed a mother to seek (albeit *not* to enforce) a maintenance order for her children before separating from him.

[104] It remained so after enactment. E. Jenks, 'Recent Changes in Family Law' (1928) 44 LQR 314, 319, rhetorically asked whether there could be 'any provision more exactly calculated . . . to turn a working-class household into a hell for the wife and children'. Jenks thought that 'virtuous wives with nagging tongues' would get an order to be kept 'in her pocket, or on the mantelpiece, as a perpetual reminder to her husband that she has it in her power to leave him and reside at his expense elsewhere, extracting from him a substantial weekly sum through the office or the police court; he, in the meanwhile, like a convict on ticket-of-leave, being required to notify each change of address in order that he may the more readily be tracked by the officers of the law'. The difficulty which women have in obtaining financial support (and even information about their husbands' means) unless they leave the family home is discussed by J. Brophy, 'Parental Rights and Children's Welfare: Some Problems of Feminists' Strategy in the 1920s', *International Journal of the Sociology of Law* 1982, 10, 149–68; whilst the most recent legislation still limits the extent to which liability under child maintenance orders accrues while parents live together: see Children Act 1989, Sch. 1, para. 3(4); and assessments under the Child Support Act 1991 can only be made against an 'absent' parent, i.e. a parent who is not living in the same household as the child: see s. 3.

[105] As was pointed out, such an order could only be enforced by seizure of property in the home or by the imprisonment of the husband; and such a proposal was therefore thought to be open to serious objections: Notes for Speech on Second Reading, HO45/12054/474998. Both Conservative and Labour administrations had, for different reasons, refused to support proposals which would have allowed wages to be attached.

mother and father continued to reside together for a period of three months.[106] Mrs Hubback protested at this further weakening of the mother's position;[107] but was rewarded with a magisterial rebuke from Sir John Anderson,[108] the Permanent Under-Secretary of State at the Home Office:[109]

[The provision] allows ample time for the wife to secure her position before actually leaving her husband. The other object to which your Society attach importance, namely, that a wife should be able to hold an Order for a long time *in terrorem* over her husband,[110] was never contemplated, would be highly controversial, and is not one which the Government could countenance. Indeed, I do not hesitate to say that if that argument were seriously advanced, the whole Bill would be imperilled . . . We have been at great pains to secure the acceptance by Parliament of the principles agreed upon last year and I really thought that your Society would have been well satisfied with the result[111]

Notwithstanding this rebuff, Mrs Hubback continued to lobby for the Bill, and wrote to peers[112] urging that the Bill would be of 'untold value' to married women. The Guardianship of Infants Act eventually received the Royal Assent on 31 July 1925.[113] The Act was thus at last safely in port;[114] and although there were those

---

[106] This provision was enacted as Guardianship of Infants Act 1925, s. 3(3). The Summary Jurisdiction (Separation and Maintenance) Act s. 1(4) made similar provision in respect of orders made by magistrates' courts under the Summary Jurisdiction (Married Women) Act 1895. Sir Claud Schuster had said in 1924 (see PRO LCO2/757, 4 June 1924) that the provision for an unenforceable order was 'nonsense . . . [but] the price of peace'; and he had put this frankly to one of the Bill's opponents who had 'practically agreed to be silent on it in future'.

[107] See her letter to Schuster dated 2 Apr. 1925: PRO LCO2/757: 'I think the point of view of the Home Office is that three months is sufficient to enable a woman to look about and make arrangements for removing the children and living apart. This fails to take into consideration the reason why we were so anxious to see some such clause included in the Bill. This is, as you know well, that the obtaining of an order by the mother will, in many cases, act as a warning to the father, and should prevent the breakup of the home altogether. To limit the enforceability of the order to three months would, in many cases, result in not giving enough time for the husband to mend his ways, or, on the other hand, might permit of his amending his ways for three months and then relapsing into bad ways again. It is obviously undesirable and impracticable that the woman should go to the courts to obtain a fresh order at such a short interval of time.'

[108] Anderson (1882–1958), one of the most remarkable figures of his time, had already served as Chairman of the Board of Inland Revenue when appointed Permanent Under-Secretary of State at the Home Office in 1922 at the age of 39. After a period as Governor of Bengal, he entered Parliament as Member for the Scottish Universities in 1938 and served in the War Cabinet during World War II.

[109] Departmental responsibility for the Bill was allotted to the Home Office in 1925.

[110] Mrs Wintringham described a similar argument as a 'magnificent bogy' in a letter to *The Times* published on 26 Mar. 1925.

[111] Schuster had in a letter dated 2 Apr. 1925 asked to be put in a position to send a civil answer to Mrs Hubback, commenting that it was 'desirable to keep these people on our side for as long as possible'; but Anderson evidently preferred to reply himself.

[112] Her commitment to the Bill did not prevent her from seeking further detailed amendments on such matters as the enforceability of maintenance orders during cohabitation—prompting Schuster to write, with apparent admiration, that she 'appeared to have been more successful in the House yesterday than I had anticipated to be possible': 19 June 1925, PRO LCO2/757.

[113] The Summary Jurisdiction (Separation and Maintenance) Act 1925, which—in so far as it allowed a wife to obtain (but not to enforce) a matrimonial order notwithstanding the fact that she was still living with her husband—was in some ways a counterpart to the Guardianship of Infants Act, received the Royal Assent on the same day.   [114] NUSEC Annual Report 1925–6, p. 7.

who saw its restricted scope as an insult to women,[115] the conventional view persuasively put by Ministers was that the compromise nature of the Act was a virtue.[116]
For NUSEC, although the Act was a poor substitute for the original equal authority Bills,[117] the compromise did effect substantial improvements.[118] Incomplete
though it was, the Act would successfully remove most cases of hardship, and
substantially improve the legal status of the mother. In a prophetic passage NUSEC
expressed its confidence that:

the near approach to equality that the new Bill provides will involve few of the difficulties that its enemies anticipate, and that when the passage of time will have given an opportunity for the remaining injustices to mothers to be generally realised, the present Bill
will form a firm foundation for the passage of an amending Bill which will give the full
equality desired[119]

It seems that Mrs Hubback and her colleagues succeeded in convincing many
that the Act had 'at last completed the work which Caroline Norton had begun
a hundred years earlier, and put fathers and mothers[120] into an equal position in
regard to their rights and powers over their offspring'.[121] But were their expectations justified?

---

[115] As *Time and Tide* ('the feminist weekly') and others (branded as 'upholders of the pure milk
of feminism' in the NUSEC Annual Report for 1925–6, p. 7) put it. What do such people 'reck of
the long struggle to obtain the substantial improvements it provides?' NUSEC rhetorically enquired.

[116] G. Locker Lampson, *Hansard* (HC) 4 Mar. 1925, vol. 181, cols. 533–4.

[117] *The Government's Guardianship of Infants Bill, 1924*, by Eva M. Hubback published by NUSEC
in Sept. 1924, price 1d. The Act would leave 'certain real grievances' while the legal status of the
mother will 'still—though somewhat intangibly—be lower than that of the father'.

[118] i.e. 'equal rights for mothers and fathers in any disputes affecting the child brought before the
courts, equal rights for parents with regard to the appointment of guardians after death, the right of
a mother to receive maintenance from the father for the child when given its custody, the right to
bring cases in the summary courts, a preamble which lays down the general principle of equal rights
and responsibilities over their children between parents': ibid.

[119] Ibid. At the 1929 meeting with the Prime Minister and Chancellor (n. 1 above) Mrs Hubback
expressed gratitude for the fact that their Government had been 'kind enough to pass' the 1925 Act
(and the Married Women (Separation and Maintenance) Act) into law as government measures. At
that meeting she advocated legislation giving wives and children rights of inheritance; and once again
the feminist claim for fixed legal rights was met by conferring on the court a discretion to make provision: see Ch. 10, below.

[120] Provided they were married. The Act was only extended to give the parent of an illegitimate
child the right to seek custody orders in 1959: see Legitimacy Act 1959, s. 3, reversing the effect of
the decision in *Re CT (An Infant)* [1957] Ch. 48. PRO file LCO2/5641 contains interesting material
on this issue.

[121] R. Strachey, *The Cause* (1928) p. 383. Even lawyers seem to have taken the view that the 1925
Act effectively remedied women's grievances in this field: see E. Reiss, *Rights and Duties of
Englishwomen* (1934) Ch. III, 'Woman as Mother 1837–1933' (1925 Act 'swept away the remaining vestiges of inequality' at p. 103); and the same author in *Our Freedom and its Results* by five
women (ed. R. Strachey, 1936) Ch. 2, 'Changes in Law', p. 91—'another long fight which had begun
as far back as 1839 came to an end'. As recently as 1982 the Act was said to have made spouses
'equal as guardians of their children': see D. M. Stetson, *A Woman's Issue: the Politics of Family
Law Reform in England* (1982) p. 112.

6. THE GUARDIANSHIP OF INFANTS ACT 1925 AND THE COURTS

Interpreting the Act

The 1925 Act was the result of a delicate compromise; but the decision of the House of Lords in the landmark decision of *J* v. *C*[122] suggests that in two respects the Act did not wholly give effect to what had been agreed.

(i) Child's Welfare the Only Consideration?

Section 1 of the 1925 Act required the court deciding any question relating to a child's custody or upbringing[123] to regard the child's welfare as the 'first and paramount consideration'; and directed the court not to 'take into consideration whether from any other point of view the claim of the father' was superior to that of the mother, or the claim of the mother was superior to that of the father.[124] In *J* v. *C*[125] the House of Lords held that this requirement meant more than treating the child's welfare as the 'top item in a list' of relevant items; and that the 'course to be followed' would be that which would most serve the interests of the child's welfare, that being 'the first consideration because it is of first importance and the paramount consideration because it rules upon or determines the course to be followed'.[126] Although the precise interpretation of the language used in the Law Lords' opinions is itself a matter of some difficulty[127] it was difficult to controvert the view that the child's welfare was ultimately to be the only relevant consideration.[128]

It is doubtful whether this interpretation—which certainly brought to an end any presumption of law[129] regarding parental rights and wishes so far as the test

---

[122] [1970] AC 668. The House of Lords held that the application of the principle that the child's welfare was to be the 'first and paramount' consideration justified the retention of a ten-year-old Spanish Roman Catholic boy in the care of English Protestant foster parents notwithstanding the wishes of the boy's unimpeachable parents to bring him up in Spain.

[123] These words impose a significant limitation on the range of issues in which the child's interests are to be regarded as decisive, since the paramountcy principle only applies to cases in which the specified matters are directly in issue: *Richards* v. *Richards* [1984] AC 174, HL (child's welfare not paramount in application for order excluding spouse from matrimonial home).

[124] The drafting of s. 1 of the Act gave rise to different opinions: in *J* v. *C* [1970] AC 670, 726, Lord Donovan said that this statutory provision was 'almost refreshing in its clarity'; whereas F. A. R. Bennion (at one time a parliamentary draftsman) regards 'first and paramount' as a 'meaningless expression' and considers that the 'first and paramount' formula is simply an example of the use of resounding adjectives: (1976) 126 New LJ 1237; and *Statutory Interpretation* (2nd edn. 1992) p. 848.

[125] [1970] AC 668. [126] Per Lord MacDermott, at 710–11.

[127] See the discussion in the Law Commission's Working Paper No. 96, *Review of Child Law: Custody* (1986) paras. 6.9–6.12.

[128] See H. K. Bevan, *Child Law* (2nd edn. 1989) pp. 86–7. Surprisingly, in *Re M (Child's Upbringing)* [1996] 2 FLR 526, the Court of Appeal (without referring to *J* v. *C*) ordered the return of a ten-year-old boy to his parents in South Africa on the basis that other things being equal it was in a child's interests to be brought up by the natural parents. Subsequent events suggest that this may not have been in the child's best interests, and this appears to have been the view of another division of the Court of Appeal: *Note: Re O (Family Appeals: Management)* [1998] 1 FLR 431.

[129] It is not easy to be confident of understanding how the wardship jurisdiction was applied 'behind the closed doors of the Chancery Division' (per Lord Upjohn [1970] AC 688, 723) and it may be

of welfare is concerned[130]—correctly reflects the intentions of those responsible for the terms in which the Guardianship of Infants Act finally reached the statute book; and it certainly gave no weight to the way in which the text of the statute emerged. In fact, all the Bills presented to Parliament down to and including the Labour Government's 1924 compromise measure did expressly provide that in deciding questions as to the custody or upbringing of a child, the court should have regard *solely* to the welfare of the child;[131] and this provision was seen not only as a great advance on the 'much more vaguely worded discretion' governing custody applications made by a mother under the Guardianship of Infants Act 1886[132] but also as justifying acceptance by the women's groups of the rule that a mother would only have parental authority as and when a court conferred it on her. But at a late stage in the debates on the 1924 compromise, Viscount Cave put down an amendment substituting the 'first and paramount' principle. His reasoning was clear and simple:

The Act of 1886 provides that the Court shall consider the conduct of the parents, and the wishes as well of the mother as of the father. I do not see why those considerations should be excluded, as they would be excluded I think by this Bill. The conduct of the parents is surely material in considering what is to become of their children. The wishes of the parents, who may possibly agree, ought also to be considered, and may very likely be of more value than the opinions of the Judge himself not guided by those wishes. There are other matters which also ought to be considered, such as the responsibility of the father for his children, the special suitability of a mother to have charge of young children, questions of religion, and matters of that kind; indeed, all the facts ought to be before the Judge, and he ought to be entitled to take them into his mind in coming to a decision. I, therefore, propose, instead of saying that the sole consideration shall be the welfare of the infant, that the welfare of the infant shall be the first and paramount

that (as Lord Upjohn put it) in the presence of the early Victorian paterfamilias 'equity too dutifully followed the law' so that the extent to which welfare considerations would override the wishes of the father was unclear and unpredictable: see further the discussion by J. C. Hall, 'The Waning of Parental Rights' [1972B] CLJ 248. It may be that the early 20th-century practice can be ascertained from evidence to the Joint Select Committee on the Guardianship of Infants Bill, Minutes of Evidence 25 July 1922, pp. 64–5, by P. O. Lawrence J. Whilst asserting that there was 'no jurisdiction better known to us judges of the Chancery Division than this, that if a father becomes unfit by conduct to have the custody of his children, the Court has no hesitation in ordering that custody to be taken from him and transferred to the mother or to any other person', he also accepted that where the wardship court had to resolve questions of upbringing it was 'well recognised that the judge . . . would all things being equal, say that the father who is recognised as the guardian by nature and nurture of his children would have the last say in the matter, if it came to a dispute'. He also accepted that the father had a right to dictate the child's religion, and that the father's wishes continued to govern that matter after his death.

[130] See per Lord MacDermott, at 714.

[131] This provision appears as cl. 1 in all the legislative texts; and note that the Lord Chancellor (Haldane) introducing the 1924 compromise Bill stated that 'the interest of the infant is to be looked at exclusively in judging what is right to be done': *Hansard* (HL) 3 June 1924, vol. 57, col. 794.

[132] 'The [High Court or County Court] may . . . make such order as it may think fit regarding the custody of such infant and the right of access thereto of either parent, having regard to the welfare of the infant, and to the conduct of the parents, and to the wishes as well of the mother as of the father . . .': s. 5.

consideration, and that we should leave the Judge at liberty to consider the other matters also . . .[133]

Lord Haldane, the Lord Chancellor, accepted[134] that the amendment would be an improvement:[135]

. . . we ought not to look solely at the welfare of the infant, because there may be other considerations which affect the welfare of the infant which should be taken into account. After all, the infant is a member of a social unit, the family[136]

It was, therefore, Cave's formulation[137] which was adopted in the 1924 compromise and which eventually passed into law in 1925. The legislative history thus makes it clear beyond doubt that the Guardianship of Infants Act 1925 was *not* intended to make the welfare of the child the sole consideration[138] and must indeed cast serious doubt on whether the 1925 Act was intended to give greater weight than in the past[139] to the welfare of the child in deciding disputes about upbringing.[140]

---

[133] *Hansard* (HL) 9 July 1924, vol. 58, col. 349. It was said to be 'common knowledge' that custody of a child would, unless cause to the contrary were shown, be given to a successful petitioner for divorce or judicial separation and this practice evidently survived the enactment of the 1925 Act; but the same practice was not followed in applications for Restitution of Conjugal Rights: see *W* v. *W* [1926] P. 111, per Lord Merrivale, P.

[134] Notwithstanding the fact that Mrs Hubback had stated her view that the Bill 'which already from our point of view, constitutes a compromise, would be very seriously weakened' if the amendment were carried: Hubback to Haldane, 7 July 1924, PRO LCO2/758.

[135] In contrast, Sir Claud Schuster had been reluctant to accept modifications suggested by Parliamentary Counsel to cl. 1 'the wording of which was hammered out inch by inch between ourselves and the promoters of Mrs Wintringham's Bill': see Schuster to Greer, 30 May 1924, PRO LCO2/758.

[136] *Hansard* (HL) 9 July 1924, vol. 58, col. 350; and compare his statement in introducing the compromise 1924 Bill that, in its original form, it was intended that the interest of the infant should be 'looked at exclusively in judging what is right to be done': *Hansard* (HL) 3 June 1924, vol. 57, col. 794.

[137] Note that the Children Act 1989 did not follow the Law Commission's recommendation (*Review of Child Law, Guardianship and Custody*, Law Com. No. 172, 1988, para. 3.15) that the welfare of any child likely to be affected by a decision about upbringing should be the court's *only* concern: see Children Act 1989, s. 1(1)—child's welfare to be court's *paramount* consideration.

[138] See per Eve J, *Re Thain* [1926] Ch. 676. It is also to be noted that on 6 May 1924 Lord Cave had delivered the leading opinion in the case of *Ward* v. *Laverty* [1925] AC 101, in which he accepted that since the enactment of the Guardianship of Infants Act 1886 greater stress had been laid on the welfare and happiness of children than in the past, but said that it was none the less still true that 'a sufficient case must be made for going contrary to the father's wishes' in dealing with cases about a child's religion (and, it would seem, other aspects of the child's upbringing). It seems scarcely credible that Lord Cave did not have this view of the proper weight to be attached to a parent's views when he moved his amendment on 9 July of the same year.

[139] Support for the view that the provision was declaratory of the existing law could be found in case law, see e.g. *Re Thain, Thain* v. *Taylor* [1926] Ch. 676, 691 (per Sargant LJ) and at 689 per Lord Hanworth; *McKee* v. *McKee* [1951] AC 352 (PC), per Lord Simonds; *Re R(M) (An Infant)* [1966] 1 WLR 1527 (in which foster parents unsuccessfully urged that *Thain* was an 'old-fashioned case'); *Re Adoption Application 41/61* [1963] 1 Ch. 315, 328, per Danckwerts LJ. Note also that in the course of the parliamentary debates on the unamended 1924 Bill Lord Phillimore asserted that the original cl. 1 should be seen as 'only stating the law as it at present stands, as I had occasion, as a Judge in the King's Bench Division to administer it . . .': *Hansard* (HL) 3 June 1924, col. 802. The application of the welfare principle could, of course, produce strikingly different results at different times: see n. 128 above.

[140] Cf. the view taken by J. C. Hall, 'The Waning of Parental Rights' [1972B] CLJ 248, 251–3.

(ii) The End of Family Rights?

But perhaps the more important issue in *J* v. *C* was whether to confine the paramountcy of the child's welfare to disputes arising between the parents, or whether—as the House of Lords unequivocally decided in that case—the same principle should extend even to a dispute between an 'unimpeachable' parent and a third party. In reaching that conclusion the House of Lords considered the wording of the preamble[141]—which might have suggested that the Act was only concerned to extend to custody disputes the principle of equality between the sexes—to be irrelevant[142] to the interpretation of the wording of the Act; whilst their Lordships were—understandably given the rules which then governed the admissibility of evidence about parliamentary proceedings—evidently wholly unaware that in the course of the five-year gestation of the Act no one had suggested (whether in parliamentary debate, or in the extensive proceedings of the Joint Select Committee, in the departmental papers, or indeed in the claims made by the promoters) that the legislation could be pressed into service to justify an outsider's claim to the upbringing of a child merely on the basis that the claimant knew better than the parents how his or her welfare might best be promoted.

Moreover, in overruling the decision of the Court of Appeal in *Re Carroll (No. 2)*[143] that the statutory welfare principle was confined in its application to questions as between the father and mother, the House of Lords was evidently— and again understandably—unaware[144] that Slesser LJ (who had delivered the 'lengthy and erudite'[145] leading judgment[146] in that case) was particularly well-informed about the intentions underlying the legislation: it was he who (as Solicitor-General in the 1924 Labour Government) had chaired the meetings at which the

---

[141] See text to n. 88, above.

[142] Following the principle laid down in *A-G* v. *HRH Prince Ernest Augustus of Hanover* [1957] AC 436, 463, HL, that the preamble to a statute cannot be allowed to override the plain words; but this is not to say that the preamble cannot be used in appropriate circumstances as a guide to interpretation: see *Siu Yin Kwan* v. *Eastern Insurance Co. Ltd.* [1994] 2 AC 199, 211, PC; and see generally F. A. R. Bennion, *Statutory Interpretation* (2nd edn. 1992) p. 500.

[143] [1931] 1 KB 317; see particularly the discussion of the effect of the 1925 Act by Slesser LJ at 355–6. The headnote states that save 'as regards the respective claims of married parents as against one another, there has been no change of attitude on the part of the legislature between the years 1891 and 1926 in respect of the wishes of the parents with regard to the custody of infant children. Notwithstanding that the Guardianship of Infants Act 1925 has provided that the welfare of the infant is the first and paramount consideration for the Court . . . [it] cannot disregard the desire of [the child's] . . . parent unless that parent has so neglected his or her duty as no longer to deserve consideration.'

[144] In contrast, Lord Upjohn relied on the professional and judicial career of Lord Cave to support his view that Cave's judgment in *Ward* v. *Laverty* represented an authoritative statement of the practice of the Chancery Division in 1925; but—again not surprisingly—it was not appreciated that Cave had been responsible for ensuring that the legislation should *not* make the child's welfare the only consideration.   [145] J. C. Hall, 'The Waning of Parental Rights' [1972B] CLJ 248, 253.

[146] Slesser's autobiography, *Judgment Reserved* (1941), at pp. 254–5, confirms that he had no doubt at all about the principle that the rights of the parent to the custody and religious education of the child were paramount, notwithstanding the fact that the result of applying that principle might be that a child was taken from a good home with foster parents and handed over to an institution.

compromise between the women's organisations and the Government had been worked out and translated into statutory form, and it was he who had secured the approval of the Home Affairs Committee and of the Cabinet to that compromise.

It is many centuries since the judiciary were so involved in the legislative process that they could say 'Do not gloss the statute; we know it better than you for we made it';[147] but *J* v. *C*—whatever its merits as an exercise in creative judicial law-making—certainly demonstrates the hazards of seeking to ascertain the mischief at which legislation is directed or its intended purpose and likely effect without detailed consideration of the historical context.[148] It seems inconceivable that legislation which would have resulted in a child being kept from his family by an outsider able to offer a better upbringing would have been well received in 1925; and this outcome was certainly unforeseen by anyone involved in drafting the 1925 Act.[149]

People's Courts for the People?

These issues of policy are undoubtedly important; and yet in some ways it could be argued that it was the—comparatively little noticed[150]—fact that proceedings under the 1925 Act could be started in the magistrates' courts which had most impact on the relationship between the law and the family in the years following the enactment of the 1925 Act. It appears (according to the notoriously unreliable statistics[151]) that there were 629 Guardianship of Infants applications

[147] Per Hengham CJ (1305) YB 33–5 Edw. I (RS) 1305. (The author is grateful to Professor J. H. Baker for providing the reference for this dictum.) *Ash* v. *Adby* (1678) 3 Swan. 644 (in which Lord Nottingham referred to his part in introducing the Statute of Frauds 1677) provides a later example of judicial reliance on personal knowledge of parliamentary history.

[148] Cf. *Pepper* v. *Hart* [1993] AC 593; and see generally T. St J. N. Bates, 'The Contemporary Use of Legislative History in the United Kingdom' [1995] CLJ 127; F. A. R. Bennion, *Statutory Interpretation* (1993 Supplement to 2nd edn., Part II). The author is not to be taken as advocating an extension of the *Pepper* v. *Hart* principle; but possibly *J* v. *C* illustrates that it constitutes something of an unsatisfactory halfway house.

[149] More than sixty years later the provisions of the Children Act 1989 prevent a local authority from keeping a child from its parents merely because the authority could better promote the child's welfare: see ss. 31(2), 100 and generally *Re M (A Minor) (Care Order: Threshold Conditions)* [1995] 2 AC 424, HL. Although the welfare principle does apply in 'private law' cases there are some restraints on its application since the court cannot hear an application under its statutory jurisdiction unless the requirements relating to the applicant's standing imposed by s. 10 are satisfied; and, in deciding an application for leave to make an application by a person not entitled under the terms of the Act to do so, the court is to follow the specific guidance given in s. 10(9) rather than the principle that the child's welfare is paramount: see *Re A and Others (Minors) (Residence Orders: Leave to Apply)* [1992] Fam. 182, CA.

[150] Although Mrs Hubback had claimed (*The Government's Guardianship of Infants Bill, 1924*) that this provision threw 'the benefits of the Bill open to all classes'; whilst Lord Askwith (*Hansard* (HL) 3 June 1924) regarded the magistrates' jurisdiction as 'the key to giving to the masses of the women of this country . . . for the first time . . . the power to have something to say in regard to the welfare of their children'.

[151] For long they were to be found only under the heading 'Certain other proceedings' in the annual volumes of Criminal Statistics.

in magistrates' courts in 1928, but this number rose steadily—to 1,169 in 1938, and 6,066 in 1948.[152] Although in theory it had always been open to a mother or other person to institute wardship proceedings and thereby have a court resolve questions about a child's upbringing by reference to the principle long applied in wardship, the absence of legal aid[153] for long confined the use of wardship to the affluent;[154] and it seems that opening the summary courts to parental custody applications must have been a factor in facilitating more widespread recourse to the courts for the resolution of family disputes than many would have thought tolerable in 1925.

7. EQUALITY AT LAST—HALF A CENTURY LATER

The 1925 Act was thus successful in providing machinery whereby family disputes about the upbringing of children could be dealt with by the courts; but the complaint that the law continued to deny equal parental authority to wives did not go away. There was no legislative initiative until 1965; but in that year, Dame Joan Vickers[155] obtained leave[156] under the ten-minute rule to being in a Bill to remove this manifestation of continued discrimination against women.[157] She claimed that to deny any legal right to a mother in the upbringing of her children was not only wrong in principle but also created a host of more mundane

---

[152] The figures appear in Table XI each year. In contrast, in the early years little use was made of the County Court with fewer than twenty applications each year until the late 1960s (when the number of County Court custody cases increased rapidly, as did recourse to the High Court's wardship jurisdiction: see below).

[153] Until 1949 wardship was initiated by proceedings to administer the child's property; but the *Final Report of the Committee on Procedure in Matrimonial Causes* under the chairmanship of Denning J (Cmd. 7024, 1947, para. 34(ix)) considered that this involved unnecessary expense and made it 'possible for an interfering person to make another person's child a ward of court without either the child or its parents or a Judge being aware of the fact'. According to Lord Merriman, P (*Hansard* (HL) 28 July 1949, vol. 164, col. 671) it had come to be realised that anyone could make a child permanently a ward by settling a small sum of money with the result that the 'thing has become absolutely farcical . . . it used to be thought that the minimum tariff should be £5 . . . but that has recently been reduced to half-a-crown . . .'. The Law Reform (Miscellaneous Provisions) Act 1949 accordingly provided that a child should only become a ward by court order to that effect; but this seems not to have inhibited the increased recourse to wardship.

[154] In evidence to the Joint Select Committee on the Guardianship of Infants Bill, Minutes of Evidence 25 July 1922, p. 64, P. O. Lawrence J (who had chaired the Committee to Enquire into the Poor Persons' Rules, Cmd. 430, 1919) had suggested that wardship might be available to the poor under those Rules; see generally R. I. Morgan, 'The Introduction of Civil Legal Aid in England and Wales, 1914–1949' (1994) 5 *Twentieth Century British History* 38. But it was only in 1950 (when legal aid under the Legal Aid Act 1949 became available for wardship proceedings) that there was any widespread use of wardship: see N. V. Lowe and R. White, *Wards of Court* (2nd edn. 1986) Ch. 1. The fact that legal aid was not made available for representation in magistrates' courts family proceedings until 1961 also no doubt affected the choice of forum.

[155] (1907–1994), Conservative MP for Plymouth, Devonport.

[156] *Official Report* (HC) 7 Apr. 1965, vol. 710, col. 486.

[157] According to *The Times* obituary published on 25 May 1994 she had declared that anti-feminism was as serious a problem as racialism or any other prejudice.

practical problems. For example, the mother had no legal right to permit her child to marry, no legal right to authorise withdrawals from the child's Post Office Savings Bank, and she had no legal right to consent to surgery on the child. In particular, the requirement of the Passport Office that any application for a passport in the name of a child should be accompanied by the explicit consent of the child's legal guardian caused particular resentment, since it prevented a separated mother from independently obtaining a passport for her child.

The grievance about the issue of passports could be and was soon dealt with by administrative action;[158] but more fundamental reform was needed. In sharp contrast to the situation in the 1920s, there was no real disagreement; and both Labour[159] and Conservative[160] parties published reports urging that the issue of principle—the legal inequality of wives—be remedied. In 1973 the Conservative Government eventually introduced legislation providing that a mother should have the same rights and authority as the law allowed to a father and that the rights and authority of mother and father should be equal.[161] The Act did not require both parents to agree on a particular course of action; instead it empowered mother or father to act alone[162] but provided that the court could resolve any specific issue on which the parents did not agree.[163]

However, the most dramatic shift in legislative policy did not occur until 1989. The Children Act is based on the principle that a person should not cease to have

---

[158] See *Official Report* (HC) Written Answer 27 Jan. 1966, vol. 723. cols. 137–8: the Minister of State at the Foreign Office stated that the prior and explicit consent of the child's legal guardian would no longer be required for the issue of a passport; but it would remain open to the legal guardian or to any person awarded the custody or the care and control of a minor to enter a caveat against the grant of passport facilities (and a decision would then be taken in the light of all the available information). Precautions were also to be taken against the danger that minors would be enabled to travel anywhere in the world without the knowledge of their parents.

[159] In its report on *Discrimination against Women*: see per Baroness Bacon, *Official Report* (HL) 20 Feb. 1973, vol. 339, col. 28.

[160] *Fair Shares for the Fair Sex*: see per Viscount Colville of Culross, *Official Report* (HL) 20 Feb. 1973, vol. 339, col. 19. The issue had been investigated by a group of Conservative women under the chairmanship of Lord McCorquodale as long ago as 1949, but Baroness Emmet of Amberley and her colleagues had to wait twenty-four years for what she described as this 'dear little Bill': *Official Report* (HL) 20 Feb. 1973, vol. 339, col. 34.

[161] Guardianship Act 1973, s. 1(1). It remains a matter of some difficulty to define the extent of parental authority: see J. M. Eekelaar, 'What are Parental Rights' (1973) 89 LQR 210; H. K. Bevan, *Child Law* (2nd edn. 1989) pp. 13–36; and the discussion in *Bromley's Family Law* (8th edn. by P. M. Bromley and N. V. Lowe, 1992) pp. 310–12; and note the comments in the Law Commission's Working Paper No. 91 (1985) *Review of Child Law, Guardianship*, para. 1.10, and the Commission's *Report* on *Guardianship and Custody* (Law Com. No. 172, 1988) para. 2.9.

[162] Guardianship Act 1973, s. 1(1). Subsequently, the Children Act 1975, s. 85(3), provided that where two or more persons had a parental right jointly either might exercise it without the other if the other had not 'signified disapproval' of such exercise; and the Children Act 1989, s. 2(4), provides that where more than one person has parental responsibility for a child, each of them may act alone and without the other in meeting that responsibility. But the extent to which one parent may act unilaterally is not altogether clear: see *Re PC (Change of Surname)* [1997] 2 FLR 730, Holman J, and the critical comments of J. Eekelaar (1998) 114 LQR 337.

[163] Guardianship Act 1973, s. 1(3).

parental authority[164] solely because some other person acquires such authority by court order or otherwise and it follows that there may now be an almost indefinite multiplication of persons—parents, those with whom the child is to live under a residence order and so on—each entitled to exercise parental authority alone and without the concurrence of any other person.[165] We have seen that fifty years ago Sir Claud Schuster, Sir John Anderson and other eminent persons foresaw very serious problems arising from a division of parental authority between two people; and their reaction had they then been confronted by the provisions accepted without reservation in 1989 would presumably be one of astonishment if not disbelief.

8. CONCLUSION

Perhaps it is surprising that it should have taken more than fifty years[166] to achieve in 1973 the legislation for which NUSEC had begun to campaign in 1920. But the notion that parental authority is of real significance[167] remains powerful. It was precisely because of fears that the father of an illegitimate child might abuse such authority[168] that the Family Law Reform Act 1987 denied him equality with the child's mother in this respect even at the price of making it impossible to achieve the Law Commission's desired objective of ending all legal distinctions which stem from the nature of the relationship between a child's parents; whilst the significance of legal status within the family is evidenced both by the large number of applications[169] for orders[170] conferring parental authority[171] made by fathers of illegitimate children and by the willingness of the courts to accept that

---

[164] Described in the Act as 'parental responsibility': see below.   [165] S. 2(7).

[166] See per Viscount Colville of Culross, *Official Report* (HL) 20 Feb. 1973, vol. 339, col. 20.

[167] It has been said that entitlement to parental authority has 'real and tangible value, not only as something [the parent] can cherish for the sake of his own peace of mind, but also as a status carrying with it rights in waiting'; and that to give a father parental authority gives him an appropriate legal status: see *Re C (Minors) (Parental Rights)* [1992] 1 FLR 1, 3, 8, per Waite J.

[168] '. . . the position of the natural father can be infinitely variable; at one end of the spectrum his connection with the child may be only the single act of intercourse (possibly even rape) which led to conception and at the other end of the spectrum he may have played a full part in the child's life from birth onwards, only the formality of marriage to the mother being absent. Considerable social evils might have resulted if the father at the bottom end of the spectrum had been automatically granted full parental rights and duties . . .': *Re H (Minors) (Local Authority Parental Rights) (No. 3)* [1991] Fam. 151, 158, per Balcombe LJ.

[169] The *Judicial Statistics Annual Report 1995*, Table 5.3, states that 4,475 orders were made in that year. A large number of applications (2,284) were withdrawn. The Lord Chancellor's Department has published a consultation paper (1998) on whether the law denying equality of parental responsibility to fathers of illegitimate children should be changed.

[170] A substantial number of parental responsibility agreements, which under the Children Act 1989, s. 4, are effective to confer parental authority on both parents, are also made.

[171] i.e. parental responsibility orders under Children Act 1989, s. 4(1)(a). 'Parental responsibility' is defined by s. 3 of that Act as meaning all the rights, duties, powers, responsibilities and authority which by law a parent of a child has in relation to the child and his property.

to make such an order will—even if the circumstances are such that the father has no immediate prospect of exercising that authority or having any relationship with the child[172]—often be in the child's interests.[173]

With the benefit of hindsight, Sir Claud Schuster's fear[174]—that the net result of giving both parents equal authority over their children would be 'to substitute a legal for a domestic forum in every household; to multiply causes of strife, and to bring into the courts, to the encumbrance of their proper business, a multitude of trivial disputes'—can be demonstrated to have been unfounded. There is no reported example of an application to the court to resolve particular issues in dispute between parents living together in the same household[175] and no doubt the Law Commission[176] were more in touch with reality than Schuster had been in believing that parents 'who are not separating are unlikely to ask the court to resolve a disagreement, and if they are separating the appropriate orders will usually be for custody and access'. It is, of course, true that the diffusion of parental authority does from time to time cause difficulties;[177] but such difficulties can be well dealt with by the courts as they arise and do not threaten the administration of justice (much less the fabric of society). Mrs Hubback's view that the 1925 compromise would provide a firm foundation for the passage of legislation giving full equality has indeed been triumphantly vindicated.[178] What she could not have foretold was how complex the legal structure would have to become in order to reflect the changes in family structures and social values which have occurred since 1925.

---

[172] See, e.g., *Re H (A Minor) (Parental Responsibility)* [1993] 1 FLR 484, CA (Judge correctly denied father contact with his child, but wrong to refuse to make parental responsibility order in his favour); and *Re S (A Minor) (Stay of Proceedings)* [1993] 2 FLR 912, 917–91 (father who has no prospect of being able to exercise parental rights in the immediate future entitled to ask court to 'recognise his position as the father of the child, irrespective of any question of maintenance or contact. It is a matter to which the father may well attach importance for its own sake').

[173] Provided that he has shown a degree of commitment to the child, and that his reasons for applying for the order are not demonstrably improper or wrong: see *Re G (A Minor) (Parental Responsibility Order)* [1994] 1 FLR 504, 508, per Balcombe LJ.

[174] Expressed 'with somewhat more freedom than is usual in an official memorandum' in response to a request (presumably from the Lord Chancellor) for his personal view on the 1923 Bill: see PRO LCO2/757, 24 Mar. 1923.

[175] There are, of course, many applications in divorce and other proceedings associated with the breakdown of parents' relationships.

[176] *Review of Child Law: Custody* (Working Paper No. 96, para. 2.3).   [177] See n. 162 above.

[178] See *The Government's Guardianship of Infants Bill, 1924*, by Eva M. Hubback published by NUSEC in Sept. 1924, price 1d; and note to the same effect the NUSEC Annual Report 1925–6, pp. 7–8.

8

Adoption—from Contract to Status?

INTRODUCTION—THE ISSUES

In English law, adoption is a legal institution intended to give a child the security of belonging to a family other than the one into which he or she was born. But how far should adoption depend exclusively on the agreement of the two families concerned? There are obvious problems—at one end of the scale, even the most enthusiastic believers in market forces draw the line at a market developing in human beings (particularly when the human being concerned is lacking in capacity and is in need of protection). But, at the other extreme, to allow adoption without the agreement of the parents simply on the basis that someone else can better care for the child may constitute a threat to the integrity and security of the family unit, and thus be considered by many to constitute an unacceptable interference with human rights.

The general question of how far the law should permit family relationships to be regulated by the private agreement of the parties has become an issue of great relevance for lawyers in recent years; and in many respects—not least in relation to marriage and its consequences—modern family law seems to have been evolving[1] towards what Maine[2] described as a phase of social order in which family relationships arise from, and are governed by, the free agreement of individuals rather than a status[3] with incidents prescribed by law. For example, the fact that a married couple had made their own agreements about the financial and other consequences of divorce was until the 1960s regarded with grave suspicion;[4]

---

* This Chapter was first published as part of 'From Status to Contract?' in *Consensus ad idem, Essays on the Law of Contract in Honour of Guenter Treitel*, F. D. Rose, ed. (Sweet & Maxwell, 1996).

[1] 'The concept of marriage seems to me to be evolving from status towards contract, in accordance with Maine's generalisation . . . but it is not yet by any means complete. At this stage, therefore, the task of reconciling concepts, arising from the law of contract, which are second nature to all common lawyers, with an institution which has not yet detached itself from its ancient roots in the quite different system of the canon law, is bound to be extremely difficult . . .': Ormrod J, *Messina* v. *Smith* as cited in *Vervaeke* v. *Smith (Messina and Attorney-General Intervening)* [1981] Fam. 77, 111.

[2] H. J. S. Maine, *Ancient Law* (10th edn. with introduction by Sir F. Pollock, 1909) p. 172. Pollock's comments on this passage at pp. 183–4 are illuminating.

[3] The 'condition of belonging to a class in society to which the law ascribes peculiar rights and duties, capacities and incapacities', per Lord Simon of Glaisdale, *The Ampthill Peerage* [1977] AC 547, 577.

[4] Until the enactment of the Matrimonial Causes Act 1963 'collusion' was an absolute bar to divorce; and it was rightly said that the posture of a petitioner for divorce had to be that of 'an innocent party willing to perform his or her side of the contract, neither conniving at nor condoning the wickedness of the other party, and above all seeking no deal or understanding with him or her to let the divorce through': see H. S. Kent, *In on the Act* (1979) pp. 78–84.

whereas the policy of divorce law embodied in the Family Law Act 1996[5] is to encourage the parties to negotiate their own arrangements about the future upbringing of the children[6] and financial matters.[7] In some areas, it is true, the policy of the law remains ambiguous;[8] but in general what may be called the 'contract' model has become increasingly dominant in family law.

However, adoption of children—involving as it now does the 'complete severance of the legal relationship between parents and child and the establishment of a new one between the child and his adoptive parent'[9]—is different. Indeed, the trend of the law is in the other direction. Whereas in 1926 (when the Adoption Act first empowered the superior courts to make adoption orders) adoption was essentially a process whereby, under minimal safeguards supervised by the court, a civil contract was registered and recognised,[10] it has now become a process, largely administered by welfare agencies, from which contractual elements have almost disappeared. Conversely, whereas the 1926 adoption order had only a limited effect on the child's legal status and could perhaps best be classified as the creation of a special kind of guardianship,[11] the law has slowly moved towards the principle that an adopted child is to be treated as if born to the adoptive parents as a child of their marriage.[12] While, therefore, adoption now undoubtedly creates legal status, that status seems less and less to originate in the natural parents' consent. In this changing scene, the only constant has been the involvement of a court; but the court's role has itself greatly changed over the years.

This Chapter explores two aspects of adoption law (the significance of parental agreement in the adoption process; and the consequences of adoption in terms of the parties' legal status); and it also touches on issues raised by the

---

[5] See generally S. M. Cretney and J. M. Masson, *Principles of Family Law* (6th edn. 1997) pp. 324–83. [6] Family Law Act 1996, s. 11.

[7] See e.g. Family Law Act 1996, s. 7(1)(b)—period for consideration of the arrangements to be made for the future which may be incorporated in a negotiated agreement about financial matters (s. 9(2)(b)).

[8] Notably in respect of the extent to which the terms which the parties have agreed are subject to monitoring by the court: see e.g. *Pounds* v. *Pounds* [1994] 1 FLR 776, CA.

[9] *Report of the Departmental Committee on the Adoption of Children* (1972) Cmnd. 5107, para. 14. For an analysis of the various legal techniques whereby parentage is created in contemporary English law, see G. Douglas and N. V. Lowe, 'Becoming a Parent in English Law' (1992) 108 LQR 414.

[10] G. Rentoul MP in the Second Reading Debate on the Adoption of Children Bill, *Hansard* (HC) 26 Feb. 1926, vol. 192, col. 930.

[11] *Report of the Departmental Committee on the Adoption of Children* (Chairman: HH Sir Gerald Hurst QC) (1954) Cmd. 9248, para. 196.

[12] Adoption Act 1976, s. 39(1). However, this assimilation is not in all respects complete: see text to n. 100 below. The statement (per Lord Upjohn, *J* v. *C* [1970] AC 668, 719, HL) that adoption severs the family ties with the true parents 'completely and for ever', and that the 'adopting parents stand for all purposes in the position of the true parents' is somewhat exaggerated; whilst Lord Upjohn's assertion that after adoption the 'infant does not see or have any communication with his true parents [and that] in the normal case, the true parents and the adopting parents are and remain in total ignorance of one another's identity, and the infant, if adopted as usual in earliest infancy remains wholly ignorant of his true parents' no longer reflects adoption practice.

involvement of the court in the adoption process. To put these matters in context it is necessary first to say a little about the background to the 1926 Act.

THE ADOPTION OF CHILDREN ACT 1926:
SOCIAL AND LEGAL BACKGROUND

'Adoption' was a familiar social institution in the eighteenth century[13] and no doubt earlier; yet the law for long gave it no formal legal recognition. Two factors go some way to explain this apparently surprising fact. First, so far as the property-owning classes were concerned, freedom of testation made it possible to arrange financial provision[14] for a child, irrespective of legal parentage; and thus the need for a formal change of status was much less evident than in civil law countries whose legal systems restrict the making of provision by will or otherwise for those outside the legal family. Secondly—albeit only towards the end of the nineteenth century—the Poor Law gave some protection to those working-class families who had cared for a child against the risk that the natural parents would exercise the common law right to retrieve a child of an age to work simply in order to take its earnings.[15]

'Adoption' first appears in the statute book in the context of the Poor Law: the Poor Law Act 1899[16] provided that the Guardians could in certain circumstances[17] assume by resolution all the parents' rights and powers until the child reached the age of eighteen; and the Guardians were then empowered to arrange for the child to be 'adopted'.[18] In this way, although there was no change in the child's legal status in the strict sense of that word, the 'adopters'[19] acquired a measure of protection against any claim by the child's natural parents.[20] It is true that this protection was inadequate not least because the Poor Law powers were not always exercised even in cases in which they would clearly have been

---

[13] See G. H. Treitel, 'Jane Austen and the Law' (1984) 100 LQR 549, 574.

[14] Provision could also be made by lifetime settlement, the only relevant restriction being the rule of public policy (eventually abolished by Family Law Reform Act 1969, s. 15(7)) prohibiting settlements in favour of the settlor's own after-born illegitimate children.

[15] Evidence given by witnesses to the *Committee on Child Adoption* (1921) Cmd. 1254, para. 13.

[16] Extending powers first conferred by Poor Law Act 1889, s. 1.

[17] Poor Law Act, 1899, s. 1. The power to assume parental rights over a child by resolution became vested in local authorities by the Poor Law Act 1930, s. 52; and such resolutions could be and were passed until the coming into force of the Children Act 1989.

[18] Poor Law Act 1899, s. 3. For the practice of local authorities under the provisions of the Poor Law Act 1930 see *Report of the Departmental Committee on Adoption Societies and Agencies* (1937) Cmd. 5499, para. 8(iii).

[19] At much the same time, the Custody of Children Act 1891 gave the court in habeas corpus proceedings a discretion to refuse to enforce a parent's legal right to recover a child the parent had abandoned or deserted: cf. *R* v. *Barnardo* (1889) 23 QBD 305; *R* v. *Barnardo* [1891] 1 QB 391; *Barnardo* v. *McHugh* [1891] AC 388; *Barnardo* v. *Ford* [1892] AC 336.

[20] The adoptive parents were not protected from a decision by the Guardians—who were empowered to revoke their consent to such adoptions—to remove the child.

available;[21] and the most powerful single factor influencing demand for a more general legal recognition of adoption seems to have been the failure of the legal system to protect those who had undertaken the care of a destitute child.

THE HOPKINSON AND TOMLIN COMMITTEES

The First World War created further pressure;[22] and in 1920 Home Office officials noted that the situation was being exploited by organisations which had 'sprung up in the last year or two'.[23] In response, the Home Secretary appointed a committee under the chairmanship of Sir Alfred Hopkinson KC;[24] and the Hopkinson Committee duly recommended that binding legal effect should be given to agreements for the adoption of children, provided that—in order to protect the welfare of the child concerned—the 'sanction of some responsible judicial or other public authority' were given.[25]

The Hopkinson Committee's Report was not well received within the Home Office.[26] But it had become difficult to resist demands from inside Parliament and outside for something to be done. In 1922 a private member introduced what a Home Office official described as a 'delightfully simple' Bill which would have empowered parents to transfer, with the approval of the court, their rights and

---

[21] Report of the *Royal Commission on the Poor Law* (1909) Cd. 4499, para. 394—children rescued from indigent parents often reclaimed and again 'subjected to evil influences and degrading surroundings'. The Royal Commission (paras. 395–6) thought the Poor Law authorities should make greater use of 'adoption'; and even after the enactment of the Adoption Act 1926 (see p. 189 below) the Departmental Committee on Adoption Societies and Agencies (1937) Cmd. 5499 commended the use of the Poor Law procedure in suitable cases.

[22] The *Report of the Child Adoption Committee* (1924–5) Cmd. 2401, para. 4 recorded that the 1914–18 war led to 'an increase in the number of de facto adoptions but that increase has not been wholly maintained'.

[23] One was said to be 'run by rather doubtful people'; but another was said to place out 'vast numbers of babies'. However, no statistics were available: see the Report of a conference of officials held on 28 Nov. 1921 to consider whether to advise the Home Secretary to introduce legislation: PRO HO45/11540.

[24] (1851–1939), lawyer, educationist and Unionist MP (1926–9 for the Combined English Universities). For some years Hopkinson combined the duties of Professor of Law at Manchester with practice at the Bar; and he served as Vice-Chancellor of the Victoria University of Manchester from 1900–13. Neville Chamberlain MP (1869–1940), remembered chiefly for the policy of appeasement he unsuccessfully pursued as Prime Minister (1937–40) but at this period playing an active and effective part in social policy issues, was a member of the Hopkinson Committee.

[25] *Report of the Committee on Child Adoption* (1921) Cmd. 1254, para. 19.

[26] The Permanent Under-Secretary of State (Sir E. Blackwell) told the conference of officials held on 28 Nov. 1921 (see n. 23, above) that although the Hopkinson Committee had 'regarded the legalisation of adoption as an urgent matter' it had given 'little or no information in support of their recommendation'. On 7 Apr. an official had minuted that the Report was 'not a very good one' not least because it made recommendations which were outside its terms of reference—possibly a reference to the Committee's recommendation that assisting necessitous mothers in the bringing up of their children by some form of allowance be actively considered—and had also advocated other reforms (including consolidation of the legislation relating to children) which would 'never have been made if they had examined any witness from the administrative staff of the Home Office . . .'.

duties over a child under seven to a named individual. The Home Office concluded that it would be 'disastrous' to allow the enactment of a Bill which 'ignores all the difficulties',[27] and ensured that it (and similar Bills introduced in 1923 and 1924) were blocked.

The decisive action in introducing adoption into English law was taken by Arthur Henderson, Home Secretary in the 1924 Labour Administration. He appointed a committee chaired by Tomlin J—a Chancery Division judge who enjoyed the confidence of the Lord Chancellor's Permanent Secretary[28]—'to examine the problem of child adoption from the point of view of possible legislation and to report upon the main provisions' to be included in any Bill.

The Tomlin Committee benefited from a strong official presence;[29] and—possibly reflecting that fact—its Report was less than enthusiastic about the need for legislation.[30] But, albeit somewhat grudgingly, the Committee did accept that people who cared for children as if they were their own ought to be able to have some legal security for their relationship; and the Committee—adopting a then[31] unusual practice—drafted the Bill which (with remarkably few amendments[32])

---

[27] The comments are those of S. W. Harris, then the Assistant Secretary in charge of the Children's Branch: for his career see Ch. 5, n. 23, above. For the decision to block the Bills see e.g. minute of 5 June 1923, PRO HO45/12642. The Bill's promoters were told that the Lord Chancellor objected to the County Courts being required to approve adoption orders (in part because of pressure of other work and in part because they lacked the machinery to make any enquiries); that baby-farmers would be able to use the legislation as a cloak for their operations; and that the Bill said nothing about succession rights.

[28] Sir Claud Schuster. Schuster relied heavily on Tomlin's advice, for example in connection with proposals (eventually coming to fruition in the Legitimacy Act 1926) to introduce legitimation by subsequent marriage into English law; and Tomlin was called in on occasion to mediate between Benjamin Cherry (the freelance draftsman of much of the 1925 property legislation) and Sir F. J. Liddell, the First Parliamentary Counsel (and—perhaps it is worth a footnote mention—younger brother of Alice Liddell, the inspiration of Lewis Carroll's *Alice* novels). In 1929 Tomlin was promoted direct to the House of Lords.

[29] Three of the six members were civil servants from the Departments most affected: W. R. Barker CB (Education), M. L. Gwyer (Health) and S. W. Harris (Home Office).

[30] 'The people wishing to get rid of children are far more numerous than those wishing to receive them and partly on this account the activities in recent years of societies arranging systematically for the adoption of children would appear to have given to adoption a prominence which is somewhat artificial and may not be in all respects wholesome': *Report of the Child Adoption Committee* (1924–5) Cmd. 2401, para. 4. The Committee rejected suggestions that institutionalising adoption would curb the practice of trafficking in children: '. . . some of those who have given evidence . . . suggested that a legal system of adoption should be supplemented by a prohibition of all transactions involving the bringing up of other people's children unless they are legalised by the forms prescribed by the Adoption Acts. This is a proposal the mere statement of which is sufficient to disclose its impracticability': ibid. para. 7. (The Committee obtained a further reference on 13 Mar. 1925 to deal with extensions to the child protection legislation; and its *Third and Final Report* (1926) Cmd. 2711 made proposals on this subject.)

[31] Since 1965 the Law Commission has routinely annexed draft legislation to its law reform proposals: see Ch. 1, n. 47, above. This practice is thought to increase the likelihood that the Commission's reform proposals will be implemented.

[32] Although some of those amendments—particularly that dealing with the circumstances in which the court could dispense with the requirement of parental consent: see the provisos to Adoption Act 1926, s. 2(3),(4)—are significant in the long-term development of the law. This is discussed further in the text to n. 59, below.

became the Adoption of Children Act 1926. This governed the substantive[33] law of adoption until 1949.

ADOPTION AS A COURT-RATIFIED CONTRACT: THE ADOPTION ACT 1926

For the Tomlin Committee the informed consent of the child's parents[34] was to be a prerequisite[35] to an adoption; and it was primarily to ensure that the parties understood the nature and effect of the proposed transaction and were acting of their own free will that the Committee recommended that adoption be a matter for judicial decision[36] and court order.[37] It was intended in this way to provide an effective safeguard against the possibility that social and economic pressures dictated by circumstances might compel a mother to 'make a surrender of her child final in character though she may herself, if a free agent, desire nothing more than a temporary provision for it'.[38] Moreover, the requirement of a 'judicial sanction' would ensure a 'competent independent consideration of the matter from the point of view of the welfare of the child'[39] and thus provide a safeguard against the possibility that legal adoption could be used as a means of legalising trafficking in children.[40] For this reason, although the making of an adoption order was to depend on the consent of the parties,[41] there was to be a real adjudication rather than a mere registration of the will of the parties seeking to part with and take over the child.[42]

---

[33] But the Adoption of Children (Regulation) Act 1939 made changes of great importance relating to the activities of adoption agencies and the making of arrangements for adoption: see further text to n. 53, below.

[34] The consent of every person who was a guardian of, or had actual custody of, or who was liable to support, the infant was also required: cl. 2(3).

[35] The Tomlin Committee recommended that the court should have power to dispense with agreement in certain restricted circumstances: see further p. 190 below.

[36] *Report of the Child Adoption Committee* (1924–5) Cmd. 2401, para. 16.

[37] The Tomlin Committee accepted the arguments strongly held within the Lord Chancellor's Office against conferring adoption jurisdiction on the County Courts; and its draft Bill provided for the High Court and magistrates to have jurisdiction. But as the Hon. A. E. Napier ((1881–1973), then Assistant Secretary in the Lord Chancellor's Office and Deputy Clerk of the Crown in Chancery; subsequently Permanent Secretary) wrote to the County Court judge eventually asked to help with drafting Rules, an amendment giving the County Court jurisdiction in 'this troublesome business' was carried on Report stage in the House of Commons 'in spite of our efforts': Napier to Cann, 9 July 1926, PRO LCO2/1120.   [38] *Report of the Child Adoption Committee* (1924–5) Cmd. 2401, para. 11.

[39] Para. 11.

[40] The papers make it clear that M. L. Gwyer, then Legal Adviser and solicitor to the Ministry of Health (the onerous duties of which post did not prevent him from editing Sir W. Anson's *Law and Custom of the Constitution* (1922)), was particularly concerned about this aspect of legalising adoption: see n. 102, below.

[41] For the court's power to dispense with consent, see text to n. 66, below.

[42] *Report of the Child Adoption Committee* (1924–5) Cmd. 2401, para. 15. It was proposed that a guardian *ad litem* should be appointed in every case 'with the duty of protecting the interests of the child before the tribunal'.

ADOPTION DEPENDENT ON AN INFORMED CONSENT

Contractual analogies clearly weighed heavily with the Lord Chancellor's officials who had the unwelcome responsibility of preparing the rules of court necessary to regulate the procedure in adoption cases. In their view, the court's task was to ensure that the parent's consent[43] was real and informed;[44] and accordingly it followed both that the court should see the natural parent and that the natural parent should know what was to happen to his or her child.[45] Would not a mother proposing to hand over her child to a stranger wish to be satisfied about the character and personality of the adopters? Would she not wish to know something about the home in which her child was to be brought up?

These considerations were evidently influential in determining the content of the Adoption Rules,[46] which provided that the name and address of the adoptive parents should be inserted on the form prescribed for the giving of parental consent; but it soon became apparent that such requirements were found extremely troublesome, particularly by adopters who had found a child through an intermediary (such as the proprietor of a maternity home or a doctor) or by using the services of one of the adoption agencies which came into existence to meet the demand for babies. In particular, there was a real fear that if the mother came to know the child's whereabouts she might disturb the child or blackmail the adopters;[47] and this fear was sufficiently strong to deter some adopters[48] from using the procedure of the 1926 Act. A significant number of *de facto* adoptions remained unlegalised; and it appears that ten years after the coming into force of the 1926 Act only a third of the 'adoptions' organised by one of the three largest adoption agencies in the country were given legal sanction under the 1926 Act.[49]

The practices of some of the agencies and others who arranged adoption placements gave rise to increasing concern in the decade after the introduction of legal adoption in 1926; and eventually Sir John Simon,[50] when Home Secretary, set up a committee[51] (chaired by Florence Horsburgh MP[52]) to consider their

[43] Required by Adoption of Children Act 1926, s. 2(3).

[44] Evidence by the Hon. A. E. Napier to the *Departmental Committee on Adoption Societies and Agencies* (1937) Cmd. 5499 as recorded in a note on PRO LCO2/1162.

[45] Sir C. Schuster, PRO LCO2/1120, 21 Dec. 1926.

[46] There were differences of detail between the rules applicable to the High Court, County Court, and magistrates' courts.

[47] *Report of the Departmental Committee on Adoption Societies and Agencies* (1937) Cmd. 5499, para. 17.

[48] But the extent to which legal adoption was used should not be underestimated: in 1936 there were more than 5,000 adoption orders, the great majority made in juvenile courts: *Report of the Departmental Committee on Adoption Societies and Agencies* (1937) Cmd. 5499, para. 3.

[49] *Departmental Committee on Adoption Societies and Agencies* (1937) Cmd. 5499, paras. 3 and 16. [50] See nn. 57 and 58, below.

[51] The *Departmental Committee on Adoption Societies and Agencies* (1937) Cmd. 5499.

[52] (1889–1969). At the time, Conservative and Unionist MP for Dundee. Subsequently, as Minister of Education in Churchill's administration, she became in 1953 the first woman to hold Cabinet Office in a Conservative Government, and was made a life peer in 1959.

activities. The Adoption of Children (Regulation) Act 1939[53] gave effect to the Committee's recommendations. Generally the Act imposed constraints on those who arranged adoptions. Specifically it sought to prohibit the evasion of the requirement that the court approve adoptions, by imposing a requirement on prospective adopters[54] to make an application to the court for an adoption order within a specified time from the placement of the child by an agency. But adopters and agencies, concerned about the dangers of the mother knowing the adopters' identity and the whereabouts of the children resorted to other methods of concealment; and there is evidence that adoption agencies routinely got mothers to sign a consent form in blank sometimes even before the child's birth;[55] while many courts did not insist on the mother appearing in court to confirm her agreement to the making of an adoption order.[56] It became clear that the conflict between adopters' wish for complete secrecy and the Lord Chancellor's officials' lawyer-like preoccupation with the need for the mother's consent to be demonstrably freely given and informed could only be resolved by more fundamental changes in the governing statute.

THE END OF THE REQUIREMENT FOR INFORMED CONSENT: THE ADOPTION ACT 1949

The decisive shift was made in the Private Member's Bill[57] which became the Adoption Act 1949. After debate—sometimes heated[58]—it was provided that

---

[53] S. 6(3).   [54] Adoption of Children (Regulation) Act 1939, s. 6(3).

[55] Notwithstanding the clear statement in *re JM Carroll (An Infant)* [1931] 1 KB 317, 329, per Scrutton LJ (form in which a mother consents to adoption by anyone to be nominated by an adoption agency should not be acted upon by any court), and the assertion by the *Departmental Committee on Adoption Societies and Agencies* (1937) Cmd. 5499, paras. 18–19, that a mother should be given the information to enable her to decide whether to give or withhold her consent and that it was most important that parents should be made aware that they had a right and duty to attend court and by attending have an opportunity to satisfy themselves personally as to the suitability of the prospective adopters, it appeared that it remained 'by no means uncommon' for the form of consent to be signed and witnessed in blank: *Report of the Departmental Committee on the Adoption of Children* (1954) Cmd. 9248, para. 98.

[56] Eventually, power was taken to dispense with the requirement that the mother attend court, and provision made for her to give a written consent.

[57] Introduced into the Commons by Basil Neild QC and carried through the Lords with the support of the former Lord Chancellor, Viscount Simon. The Bill was largely based on the report *In Loco Parentis* by an unofficial committee under the chairmanship of Judge Gamon: see Dobson to Vaisey, PRO LCO2/4483, 18 Mar. 1949.

[58] See in particular Lord Simon's speech on the Committee stage in the House of Lords, *Official Report* (HL) 21 July 1949, vol. 164, col. 358. Simon (who, as noted above, had appointed the *Departmental Committee on Adoption Societies and Agencies* in 1936 and evidently continued to interest himself in the subject) had the carriage of the Bill in the House of Lords. The papers reveal that he was more than a match for an outstandingly able Parliamentary draftsman, Sir Noel Hutton; whilst his understanding of how adoption was operated in the magistrates' courts was increased by advice from his daughter, Mrs Edwards JP.

consent to the making of an adoption order in pursuance of an application could be given without knowledge of the applicant's identity;[59] and that if such a consent were subsequently withdrawn on the ground only of ignorance of the adopter's identity the parent's consent should be deemed to be unreasonably withheld.[60] In practice—although not in legal theory—consent could now be given to an adoption by persons about whom the mother knew nothing;[61] and the emphasis originally placed on the need for her to take a personal decision about the adopters' suitability had disappeared. In reality, the task of deciding whether the mother had indeed given a true consent to the adoption of her child was transferred from the courts to the JP or other person who was now required to attest the parent's signature on a printed form.

These changes paved the way for subsequent changes culminating in the 'freeing for adoption' provisions of the Children Act 1975 (which allowed a parent, in proceedings started by an adoption agency, to agree 'generally and unconditionally to the making of an adoption order' whether or not the child had been placed for adoption). In such cases the court's order declaring the child free for adoption effectively divests the mother of her legal authority[62] in respect of the child in favour of the applicant adoption agency. This transfer of responsibility

---

[59] Adoption of Children Act 1949, s. 3(2). But the mother's consent to the making of an order was not to be admissible unless the child was at least six weeks old on the date of the execution of the document; and—although suggestions (see notably the speech of Lord Faringdon on the Report stage, *Official Report* (HL) 28 July 1949, vol. 164, col. 680) that a consent should be irrevocable after three months were rejected—the Act provided that a person who had consented to the making of an adoption order was not to remove the child from the applicant's care and possession without leave of the court: s. 3(4). Thus, for the first time, the legal consequences of giving a consent before the court hearing affected, albeit indirectly, the prospects of the mother being able to recover her child if she changed her mind: on deciding an application for leave the court would be guided by considerations of the child's welfare and the decision would not be concluded by the parent's common law entitlement to custody.

[60] And the court could accordingly dispense with the consent: s. 3(1)(c); see p. 193 below.

[61] Simon regarded the question of whether a general consent should be sufficient as the most difficult point in the Bill; and he himself favoured allowing a general consent because 'it helps so much to secure that the natural mother will not know who the adopter is . . .' (Simon to Jowitt, PRO LCO2/4483, 13 July 1949). Reflecting this view, the Bill at one stage provided in terms that consent could be given whether or not an application was pending and could be given *either* generally *or* only in respect of adoption by a specified person. But eventually the less drastic provision set out in the text was agreed. In many cases, prospective adopters took advantage of a procedure prescribed by Rules (see Adoption of Children (County Court) Rules 1952) whereby the applicant's identity was concealed by the use of a serial number; and, although the *Departmental Committee on the Adoption of Children* (1954) Cmd. 9248, para. 93 stated that some courts declined to allow applicants to use this procedure, the Committee considered that it gave a very valuable protection for the adopters and for the child and that no attempt should be made to thwart applicants who wished to take advantage of a right 'deliberately conferred by Parliament'.

[62] But a freeing order—in contrast to the adoption order which should normally follow—does not affect the parent's status as such. The legislation provides some protection for a parent who is concerned about the risk that no adoption will ever be made, but these provisions have given rise to difficulties: see *Re G (A Minor) (Adoption: Freeing Order)* [1997] AC 613; and (for a full consideration of the problems to which the freeing procedure had given rise) N. V. Lowe, 'Freeing for Adoption: The Experience of the 1990s' [1990] JSWL 220.

from a parent to a local authority[63] or state licensed agency[64] would surely have seemed remarkable to those responsible for the introduction of legal adoption in 1926.[65] Certainly, it has become quite impossible to regard legal adoption as any longer primarily founded on contract.

ADOPTION AGAINST THE PARENT'S WILL

Notwithstanding the Tomlin Committee's view of adoption as a court-sanctioned contract—and thus necessarily founded on the consent of the parties—the court has from the outset had power in certain circumstances to make an adoption order in spite of the complete absence of parental agreement. But the Tomlin Committee's draft Bill[66] envisaged that consent would only be dispensed with in wholly exceptional circumstances (reflecting the grounds upon which the Poor Law Guardians had been able to assume parental rights over a child): the court could dispense with consent if satisfied that the person concerned had abandoned or deserted the child or could not be found or was incapable of giving a consent or had persistently neglected or refused to discharge his liability to support the child. The 1926 Act[67] in fact went somewhat further than this, giving the court what might be construed as a general power to dispense with consent;[68] but for twenty

---

[63] All local authorities were empowered to act as adoption agencies by the Children Act 1958, s. 30; whilst the Children Act 1975, s. 1 (in a provision which long remained unimplemented because of concern about its financial implications) imposed a duty on local authorities to establish and maintain a comprehensive adoption service: see now Adoption Act 1976, s. 1(1). It appears that voluntary agencies now play only a small part in arranging adoptions and that local authorities have come to dominate adoption practice: see *Inter-Departmental Review of Adoption Law Discussion Paper Number 3, The Adoption Process* (1991) para. 101; P. Morgan, *Adoption and the Care of Children* (1998) pp. 12–14.

[64] Early concern about the activities of agencies resulted in a statutory requirement for registration (see Adoption of Children (Regulation) Act 1939—giving effect to the recommendations of the *Departmental Committee on Adoption Societies and Agencies* (1937) Cmd. 5499, see text to n. 51 above); and the Children Act 1975 required them to be approved by the Secretary of State: see now Adoption Act 1976, s. 3.

[65] Even the limited registration provisions of the Adoption of Children (Regulation) Act were opposed by a member of the *Departmental Committee on Adoption Societies and Agencies* for fear that such arrangements would be seen to relieve the parent of his or her own clear duty and responsibility to take decisions relating to the child: Note of Reservation by Mr G. W. Russell (who, a decade earlier, had been a member of the Tomlin Committee).

[66] *Child Adoption Committee, Second Report* (1925) Cmd. 2469.   [67] S. 2(3) proviso.

[68] S. 2(3) provided that the court might 'dispense with any agreement required' on the part of a parent, guardian, person with actual custody, or person liable to contribute to the support of the child if satisfied 'that the person whose consent is to be dispensed with has abandoned or deserted the infant or cannot be found or is incapable of giving such consent, or, being a person liable to contribute to the support of the infant, either has persistently neglected or refused to contribute to such support *or is a person whose consent ought, in the opinion of the court and in all the circumstances to be dispensed with*'. The italicised words were an inelegant addition to the Tomlin Committee's draft (see *Child Adoption Committee. Second Report* (1925) Cmd. 2469) made perhaps to empower the court to dispense with consent in cases such as those postulated by Lord Goddard in *H* v. *H* [1947] KB 463 in which a child had been kidnapped or in which a child's mother refused agreement to adoption by a relative of her husband 'purely to annoy her husband'.

years the courts interpreted the dispensing power narrowly. However, in 1947[69] the Divisional Court held that the court could dispense with the consent of a parent or other person in any circumstances in which it deemed it appropriate to do so.[70]

Those concerned with the drafting of the Adoption of Children Act 1949 considered such a discretion to be too wide;[71] and accordingly the conditions were redefined.[72] But linguistic change did not remove doubts, and there was a divergence of judicial approach to the interpretation of the statutory provision.[73] In particular there was a conflict between those who thought that dispensation on this ground could only be based on the parent's culpability or self-indulgence[74] and those prepared to accept a broader interpretation in which the weight a reasonable parent would give to the child's best interests would be particularly significant in determining the reasonableness or otherwise of the parent's refusal.[75] Eventually in 1971 the House of Lords took[76] the latter view. Although there remains a distinction between adoption and custody[77] cases, a reasonable parent faced with a decision as to whether to give his or her consent to the making of an adoption order would pay regard to the welfare of his child, and accordingly

---

[69] *H* v. *H* [1947] KB 463, 466 (court has 'widest possible discretion', per Lord Goddard). According to the *Departmental Committee on the Adoption of Children* (1954) Cmd. 9248, para. 114, the decision was rather unexpected.

[70] The Divisional Court rejected the argument that the power to dispense with consent on the grounds that it was unreasonably withheld did not apply to parental consent but only to those cases in which the consent of a person liable to support the child was required.

[71] See in particular Lord Simon's speech, *Official Report* (HL) 11 July 1949, vol. 163, col. 1048; and note his heavily sarcastic comments about the views expressed at cols. 1068–71 by his predecessor as Lord Chancellor, Viscount Maugham.

[72] It was provided that the court could dispense with the consent of a parent or guardian who had abandoned, neglected or persistently ill-treated the child and of any person who could not be found or was incapable of giving consent and with the consent of any person which was 'unreasonably withheld': Adoption Act 1949, s. 3(1)(a), (c). The consent of a person liable to maintain a child by virtue of an order or agreement—usually the natural father of an illegitimate child—could be dispensed with if he had persistently neglected or refused to contribute to the child's maintenance: s. 3(1)(b).

[73] For a brief account, see S. M. Cretney, *Principles of Family Law* (4th edn. 1984) pp. 449–55. The belief that the courts were interpreting the provision to mean that they could only dispense with consent if the parent was maintaining an attitude which it was unreasonable to hold *as a parent* (rather than considering the parent's attitude to the impact of the refusal on the child's welfare) led the *Departmental Committee on the Adoption of Children* (1954, Cmd. 9248, para. 120) to recommend that the ground of unreasonable withholding should be removed and that there should be a further specific ground allowing the court to dispense with consent by a parent who had 'made no attempt to discharge the responsibilities of a parent'. This would have been very much narrower than the formulation which eventually emerged from the decision of the House of Lords in *Re W (An Infant)*, as to which see below.

[74] *Re C(L) (An Infant)* [1965] 2 QB 449, 471, per Diplock LJ; *Re W (An Infant)* [1970] 2 QB 589, 600, CA.

[75] Notably Lord Denning MR in *Re L (An Infant)* (1962) 106 SJ 611; and see *Re B (CHO) An Infant)* [1971] 1 QB 437, 454, per Winn LJ.   [76] *Re W (An Infant)* [1971] AC 682, HL.

[77] In which the child's welfare was the paramount consideration: see generally *J* v. *C* [1970] AC 668, and (on the distinction between adoption and other cases) at 719, per Lord Upjohn reproduced (and the subject of comment) at p. 185 above.

the effect on the child's welfare of the parent's withholding agreement to adoption would be relevant in all cases if and to the extent that a reasonable parent would take it into account, and decisive in those cases where a reasonable parent would so regard it.[78] In effect, the question was not whether a reasonable parent would refuse to agree to the adoption; it was whether any reasonable parent could refuse to do so.[79]

This ruling appears to have had a significant effect on practice: whereas it had been considered an accepted fact that courts would 'almost always' refuse an adoption order if a parent withheld consent[80] there has been an increasing tendency for the courts to dispense with parental agreement in cases in which the evidence of welfare professionals[81] indicates that the child's welfare would best be served by that course—notably where a child has been in local authority care for some time,[82] and the parent has had no contact.[83]

Concern has been expressed as to whether the law gives sufficient weight to the parent's refusal to agree to adoption[84] and as to whether in practice the courts

---

[78] *Re W (An Infant)* [1971] AC 682, 699, per Lord Hailsham.

[79] *Re W (An Infant)* [1971] AC 682, 700, per Lord Hailsham.

[80] See (1981) *Adoption and Fostering* 24.

[81] Employed in local authority Social Services Departments, and in that capacity deciding whether adoption is to be the preferred option for a child in local authority care. Local authority social workers may also be involved in preparing the elaborate reports to the court now required by the Adoption Agencies Regulations 1985. Private placements for adoption have been prohibited since the coming into force of the relevant provisions of the Children Act 1975 on 15 Feb. 1982, and the prohibitions are drawn in startlingly wide language: see e.g. *Re W (a minor)(adoption: mother under disability)* [1995] 4 All ER 282 (where a District Judge held that they prohibited the child's maternal grandmother from making arrangements on behalf of her mentally incapable daughter with an adoption agency). However, not all placements will have been arranged by agencies—adoptions by relatives, and adoptions of children brought to this country by intending adopters are common examples of non-agency adoptions. In such cases, the local authority must be notified of the intended adoption; and the local authority will make the extensive enquiries and reports which are now required: see Adoption Act 1976, s. 22; Adoption Rules 1984, Schs. 2 and 3. It is interesting to note that one of the reasons for the Lord Chancellor's officials' objections to conferring adoption jurisdiction on the County Court was the lack of any suitable provision for the making of enquiries on the court's behalf; and although the Adoption Act 1926, s. 7(3), required the appointment of a guardian *ad litem* 'with the duty of safeguarding the interests of the infant before the court' in every case, the rules were undemanding and unspecific about the guardian's qualifications: see Adoption (County Court) Rules 1926. (It appears that in many cases the guardian was an official of the Local Education Department, and that in some cases the clergy or even members of the court staff performed this role). The contrast with the requirements now imposed by the Guardian ad Litem and Reporting Officers (Panels) Regulations 1991 (SI 1991/2051) is striking.

[82] Note, however, that on one view local authorities are often excessively concerned to preserve the family link and accordingly reluctant to place children for adoption: see generally P. Morgan, *Adoption and the Care of Children* (1998) (and note in particular the view that more than 12,000 children currently in local authority care might be 'adoptable': p. 149 and Ch. 15, *passim*).

[83] The crucial question in many cases is whether the court, having made a care order under the provisions of the Children Act 1989, s. 31, denies the parent contact under the powers conferred on it by the Children Act 1989, s. 34. This latter issue is resolved by reference to the child's welfare; and thus on one view that issue has effectively become dominant in determining whether a child is to be adopted notwithstanding the opposition of the parent.

[84] *Review of Adoption Law* (1992) para. 12, cited with approval by Balcombe LJ in *Re C (A Minor) (Adoption: Parental Agreement: Contact)* [1993] 2 FLR 261, 270, CA.

have not come to regard the test as being that the child's welfare is paramount. But it can also be argued that the notion of the reasonable parent reflects the 'anthropomorphic conception of justice' familiar in the context of the contractual doctrine of frustration,[85] and that it does no more than to provide machinery whereby the court can decide whether, having regard to the evidence and applying the current values of our society, the advantages of adoption for the welfare of the child appear sufficiently strong to justify overriding the views and interests of an objecting parent.[86] It seems improbable that those responsible for the enactment of the first adoption legislation—or those responsible for the reformulation effected in 1949—contemplated that the need for parental agreement would ever have been allowed to be eroded to this extent.

STATUS OF THE ADOPTED CHILD

The Adoption Act 1926 left the legal status of the adopted child somewhat ambiguous. It is true that the Tomlin Committee rejected suggestions that the court should have power to revoke an adoption order once made; and the 1926 Act contained no such provision.[87] It is also true that the 1926 Act defined the effect of an adoption order in resounding language.[88] But that language could not conceal the fact that the 1926 Act (unsurprisingly, given that the most important failing of the common law had been identified as its failure to give 'adoptive parents' any legal security in their possession of the child) virtually confined the effect of an

---

[85] Per Lord Radcliffe, *Davis Contractors* v. *Fareham UDC* [1956] AC 696, 728–9; and see generally G. H. Treitel, *The Law of Contract* (9th edn. 1995) pp. 832–7; G. H. Treitel, *Frustration and Force Majeure* (1994).

[86] *Re C (A Minor) (Adoption: Parental Agreement: Contact)* [1993] 2 FLR 261, per Steyn and Hoffmann LJJ at 272–3, CA.

[87] Tomlin Report, para. 26. The Committee thought the notion of revocation would be inconsistent with adoption; but recent cases have demonstrated the potential for hardship which is inherent in the irrevocability of an adoption order: see notably *Re B (adoption order: jurisdiction to set aside)* [1995] Fam. 239, CA. (Child of Kuwaiti Muslim Arab father and Roman Catholic mother adopted by orthodox Jewish couple who believed him to be Jewish and brought him up as such. Applicant wished to settle in Israel but suspected of being Arab spy; and, having traced his father, found it impossible to settle in Kuwait either. *Held*: no power to revoke the order.) Compare *Re M (Minors) (Adoption)* [1991] 1 FLR 458, CA (Children's father consented to their adoption by stepfather and mother—mother, unknown to father, suffering from terminal cancer and died three months later. *Held*: father's agreement to adoption could be set aside as a 'classic case of mistake' which (per Glidewell LJ at 459) vitiated his consent. It appears that the distinction between the two cases lies in the fact that the latter case was one dealt with by way of appeal (albeit leave to appeal out of time was necessary).

[88] S. 5(1) provided that upon the making of an adoption order, 'all rights, duties, obligations and liabilities of the parent or parents, guardian or guardians of the adopted child, in relation to the future custody, maintenance and education of the adopted child, including all rights to appoint a guardian or to consent or give notice of dissent to marriage shall be extinguished, and all such rights, duties, obligations and liabilities shall vest in and be exercisable by and enforceable against the adopter as though the adopted child was a child born to the adopter in lawful wedlock, and in respect of the same matters and in respect of the liability of a child to maintain its parents the adopted child shall stand to the adopter exclusively in the position of a child born to the adopter in lawful wedlock'.

adoption order to transferring guardianship, custody[89] and maintenance obligations to the adopters. The Act stopped far short of creating a legal transplant from birth to adoptive family. In particular, for purposes of succession rights and of the prohibited degrees for marriage, an adopted child was to remain within his or her natural family.[90]

This approach may today seem timid, but at least it can be defended on the grounds of intellectual coherence; and in fact the only technical flaws of the Tomlin legislation seem to have resulted from failure to hold fast to its first thoughts about the effect of adoption on the child's name. The Committee originally asserted that in law 'a surname is a matter of reputation and nothing else'. It followed that there was no need for any statutory provision to enable an adopted child to be called by the surname[91] of the adopting parent.[92] However, the Registrar-General considered that adoption would be an act 'of civil status having legal consequences as regards the rights of the individuals concerned'[93] and that there ought accordingly to be an entry in the Register 'to afford an accessible record of the change of status involved'. The Adoption Act accordingly made provision for registering the name;[94] but unfortunately this caused immense difficulties which were not wholly resolved until 1958. Those difficulties—far too complex to be explored in a short essay—could be regarded as revealing an ambivalence about the nature of adoption:[95] how far was adoption under the Adoption Act 1926 really an 'act of civil status'?

---

[89] Including consent to marriage.

[90] See Tomlin Report, paras. 18–21, 27; Adoption of Children Act 1926, s. 5(2).

[91] The position about changing forenames might be thought to be more difficult.

[92] Tomlin Report, para. 21.   [93] PRO HO45/12462.

[94] Adoption of Children Act, 1926, s. 11, and Sch. From 1928 there was heated controversy (see PRO file PRO LCO2/1159) involving the Chancery judges, the Lord Chancellor's Office, and the Registrar-General S. P. Vivian about the meaning of these provisions; but the issues were not fully addressed in public until the *Report of the Departmental Committee on the Adoption of Children* (Cmd. 9248, 1954, paras. 205–20) made recommendations (carried into effect by Children Act 1958, s. 25) which effectively allowed the applicants to use the adoption to register the forenames and surnames of the child as they wished. The entries to be made are now prescribed by delegated legislation: Forms of Adoption Entry Regulations 1975, SI 1975/1259.

[95] Tomlin's original proposal was that the entry in the Adopted Children Register should state the 'name and surname' of the child, but such an entry might enable the original birth registration to be traced and thus break the secrecy principle to which adoption societies (and others concerned to prevent disclosure of the fact that a child had been born illegitimate) attached great importance. Accordingly the Act merely required the child's 'name' to be entered. This provision caused problems, not least because the High Court routinely gave directions for the surname to be included. The Registrar-General considered that high matters of constitutional principle were involved; but Sir Claud Schuster was 'very unwilling to stimulate (the Registrar-General) into any further correspondence, principally for the reason that, being a very conscientious man and a very ingenious man, he usually writes at enormous length and I find it very difficult to follow what he writes': Schuster to Luxmoore, 15 Mar. 1929, PRO LCO2/1159. Schuster was also reluctant to give the matter any publicity ('if we do, all the people who get excited on this subject (and they are many) will think they see an opportunity for airing their views': (Schuster to Luxmoore, 18 Dec. 1929) while the prospect of legislation on the subject was unappealing 'both because the Government appear to have formed legislative plans which . . . are likely to occupy Parliament for the rest of our lifetime and because there is a risk lest, if the matter arises again in Parliament, it may be difficult to confine the amendments to those which you would consider necessary or desirable' (Schuster to Luxmoore, 29 July 1929).

Whatever the answer to that question may be, it is today clear beyond doubt that an adoption order does indeed create a new legal status. Part IV of the Adoption Act 1976[96] is entitled 'Status of Adopted Children'; and declares[97] that an adopted child is to be treated in law as the child of the adoptive parents' marriage and not the child of any other person;[98] and it is expressly provided that these provisions prevent an adopted child from being illegitimate.[99] But an examination of the effect of adoption on some of the normal incidents of legal status suggests that—although the 1949 Act did mark a decisive shift from contract to status in relation to the legal nature of adoption—there are still some anomalies and inconsistencies.

(i) Succession Rights

In respect of succession rights,[100] the Tomlin Committee asserted that it did not require any profound knowledge of the law of succession to bring home to an inquirer (1) the impracticability of putting an adopted child in precisely the same position as a natural child in regard to succession;[101] and (2) the grave difficulties which would arise if any alterations were to be made to the law of succession for the purpose of giving an adopted child more limited rights. Accordingly the Committee thought the best solution—given the concern evidently felt[102] by some (including members of the Committee) about exploitation of adopted children as a source of cheap labour—would be to leave the adopted child's succession rights unchanged, but to give the court power to require the adopter to provide for the child (for example, by imposing terms and conditions in an

---

[96] The 1976 Act was a consolidation measure. As explained below, the most important changes in the substantive law were, in the present context, made by the Adoption Act 1949 and the Children Act 1975.

[97] S. 39 (1)(a), dealing with adoption by a married couple. In other cases, the child is to be treated as if he had been born to the adopter in wedlock (but not as a child of any actual marriage of the adopter): s. 39(1)(b). The Act does recognise some exceptions to the general principle (notably in relation to the descent of peerages); and see text to nn. 108 and 116 below in relation to the prohibited degrees, citizenship and immigration status.

[98] S. 39(2). The Act (s. 41) provides that relationships existing by virtue of s. 39 may be referred to as an adoptive relationship, that a male adopter may be described as the adoptive father and a female adopter as the adoptive mother, and 'any other relative of any degree under an adoptive relationship may be referred to as an adoptive relative of that degree'.   [99] S. 39(4).

[100] The Adoption of Children Act 1926 included express provision declaring (in effect) that an adoption order should neither deprive an adopted child of any interest in property to which, but for the order, he would have been entitled, nor should it confer any interest on him. Moreover, the expressions 'child', 'issue', etc. used in wills, settlements, etc. were not to include adopted children whether the disposition was made before or after the making of an adoption order: s. 5(2).

[101] It is to be assumed that the Committee had in mind such questions as the respective seniority of adopted and natural children, which did indeed cause problems to the draftsman concerned with the 1949 legislation: see n. 107 below.

[102] Notably by the Legal Adviser to the Department of Health, M. L. Gwyer, who wrote on 18 Mar. 1926 (PRO file HO45/11540) to S. W. Harris at the Home Office: '. . . it is the transfer of the bodies of helpless children which moves me most, and the powers arrogated by the existing Societies seem to me emphatically against public policy'.

adoption order or requiring the adopter by bond to make such provision for the adopted child as was just and expedient[103]).

Only in 1949 (and against opposition[104]) did legislation accept[105] the broad principle that the adopted should be treated as children of the adopters for the purposes of the devolution or disposal of real and personal property; and the development of the law reflects not only the (often insoluble) conundrums with which a draftsman may be faced but the property lawyer's legitimate concern that changes in the devolution of property should not be imposed retrospectively. In fact the 1949 Act did not achieve[106] total integration of the child into the adoptive family for succession purposes—this had to wait until the Children Act 1975[107]—but the 1949 Act did assert and establish the principle that adoption changed the child's legal status in terms of succession rights.

(ii) The Prohibited Degrees

The Tomlin Committee's reasons for rejecting the 'introduction of artificial prohibitions'[108] on marriage throw considerable light on the Committee's view of the nature of adoption as a social institution:

[103] In fact there is no evidence that the power to impose conditions relating to financial matters was ever exercised on any significant scale. Latterly the power to impose conditions has occasionally been invoked to require the adoptive parents to allow the natural parents a measure of contact with the child; but this (so it has been held) should only be done in exceptional circumstances: see *Re C (A Minor) (Adoption: Conditions)* [1989] AC 1, HL; *Re S (a minor) (adoption order: conditions)* [1995] 2 All ER 122, CA.

[104] The Lord Chancellor's Office consulted Vaisey J and Lord Morton of Henryton. These two judges opposed any change which might cause the devolution of an intestate's property to be affected by an adoption about which the intestate had been unaware. Many possible permutations were discussed (see notably the letter from Napier to Simon, 30 June 1949, PRO file PRO LCO2/4483, and the copy letter dated 13 July 1949 on the same file from the draftsman (Hutton) to Simon). Eventually—and in large part because of the great technical difficulty of drafting compromise provisions—it was decided to accept the principle stated in the text, but only in respect of intestacies occurring and wills and settlements made after the date of the adoption order: see the notably ill-humoured exchange between Simon and Maugham on the Committee stage: *Official Report* (HL) 21 July 1949, vol. 164, col. 374.   [105] Adoption of Children Act 1949, s. 9(1).

[106] By reason of the exclusion of the adopted child from succeeding as a child of the deceased under dispositions made before the date of the order: see the discussion in the *Report of the Departmental Committee on the Adoption of Children* (Cmd. 9248, 1954, paras. 155–60). The Children Act 1958, s. 22, dealt with one problem by providing that a will was for this purpose to be treated as made on the date of the testator's death; but did not remove the inability of the adopted child to take as the adoptive parent's child under (for example) a settlement made before the adoption in favour of the settlor's grandchildren.

[107] Sch. 1, paras. 3, 5 (giving effect to the recommendations of the *Departmental Committee on the Adoption of Children* (1972, Cmnd. 5107, para. 328). The draftsman had to include provision (to be found in Sch. 1, para. 6) to deal with the seniority of adopted children in cases (such as those envisaged by Hutton in 1949: see his letter to Simon dated 13 July 1949, PRO LCO2/4483) in which a testator's will leaves his estate to A for life with remainder to A's eldest child living at his death, and A is 'sufficiently inconsiderate to die leaving surviving him a natural child aged 20' born in 1950 and an adopted child aged 25 adopted in 1951. As mentioned at n. 104 it was eventually decided not to include such a provision in the 1949 Act because that Act was confined to dispositions made after the adoption order, and a testator or settlor 'who had his wits about him' would not set the courts this particular problem.

[108] *Report of the Child Adoption Committee* (1924–5, Cmd. 2401) para. 20.

The blood tie cannot be severed . . . [The] existing prohibitions . . . must remain and it is repugnant to common sense to make artificial offences the result of a purely artificial relationship [*sic*]. The relationship of guardian and ward does not to-day preclude inter-marriage and the adopting parent will only hold the position of a special guardian . . . [Accordingly,] legalised adoption should have no effect in this regard at all.[109]

This policy was followed in the 1926 Act, which made no provision at all about the prohibited degrees. Perhaps, from the perspective of the 1990s, the Tomlin Committee may be thought not to have taken sufficient account of the distinction between prohibited degrees arising out of consanguinity (where there is a genetic case for preserving a prohibition) and those based on a factual social relationship[110]—for example, stepfather and stepchild or brother and sister—such as would seem to be incompatible with the creation of the relationship of husband and wife[111] between the two persons concerned). But the adoption legislation has not fully recognised this. Although the 1949 Act provided that an adopted child could not marry the adoptive parent,[112] there is no bar on marriage with an adoptive brother or sister. As Lord Chancellor Jowitt observed in 1949 this seems rather curious;[113] but there seems little enthusiasm[114] for changing the law, and the fact that many adoptions are now of older children may well put a different complexion on the matter—the considerations which might make it repugnant to contemplate the marriage of two people brought up from infancy to maturity as brother and sister clearly would not apply to the marriage of a young woman adopted at age sixteen and her adoptive brother who had never been a member of the same household.[115]

---

[109] Ibid.

[110] See S. M. Cretney and J. M. Masson, *Principles of Family Law* (6th edn. 1997) pp. 44–50.

[111] This distinction is recognised by the Marriage (Prohibited Degrees of Relationship) Act 1986 which permits marriages between persons formerly within the prohibited degrees created by affinity, subject to certain conditions: see S. M. Cretney and J. M. Masson, *Principles of Family Law* (6th edn. 1997) pp. 46–9.

[112] S. 11(1). The validity of any such marriages solemnised before commencement was expressly preserved.

[113] *Official Report* (HL) 11 July 1949, vol. 163, col. 1083. Jowitt received a letter from a man who had been happily married to his adoptive sister for thirty-five years: see PRO file PRO LCO2/4483. Simon wrote to Jowitt on 13 July 1949 that, although he quite saw Jowitt's point, 'I doubt whether we can go the whole way in this matter. A step-brother can marry his step-sister. Moreover, if we go the whole way, the brother of the adopter could not marry the adopted child, for an uncle cannot marry his niece . . . The Home Office are anxious about the proposed extension because it might increase cases of incest.'

[114] The *Departmental Committee on the Adoption of Children* (1972) Cmnd. 5107 had originally been minded to favour extending the prohibition to all relatives whom the adopted child would have been debarred from marrying had the child been born into the adoptive family, subject to the power of a court to permit marriage in any particular case. But the Committee's Report rejected this provisional view, in part because few adoptive parents favoured a complete ban on sibling marriages, and it was difficult to see on what basis a court could identify cases in which it would be proper to refuse permission: see paras. 329–33.

[115] The adopted child remains within the prohibited degrees to all the members of his natural family: Adoption Act 1976, s. 47(1). However, the impact of this rule, in cases of affinal relationships, is reduced by the provisions of the Marriage (Prohibited Degrees of Relationship) Act 1986; see

(iii) Other Consequences of Adoption: Citizenship

The Adoption Act 1926 did not affect the citizenship of the adopted child; but the 1949 Act—consistently with its general approach—included what Lord Simon described as 'an interesting little clause'[116] dealing with citizenship,[117] the effect of which was to confer United Kingdom citizenship on a child adopted by a citizen. Simon accurately predicted that there would be no opposition[118]—a fact which may indicate not only how far Parliament in 1949 was prepared to accept a much more far-reaching notion of the effects of adoption than had been thought appropriate a quarter of a century earlier, but also the extent to which attitudes to immigration and citizenship have changed since 1949.

A ROLE FOR THE COURT?

It has already been noted that about the only constant in the development of the adoption process over the past seventy years has been the involvement of a court; and there can be little doubt that the court serves a useful—indeed indispensable role in those, statistically rare, cases in which the making of the order is contested. But the issue is not so clear cut in the great majority of cases in which there is no dispute. Certainly, the justification advanced by the Tomlin Committee[119] in 1925 that judicial investigation was required to ensure independent investigation from the point of view of the child and to protect the mother from exploitation and pressure seems unconvincing in a system which now has such an elaborately structured system of investigation, counselling and decision taking;[120]

---

n. 111 above. The likelihood that a person will go through a form of marriage with a person who (unknown to either of them) was within the prohibited degrees has been minimised by provisions enabling an adopted person who is 18 or over to have access to his birth records (and a person under that age may enquire whether his birth records suggest that he may be within the prohibited degrees to any person he intends to marry: Adoption Act 1976, s. 51(2)).

[116] *Official Report* (HL) 11 July 1949, vol. 163, col. 1066.

[117] Adoption of Children Act 1949, s. 8.

[118] It remains the law that a child adopted by a British citizen will become a British citizen on the making of an adoption order by a UK court: British Nationality Act 1981, s. 1(5), (6). But reported cases suggest divergent approaches to the weight to be attached to nationality and immigration factors in deciding whether to make an order: compare, on the one hand, *Re A (an Infant)* [1963] 1 WLR 231, 237 (court to be circumspect in making adoption order in case of foreign child approaching majority); *Re K (A Minor) (Adoption Order: Nationality)* [1994] 2 FLR 557, CA (Home Secretary successfully appealed against the making of an order in respect of a girl eight days short of her eighteenth birthday); and *Re B (Adoption Order: Nationality* [1998] FLR 965 (CA) (Home Secretary successfully appealed against the making of an order in respect of a girl aged 16); as against *Re H (Adoption) (Non-Patrial)* [1996] 2 FLR 187, *Re J (Adoption: Non-Patrial)* [1998] 1 FLR 225.

[119] *Report of the Child Adoption Committee* (1924–5) Cmd. 2401, paras. 11–12.

[120] See Adoption Agencies Regulations 1983, SI No. 1964; Halsbury's *Laws of England* (4th edition reissue, 1993) paras. 1030–42; and (for the guardians *ad litem* and reporting officers appointed to safeguard the interests of the child, and to deal with matters relevant to the giving of parental agreement respectively) see Adoption Act 1976, ss. 65 and 65A, and the relevant Adoption Rules.

and it is not surprising that the most recent official review of adoption law[121] recorded the impression that in the great majority of cases the court hearing had a symbolic rather than a judicial function, albeit perhaps adding a sense of formality to the proceedings and thereby reducing the likelihood of the propriety of the order being subsequently questioned. But although this review recorded that adopters often found the hearing an anticlimax, the Government has firmly committed[122] itself to retaining the basic structure under which adoptions are authorised by the courts, which in turn are advised by adoption agencies, which in their own turn are advised by adoption panels.

CONCLUSION

This account of the evolution of adoption law will have demonstrated very considerable changes in its juristic nature. But the very fact that it has been seen to be related to legal status (rather than simply being one technique for dealing with the needs of children) has had sometimes unfortunate consequences—not least that adoption legislation has often been treated in isolation from other legislation affecting children—even comprehensive codifying legislation such as the Children Act 1948 and the Children Act 1989. The background to the 1948 Act is the subject of the next Chapter of this book; and the fact that adoption was at that time seen as inappropriate to be dealt with in legislation dealing with child welfare will be seen to have had some long-term significance.

---

[121] *Inter-Departmental Review of Adoption Law*, Discussion Paper No. 3, 'The Adoption Process', 1991, Part 13.

[122] *Adoption: The Future*, Cm. 2288 (1993) para. 1.6. The suggestion made in *Inter-Departmental Review of Adoption Law*, Discussion Paper No. 3, 'The Adoption Process', 1991, that consensual adoptions might be dealt with on the papers by a 'special procedure' similar to that familiar in divorce has not been followed up.

9*

The State as a Parent:
The Children Act 1948 in Retrospect

INTRODUCTION

The declared objective of the Children Act 1948 was to 'provide a comprehensive service for the care of children deprived of the benefit of a normal home
life'.[1] Local authorities were to receive such children into their care and to stand
as a parent[2] to them, exercising their powers so as to further the child's best interests. The Act has long been seen as a landmark in the history of the public care
of children,[3] and as a major element in the creation of the post-World War II
welfare state. The duties assumed by the State under the Children Act are comparable in ideological terms to the duty[4] to promote a comprehensive health
service securing improvement in the people's physical and mental health, and
to the duty to promote the people's education by providing a varied and comprehensive educational service throughout the country[5] and thereby contribute
to the community's spiritual, moral, mental and physical development.[6] But lawyers have given the Act and its background little attention,[7] and after more
than half a century it seems appropriate to re-examine the background to the
legislation.[8]

There are some curious features about the Act and the events which led up
to it. For example, it is widely known that the Children Act gave effect to the

---

* This Chapter was first published as an article in (1998) 114 LQR 419. The author is grateful
to those who assisted by reading drafts, supplying materials and making helpful comments, including Mrs Anne Bull, Archivist of Newnham College, Cambridge; Rupert Hughes, formerly of the
Department of Health and Social Security; Pamela Hardiker, Senior Lecturer, School of Social Work,
University of Leicester; Professor Jane Lewis, Director, Wellcome Unit for the History of Medicine,
Oxford University; and Professor Roy Parker, Centre for Social Policy, Dartington. His greatest debt
is to Dr Charles Webster, Fellow of All Souls College, Oxford, whose encyclopaedic knowledge
was unstintingly placed at the author's disposal.
[1] *Summary of the Main Provisions of the Children Bill*, 1948, Cmd. 7306, para. 1.
[2] *Summary of the Main Provisions of the Children Bill*, 1948, Cmd. 7306, para. 5.
[3] Per Lord Listowel, the government spokesman, *Official Report* (HL) 12 Dec. 1946, vol. 144
col. 900.   [4] National Health Service Act 1946, s. 1.
[5] Education Act 1944, s. 1(1).   [6] Education Act 1944, s. 7.
[7] The Children Act 1948 is mentioned only once in Graveson and Cranes's *Century of Family
Law 1857–1957* (1957).
[8] The background to the gestation of the Children Act 1948 has already been greatly clarified
by Professor Roy Parker's archival research: 'The gestation of reform: the Children Act 1948', by
R. A. Parker, in *Approaches to Welfare*, eds. Philip Bean and Stuart Macpherson (1983).

Report of the Care of Children Committee[9] ('the Curtis Committee'[10]) and that
this Committee has its own place in history as the first inquiry in this country
directed specifically to the care of all children deprived of a normal home life and
covering all groups of such children;[11] and it is often assumed that it was the
death of Dennis O'Neill (a twelve-year-old child boarded out by a local authority[12]
with foster parents) which led to the establishment of the Curtis Committee.[13]
Yet in fact[14] the war-time Coalition Government had announced its decision
to establish the Committee on 7 December 1944[15]—a month before Dennis
O'Neill's death.[16] Again, it seems strange that a disastrous failure in the system
of boarding out children in need of care should have led to the provision in the
Children Act 1948 which in terms required local authorities to board children
out unless this could be shown to be not practicable or desirable.[17] The reality—
as this Chapter shows—is that the background to the legislation is much more

   [9] (1946) Cmd. 6922.
   [10] After its chairman, Myra Curtis (1886–1971). For someone with a secure place in the history
of social reform, recognised as the founder of a new social service (see *The Times*'s obituary,
29 June 1971), she is poorly served by reference books, having no memoir in the *Dictionary of National
Biography*. It is appropriate therefore to record that her forebears were said to be 'north country
working class' but her Post Office father and elementary schoolteacher mother were able to ensure
that she received the secondary education which qualified her for an entrance award to Newnham
College Cambridge (of which she was Principal from 1942–54). After seven years as an Assistant
Editor of the *Victoria County History*, she entered the Civil Service in 1915 and, having served as
Superintendent of the Post Office Savings Bank, Director of Women Establishments in the Treasury,
and Principal Assistant Secretary in the War Damage Commission, she ended her civil service career
in 1942. A vigorously reforming Principal of Newnham, it has been doubted whether she ever reconciled herself to the indecisiveness of much academic administration and seems to have found
young peoples' changes of mind 'somewhat exasperating': *Newnham College Roll Letter 1972*,
p. 55. As Chairman of the Committee appointed by Cambridge University to investigate the case for
a third women's college she played a major part in the establishment of New Hall (which received
its first undergraduates in the year she retired from Newnham). She was appointed CBE in 1942 and
promoted DBE in 1949. The judgement that she was at work 'certainly a formidable figure' is cor-
roborated by Lady Allen of Hurtwood's experience giving evidence to the Curtis Committee in 1946:
Memoirs of an Uneducated Lady by M. Allen and M. Nicholson (1975) pp. 190–1.
   [11] *Report of the Care of Children Committee*, 1946, Cmd. 6922, para. 3. The Committee's terms
of reference were 'to inquire into the existing methods of providing for children who from loss of
parents or from any cause whatever are deprived of a normal home life with their own parents or
relatives; and to consider what further measures should be taken to ensure that these children are
brought up under conditions best calculated to compensate them for the lack of parental care'.
   [12] The Newport County Borough Council to whose care as a 'fit person' Dennis O'Neill and his
brother Terence had been committed by a juvenile court on the grounds that they were, by reason
of parental neglect, in need of care and protection.
   [13] See e.g. *A Child in Trust, the Report of the Panel of Inquiry into the circumstances surrounding
the death of Jasmine Beckford* (Chairman, Louis Blom-Cooper QC) (1985) p. 3.
   [14] As Professor R. A. Parker demonstrated as long ago as 1983: see 'The gestation of reform: the
Children Act 1948' in *Approaches to Welfare*, eds. Philip Bean and Stuart Macpherson (1983).
   [15] *Official Report* (HC) 7 Dec. 1944, vol. 406, col. 732. It is true that the Committee's Warrant
of Appointment was not signed until 8 Mar. 1945: see n. 110, below.
   [16] On 9 Jan. 1945. Unless otherwise indicated in the text, statements about the O'Neill case are
taken from *Report by Sir Walter Monckton KCMG, KCVO, MC, KC on the circumstances which led
to the boarding out of Dennis and Terence O'Neill . . .* , 1945, Cmd. 6636.
   [17] Children Act 1948, s. 13(1).

complex than is often assumed; and the response to the pressures for change is reflected in various ways in the provisions of the Children Act and in the omissions from it.

Four factors influenced the decision that some governmental action was necessary to deal with the problem of orphans and other children in need. First, there was the plight (perceived by officials as early as 1943) of children left homeless when the war-time evacuation schemes were wound up. Secondly, there was the realisation within the Ministry of Health that implementation of the 1942 Beveridge Report's recommendation to abolish the Poor Law had consequences for the 37,000 children cared for by public assistance authorities. Thirdly, there was the public campaign (associated in particular with Lady Allen of Hurtwood) focusing on the need to compensate orphans and other children deprived of a normal family life. Fourthly, there were the highly publicised complaints made by John Watson JP and other juvenile court magistrates about the conditions in London County Council remand homes, and the Report of a Committee appointed to investigate. It was the publicity given to the Allen and Watson campaigns which led the war-time Coalition to decide that the question of child care should be investigated by an independent committee, rather than leaving matters to be handled entirely within the government machine.

After that decision had been announced, the death of Dennis O'Neill led the Home Secretary to appoint Sir Walter Monckton to carry out an inquiry; and different views have been expressed about the extent to which that inquiry influenced the course of events.

These matters are best examined in turn.

1. Bureaucratic Pressures: (i) The Problem of the Homeless Evacuees

In August 1943 an informal committee was set up in the Ministry of Health to consider the problems arising from the return of evacuees to their homes. The Committee gave examples[18] of the problems[19] which would have to be faced,

---

[18] 'A boy of 12, illegitimate, who has never had a proper home but was boarded out by his mother until the war with a succession of foster mothers with whom he was unhappy. Is now in a good billet happy and secure, but asks what will happen to him at the end of the war. A boy of 13 whose mother married after his birth and has never told her husband of his existence; brought up in a public assistance home until 1938, when his mother was told that she must provide for him; she arranged for his admission to a voluntary home from which he was evacuated and billeted in 1939. Mother says she cannot have him home': see the Appendix to the Committee's Report, PRO MH102/1157, *Report of Informal Committee on consequences of ending wartime evacuation scheme.*

[19] The Committee's major concern was that some of the cases seemed to fall neither within the provisions of the Poor Law Act 1930 nor of the Children and Young Persons Act 1933 (which empowered juvenile courts to commit children to the care of fit persons in certain circumstances).

pointed out that the voluntary organisations caring for children were in serious difficulties because of the uncertainty, and concluded that 'the creation of some machinery to undertake the general care of children and adolescents' was a matter requiring urgent examination.[20]

2. Bureaucratic Pressures: (ii) The Break-up of the Poor Law

Lord Scarman has said that it was the Poor Law which constituted the 'historic base from which Parliament advanced to meet the needs of the orphan, the deserted, and the abandoned child';[21] and in 1944 there remained some 27,000 children in the care of the Poor Law authorities.[22] It is true that the administration of the Poor Law had, as part of the reforms effected during Neville Chamberlain's time as Minister of Health,[23] been entrusted to local authorities;[24] and it is equally true that statute required the growing welfare functions of local authorities[25] to be used in preference to Poor Law relief wherever possible; but even at this distance of time it seems remarkable that those authorities' duty to what was in fact numerically the largest group of children deprived of a normal home life was expressed simply in terms of an obligation to set them to work or to put them out as apprentices.[26]

This state of affairs could not continue; and the projected abolition of the Poor Law[27] made it imperative to find some other method of dealing with the children concerned.

A committee of officials was established in the Ministry of Health[28] to consider the impact of the impending changes; and the Committee recommended

---

[20] The Committee recommended that an interdepartmental inquiry be established; and its papers support the view that credit for being the first to recommend—in 1938—a more co-ordinated government policy in relation to children should go to a Home Office official S. W. Harris who advocated regular interdepartmental conferences chaired by the Permanent Under-Secretary of State at the Home Office, Sir Alexander Maxwell; but the outbreak of World War II prevented action from being taken. For S. W. Harris's career see Ch. 5 n. 23, above.

[21] *Leeds City Council* v. *West Yorkshire Metropolitan Police* [1983] 1 AC 29, 41.

[22] Including 1,433 in Public Assistance Institutions (i.e. workhouses), 2,582 in Public Assistance residential nurseries, 10,312 in cottage homes, 4,720 in other Public Assistance children's homes, whilst 4,270 were boarded out. These figures (which are estimates taken from the Ministry of Health's Memorandum (PRO MH102/1378) *The Break Up of the Poor Law and the Care of Children and Old People*, para. 5) show a sharp fall since the beginning of the War in the number of children (6,324 on 1 Jan. 1939) in workhouses but the small number boarded out is striking given that informed opinion—as evidenced by the Advisory Committee on Mothers and Young Children—had come to favour boarding out as the most satisfactory way of providing for homeless children.

[23] For an account of Chamberlain's role, see D. Dilks, *Neville Chamberlain, vol. 1, 1869–1929* (1984) Ch. 34.

[24] By the Local Government Act 1929, in this respect giving effect to the recommendations of the majority of the Royal Commission on the Poor Laws (Cd. 4499, 1909).

[25] See notably the provisions of the Public Health Act 1936, Part VII.

[26] Poor Law Act 1930, s. 15(1)(c), employing language dating back to the original Poor Relief Act 1601.   [27] Effected by the National Assistance Act 1948, s. 1.

[28] Its draft report, *The Break Up of the Poor Law and the Care of Children and Old People*, was sent to the Home Office on 9 May 1944: PRO MH102/1378.

—notwithstanding the formidable transitional problems involved—a Bill[29] co-ordinating and modernising the legislation relating to children, and bringing under a single well-qualified and sympathetic administration the selection and control of foster parents and the supervision of children cared for by foster parents or in publicly provided or voluntary homes.[30] In this way, all the functions of lodging and caring for children not otherwise provided for would be taken out of the Poor Law, and transferred to local authorities;[31] whilst in order to cope with the personal problems involved in boarding out children satisfactorily and in supervising foster parents and foster homes it was proposed[32] to require local authorities to establish children's committees[33] able to supply local and personal knowledge,[34] and to encourage the employment of welfare staff—especially women with recognised training and practical experience of home visiting and children's problems. Finally, in order to ensure the maintenance of proper standards, central government should have power to carry out inspections of children's homes (whether voluntary or directly run by the local authority); and these steps[35]—so the officials thought—were 'well calculated to produce a strong sense of local responsibility and therefore an effective, understanding and sympathetic control in the true interests of children'.[36]

These proposals—worked out as they were in suggested heads of a Bill—look[37] in many respects uncannily like the system recommended by Curtis and put into legislative form by the Children Act four years later. Why then did it take so long—and so much additional pressure—to get the Children Act 1948 onto the statute book?

The explanation, in part at least, lies in the 1944 Committee's view that it would be in the best interests of orphans and children whose parents were unable or unwilling to look after them properly to 'break away as soon as may be from any association, however slight, with the authorities responsible for the police and the prevention and punishment of crime'.[38] This led ineluctably to the

---

[29] Falling 'readily and without overlap into the pattern formed by the [Education Act 1944], the proposals in the White Paper on a National Health Service, and the Social Insurance Plan, when these come into operation': *The Break Up of the Poor Law and the Care of Children and Old People* (op. cit. n. 22 above) para. 3.

[30] There were overlapping provisions and divided responsibilities for inspection and supervision under the Public Health Act 1936, ss. 206–19, and the Children and Young Persons Act 1933, ss. 92–5. [31] i.e. counties and county boroughs.

[32] *The Break Up of the Poor Law and the Care of Children and Old People* (n. 22 above) paras. 13–20.

[33] The committees were to have power to co-opt members with special knowledge and experience; and at least one-quarter of the committee were to be women: *The Break Up of the Poor Law and the Care of Children and Old People* (n. 22 above) para. 20.

[34] It was recognised that an organisation centred on a county town was 'not qualified, unaided' to deal with these matters involving personal judgement.

[35] And specifically the supervision of voluntary children's homes.

[36] *The Break Up of the Poor Law and the Care of Children and Old People* (n. 22 above) para. 21.

[37] In fact there are significant differences of emphasis: see text to n. 117, below.

[38] The annotations on the Home Office copy describe this as 'the old M/H view!'

conclusion that the Home Office,[39] whilst retaining its responsibilities for the juvenile delinquent, should not have any part to play in the provision of child care for other children. To say the least, this view was not welcome in the Home Office;[40] and the question of central government responsibility was not resolved until after the Curtis Committee had reported.[41]

3. The Public Campaigns: (i) The Role of Lady Allen of Hurtwood

This activity within Whitehall remained unknown even to those outsiders interested in children's welfare. Some weeks before the Department of Health's blueprint for a comprehensive child care system was circulated in Whitehall, Lady Allen of Hurtwood—long interested in education matters, perplexed by the administrative overlaps she had observed in the arrangements for children in residential care,[42] and concerned that the plight of such children had not been addressed in published government reconstruction plans for health and education, sent a lengthy memorandum on the subject to the Home Secretary, Herbert Morrison. Subsequent events were summarised by Sir William Haley:[43]

Getting no response from Government, she wrote a letter to *The Times* . . . The response was staggering . . . Here was a classic case of how one person can influence opinion, stir a government into action by setting up a committee of inquiry . . . and pass a Bill[44]

Whilst it is certainly true that Lady Allen received no open encouragement from Whitehall,[45] the situation behind the scenes was very different. Morrison

---

[39] Which had powers of inspection (of voluntary homes) under the Children and Young Persons Act 1933, ss. 92–5.

[40] The copy of the 1944 Report on the Home Office files in the Public Record Office is emphatically annotated to record dissent from the view that powers in respect of children had been vested in the Home Secretary because a minority of children in residential care had been committed by court order: see para. 21.   [41] See text to n. 193, below.

[42] *Memoirs of an Uneducated Lady*, by Marjory Allen and Mary Nicholson (1975) p. 170 (hereinafter Allen: *Memoirs*) records Lady Allen's impression of the 'fat, flabby and listless appearance' of children in Poor Law institutions as always noticeable and their 'heavy, ill-fitting clothes and boots so clumsy they could only shuffle along'. She saw the root of the problem as lying in poor administration.

[43] Editor of *The Times* (1952–66) in the 1958 *Haldane Memorial Lecture* on 'The Formation of Public Opinion' as cited by *The Times* in its obituary of Lady Allen published on 13 Apr. 1976. A similar assessment had been made ten years earlier by the Home Secretary, J. Chuter Ede, in the debates on the Bill for the Children Act 1948 (*Official Report* (HC) 28 June 1948, vol. 452, col. 1889): 'It is some tribute to the work that may still be done by enlightened people using the more respectable parts of the Press for the ventilation of public grievances, that this great Measure has virtually flowed from a letter that was written to *The Times* by Lady Allen . . .'

[44] Lady Allen's letter, eventually published by prior arrangement with the then editor R. Barrington-Ward on 15 July 1944 stated (contrary to the facts as they are now known) that the plight of children in public or voluntary care had been 'entirely forgotten' in planning for post-war reconstruction. She urged a public inquiry to 'ascertain whether the public and charitable organisations concerned were enabling these children to lead full and happy lives and to make recommendations how the community can compensate them for the family life they have lost'.

[45] Morrison did not reply to her letter for more than three months; and then, on 4 July 1944, wrote that the problem was already under consideration within the Home Office, and that he was not convinced any inquiry was necessary: PRO MH102/1293. It was presumably the receipt of this letter

instructed his officials to treat her letter to him on the 'basis of a genuine person anxious to be right about the facts';[46] and it soon became clear that although—as we have seen—the main issues had been fully considered within the Civil Service it was Lady Allen's published letter (and the publicity[47] which followed[48]) which made it seem politically essential to establish a public committee of inquiry,[49] however little the officials concerned believe this to be necessary.[50] It is true that this decision was not taken for nearly six months; but that delay was at least in part attributable to the fact that the question had become one of the machinery of government; and this was in reality the only matter on which there was any significant disagreement.

Lady Allen was indignant and angered that she herself was not invited to serve on the Curtis Committee;[51] but her role in the history of the development of child

which prompted Lady Allen to arrange for the publication of the letter in accordance with her agreement with Barrington Ward.

[46] PRO MH102/1293.

[47] As well as Lady Allen's continued pressure on senior officials. As she recounts in Allen: *Memoirs*, p. 183: '. . . I had been much too timid in my manner of putting questions to civil servants: a polite letter obviously got nowhere. And why should I plead with them? They were there to serve the public, and as a member of the public I was entitled to be served. From this moment my whole attitude changed. Instead of writing to government departments, I arranged to see someone fairly high up. This method was much more successful. My new contacts were most willing to tell me what I wanted to know. The only difficulty was that they did not always know it themselves.' She also inspired a parliamentary campaign, culminating in an Early Day Motion in Nov. 1944 signed by 158 MPs; and a request on 20 Nov. 1944 for the Minister of Reconstruction (Lord Woolton) to receive a deputation of MPs. (In fact by this time the Government had decided to appoint a committee, and this was delicately conveyed to those concerned by Woolton's Private Secretary.)

[48] Sir William Haley stated that the response to her letter was 'staggering', and that 'day after day and week after week the letters [many from persons of considerable standing] poured in'; and in a leading article concluded that the support for an inquiry was 'too impressive to be ignored': see Allen: *Memoirs*, p. 182. Lady Allen continued to publicise her concerns, notably by means of a pamphlet, *Whose Children?* (1944) intended as a 'disquieting document' describing the living conditions and treatment of children deprived of a normal home life because they were orphaned, illegitimate, destitute or on probation' and recounting her 'painful experiences of departmental confusion'. 'I wrote it' (Lady Allen concluded) 'to stir the human heart': see Allen: *Memoirs*, p. 185.

[49] The papers on PRO file MH102/1161 make it clear that, although the Minister for Health H. U. Willink considered that a Royal Commission would be the appropriate form of inquiry, the view of his Permanent Secretary (Sir John Maude) that the issue 'hardly warranted the heavy machinery of a Royal Commission' which in any event was likely to take longer to report carried the day: see Maude to Maxwell, 15 Nov. 1944.

[50] Maxwell told Sir Arthur Rucker (Deputy Secretary at the Department of Health) on 10 Aug. 1944 that he personally would 'have been very glad to postpone an enquiry of this kind; but the Home Secretary feels that in view of the correspondence in *The Times* and the pressure which will no doubt be exerted in Parliament . . . it will probably be impracticable to avoid taking early action'; whilst Sir Norman Brook, Permanent Secretary at the Ministry of Reconstruction, told Sir Frank Newsam (Deputy Under-Secretary of State at the Home Office) on 21 Sept. 1944 (PRO CAB 124/780) that Ministers would have to decide whether it would be 'politically practicable to postpone' holding an inquiry.

[51] 'It had been taken for granted by the press, and by my friends and colleagues, that I would be a member of the committee . . . I was upset and angry.' Morrison told her she had been excluded because she had taken a position about the activities of some of the voluntary children's societies and would therefore not be objective: Allen: *Memoirs*, p. 189.

care had been secured.[52] Had it not been for her campaign it seems very doubtful whether the Curtis Committee would ever have been established. In the circumstances, Clifford Allen's assessment of his fiancée as 'a girl with few brains— no knowledge of politics—so shy that she can hardly say Boo to gooses . . . [and] with no modern ideas'[53] must rank as one of the most remarkable misjudgements ever made.[54]

There is one aspect of Lady Allen's role which seems to have escaped attention: this is that she had for long been on close terms of personal friendship[55] with Morrison (and indeed that some years[56] later he proposed marriage to her). It is tempting to speculate on whether the official correspondence reveals the whole story of the influence she brought to bear on the Home Secretary.[57]

4. The Public Campaigns: (ii) The London Remand Homes Inquiry

The public interest in the fate of children in public care aroused by Lady Allen's campaigning subsided for the time being.[58] But on 14 November 1944 John Watson—a well-known juvenile court magistrate—deliberately fanned the flames[59] and gave fresh stimulus to the campaign.[60] For some years, juvenile court magistrates had protested about defects which they had observed in the remand homes[61]

---

[52] As *The Times* recorded in its leading article on 25 Mar. 1947 welcoming the Government's acceptance of the Curtis recommendations.

[53] Informing R. E. Trevelyan on 7 Aug. 1921 of his engagement: *Plough my own Furrow, The Story of Lord Allen of Hurtwood . . .* , by M. Gilbert (Longmans, 1965).

[54] Allen's judgment in international politics was also questionable: see the biography by A. Marwick, *Clifford Allen: the open conspirator* (1964); and the materials collected in M. Gilbert, *Plough my own Furrow, The Story of Lord Allen of Hurtwood . . .* (1965).

[55] Lady Allen was the widow of Clifford Allen (1889–1939) whose friendship with Morrison dated back to 1914 and their joint involvement in the management of a short-lived left-wing newspaper *The Daily Citizen*. Allen was a prominent conscientious objector during World War I, and was thereafter active in Labour Party politics until ostracised ('Barony—Reward for Betrayal' was the *Daily Worker's* headline) for accepting a peerage in 1932 on the recommendation of Ramsay MacDonald, Prime Minister in the National Government. Morrison unlike most of his Labour colleagues remained in touch with MacDonald (towards whom his attitude appears to have been equivocal) and no doubt for that reason he remained on close terms as a frequent house guest of the Allens. During World War II Morrison lived what his biographers describe as a 'strange nomadic life' frequently making unannounced weekend visits to Lady Allen's house where he spent happy evenings dancing between Air Raid alerts: see B. Donoghue and G. W. Jones, *Herbert Morrison, Portrait of a Politician* (1973) p. 312.

[56] In 1952. He apparently told Lady Allen that his marrying a MacDonaldite might damage his political career 'but never mind I'll do it'; and it is perhaps not surprising that she declined: see B. Donoghue and G. W. Jones, *Herbert Morrison, Portrait of a Politician* (1973) p. 528.

[57] Although this is not to suggest that Morrison always gave way to her demands—in particular that she should be a member of the Curtis Committee: see above.

[58] As Sir Norman Brook put it to Sir Frank Newsam on 28 Oct. 1944, PRO MH102/1161. But Brook presciently observed that Lady Allen was only 'holding off temporarily'.

[59] A full account from his own viewpoint is given in Ch. 9 of *Which is the Justice?*, by J. A. F. Watson (1969).

[60] Watson had written to *The Times* supporting the call for a general inquiry.

[61] Established under the Children and Young Persons Act 1933, s. 61.

administered by the London County Council; and Watson, having failed to get a response from the Home Office[62] about the case of a seven-year-old girl found to be in need of care and protection, and accommodated by the LCC in Marlesford Lodge Remand Home,[63] decided to make an open court statement in dramatic terms. Watson's specific complaint was that a child of that age should never have been put into the company[64] of forty-three adolescent girls, some of immoral character, and some with criminal convictions.[65] The press had been primed to expect a newsworthy event, and duly obliged. The Home Secretary, Herbert Morrison,[66] felt obliged to set up an inquiry[67] into the complaints made by Watson and his colleagues.

In fact the ensuing report was not particularly critical of the LCC.[68] Instead it criticised Watson and his colleagues for their lack 'of that moderation of statement and steadiness of judgment which might have been expected of persons in their position' in alleging publicly that the LCC had been guilty of a 'grave dereliction of duty' and for having deliberately secured the co-operation of the press, promoting 'a type of publicity which caused much undeserved distress to the

---

[62] In *Which is the Justice?* (n. 59, above), p. 156, Watson recounts that he came away from the meeting with Sir Sidney Harris (as to whom see Ch. 5 n. 23, above) with the impression that the 'chances of anyone taking positive action were negligible' and that it was for this reason that he decided to publicise the case.

[63] Watson described Marlesford Lodge—a recently opened Home in Hammersmith—as 'a grim soulless place' and claimed that the 'girls had little to occupy their time, they had scarcely any outdoor exercise because of the danger of their scaling the wall and running away . . .': *Which is the Justice* (n. 59 above) p. 156.

[64] Watson argued for the separation of offenders from those in care because of neglect or need. The Inquiry Report accepted the long-standing Home Office view that separation of the 'deprived' from the 'depraved' would be 'inconsistent with the spirit and intention of the' legislation; and it did not accept Watson's view that 'girls of sexually immoral character should be kept separate from girls who were innocent in that respect'. The Inquiry did favour a somewhat more stringent classification, but this was to be based on age: see *London County Council Remand Homes*, Report of a Committee of Enquiry (1945) Cmd. 6594, para. 35, and *Which is the Justice?* (n. 59, above) pp. 155–62.

[65] He complained that the LCC evidently considered the 'society of young prostitutes and thieves' suitable for a child of seven; and complained that it was a 'crying scandal' for the 'greatest local authority in the country' to have allowed this state of affairs to continue: see para. 13.

[66] According to his biographers, Morrison was not at ease with such matters, and was in any event reluctant to believe that 'do-gooders' such as Watson and Lady Allen 'had a case against the LCC and his Home Office': B. Donoghue and G. W. Jones, *Herbert Morrison, Portrait of a Politician* (1973) p. 308.

[67] The members of the Committee were Sir Godfrey Russell Vick (Chairman) and Miss Myra Curtis. The involvement of Myra Curtis in what was regarded by some—including the *Daily Telegraph*'s headline writer—as a 'whitewashing' exercise made her subsequent appointment to chair the Care of Children Committee somewhat controversial: see text to n. 106 below. The Inquiry into LCC remand homes heard evidence from fifty-two witnesses at a twelve-day private hearing and reported on 14 Feb. 1945 (*London County Council Remand Homes*, Report of a Committee of Enquiry (1945) Cmd. 6594) and extensive press publicity was given to it on the following day when the press also carried stories of the committal proceedings against Dennis O'Neill's foster parents: see below.

[68] It did find 'that there must have been a certain indifference and lack of enterprise' about the administration of the girls' remand homes (see para. 28) and noted the failure to give children sufficient activity of a 'cultural or recreational kind': para. 32. The Report also noted the inadequacy of Home Office inspections in this case.

workers in the homes and to the girls themselves and their parents . . .'.[69] But from the point of view of those campaigning for a wide-ranging inquiry into public care of children the case had already served its purpose.[70] As Sir John Maude observed, this 'unfortunate incident between John Watson and the LCC' had made it 'still more difficult to hold up' a general inquiry into the care of children;[71] and on 7 December 1944 the Government announced its decision to set up the inquiry for which Lady Allen had campaigned. Its terms of reference were to 'inquire into existing methods of providing for children who from loss of parents or from any cause whatever are deprived of a normal home life with their own parents or relatives; and to consider what further measures should be taken to ensure that these children are brought up under conditions best calculated to compensate them for the lack of parental care'. The matter had passed from the private world of Government Departments to the openness of a public inquiry.

AROUSING THE PEOPLE'S CONSCIENCE: THE DEATH OF DENNIS O'NEILL AND THE MONCKTON INQUIRY

Dennis O'Neill—a twelve-year-old boy in local authority care—died at Bank Farm, Minsterley, Shropshire on 9 January 1945, a month after the Government's decision to set up a Committee into the Care of Children had been announced. The chronology thus makes it clear beyond any doubt that his death cannot have influenced the decision to establish the Curtis Committee. But it does not necessarily follow that the O'Neill case influenced neither the process nor the content of reform.[72] To form a judgement on these matters it is necessary to give a brief account of the O'Neill case; and of the public response to it.

Dennis O'Neill was one of the eleven children[73] born to an unemployed labourer and his wife who made unsuccessful attempts to bring up their family in one

---

[69] *London County Council Remand Homes*, Report of a Committee of Enquiry (1945) Cmd. 6594, para. 37. This criticism of press publicity was not surprisingly resented by the newspapers concerned; and on 20 Mar. 1946 the *Daily Mail* cited the 'measured words' of Wrottesely J at the end of the trial of Dennis O'Neill's foster parents ('nothing to be ashamed of' in publicising child abuse cases) as an answer to those who had 'deprecated the prominence given by the newspapers to cases of distressed children—including the committee who inquired into the London remand homes. Full publicity [the paper asserted], never secrecy, is the way to remedy abuses.'

[70] The *Daily Mail* was able to conclude (notwithstanding what it described as the Report's 'almost painfully tactful' language) that the Report constituted a 'serious indictment of administrative methods' from which neither the Home Office nor the LCC emerged with credit. The *Daily Mail* took pride in the readiness of the press to publicise the magistrates' statements thereby bringing the matter into the open. Officials should (the paper concluded) realise that they were 'the public's servants, not their masters'.

[71] Postscript to Maude's letter to Maxwell, 15 Nov. 1944, PRO file MH102/1161.

[72] Cf. S. M. Cretney and J. M. Masson, *Principles of Family Law* (6th edn. 1997) p. 769, fn. 13.

[73] His older brother Tom (who had been in an approved school in 1945) became a residential social worker for Kent County Council, and wrote *A Place Called Hope* (1981) which gives some account of the parents' background in Newport but contains disappointingly little first-hand information.

room on an income of £2[74] weekly. Hardly surprisingly, they failed. The NSPCC initiated a prosecution for neglect; the parents served a jail sentence imposed in default of payment of a fine; and eventually Dennis was committed to the care of the Newport County Borough Council[75] as a child in need of care and protection. The Council was under a duty to board him out.[76] There had always been difficulty in finding suitable foster parents, however, and these difficulties had been particularly acute[77] at the time when a new foster home had to be found for Dennis in June 1944.[78] More or less by chance (but as it no doubt seemed at the time, happily) the Local Authority School Attendance Officer,[79] found a placement for the boy and his brothers with Reginald and Esther Gough at their seventy-acre Bank Farm.[80] The Officer formed a favourable view of the Goughs:[81] 'the lad has gone to a very good home and will be brought up well'.[82] There were, however, things that the authorities did not know: perhaps the fact that as a teenager Gough had been convicted of assault would not after thirteen years carry too much weight, but the fact that two years earlier his wife had only withdrawn an application based on persistent cruelty for a magistrates' separation order

---

[74] Some £30 in 1998 values.

[75] Under the provisions of the Children and Young Persons Act 1933, s. 61(1)(a).

[76] The Children and Young Persons (Boarding Out) Rules 1933, SI 1933/787, rule 4 (giving effect to a preference expressed in the *Report of the Committee on the Treatment of Young Offenders*, chairman Sir T. F. Molony, Bart., Cmd. 2831, 1927, p. 64).

[77] As a result of the resumption of air raids on London and other cities.

[78] *Report by Sir Walter Monckton KCMG, KCVO, MC, KC on the circumstances which led to the boarding out of Dennis and Terence O'Neill . . .* , 1945, Cmd. 6636 (hereinafter *The Monckton Report*) paras. 12, 21.

[79] Responsibility for children in care under fit person orders was vested in the Local Authority's Education Committee.

[80] A 'lonely farm in a wild part of Shropshire', as *The Times* put it in its report on 6 Feb. 1945. Life for people such as the Goughs was difficult; and in evidence at her trial Mrs Gough gave a telling account of her daily routine: see *The Times* 19 Mar. She was always first up in the morning to light the fire. Then came the milking, and very often she had to bring the horses up. She helped to clean the cow house, sometimes turned out the cows and looked after 100 poultry and 20 ducks and then suckled the calves. She helped with the milking at night. She had to do the housework and get the meals in the house. But although Mrs Gough's life was undoubtedly hard, it needs to be set in historical context. The *Report on Post-War Organisation of Private Domestic Employment*, 1945, Cmd. 6650, reported at para. 20 that certain tasks had to be performed in every household, whether rich or poor. ('The breakfast must be prepared, cooked and washed up. Coal fires must be cleared out, grates relaid and scuttles filled. The front step must be swept and cleaned if necessary. Slops must be emptied, beds aired and made. The daily work of dusting, cleaning and scrubbing must be done in bedrooms, bathrooms, lavatory, landing, stairs and hall . . . there should be a thorough turnout at least of one room which makes the special work of the day. Subsequent meals must be prepared, cooked, laid, served and washed up.') But as the Committee pointed out, at para. 15, the burdens placed on the working-class housewife (who in sickness as in health knew 'no respite from household drudgery and family cares') had for long been notorious, and public opinion would insist on their being lightened.   [81] *Monckton Report*, para. 20.

[82] The *Daily Mail*, 13 Feb. 1945. The official concerned had good grounds for this favourable assessment since (according to a full account of the case and its background by Montague Smith published in the *Daily Mail* on 20 Mar. 1945) Mrs Gough was not only a trained nurse but had two years' experience as nurse to the children of Captain Sir Offley Wakeman (by coincidence subsequently chairman of the bench which heard the committal proceedings).

after conciliation by a probation officer[83] would surely have suggested the need for some further investigation.

As it was, Dennis O'Neill—as the coroner's jury found—was in a state of under-nourishment due to neglect, and died from acute cardiac failure following violence applied to the front of the chest and being beaten with a stick. The jury added a rider that there had been a serious lack of supervision by the local authority.

Within a week of the end of the foster parents' trial[84] the Home Secretary had appointed Sir Walter Monckton KCMG KCVO MC KC[85] to inquire into and report upon the circumstances which led to the boarding out of the O'Neill brothers and the steps taken to supervise their welfare; and six weeks later Monckton reported.[86] For present purposes, it is not necessary to go beyond the comments made by *The Times*.[87] Monckton's task had been to find out how it came about that 'two children for whom public authority had been constituted the trustee, were ever placed in the charge of a man who, as a little inquiry would have shown, was known to the police as a blackguard; . . . and why no adequate inquiry was made into their state of health and the treatment they were receiving'. But in reality Monckton's conclusions were undramatic; and the style of the Report serves to remind the reader that unkind contemporaries nicknamed Monckton 'the oil-can'. There had indeed been administrative failings;[88] but no single person had been 'found very much to blame'. All the officials involved had done their duty fairly well according to their lights 'though these were sometimes dim'. Some of those concerned lacked sufficient skill and experience, and there was administrative friction; but all the errors and omissions were petty.

All this must have seemed a damp squib for those who were looking for a sacrificial victim, or even for radical change; but even so the case—and the ex-

---

[83] In 1944 the fact that responsibility for the Probation Service could not sensibly be removed from the Home Office, and that the 'conciliation and advisory work of probation officers [was] designed to prevent the broken home (itself so often a cause of neglect and delinquency) whenever proper', was regarded within the Home Office as a powerful argument in favour of Home Office responsibility for child care generally: see e.g. Maxwell to Harris, 23 Sept. 1944, PRO MH102/1378.

[84] In a timetable which by the standards of the 1990s seems incredible, the Goughs's trial at Stafford Assizes ended—after full committal proceedings and a full trial on indictment—only eleven weeks after the boy's death. Reginald Gough was sentenced to six years' penal servitude for manslaughter; and his wife to six months' imprisonment for neglect. In sentencing Mrs Gough, Wrottesley J told her that 'it was hard perhaps to be tied to such a man in charge of such children, but your upbringing told you what your duty was and you did not do it . . .': *The Times* 20 Mar. 1945.

[85] One of the most highly regarded lawyers and negotiators of his day, Attorney-General to the Prince of Wales 1932–6 (and thereafter deeply involved in the negotiations surrounding King Edward's abdication in Dec. 1936), acted for the Nizam of Hyderabad in relation to constitutional issues arising from Indian independence, subsequently a Cabinet Minister in Conservative administrations 1951–7 (resigning as Minister of Defence in Oct. 1956 because of disagreement about the Eden Government's policy of armed intervention in the Middle East, but retaining Cabinet Office apparently to preserve the appearance of ministerial solidarity). There is no mention of the O'Neill Inquiry in the biography by the 2nd Earl of Birkenhead, *Walter Monckton: the life of Viscount Monckton of Brenchley 1891–1965*.

[86] *Report by Sir Walter Monckton KCMG, KCVO, MC, KC on the circumstances which led to the boarding out of Dennis and Terence O'Neill . . .*, 1945, Cmd. 6636.   [87] 29 May 1945.

[88] *Monckton Report*, para. 47.

tensive[89] (and sometimes well-informed[90]) press treatment[91] of it and other child care[92] issues[93]—does seem (as the *Daily Mail* put it) to have aroused 'the conscience of the British people'. Sir Walter Monckton's unemotional prose did not prevent the *Mail* from declaring that there were now 'three principal defendants before the court of public opinion', and that they were the three Whitehall Departments 'jointly responsible for the existing system of child care'. The message from the O'Neill case was, it seemed, that the whole system under which local authorities look after children committed to their care had been on trial and found wanting.

Something had to be done, and the Government had appointed the Curtis Committee to do it.[94] The O'Neill case had 'grimly underlined' the need for an investigation;[95] whilst the case is repeatedly referred to in the Curtis Committee's report;[96]

[89] Especially remarkable in view of the restricted space available in the newspapers of the time— *The Times* had no more than eight pages, for example—and the pressure of other even more dramatic events as the war in Europe moved to its end with the German capitulation on 8 May 1945. V2 rockets —the precursors of Intercontinental Ballistic Missiles—were bringing sudden death without warning to civilians in Britain and on 3 Mar. 1945 an unsophisticated bombing raid intended to destroy the rockets' fuel sources in The Netherlands killed more than 500 Dutch civilians and led to protests by the Dutch Government: see M. Gilbert, *Road to Victory, Winston Spencer Churchill 1941–1945* (1986) p. 1256; whilst shortly before publication of the Monckton Report, a Parliamentary Delegation concluded its report on *Buchenwald Camp* Cmd. 6626 (Apr. 1945) para. 15 (the first of the major German concentration camps to be liberated) with the 'considered and unanimous opinion . . . that a policy of steady starvation and inhuman brutality was carried out at Buchenwald for a long period of time; and that such camps as this mark the lowest point of degradation to which humanity has yet descended. The memory of what we saw and heard will haunt us ineffaceably for many years.'

[90] On 9 Feb. 1945—three days after its report on the inquest on Dennis O'Neill—*The Times* carried a letter from Helen Waugh and others writing from an address in Hampstead asking six very pointed questions about the facts which the inquest revealed—for example, what action did the Newport Borough Council take to satisfy itself that Dennis was being properly looked after, how did it satisfy itself that he would be better looked after there than by his parents, and why he was so far away from his parents and the county of Monmouthshire? The *Monckton Report* reproduced the answers given by the local authorities involved and others to some of these questions.

[91] *The Times* on 13 Feb. 1945 headlined its account of the committal proceedings 'Neglect and violence—practically starved—thrashed nightly' and reported that there was 'no fat on him' (he weighed only 60 pounds at death) whilst prosecuting counsel was reported as saying that the photographs of the body were the 'most revolting pictures I have ever seen'.

[92] But whilst there may have been problems in Britain these were insignificant compared with those in parts of Europe: the newspapers which carried accounts of the failings at Marlesford Lodge also noted that 2,000 Dutch children brought to England after a four-day journey from famine-riven Holland had 'after a meal of Irish stew and milk pudding at a local school' been sent to homes in the Midlands.

[93] The Report into the LCC Remand Homes (see n. 69 above) was published on the third day of the Goughs's committal proceedings, and was given prominent press coverage.

[94] Note that in responding to criticism of supposedly lenient sentencing of parents convicted of neglect or cruelty the Home Secretary specifically referred to the appointment of the Curtis Committee: *Official Report* (HC) 15 Feb. 1945, vol. 407, col. 222—a statement which *The Times*, 16 Feb. 1945, relied on in a leading article to make the point that the appointment of the Committee after 'long public agitation' was a more important matter.

[95] Home Office Briefing Note for the Second Reading Debate on the Bill for the Children Act 1948 in the House of Lords, 10 Feb. 1948.

[96] The Report states, for example, that 'even the most complacent Local Authorities had been given a jolt by recent publicity': para. 129; that 'the O'Neill case had put authorities on their guard against slackness in administration' but that 'only the generally high standard of the [foster] homes chosen ensured protection from another O'Neill tragedy because in many cases exactly the same conditions of supervision prevailed . . .': para. 371.

and the Committee recorded[97] a general impression amongst the officials and foster parents visited that the reason for the inquiry was to prevent a repetition of the O'Neill case. As will be seen, the rather bland language of the Monckton Report was cited as the justification for a new and positive ideology and a radical restructuring of child care services; whilst the decision to legislate was strongly influenced by politicians' perception of the climate of opinion[98] which the O'Neill case had done so much to create.[99] Dennis O'Neill was the victim whose death put reform onto the urgent agenda of practical politics.

THE CURTIS COMMITTEE'S WORK

A Controversial Appointment

The decision to set up a committee, announced on 7 December 1944,[100] immediately prompted speculation and controversy about its membership.[101] Although the Ministers concerned all felt that 'for a Committee of this character it would be right to find a suitable woman as Chairman',[102] such a person proved difficult to find.[103] Eventually it was agreed[104] to approach Myra Curtis and she accepted the offer.[105]

[97] At para. 427.

[98] This is also confirmed by officials' records, e.g. PRO ED 136/720 15 Dec. 1946: the 'main difficulty with public opinion has been that the Dennis O'Neill and Marlsford [*sic*] Lodge cases' created an impression that LEAs and Directors of Education 'do not take a keen interest in their present duties of supervising deprived children, and regard them as not really their main job'.

[99] The existence of such a link in the minds of even well-informed people can be seen, for example, in the debate on the Curtis Report initiated by the Earl of Iddesleigh in the House of Lords on 12 Dec. 1946 (*Official Report* (HL) vol. 144, col. 886) in the course of which he said that the House had been 'prepared for these revelations by the Report on the O'Neill case'. But the Curtis 'revelations' were about residential homes, the management of which was in issue neither in the O'Neill case nor in Sir Walter Monckton's Report. Again, a clear link was drawn by the Lord Chancellor. Moving the Second Reading of the Children Bill (*Official Report* (HL) 10 Feb. 1948, vol. 153, col. 915) he referred to the anxiety caused by Lady Allen's campaign and the O'Neill case, and the Monckton Report's criticism of the fact that 'there were many people who had administrative responsibility [for children in care] but there was no one really concerned in the personal welfare of that child. And so we appointed the Curtis Committee . . .'. In fact the Committee had been appointed by the Coalition Government (rather than the Labour Government which took office on 26 July 1945) and the decision to appoint the Committee had been taken before Dennis O'Neill's death: see above.

[100] *Official Report* (HC), vol. 406, col. 732.

[101] In the House of Commons the Communist MP W. Gallacher had urged the appointment of a working-class chairman on the grounds that most of the children concerned were working class. He was quite clear that 'we do not want another lawyer as chairman of the Committee': *Official Report* (HC) 7 Dec. 1944, vol. 406, col. 735.

[102] Memorandum by the Home Secretary to the War Cabinet, WP (45) 101, 16 Feb. 1945, PRO CAB 66/62.

[103] 'It is essential that the Chairman should bring to the Committee not only interest and a sound judgment, but should be capable of guiding the deliberations of the Committee and producing a report which will lead to practical measures': ibid.

[104] There was a distinct lack of enthusiasm for the appointment on the part of two of the three Ministers responsible: see n. 108 below.

[105] Memorandum by the Home Secretary to the War Cabinet, 16 Feb. 1945, WP(45) 101, PRO CAB 66/62.

But the publication of the London Remand Homes Report[106] under Myra Curtis's signature on 14 February—a report criticised by some as 'a white-washing report instigated by the Home Office'[107]—raised doubts about the wisdom of the appointment; and the Home Secretary decided to take the matter to the War Cabinet. Although there were influential voices[108] favouring second thoughts, the majority were persuaded that to look elsewhere for a chairman 'might be interpreted as implying that the Government was impressed with the criticisms which had been directed against [Curtis] as joint author of the report on the London Remand home question'. Morrison announced the appointments[109] in the Commons,[110] and vigorously defended the choice of Chairman.[111]

The Committee's Work

The full Committee met on 64 days and examined 229 witnesses;[112] and no less than 451 institutions (and 58 local authorities) were visited.[113] The Committee's Report[114]

[106] *London County Council Remand Homes*, Report of a Committee of Enquiry (1945) Cmd. 6594.

[107] Home Secretary Morrison told the Cabinet that there was not the slightest foundation for such an allegation, and that 'but for the spirit of controversy which has surrounded this incident from the outset, the conclusions in the report would be generally accepted as sensible and right': Memorandum by the Home Secretary to the War Cabinet, 16 Feb. 1945, WP(45) 101, PRO CAB 66/62. He subsequently made an equally vigorous defence in public: see *Official Report* (HC) 22 Feb. 1945, vol. 408, col. 941.

[108] The opposition to upholding the original decision came from the two Ministers who, with Morrison, had had the responsibility for selecting her, i.e. Willink (Health, who stated that, although not wishing to press his views, 'he had never been satisfied that Miss Curtis would be an altogether suitable Chairman for the Committee') and Butler (Education, who 'had no doubt that Miss Curtis had the ability and experience necessary' but felt that 'in the present circumstances some other appointment might be advisable'): War Cabinet Conclusions, 19 Feb. 1945, WM(45) 21st Conclusions, PRO CAB 65/49. The fact that the Cabinet preferred Morrison's judgement is striking evidence of his influence.

[109] The Committee had what at the time was considered the appropriate 'balanced' membership —three MPs, the Chairman of the LCC, a Chancery Silk, a Public Assistance Officer, a Professor of Child Health and the Director of a course for Psychiatric Workers at the London School of Economics, the Secretary of the Council of the Associated Children's Homes, two members of Local Authority committees, the Head of a Camp School, the widow of an Archbishop of Canterbury, and a Trade Unionist: see the details given in *Official Report* (HC) 22 Feb. 1945, vol. 408, col. 940.

[110] The Committee was formally appointed on 8 Mar. 1945.

[111] He claimed that much of the press criticism of the 'two eminent persons' who had made the remand homes Report was 'disgracefully unfair, if not libellous'. Had the Government decided to reverse its decision to appoint Myra Curtis 'in the light of statements of that sort, we should not have been very upright in our conduct': *Official Report* (HC) 22 Feb. 1945, vol. 408, col. 942.

[112] The Committee did not commission research in the way that subsequently became routine for such bodies; but some prominent workers in the child care field—including John Bowlby (then a Lieutenant-Colonel in the Royal Army Medical Corps; subsequently the author of many works on attachment theory and the effects of deprivation of maternal care); Dr Susan Isaacs (author of *The Cambridge Evacuation Survey*); Dr Donald Winnicott (an eminent child psychiatrist); and Clare Britton (subsequently in charge of the child care training course at the London School of Economics)—gave evidence and their views were evidently influential. Lady Allen was also prominent amongst the lay witnesses: see Allen: *Memoirs*, pp. 190–2.

[113] *Report of the Care of Children Committee*, 1946, Cmd. 6922, paras. 1–2.

[114] *Report of the Care of Children Committee*, 1946, Cmd. 6922. The Report was completed in Aug. 1946 and reached Ministers on 13 Sept. 1946: see *Official Report* (HL) 12 Dec. 1946, vol. 144, col. 884. (An *Interim Report* dealing with the urgent question of Training in Child Care, Cmd. 6760, had been published in Jan. 1946).

devoted 135 of its 182 pages to an analysis of the existing arrangements, and some of the descriptive writing[115] has, even at this distance of time, lost little of its power to shock. As the Finer Report[116] put it more than a quarter of a century later, the Curtis Committee's description of the physical, emotional and intellectual deprivation suffered by some of the children in public care 'shocked public opinion'.

It was easy enough to highlight deficiencies in the existing arrangements for public child care; but what was the solution? The Committee made sixty-two recommendations, but it is possible to identify a number of underlying themes:

(i) The Need for Personal Care

The worst feature which Curtis identified in the existing arrangements for children in public care was the 'complete failure to provide any kind of individual interest or notice'[117]—or, as Lord Listowel[118] (the government spokesman in a subsequent House of Lords debate[119]) put it:[120] 'what the normal parent gives the normal child almost without knowing it—a strong and constant flow of personal affection and a sense of security that comes from long and habitual experience of the same familiar faces in the same familiar surroundings'. The Committee had 'been increasingly impressed by the need for the personal element in the care of children, which [it said[121]] Sir Walter Monckton emphasised in his report

---

[115] For example, in the children's ward of one workhouse, 'was an eight year old mentally defective girl . . . she could not use her arms or legs. There were two babies with rickets clothed in cotton frocks, cotton vests and dilapidated napkins, no more than discoloured cotton rags. The smell in this room was dreadful. A premature baby lay in an opposite ward alone. . . . The healthy children were housed in the ground floor corrugated hutment which had been once the old union casual ward . . . The children fed, played and used their pots in this room. They ate from cracked enamel plates, using the same mug for milk and soup. They slept in another corrugated hutment in old broken black iron cots some of which had their sides tied up with cord. The mattresses were fouled and stained . . . The children wore ankle length calico or flannelette frocks and petticoats and had no knickers . . . Most of [the children] had lost their shoes; those who possessed shoes had either taken them off to play with or were wearing them tied to their feet with dirty string. Their faces were clean; their bodies in some cases were unwashed and stained': *Report of the Care of Children Committee*, 1946, Cmd. 6922 (hereinafter *Curtis Report*), para. 144. This passage (dealing with the institution which had 'sunk to the lowest level of child care which has come under out notice': para. 144) was quoted by the Earl of Iddesleigh in the House of Lords debate on 12 Dec., *Official Report* (HL), vol. 144, col. 883.   [116] *Report of the Committee on One-Parent Families*, 1974, Cmnd. 5629, para. 8.21.
[117] *Curtis Report*, para. 155.
[118] For the career of Lord Listowel (1906–97) see Ch. 5, n. 22, above. Listowel would no doubt have played a more prominent role in the debates on the Children Bill in 1948 had the vagaries of politics not interfered: Morrison reminded the Lord Chancellor (Jowitt) that Listowel took a keen interest in child care matters and might be useful as a helper during the Bill's passage through the Lords, but added a manuscript private note, 'Of course, this assumes he is still a Minister—you would wish to wait a bit and see' (see PRO LCO2/4473), and in fact in Jan. 1948 Listowel accepted demotion from the Cabinet to the junior post of Minister of State at the Colonial Office.
[119] Initiated by the Earl of Iddesleigh in order to draw attention to the delay in implementing the Curtis proposals: *Official Report* (HL) 12 Dec. 1946, vol. 144, col. 881.   [120] At col. 901.
[121] In fact, the *Monckton Report* is couched in remarkably measured terms, and the statement that the Report 'emphasised' this need is surprising. It is true that Monckton states that a 'fit person'— often in fact a local authority—to whose care the court commits a child 'must care for the child as his own: the relation is a personal one' (para. 46); that the Report concluded the local authorities involved in the O'Neill case had failed to realise the 'direct and personal nature of the relationship

on the O'Neill case . . .'. Substitute homes should compensate to the greatest possible extent for the psychological and material advantages derived by the ordinary child from a family background.[122]

(ii) Appointment of Local Authority Children's Officers

The belief that no office staff dealing with children simply as 'cases' could establish this vital personal link was the foundation on which the Curtis Report based its conclusion that every local authority should be required to appoint a Children's Officer of high standing and qualifications[123] who would be the pivot[124] of the whole organisation of child care:

She[125] . . . will be a specialist in child care as the Medical Officer of Health is a specialist in his own province and the Director of Education is in his; and she will have no other duties to distract her interests[126]

Such a person (the Committee thought) would not only discharge administrative functions, but would also carry out field work 'involving many personal contacts and the solution of problems by direct methods, in particular the method of interview rather than official correspondence'.[127] In this way all the persons who deal with the child would be known to the 'officer of the authority to whom the care of that particular child has been assigned'.[128]

---

between a supervising authority and boarded out children' (para. 50); and that Monckton took the view he need not make recommendations for change to the principles applied in the Children and Young Persons Act 1933 since what was needed was that 'the administrative machinery should be improved and informed by a more anxious and responsible spirit' and that the 'personal relationship in which the local authority . . . stands to the child should be more clearly recognised' (para. 54). It also appears that Monckton made some remarks at the conclusion of his hearing which were interpreted as favouring a new approach, ('KC's Pledge on Children's Care' as the headline in the *News of the World* put it).

[122] Per Lord Listowel, *Official Report* (HL) 12 Dec. 1946, vol. 144, col. 901.

[123] '. . . highly qualified academically, if possible a graduate who has also a social science diploma. She should not be under thirty at the time of appointment and should have had some experience of work with children. She should have marked administrative capacity . . . Her essential qualifications, however, would be on the personal side. She should be genial and friendly in manner and able to set both children and adults at their ease. She should have a strong interest in the welfare of children and enough faith and enthusiasm to be ready to try methods new and old of compensating by care and affection those who have had a bad start in life. She should have very high standards of physical and moral welfare, but should be flexible enough in temperament to avoid a sterile institutional correctness': *Curtis Report*, para. 446. [124] *Curtis Report*, para. 443.

[125] The Committee did not wish to exclude men from consideration, but thought that women would fill most of the vacancies: *Curtis Report*, para. 443. This was certainly the view of Ministers: the briefing notes for the Press Conference introducing the Children Bill on 15 Jan. 1948 stated that children's officers would be 'preferably a woman . . . over thirty years': PRO MH102/1523.

[126] *Curtis Report*, para. 443. [127] *Curtis Report*, para. 421.

[128] Ibid. The Committee accepted that it would not be practicable for the Children's Officer in a large authority to know and keep in personal touch with all the children under her care, and she should therefore aim at allocating a group of children definitely to each of her subordinates. These subordinates would 'be the friend of those particular children through their childhood and adolescence': *Curtis Report*, para. 445.

(iii) Preferred Means of Caring for Children

The Committee had no doubt[129] that every effort should be made to keep a child in the family home.[130] But if this was not possible, the aim of the local authority had to be to 'find something better—indeed much better . . .'.[131] In order of preference, the Committee favoured adoption, then boarding out, and last, residential care.[132]

Curtis's preference for adoption is often overlooked. But the reason why adoption does not figure in the Children Act 1948 has nothing to do with the merits. It is simply that adoption was regarded as primarily concerned with legal status and thus not within the scope of a child welfare Bill[133]—a remarkable illustration of the way in which policy may effectively be determined by considerations of legal classification and departmental responsibility. Even the common belief that the Curtis Committee 'argued in favour of fostering as the best possible form of substitute care for deprived children (barring adoption)'[134] represents something of an oversimplification; for in fact the Report's enthusiasm was carefully qualified. Although the Committee accepted evidence 'that in the free conditions of ordinary family life with its opportunities for varied human contacts and experiences, the child's nature develops and his confidence in life and ease in society are established in a way that can hardly be achieved in a larger establishment living as it must a more strictly regulated existence'[135] this could only be true if the foster home were entirely satisfactory. No risks should be taken in this respect, not least because there were more difficulties in supervising individual children in private houses than in institutions. The Committee believed that it would be 'quite wrong' to establish a statutory policy of boarding out particular categories of child (as had been done in dealing with children found by the court to be 'in need of care and protection') since such a policy inevitably led to sub-standard homes being too readily accepted: the 'O'Neill case supplies an example'.[136] For this and other reasons the Committee accepted the continuing role of institutional (or 'residential community') care; and made detailed recommendations about the general principles to be adopted (and enforced by inspection) in such homes. It also emphasised the need for effective inspection, supervision and enforcement of proper standards in all aspects of child care. The Committee evidently had considerable faith in what could be achieved by such administrative measures; but it still seems to have been a bold step to commend the very system which

---

[129] *Curtis Report*, para. 447. [130] 'or with its mother if it is illegitimate': para. 447.
[131] *Curtis Report*, para. 447. [132] Ibid. [133] See Ch. 8 above.
[134] J. Packman, *The Child's Generation* (2nd edn. 1981) p. 20. This preference was hardly radical: the Royal Commission on the Poor Laws (Cd. 4499, 1909, para. 389) had in 1909 strongly advocated the extension of boarding out subject to stringent controls on the suitability of the foster home. (The Minority Report signed by Beatrice Webb and others agreed that boarding out under careful and continuous supervision had much to recommend it in appropriate cases, but did not accept that the Poor Law authorities had the resources to provide such supervision: see Royal Commission on the Poor Laws (Cd. 4499, 1909, vol. 2, pp. 168–9).) [135] *Curtis Report*, para. 461.
[136] *Curtis Report*, para. 461.

had so disastrously failed Dennis O'Neill. It may seem even bolder for the drafts-man to cast this preference into the prescriptive language of a statute.[137]

(iv) Co-ordinated and Simplified Administrative Structure

The Curtis Committee presented a detailed indictment of the jungle of com-mittees and agencies with responsibility for child care; and no one disputed the need for co-ordination and simplification.[138] The Committee was clear that the central government responsibility should be vested in a single Department[139] but—in accordance with the view forcefully communicated to it[140]—did not seek to make any recommendation about which Whitehall Department should assume that responsibility.

The central department of State—whichever it was—would have the import-ant responsibility[141] of defining requirements, maintaining standards, advising and assisting those immediately responsible for the care of children, and acting as a clearing house for progressive ideas. But the role of central government, albeit important, was limited. The Committee believed that constant 'local inter-est in the children of a locality' was a very important element in their welfare;[142] whilst the fact that many of the services on which the responsible agency would need to draw to meet the child's needs were already the responsibility of local government also pointed away from centralisation.[143] Hence the Committee rejected the notion that children in need of care should be the *direct* respons-ibility of a central government department.

Local involvement was thus vital; but the Committee concluded that the exist-ing confusion[144] in local authority responsibility was inconsistent with the devel-opment of sound practice and was indeed 'acute and dangerous'.[145] The solution was that local authorities[146] should be required to appoint a single *ad hoc* Chil-dren's Committee[147] reporting direct to the council and assuming responsibility[148]

---

[137] Children Act 1948, s. 13(1)(a).

[138] Per Lord Listowel, *Official Report* 12 Dec. 1946 (HL) vol. 144, col. 902.

[139] See further, below. The Home Office Notes for Legislation and Administrative Action went so far as to describe this as the 'pivot round which the other recommendations revolve': PRO MH102/1490. [140] See n. 206, below.

[141] To use the language of the *Report of the Care of Children Committee*, 1946, Cmd. 6922, para. 432. [142] *Curtis Report*, para. 431.

[143] For a critical assessment of the philosophy of localism, see R. M. Titmuss, *Official History of the Second World War, Problems of Social Policy* (1950, revised 1976) Ch. 12.

[144] 'The local authority for one purpose, e.g., child life protection, may be different from the local authority for another purpose, e.g., public assistance, and under a particular authority there may be a division of responsibility among these committees': *Curtis Report*, para. 438.

[145] This was the lesson perhaps to be drawn from the O'Neill case: see *The Monckton Report* paras. 47–54.

[146] i.e. county councils and county borough councils.

[147] But the co-option of voluntary agencies' representatives to serve on the committee would be 'most desirable' and it was to be open to the committee to co-opt 'within narrow limits of numbers' other skilled and experienced persons: *Curtis Report*, para. 438.

[148] Local authorities were no longer to be allowed to refuse to accept nomination as a 'fit person' to assume the care of a child under a court order: *Curtis Report*, para. 440.

for all the council's child care functions.[149] There should be provision for the
responsible Minister to declare a local authority in default, and give directions
enforceable by mandamus.[150]

(v) Training

The Committee noted that large sections of the staff caring for children were
without any special training for the task; and identified this as a factor in part
responsible for unsatisfactory standards.[151] A Central Training Council in Child
Care should be established; and training courses should be established for the
staff of children's homes and for the Boarding Out Officers—i.e. in effect the
Children's Officers' assistants.

(vi) Control over Voluntary Homes

The Curtis Committee was faced with something of a dilemma over children's
homes run by voluntary organisations. 'Voluntary homes' cared for large numbers of children, and some (such as Dr Barnardo's) had established a favourable
public image[152] fulfilling their founders' desire to do good to the disadvantaged
at a time when state provision was not developed.[153] On the other hand, there
were those who associated voluntary homes—which were only subject to government inspection if they solicited contributions from the public or received poor
law children—with low standards of care, whilst the fact that many of those which
were exempt from inspection owed their inspiration to religious conviction was
also a source of disquiet. These differences reflected the more general conflict
of ideology between those predisposed to centralised state planning and control
on the one hand and those taking a more traditional attitude towards the proper
function of government on the other. Thus Lady Allen in particular was known
to be critical of the voluntary organisations not least because of the 'stigma' attaching to charity; and she believed that all children deprived of a normal home life

---

[149] As enumerated in *Curtis Report* para. 440.

[150] *Curtis Report*, para. 432. This recommendation was not implemented: a long note on PRO
MH102/1490 points out that mandamus was available only to compel performance of absolute duties;
and it was decided to deal with this matter by providing for local authorities to act in accordance
with ministerial guidance: see further n. 271 below.

[151] The Committee presented an *Interim Report* on Training in Child Care (Cmd. 6760) on 6 Jan.
1946. Although the Interim Report was primarily concerned with the training of 'residential staff of
the House Mother type in charge of groups of children in small cottage or independent . . . homes',
it summarised all the training available for child care workers of all kinds, and emphasised as a matter 'of great importance and urgency' the need to attract suitable recruits from the men and women
then leaving the armed forces.

[152] '. . . the Curtis Committee's Report does not recommend the extinction of the great voluntary
services which, indeed, they most strongly commend', per Viscount Simon, *Official Report* (HL)
12 Dec. 1946, vol. 144, col. 904. Nevertheless, Barnardo's (like other voluntary agencies, at a low
ebb after World War II) was equivocal in its approach to Curtis, particularly since the possibility of
State interference by inspectors threatened their historic 'freedom of action': see J. Rose, *For the
Sake of the Children* (1987) p. 199.   [153] *Curtis Report*, para. 227.

should become 'wards of the state'[154]—albeit the direct responsibility of an identified individual.[155]

The Curtis Committee was not sparing in its criticisms of some voluntary homes;[156] but concluded that 'as a group' the voluntary homes did not fall below 'the general level of child care now obtaining throughout the country' and indeed that in 'many instances they were well above it'.[157] Hence the Committee adopted one of those compromises which have for long characterised the provision of welfare services in this country: such homes (whatever their status) should be required to comply with Regulations made by the responsible Minister, and they should be registered with and inspected by the relevant department of central government; but, provided that they could be brought up to the appropriate standard, they should be allowed to continue their activities in the care of children.[158] If not, they should be closed down.

(vii) Child Neglect: Compulsion

The Committee accepted that children suffering from neglect, malnutrition or other evils might indeed be said to be deprived of a 'normal' home life,[159] yet 'the difficulty of drawing the line among children in their own homes is obvious'. For this reason, the Committee concluded that the problem of child neglect in the child's own home was not one with which they had been asked to deal; and the Committee did not consider the question of the basis upon which the courts could order that a child be removed[160] from his parents against their will.[161] The

---

[154] The Permanent Under-Secretary of State at the Home Office Sir A. Maxwell referred to 'Lady Allen's campaign against voluntary homes'; and her autobiography (Allen: *Memoirs*) did not conceal her regret that the State had not assumed direct responsibility for children in voluntary homes ('... the state is responsible for the sick, the old and the unemployed. It would have been a fine thing to abolish for ever the necessity for any child to be dependent on charity': p. 208). Although she hailed the Children Act 1948 as a 'Children's Charter' in an article in the *News of the World* on 25 Jan. 1948, she continued to criticise the lack of safeguards for children being cared for by voluntary organisations, and painted a horrifying picture of one 'wealthy foundation' which 'admitted only the illegitimate, allowed no parental contact, and rebaptized and renamed the children ...'.

[155] See Allen: *Memoirs*, Ch. 14.   [156] See *Curtis Report*, para. 225 ff.

[157] *Curtis Report*, para. 227.   [158] *Curtis Report*, para. 433.

[159] In the House of Lords debate (*Official Report* (HL) 12 Dec. 1946, vol. 144, col. 892) the Bishop of Sheffield pointed out that there were a 'very considerable number of children living with parents who are vicious or mentally deficient, under conditions of bestial squalor which are quite shocking'. Parents might be prosecuted and imprisoned, and their children lodged in the Poor Law Institution; but the parents received no psychiatric treatment and no education in parentcraft. At the end of the parents' sentence, the family would return to the 'previous conditions unchanged'. He considered that legislation as well as vigorous administration was needed.

[160] The Committee did, however, recommend that if a court wished to commit a child to the care of a local authority as a fit person the local authority should be obliged to undertake the child's care: *Curtis Report*, para. 425.

[161] The courts had power under the Children and Young Persons Act 1933, Part III, to commit a child to the care of a fit person (including a local authority) willing to receive the child if the child had committed an offence, was beyond parental control, or was in need of care and protection. The Home Office view was that it 'was often an accident' whether a child came before the court as a delinquent or as a neglected child; and for this reason the Committee accordingly concluded that 'the same methods of treatment should be equally available in either case': *Curtis Report*, para. 38.

world with which the Curtis Committee was concerned was the world of social administration not legal action;[162] its Terms of Reference required it to deal with children who had in fact been deprived of a normal home life with their own parents. Statutory provision specifically focusing on preventive work had to wait for another committee[163] and other legislation;[164] whilst the circumstances in which the State could properly remove a child from its parents remained controversial. Another twenty years would elapse before a government was prepared to bring forward legislation seeking to remedy the defects in the relevant statutory provisions.[165]

(viii) Guardians for the Orphan?

Although the Curtis Committee did not consider the circumstances which might justify removing a child from the family, it did consider the question of legal authority in respect of the child who had in fact come into care. As we have seen the Committee's starting point was that an identifiable person should be responsible for the child's care;[166] and to this end the Committee thought it desirable that every orphan or deserted child maintained or supervised by a local authority should have a legal guardian—preferably a relative, but otherwise the Head of an approved voluntary home, or the local authority itself[167]—able to take the major decisions in the child's life and 'to feel full responsibility' for the child's welfare. The Committee accordingly recommended that County Courts and magistrates' courts should be empowered to appoint a guardian for any child who had no natural or testamentary guardian, and it considered that the authority should raise the question of guardianship in all cases in which it took responsibility for the child's welfare.[168] The Committee thought this procedure would help to give foster parents a measure of security: 'if this simple procedure were available it might often make possible a stable relation short of adoption between a good foster parent and a child'.[169] But as we shall see, the implementation of this policy gave rise to difficulty; and

---

[162] See *Lewisham London Borough Council* v. *Lewisham Juvenile Court Justices* [1980] AC 273, 306, per Lord Scarman.

[163] *Report of the Committee on Children and Young Persons* (The Ingleby Committee) (Cmnd. 1191, 1960).   [164] Children and Young Persons Act 1963, s. 1.

[165] Amendment of the relevant 'care and protection' provisions of the Children and Young Persons Act 1933 was recommended by the Ingleby *Committee on Children and Young Persons* (Cmnd. 1191, 1960): see paras. 83–94 and App. III. But the relationship between prosecution of the delinquent and care of the neglected became the subject of much discussion in the 1960s (see notably *The Child, the Family and the Young Offender* (Cmnd. 2742, 1965) and *Children in Trouble* (Cmnd. 3601, 1968)) and it was not until 1969 that the Children and Young Persons Act 1969 reformulated the principles upon which compulsory protective measures could be taken in respect of children. Those provisions remained the basis of the law until the coming into force of the Children Act 1989 in 1991 which adopts a clearly principled (albeit still controversial) approach, and has engendered a mass of case law.

[166] See text to n. 123, above.   [167] *Curtis Report*, para. 425(ii).

[168] The Committee contemplated that 'failing a suitable relative, for whom enquiry should be made, or the Head of an approved voluntary Home which has the child under care, the local authority itself should apply for appointment as a guardian'. This recommendation prompted some modification to the powers of local authorities under the Poor Law Act 1930, s. 52, to assume parental rights over a child by resolution: see below.   [169] *Curtis Report*, para. 425(ii).

the question of how best to create a secure legal status[170] for the long-term foster parent remained troublesome for years to come.[171]

(ix) Assumption of Parental Rights?

The proposal for court-appointed guardians was to be restricted to cases in which the child had no natural or testamentary guardian; but—in a somewhat confused passage in its Report[172]—the Committee seemed to suggest that the appointment of a guardian by the court under this procedure would also supplant the proced-ure derived from the Poor Law[173] whereby local authorities could by adminis-trative means assume the parents' rights over a child[174] in their care in certain circumstances.[175]

As a Home Office official had put it in 1944,[176] it was a 'subject for wonder how [this procedure] ever passed the scrutiny of Parliament';[177] and apparently

[170] And how far adoption should be favoured over other methods of care: see most recently P. Morgan, *Adoption and the Care of Children* (1998).

[171] On 23 Apr. 1948 Lord Chancellor Jowitt wrote to the Home Secretary expressing concern about the position of small children deserted by their natural parents and boarded out with foster parents: 'it frequently happens—and God be praised that it does—that these foster-parents become really attached to the children and would, if they could, be only too ready to adopt them so that they might have them "for keeps" and give them the benefit of a real home life . . . Would it not be possible to pro-vide in the case of a child deserted by its parents that, after a certain time and of course with the approval of the Home Office . . . an adoption might be allowed?' The response, as Jowitt had expected, was that such a proposal was not within the scope of the Bill. The Children Act 1975 eventually permitted a local authority to pass a parental rights resolution on the ground that the child had been in care for three years or more, thereby facilitating a placement for adoption; whilst statute and judicial interpretation facilitated the making of adoption orders notwithstanding opposition from the birth parents: see Ch. 8 above. [172] Para. 425(iii).

[173] The Poor Law Act 1889, s. 1 first gave the guardians powers to assume parental rights over a child deserted by a parent (although a parent imprisoned for certain offences against the child was to be treated as having deserted the child). This power was extended by the Poor Law Act 1899, s. 2, to cases in which the parent was of vicious habits, detained under the legislation dealing with inebriates and cases in which the parent was permanently bedridden or disabled. It was intended that the guardians would then arrange for the child to be 'adopted' by foster parents, and although such adoptions did not affect the child's legal status (and did not protect the foster parents against a decision by the guardians to remove the child) they did give the 'adopters' a measure of protec-tion against claims by the natural parents to resume the care of the child as soon as he was able to earn wages. Although the resolution procedure was criticised, it had its supporters: the *Royal Com-mission on the Poor Law*, Cd. 4499 (1909), considered that greater use should be made of such 'adop-tions'; and even after the creation of statutory machinery for adoption in the modern sense (Adoption Act 1926) the *Report of the Departmental Committee on Adoption Societies and Agencies*, Cmd. 5499 (1937), commended the use of poor law adoptions: see further Ch. 8 above.

[174] For these purposes a 'child' was a person under 18; and the assumption was that the years between 16 to 18 were critical 'because during them the young people's earnings will usually need to be supplemented, friendly advice is of special importance to them, and undesirable relatives attempt to resume control of them, either to claim their earnings or to corrupt their morals': *The Break Up of the Poor Law and the Care of Children and Old People* (n. 22 above) para. 23.

[175] i.e. if the child was an orphan (or, if illegitimate, motherless), or had been deserted by the parent, or if the parent (because of mental deficiency or habits or mode of life) was unfit to have control of the child: Poor Law Act 1930, s. 52.

[176] S. W. Harris's Memorandum dated 13 June 1944, PRO MH102/1378, para. 8.

[177] The short answer may be that Parliament gave the matter almost no scrutiny: see *Hansard's Parliamentary Debates, 4th series* 29 June 1899 vol. 73, col. 951.

(notwithstanding the fact that the Authorities used the power 'with discretion and a proper sense of responsibility'[178]) complaints by parents about its use 'were not uncommon'. The Curtis Committee agreed with these criticisms, considering that to extinguish the rights of a parent or other guardian by a mere resolution of a council was fundamentally objectionable.[179] Accepting that public opinion was critical of interference with parental rights and personal liberty,[180] the Curtis Report favoured requiring judicial decision in such cases. Even 'if extra publicity and work were involved in court proceedings, we are of opinion that they would be more than counterbalanced by the value of an impartial and detached judicial inquiry at the outset directed to the paramount welfare of the child'.[181]

It would seem to follow that the Curtis Committee favoured the abolition of the parental rights resolution, but as we shall see the Committee's views on court-appointed guardians and parental rights resolutions were not fully elaborated and gave rise to considerable difficulty[182] when legislation came to be drafted. In fact the parental rights resolution not only survived until 1991[183] but was given an extended application by the Children Act 1975.[184]

PUBLICATION OF THE CURTIS REPORT

The Curtis Report was signed in August 1946[185] and delivered to Ministers on 13 September.[186] Although it was clear that legislation would be necessary to

---

[178] *The Break Up of the Poor Law and the Care of Children and Old People* (n. 22 above) para. 24. Although this Report accepted the case for modification and the imposition of a requirement for a judicial decision, it also pointed out that the provisions of the Children and Young Persons Act 1933 had not always succeeded in giving children the necessary care and protection 'because the courts are too reluctant to deprive a parent of the control of his child' and suggested there might be a case for applying the criterion—then embodied in the Guardianship of Infants Act 1925, s. 1, and retained (albeit only as a necessary and not as a sufficient justification for removing a child from its parents) in the Children Act 1989, s. 1—that the child's welfare be the paramount consideration.

[179] The Home Office had also regarded proposals to commit children to the care of local authorities without any indication of what course was to be taken as open to 'serious objection': S. W. Harris's Memorandum (see n. 176 above) para. 12(i).

[180] As the Report on *The Break Up of the Poor Law and the Care of Children and Old People* (n. 22 above), para. 24, had put it.   [181] *Curtis Report*, para. 425(ii).

[182] The Committee seems not to have appreciated that their proposal for court-appointed guardians would not cover all the cases in which parental rights resolutions were available (e.g. cases in which the child had been deserted but still had a 'natural guardian'); nor did the Committee consider the difficulties (highlighted in S. W. Harris's Memorandum dated 13 June 1944, PRO MH102/1378, paras. 8–9 (see n. 176 above)) arising from the interrelationship of the resolution procedure (and any substitute for it) and the powers of the court under the Children and Young Persons Act 1933 to commit a child to the care of a fit person.

[183] With the coming into force of the Children Act 1989.   [184] See below.

[185] Six members of the Committee signed a note of Reservation dissenting from the majority view that the existing Poor Law rule prohibiting the boarding out of a child with foster parents of a different religious persuasion be abolished: see *Curtis Report*, para. 472, and p. 183.

[186] *Official Report* (HC) 12 Dec. 1946, vol. 144, col. 884.

deal with the consequences of the ending of the Poor Law—and indeed the Minis-try of Health had jumped the gun by delivering Instructions to Parliamentary Counsel[187]—there remained uncertainty about how extensive that legislation would need to be. There was some emotive press comment about the treatment of chil-dren in voluntary homes;[188] but even here the newly elected Labour Government was cautious. It would be wrong (Health Minister Aneurin Bevan told the Commons[189])to run the risk of losing many devoted workers in voluntary homes who might feel tainted by the general atmosphere. There were some who thought that the—overwhelmingly Conservative—press were using the delay in introducing legislation as a stick with which to beat a Government[190] preferring (so it was said) to introduce doctrinaire nationalisation legislation rather than pro-tecting the nation's children. But making all necessary allowances, it still seems true that there was strong parliamentary pressure for legislation[191] and criticism when no commitment to legislate was given in the King's Speech in October 1946. The Government's response was to point to what could and was being done by administrative action;[192] but the truth of the matter was that delay was at least in part attributable to the continuing dispute about which Whitehall Department was to assume responsibility for child care.

[187] See the copy on PRO MH102/1491. Para. 71 of the Instructions stated that provision should be made for central responsibility remaining with the 'Minister of Health (Secretary of State)' but the Instructions presciently went on that this was 'a point on which there may later be a different Ministerial decision'.

[188] In the House of Lords debate on 12 Dec. 1946 (*Official Report* (HL) vol. 144, col. 889) Lord Iddesleigh urged the Government immediately to introduce legislation extending powers of inspec-tion and, in an attempt to raise the standards of others, the exemplary closure of some institutions. He highlighted the case of a 'very shocking convent laundry where the children are grossly over-worked and underpaid . . . the children have to rise at six o'clock, do an hour's housework and half an hour's spiritual meditation before breakfast' and claimed that there were 'many other extraordin-ary examples of old-fashioned, ill-run, voluntary homes, sometimes . . . run by untrained people and quite out of touch with modern ideas'.

[189] *Official Report* (HC) 31 Oct. 1946, vol. 428, col. 778.

[190] See, for example, Paul Winterton in the (liberal) *News Chronicle* 11 Dec. 1946, arguing that the problems which Curtis had highlighted were attributable to a period when the country had been ruled by 'hard-headed businessmen bent primarily on the pursuit of gain and semi-feudal squires with semi-feudal ideas'.

[191] See notably Wilson Harris's remarks (*Official Report* (HC) 19 Nov. 1946, vol. 430, col. 763) in the debate on the King's Speech; and note in the House of Lords debate, *Official Report* (HL) 12 Dec. 1946, vol. 144, col. 881.

[192] See, for example, the Prime Minister's statement in the House of Commons, *Official Report* (HC) 28 Nov. 1946, vol. 430, col. 329; whilst in the full House of Lords debate (*Official Report* (HL) 12 Dec. 1946, vol. 144, cols. 903–907) Lord Listowel was able to point to a substantial body of administrative measures: (1) Publication of a Circular to Local Authorities requiring them to review arrangements in the light of recommendations and criticisms in the *Curtis Report*; (2) Strengthening of the Home Office and Ministry of Health Inspectorates; (3)Establishing training courses for house mothers and senior staff; and the creation of a Central Council on Training and Child Care; (4) Making of new Rules on boarding out and fostering, and publication of detailed directions and guidance about the procedures to be followed; (5) Publication of Guidance on improved administrative procedures including placing responsibility for finding foster homes and the supervision of foster homes on a single officer.

THE MACHINERY OF GOVERNMENT ISSUE

The three Whitehall Departments with child care responsibilities had, as we have seen,[193] been aware at least since 1944, of the need to grapple with the machinery for dealing with the care of children. If there was—as had been suggested at that time—to be a single Department[194] responsible for these matters should this be the Home Office, the Ministry of Health or the Department of Education,[195] or even a specially created Ministry for Children?

From the start, the Home Office had vigorously resisted the suggestion[196] that its responsibilities for the police and the administration of the prisons and criminal justice disqualified it from assuming overall responsibility for child care. In part, the Home Office case was founded on the constitutional position of the Secretary of State, from which it followed that the Home Office had central responsibility for the protection of children (as for other internal affairs) except so far as responsibilities had been specifically allotted to the Ministry of Education or (in the case of public health and public assistance) to the Ministry of Health.

At the heart of the Home Office case was the view that the nature of its constitutional responsibilities had led to the establishment of a tradition of case by case consideration of individual problems. Dealing 'with human life and happiness [required] the human touch of a single person' who could be held individually responsible for his administration rather than a 'soulless instrument';[197] and Home Office officials and Ministers convinced themselves that only the Home Office[198]

---

[193] For a full analysis see R. A. Parker, 'The gestation of reform: the Children Act 1948', n. 8 above.

[194] For the possibility of joint departmental responsibility, see n. 198 below.

[195] All these Departments had responsibilities in respect of certain categories of children, while the Ministry of Pensions and Service departments also took responsibility in some circumstances. Press comment had tended to assume the Ministry of Education should be the preferred central department (see e.g. the *Daily Mail*, 20 Mar. 1945); and almost forty years earlier the Minority Report of the Royal Commission on the Poor Laws (Cd. 4499, 1909, vol. 2, p. 169) had asserted that 'one Local Authority in each district, and only one [should be] responsible for the whole of whatever provision the State' chose to make in respect of children of school age, and that only Local Education Authorities under the supervision of the Board of Education (with 'their extensive staffs of teachers, their residential and their day feeding schools, their arrangements for medical inspection and treatment, their School Attendance Officers and Children's Care Committees') had the 'machinery requisite for searching out every child destitute of the necessaries of life, for enforcing parental responsibility, and for obviating, by timely pressure and assistance, the actual crisis of destitution'.

[196] Advanced in the Ministry of Health's Memorandum on *The Break Up of the Poor Law and the Care of Children*: see n. 22 above.

[197] See the Officials' Minute commenting on the Ministry of Health Memorandum to the Machinery of Government Committee, 1 Jan. 1945.

[198] S. W. Harris did produce a Memorandum, *First Thoughts on the Pooling of the Children's Problem*, which considered the possibility of joint Home Office (Juvenile Court and Probation Service) Ministry of Health (Poor Law and other infants) service; but in a covering manuscript note to Maxwell dated 18 Aug. 1944 (PRO MH102/1378) he made clear his view that he would '*greatly* prefer to tackle the whole problem ourselves', that to agree to the Ministry of Health proposals would 'be fatal to recent progress', but that if 'we must give in, a joint solution may be best for the children concerned but it will be difficult to run without creating new troubles'.

was equipped to provide this level of individualised care.[199] The Home Office had been given the right to enter and inspect[200] children's homes by the Children Act 1908 and the work of the Home Office Children's Department[201] was well known and highly regarded.

Another aspect of the Home Office case for recognition as the single Department responsible for child care issues was founded on a bold refutation of the alleged association of the Home Office with criminality. It was true that none of the other Departments concerned could properly assume responsibility for the juvenile courts because those courts had coercive powers. But the courts dealt equally with care and protection and delinquency cases, and in reality children committed because they were in need of care and protection often presented 'more serious behaviour problems than are presented by the high-spirited boy who has robbed an orchard or broken windows'. In this view, the juvenile courts—which were 'as much civil as they are criminal in the technical sense'[202]—dealt with all children coming before them simply on the basis of their needs and future welfare rather than on what had brought them before the court. In particular, the Home Office strongly resisted the suggestion that 'delinquent children form a class apart, who must not be associated with other children'.[203] The Home Office official[204] in charge of the Children's Department regarded the inevitable isolation of the juvenile delinquent as the 'worst feature' of the proposal to deprive the Home Office of its general responsibility for children:

[199] The Reports on the work of the Children's Department contain much evidence of current attitudes to child care—the Fifth Report for example comments at p. 82 on the need for attention to 'the regular action of the bowels' since 'impairment of physical and mental vigour may result from the neglect of it'. The Department considered that 'careful instruction and supervision' could lead to the establishment of regular habits.

[200] The papers reveal the strong conviction of Home Office officials that Home Office inspections had 'been much closer and more sympathetic than that of the Ministry of Health over the institutions they inspect' and that 'this important function in the interest of children ought not to be lightly abandoned': S. W. Harris, Memorandum on Ministry of Health Proposals, 13 June 1944, PRO MH102/1378, para. 10. PRO MH102/149 contains further criticisms of the 'low standards' of Health inspections, sometimes amounting to little more than 'casual notes of a brief walk round'.

[201] The Children's Branch of the Home Office had published Reports spasmodically—the first three annually in 1923, 1924 and 1925. The *Fourth Report* in 1928 stated that it was preferable to publish Reports periodically 'as often as changing circumstances or new developments' required; but it was ten years before the next Report appeared in 1938. (The delay was attributed to the heavy burden in preparing for the 1933 Act and in dealing with the new problems to which it gave rise.) In its 1944 Memorandum to the Machinery of Government Committee the Home Office stated that the series would have continued 'but for the war'.

[202] *Home Office Memorandum to the Machinery of Government Committee*, Dec. 1944, PRO MH102/1379.

[203] Maxwell to Maude, 13 July 1944, PRO MH102/1378. The same view was expressed more provocatively by Norman Brook in marginal annotations to a Ministry of Health memorandum (PRO MGO 62 12/40): 'Almost all children are delinquents—some are caught—others aren't. The young criminal is a very rare bird'.

[204] S. W. Harris, Memorandum to Maxwell dated 13 June 1944, PRO MH102/1378, commenting on the Ministry of Health's 'Break up of the Poor Law' proposals. Harris thought transfer of responsibility to the Ministry of Health would be 'fatal to recent progress': manuscript postscript to minute, Harris to Maxwell, 18 Aug. 1944, PRO MH102/1378.

[The] idea that a young person or adolescent who, often through no fault of his own, commits an offence should be regarded as necessarily needing segregation from other children is no longer tenable. It is completely opposed to the principles embodied in the Children and Young Persons Act [1933], which prescribes both for the neglected and the delinquent treatment which should ensure the 'welfare of the child'.

The dispute dragged on behind closed doors for more than three years. The one thing about which all those involved were agreed was that it would be 'unhelpful and might even be embarrassing' if the Curtis Committee were to go beyond questions of the treatment of children but also concern itself with such questions of central administration;[205] and this was made clear[206] to the Committee. The decision on departmental responsibility was one for government, and it appeared at long last to have been settled in April 1945 when the Cabinet accepted the advice of the Machinery of Government Committee[207] in favour of the Home Office.[208]

---

[205] The quotation is taken from a draft Memorandum to the Reconstruction Committee, 6 Nov. 1944, PRO MH102/1161, p. 3.

[206] The Curtis Committee's Terms of Reference did not preclude consideration of this sensitive issue: cf. R. A. Parker, 'The gestation of reform: the Children Act 1948', n. 8 above—indeed Sir John Maude took the view that the use of language directly excluding the machinery of government issue from the Committee's terms of reference might 'offend both Parliament and the proposed Committee' and agreed that the 'better course' would be to 'use language of quite a wide kind but to intimate to Parliament, when the announcement is made, that the Government already have under consideration the question of central machinery' and 'hope to make their views on this point known to the Committee at the outset of the inquiry' (Maude to Maxwell, 15 Nov. 1944, PRO MH102/1161, para. 1). Morrison's statement to the House of Commons on 7 Dec. adopted this approach; and Myra Curtis was 'confidentially informed' of the position at an early stage: PRO ED136/720. The Curtis Committee accepted that the identification of the particular department concerned 'must be settled on another level' (para. 434) but did consider the *distribution* of responsibility among Government Departments for the care of children (as distinct from the question of which particular department should assume any particular function) (see *Curtis Report*, paras. 429–32): as noted above, it rejected the notion that the upbringing of all deprived children should be a direct State responsibility exercised through officers of a central department (para. 429) but recommended that the Government Department concerned should 'define requirements, maintain standards, advise and assist those taking immediate responsibility for the care of children and act as a clearing house for progressive ideas': para. 432. The Committee also urged 'that whichever department undertakes the work, it should have a Children's Branch making a special study of child welfare on the side of the home, without specialist bias on any side, and an inspectorate able to judge whether the conditions for the child's total welfare as a human being exist in a particular case': para. 434. Moreover, the responsible Minister 'might be well advised to appoint an Advisory Council to keep him in touch with developments in outside expert opinion on the subject of child care': para. 435.

[207] To which it had been referred in Dec. 1944: see R. A. Parker, op. cit. n. 8 above, at p. 202.

[208] The Committee reached this conclusion 'not because [the Home Office] is a specialist Department in respect of delinquents but because, being in general a wide-ranging and non-specialist Department, it is well placed for giving that general consideration to the domiciliary problems of children as human beings, rather than as medical or educational units, which is essential for the balanced development of policy': *Further Report by the Committee*, MGO 72, 26 Apr. 1945, PRO CAB 87/71. (It appears that the Committee had been impressed by the argument that the Home Office should not be shorn of too many functions not 'purely repressive in character', and that the 'development of a progressive policy manifestly founded on a sympathetic appreciation of the whole problem would constitute an admirably stimulating administrative aim for an enlarged Children's Branch in the Home Office': para. 12 of the Committee's draft Report as discussed with Sir A. Maxwell on 8 Mar. 1945: PRO MH102/1382). The Machinery of Government Committee was opposed to the notion

But the change of government after the 1945 election allowed the matter to be reopened.[209] Once again the Home Office's case[210] triumphed over the well-prepared claims of Health[211] and the increasingly[212] strongly asserted[213] claims[214]

of a separate Children's Ministry as being inconsistent with the doctrine laid down by the Haldane Committee that responsibility should be based on the services provided rather than by reference to the class of persons using those services. See further R. A. Parker, 'The gestation of reform: the Children Act 1948' op. cit. n. 8 above, at pp. 205–6.

[209] The Labour Government at first set up a Social Services Committee which gave some consideration to children's services; but on 15 Nov. 1946, after delivery of the Curtis Report, the Prime Minister set up a Care of Children Committee specifically to consider the matters to which the Curtis Report (and its Scottish counterpart, the Clyde Report: see n. 230 below) gave rise. The fact that the Committee was chaired by Morrison, who was strongly committed to the Home Office's children's work, and that Morrison was advised by a former Home Office official of exceptional ability (Sir Norman Brook) may have been one of those accidents of history which affects its course. Morrison took the view at the first meeting of the Care of Children Committee on 6 Dec. 1946 that the onus lay on those who disagreed with the Coalition Government's decision to make their case: see PRO CAB 130/15. See generally the account in R. A. Parker, 'The gestation of reform: the Children Act 1948', n. 8 above, at pp. 207–11.

[210] Some informal lobbying also went on: Maxwell told the Home Secretary, Chuter Ede, that a dinner table conversation with Henry Salt KC (a member of the Curtis Committee) had convinced him that all but one of the members of the Committee favoured the Home Office as the appropriate central government department: Maxwell to Home Secretary, 13 Dec. 1946, PRO MH102/1393. Chuter Ede asked that this information be conveyed to the Lord President.

[211] For more detail, see 'The gestation of reform: the Children Act 1948', by R. A. Parker, op. cit. n. 8 above, at pp. 209–10. The case for conferring central authority on the Ministry of Health was put by Lord Amulree in the House of Lords debate on the Curtis Report (*Official Report* (HL) 12 Dec. 1946, vol. 144, col. 894) 'because it has . . . a large number of very well-trained men and women inspectors and a trained medical staff . . .'; but the tendency of those who had served as Home Secretary to defend the Home Office's role was exemplified by Lord Simon (Home Secretary 1935–7) at col. 899.

[212] D. N. Chester and F. M. G. Wilson, *The Organisation of British Central Government 1914–1956* (1957), p. 176, state that although some believed that the Ministry of Education was the only agency which could be relied on to administer child care work in a humane way, the Ministry was 'not particularly keen to accept the work'; and the records suggest some uncertainty of purpose within the Ministry: see the papers on PRO ED 136/719 and 720.

[213] The Minister had recorded at a meeting of the Social Services Committee on 12 July 1946 that she took 'strong exception' to proposals which took 'no account of the new conception of the responsibilities of the Ministry of Education': see PRO MH102/1390. The sharpness of the rivalry is evidenced by a criticism made at the meeting of the Cabinet Care of Children Committee on 6 Dec. 1946 when the Minister of Education referred to one named Home Office Inspector whose only qualification (so the Minister alleged) was a certificate in gardening. The Home Secretary (Chuter Ede) found it necessary to write personally to Morrison recording that the person in question had indeed at one stage been a Lecturer at an agricultural college but that she had thereafter proved herself so successful as Head of an LCC approved school that she was selected as an inspector.

[214] The case for transfer to the Ministry of Education was also put publicly: see e.g. *Official Report* (HC) 31 Oct. 1946, vol. 428, col. 778. The Labour Party's Standing Joint Committee of Working Women's Organisations made representations to the same effect; and in Feb. 1946 Morrison evidently judged it necessary to send a detailed *Memorandum* to the Party's National Executive: see PRO MH102/1386. This argued that the 'function of guarding the interests of [homeless] children ought to be recognised as a distinct subject ranking in importance with the subjects of education and health, and assigned to a Minister who should be specifically responsible for seeing not merely that the educational and medical needs of the homeless child are met, but that he is provided for the fullest possible extent with those elements of child welfare which the good parent or guardian provides'. Morrison argued that the Home Secretary would be the appropriate Minister; and recorded that his 'experience

of the Ministry of Education.[215] The Cabinet decided[216] that the central responsibility for the care of deprived children should be concentrated in the Home Office,[217]
and on 24 March 1947[218] the Prime Minister (in a statement telling the Commons
that the Government accepted the main Curtis recommendations) also announced
the decision that the Home Office was the central Department best fitted to assume
the responsibility for supervising arrangements made for children deprived of a
normal home life.[219]

   This decision may have come as a surprise and disappointment to some;[220]
and it seems that it was a result less of any dispassionate assessment of the competing arguments and more to the considerable political and tactical skills of Herbert Morrison (Home Secretary in the war-time Coalition but at the time Lord

of the Home Office showed . . . that there is in this Department a tradition of care for the interests
of the individual child which would be helpful to the Minister charged with developing a
policy of far-reaching reforms in this field. Amongst the many constructive activities of the Home
Office, extending over a wider field as they do than those of any other Department, I think it can be
said there is none in which it has been more successful than child welfare . . . [The Home Office
had] stood emphatically for the view that every child must be dealt with as an individual, and that
the welfare of the individual child must be the primary consideration.' Morrison copied this under
a personal 'My Dear Ellen' letter (21 Mar. 1946, PRO ED137/719) to the Minister of Education
(with whom he was on close terms: see n. 215 below).

   [215] Until her death from a drug overdose on 6 Feb. 1947 the formidable Ellen Wilkinson, for long
a close friend of Morrison (whom, his biographers record, she had admired 'to the point of love').
It appears that the BBC was persuaded not to broadcast news of her death until Morrison—who was
in hospital at the time—had been told: see B. Donoghue and G. W. Jones, *Herbert Morrison, Portrait
of a Politician* (1973) p. 392; and see also B. D. Vernon, *Ellen Wilkinson* (1982) p. 128.

   [216] On 18 Mar. 1947: PRO CAB 128/9.

   [217] The main argument recorded in the Cabinet Minutes against Home Office involvement was
that it would be seen as handing over the care of deprived children to Departments mainly concerned
with offenders; and it was agreed that the Cabinet's decision should be announced 'in such a way
as to give no ground to the suggestion that deprived children were being handed over to the police'.
The Cabinet Secretary's *Notebook* for 1947 (CM (47)29) makes it clear that there was a full debate,
and in particular the Minister of Education 'argued [his Department's case] at great length'.

   [218] *Official Report* (HC) vol. 435, col. 853. The terms of the statement differ in one interesting
respect from the draft contained in an annex to Morrison's Memorandum to the Cabinet: references
to the need to provide for delinquent children was removed.

   [219] A new and enlarged Children's Branch was to be created, with an expanded inspectorate organised on a regional basis. The primary function of the Children's Branch would be to ensure that
everything possible was done to give homeless children, not only the material care, but also the sense
of security and status which a normal home provides. A Standing Advisory Committee, widely representative of the many interests involved, and including representatives of the Ministries of
Education, Health and Labour, was to be appointed to assist the Home Office in its administration.
The need for the Home Office to 'rise to its new responsibilities' had been emphasised by Norman
Brook in his memorandum of 13 Dec. 1946; but in the event the heavy reliance on the Inspectorate
led to some criticism that Home Office guidance to Children's Officers was not adequate: see
J. A. G. Griffith, *Central Departments and Local Authorities* (1966) (and for the traditional role of
Home Office Inspections, J. Pellew, *The Home Office 1848–1914: from clerks to bureaucrats* (1982)
pp. 164–82).

   [220] *The Times*, in a leading article, 25 Mar. 1947, commented that 'not everyone' would agree
with the decision on the central role of the Home Office. But it considered that any reservations on
this score had to be balanced by satisfaction at the various procedures intended to ensure collaboration between all agencies with an interest in child care.

President of the Council) and the eminent civil servant Sir Norman Brook.[221] Brook had produced two exceptionally powerfully argued papers[222] for Morrison; Morrison then arranged an 'informal meeting' of the three Ministers on the Cabinet Committee 'who had no Departmental interest in the question of administrative responsibility'—i.e. himself (Lord President of the Council), the Lord Privy Seal and the Chancellor of the Exchequer—and secured their agreement to his drafting a paper for the Cabinet[223] (leaving it to the dissenting Ministers of Health and Education[224] to argue their case[225] at Cabinet[226] from a position of manifest

[221] Brook was at the time Additional Secretary to the Cabinet. He had entered the Home Office in 1925, and remained there until appointed to assist Sir John Anderson in 1938. He subsequently became Secretary to the Cabinet in 1947, and Head of the Home Civil Service in 1956.

[222] The first (PRO CAB 124/781, 3 Dec. 1946) states the positive points—(i) the Home Office tradition of individual case work, mirroring Curtis's emphasis on the need for *individual* treatment, as compared with the disposition of other Ministries 'concerned with large scale administration' and thus likely to treat children as 'medical or educational units rather than human beings'; (ii) the fact that the 'delinquent' children for whom the Home Office was responsible were (in accordance with the requirements of the Children and Young Persons Act 1933 s. 44) catered for on the basis of their *needs*; and (iii) the desirability of responsibility for young offenders going hand in hand with responsibility for adult offenders. The second (13 Dec. 1946) seeks to rebut arguments put forward by the other Departments—for example, that the Home Office lacked suitably qualified staff (the task was to provide parental care, in which paper qualifications were of little value—the staff would use experts when appropriate but 'need not themselves be expert in anything but the job of seeing that these children are provided with an adequate substitute for home life'). Brook described other arguments put forward by the Ministries as 'going much too far' and 'nonsense'.

[223] See Note dated 7 Jan. 1947 of a Meeting in the Lord President's Room, 17 Dec. 1946: PRO CAB 124/781. The Lord President's Memorandum to the Cabinet (PRO CAB 129/17) canvassed the different arguments put forward by the three Departments competing for central responsibility but —drawing heavily on Brook's minutes—accepted the arguments in favour of the Home Office (although it also recorded the need for a new and enlarged Children's Department, institutionalised procedures for consultation between the relevant Departments about the services to be provided for children, and that delinquent 'children for whom it is necessary to provide substitute homes will be treated as an incidental section of the larger class of deprived children'). In relation to the discharge of local responsibility for child care services, the Memorandum noted but rejected the view of the Minister of Education that a subcommittee appointed jointly by the maternity and child welfare and educational committees should be preferred to the *ad hoc* children's committee proposed by the Curtis Report.

[224] Ellen Wilkinson's copy of the paper is adorned with outspoken comments ('This is really the limit . . .' in the margin by a reference to the humane policies pursued by the Home Office in approved schools). Minutes by her officials record the 'indignation we all feel' about what the 'three impartial prefects' had produced, which (they considered) accepted Home Office arguments 'hook, line and sinker': see PRO ED136/721.

[225] Each also dissented from the Curtis recommendation for a separate children's committee (which, it was said, would be regarded as Public Assistance Committees in a new guise). For Education, it was argued that Local Education Authorities were to be preferred; whilst the Minister of Health, Bevan, was able to point to the friendly associations between the Ministry of Health and Local Authorities' Child Welfare Subcommittees; and he emphasised the role played by Health Visitors (who went into the homes of 97 per cent of newborn babies and thereby had unequalled opportunities for discreet and unstigmatising visits, effective educative and preventive work and for recruiting suitable foster parents).

[226] This they did, and the memoranda they submitted, CP(47)85 and 88, are to be found on PRO CAB 129/17. The Minister of Education, George Tomlinson urged that the present tendency was to widen the scope of education so as 'to include the whole life of the child' and the care of deprived children would thus be a natural addition to the Ministry's existing work. In the oral discussion in

weakness compared with the powerful and senior group now backing Morrison). Finally, Morrison wrote a personal letter to the Prime Minister[227] explaining why the Home Office should take charge. In the circumstances, the outcome was unsurprising.[228]

LEGISLATION OR ADMINISTRATIVE ACTION:
SETTLING THE TERMS OF THE CHILDREN ACT

The Government had thus accepted the main Curtis recommendations, and the issue of departmental responsibility was settled. It was clear that legislation of some sort would be necessary; but little serious detailed discussion about the contents of the Bill seems to have been given until the Cabinet had resolved the question of ministerial responsibility on 18 March 1947.[229] As late as August 1947

Cabinet he was even driven to say that there would be no 'insuperable difficulty' in his Department assuming responsibility for the juvenile courts. The Minister of Health, Aneurin Bevan, claimed that the 'political consequences of placing responsibility on the Home Office would be grave. There would be widespread indignation throughout the country generally and among Government supporters in particular . . .' Bevan's view of the role of the juvenile court was much closer to thinking in the 1990s than that of his colleagues: it was to ensure that 'while any necessary and appropriate reforming influences are brought to bear on delinquent children and those who are beyond their parents' control, ordinary homeless children are passed by those courts back to the care of the comprehensive welfare authority'.

[227] Morrison's 'Immediate and Personal' letter to Attlee dated 17 Mar. (PRO CAB 124/781) addressed to 'My dear Clem' states the 'unanimous conclusion' of the three senior Ministers that central responsibility should remain with the Home Office, and goes on: 'I would just like to add to this with a considerable experience of machinery of government questions both centrally and in local government, I am convinced that this is administratively the most satisfactory solution and the one calculated to serve the best interests of the children. To approach the problem as if it were educational is to ignore the real point, which is that in these cases the job of the State is to see that the children have the equivalent of the parental care which they lack at home. This is, of course, a field in which the Children's Branch of the Home Office have a long and distinguished record, and it is absurd, as I know from my own experience, to suggest that they are influenced by the police approach to the problem . . . And, if it is agreed [*sic*] that the decision would be unpopular with some people, I would reply firstly that the interests of the children must be paramount, secondly that the Government is the best judge on a matter of Departmental organisation, and thirdly that I believe that the amount of likely opposition is greatly exaggerated. There is a strong body of informed opinion in Parliament and in the country which favours the Home Office . . .'

[228] But the files reveal continuing anxiety on Morrison's part about 'possible hostility amongst Government supporters' and the need to draft the statement made to the Commons with 'special care': see CAB 124/781, 20 Mar. 1947, 'JARP' to Maxwell.

[229] For the official discussions on policy see PRO file MH102/1490 (Recommendations of the Care of Children Committee; Note for legislation and administrative action); MH102/1491 (Implementation of the recommendations of the Care of Children Committee; The break up of the Poor Law, Instructions for Parliamentary Counsel); MH102/1504 (Children Bill 1947/1948: Essential Legislation); MH102/1506 (Children Bill 1947–48, Scope of the Bill); MH102/1508 (Children Bill: Memorandum for the Lord President's Committee); MH102/1510 (Children Bill: Implementation of recommendation 4 of Curtis Report; and no new voluntary home to be opened without consent of SoS). For the successive drafts, see MH102/1513 (Children Bill: Drafts—consideration of points arising between submission of Instructions . . . and receipt of first draft); MH102/1518 (Children Bill: Consideration of First Draft); MH102/1519 (Children Bill: Consideration of Second Draft); MH102/1520

both the Home Secretary and the Secretary of State for Scotland[230] were taking the view that the Bill should be restricted to provisions essential by reason of the impending abolition of the Poor Law;[231] and officials initially proposed that forty-two out of the sixty-two recommendations made by Curtis should not be dealt with in forthcoming legislation. Although it is true that in some cases[232] the decision against legislation was taken on policy grounds, in many others the official view was that Curtis's recommendations—even some as central to the Committee's thinking as the codification of local authority duties and powers[233] and the preference for boarding out[234]—could best be left to administrative action.[235] But in the event, the Children Act 1948 (which received the Royal Assent on 30 June 1948) was very different from the low-key measure originally envisaged.

Eight printed drafts[236] were circulated before the first parliamentary debate[237] on the Bill (which was introduced into the House of Lords[238]); and a number of

---

(Children Bill 1947–1948, Memorandum on submission to legislation committee); MH102/1521 (Children Bill: Consideration of Third Draft); MH102/1522 (Children Bill: Consideration of Fourth Draft); MH102/1524 (Children Bill: Consideration of Fifth Draft); MH102/1525 (Children Bill: Consideration of Sixth Draft). Additional pressure was placed on officials by a ministerial decision to publish a White Paper and hold a press conference immediately prior to the Bill's introduction into the House of Lords: see on this and events: MH102/1523 (Children Bill 1947–1948, Issue of a White Paper—Memo. by the Secretary of State).

[230] A Committee under the chairmanship of J. L. Clyde KC had been set up, with identical terms of reference, to consider the situation in Scotland. Its report (*Report of the Committee on Homeless Children*, Cmd. 6911, 1946) was much more succinct than the Curtis Report, but the conclusions were similar in effect.

[231] This view, put forward by Chuter Ede in Nov. 1946 (see PRO MH102/1504, minute of 9 May 1947), was reiterated in a paper put by the two Ministers to the Lord President's Committee on 1 Aug. 1947: see PRO MH102/1508.

[232] For example, Curtis's proposal that the courts be empowered to appoint a guardian for children in local authority care: *Curtis Report, Summary of Recommendations*, para. 4.

[233] PRO MH102/1490(1) 47 records that 'no special action' was required to give effect to Curtis's recommendations in this area.

[234] *Curtis Report, Summary of Recommendations*, paras. 16, 21.

[235] An Interdepartmental Meeting of Officials provisionally agreed what should be, and what should not be, in the Bill on 25 June 1947 (PRO MH102/1506).

[236] The two draftsmen were P. H. See (1910–63) and Sir J. Rowlatt (1898–1956).

[237] The first draft—and that only 'a basis for discussion'—was not printed until 8 Nov. 1947. Many important points of policy remained unsettled—for example, the provision (eventually Children Act 1948, s. 1(3)) that a local authority could not retain a child against the wishes of its parent was only agreed on 4 Dec.—for some time. Because of these and other difficulties the Bill was originally introduced 'in dummy' (i.e. with only Short and Long Titles) on 18 Dec. 1947. Even then, Parliamentary Counsel had to inform the Lord Chancellor's Office that the print which had been supplied 'was wrong, not merely as to the main content of the Bill, but also as to the long title . . . Could you make quite certain that the document off which the Lord Chancellor reads the title of the Bill when he introduces it . . . states the long title and the short title of the Bill [correctly]. It would probably be as well to deprive the Lord Chancellor, if possible, of the copy of the Bill which he received as a member of the Legislation Committee . . .': Rowlatt to Mayell, PRO LCO2/4473, 17 Dec. 1947.

[238] It appears that the decision to introduce the Bill in the House of Lords was taken because the Home Secretary was preoccupied with securing the passage of the Bill for the Criminal Justice Act 1948 through the House of Commons.

significant changes were made in policy[239] as the successive drafts were debated. From the lawyer's perspective, perhaps the most interesting are those reflecting the difficulties experienced by Parliamentary Counsel[240] in giving legislative effect to what was proposed. In particular, the question of legal authority in respect of the children concerned was a source of considerable difficulty. How could a local authority care properly for a child unless the authority had at least some parental authority? The answer was found in a delicate compromise: a local authority which had received a child into care was under a duty to keep the child in care for so long as the child's welfare required,[241] and the local authority's statutory powers and duties then applied;[242] but that provision was not to authorise a local authority to keep a child in care against the wishes of a parent or guardian.[243] In this way, the Act could be presented as intended to safeguard the rights of parents.[244] But what was to happen if a parent insisted on exercising the right to remove a child from care in circumstances which the local authority judged to be inconsistent with the child's welfare? The solution which finally[245] emerged[246] was a

---

[239] A striking example—involving a ministerial rejection of emphatic official advice—was in connection with local authorities' powers to arrange the emigration of children in their care. The comparable provisions in the Poor Law Act 1930, s. 58, had required the consent of a Justice of the Peace in such cases. Early drafts of the new Bill required the consent of a child aged 8 or over, but Home Office officials regarded such a requirement as dating 'from the days of bumbledom' and being quite inappropriate in modern conditions, not least because they thought it would be wrong to 'put the responsibility for a *decision*' on a 13- or 14-year-old child, whilst it might well be in the 'interest of one of the black babies to send him to relatives in America'. But Home Secretary, Chuter Ede, disagreed: twenty years earlier as a JP he had been asked to sign the relevant documents but had insisted on seeing the young teenage children concerned and 'asking them if they wanted to go; They all said they did not. The Relieving Officer who brought them was very indignant and said I only had to sign and not to ask questions. I refused to sign and the children did not go . . .' Ede insisted (see PRO MH102/1521, 10 Dec. 1947; and see also Standing Committee Session 1947–8 *Official Reports* vol. 111) that the Bill incorporate a requirement for the child to consent unless too young to do so: see Children Act 1948, s. 17.   [240] See to Brass, 8 Nov. 1947, PRO MH102/1518.

[241] Children Act 1948, s. 1(2).   [242] Children Act 1948, Part II.

[243] Children Act 1948, s. 1(3) (which also imposed a duty on the local authority to endeavour to secure that care of the child be assumed by a parent, guardian, relative or friend if that would be consistent with the child's welfare).

[244] See per Lord Jowitt LC, *Official Report* (HL) 10 Feb. 1948, vol. 153, col. 918; and note *Lewisham London Borough Council* v. *Lewisham Juvenile Court Justices* [1980] AC 273, 306, per Lord Scarman.

[245] The policy was only finally settled at a desperately late stage with the circulation of the fifth draft (which gave rise to nine pages of drafting points) on 24 Dec. 1947: see MH102/1524. The draft was accompanied by a despairing note to the effect that the Secretary of State wished to hold a press conference before 15 Jan. Even on the sixth draft vital points about the funding of education of children in care were raised, as well as four pages of minor drafting points. The Children Act 1948 (which had in one form or another been in preparation for four years) provides a striking example both of the need for close attention to detail, and of the fact that issues of policy are often to be found secreted in the details.

[246] Ministers (notably Morrison: see his letter to Ede, 1 Sept. 1947, MH102/1510) had been concerned at the initial decision not to give effect to the Curtis recommendation—which seems to have been based on a misapprehension about the likely scope and effect of the proposed provision: see text to n. 169, above—that all orphans and deserted children should have court-appointed guardians. The retention of the resolution procedure to some extent met that concern; but it was eventually decided to give the courts a general power to appoint a guardian for any child who had no parent, no guardian of the person, and no other person having parental rights over him: Children Act 1948, s. 50, inserting

reformulation of the power—which Curtis[247] had wanted to scrap—for the local authority to assume parental rights over a child in care[248] by resolution.[249] The Authority was required to inform the person whose rights[250] were to be acquired in this way of the fact that the resolution had been passed;[251] and that person could then apply to the juvenile court. If such an application was made, the resolution would lapse[252] unless the local authority satisfied the court that the applicant had abandoned the child or was 'unfit to have the care of the child by reason of unsoundness of mind or mental deficiency or by reason of his habits or mode of life';[253] and in this way the legislation carefully preserved the principle that a parent was not to be deprived of his rights without having the opportunity to bring the matter before a court.[254] The Bill tried to draw a happy mean between interference with parental rights[255] and ensuring that local authorities were able to act effectively against neglect.

Such provisions are of great concern to lawyers; and became of importance in practice as—facilitated by legal aid—parents became readier to challenge local authority decision taking.[256] But they were not the provisions which appeared of

s. 4(2A) into the Guardianship of Infants Act 1925. In fact this provision was normally used to give a legal status to a relative or other person taking over the care of an orphaned child, and seems to have been largely irrelevant in the local authority context.

[247] See above.

[248] The fact that a resolution could only be passed with respect to a child in the local authority's care under s. 1 of the Act meant that there was no power under this provision to *remove* a child from the parents: see *Lewisham London Borough Council* v. *Lewisham Juvenile Court Justices* [1980] AC 273, HL. In some circumstances, the courts had powers to order the removal of neglected children under the Children and Young Persons Act 1933.

[249] The grounds upon which such a resolution could be passed were that the child's parents were dead and he had no guardian, or that a parent or guardian of his had abandoned him or suffered from some permanent disability rendering him incapable of caring for the child, or was of such habits or mode of life as to be unfit to have the care of the child: Children Act 1948, s. 2(1).

[250] It had originally been envisaged that all parental rights over the child would pass to the local authority, but this was reversed: s. 2(1) of the Children Act 1948 provided that 'all the rights and powers of the person on whose account the resolution was passed' should vest in the local authority. Hence it might be that one parent would retain parental rights in respect of a child subject to a resolution: see *R* v. *Oxford City Justices, ex parte H* [1975] QB 1, and for an account of the difficulties to which this could give rise, S. M. Cretney, *Principles of Family Law* (4th edn. 1984) pp. 516–17.

[251] Unless that person had consented in writing to the resolution being passed: Children Act 1948, s. 2(2). The comparable provision of the Poor Law Act 1930, s. 52, allowed a juvenile court to revoke a parental rights resolution, but contained no provision for notifying the parent or other person concerned that a resolution had been passed.

[252] The Act also provided for the local authority to rescind a resolution if that would be for the child's benefit; and for the parent to apply to the court for the resolution to be determined: Children Act 1948, s. 4(2), (3). Otherwise a resolution remained in force until the child attained 18—this age eventually being preferred to 16 because it was thought the years 16 to 18 were of especial importance in young peoples' personal development: see n. 174 above.

[253] Children Act 1948, s. 2(3).

[254] *Lewisham London Borough Council* v. *Lewisham Juvenile Court Justices* [1980] AC 273, 307, per Lord Scarman; and see per Lord Jowitt LC, *Official Report* (HL) 10 Feb. 1948, vol. 153, col. 918.

[255] Lord Chancellor Jowitt subsequently told the House of Lords that his experience convinced him such interference would very seldom be justified: *Official Report* (HL) 10 Feb. 1948, vol. 153, col. 918.   [256] See S. M. Cretney, *Principles of Family Law* (4th edn. 1984) pp. 518–22.

most importance to those who had campaigned for effective help for children
deprived of a normal home life. For them the fact that the Act would articulate
and codify many of the child care practices—not least the preference for boarding out[257]—supported by Curtis was a great step forward; whilst the fact that the
Act would oblige local authorities to receive needy[258] children into care, to further children's best interests and give them the opportunity to develop their abilities[259]—an obligation supported by the power to assist young people who had
been in local authority care to meet educational and training expenses until the
child was twenty-one or even beyond that age[260]—was of enormous importance,
both symbolic and practical. The Act seemed to establish the principle that children in care were to have exactly the same opportunities, for example, for further education[261] as children living with their parents; and it was provisions such
as those which enabled Lady Allen to claim[262] that if a child wished and had the
aptitude to become a doctor, a lawyer, or a musician, or to pursue any other career
of his choice, 'the local authority would see him through . . .'. The prominence
given to the local authority's duties gave credibility to the description of the Bill
as a Children's Charter; and they were certainly inspired by a totally different
philosophy from the statutory provision previously in force requiring that orphan
and other destitute children be 'set to work'.[263]

THE ACT ON THE STATUTE BOOK—AND IN FORCE

The Bill had a largely trouble-free passage through Parliament,[264] with only the
question—which had divided the Curtis Committee—of the religious upbringing

[257] For the failure to give statutory effect to Curtis's preference for adoption in appropriate circumstances, see above.

[258] i.e. abandoned, lost and parentless children, and children whose parents or guardian were 'for
the time being or permanently, prevented by reason of mental or bodily disease or infirmity or other
incapacity or any other circumstances from providing for [the child's] accommodation, maintenance
and upbringing': Children Act 1948, s. 1. The extension of local authority responsibility far beyond
destitution (the only basis for intervention under the Poor Law) was not in terms envisaged by the
Curtis Committee: cf. *Curtis Report*, para. 424 (which recommended the extension of public care
and supervision only to certain specified groups of children in need of care and supervision); but the
need to clarify the basis for assuming responsibility had been foreseen by Home Office officials from
the outset: see Maxwell to Maude, 13 July 1944, para. 6, PRO MH102/1378.

[259] Children Act 1948, s. 12(1).   [260] Children Act 1948, s. 20.

[261] See the discussion of what was intended to be the final version of the Bill discussed at
the Cabinet Legislation Committee, 16 Dec. 1947: HPC (47) 28th Meeting, as extracted on
MH102/1520; and note that the Act empowered local authorities to use private sector facilities (speech
therapy being an example quoted) when appropriate: Children Act 1948, s. 12(2). Although the
Committee gave general approval to the Bill, it was accepted that the draft still required 'a good
deal of amendment' and it was to allow publication of the substantive provisions to be deferred that
the decision, noted at fn. 237 above, to introduce the Bill 'in dummy' was taken.

[262] In an article in the *News of the World* 25 Jan. 1948, headlined 'A Triumph for Public
Opinion—Blameless Children Get a New Charter'.   [263] Poor Law Act 1930, s. 15(1)(c).

[264] For parliamentary debates see (House of Lords) *Official Report* 10 Feb. 1948, vol. 153, col. 913
(Second Reading); 9 Mar. 1948, vol. 154, col. 531 (Committee); 13 Apr. 1948, vol. 155, col. 3 (Report);
20 Apr. 1948, vol. 155, col. 156 (Third Reading); 30 June 1948, vol. 157, col. 92 (Consideration of

of children in care giving rise to much debate.[265] Lord Chancellor Jowitt emphasised that the Bill did not permit children to be removed from parents against the parents' will;[266] and the Conservative Opposition expressed doubts about the scale of central control implicit in the Home Office's inspection powers. The Opposition also pointed to the danger that children's officers would not be able to give of their best if they had to spend most of their time dealing with the Home Office and in seeing that the various forms were correctly completed.[267] But generally there was little opposition to a measure which was intended to ensure that children cared for by the State should get the personal sympathy and human understanding so necessary to the well-being of children who lacked the love and affection of parents.[268] In the welfare state there was to be no shame attached to need;[269] and the State would ensure, through the centralised administration of the National Assistance Board, that adequate financial resources were available to wipe out poverty as it had been known. But the welfare of the individual was best left to local administration. As the Minister of Health, Aneurin Bevan, put it:[270]

Where the individual is immediately concerned, where warmth and humanity of administration is the primary consideration, then the authority which is responsible should be as near to the recipient as possible.

The Children Act 1948 sought to give effect to this approach.[271]

Commons Amendments). (House of Commons) *Official Report* 7 May 1948, vol. 450, col. 1609 (Second Reading); Standing Committee Session 1947–8 *Official Reports* vol. 111; *Official Report* 28 June 1948, vol. 452, col. 1844 (Report); 28 June 1948, vol. 452, col. 1858 (Third Reading).

[265] The Archbishop of Canterbury had written to the Lord Chancellor urging that that Act make it clear that children in care should attend church: see PRO LCO2/4473. In the event, the Act referred to arrangements being made for children to 'receive a religious upbringing appropriate to the persuasion to which they belong': see e.g. s. 15(4). It was also thought necessary to prohibit the cremation of deceased children where cremation was not in accordance with the practice of the child's religious persuasion: s. 18(1) proviso.

[266] *Official Report* (HL) 10 Feb. 1948 vol. 153, col. 918.

[267] Lord Llewellin, *Official Report* (HL) 10 Feb. 1948, vol. 153, col. 929.

[268] Kenneth Younger, Parliamentary Under-Secretary of State at the Home Office, *Official Report* (HC) 7 May 1948, vol. 450, col. 1611.

[269] A. Woodburn, Secretary of State for Scotland, in the debates on the Bill for the National Assistance Act 1948 (s. 1 of which provided that 'the existing poor law shall cease to have effect'): *Official Report* (HC) 24 Nov. 1947, vol. 444, col. 1653.

[270] *Official Report*, 24 Nov. 1947, vol. 444, col. 1604. This philosophy underlay the provisions empowering local authorities to provide residential accommodation (so-called Part III accommodation) for some groups unable to care for themselves. Although these are the only provisions of the National Assistance Act 1948 still in force, it appears that much of the work of social services departments is still based on powers first taken in the 1948 Act: *Social Services: Achievement and Challenge* (Cm. 3588, 1997) para. 1.6.

[271] Central supervision was exercised through the Home Office's inspectorial role; and by the obligation imposed on local authorities to exercise the relevant functions 'under the general guidance of the Secretary of State': Children Act 1948, s. 45(1) (now repealed and replaced by Local Authority Social Services Act 1970, s. 7). This provision, apparently—for the reasons set out at n. 150 above—much weaker than Curtis's recommendation (para. 432) that mandamus be available as the sanction for default, has over the years proved an effective means whereby central government formulates standards and determines general policy—notably in the context of the volumes of Guidance relating to the Children Act 1989.

Although the 1948 Act[272] remained the basis for the provision of care for children until its provisions were finally swept away by the comprehensive reforms brought about by the Children Act 1989, there were over the years many changes of child care policy. This is not the place for an attempt to summarise even the more important of those changes; but certain developments directly related to the main structure created in 1948 should be briefly recorded.

The Rise and Fall of the Children's Officer

The Children Act was founded on the principle that care work be in the hands of an identifiable individual. It is reasonable to suppose that many of the women taking office as Children's Officers[273] in 1948 were inspired by a sense of mission in rescuing the deprived child, and giving 'all those public waifs' a 'new square deal';[274] and over the years they acquired a status comparing favourably with any other social service professional.[275] But it soon began to be thought that the problem of ensuring that children received the most appropriate form of help available from the social services was much more complex than had been seen in the immediate aftermath of World War II. In 1968 the Seebohm Committee[276] rejected the assumption underlying the 1948 Act that the 'needs of children differ so much from those of old people'[277] and the corollary that organisationally distinct arrangements were necessary in order to ensure proper arrangements.

[272] The Act was amended over the years—perhaps most notably by the Children and Young Persons Act 1963, which sought to reinforce local authority powers to undertake work designed to forestall the need for children to be received into care; and the legislation was eventually consolidated in the Child Care Act 1980.

[273] Local authorities were required to submit the shortlist of candidates to the Home Secretary who had power to prohibit the appointment of anyone considered not to be a fit person: Children Act 1948, s. 41(2). It appears that some local authorities sought the Home Secretary's consent under the Children Act 1948 s. 41(3) to the Children's Officer performing other functions; but the official view was that although such proposals would 'of course, be judged on their merits, . . . it is clear enough that we shall have to maintain a firm front if we are to ensure that the children's officers posts are filled by suitable people possessing the requisite qualifications, and devoting their whole time to the work in those areas where there is a full-time job': Ross to Mayell, 20 Apr. 1948, PRO LCO2/4473.

[274] J. Stroud, *The Shorn Lamb* (1960) pp. 242–3. It is not easy to imagine the reaction of such people to the statement that the primary function of a social services department should be 'to assess the social care needs of its population; to plan the provision required to meet those needs over a period of years; and, in the light of the resources likely to be available in the community as a whole, to decide how to deploy its own resources most effectively to contribute towards that plan': *Social Services: Achievement and Challenge* (1997, Cm. 3588, para. 2.21).

[275] This is the assessment made in the far from uncritical analysis by J. A. G. Griffith, *Central Departments and Local Authorities* (1966) pp. 430–1.

[276] *Report of the Committee on Local Authority and Allied Personal Social Services* (1968) Cmnd. 3703.

[277] *The Break Up of the Poor Law and the Care of Children and Old People* (n. 22 above) para. 20.

Inspired by a belief in the capacity of the State to provide personal social services to all those in the need on the basis of the total requirements of the individual and the family concerned, the Seebohm Committee recommended the creation of a new local authority department, providing a community based and family oriented service available to all.

The Local Authority Social Services Act 1970 gave effect to this philosophy.[278] The Act provided for the unification under one committee and one chief officer of the social services responsibilities previously divided between children's, welfare and health services; and accordingly children's committees and children's officers were supplanted by Social Services Committees and the specialist children's officer and boarding out officer by the generic social worker.[279] The day of the Children's Officer, with a personal knowledge of all her charges, has gone beyond recall. But in one respect at least Curtis can claim to have left an enduring legacy: the Committee's concern to refute the belief that 'a good character and a little domestic experience'[280] was sufficient qualification (at least for residential care staff) and its commitment to the need for training had its impact at the time;[281] and played a part in professionalising social work.[282] Although the provision of an adequate stock of trained workers has remained a problem, it is accepted even in the climate of the late nineties[283] that the 'delivery of social care to children often requires particularly difficult judgments' and that accordingly those undertaking this task should have a more extensive training commitment than other social workers.

Central Government Responsibility

The Seebohm Committee, committed as it was to the view that organisational change could bring about substantial improvements to the delivery of personal social services—and assuming that resources would be available as required —regarded it as essential that one central government department should be

---

[278] The relevant provisions came into force on 1 Jan. 1971.

[279] The reorganisation did not resolve all the administrative problems of catering for families in need, not least because housing decisions were not within the remit of the social services committee: see *R* v. *Northavon District Council, ex parte Smith* [1994] 2 AC 402, HL.

[280] As Lord Listowel put it: *Official Report* (HL) 12 Dec. 1946, vol. 144, col. 905.

[281] The Government was criticised at the time for delay in giving effect to the Curtis Committee's recommendations (see *Official Report* (HL) 12 Dec. 1946, vol. 144, col. 882); the Central Council was established in 1947, and some staff, qualified in residential care and as boarding out officers, were available when the Children Act 1948 came into force: see J. Packman, *The Child's Generation* (2nd edn. 1981) p. 10.

[282] 'The work done by "social workers" is not new, but until modern times was undertaken by voluntary organisations, family doctors, the clergy and neighbours. The change to paid and trained workers and the growth of their professionalism are of recent origin . . .': *R* v. *City of Birmingham District Council, ex parte O* [1982] 2 All ER 356, 361, per Donaldson LJ. Specifically on the impact of the Committee's approach see 'The gestation of reform: the Children Act 1948', by R. A. Parker, in *Approaches to Welfare*, eds. Philip Bean and Stuart Macpherson (1983), at p. 212.

[283] See *Social Services: Achievement and Challenge* (1997, Cm. 3588, para. 1.7 g).

responsible for providing the overall national planning of social services, social intelligence and social research;[284] and it was axiomatic that central government should play a decisive role in deciding policy and that it should assume responsibility for ensuring the availability of trained personnel.[285] This approach was consistent with both the 1964–70 Wilson Labour Governments'[286] belief in the planned economy and with the business inspired management philosophy of the 1970–4 Heath Conservative administration.[287] It was clear that the Ministry of Health was in a strong position to claim responsibility for the social services,[288] and (notwithstanding a determined fight by Wilson's Home Secretary, James Callaghan,[289] to preserve the Home Office Children's Department) those functions were transferred to the enlarged Department of Health and Social Security in 1971.[290] Although there were certainly problems in assimilating the work of the children's department,[291] subsequent experience—not least in commissioning

---

[284] *Seebohm Report*, para. 637.   [285] *Seebohm Report*, paras. 646–7.

[286] The Local Authority Social Services Act 1970 was rushed through its final parliamentary stages because of Wilson's decision to call an election on 18 June 1970. Royal Assent was given on 29 May 1970, the day on which Parliament was dissolved.

[287] The White Paper, *The Reorganisation of Central Government* (Cmnd. 4506, 1970), took as its starting point the belief that government had been 'attempting to do too much', asserted that the outcome of the review would be 'less government, and better government carried out by fewer people', and adopted the principle that functions should be grouped together in departments with a wide span, so as to provide a series of fields of unified policy. Consistently with this approach, it considered that the 'effective development of a new, broadly based service to deal with family needs in accordance with the objectives of the Seebohm Committee [already being carried out at local level under the provisions of the Local Authority Social Services Act 1970] calls for the support, encouragement and guidance of a single minister'; and concluded that the Home Secretary's child care responsibilities should be transferred to the Secretary of State for Social Services (although the Home Secretary was to retain his existing responsibilities in relation to the juvenile courts and the problems of juvenile delinquency 'since these are integral to his overriding responsibility for protecting the public and ensuring the rights and liberties of the individual': para. 35).

[288] A full account of the negotiations, making use of documents not yet in the public domain, is given by C. Webster, in the official history of *The Health Services since the War Vol. 2* (1996) pp. 304–10. Reference may also be made to P. Hall, *Reforming the Welfare. The politics of change in the Personal Social Services* (1976) and J. Cooper, *The Creation of the British Personal Social Services 1962–1974* (1983).

[289] Callaghan not only got an undertaking from Wilson that the Children's Department would not be transferred so long as Callaghan remained Home Secretary (R. H. S. Crossman, *The Diaries of a Cabinet Minister, Vol. 3, Secretary of State for Social Services, 1968–1970* (1977), pp. 147, 150, 160, 553) but also subsequently made 'private representations' (unsuccessfully) to R. Maudling, his Conservative successor at the Home Office: see J. Callaghan, *Time and Chance* (1987) p. 235. Callaghan (whose views on this issue were shared by the long-serving Permanent Under-Secretary of State Sir P. Allen) wrote that 'After many years spent building up one of the best services of its kind, the work has to my everlasting regret been swallowed up by the Department of Health and Social Security. One of the brightest jewels in the Home Office crown is now submerged in the general work of the DHSS, without any improvement that I can detect' (see 'Cumber and Variableness' in *The Home Office, Perspectives on Policy and Administration, Bicentenary Lectures 1982* (Royal Institute of Public Administration) (1982), pp. 10, 24, 33.

[290] The decision to make the transfer was announced in the Heath Government's White Paper, *The Reorganisation of Central Government* (Cmnd. 4506, 1970) and effected on 1 Jan. 1971.

[291] There was physically no room available for the children's department staff taken over by the DHSS for a year or more after the formal transfer: see Cooper op. cit. n. 288 above, p. 113.

research and disseminating its results and in the massive commitment to publicising and issuing guidance on the structural and legal changes effected by the Children Act 1989—refutes the post-World War II Home Office fears that child-related work would be given low priority in so large a department. But those who believed so passionately in the virtues of an individualised casework approach to children's problems, and in the effectiveness of a specialist inspectorate, might be sceptical about the virtues of more recent proposals[292] to bring together all local authority social services regulatory responsibilities into a single statutory body formed by consortia of local and health authorities. At a more fundamental level, an apparently never-ending series of child care scandals[293] has been a factor leading some to question how far the State can ever really provide effective 'care' for children. In this view, adoption deserves much more emphasis than foster or residential care as an effective means of providing for the needy child[294]—a view which (it is often forgotten) would have had some appeal for the Curtis Committee.

Deprived or Depraved

The belief—as we have seen, held in the Home Office well before World War II—that 'whether a young child commits an offence, goes out on the loose, or is just unruly or naughty is purely fortuitous'[295]—only began to be seriously questioned in the 1970s.[296] Those responsible for the formation of policy over those years would view with disbelief the apparent consensus of the nineties on the need for a punitive approach to young delinquents.[297] It is in this respect that the philosophy of the 1948 legislation has been most dramatically overturned. For the Curtis Committee the emphasis was not to be on what a child had done in the past but on what the child's needs were at present; fifty years later, opinion seems (in the author's view, regrettably) to have shifted so that what is done to a delinquent child is influenced almost entirely by the child's past behaviour,

---

[292] *Social Services: Achievement and Challenge* (1997, Cm. 3588, para. 4.8).

[293] See the *Report of the Review of the Safeguards for Children Living Away from Home, People Like Us* (Sir W. Utting) (1998).

[294] See P. Morgan, *Adoption and the Care of Children* (1998).

[295] *Seebohm Report* (1968) para. 188.

[296] The Children and Young Persons Act 1933 did make a clear distinction between prosecution and protection measures, and the anomalies to which this was thought to give rise were analysed by the Ingleby *Committee on Children and Young Persons* (Cmnd. 1191, 1960) which (*inter alia*) recommended amendments to the 'care and protection' provisions of the Children and Young Persons Act 1933, s. 61 (see paras. 83–94 and App. III); and further discussion (*The Child, the Family and the Young Offender* (Cmnd. 2742, 1965) and *Children in Trouble* (Cmnd. 3601, 1968)) formed the background to the enactment of the Children and Young Persons Act 1969. That Act reformulated the principles upon which compulsory protective measures could be taken in respect of children, and they remained the basis of the law until the coming into force of the Children Act 1989 in 1991; but attempts to reform the treatment of delinquents remained controversial.

[297] However, the speeches in *R* v. *Secretary of State for the Home Department, ex parte Thompson and Venables* [1997] 2 FLR 471, HL, have served as a reminder that statute still requires the courts and others in dealing with delinquents to have regard to the child's welfare: Children and Young Persons Act 1933, s. 44.

and little thought is given as to how best to take advantage of the fact that children (unlike adults) develop over the years and may indeed be truly rehabilitated by appropriate treatment.

Judicialisation of Child Care Decisions

The Curtis Report, as we have seen, gave little attention to compulsory measures of child care; and for many years the superior courts were hardly troubled with cases involving children who were, or might be, placed in care. The trickle of cases in the 1960s has now become a flood, and child care law is a recognised forensic specialty. But in one respect the philosophy of 1948 remains untouched. The question of whether compulsory intervention in a child's upbringing is justified has been firmly allotted to the courts; and in contrast the question of how the child in care should be treated if and when the court decides to make a care order has been[298] equally firmly allotted to the local authority. The courts have shown a marked reluctance to scrutinise local authority decisions.[299]

CONCLUSION

With the benefit of fifty years' hindsight it is tempting to take a somewhat dismissive view of the Children Act 1948 and the events which led up to its enactment. Could anyone seriously believe, for example, that—as Lady Allen of Hurtwood[300] put it—the happiness of children could be promoted by better administration?[301] But the reality is that the 1948 Act did enable a coherent and rational structure for this particular social service to be established; and that the bold assertion on the face of an Act of Parliament of the State's duty to provide for children in need—and not merely for the destitute—established a tradition which still survives[302] in a very different[303] social, political and economic

[298] Subject to (a) the court's role in scrutinising the local authority's care plan in order to decide whether it would be in the child's interests to make an order; (b) the court's power to control the contact to be allowed between parent and child; and (c) the court's powers to make directions for assessments in some circumstances.

[299] *X v. Bedfordshire County Council* [1995] 2 AC 633. In some circumstances (see e.g. *Re T (accommodation by local authority)* [1995] 1 FLR 159) judicial review may be available; but the courts have shown a strong preference to leave complainants to the statutory grievance procedures established by the Children Act 1989.   [300] *Memoirs*, p. 168.

[301] Lord Listowel, the government spokesman in the 1946 House of Lords debate on the implementation of the Curtis Report (*Official Report* (HL) 12 Dec. 1946, vol. 144, col. 904) did urge peers to ask themselves whether 'any Statute, however carefully framed, [could] give the homeless child the sort of substitute home and substitute parents we all desire'.

[302] See e.g. Children Act 1989, s. 17(1) imposing a 'general duty' on local authorities to safeguard and promote the welfare of children within their area who are in need, and (so far as is consistent with that duty) to promote the upbringing of such children by their families by providing a range and level of services appropriate to those children's needs.

[303] Compare the 1948 emphasis on the need for local involvement in child care (p. 221 above) with the situation in 1997 as described in *Social Services: Achievement and Challenge* (1997, Cm. 3588) para. 3.22: 'Local authority social services provide direct help to a small proportion of

climate.[304] No doubt it is true that the war-time decision finally to abolish the last traces of the Elizabethan Poor Law would have necessitated alternative provision for orphans and some other deprived children; but although a comparison of the reforms worked out in Whitehall in 1944 and the system of child care eventually established under the 1948 Act reflects well on the administrative skills, foresight and humanity of the officials concerned, it also demonstrates the much wider ambitions put into statutory form in the 1948 Act. The detailed work of the Curtis Committee was a powerful influence on the legislation; but the Act might well never have taken the form that it did had it not been for the climate of opinion engendered at least in part by the campaigning zeal of Marjory Allen and by the publicity given by the press to the death of Dennis O'Neill.[305]

children in their localities. There is not the same degree of continuing public interest in them and knowledge of them as there is, for example, in social services for older people or education services for children. There is therefore a risk that in the children's field democratic influences and account-ability may be less strong, and that the services themselves may suffer from professional isolation. It is for local authorities to decide how best to make arrangements to enable the wider public . . . to understand and influence their policies for children.'

[304] Foster carers now look after some 60 per cent of children in local authority care—historically a very high proportion: *Social Services: Achievement and Challenge* (1997, Cm. 3588) para. 4.8; and see also para. 3.5.

[305] It is a saddening reflection that the three major child law reforms since the end of World War II —the Children Act 1948, the Children Act 1975, and the Children Act 1989—can all be associ-ated with a highly publicised child abuse scandal (Maria Colwell in the case of the 1975 Act and the events in Cleveland in 1987). It is also striking that the particular facts of the scandal do not necessarily bear any close relation to the contents of the legislation for which they provided the stimulus.

10*

Dividing Family Property on Death: Approaches to Reform of Intestacy

INTRODUCTION

The law of intestacy is of great practical importance and considerable social, economic and political significance. For it is the law of intestate distribution which determines how property should be divided on the owner's death in those —numerous[1]—cases where there is no effective will. In substance, the State then does what the deceased has failed to do.

The rules of intestate distribution can arouse strong feelings. For example, the new code introduced as part of the fundamental reform effected by the 1925 property legislation[2] was criticised by some[3] as threatening the traditional landed estates; whilst seventy years later the authors of a standard practitioners' textbook denounced reform proposals made after prolonged investigation by the Law Commission[4] as 'naive and simplistic'[5] and the proposals were rejected[6] by the Government of the day (notwithstanding the Commission's protests at this response to what the Commission regarded as the 'overwhelming'[7] case for reform).

---

* This Chapter draws on two previously published articles: 'Intestacy Reforms—the Way Things Were' [1994] *Denning Law Journal* 35–51, and 'Reform of Intestacy: The Best We Can Do?' (1995) 111 LQR 77.

[1] Only a third of a sample of people interviewed for the Law Commission had made wills (although almost two-thirds of people aged 60 or over had done so). On the significance of intestacy in relation to the transfer of wealth, see J. M. Masson, 'Making Wills, Making Clients' [1994] Conv. 267, 268–70, and generally J. Finch, J. Mason, J. Masson, L. Hayes and L. Wallis, *Wills, Inheritance, Families* (1995).

[2] Administration of Estates Act 1925, consolidating provisions first enacted in the Law of Property Act 1922.

[3] Walter Hume Long (1854–1924), widely regarded as the leader of the country party amongst the Unionists and at the time First Lord of the Admiralty, had his expressed concerns about the possible impact of the reforms on the landed interest allayed by a twelve-page letter from the Permanent Secretary, Sir Claud Schuster; and Long's specific concern that the ending of primogeniture would lead to the break up of the old family estates was met by the argument that such estates were usually held in settlements which would regulate devolution irrespective of the law of intestacy: see letters of 1, 9, 10 and 12 Feb. 1920, PRO files LCO2/443.

[4] *Distribution on Intestacy*, Law Com. No. 187 (1989). The Report had been preceded by a Working Paper (No. 108, 1988).

[5] Sherrin and Bonehill, *Law and Practice of Intestate Succession* (2nd edn. 1994) p. 24. For more temperate criticism, see R. Kerridge, 'Distribution on Intestacy, the Law Commission's Report' (1990) 54 Conv. 358.   [6] See below, p. 272.

[7] Law Com. No. 187, para. 23.

This Chapter is concerned with significant episodes in the recent history of intestacy reform. In particular, it examines the work of a small *ad hoc* committee chaired by a Law Lord[8] which made the recommendations embodied in the Intestates' Estates Act 1952; and it analyses the developments which, some three decades later, led to the rejection of the Law Commission's proposals. It concludes by considering the options for further reform.

THE BACKGROUND: FUNDAMENTAL ISSUES

Decisions about reform of intestacy law necessarily involve consideration of the purposes to be served by the law governing property transfers, whether by life-time gift, by will, or by intestate succession. Should the law, for example, favour unfettered freedom of disposition as a necessary[9] or desirable[10] incident of the economic power inherent in the ownership of property? Or does it attach greater importance to the notion that family property ought to be preserved within the family and serve as an endowment to successive generations?[11] How far is the State prepared to interfere with property rights, whether to promote democratic[12] or egalitarian[13] ideals or simply—perhaps in self-interest—to impose a duty to support an owner's dependants?[14] And then there are difficult questions which relate specifically to the function of the code of intestate succession. Is it, for example, to be seen primarily as a safety net or default system[15] for those who have, or think they have, little to leave, or who have not thought about the

---

[8] *Report of the Committee on the Law of Intestate Succession* (chairman: Lord Morton of Henryton) (Cmd. 8310 (1951)).

[9] Contrast Montesquieu's view that 'ownership dies with the man', *Esprit des lois* 26.6.15 (as cited by A. G. Guest, 'Family Provision and the *Legitima Portio*' (1957) 73 LQR 74).

[10] The preference for freedom of testation seems to have become dominant in England in the 18th century; and when in 1724 the customary succession rules of the City of London (which prevented citizens and freemen of the City from freely willing their personal estates) were abolished the change was justified on the ground that a citizen would be less likely to amass wealth if he was bound to leave it to an 'ill-deserving wife or to idle and uninstructed children': see F. Pollock and F. W. Maitland, *The History of English Law* (2nd edn. reissued with new introduction etc. by S. F. C. Milsom, 1968) Vol. 2, p. 350.

[11] 'Les hommes passent, la famille et son fondement matériel demeurent . . .': H. Fulchiron in Meulders-Klein and Thery, *Les Recompositions Familiales Aujourd'hui* (Paris, 1993) p. 282, succinctly expressing the view traditionally taken in many continental systems.

[12] See J. M. Morton, 'The Theory of Inheritance' (1894–5) Harv. LR 161, 163; L. Miraglia, *Comparative Legal Philosophy* (tr. J. Lisle, Boston, 1912) Chs. 21 and 22; and note the problems faced in the early history of the United States in deciding how far to reject concepts of the English law of property: see Shammas, 'English Law of Inheritance and its transfer to the Colonies' (1987) 31 Am. J Legal Hist. 145.

[13] See D. Bradley, 'Marriage, family, property and inheritance in Swedish law' (1990) 39 ICLQ 370 at 371 for an account of reforms said to reflect socialist hostility to inherited wealth and a diminished importance for the family and traditional values in society.

[14] See R. Atherton, 'New Zealand's Testator's Family Maintenance Act of 1900—the Stouts, the Women's Movement and Political Compromise' (1990) 7 Otago LR 202 at 204–5.

[15] See L. W. Waggoner, 'Marital Property Rights in Transition' (1994) 59 Missouri L Rev. 21.

matter[16] or who die prematurely?[17] Or is it rather to be seen as an attempt to create a fair and rational system reflecting the wishes of the great majority about the disposal of their property?[18]

These are difficult issues; and it is not surprising that different legal systems have adopted a bewildering variety of solutions[19] reflecting their diverse economic and cultural assumptions and legal traditions.

In the course of the twentieth century, the most distinctive development in English intestacy law has been the increasing recognition for the claim of the surviving spouse as against the claim of the deceased's children; and the erosion of the succession rights of remote kin. The decisive step was taken by the 1925 property legislation.

PREFERRING THE SURVIVING SPOUSE

The assimilation of the law of real[20] and personal property[21]—a central feature of the 1925 property reforms—made it essential to substitute a uniform set of rules to govern the devolution of all forms of property on death. For this purpose, the content of the rules did not matter; what was important was that the same rules should apply to all the property which passed as part of a deceased person's estate. This explains how it came about that what in retrospect is clearly

[16] The Church for long took pains to instil what Pollock and Maitland call an 'intense and holy horror of intestacy' even to the lengths of denying the intestate burial in consecrated ground: F. Pollock and F. W. Maitland, *The History of English Law* (2nd edn. reissued with new introduction etc. by S. F. C. Milsom, 1968) Vol. 2, p. 356; and note the exhortations in the Book of Common Prayer rite for the Visitation of the Sick. But today the role of encouraging testacy seems to have passed to charities and others who no doubt also have a measure of self-interest in encouraging the making of wills.

[17] *Distribution on Intestacy* (Law Com. No. 187 (1989)) para. 5. The evidence suggests that will making is often deferred until late middle age: see n. 1 above.

[18] 'as in France . . . the heads of families . . . generally save themselves the trouble of executing a Will and allow the law to do as it pleases with their assets' (H. Maine, *Ancient Law* (Everyman's Library edn., 1954) p. 129.

[19] For an excellent analysis of the issues and of the approaches of different legal systems see the title 'Wills and Succession' by D. B. Walters and E. Clive in *The Laws of Scotland, Stair Memorial Encyclopaedia*, Vol. 25 (1989).

[20] Governed by the common law rules of descent, as lucidly expounded in R. E. Megarry and H. W. R. Wade, *The Law of Real Property* (3rd edn. 1966). In theory these rules gave some protection to a widow, who was entitled to a life interest in one-third of the deceased's real property. However, there were conveyancing techniques enabling the widow's right to be barred *inter vivos*, whilst the Dower Act 1833 allowed the widow's right to dower to be barred by will. It was said that even in the early 19th century dower was rarely encountered save in cases of 'inadvertency or unskilfulness, or from short sighted economy': Real Property Commissioners, *First Report* (1829), BPP Vol. 10, p. 17.

[21] Succession to which was governed by the Statute of Distributions 1670 (or by the local custom which that Act preserved: see s. 4). The scheme of the Statute was that the widow took one-third of the deceased's personal property, the balance going to the deceased's children and issue. If there were no issue, the widow's share was increased to one-half, the balance going to the next of kin: s. 6.

a decisive change in the policy of the law was carried through with very little discussion or consideration.[22] As a result of the 1925 legislation, for the first time, the intestate's spouse was—save in the case of the largest estates—to be preferred to other relatives; and the legislation finally abandoned the principle[23] under which both spouse and children were entitled to a share of even the smallest estate. Under the new regime, husband and wife were to be put on an equal footing, and the surviving spouse was to be entitled to the personal chattels[24] absolutely, to a statutory legacy[25] of £1,000, and to a life interest in any residue.[26] The statutory legacy was fixed at £1,000[27] because wills of small estates almost invariably gave the surviving spouse the whole estate and the £1,000 legacy would produce the same result in the great majority of intestacies.[28] Even with somewhat larger estates a £1,000 legacy would usually enable the deceased's house to be retained for occupation by the survivor.[29] The 1925 legislation thus established the related policies of allowing the whole of all but the largest estates to pass to the widow and ensuring that she should be able to go on living in the family home after her husband's death.

[22] The legislation has its immediate origins in the Report of the Acquisition and Valuation of Land Committee, established in 1919 by the Minister of Reconstruction to consider Land Transfer in England and Wales and to advise on action to facilitate and cheapen the transfer of land. The Committee considered draft legislation (including an Intestacy Bill drafted by Charles Sweet); and recommended that there be no distinction between devolution and the methods of dealing with real and personal estates: Fourth Report (Cmd. 424, 1919) para. 26. The Committee put forward for consideration on the merits clauses drafted by Sir Benjamin Cherry but it accepted that the changes envisaged in the distribution of property on intestacy were incidental and not essential to the main purpose of its inquiry.

[23] Embodied in respect of personal property in the Statute of Distributions 1670.

[24] The *Report from the Joint Select Committee on the Law of Property Bill* (1920) BPP Vol. 7, p. 131, had proposed that the personal representatives be empowered to allow a surviving spouse who did not take the whole estate absolutely the use and enjoyment of furniture and 'other like chattels (including consumable stores)' for life: amendment to cl. 138(1)(ii).

[25] The origins of the statutory legacy are to be found in the Intestates' Estates Act 1890 which in effect provided a legacy of £500 for the widow of an intestate who left no issue; and, for the first time, English law gave a preference to a widow as against her husband's kin. Notwithstanding the significance of this change, the Act seems to have been uncontroversial: the Second Reading Debate in the House of Lords on 8 July 1890 is extremely brief, and there was virtually no discussion in the House of Commons.

[26] One-half if there were surviving issue. The legislation gave the personal representatives power to redeem any life interest with the consent of the life tenant or leave of the court; but this power was apparently little used.

[27] It had originally been proposed that the statutory legacy should be fixed at £500 (in line with the recommendation of the Acquisition and Valuation of Land Committee and reflecting the sum in respect of which a widow had been given priority by the Intestates' Estates Act 1890): see the speech of Lord Birkenhead LC on the Second Reading of the Law of Property Bill 1920, *Official Report* (HL) 3 Mar. 1920, vol. 39, col. 255. But in fact £1,000 in 1922 corresponded in purchasing power to £500 in 1890; and the lengthy gestation period of the Birkenhead legislation allowed time for further reflection on the amount of the legacy: see notably the *Report from the Joint Select Committee on the Law of Property Bill* (1920) BPP Vol. 7, p. 131, amendments to cl. 138.

[28] According to the Lord Chancellor, in 97 per cent of cases the surviving spouse 'either takes the whole or some substantial life or other interest': *Official Report* (HL) 17 Mar. 1921, vol. 44, col. 650; and according to the Solicitor-General, about 98 per cent of intestacies were of less than £1,000, so that in the great majority of cases the survivor would take the whole estate: *Official Report* (HC) vol. 154, col. 93. [29] See *Official Report* (HC) 15 May 1922, vol. 154, col. 99.

PROTECTION AGAINST DISINHERITANCE:
DISCRETION RATHER THAN ENTITLEMENT

These policies could, however, be defeated if a testator exercised the right to make a will. There was acute controversy;[30] but eventually after prolonged campaigning[31] the Inheritance (Family Provision) Act 1938[32] ended the short[33] era of complete testamentary freedom in English law by giving the High Court power to order reasonable financial provision for the maintenance of certain specified dependants—spouse, infant sons, and disabled adult sons or married daughters who could show that their disability prevented their maintaining themselves— of a deceased testator. (It was not thought necessary to give any power to depart

[30] For a full account of the history, making use of the Lord Chancellor's Department's records, see *Tyler's Family Provision* (3rd edn. by R. D. Oughton, 1997) Ch. 1. The Labour Lord Chancellor, Sankey, had favoured legislation even on the lines of the much more radical legislation proposed by the National Council of Societies for Equal Citizenship in 1929 (see Sankey to Parmoor, 14 Oct. 1929, LCO2/1185) but there had been disagreement between Conservative Lord Chancellors: the first Lord Hailsham had been, and remained, an implacable opponent of the legislation; whereas Lord Maugham (whose view was finally that which prevailed in Cabinet) had been prepared to allow Parliament a free choice. The departmental papers reveal that the opposition was not confined to politicians: Parliamentary Counsel stated in a letter to George Coldstream of the Lord Chancellor's Office on 6 Aug. 1941 that 'I never ceased to say at every opportunity throughout the time whilst I was dealing with it that it appeared to me to be wrong both in conception and in drafting. Consequently no attacks upon it are likely to offend my *amour propre*': PRO file LCO2/1516.

[31] Eleanor Rathbone MP (author of *The Disinherited Family, A Plea for the Endowment of the Family* (1924)) was an eloquent voice for reform; but the skilled lobbying carried out by Mrs Eva Hubback (Parliamentary Secretary to the National Union of Societies for Equal Citizenship)—and whose views on this matter seem to have been sympathetically received by the Lord Chancellor's Permanent Secretary, Sir Claud Schuster: see, for example, her letters to him of 2 and 18 May 1928 on file LCO2/1185—seems to have been by far the most important factor in overcoming opposition from within the judiciary and the Cabinet.

[32] For the historical background, see R. D. Oughton, *Tyler's Family Provision* (3rd edn. 1997) Chs. 1 and 2; and see also G. W. Keeton and L. C. B. Gower, 'Freedom of Testation in English Law' (1934) 20 Iowa L Rev. 326; J. Dainow, 'Limitations on Testamentary Freedom in England' (1940) 25 Cornell LR 337. For discussions of the principles underlying English and comparable legislation, see E. N. Cahn, 'Restraints on Disinheritance' (1936) 85 U Pa. L Rev. 139; J. Dainow, 'Restricted Testation in New Zealand, Australia and Canada' (1938) 36 Mich. L Rev. 1107; J. Unger 'The Inheritance Act and the Family' (1943) 6 MLR 215; J. Laufer, 'Flexible Restraints on Testamentary Freedom—A Report on Decedent's Family Maintenance Legislation' (1955) 69 Harv. LR 277; A. G. Guest, 'Family Provision and the *Legitima Portio*' (1957) 73 LQR 74; R. Atherton, 'The Family Provision Act 1982 (NSW): A New Deal for the Family' (1984) 58 ALJ 274; J. G. Miller, 'Provision for a Surviving Spouse' (1986) 102 LQR 445; S. Green, 'The Englishwoman's Castle—Inheritance and Private Property Today' (1988) 51 MLR 187; R. Atherton, 'The Testator's Family Maintenance and Guardianship of Infants Act 1916 (NSW): husband's power v. widow's right' (1990) *Australian Journal of Law and Society* 97; R. Atherton, 'New Zealand's Testator's Family Maintenance Act of 1900 . . .' (1990) 7 Otago LR 202; W. M. Patterson, *The Law of Family Protection and of Testamentary Promises in New Zealand* (Wellington, 1985); A. Dickey, *Family Provision after Death* (Sydney, 1992). The Irish experience in striking a balance between discretion and entitlement is particularly interesting: see Mark Cooney, 'Succession and Judicial Discretion in Ireland: The Section 117 cases' (1980) 15 Ir. Jur. 62.

[33] As pointed out by M. Albery, *The Inheritance (Provision for Family and Dependants) Act, 1938* (1950) p. 1, complete freedom of testation had only existed for the forty-seven years between the Mortmain and Charitable Uses Act 1891 and 1938.

from the statutory provisions governing the division of a deceased *intestate's* estate.[34])

The discretion conferred by the 1938 Act was restricted—not only by allowing only a narrowly defined category of relative to apply, but also by founding the court's[35] power to award financial provision on relieving the applicant's need for *maintenance*,[36] rather than on redistribution to achieve fairness in the division of the deceased's assets. But the debates leading up to the legislation also evidenced the strength of opposition[37] to any remodelling of English succession law so as to give fixed rights[38] of inheritance, whether on the pattern of the *jus relictae* and *legitim* of civil law systems or the system of elective shares now embodied in the American Uniform Probate Code.[39] Thus, although the

[34] The 1938 Act applied where a person died 'leaving a will', and was thus manifestly inapplicable to cases of total intestacy; but it was an open question whether it applied in cases of partial intestacy: see the discussion in the *Report of the Committee on Intestate Succession* (Cmd. 8310 (1951)). For the effect of the Intestates' Estates Act 1952 see text to n. 100, below.

[35] 'Unqualified hostility' to any provision conferring jurisdiction on the County Court was expressed by Lord Chancellor Hailsham (see the agreed minute of his discussion with the Solicitor-General, 18 Nov. 1937, PRO file LCO2/1189); and the case against extending the jurisdiction from the Chancery judges (with a 'proper opportunity for them to be continuously in touch with one another and as a result to evolve the necessary guiding principles' as against distributing jurisdiction 'amongst the sixty or so county court judges') was put by officials in 1941 in response to an MP's suggestion: see PRO file LCO2/1516. The County Court was eventually given jurisdiction in the case of small (i.e. less than £5,000) estates by the Family Provision Act 1966 (see *Official Report* (HL) 16 June 1966, vol. 275, col. 208); and now has jurisdiction whatever the size of the estate: Courts and Legal Services Act 1990, s. 1; High Court and County Courts Jurisdiction Order 1991, arts. 2(1), 7.

[36] The court had to be satisfied that the disposition of the deceased's estate was not such as to make 'reasonable provision for [the applicant's] maintenance'; whilst an adult son or unmarried daughter could not apply unless they were incapable of maintaining themselves by reason of physical or mental disability: Inheritance (Family Provision) Act 1938, s. 1.

[37] See the account, drawing on papers from the Lord Chancellor's Office held in the Public Record Office, in R. D. Oughton, *Tyler's Family Provision* (3rd edn. 1997).

[38] Private Members Bills, introduced under the aegis of the National Council of Societies for Equal Citizenship in 1928, 1929 and 1931, had been influenced by the Scottish system of providing fixed entitlements for spouses and children. A Joint Committee under the chairmanship of Lord Thankerton reported on 17 June 1931 that it was satisfied that there was a substantial number of cases in which families had been unjustifiably left unprovided for, but that legislation based on any 'arbitrary or fixed standard' would be complicated and lead to expense and for those reasons was not justified. The Committee did consider that a Bill which would entitle a surviving spouse or child left without adequate means of support to apply for a court order would be worthy of serious consideration. Disagreement within government and the judiciary about legislation remained: the Attorney-General, Sir Donald Somervell, was favourably disposed to legislation on the discretionary pattern (whilst expressing the view to Sir John Simon, the Home Secretary, that 'it may well be the Scotch form [of fixed entitlement] is really the better': see his letter of 1 Dec. 1936 in PRO file HO45/16479/176695; and compare his much more muted letter to Lord Chancellor Hailsham—a strong and consistent opponent of legislation—on 25 Mar. 1936: PRO file LCO2/1189). Eventually, on 2 Nov. 1937 the Cabinet agreed to adopt an attitude of neutrality to a Bill based on the discretionary principle; and amendments designed to confer an entitlement to a statutory allowance for maintenance were defeated.

[39] For a perceptive account of the difficulties caused to the drafters of the 1969 Code by the growth in the number of stepfamilies, see W. F. Fratcher, 'Towards Uniform Succession Legislation' (1966) 41 NY Univ. LR 1037; and for the revisions made in 1990 see J. W. Fisher and S. A. Curnutte,

introduction of judicial discretion into the allocation of family property was unwelcome to many, it was none the less clear that thenceforth cases of hardship had to be remedied—if at all—by empowering the court to exercise discretionary adjustive powers to order reasonable provision for those affected.

COPING WITH INFLATION

The policy of the law governing distribution on intestacy was thus clear, but changing economic factors made it seem doubtful whether the legislation was effective in securing adequate protection for the widow. Shortly after the end of World War II—notwithstanding the fact that inflation had been, by more recent standards, modest—concern began to be expressed (both officially[40] and otherwise[41]) about whether, given the changes in the value of the currency[42] and the inflation of house prices,[43] the rules of intestate distribution still met its objectives, in particular in the case of the widows of men of modest means.[44] A particular problem was that the matrimonial home might have to be sold to provide funds to satisfy the entitlement of children to half of the residue in cases which could no longer be described as large. Eventually a Parliamentary Question[45] by Iain Macleod[46]

'Reforming the Law of Intestate Succession and Elective Shares . . .' (1990) 93 W Virginia LR at pp. 61–146; L. H. Averill, 'An Eclectic History and Analysis of the 1990 Uniform Probate Code' (1992) 55 Albany LR 891; L. W. Waggoner, 'Marital Property Rights in Transition' (1994) 59 Missouri LR 21.

[40] The Law Society, responding to letters from solicitors, inserted a notice seeking views in the *Gazette* in Nov. 1948; and the Council concluded that a surviving spouse should receive £5,000 irrespective of whether there were children of the marriage: H. Boggis-Rolfe (Lord Chancellor's Office) to the Treasury Solicitor Sir Thomas Barnes (1873–1967) 22 May 1950, LCO2/4440.

[41] A correspondent informed the Lord Chancellor's Office (see LCO2/4441) that he had had the 'painful duty of having to turn the widow out of the family home on the death of a husband . . . and I have just dealt with a case where the husband had to leave the home arising out of the death of the wife. I could recite other tragedies, if necessary.'

[42] According to official indices, it would have been necessary to spend £1,700 in 1948 to buy goods which had cost £1,000 (the amount of the statutory legacy to a surviving spouse) in 1925.

[43] The 'inflated value of house property' was referred to as a relevant factor in the *Report of the Committee on the Law of Intestate Succession* Cmd. 8130 (1951) para. 10; but Lord Chancellor Simonds appears to have deleted the reference to this factor from his officials' draft of the paper recommending legislation to be submitted to the Home Affairs Committee on 28 Nov. 1951: see the manuscript amendments to the draft in file LCO2/4451.

[44] Changes in attitudes to the role of the sexes over the past half century are vividly demonstrated by a World War II poster preserved in the Public Record Office which sought to increase security consciousness by the slogan 'Be like Dad, Keep Mum!'   [45] 16 Apr. 1950.

[46] He asked the Attorney-General to set up a committee on intestacy 'particularly in relation to the widow's right to purchase the home where she and her deceased husband have lived'. He had earlier written to the Attorney-General, Sir Hartley Shawcross (b. 1902) referring to a constituency case in which the deceased's daughter was insisting that the house be put up for auction 'which is, I believe, within her rights . . . although the widow's money contributed greatly to the buying of the house'. Macleod, elected an MP in 1950, was a powerful orator who had a meteoric rise to office (becoming Minister of Health in 1952 at the age of 38 on promotion direct from the backbenches) but he was not popular with influential right-wing Conservatives (who not only opposed his attitude

led the Lord Chancellor[47] to favour the appointment of a committee under Lord Morton of Henryton[48] to investigate the issues.[49] The way in which that Committee was established and worked, and the events which led up to the enactment of the Intestates' Estates Act 1952 (which is still, more than fifty years later, substantially in force) provide a textbook illustration of how issues of law reform were handled at the time.

THE MORTON COMMITTEE: MEMBERSHIP

The Government intended that the Committee should reflect a broad range of interests; and the official files show a high level of political involvement in the process of choosing those to be appointed. Advice was taken from a number of Ministers. Herbert Morrison[50] urged[51] that Members of Parliament should be appointed (in part because this could be of considerable assistance when the

---

to self-rule for Britain's colonies but thought him 'too clever by half' and evidently sometimes found it difficult to accept a man who had earned an income by playing bridge). His sudden death on 20 July 1970, shortly after being appointed Chancellor of the Exchequer in the Heath Government, left (in the words of his biographer) a 'gaping crater in the Conservative Party': see R. Shepherd, *Iain Macleod* (1994) p. 550.

[47] Viscount (subsequently Earl) Jowitt (1855–1957). Elected as a Liberal MP in the Apr. 1929 General Election, he immediately accepted the post of Attorney-General in the Labour Government and joined the Labour Party (as Lord Birkenhead put it, 'hurling himself upon the Socialist omnibus as it was turning at full speed into Downing Street'). He was expelled from the Labour Party in 1931 for accepting office in Ramsay MacDonald's National Government: see for a full account, R. F. V. Heuston, *Lives of the Lord Chancellors 1940–1970* (1987) Ch. II. In the circumstances, it is not surprising that Jowitt was thought by some to lack political principle, and his choice of the motto 'tenax et fidelis' when raised to the peerage on appointment as Lord Chancellor in the 1945 Labour Government was undoubtedly provocative: see further, n. 130, below. But his tenure of the Great Seal (1945–51) was distinguished by considerable achievements in law reform.

[48] (1887–1973). Appointed to the Chancery bench in 1938, Morton had had previous experience of public service as deputy chairman of the contraband committee at the Ministry of Economic Warfare and as Chairman of the Council of Legal Education. He was created a Lord of Appeal in Ordinary in 1947. It has been said (by Sir Denys Buckley in *The Dictionary of National Biography 1971–80*) that 'he possessed a ready and impish sense of humour which won him general friendship and affection . . . His advocacy was consistently careful, constructive, concise and cogent, and in his judicial judgements he never seemed to find any difficulty in reaching a clear and convincing conclusion lucidly expressed. He was a delightful judge to whom to present an argument but a testing one.' But his role as Chairman of the Royal Commission on Marriage and Divorce (as to which see Ch. 2, above) prompted much criticism in some quarters.

Morton accepted the invitation; and it was thus unnecessary to approach Denys Buckley (b. 1906; Treasury Junior Counsel 1949–60, and subsequently a Chancery Division judge and Lord Justice of Appeal) or Raymond Jennings QC (1897–1995; subsequently Master of the Court of Protection) who had also been regarded as suitable by the Department.

[49] See the letter from H. Boggis-Rolfe (b. 1911) of the Lord Chancellor's Office (subsequently Deputy Permanent Secretary and at one time Secretary to the Law Commission) to Sir Thomas Barnes (1888–1964—the first solicitor to be appointed Treasury Solicitor).

[50] (1888–1965). Morrison, then Lord President of the Council and as such responsible for the co-ordination of the Labour Government's policies, was a powerful figure in the Labour party: see below.

[51] Morrison to Jowitt, 12 July 1950, PRO file LCO2/4440.

time comes to give effect to the Report). Morrison also thought that there must be 'at least one woman',[52] and that it was always an advantage 'to put on somebody from Wales'. His specific proposal[53] of the Labour MP and former schoolteacher Mrs Dorothy Rees (whom he described as 'a sensible and practical woman') was no doubt welcome.[54] She was balanced politically by the Conservative MP for Northwich, John Foster KC[55] (a lawyer of renowned brilliance); and further legal input was provided by the barrister Michael Albery[56] and by the solicitor and Labour MP, Eric Fletcher.[57] Considerable difficulty was experienced in finding a suitable trade unionist: Arthur Deakin[58] the powerful General Secretary of the then 1.3 million strong Transport and General Workers' Union refused[59] to allow Morrison's first suggestion to be appointed, and eventually Lord Kershaw[60] (to whom Deakin had 'no objection') was nominated. Harold Wilson[61] put forward a number of names of possible employers' representatives and his first choice (Sir Hugh Chance,[62] chairman of a family glass manufacturers 'who manages to find time for a good deal of social work') was appointed.

THE MORTON COMMITTEE'S TERMS OF REFERENCE

The Committee's Terms of Reference were a matter of great importance—and difficulty—to the Lord Chancellor's officials. They realised that any increase in the provision to be made for a surviving spouse on intestacy would inevitably increase the number of cases in which hardship might be caused to others who

[52] When the names of the Committee were announced there was adverse comment on the fact that only one woman had been appointed. The National Council of Women of Great Britain had previously urged that a representative be appointed, but were politely rebuffed: 10 Aug. 1950. Ambrose Appellbe, a prominent solicitor of progressive views, wrote on behalf of the Married Women's Trust and protested at the gender imbalance (31 Oct. 1950), as did the Women's Group on Public Welfare (14 Dec. 1950).

[53] Jowitt had doubted whether it was really necessary to have someone from Wales, but said he was prepared to appoint a Welshman who was either a lawyer or had experience of social work: Jowitt to Morrison, 28 June 1950.

[54] Mrs Rees (born 1898) was subsequently engaged in much public work and was appointed DBE.

[55] (1903–82). Fellow of All Souls College, Oxford, 1925–82.

[56] (1910–75). Albery was the author of a work, evidently admired within the Lord Chancellor's Office, on the Inheritance (Provision for Family and Dependants) Act 1938.

[57] (1903–90), subsequently ennobled as Lord Fletcher of Islington. Prominent on the right wing of the Labour Party, he became Minister without Portfolio with special responsibility for law reform in the Wilson administration (see Ch. 1, n. 102, above) although his conservative approach to divorce law reform was a source of tension: see Ch. 2, nn. 83 and 84 above, E. G. M. Fletcher, *Random Reflections* (1968) and R. F. V. Heuston, *Lives of the Lord Chancellors 1940–1970* (1987).

[58] (1890–1955).

[59] On the ground that the person concerned was indispensable to the Union.

[60] (1881–1961). Kershaw had served as Chairman of Courts of Referees under the Unemployment Insurance Acts.

[61] Then President of the Board of Trade: see Wilson to Jowitt 14 Sept. 1950, LCO2/4440.

[62] (1896–1981).

had been dependent on the deceased; yet they had no wish[63] to reopen discussion on what had in the recent past proved the exceedingly controversial matter of giving the court a discretion to override a testator's wishes[64] or even to override the provisions laid down by law on intestacy in such cases. In the end, pressure from within the government machine[65] made it impossible altogether to exclude this topic from the terms of reference; but they were skilfully crafted to confine the issues as narrowly as possible. The Committee was:

1. To consider the rights[66] of a surviving spouse in the residuary estate of an intestate;
2. To consider whether, and if so to what extent and in what manner, the provisions of the Inheritance (Family Provision) Act 1938 ought to be made applicable to intestacies;
3. To report whether any, and if so what, alteration in the law is desirable.[67]

THE MORTON COMMITTEE'S[68] DELIBERATIONS

The Committee worked with what today seems astonishing speed; and the Chairman was able to submit the Report to the Lord Chancellor less than eight months after the Committee had been established.[69] The Committee's Secretary[70] was evidently knowledgeable and formidably efficient; and the Chairman did not encourage lengthy discussion.[71] But the main factor influencing such a

---

[63] The draft terms of reference put by Boggis-Rolfe to the Treasury Solicitor (LCO2/4440, 22 May 1950) were confined to a consideration of the rights of a surviving spouse on intestacy, and stated that Coldstream and he had 'not been able to think of any other subject which could conveniently be considered simultaneously'.

[64] Under the powers conferred by the Inheritance (Family Provision) Act 1938 which had only been enacted after prolonged and sometimes almost bitter controversy: see above, p. 250.

[65] Notably from the Treasury Solicitor.

[66] Under Administration of Estates Act 1925, s. 46.

[67] *Report of the Committee on the Law of Intestate Succession* Cmd. 8130 (1951) (hereafter referred to as '*Morton Report*') para. 1.

[68] The membership was announced in *The Times*, 18 Oct. 1950. B. E. Astbury and A. W. Brown were appointed to the Committee in addition to those mentioned in the text.

[69] The Report is dated 5 June 1951 and was submitted on 25 June. In contrast, the Law Commission evidently began its study of Distribution on Intestacy in 1987, and completed a Working Paper (No. 108) for consultation on 10 June 1988. Its Report (Law Com. No. 187) dated 27 Oct. 1989 was laid before Parliament on 18 Dec. 1989.

[70] D. R. Holloway (b. 1917). An official in the Probate Registry he subsequently served as Assistant Secretary to the Royal Commission on Marriage and Divorce (see Ch. 2, above) and, from 1966 to 1983, as a Registrar of the Principal Registry of the Family Division. Holloway produced briefing memoranda which may still be regarded as models of their kind; and also marshalled the statistical evidence (collected in PRO file LCO2/4445) on which the Committee placed some reliance, see text to n. 76 below.

[71] The Committee met on only six occasions. The minutes of the fifth meeting give some flavour of the Chairman's style. After a 'long discussion' on whether the provisions of the Inheritance (Family Provision) Act 1938 should be extended to total intestacies (see text to n. 100, below) 'the Chairman put the following question to the Committee: Do you think that some provision should be made by

rapid disposal of what might have been thought complex issues is the Committee's confidence in its ability to interpret what it described[72] as the spirit of the age. Moreover, the Committee accepted[73] the philosophy (previously adopted in framing the 1925 legislation[74]) that the provision in fact made by testators provided a sound basis upon which intestate distribution could be based;[75] and it did have available to it a survey of wills proved over a five-week period.[76] The Committee received advice[77] on the law of intestacy in foreign countries, and written memoranda from seven organisations,[78] and it received a large number of written suggestions[79] (including a petition signed by 3,202 persons urging improvement in the widow's position[80]); but the Committee did not seek to dramatise the problems,[81] and did not even consider carrying out an attitude or other public opinion survey.

statute for mitigating cases of hardship which might arise' if the proposal significantly to increase the surviving spouse's rights were adopted? 'All the members with the exception of Mr Eric Fletcher thought that some provision should be made. Mr Fletcher then said that in view of the general opinion of the other members he was prepared to support the recommendation put forward by the Chairman in the outline of the report. (Mr Fletcher left the meeting at this stage).': PRO file LCO2/4448.

[72] *Morton Report*, para. 10.

[73] As had The Law Society: see Boggis-Rolfe to Barnes, 22 May 1950, LCO2/4440.

[74] See n. 28 above. The Notes for Ministers prepared by Officials on the Bill which became the Intestates' Estates Act 1952 state that the draftsman of the 1925 Act, Sir Benjamin Cherry, 'incorporated what he believed to be general intention of persons dying intestate. In doing so he acted mainly on his personal knowledge, no comprehensive statistics of disposals by will being available at the time'. But it appears that in fact statistics were obtained from the Estate Duty Office in 1921 and that they confirmed the view taken by Cherry: see Memorandum No. 1 to the Morton Committee (PRO file LCO2/4447) p. 2.

[75] Contrast the cogent criticism of this approach by the Law Commission, *Distribution on Intestacy* Law Com. No. 187, para. 4.   [76] *Morton Report*, para. 18.

[77] Prepared by Sir David Hughes Parry (1893–1973), Director of the Institute of Advanced Legal Studies, London University, and author of a still widely used student's text: Parry and Clark, *The Law of Succession* (10th edn. 1996 by R. Kerridge).

[78] The General Council of the Bar and the Council of the Law Society (who both also gave oral evidence); the Solicitors' Managing Clerks' Association; the Committee of London Clearing Bankers; the Married Women's Association; the National Council of Women of Great Britain; and the Marriage Law Reform Society. The Society did not disguise the fact that its primary objective was to reform the divorce law so as to permit divorce after the spouses had lived apart for two years rather than to reform the law of intestate succession, but it did prophetically favour giving a person who had lived with the deceased as a spouse for three years the right to make a claim under the 1938 Act (cf. Law Com. No. 187, para. 63—two-year cohabitants to be eligible).

[79] Although the *Morton Report* states that most of the private individuals' comments were about particular cases of hardship (para. 2) it should be recorded that Professor Glanville Williams presciently identified the demographic changes reflected in an increasing number of step-parent relationships as a matter which should be taken into account in any reform; and that a particularly powerfully argued letter from a Halifax solicitor, E. Maurice Drake, foreshadowed the recommendation ultimately made by the Law Commission in 1989 that the whole estate should go to the widow leaving other dependants to an application for the exercise of the court's discretion under the Inheritance legislation.   [80] *Morton Report*, para. 2.

[81] The Secretary found it necessary to write on 30 Nov. 1950 to the editor of the *Daily Graphic* stating that whilst he welcomed 'to a limited extent' the publicity which the newspaper had given to the Committee's work, it was 'not correct to say that I hear daily of tragedies caused by persons dying intestate. I have no recollection of making a statement of this nature to your reporter and in any event it is not true.'

THE COMMITTEE'S GENERAL POLICY:
IMPROVING THE RIGHTS OF THE SURVIVING SPOUSE

The Committee did not find it difficult to reach agreement on its general policy. It accepted the argument that there had been a considerable depreciation in the value of sterling since the 1925 reforms; and that the matrimonial home[82] was often worth a sum 'greatly in excess' of the statutory legacy. It accepted that, in consequence, the surviving spouse might be forced to leave the home, which would have to be sold to satisfy the claims of the deceased's children. For these reasons, there was no longer any similarity between the provision made for the surviving spouse by the average testator and that made for the spouse by the law of intestate succession.[83] In the Committee's view it followed that the surviving spouse's share should be increased.

It would hardly have required the appointment of a Committee to reach this conclusion; but deciding on the nature and scale of the increase was much less easy. The Committee drew a distinction between cases where the intestate left surviving issue and other cases. Where there were surviving issue, the Committee decided that a fivefold increase (to £5,000[84]) in the amount of the statutory legacy payable to a surviving spouse[85] would be appropriate.[86]

The Committee also made two ancillary proposals intended to improve the surviving spouse's position. First, the survivor should be given an option to purchase the matrimonial home at its open market value as at the date of the deceased's death;[87]

---

[82] Considerable difficulty was caused to the Committee and to officials by the existence of a concession which often led to the home being valued *for estate duty purposes* at its pre-World War II value: see e.g. *Morton Report*, para. 25. But unless the contrary is indicated references in this text are to the market values current at the time.   [83] *Morton Report*, para. 16.

[84] Free of death duty and costs; and the survivor would retain the entitlement to the deceased's personal chattels. The recommended increase in the amount of the statutory legacy was substantially more than would have resulted from adjusting the £1,000 provided by the 1925 Act to take account of general inflation, and was at the upper end of the range of suggestions made by witnesses. Indexation—which would have justified an increase to £2,000—was evidently a comparatively little understood concept; and the Committee does not seem to have been influenced by it. The Bar Council (virtually alone) had recommended that the legacy remain unchanged, the spouse's position being improved by conferring a life interest in the whole of the deceased's residuary estate: *Morton Report*, para. 17.

[85] The rate of interest payable on this statutory legacy was to be reduced from 5 per cent to 4 per cent: *Morton Report*, paras. 16–22.

[86] The statement by Lord Gardiner in moving the Second Reading of the Family Provision Bill 1966 (see *Official Report*, 16 June 1966, col. 202) that the Morton Committee had 'pointed out that the object of the statutory legacy was to enable the widow to buy the house', that the Committee said that '£1,000 for this purpose was no use in 1952' and that the proper equivalent, 'judged in terms of the increase in the price of houses' was £5,000 does not accurately reflect the Committee's expressed views (see *Morton Report*, paras. 10–21) which took account of inflation in house prices as merely one relevant factor. The Committee (following the precedent of those responsible for the 1925 legislation) was much more influenced by the pattern of testators' wills.

[87] *Morton Report*, paras. 23–7.

and, secondly, the spouse should be entitled[88] to redeem the life interest in half the remaining estate to which (the Committee proposed) the survivor should continue to be entitled.[89]

In cases in which the deceased left no issue, the Committee recommended a compromise between those[90] who favoured giving the whole estate to the survivor;[91] and those who thought that the deceased's kin should also benefit. Where the deceased died without issue but left a spouse and a parent or sibling of the whole blood the spouse should take a legacy of £20,000 and half the residue absolutely. The balance of the estate should go to the surviving parent or parents, or (if neither parent survived) to the brothers and sisters of the whole blood.[92] The Committee did not think the average individual would want relatives more remote than this to benefit from the estate at the expense of the surviving spouse[93] and accordingly recommended that brothers and sisters of the half-blood and their issue, grandparents, uncles and aunts of the whole or half-blood and their issue, should lose the right[94] to share in the estate of an intestate who died leaving a surviving spouse.[95]

PROVIDING FOR CASES OF HARDSHIP

The general tenor of the Committee's proposals was thus vividly to exemplify what has been described[96] as the amputation of the blood stock and of the movement of marriage (as against genetic kinship) into the foreground.[97] But the Committee was conscious[98] that the increased provision which it proposed for

[88] Under the Administration of Estates Act 1925, s. 48(1), the intestate's personal representatives were empowered to redeem the life interest in accordance with tables they selected; but this procedure was not much used: *Morton Report*, para. 32. The Committee's proposal conferred the right of redemption on the surviving spouse in accordance with a 'simple table' incorporated in the legislation: *Morton Report*, para. 32.   [89] *Morton Report*, paras. 28–32.

[90] Notably, the Council of the Law Society: *Morton Report*, para. 34.

[91] 'This seems rather a striking proposal. It means that the spouse would take the whole estate even if the intestate left a very large estate . . . We feel that under such circumstances a childless person, dying intestate, would wish that close relatives . . . should take some benefit from the estate, subject always to adequate provision being made for the spouse. It often happens that a large portion of the intestate's estate has been derived from his family and it seems just, therefore, that the family should have an opportunity of sharing in it after the intestate's death.' (*Morton Report*, para. 34.)

[92] On the statutory trusts defined by the Administration of Estates Act 1925, s. 47, which also provide for substitution of issue of deceased siblings.

[93] *Morton Report*, para. 36. The surviving spouse was to take the whole estate absolutely if no relatives within the defined class survived.   [94] Administration of Estates Act 1925, s. 46.

[95] *Morton Report*, para. 36. Such relatives were to retain the right to succeed if there were no surviving spouse.

[96] By Sundberg, cited by D. Bradley, 'Marriage, family property and inheritance in Swedish law' by D. Bradley (1990) 39 ICLQ 370.

[97] This thesis is persuasively developed by M. A. Glendon, *The New Family and the New Property* (Toronto, 1981).

[98] Although this was one of the few matters on which the Committee found difficulty in reaching agreement: see text to n. 64 above.

a surviving spouse might well work injustice in many cases where there were stepchildren by another marriage. After considerable debate,[99] the Committee decided to recommend that the Inheritance (Family Provision) Act should be made to apply to cases of intestacy.[100] This acceptance of the view that no code of distribution could provide adequately for all the complexities of modern family structures, and that recourse to judicial discretion was necessary to obviate hardship was controversial; and had important implications for the future development of the law. The Committee knew that its terms of reference had been deliberately restricted[101] so as to prevent it from reopening the issues which had proved so difficult in the thirties, and it clearly found this constraint embarrassing.[102]

FROM REPORT TO STATUTE

British constitutional practice allows Ministers to seek advice (whether from bodies such as departmental and other advisory committees[103] or from their own departmental officials or from others); Ministers[104] decide whether to take such advice and whether and when to promote legislation;[105] and Parliament decides whether to enact the measures placed before it.

The relationship between the different actors in this scenario can be subtle: the power of officials to influence matters has been a source of much comment but seems inevitable given their long-term involvement in the executive machine. On the other hand, Ministers will have declared policies on some matters (albeit rarely on matters of lawyer's law reform) and certainly cannot routinely force through legislation which their officials support without regard to opinions expressed in either House of Parliament. The passage of the Intestates'

---

[99] See n. 71 above.   [100] *Morton Report*, paras. 41–51.

[101] At its first meeting on 9 Nov. 1950 the Committee discussed whether to seek to have the terms of reference extended to enable it to consider the working of the 1938 Act. But only John Foster KC dissented from the general consensus not to do so: see Minutes, PRO papers LCO2/4448.

[102] The Morton Report suggested, 'at the risk of travelling outside our terms of reference', that if the Inheritance Act were to be extended to cover cases of intestacy 'opportunity might advantageously be found to remove some of the defects which have come to light in the course of' experience of its working (in particular the restrictions imposed by s. 1(3) and (4)): *Morton Report*, para. 49. The Committee also noted that the class of dependants eligible to apply under the Act was restricted— for example, an adult son of the deceased's could only do so if disabled—and expressed the view that it would 'obviously be necessary' to review the whole of the Act closely if it were extended to intestacies, and that it might be thought desirable to enlarge the class of 'dependants': *Morton Report*, para. 51. In the event, no comprehensive review took place until the Law Commission undertook the Review (*Second Report on Family Property: Family Provision on Death*, Law Com. No. 61, 1974) which formed the basis of the Inheritance (Provision for Family and Dependants) Act 1975: see text to n. 158, below.

[103] For the special responsibilities of the Law Commission in this context, see Ch. 1 above.

[104] Assuming collective responsibility for Cabinet decisions. In practice, crucial decisions will usually be taken by Cabinet Committees—in the present instance the Home Affairs Committee.

[105] Or whether to block, preserve neutrality (benevolent or otherwise), or actively to support Bills introduced by private members: see e.g. Ch. 3, above.

Estates Act 1952 illustrates the working of these relationships in the context of what appeared to be a Bill devoid of almost any political content.[106]

Technicalities (i) *Commorientes*

The first stage in the decision-taking process was for the Lord Chancellor's officials to consult with other officials on the Morton Report's proposals; and, immediately, problems were raised. On one view, the most difficult[107] was whether the Committee had fully considered the implications of the rule[108] that the younger of two persons who died in circumstances rendering it uncertain which had survived should be deemed to have survived. The larger the surviving spouse's entitlement on intestacy the more likely it was (for example) that the family of a young bride killed with her husband in an air crash would inherit substantial wealth, perhaps derived from his family. Lord Morton candidly told[109] Coldstream that his Committee had never considered the point[110] and that he did not want to do so. To deal with this problem, the Lord Chancellor eventually agreed[111] that legislation should nullify the statutory presumption for the purposes of intestate succession;[112] and the Lord Chancellor's Memorandum to the Home Affairs Committee was settled accordingly.

Technicalities (ii) The Right to Buy the Matrimonial Home

Although it may sometimes be difficult to secure agreement on broad issues of policy (even in 'uncontroversial' and technical legislation) such difficulties often pale into insignificance when the agreed policy has to be formulated with the precision required by the English tradition of statutory drafting. The Intestates' Estates Act 1952 provides a striking example of this phenomenon.

[106] The Morton Committee had been appointed by, and reported to, the Labour Government's Lord Chancellor (Jowitt: see n. 47 above). But that Government was defeated at the General Election on 25 Oct. 1951 and decisions as to implementation fell to Lord Simonds (1881–1971), a man of no political experience who was evidently mystified by Winston Churchill's action (in his last administration) in offering him the post: see the account in R. F. V. Heuston, *Lives of the Lord Chancellors 1940–1970* (1987) pp. 147–9. Simonds was a great Chancery lawyer, who sadly is now best known for his vigorous criticisms of Lord Denning (see the *Midland Silicones* case [1962] AC 446, 459: 'heterodoxy, or, as some might say, heresy, is not the more attractive because it is dignified by the name of reform'). [107] Raised by the Treasury Solicitor.

[108] Law of Property Act 1925, s. 184.

[109] According to a note endorsed on a letter from Coldstream to Morton dated 19 Nov. 1951 marked 'not to be sent'.

[110] Although the point had in fact been put to the Committee by the Quain Professor of Jurisprudence at London University, Professor Glanville Williams (1911–97).

[111] Simonds's manuscript note on a minute from Dennis Dobson dated 26 Nov. 1951: file LCO2/4457.

[112] See now Administration of Estates Act 1925, s. 46(3), as added by Intestates' Estates Act 1952, s. 1(4). Following consideration by the Law Commission (*Distribution on Intestacy*, Law Com. No. 187, 1989, para. 57) it is now also provided that a spouse who *does* survive should only inherit on intestacy if he or she survives the deceased for a period of twenty-eight days: see Administration of Estates Act 1925, s. 46(2A) inserted by Law Reform (Succession) Act 1995.

What, for example, could be simpler than to draft legislation giving effect to the Morton Committee's recommendation that a surviving spouse should have an option to purchase the deceased's interest in the matrimonial home? And yet . . . How was matrimonial home to be defined? How were the interests of purchasers and creditors to be protected? What was to happen if the survivor were under twenty-one or of unsound mind?

The draftsman[113] did his best but was not satisfied with the result: it is not, of course, the draftsman's job to take views on policy but the draftsman wrote that the difficulties were so great that 'the whole of this option' might best be omitted from the Bill. After all (he wrote) 'the Committee were luke warm about it particularly, as I read between the lines, the legal members'. There would be no problem in keeping the house for the widow's occupation where the family was harmonious, and so 'one is probably legislating for the cases where either side are ready to take any obstructive point, and this subject fairly bristles with debatable points which the drafting must leave open'. It seems clear that issues of policy could not easily be segregated from technicalities: the grant of an option to purchase would[114] 'simply encourage old ladies to insist on going on living in houses which were far too large for them and against their real interests'.[115]

In the result, the officials came to agree that it was impossible to draft legislation to give effect to the proposal, and the Bill as first presented to Parliament did not seek to deal with the matter. But—to anticipate—in the end the practical experience of the solicitors' profession came to the rescue:[116] the surviving spouse was to be given the right to require the personal representatives to exercise the 'well-tried' powers of appropriation[117] in respect of the matrimonial home;[118]

---

[113] A. N. Stainton (1913–88), who subsequently became First Parliamentary Counsel and (according to the obituary published in *The Times* on 12 Nov. 1988) was responsible for drafting much tax legislation. His obituarist refers to his analytical mind and prodigious intellect, and to the fact that, although he did not suffer fools gladly, 'he would at least allow the fool to leave the room before expressing exasperation'. For some deeply felt remarks about difficulties encountered in collaboration between some Law Commission staff and Parliamentary Counsel, see R. T. Oerton, *A Lament for the Law Commission* (1987) Ch. 6, particularly pp. 54–6.

[114] Coldstream to the Solicitor-General Sir Reginald Manningham Buller, 7 Mar. 1952. The draftsman's attempt to produce clauses conferring an option to purchase had been referred to the Senior Chancery Judge, Vaisey J (1877–1965), and he had made 'the most devastating criticism of the proposal' and advised the Lord Chancellor to drop it because legislation would do more harm than good.

[115] See to the same effect H. Hylton-Foster's speech on the Second Reading of the Bill: *Official Report* (HC) 28 Mar. 1952, vol. 498, col. 1078.

[116] See the correspondence between Coldstream and Horsfall-Turner from 13 Mar. 1952.

[117] Administration of Estates Act 1925, s. 41. It was held in *Lall* v. *Lall* [1965] 1 WLR 1249 that the survivor has, prior to appropriation, no equitable interest in property such as to give standing in a possession action brought by registered proprietor; and note the draftsman's concern about the difficulties of deciding how far the Morton Report's 'option' would bind third parties.

[118] But if the widow were to be given a right to keep the matrimonial home, should she not also be given a right to keep the family business? An amendment to this effect was successfully moved by Barnett Janner MP (later Baron Janner—a solicitor and President of the Board of Deputies of British Jews and himself the son of a small shopkeeper) *Official Report* 15 July 1952 vol. 503 col. 2106; but a firm stand was taken against what Lord Mancroft described as a 'perfectly horrible

and the resultant provisions seem to have given rise to few problems[119] in practice.[120]

The fertile mind of the draftsman found[121] many other difficulties;[122] but a Bill was eventually drafted.[123] Further amendments[124] were made to take account of

clause' (*Official Report* 29 July 1952, vol. 178, col. 394). As the draft prepared by officials, explaining to Janner why the clause was to be removed, put it, leaving the technicalities on one side, 'widows are often not the best judges of their own business capacity': LCO2/4452.

[119] But see *Re Phelps dec'd*. [1980] Ch. 275, CA overturning the decision of Foster J [1978] 1 WLR 1501 to the effect that the right could not be exercised where the house was worth more than the amount of the statutory legacy. And note the view of the Law Commission (Law Com. No. 187, para. 34) that the interpretation put on this provision in *Robinson* v. *Collins* [1975] 1 WLR 309 (value of house to be calculated at date of appropriation rather than at death) had caused problems. The *Morton Report* envisaged that the survivor's right should be to purchase at the death valuation: para. 25.

[120] See the discussion in Sherrin and Bonehill, *The Law and Practice of Intestate Succession* (2nd edn. 1994). It is to be noted that officials were worried that the exercise of the power might be 'catastrophic' in some cases (e.g. where the matrimonial home had been a farmhouse) and that accordingly in certain defined cases the right to require appropriation is not exercisable unless the court is satisfied that doing so would not be likely to diminish the value of other assets or make them more difficult to dispose of: see Intestates' Estates Act 1952, Sch. 2, para. 2. But it was decided (contrary to tradition) that 'the attempt to legislate for every case should be abandoned': see Notes on Clauses, LCO2/6671, p. 24.

[121] Unfortunately, he did not identify some problems which arose in practice. The drafting of the 1952 Act was criticised by academic writers (see Sherrin and Bonehill, *The Law and Practice of Intestate Succession* (2nd edn. 1994); and in the debate on the amending Family Provision Act 1966 the Conservative spokesman took the possibly unprecedented step of apologising for the 'considerable errors' which were made: see *Official Report* (HL) 16 June 1966, vol. 275, col. 210.

[122] See in particular the six-page letter dated 4 Jan. 1952. Amongst the difficulties raised were: (i) the application of the rule in *Allhusen* v. *Whittell* (1867) LR 4 Eq. 295 to the surviving spouse's legacy; (ii) the position if the court made an order under the 1938 Act on the basis of provisions which turn out not to be those made in the will (e.g. where a new will is discovered); (iii) were purchasers to be affected by notice that chattels should have gone to spouse?; (iv) difficulties which were perceived as likely to arise in relation to the requirement that one spouse be proved to have survived the other. The draftsman's comments caused some irritation to the Lord Chancellor's officials: in particular, Stainton's suggestion that the Committee be asked whether they had taken account of the implications of the rule in *Allhusen* v. *Whittell* prompted a great deal of departmental research; but ultimately Dobson told the private member to whom the Bill had been allotted (Sir Hugh Lucas-Tooth: see n. 125 below) that he was not sure that the problem was quite as difficult as Stainton had made it appear 'because . . . I think one would find that little notice was taken of the rule in *Allhusen* v. *Whittell*': Dobson to Lucas-Tooth, 7 Jan. 1952.

[123] The Bill as drafted departed from one recommendation of the Morton Committee (which had taken the view that there should be no special rules for partial intestacies). It was decided that, in the light of the increased size of the statutory legacy, the spouse should be required to bring any benefit taken under the will (or in exercise of any general power of appointment) into account against that provision; but the Law Reform (Succession) Act 1995, s. 1(2), repealed this provision in an attempt to reduce difficulties caused to lay personal representatives.

[124] For example, on the method of calculating the amount to be paid by way of redemption of the surviving spouse's life interest: see the Notes on Clauses, pp. 15–19, LCO2/6671. Following advice from the Government Actuary a simple scheme for valuation by reference to the cost of a Post Office Annuity was incorporated into the legislation: Intestates' Estates Act 1952, s. 2(2). Subsequently, the withdrawal of Post Office annuities required the scheme to be amended; and it is now provided that the capital value is to be reckoned in such manner as the Lord Chancellor may direct: see Administration of Justice Act 1977, s. 28(3), and the tables laid down in the Intestate Succession (Interest and Capitalisation) Order 1983 (SI 1374).

comments on the draft from Departments; but the Bill was eventually introduced,[125] and its passage through both Houses of Parliament was skilfully handled by the private members entrusted with its carriage. Although there were in fact a number of serious issues of principle which might have been discussed, the Commons spokesman, Hylton-Foster[126] decided that[127] 'speed and joviality looked like the easiest way'. In the result the few members who attended the debates[128] were regaled with accounts of 'elderly gentlemen who marry little blonde creatures much younger than themselves in the autumn of their days'[129] and similar witticisms;[130] and there was little critical probing of legislative policy or detail.

Passing over the Difficulties

The parliamentary debates certainly understate the concern—recognised by Morton,[131] echoed by the Cabinet's Home Affairs[132] and Legislation[133] Committee, and forcefully expressed by the President of the Probate, Divorce and Admiralty

---

[125] It was thought better that it should be handed to a private member who had a good place in the ballot for Private Members' Bills and lacked any Bill of his own (rather than being introduced as part of the Government's legislative programme). It had originally been intended that the Bill would be taken through the Commons by the barrister Conservative MP for Hendon South, Sir Hugh Lucas-Tooth (1903–85); but he was appointed Parliamentary Under-Secretary at the Home Office and a substitute had to be found.

[126] Harry Hylton-Foster (1905–65) had been elected Conservative MP for York in 1950, and subsequently became Solicitor-General (1954–9) and Speaker of the House of Commons (1964–5).

[127] To Coldstream, 29 Oct. 1952.

[128] Officials voiced concern about the unrepresentative nature of the debates: the House of Commons Second Reading Debate was 'a very thin house' with few speakers. (In fact the House was counted out on 28 Mar., but the Second Reading was carried 'on the nod' in the following week. The Committee debate was 'very meagre'; and officials regretted that the Bill had had so little consideration because there were 'many questions of principle' on which any government would want a free vote (e.g. the size of the statutory legacy). The only point of principle urged with any conviction was by Charles Fletcher-Cooke (b. 1914), the barrister Conservative MP for Darwen, who successfully objected to the further discrimination proposed by the Morton Committee against relatives of the half-blood: the Bill was amended to allow brothers and sisters (and uncles and aunts) of the half-blood to retain their right to succeed in default of any spouse, issue, or parent of the deceased, ranking after relatives of the whole blood in the same degree.

[129] H. Hylton-Foster, *Official Report* (HC) 28 Mar. 1952, vol. 498, col. 1083.

[130] The Conservative peer Lord Mancroft (1914–87) (at the time a Member of the Bar Council) was entrusted with the carriage of the Bill in the House of Lords. His light-hearted speech on the Second Reading Debate in the House of Lords was evidently skilfully attuned to the mood of the House. The Administration of Estates Act had, he said, been drafted by the late Sir Benjamin Cherry, and contained a table of 'a complexity and confusion equal only to that in the Table of Affinity in the Prayer Book, concluding with certain nefarious characters which could have stepped only from the pages of Saki or P. G. Wodehouse—namely, aunts of the half-blood. I never met a case of a man being disinherited by a half-blooded aunt, but presumably Sir Benjamin Cherry did not want to take any risks!' (*Official Report* 29 July 1952, vol. 178, col. 390.) A humorous reference to the possibility that Lord Chancellor Jowitt (see n. 47, above) might solve his housing problems by moving into the vicarage at Bray offended Jowitt to the point that he left the Lords' chamber whenever Mancroft spoke (Heuston, op. cit. n. 106 above, p. 80); but his parliamentary skills were subsequently put to good effect in securing the enactment of the Marriage (Enabling) Act 1960 which rationalised the rules governing the prohibited degrees of marriage.   [131] *Morton Report*, para. 47.

[132] Minutes, 7 Dec. 1951.   [133] Minutes of meeting, 11 Mar. 1952.

Division[134]—that the overriding preference given to the widow on intestacy might cause very considerable hardship. In this view, too much had been sacrificed for the sake of simplicity. But—paradoxically, in the light of the sensitivity felt within the Lord Chancellor's Department about giving the court power to order reasonable provision to be made for a dependant out of a deceased's estate[135]—the Lord Chancellor relied on the extension of the 1938 Act to intestacy as the means 'to enable the courts to intervene'[136] in cases where (for example) a husband with issue by one marriage remarried late in life. It was (he said) precisely 'because of this kind of difficulty' that the 1938 Act was to be extended in its application. That was sufficient to resolve the immediate difficulty; but it was not an adequate long-term solution to the problems presented by the 1938 Act.

SIGNIFICANCE OF THE INTESTATES' ESTATES ACT 1952

Notwithstanding the lack of parliamentary interest in the Bill, it can now be seen that the Intestates' Estates Act 1952 Act is of major significance in the development of the law. First, it emphatically recognised the primacy to be accorded to the claims of a surviving spouse. Secondly, for the first time in English statute law, it recognised the family home as an asset deserving special protection. Finally —and perhaps of even greater long-term importance—is the acceptance of the principle that, since no general code for intestate distribution could achieve satisfactory results in every case, the court should be given power to vary the statutory provisions in cases in which those provisions failed to make reasonable provision for the deceased's dependants.

INTESTACY RULES STILL INADEQUATE TO DEAL WITH CHANGING CIRCUMSTANCES: INFLATION

The policy of the 1952 reforms was to improve the position of an intestate's surviving spouse; but it soon became clear that this policy was in danger of being defeated by economic factors. Inflation soon eroded the real value of the amounts fixed by the Intestates' Estates Act 1952 for the surviving spouse's statutory legacy: between 1952 and 1966 the purchasing power of the statutory legacy fell by 50 per cent (whilst the increase in the cost of housing over that period

---

[134] Merriman to Coldstream, 5 Mar. 1952, LCO2/4451. Lord Merriman (1880–1962) had had a difficult relationship with the Department, no doubt in part because of his bitter opposition to the proposals for reform of divorce law and procedure put forward in the Reports of the (Denning) *Committee on Procedure in Matrimonial Causes* (1946–7): see Ch. 6, above. Merriman's letter reveals his resentment at not having been consulted about the intestacy reforms at an earlier stage—and this failure is all the more surprising in the light of Coldstream's expressed view that inquiries of this kind should not 'be allowed to be started unless we are quite sure that it is one which is likely to have the approval of the head of the division concerned': LCO2/3951.　　　　　[135] See text to n. 64, above.

[136] Minutes of Home Affairs Committee, 7 Dec. 1951.

had been somewhere between 60 and 80 per cent[137]). Eventually, in 1966 (on the basis of Lord Chancellor Gardiner's not entirely accurate assertion[138] that the original intention of the statutory legacy had been to enable a widow to buy the matrimonial home[139]), the £5,000 legacy was increased by 75 per cent to £8,750 in line with the increase in house prices, while the £20,000 legacy was increased by only 50 per cent to £30,000 in line with the cost of living.

Housing considerations thus came to have an even greater prominence; while the Government met the need to respond comparatively speedily to changing money values by taking power[140] to increase the amount of the statutory legacy by order. This power was used five times between 1966 and 1993;[141] and now a surviving spouse is entitled to £125,000 if the deceased left issue and £200,000 if he or she did not. The policy remains[142] that the surviving spouse should take the whole of all save the largest estates and be enabled to 'remain in the former matrimonial home[143] and to have a sufficient surplus on which to live'.[144] It is true that the technique of leaving it to the Government to increase the amount of the statutory legacy is a crude method of dealing with changes in the value of money and other assets; and there is something of a mystery surrounding the taking of decisions on the exercise of the power to increase the amount of the legacy. (Lord Chancellor Gardiner's answer to a question[145] about the machinery necessary to inform decisions on these matters[146] had the merit of candour[147]

---

[137] *Official Report* (HL) 16 June 1966, vol. 275, col. 202.

[138] See *Official Report* (HL) 16 June 1966, vol. 275, col. 202.

[139] The problem of a widow having to give up the matrimonial home was merely an incidental factor in settling the policy of the 1925 legislation; the determining element was the provision made by testators in wills: see n. 28 above. Housing was a more significant consideration in the 1952 legislation but hardly to the decisive extent suggested.   [140] Family Provision Act 1966, s. 1(1).

[141] The changes in the amount of the surviving spouse's statutory legacy are conveniently summarised in Sherrin and Bonehill, *Law and Practice of Intestate Succession* (2nd edn. 1994) pp. 217–18.

[142] In terms of the overall purchasing power of the pound, computed according to the official statistics, the position of the surviving spouse of an intestate who leaves issue has improved dramatically (and the interests of the intestate's issue correspondingly eroded) over the years: the 1994 equivalent of the 1925 £1,000 is some £28,000; and the equivalent of the 1952 £5,000 would be £76,737— i.e. substantially *less* than the £125,000 now payable. In contrast, the 1994 equivalent of the £20,000 legacy provided for a surviving spouse in 1952 in cases where the intestate left no issue but did leave a parent or a sibling would be £306,949—i.e. substantially *more* than the £200,000 provided for under the statute. The outcome appears to be that the benefits to which the parents or other kin of a 'childless' but wealthy intestate are entitled have been comparatively increased over the years— an outcome which may be thought paradoxical given that a 'childless' intestate may in fact have stood *in loco parentis* to stepchildren for many years: see text to n. 182, below.

[143] These figures should be seen in the context of a housing market in which estimates of the average price of a detached house range from £86,588 in Wales to £206,517 for an 'older' detached house in Greater London: Nationwide Building Society, *Housing Finance Review* (Jan. 1998).

[144] *Official Report* (HL) 1 July 1993, vol. 547, col. WA 38.

[145] *Official Report* (HL) 16 June 1966, vol. 275, col. 210.

[146] The Law Commission thought that the most recent changes, made in 1993, still caused 'serious injustice': *Law Commission 28th Annual Report 1993* (Law Com. No. 223, 1993) para. 3.8.

[147] 'Frankly, I have not yet settled a future policy. Wherever there is such a sum of money which can be altered by an order under an Act, it ought to be looked at once a year. Whether some other period would be better, I am not sure. Where you get the information from depends entirely, of course,

but little else.) But at least the problem of changing asset values has been addressed. As we shall see, other problems have not.

As already noted,[148] the Morton Committee had—notwithstanding the restrictions imposed by its terms of reference[149]—identified a number of difficulties in the operation of the Inheritance (Family Provision) Act 1938; but the Government had opposed any profound investigation of that legislation. Twenty years after Morton there was a different climate. The Law Commission had been established;[150] and—much influenced[151] by the feeling, strongly expressed in the discussions leading up to the 1969 divorce reforms, that the regimes of separation of property and freedom of testation did not give adequate recognition to the claims of married women—embarked on a comprehensive review of family property law.[152] The Commission's early preference was for radical change: the succession code should be founded on fixed rights of inheritance[153] only to be overridden in exceptional cases. But this was—in the light of professional and other hostility[154]—abandoned.[155] However, the Commission accepted[156] that the claim of a widow or widower on the 'family assets' should be at least equal to the claim which a divorced spouse enjoyed under the very wide powers contained in the Matrimonial Proceedings and Property Act 1970.[157]

on the nature of the sum of money. What has happened is that if it is a question of a fall in the value of money, I get the information from the Treasury, who know all about that; and if it is a question of the price of houses, there are various building societies which publish information . . .' (*Official Report* (HL) 16 June 1966, vol. 275, col. 220). It is not clear whether an annual review has in fact been carried out; changes in the prescribed amount have been made at approximately five-yearly intervals (see n. 141, above), and they have been considerable. As the Law Commission pointed out: 'someone whose spouse died leaving issue on 31 May 1987 will receive £40,000 and a life interest in half the rest, whilst someone whose spouse dies a day later' will be entitled to a legacy of £75,000: *Working Paper No. 108* (1988) para. 3.2.

[148] See n. 102, above.   [149] See n. 101, above.   [150] See Ch. 1 above.

[151] For a perceptive discussion, see O. Kahn-Freund, 'Recent Legislation on Matrimonial Property' (1970) 33 MLR 601.

[152] See in particular *Family Property Law* PWP No. 42, 1972, Part III, *Family Provision*, and Part IV, *Legal Rights of Inheritance*; the *First Report on Family Property: A New Approach*, Law Com. 52; and the *Second Report on Family Property: Family Provision on Death*, Law Com. No. 61 (1974).

[153] See PWP No. 42, Part IV.

[154] There was 'marked lack of support for the principle of legal rights of inheritance for a surviving spouse among members of the legal profession (practising and academic); and the preponderance of opinion among women's organisations and members of the public was against it': *First Report on Family Property: A New Approach* (Law Com. No. 52, 1973, para. 2(c)).

[155] *Second Report on Family Property: Family Provision on Death*, Law Com. No. 61 (1974) para. 2(c).

[156] *Second Report on Family Property: Family Provision on Death*, Law Com. No. 61 (1974) para. 2(b).   [157] Subsequently consolidated in the Matrimonial Causes Act 1973.

The Commission's Report led to the enactment of the Inheritance (Provision for Family and Dependants) Act 1975; and that Act confers exceptionally wide powers on the court to make financial orders in cases in which the disposition of a deceased person's estate whether 'effected by his will or the law relating to intestacy' is not 'such as to make reasonable financial provision' for an applicant.[158]

There are, however, important limitations on the scope of the Act. In particular, only persons who fall within one of the categories of 'dependant' defined by the Act[159] can apply to the court; and it has been held that the court's function is not to remedy unjust enrichment or decide how the assets should be 'fairly' divided.[160] Moreover, whilst the court's powers in favour of the deceased's widow or widower are exercisable 'whether or not that provision is required for his or her maintenance',[161] in the case of the other specified categories of 'dependant' the court is still only to be concerned with financial provision which it would be reasonable for the applicant to receive for maintenance.[162]

INTESTACY RULES STILL INADEQUATE TO DEAL WITH
CHANGING CIRCUMSTANCES: DEMOGRAPHIC FACTORS

Where do these changes leave the law governing intestate distribution? As noted above, a crude (but, within its limits, effective) remedy has been found for the impact of inflation on the surviving spouse's statutory legacy. But how satisfactorily has it dealt with other social changes?

Intestate Succession and Changing Family Structures

The system of intestate succession based on the Administration of Estates Act 1925 and the Intestates' Estates Act 1952 makes provision only for the deceased's spouse (i.e. the person who was legally married to the deceased at the date of death) and those other members of the family who fall within the

---

[158] The Act (and the background to it) is considered in detail in R. D. Oughton, *Tyler's Family Provision* (3rd edn. 1997).

[159] i.e. the deceased's spouse, former spouse, or child; any person treated by the deceased as a child of the family in relation to any marriage to which the deceased was at any time a party; and any person who was being maintained wholly or partly by the deceased immediately before the death: Inheritance (Provision for Family and Dependants) Act 1975, s. 1(1). This provision has been extended by the Law Reform (Succession) Act 1995: see below, p. 272.

[160] *Re Coventry (Dec'd.)* [1980] Ch. 461, 486, per Goff LJ.

[161] S. 1(2)(a). In deciding whether such provision has been made (and if not what orders should be made) the court is also directed to consider the provision which the applicant might reasonably have expected to receive if the marriage had been terminated by divorce rather than death: s. 3(2). For the radical consequences of the abolition of the restriction of the surviving spouse's claim to a claim for maintenance, see e.g. *Moody* v. *Stevenson* [1992] Ch. 486; but note that it does not follow that a surviving spouse will receive a capital payment from the estate merely because he or she might have expected one on divorce: *Davis* v. *Davis* [1993] 1 FLR 54, CA.

[162] S. 1(2)(b). For the effect of this distinction, see text to n. 231, below.

statutory definitions of children, issue, and so on. Yet in recent years kinship networks have become so complex as to make such rigid statutory definitions inapt to reflect the reality of modern family life.

Two demographic developments are especially important: the growth in the divorce rate, and the increase in extramarital cohabitation and child bearing.

(i) Intestacy in a Divorcing Society[163]

In 1925, there were only 2,657 divorces in England and Wales;[164] in 1952 there were 31,966;[165] today there are some 160,000 divorces each year.[166] For present purposes, these figures are significant not so much because of the vastly increased probability that an intestate will leave more than one former spouse[167]— the divorce court has extensive powers to reallocate property at the time of divorce[168]—but because of the likelihood that the deceased's widow[169] may never have had any parental relationship with the children of his first marriage,[170] and may not feel under any obligation to pass on to them[171] any of the property she inherits from their father.[172]

(ii) Intestacy in a Cohabiting Society

The phenomenon of extramarital cohabitation is now well documented;[173] and it seems that amongst the young it has gone a long way to replace formal legal

---

[163] 'The current trend towards multiple marriages is apparently unremitting. Probate laws must respond intelligently to those changes': L. H. Waggoner, 'The Multiple-Marriage Society and Spousal Rights under the Revised Uniform Probate Code' (1991) 76 Iowa LR 223, 255.

[164] *Royal Commission on Marriage and Divorce, Report 1951–5*, Cmd. 9678, App. II, Table 2.

[165] Ibid. The Royal Commission calculated that the number of divorces per 1,000 total population was 0.76 compared with 0.07 in 1925.

[166] Figures are given annually in the *Judicial Statistics, Annual Report*; and for tables showing recent trends see *Social Trends 28* (1998) pp. 50–1.

[167] More than 80,000 divorced males and 78,000 divorced females remarried in 1990: see (1992) *Population Trends* (No. 70) Table 22; and in 1991, 37 per cent of marriages were remarriages for one or both partners: (1993) *Population Trends* (No. 71) p. 11. The marriage rate for divorced men and widowers has overtaken the rate for bachelors: *Social Trends 23* (1993) p. 29.

[168] See Matrimonial Causes Act 1973, Part II. The court's powers extend to excluding the right of a divorced spouse to apply to the court on the former spouse's death for provision out of the estate: Inheritance (Provision for Family and Dependants) Act 1975, s. 15; *Whiting* v. *Whiting* [1988] 2 FLR 189, CA.

[169] The desirability of using gender neutral language has on occasion to yield to the need for clarity and brevity.

[170] The incidence of remarriage also greatly increases the prospect of an intestate being survived by a half-brother or half-sister; and it is not clear that the rule (Administration of Estates Act 1925, s. 46(1)(v)) which prefers the whole to the half-blood can still be justified.

[171] Particularly if—as will often be the case—she has had children by her marriage to the intestate: there are some 40,000 births to remarried women—about 5 per cent of all births within marriage—each year: see (1992) *Population Trends* (No. 70) Table 11.

[172] It has been estimated that half of all the children of divorcing parents live with the mother and her new husband (and that one in fifteen live with their mother and the man with whom she is cohabiting): J. Haskey, 'Children in Families Broken by Divorce' (1990) *Population Trends* (No. 61) p. 42.

[173] See *Social Trends* (1998) Table pp. 48–9; and generally J. Haskey, 'Pre-marital cohabitation and the probability of subsequent divorce' (1992) *Population Trends* (No. 68) 10.

marriage.[174] Many children are born to parents who are not married: more than a third[175] of all live births in England are to such parents, and many of these parents seem likely to be cohabiting on a more or less stable basis.[176]

The law draws a sharp distinction between the succession rights of the partners to a cohabiting relationship and their children. Whilst the cohabitants have no legal right to succeed on a partner's intestacy,[177] the fact that a persons's parents are unmarried is now irrelevant in determining legal relationships for succession as for other purposes.[178] An illegitimate child thus has a right to be supported by both his parents during their lifetimes,[179] a right to take on the intestacy of both parents, and a right to apply for reasonable financial provision out of a parent's estate. But in one significant respect children brought up by unmarried partners are treated unfavourably: the definition of 'child of the family' in the Inheritance (Provision for Family and Dependants) Act 1975[180] requires that the child should have been treated by the deceased as a child of the family *in relation to a marriage*; and it follows that a child cannot claim reasonable financial provision as a child of the family[181] out of the estate of his mother's cohabitant notwithstanding the fact that the cohabitant may have been the only father figure in the child's life.[182]

Disinherited Children?

These legal rules may have a particular effect on three groups of children:

---

[174] See K. E. Kiernan and V. Estaugh: *Cohabitation, Extra-Marital Childbearing and Social Policy* (Family Policy Studies Centre, Occasional Paper 17, 1993) Ch. 2; and J. Haskey and K. Kiernan, 'Cohabitation in Great Britain—Characteristics and Estimated Numbers of Cohabiting Partners' (1989) *Population Trends* (No. 58).   [175] See *Social Trends* (1998), pp. 52–3.

[176] Eighty per cent of illegitimate births are registered by both parents; and three-quarters of these were living at the same address: *Social Trends* (1998) p. 52.

[177] A cohabitant may, however, have the right to apply to the court for reasonable financial provision out of a deceased partner's estate: see below, p. 272.

[178] Legislation to this effect culminated in the Family Law Reform Act 1987.

[179] Both under the Children Act 1989, Sch. 1 and under the Child Support Act 1991. It is now well established that the power to order support under the 1989 Act extends to making provision for the child's housing (see *K* v. *K (Minors: Property Transfer)* [1992] 1 WLR 530, CA); but it has been held that—following the principles applied by the divorce court (see *Chamberlain* v. *Chamberlain* [1973] 1 WLR 1557, CA; *Lilford (Lord)* v. *Glynn* [1979] 1 WLR 78, CA; *Kiely* v. *Kiely* [1988] 1 FLR 248, CA)—the discretion should not be exercised to create a long-term capital endowment for the child: *A* v. *A (A Minor) (Financial Provision)* [1994] 1 FLR 657.

[180] The concept of a 'child of the family' was originally developed in the divorce legislation: see Matrimonial Causes Act 1973, s. 52(1); but the definition in the Inheritance (Provision for Family and Dependants) Act 1975, s. 1(1)(e)—'any person . . . who, in the case of any marriage to which the deceased was at any time a party, was treated by the deceased as a child of the family in relation to that marriage'—is materially different in a number of respects: see *Re Leach (dec'd.)* [1986] Ch. 226, 234, per Slade LJ.

[181] It is possible that such a child would be able to claim on the basis of being a person who 'immediately before the death of the deceased was being maintained, either wholly or partly, by the deceased': Inheritance (Provision for Family and Dependants) Act 1975, s. 1(1)(e).

[182] *J* v. *J (Property Transfer)* [1993] 2 FLR 56.

(i) Children of a Divorced Father

The first category consists of the children of a marriage who live with the mother after divorce,[183] perhaps having little contact with the father or the person he subsequently marries.[184] Such children of course are still legally the father's children and are entitled, as the law now stands, to share in his estate on intestacy; but, if he remarries, the size of the widow's statutory legacy means that this right will be valueless in all save very substantial estates. Moreover, the deceased's children by his divorced wife have no right to share in the estate of the widow on her subsequent death, nor do they have any right to seek provision out of the widow's estate notwithstanding the fact that the whole or a substantial part of it may have been derived from their father.[185]

The deceased's children remain entitled to share in the intestacy of their mother but, if she remarries, her surviving husband will take the first £125,000 of her estate, and the children will have no right to share in the intestacy of their stepfather (because they are not his children for the purpose of the laws of intestate distribution).[186]

It is true that a child who is dissatisfied with the effect of the rules in these cases may apply to the court under the Inheritance (Provision for Family and Dependants) Act 1975 for reasonable financial provision out of the estate of the father, mother, or stepfather;[187] but such an application will only succeed if provision is required for the applicant's maintenance, i.e. to meet the cost of daily living at an appropriate standard.[188]

(ii) Children of a Non-Marital Relationship

Such children will be in the same position in respect of intestate succession to each parent as the children of a marriage; and they are equally entitled to claim reasonable financial provision—limited to maintenance—out of the estate of their father, mother, or[189] mother's husband. But, as already pointed out,[190] there is no right to claim provision from the estate of a man—a 'de facto stepfather'—who

---

[183] The father will have remained under an obligation to support the children under the provisions of the Child Support Act 1991; and the divorce court has extensive powers to make property adjustment orders in favour of children; but the court will not normally exercise those powers so as to provide any substantial long-term capital for a child: see *Chamberlain* v. *Chamberlain* [1973] 1 WLR 1557, CA; *Lilford (Lord)* v. *Glynn* [1979] 1 WLR 78, CA; *Kiely* v. *Kiely* [1988] 1 FLR 248, CA.

[184] See, for example, the poignant situation in *Re Jennings (dec'd.)* [1994] Ch. 286, CA: see p. 277 below.

[185] In contrast, children by the woman who became the father's widow will be entitled on her intestacy (and thus in anything which remains of the fund she inherited).

[186] Unless they have been adopted by him.

[187] Assuming that the stepfather has treated the child as a child of the family: see n. 180 above.

[188] *Re Jennings (dec'd.)* [1994] Ch. 286, CA.

[189] Assuming that they have been treated as a child of the family in relation to the mother's marriage to the deceased.   [190] See n. 180, above.

has lived with the mother outside marriage, however strong may have been the factual parenting link.[191]

If the parents' relationship ends by death (rather than breakdown) the children may well be in a better financial position than the children of married parents, since the surviving parent will be entitled to nothing on the partner's intestacy, whilst the children will be entitled to the whole of the deceased parent's estate.[192]

(iii) Children of the Deceased's Widow

Almost half of the 160,000 children involved each year in a parental divorce will live with their mother and the man she subsequently marries.[193] Again, a significant number of married women may have children by a previous non-marital relationship. In either case, the children may well have lived for almost the whole of their childhood in their stepfather's household.[194] But they do not qualify as the stepfather's children for the purpose of intestate succession to his estate[195] although they will have a right to apply to the court[196] for reasonable financial provision—restricted to maintenance—out of his estate. They will, of course, be entitled to share in the estate of their mother if she subsequently dies intestate, and in this way it is possible that they will eventually inherit the property built up during their childhood by their mother and stepfather.

Changing Modes of Wealth Holding

It is not only changes in social structures which make the task of formulating a rational code of intestate distribution difficult: changes in the methods whereby wealth is held and transmitted add to the problems. This is because it is only the deceased's 'real and personal estate' which is distributed under the intestacy rules;[197] and increasingly wealth is held in forms (or subject to legal regimes) which fall outside this definition.[198] As the Law Commission pointed out in 1988,[199] if a

---

[191] *J v. J (Property Transfer)* [1993] 2 FLR 56, Eastham J (where the child had lived with her mother and her cohabitant for ten years).

[192] Assuming that the parent did not leave a spouse, and subject to any claim by the surviving cohabitant under the Inheritance (Provision for Family and Dependants) Act 1975, as amended.

[193] See text to n. 172, above.

[194] See generally S. H. Ramsey and J. M. Masson, 'Step-Parent Support of Step-Children: A Comparative Analysis of Policies and Problems in the American and English Experience' (1985) 36 Syracuse LR 659; J. Masson, D. Norbury and S. G. Chatterton, *Mine, Yours or Ours, A Study of Step-parent adoption* (1983).

[195] Accordingly, if the deceased left no other issue half his estate (after paying the enhanced statutory legacy of £200,000) would pass immediately to his parents, or to his brothers and sisters. The stepchildren would get nothing.   [196] As children of the family: see n. 180, above.

[197] See Administration of Estates Act 1925, s. 33.

[198] In this country—in contrast to the situation in the United States—it seems that avoidance of the need to have recourse to probate is not a significant factor in determining how wealth should be held: see J. H. Langbein, 'The Non-Probate Revolution and the Future of the Law of Succession' (1984) 57 Harv. L Rev. 1108.

[199] *Distribution on Intestacy*, Law Com. No. 187 (1989) para. 19.

couple own the family home jointly, the survivor acquires the deceased's interest automatically and will receive not only the home but a full statutory legacy; whereas if the couple were tenants in common the deceased's interest forms part of the estate and its value counts towards the statutory legacy. Again, many benefits under pension schemes—for example, the death in service benefit often amounting to twice the deceased's annual salary—do not fall into his or her estate and will thus not be taken into account in determining beneficiaries' entitlements on intestacy. In the result there are disparities in what survivors receive which will often seem arbitrary and unfair.[200]

FURTHER REFORM: THE ATTEMPT WHICH FAILED

When the amount of the statutory legacy was amended in 1987, the Law Commission decided—in the light of evidence that the law as it stood could give rise to hardship as well as unfairness—to undertake a comprehensive review of the law relating to intestate distribution. This review led the Commission to the conclusion[201] that a surviving spouse should in all cases have an entitlement to the whole estate; and that, whilst no attempt should be made to provide for cohabitants under the rules governing distribution on intestacy, a cohabitant[202] should be eligible to apply to the court under the Inheritance (Provision for Family and Dependants) Act 1975 for reasonable provision to be made.

The proposal to allow a cohabitant to apply under the 1975 Act has been implemented by the Law Reform (Succession) Act 1995,[203] but the Government rejected the Commission's main proposal to enlarge the surviving spouse's entitlement;[204] and there are apparently no specific plans for further review. The Government accepted that the main proposal would have the attractions of simplicity and clarity; but it considered that these were outweighed by the problems which would be caused by excluding all other members of the deceased's family from entitlement, 'particularly where the deceased left children from a previous marriage'.[205]

---

[200] Ibid.   [201] *Distribution on Intestacy*, Law Com. No. 187 (1989).

[202] Provided that he or she had been living in the same household as the deceased throughout the period of two years ending with the deceased's death: Inheritance (Provision for Family and Dependants) Act 1995, s. 1(1)(ba), as inserted by Law Reform (Succession) Act 1995. Under the 1975 Act (s. 1(e)) a person who immediately before the deceased's death was being maintained by the deceased, either wholly or partly, is eligible to apply; and that provision (which remains in force) was sometimes invoked by a surviving cohabitant: see *Bishop* v. *Plumley and another* [1991] 1 FLR 121, CA: for the relationship between the two provisions, see S. M. Cretney and J. M. Masson, *Principles of Family Law* (6th edn. 1997) pp. 208–10; R. D. Oughton, *Tyler's Family Provision* (3rd edn. 1997) pp. 80–91, 106–8.   [203] See above.

[204] *Official Report* (HL) 1 July 1993, vol. 547, col. WA 38. For other parliamentary discussion of the Law Commission's proposals, see *Official Report* (HL) 16 June 1992, vol. 538, cols. 170–8 (discussion on unstarred question by Lord Mishcon) and *Official Report* (HL) 13 Feb. 1995, vol. 561, cols. 502–11 (Second Reading of Law Reform (Succession) Bill).

[205] *Official Report* (HL) 13 Feb. 1995, vol. 561, col. 503, per Lord Mackay of Clashfern, LC.

FURTHER REFORM: WHAT DOES PUBLIC OPINION WANT?

The Government's attitude, whilst entirely understandable given the views expressed by informed commentators, is worrying given the 'unanimous agreement' amongst those consulted by the Law Commission that the present law governing distribution on intestacy was in need of reform.[206] This view was supported by an attitude survey[207] undertaken for the Commission[208] which produced two fairly clear preferences. First, as a general rule the whole estate should pass to the surviving spouse in preference to children whether adult or minor.[209] Secondly, this rule should not apply to cases in which the surviving spouse was the deceased's second wife. Less than a third of the sample[210] thought the survivor should take the whole estate in such cases.[211] It seems clear, therefore, that the survey does not support the Commission's proposal to make the surviving spouse the sole beneficiary irrespective of whether the survivor was the deceased's first, second

[206] *Distribution on Intestacy*, Law Com. No. 187 (1989) para. 17.

[207] This is not the first occasion on which a survey has been used in the context of family property rights: see the Report (by J. E. Todd and L. M. Jones) *Matrimonial Property*, commissioned by the Law Commission from the OPCS Social Survey Division and published in 1972. The response to questions on distribution on intestacy would not have supported a proposal that the surviving spouse should be the sole beneficiary: see Chs. 9 and 11. More recently, the Scottish Law Commission commissioned a survey (published as an Appendix to the Scottish Law Commission's *Consultative Memorandum No. 69*) and the findings were amongst the factors influencing the Scottish Commission against the solution of constituting the surviving spouse sole beneficiary: *Report on Succession*, Scot. Law Com. No. 124 (1990). In the United States, a telephone survey confirmed that a rule under which a surviving spouse inherited the entire estate on intestacy would be the most popular option, but not in cases in which the deceased left children by another relationship: see M. L. Fellows, R. J. Simon and W. Rau, 'Public Attitudes about Property Distribution at Death and Intestate Succession Laws in the United States' (1978) *American Bar Foundation Research Journal* 321.

[208] The Commission thought such a survey would provide a 'much more reliable guide to the wishes of those who may die intestate' than the traditional method of approaching reform by an analysis of the provisions found in wills: *Distribution on Intestacy*, Law Com. No. 187 (1989) para. 4.

[209] The survey undertaken for the Law Commission found that 72 per cent of the sample group favoured a surviving wife inheriting everything (and the proportion was higher when there were young children): see *Distribution on Intestacy*, Law Com. No. 187, App. C, para. 2.8. For the American preference in favour of a surviving spouse—notable because the Uniform Probate Code and the law of most American states in fact provide a different solution—see M. L. Fellows, R. J. Simon and W. Rau, 'Public Attitudes about Property Distribution at Death and Intestate Succession Laws in the United States' (1978) *American Bar Foundation Research Journal* 321. In contrast, the Scottish Law Commission's survey revealed much less support for universal spouse succession: only 51 per cent of the sample considered that the entire estate of a married man (who was neither poor nor wealthy) should pass to his wife; and this proportion fell to 19 per cent where the surviving spouse was the deceased's second wife and there were children surviving from the first marriage: see the Scottish Law Commission's *Consultation Paper* No. 69, *Intestate Succession and Legal Right* (1986) pp. 227–8.

[210] In the United States the proportion favouring this solution was even smaller: a distribution giving 60 or 70 per cent of the estate to the surviving spouse with the balance being shared equally by the deceased's issue would reflect most preferences: see M. L. Fellows, R. J. Simon and W. Rau, 'Public Attitudes about Property Distribution at Death and Intestate Succession Laws in the United States' (1978) *American Bar Foundation Research Journal* 321, 367.

[211] Although a quarter thought the surviving second wife should take the house (or, if there were no house, a fixed sum) whilst the residue of the estate would go to the children: *Distribution on Intestacy*, Law Com. No. 187 (1989) App. C, para. 2.13.

or even third spouse. There is indeed widespread support for improving the surviving spouse's position at the expense of the deceased's blood relatives;[212] but
there is also a wide appreciation of the problems created by the phenomenon of
divorce and remarriage.

The survey evidence would therefore support a special regime to regulate cases
in which the deceased's surviving spouse was not the only person to whom he
or she had been married; and the comparative menu offers a bewildering range
of possibilities from which a choice could be made. The surviving spouse's share
might, for example, depend on the number of children,[213] or the length of the
marriage, on whether the deceased left issue by someone other[214] than the surviving spouse[215] or on whether the survivor has children by someone other than
the deceased[216] and/or the survivor might be given special rights in respect of
the family home.[217]

But one thing emerges without possibility of contradiction from any survey
of these solutions. It is that all systems of intestate succession which have tried
to make provision taking account of the varied circumstances of second marriages are immensely complex.[218] The introduction of any such regime into English

[212] See M. A. Glendon, *The Transformation of Family Law* (1989) p. 238.

[213] In many Canadian jurisdictions the surviving spouse takes a legacy and one-half the residue
if the deceased left one child, and one-third if more than one.

[214] As the Law Commission point out, the fact that English succession law no longer distinguishes
between marital and non-marital relationships, with the corollary that any special rule would have
to refer to all cases where the deceased left issue of any other relationship, would enormously com-
plicate the administration of estates (presumably because it might involve either the making of lengthy
and embarrassing enquiries, or a provision protecting the administrators and perhaps the beneficiaries against the consequences of a claim being made by a child of whom they had no knowledge).
The Law Commission comment that 'given that adequate provision would still have to be made for
the spouse, [such a development] would benefit only a very few people overall': *Distribution on
Intestacy*, Law Com. No. 187 (1989) para. 44.   [215] See R. Kerridge (1990) 54 Conv. 358.

[216] As in the 1990 Revision of the Uniform Probate Code: see C. Fried, 'The Uniform Probate Code: Intestate Succession and Related Matters' (1992) 55 Albany L Rev. 927. The Law
Commission's consultation revealed concern lest a surviving spouse prefer her own children to her
stepchildren so that the deceased's children would end up by inheriting none of what was originally
their parents' property: *Distribution on Intestacy*, Law Com. No. 187 (1989) para. 41; and further
refinements can be introduced to seek to meet such problems: for example, it has been suggested
that the stepparent should be entitled to the whole of the deceased's estate only if the surviving stepchild
has lived in the family home for a minimum of two years: see C. R. Glick, 'The spousal share in
intestate succession: stepparents are getting shortchanged' (1990) 74 Minn. LR 631.

[217] As in the right given under English law to require the house to be appropriated in satisfaction
of the surviving spouse's share: Intestates' Estates Act 1952, Sch. 2. The Scottish Law Commission
also favour giving a surviving spouse the right to acquire the home: see *Report on Succession*, Scot.
Law Com. No. 124 (1990).

[218] See, for example, the first tentative draft revision of the Uniform Probate Code which would
have given the surviving spouse an interest in the whole of the intestate's estate only if a live child
had been born of the marriage, or the marriage had been contracted before the deceased reached the
age of 40 and had lasted at least ten years or the marriage had lasted twenty years. If these conditions were not satisfied the surviving spouse's interest would be reduced to one-third of the estate.
Moreover, the survivor's interest would be absolute only if the intestate left no issue by another spouse
or the estate was small (not exceeding $30,000); in such cases the survivor would take one-third of
the fund absolutely and a life interest in the balance: see generally W. F. Fratcher, 'Towards Uniform
Succession Legislation' (1966) 41 New Y Univ. LR 1037.

law would thus be quite inconsistent with the widely expressed preference for a system clear and simple both to operate and to understand.[219] For that reason— and also because it is exceedingly doubtful whether any such system could be wholly effective to achieve fairness given the vast range of factual situations which may arise—it seems unlikely that an attempt to recast the rules of intestate distribution in this way would be satisfactory;[220] and it is submitted that the Law Commission correctly concluded that any system providing certain, clear and simple rules which meet the great majority of cases cannot be adapted to cater properly for the enormous range of family circumstances of which a modern legal system has to take account.[221]

WHAT IS TO BE DONE?

What, then, is to be done? The Commission's preferred option—that a surviving spouse should take the whole estate—would be comprehensible and simple and would reflect public opinion in those cases—still a considerable majority —in which the intestate has been married no more than once. But what of the minority of awkward cases in which there is a conflict between the surviving spouse and others? The answer can, it is submitted, only be found in the discretionary power of the court to redistribute the estate so as to provide a reasonable share for a surviving spouse and reasonable maintenance for other dependants.[222]

EXTENDING JUDICIAL DISCRETION?

The advantages of allowing a measure of flexibility and discretion in the law of succession[223] are now increasingly appreciated in many of those countries which have a system of fixed division on intestacy; but it would be wrong to deny that

---

[219] *Distribution on Intestacy*, Law Com. No. 187 (1989) para. 25. R. Kerridge (1990) 54 Conv. 358 makes what is on the basis of principle a strong case for providing a life (rather than an absolute) interest in the estate in cases in which the intestate leaves no issue by the surviving spouse but did leave other issue. But to have recourse to life interests would sometimes involve disproportionate administrative expense (see *Kusminow* v. *Barclays Bank Trust Co. Ltd.* [1989] Fam. Law 66) and would be to reverse the trend established for that and other reasons since the Morton Report.

[220] For a different view, see R. Kerridge (1990) 54 Conv. 358.

[221] *Distribution on Intestacy*, Law Com. No. 187 (1989) para. 45.

[222] *Distribution on Intestacy*, Law Com. No. 187 (1989) para. 27. The Commission also refer to the power of the court under the Mental Health Act 1983, s. 96, to make a will for a person who is mentally incapable of doing so for himself; see for the exercise of this discretion (which the legislation leaves at large) *Re D(J)* [1982] Ch. 237 (Sir Robert Megarry).

[223] See e.g. 'Public Attitudes about Property Distribution at Death and Intestate Succession Laws in the United States' by M. L. Fellows, R. J. Simon and W. Rau (1978) *American Bar Foundation Research Journal* 321, 386.

there are serious drawbacks inherent in any such system.[224] It is said (for example) that it is difficult to predict the outcome of applications,[225] that unnecessary litigation within families is encouraged, whilst the costs of defending a claim—given that it is likely that the expense will be borne by the estate[226]—are high, so that there is strong pressure to agree to settle even an apparently unmeritorious—or blackmailing—claim.[227]

Unfortunately little hard data is available about the working of the family provision legislation in practice. The Judicial Statistics no longer provide information about the number of applications[228] (much less about how many proceed to trial rather than being settled).[229] Nevertheless, the general principle of allowing a discretionary adjustive power has survived for nearly sixty years; and—since the Government was content to allow the class of eligible dependant to be extended to include the cohabitant as such[230]—it may perhaps be inferred that the judiciary no longer perceive serious difficulty in administering the jurisdiction. No one would claim that reliance on a discretionary jurisdiction is an *ideal* solution; and there is certainly force in some of the criticisms set out above. But what is the alternative? In all the circumstances it is suggested that it seems difficult to deny that in this country—particularly given the extensive experience of administering a wide discretion in relation to the financial consequences of divorce—such a system provides a solution preferable to any other.

But there are two particular issues about the scope of the discretionary power to depart from the prescribed code of intestate distribution to which further thought needs to be given. First, is it right that the court's powers should be confined—

---

[224] A 'quick fix, an easy compromise, or a way of passing the buck to the courts on a controversial issue': M. A. Glendon, 'Fixed Rules and Discretion in Contemporary Family Law and Succession' (1986) 60 Tulane LR 1165; and see the same author's *The New Family and the New Property* (Toronto, 1981), and *The Transformation of Family Law* (1989). The case against a discretionary system is also powerfully argued by M. C. Meston, 'Succession—Rights or Discretion' [1987] JR 1; whilst the Scottish Law Commission have not pursued suggestions made in Consultation Paper No. 69, under which discretionary provision for cohabitants might in some circumstances be ordered.

[225] And note the view expressed by Lord Wilberforce, *Official Report* (HL) 20 Mar. 1975, vol. 358, col. 933 that the difficulty for a judge hearing an application under the family provision legislation 'remains intense'.

[226] But note dicta to the effect that judges should look closely at the merits of the application before ordering that the applicant's costs be met out of the estate: *Re Fullard (dec'd.)* [1982] Fam. 42, CA.

[227] For an account of the pressures experienced by parties to financial applications in the context of divorce, see Davis, Cretney and Collins, *Simple Quarrels* (1994).

[228] The *Judicial Statistics Annual Reports* give the number of applications to the Chancery Division of the High Court, but not the number of applications in the Family Division of the High Court or in the County Court (which since 1991 has had unlimited jurisdiction). For a summary of such figures as are available see R. D. Oughton, *Tyler's Family Provision* (3rd edn. 1997) App. A; and note the conclusion (based on the number of standing searches in the Probate Registry) that a total of 2,000 applications under the 1975 Act in all courts 'does not seem an unreasonable estimate'.

[229] It appears that some 1,300 applications for legal aid are granted each year: *Legal Aid Board Annual Report 1991/2*, Table Civil 7 (1,391 applications granted in that year). The statutory charge does not apply to sums recovered under the Inheritance (Provision for Family and Dependants) Act 1975: Civil Legal Aid (General) Regulations 1989, reg. 94(b).   [230] See above, text to n. 203.

as they are under the 1975 Act in the case of applicants other than a surviving widow or widower—to making provision for an applicant's *maintenance*; and, secondly, does the legislation define the class of dependants (who alone are eligible to apply) sufficiently broadly to deal with the trends in kinship patterns noted above?

'Required[231] for Maintenance'?

The courts have consistently refused to give any precise definition of this term and this is not the place for a detailed exegesis of the case law.[232] However, the general thrust is clear: although maintenance does not mean just enough to enable a person to get by[233] it does not extend to provision for everything which may be regarded as reasonably desirable for the applicant's general benefit or welfare.[234]

The decision of the Court of Appeal in *Re Jennings (dec'd.)*[235] demonstrates just how limiting[236] this interpretation may be:

The applicant was a fifty-year-old who had been brought up from the age of four by his mother and stepfather. There was no contact between father and son after the divorce and the only thing the father did for his son was to send him ten shillings in a birthday card on his second birthday. The father left the residue of his estate (which amounted to some £300,000 after payment of Inheritance Tax) to charities. The son had been successful in business; and the Court of Appeal held that accordingly no requirement for maintenance had been made out.[237]

Such an approach may be appropriate in the context of legislation which is heavily based on the ideology of freedom of testation—that 'an Englishman remains

---

[231] In *Re Jennings (dec'd.)* [1994] Ch. 286, CA, both Nourse and Henry LJJ state that the provision must be 'required' for the applicant's maintenance (following in this respect a dictum at first instance in *Re Coventry (dec'd.)* [1980] Ch. 461 at 472, per Oliver J). But the word 'required' does not appear in the Inheritance (Provision for Family and Dependants) Act 1975, s. 1(2)(*b*); and it may be respectfully doubted whether Oliver J was correct in thinking that it should be read into the relevant provision.

[232] See *Re Jennings (dec'd.)* [1994] Ch. 286; and generally R. D. Oughton, *Tyler's Family Provision* (3rd edn. 1997) pp. 222–37.

[233] *Re Coventry (dec'd.)* [1980] Ch. 461 at 485, per Goff LJ.   [234] Ibid.

[235] [1994] Ch. 286, CA.

[236] And in some respects arbitrary: in *Re Callaghan (dec'd.)* [1985] Fam. 1, Booth J (a decision evidently approved by the Court of Appeal in *Re Jennings (dec'd.)*), it was held that an adult stepson had established a need for maintenance because he wanted to buy his council house without having a mortgage debt hanging over him for the remainder of his working years.

[237] The ratio of the case was that the applicant had not demonstrated that the deceased had been unreasonable in failing to make financial provision for the applicant, it being necessary for an adult child to demonstrate some special circumstance (typically, a moral obligation) if he or she was to be eligible for consideration. The mere existence of the relationship of father and son was not a sufficient basis for the making of an order: see per Nourse LJ at [1994] 3 WLR 67, 75; and compare *Re Hancock (dec'd.)* [1998] 2 FLR 346, CA. It must be pointed out that this approach—although in accordance with the authorities—treats the statutory enumeration of the matters to which the court is required to have regard as if they were an exhaustive list of conditions, one at least of which must be satisfied by a successful applicant; but it is not clear that this approach is justified by the language of the statute.

at liberty at his death to dispose of his own property in whatever way he pleases'[238]—and which is *not* concerned to provide legacies or awards for the deserving.[239] But it seems doubtful whether the same approach is justified where it is not the deceased's will which controls the devolution of his property, but rather a default code which cannot be expected to deal adequately with the diversity of family circumstances for which the law now has to provide.[240] Under the existing law, it is established (at any rate up to the House of Lords) that the mere existence of the relationship of parent and child is not a sufficient foundation for a successful application.[241] But in intestacy cases the beneficiary's sole title to take under the code of distribution is the existence of a family relationship and it is not easy to see why, in principle, someone who can establish a comparable relationship should not be eligible to invoke the discretionary adjustive power on that basis alone without having to show a need for 'maintenance'.[242]

Those who May Apply

The addition of those who had been living with the deceased as a spouse throughout the two years before death to the class of 'dependant' entitled to apply for reasonable financial provision out of the deceased's estate does not extend the class sufficiently. Is it right to deny recognition to a child's claim against the estate of the person who has been responsible for his or her upbringing, merely because the family in which the child was reared was not founded on a legal marriage?[243] Is it right to deny a child any claim against the estate of the woman who married his or her father and took all the father's property on his intestacy?[244] A great deal more thought needs to be given to the question of who should be entitled, in cases of intestacy, to seek provision from the estate; and there may be a case for extending the class to all who can show that they were dependent on the deceased, or that they could properly be regarded as members of the deceased's family.

---

[238] *Re Coventry (dec'd.)* [1980] Ch. 461 at 474, per Oliver J.

[239] *Re Jennings (dec'd.)* [1994] 3 WLR 67 at 78, per Henry LJ.

[240] See the discussion in text to nn. 163–76 above.

[241] See notably *Re Jennings (dec'd.)* [1994] 3 WLR 67 at 75, per Nourse LJ.

[242] The Law Commission discuss the 'maintenance' restriction very shortly in recommending that a cohabitant should be eligible to apply under the 1975 Act, and conclude that the cohabitant's claim should be confined to provision required for maintenance. But since a cohabitant who was being maintained by the deceased is, under the existing law, eligible to apply as a dependant (s. 1(1)(e)) it would seem that the addition to the class will have very little effect.

[243] See *J* v. *J (Property Transfer)* [1993] 2 FLR 56; and text to n. 180, above.

[244] The exclusion of a half-brother or sister might also be considered: see n. 94, above.

CONCLUSION

In conclusion it is submitted:

1.   The Law Commission's proposal that a surviving spouse should inherit the whole of an intestate's estate has much to recommend it[245] in terms of achieving a simple code of succession law which would give effect to the intestate's presumed wishes in the majority of cases.

2.   However, social and economic changes mean that such a code would lead to injustice in some cases.

3.   Although there must be real concern about recourse to a discretionary adjustive code as a means of remedying the inability of the law to deal with changing family structures, it seems unfortunate that the Law Commission—whose statutory duty is to undertake the systematic development of the law[246]—were not able to undertake a comprehensive examination of the implications for the Inheritance (Provision for Family and Dependants) Act 1975[247] of changing the law of intestate succession. In principle, recourse to a judicial discretion would seem to be the least unsatisfactory method of providing for the inevitable cases in which the rules of intestate succession would not achieve reasonable equity between those who have some claim on the deceased.

4.   The Inheritance (Provision for Family and Dependants) Act 1975 does not, as it stands, provide a remedy to all those who might be thought to have such a claim. Amendment to the prescribed category of 'dependant' may be desirable; and consideration needs to be given to removal or amendment, at least in the case of intestacy, of the provision restricting claims under the Act to provision for 'maintenance'.

---

[245]   For a different view, see R. Kerridge (1990) 54 Conv. 358.

[246]   Law Commissions Act 1965, s. 3(1).

[247]   The absence of reliable statistical and empirical evidence about the working of the Inheritance (Provision for Family and Dependants) Act 1975 is also regrettable.

Index